D1285669

The Conquest
of the Material World

*In order to illuminate the whole we must see more deeply into the particular,
just as in order to have understanding of the particular
we must acknowledge the whole.*

Cap d'Antibes Conference, 1964
CENTER FOR HUMAN UNDERSTANDING

The Conquest
of the Material World

JOHN NEF

THE UNIVERSITY OF CHICAGO PRESS

CHICAGO AND LONDON

Library of Congress Catalog Card Number: 64-15804

THE UNIVERSITY OF CHICAGO PRESS, CHICAGO & LONDON
The University of Toronto Press, Toronto 5, Canada

A EVELYN STEFANSSON NEF

Qui m'a délivré de la tristesse

.

Preface

The recently formed Center for Human Understanding concerned itself during its last meeting in Washington with problems related to building a bridge of understanding between countries in different stages of development. The subject was chosen especially by our European members. I was enthusiastic about it, but my role as presiding officer did not determine the direction which the discussions took. Representatives of countries from Africa, Asia, and Latin America discussed papers written by representatives of Europe and the United States, each of whom chose his own theme within the general framework suggested by the subject. As it turned out, the central matter which concerned the African, Asian, and Latin American participants was the industrialization of their countries. How fast is it desirable for them to move toward mechanization and automation? What traditions do they wish to retain even if retaining them involves slower progress in achieving the material wealth which all these societies are seeking?

I had not expected that human understanding would present itself so universally as related directly or indirectly to questions raised by the coming of the industrial state. Yet this is perhaps natural because industrial civilization as we know it is a new thing in history.

As an historian I have devoted my life to its evolution in Europe, particularly in England and France. It has been the subject of the historical books and articles which I have published during thirty years, since the appearance in 1932 of my examination of the origins in Great Britain of a coal-burning economy—itself a factor in the rise of industrialism.

Nevertheless it was with surprise that I discovered, at our Washington meeting, that the conquest of the material world is the subject which raises the major issues that concern the leaders and the people of every country. I feel a little as Monsieur Jourdain did when his teacher of manners told him that his conversation was "prose." I find that, without realizing it, my primary concern as a writer has been with what seems to be the major theme of modern history.

The making of the industrialized world of our time goes far back into the past of the European, and hence the North American, societies where it was first established. So we can learn a great deal from Western history concerning its causes and consequences—much of which, if rightly interpreted, can help countries later industrialized and countries in process of industrialization with present problems. The restrictions on the coming of industrial civilization, as well as the forces which brought it into being, in Europe and the United States have taken on an unexpected interest since I began to write, because of the rapid spread of industrialism in recent decades.

I like to think that the essays assembled as chapters in this volume, and taken together, form a fragment of a new kind of history of the civilization that has emerged in Europe and America and is now penetrating every part of the world. All of these essays have been revised, chapters v and vii extensively revised, and parts of chapters ii, iii, and iv have been rewritten.

After an introduction, concerned with the origins of industrialism as far back as the Roman Empire, this book deals mainly with European history during the period from the mid-fifteenth to the late seventeenth century. A final essay brings the story down to the end of the eighteenth century. By that time the evolution of European society—especially since the Reformation—had made the triumph of industrialism virtually inevitable. So it is to the period before the American Revolution that we need to look for those factors and for those individual decisions which are responsible for the new kinds of existence all the peoples of the earth are living today.

No one could be better aware than I that this book is fragmentary in content, imperfect in detail, and tentative in its conclusions. I believe nevertheless that the subjects discussed are vital to an understanding of the modern world, because the essays touch on some of the conditions without which the industrial revolutions could hardly have come as soon as they did and might not have come at all. The essays help to reveal the nature of some of the barriers to industrialization, which were surmounted especially during two centuries preceding the 1780's, when the constitution of the United States was prepared and published. They also suggest some of the consequences of industrialization.

In the light of fresh materials gathered during years of research in European archives, my account of the origins of industrial civilization differs from that which is to be found in historical textbooks or in historical popularizations fed to college and university students or offered as nourishment to what it is hoped will be a wide public of readers. My essays were not written, and they are not now presented, to support and amplify what I regard as a correct outline of European history in its relation to the triumph of industrialism, such as the student and general reader can obtain elsewhere. They are not merely what is called in our colleges and universities "collateral reading." They were written, and they are presented, to suggest original explanations of European history, which for me at least are nearer to reality than those suggested by the history books with which I am familiar. Whether or not this is an illusion is for others to judge in the years ahead. I would only say that I offer this book to the reader in the same spirit that Montaigne offered his essays. This is a book of good faith, and it is written out of my own experience both as a human being and an historian, so that I, too, am, in my own way, "the subject of my book."

In what ways is it designed to reach readers? I like to hope that, for the scholar, the essays may offer a background against which to evaluate his research, different from the backgrounds against which firsthand learned contributions have hitherto been made. My essays are intended also to provide the student and the general reader with what is, for me, the very heart of forward instruction in European history, insofar as that is related to the world in which we find ourselves in the late twentieth century.

Their fresh outlook consists partly in tracing back to earlier times, before the eighteenth century, developments which account for the priority of Europe and North America in the mechanized, automatized economy that has now triumphed. It consists also in relating novel developments in industry to a great many other kinds of endeavor, religious, monetary, scientific, and governmental. The study of historical interrelations, which is the subject of Part 3, suggests that it may be possible to bring diverse strands of history into a new unity, hitherto missed.

The substance of this unity it seems to me might render obsolete the outlook presented by the cycle historians from Gobineau to Spengler and even Toynbee. The historical drama unfolding in the late twentieth century may not prove to be mainly, as Gobineau and Spengler expected, a repetition in new forms of an old story. My essays (taken together with my recent books, which relate the coming of industrialism to other historical developments from those with which the chapters in Part 3 are primarily concerned) help show, I believe, that the conquest of the material world has come out of human efforts never made before, and out of a new hope in human nature which the future will either destroy or partly sustain. These essays attribute to the individual a more active and nobler role in the making of what I consider, unlike the cycle historians, not just another "civilization," but potentially *civilization* itself. I derive this meaning of the word from that given it by the French and English writers who introduced it into these two languages in the eighteenth century.[1] I believe that the future of human life

[1] Cf. Nef, *Cultural Foundations of Industrial Civilization* (New York, 1960), pp. 79–80.

may well depend on the capacity of individuals to play a still more active and still nobler role than they have played before. If that is true, then the view of history which these essays present may perhaps be worthy of general attention. I publish them in the hope that this view may contribute to the moral, aesthetic, and spiritual awakening by which men and women could alone prove themselves worthy of what many of our ancestors believed to be their divine origin.

JOHN NEF

May 20, 1963

Contents

Mining and Metallurgy in Medieval Society

1

Introductory: Mining and Metallurgy
in Medieval Society

Nature endowed Europe with extraordinarily varied and abundant mineral resources. The conquest of this underground wealth by the Western peoples has been inseparable from the unprecedented power obtained by men in recent centuries over the physical world.[1]

This power has come from the solution of technical problems which earlier civilizations had never seriously faced. Many of these problems first became acute in connection with mining and metallurgy. Three examples will perhaps suffice. It was the search for adequate means of draining coal pits that led to the practical use of the force contained in jets of steam, to the invention of the steam engine. As the quantities of minerals dug out of the earth increased, their bulky character exerted increasing pressure on men's minds to discover cheaper methods of carrying them over land and water. It was the difficulty of hauling ores and coal in wagons along rough, soggy ground that led to the invention and development of the railway. The demand for larger quantities of metal for use in war as well as in peace pressed men on to discover methods of treating ores which would reduce the labor and the waste involved in separating and obtaining metals. It was the persistence of western Europeans in exploiting a discovery which had been made by earlier people[2]—that iron ore actually melted when the fires

From *The Cambridge Economic History of Europe,* Vol. II, ed. M. Postan and E. E. Rich (Cambridge, 1952), pp. 430–93. Professors Earl J. Hamilton, the late Ernst Kantorowicz, Charles H. McIlwain, Otto von Simson, Cyril S. Smith, formerly Director of the Institute of Metals at the University of Chicago, and Lynn White of the University of California have generously read this section in typescript and have helped me by their suggestions to improve it. I am deeply grateful to them.

[1] On relations between geography and the origins of industrial civilization, see Nef, *La Naissance de la civilisation industrielle et le monde contemporain* (Paris, 1954), pp. 83–104.

[2] Cf. J. Newton Friend, *Iron in Antiquity* (London, 1926), pp. 92–93, interpreting Pliny, *Natural History,* Bk. XXXIV, chap. xli.

were hot enough—which has produced metal in overwhelming quantities from cascades of liquid flame.

Upon this abundance the great industrial expansion of modern times partly depended. Had it not been for cheap iron and steel, the twentieth-century European might be giving his fiancée an iron ring as a token of their engagement, as Pliny tells us was still the custom in the rich Roman world of the first century.[3] Had it not been for the general use of coal fuel, which was no less novel than the production of large quantities of iron, the expansion of heavy industry could hardly have taken place. Fresh technical problems raised by the demand for minerals aroused the curiosity of natural scientists. Modern mining and metallurgy offered them new materials for speculative thought and experiment. Modern mining and metallurgy were among the many sources which helped to lead their minds in new directions, hitherto unexplored. Again and again their general scientific discoveries have provided theoretical foundations without which many of the technical industrial achievements of the modern world that have dazzled and also bewildered mankind would have been impossible. Indirectly, therefore, as well as directly, the development of the mining and metallurgical industries has contributed to the triumph of industrial civilization.

Early in the seventeenth century Bacon and Descartes dreamed of a paradise of material plenty. Without the treasures of the subsoil and the attraction they exercised on men's minds, these dreams would hardly have approached fulfilment at the beginning of the twentieth century.

The rich endowment of Asia and North America, as well as western Europe, with mineral resources obviously presented novel challenges to human ingenuity. But such challenges come to nothing unless someone is challenged. Vast mineral resources are now known to have been present in many parts of the earth for thousands of years. In China, moreover, a remarkable exploitation of iron ore and coal occurred in the tenth and eleventh centuries A.D., under the Sung dynasty. It failed to lead, as a somewhat similar exploitation of such resources in late sixteenth- and seventeenth-century Great Britain was destined to lead, to the triumph of industrial civilization.[4] The earlier inhabitants of Europe and North America, even the highly civilized peoples of the ancient classical world, showed little disposition to *ransack* the subsoil for these underground riches. Their existence was more a condition of the conquest of the material world than a cause for it. How did it happen that the western Europeans were the first to respond to the challenge? Why have they been less reluctant than earlier

[3] Pliny, *Natural History,* Bk. XXXIII, chap. i.
[4] I owe this information to Robert M. Hartwell who is (1963) getting his Doctor's degree with the Committee on Social Thought of the University of Chicago. His thesis is entitled "Iron and Early Industrialism in Eleventh Century China."

civilized peoples to rob the earth of its treasures? A history of the efforts to exploit mineral resources in Europe during the thousand years which ended with the Reformation is a necessary prelude to any attempt to answer such questions. How far had the technical skill and economic enterprise developed among the medieval Europeans made inevitable the phenomenal progress in modern times of mining and metallurgy, which has been an essential element in the rise of industrial civilization?

THE INDUSTRIES IN CLASSICAL TIMES

At hundreds of places in Europe seams of ores containing gold and silver, copper, lead, and zinc, tin and iron, as well as seams of coal, once broke through the surface, or lay hidden at such short depths that builders uncovered them in digging foundations, if they had not been already disclosed by the plow of some husbandman.

Some of these ores had been exploited long before the Roman conquests. A growing recognition of the value of the seams, and of the course that they followed below the surface, led miners to sink shafts and to discover further treasure at greater depths. Already in the fifth and fourth centuries B.C., thousands of workpeople, mostly slaves, were employed in mining and working the famous silver-bearing lead ore on the mountain of Laurion near Athens. A few of the pits reached down three hundred feet or more into the earth. The slopes and valleys in the neighborhood were full of men washing, breaking, and preparing the ore, or separating the silver from the lead. During the Hellenistic period of the third and second centuries mining operations were pursued with increased vigor in some of the lands surrounding the Mediterranean, so that the Romans found metallurgical enterprises in nearly all the countries they conquered.

It is not possible to determine whether the Roman conquests and the founding of the Roman Empire slowed down this progress. In any event progress continued in the sense that the production of metals went on increasing at least for several generations. Many mines were opened in Spain, Britain, Gaul, and in the Alpine regions south of the river Danube. What was lacking was the zeal, which eventually took possession of western Europeans, for driving on into the earth regardless of the cost. Like the Greeks, the Romans generally had little scientific knowledge of the nature of minerals. Many well-educated men thought that they grew like plants,[5] a view which persisted even among the intelligentsia in Europe into the eighteenth century. In 1709 the French *intendant* at Lyons actually consoled the *contrôleur-général* for the exhaustion of the surface coal at St.

---

[5] Maurice Besnier, "L'interdiction du travail des mines en Italie," *Revue archéologique*, 5th ser., X (1919), 37–38.

Etienne by telling him that these mines had "the happy property of reproducing themselves"! [6]

In classical times mining was generally regarded as a much less desirable occupation than agriculture. A law was passed by the Roman Republic, probably toward the end of the second century B.C., prohibiting the digging of ores in Italy. Modern authorities disagree about the circumstances that led to this particular enactment. It seems to reflect the distaste felt by classical peoples for labor underground, and their preference for agrarian pursuits.

As century followed century across a millennium of history in the Mediterranean lands, the readily accessible surface ores were eventually largely exhausted in the populous parts of the Roman Empire. The exhaustion of the more easily worked seams added continually to the arduous and distasteful nature of the miners' work. The difficulties of sinking shafts, draining off water, and raising ore to the surface were forever multiplying. While the classical peoples were frequently ingenious in devising machinery, they were backward about harnessing the strength of animals, of flowing streams (which were scarce and subject to drought), and even of the wind to drive it. Little wonder if labor in the mines seemed more and more intolerable. Convicts and Christians were deported to work them.[7] As a consequence of these difficulties, the costs of mining in manpower, even with slave labor, drove up the prices of the ores and the metals made from them and discouraged their extensive use.

To a modern man who has visited the coalfields of Belgium, South Wales, or Pennsylvania, with the mountains of black earth beside the shafts, or who has seen the skies aflame for miles from the fires of blast furnaces in the Ruhr, the English Midlands, or northwestern Indiana, the mines and forges of the Roman Empire would not have seemed impressive. Together with the quarries, they formed "merely small islands in a sea of fields and meadows." [8]

According to the criteria of a modern European all metals were scarce. Metal was the material of many statues, but it was never the basis for constructing ships, aqueducts, public buildings, theaters, or stadiums. It was used as sparingly as possible in making tools and machinery. Iron was almost always obtained by prolonged and patient heating in a forge fire, followed by reiterated heatings and hammerings on the anvil. Small-scale operations alone were possible and much of the iron present in the ore was lost as slag and scale. The process was very costly in firewood, char-

[6] A. M. de Boislisle, *Correspondance des contrôleurs généraux . . . avec les intendants* (Paris, 1897), Vol. III, No. 496.

[7] Evidence of this is to be found in the early litanies, Professor Kantorowicz told me.

[8] M. Rostovtzeff, *The Social and Economic History of the Roman Empire* (Oxford, 1926), p. 296.

coal, and labor. Lead was preferred to iron whenever it could serve, because less fuel was needed to produce it. Bronze and brass were derived from copper, tin, zinc, and their ores, all of which required less heat in smelting than iron ore. The greatest development of manufacturing in classical times occurred in regions bordering the Mediterranean, which were exceedingly poor in coal resources compared with the north of Europe or North America, and where the climate was very warm in summer and relatively mild in winter so that less fuel was required for heating rooms. Partly on account of these conditions, no attempt was made, except perhaps in Roman Britain, to substitute coal for firewood and charcoal either for domestic fuel or in industry. As the price of wood rose under the pressure of growing population and expanding industry, metallurgy and every other kind of manufacture requiring fuel was discouraged. Without the wholesale use of coal, oil, and hydroelectric power, without also the preliminary use of abundant wood from the thick forests of northern Europe and America, industrial changes similar to those which transformed the Western world before the middle of the twentieth century were impossible.

THE COURSE OF PRODUCTION C.300–C.1330

A decline in the output of metal began in Europe in the third century. At first it was probably slight, but it continued for hundreds of years. From the end of the sixth century until the end of the tenth, ores were taken at much shallower depths than those that had been often reached in classical times. More primitive methods of working the mines prevailed. Gone were the long shafts such as had been occasionally sunk, for example in the neighborhood of Cartagena in Spain, to depths of five or six hundred feet. Gone also—buried in debris—were pits forty feet or more in depth, such as had been fairly common during the second century. All the more ambitious mines of the Roman Empire in the West were eventually abandoned. They disappeared from the sight of the local villagers, to be rediscovered only during the last hundred years by modern archaeologists in the course of their excavations. With the decline in the population of Europe, which began after the third century, with the accompanying decay of towns, the shrinkage of trade, and the reduction of the acreage under cultivation, the descendants of the ancient inhabitants, and the Germanic invaders who settled among them, contented themselves with such ores as could be won near their village huts, mostly in the remnants of old workings accessible without the sinking of shafts. Efforts to find new seams at considerable depths ceased. In many places, forests, cut down in Roman times, grew again.

The output of iron diminished less than that of other metals. Iron was still needed by woodsmen and husbandmen for axes, knives, and spades, and even for plowshares in a few places where a knowledge of Roman methods of plowing was preserved. Iron was wanted, above all, for weapons. As it was the most abundant of the ores dug during the Middle Ages, it could generally be had with less effort than ores containing silver, lead, copper, or tin. At many places in Gaul, the Rhineland, Saxony, Bohemia, and Tuscany, and especially in Spain and possibly on the slopes and along the valleys of the eastern Alps,[9] iron in small quantities was produced throughout the early Middle Ages.[10] An increase in iron output began after the eighth century, in the Carolingian age.[11] At the end of the ninth century iron was an item of some prominence in the exports of Venice to the sophisticated Near East.[12] Its production probably increased considerably at this time, at least in the eastern Alps.

There is, by contrast, little trace in historical records of mining for copper ore between the beginning of the sixth and the end of the tenth centuries. Brass, an alloy of copper and calamine, the ore of zinc, seems to have gone largely out of use until the discovery of deposits of calamine in the Alps and the north of Europe during the fifteenth century. Bronze, an alloy in which copper is the main element, is historically the oldest of the metals to be extensively used. It was used concurrently with iron, often for the same purposes. The paucity of early medieval references to copper suggests that iron may have been taking the place of bronze to a considerable extent. It would be unreasonable to suppose, however, that the demand for bronze ceased for an extended period, or that the medieval Europeans ever lost touch altogether with the copper ores needed to supply it.

According to Tacitus, one of the considerations that prompted the Claudian invasion of England in the middle of the first century was the mineral wealth. There was perhaps no part of the Empire in which mining occupied as prominent a place in industrial life as in Roman Britain. Other provinces had more impressive mines. But the relative importance of mining in Britain, not one of the most populous provinces, was great when compared with the Empire generally. In Britain, lead ore, some of which contained silver, seems to have been worked more extensively than any other mineral. The ancient tin mines of Cornwall were revived by the

[9] There is some dispute as to whether iron was worked continuously in the eastern Alps. The principal authority on iron mining in Styria argues that when the Slavs settled this area in the sixth and seventh centuries, ironwork was abandoned (L. Bittner, "Das Eisenwesen in Innerberg-Eisenerz," *Archiv für österreichische Geschichte,* LXXXIX [1901], 458–59). But a later writer, who studied the ironmaking industry in Carniola, raises what seem to be weighty objections to this thesis (Alfons Müllner, *Geschichte des Eisens in Krain, Görz und Istrien* [Vienna, 1909], pp. 112–13).

[10] Cf. Ludwig Beck, *Die Geschichte des Eisens* (2d ed.; Brunswick, 1890–1903), I, 703 ff., 728–39.

[11] As Dr. White suggested to me. See also Ed. Salin and Alt. France-Lanord, *Le Fer à l'époque mérovingienne* (Paris, 1943).

[12] H. Pirenne, *Economic and Social History of Medieval Europe,* trans. I. E. Clegg (New York, 1937), p. 18.

Romans in the third century; copper was worked in Shropshire and Wales; iron in many places. The rich and abundant mines of coal were dug, it seems, in a number of the fields where they poked their way close to the surface.[13]

Neither the mining of tin nor of lead ore was abandoned altogether in Great Britain after the Saxon conquests of the fifth and sixth centuries, although these conquests were apparently followed by an eclipse of copper ore and coal mining. A more or less steady demand for lead, both in England and in most Continental countries, continued after the barbarian invasions, because of the use made of it in roofing the churches which were always being built, or at least repaired, during ages when the hold of Christianity tightened on all the European peoples.

In spite of the continued use of metal in small quantities, it is probable that the European production of gold, silver, copper, lead, and tin had shrunk by the early ninth century, after the Muslim conquests. Farmers of the imperial revenues from mines in Hadrian's reign, if they could have been brought back to life six centuries afterwards on the eve of the Carolingian period, might have been shocked to find how small was the yield of ores and metals. The mining districts which they had known in prosperous times might have seemed almost deserts. Pliny might have deplored the loss of interest in natural history, which had been associated by the classical peoples partly with mining and metallurgy, though he would perhaps have applauded the reluctance of men to raid underground treasure which in his eyes bred mainly luxury and vice.

The growth in the output of iron, which seems to have begun in the eastern Alps before the end of the ninth century, if not earlier, was followed in the last half of the tenth by more general progress in mining and metallurgy especially in Germany. Several new mines were discovered there. The most famous were the rich copper mines and silver-bearing lead ores of the once thickly wooded Rammelsberg, the fine hill that rises some twelve hundred feet above the town of Goslar in the Harz. In German the same word was used for miner as for mountaineer. During the eleventh and twelfth centuries mining became primarily an Alpine occupation. In the Harz, the Vosges, the Jura, and especially in the eastern Alps, the working of gold, silver, lead, copper, and iron grew in importance. After the middle of the twelfth century progress was intensified and the new interest in mining spread to other regions.

The first great period in the history of mining among the Western peo-

[13] The late Professor Collingwood accepted the evidence of modern archaeologists as proof that coal was rather extensively worked in Britain during the Roman period (R. G. Collingwood and J. N. L. Myres, *Roman Britain and the English Settlements* [2d ed.; Oxford, 1937], pp. 231–32). No other scholar gives coal in Roman times so much importance (cf. M. Rostovtzeff, *The Social and Economic History of the Hellenistic World* [Oxford, 1941], III, 1615).

ples began around 1170, with the discovery of the rich silver-bearing ores of Freiberg in Saxony. It continued until the fourteenth century. If statistics of output existed, they would probably show that during a stretch of 150 years or so there were few decades in which the production of minerals and metals in Europe failed to increase substantially.

In cultural and intellectual history this period is one of the most brilliant in the annals of Europe. The achievements were summed up in the wonderful romanesque and gothic churches. These monuments were the expression of Europe's common form of worship, at a time when the whole of life centered about religious life. The twelfth and thirteenth centuries, like the eighteenth and nineteenth, were times of extraordinary hope and extraordinary economic and social progress in which the whole of Europe shared. The hope was of a different kind, and the directions which progress took in the earlier period were less material. The efforts of the twelfth- and thirteenth-century Europeans culminated in the great cathedrals with their spires, some of which, especially in the North, seemed almost to pierce the heavens. But even structures symbolizing a transcendental conception of the destiny of man require much concrete material to build.

The increase in the production of silver, gold, and less valuable metals contributed to the growth of wealth, partly by increasing the supply of money but mainly by adding to the material available for industrial purposes. A prodigious expansion of agrarian and industrial production, combined with an even more remarkable growth of trade, transformed the economic face of western Europe between the late eleventh and the fourteenth centuries. The growth of mineral wealth helps to explain how it was possible for the people of the thirteenth century to create such magnificent and costly monuments in stone and to embellish them with equally wonderful work in glass and metal. The growth of wealth also made possible greater leisure. This facilitated the remarkable philosophical speculations which were the chief glory of the medieval universities.

How strong an influence had the expansion of mining and metallurgy upon the evolving European society from the eleventh to the fourteenth centuries? The influence apparently seemed indirect and remote to most medieval writers. Few of them mentioned it in the works they composed. Albertus Magnus, with his German background, was apparently the only famous thinker who talked much about the metallurgical development of his age. He wrote with enthusiasm of the fine quality of the silver from the great mines discovered at Freiberg shortly before his birth. The most striking progress in mining of all kinds, particularly of silver-bearing ores, took place on the frontiers of western European development, away from the chief centers of cultural and economic life. Paris and the Île-de-France, the focus from which the culture of the thirteenth century radiated, were greatly favored by nature. But their riches were of the soil rather than the subsoil.

Modern historians are often prone to read back into history conditions far more applicable to their own age than to the age about which they are writing. The progress in mining was perhaps less a cause for the economic development of medieval Europe than a result of it. Yet in the mystery of the historical process, cause and effect are so intertwined that the positive conception of them that the modern mind has derived from the natural sciences is hardly of service to truth.

Among the driving forces behind the discovery and the development of mining were the increase in population and the growth in tillage, trade, and industry. Not until after 1750, not perhaps until after 1785, were the western European peoples again to grow in numbers at as rapid a rate as during most of the twelfth and thirteenth centuries. The area of cultivation and pasturage was extended in every direction, especially into wooded, hilly, and mountainous country, hitherto sparsely populated. Frequently the plow of a husbandman struck against one of the outcropping seams of iron ore or coal with which the northern parts of Europe were so plentifully supplied. The location of more valuable ores was disclosed by the violence of nature in the forests, the Alpine valleys, and even on the slopes of high peaks. When the snows melted, rushing torrents overflowed their banks to strip off surface land and lay bare treasure underneath. Seams of rich ore were also revealed when a great wind uprooted trees, when lightning splintered rocks, or when an avalanche tore its path down some mountain side. As settlers and traveling traders streamed into the uplands and penetrated the woodlands, there were more eyes to watch these accidents, which encouraged prospectors to probe the earth for minerals. The increasing curiosity about the material world and the increasing agricultural, commercial, industrial, and artistic needs for gold, silver, iron, lead, copper, tin, and alloys of these metals made men eager to explore beneath the soil, to examine, and to exploit the substances they found. Not until the eve of the Reformation, when fresh waves of settlers pushed into the same regions, was there another comparable movement of exploration and discovery.

This newly aroused curiosity accounts for the rapid growth of the silver mines at Freiberg in the late twelfth century. Traders carrying salt happened on some argentiferous lead ore where the spring floods had washed away the earth. They took a sample to Goslar to compare with the famous ores from the Rammelsberg. Their sample yielded a larger quantity and a finer grade of silver than those. As news of their discovery spread, adventurers in considerable numbers, with picks and shovels, hurried to Freiberg. They came in a spirit of adventure not altogether unlike that of the Americans who migrated to California in the gold rush of the mid-nineteenth century.

In the late twelfth and thirteenth centuries traders and colonizers everywhere were on the lookout for ores, and especially for ores containing silver or gold. Rich veins lay waiting for them near the surface, chiefly in Central Europe. Such ores as could be readily reached were especially abundant north of the Danube—in Saxony, Bohemia, Silesia, and Hungary. The lands containing them had lain for the most part beyond the borders of the Roman Empire. Partly no doubt on that account there had been relatively little mining here in Roman times. In the Middle Ages these regions—together with greater Austria, the Harz, and the Black Forest—assumed a position of dominance in mining, like that of the Iberian Peninsula in classical times. They supplied all Europe with silver, copper, and small quantities of gold. On the slopes and along the valleys of the eastern Alps, the Carpathians, the Erzgebirge, and the Sudeten Mountains, the thick woods provided abundant lumber for building, firewood, and charcoal for fuel needed in preparing ores for the smelters, in separating them from the worthless material with which they were intermingled, and in converting them to metals. The rushing brooks and streams, in which these regions abounded, were hardly less helpful than the woods. As will appear, they came to provide the force to drive machinery that crushed and hammered the materials or blew air upon the fires. From the beginning the abundant water courses facilitated the washing away of dirt and impurities; the ore was dressed in artfully constructed containers, made to settle the heavy minerals and to remove the lighter rocky matter.

German emigrants, some of whom were bent on mining, were pushing into regions held by Slavs and Magyars in the great colonizing movement toward the east and southeast, which brought Walloons and Flemings into Saxony and Frenchmen into the western Rhineland. It was not only in eastern and southern Germany, it was in almost all Central Europe that the Germans took the leading part in mining. The movements to colonize and to mine went hand in hand. One of the strongest attractions for German settlers was the glitter of precious metals.

Ores near the surface containing silver and gold were fewer and less fruitful west of the Rhine and the Alps. It was partly the accidents of nature that made Germans, rather than other Western peoples, the leaders in mining and metallurgy from the twelfth to the sixteenth centuries. Traveling traders and explorers in France, England, and the Low Countries were no less eager to discover ores containing precious metal. Kings, princes, bishops, and other great landlords in western Europe were not backward in encouraging prospectors. Where silver-bearing ores were discovered, as in Devon and Alsace, they were exploited as vigorously as in Central Europe.

While the search for precious metal had a special fascination for the Europeans throughout the later Middle Ages, the demand for minerals of every kind grew rapidly with the rapid growth of population, industry, and trade. The boom in mining extended to ores containing only base metals—copper, lead, tin, and iron. It extended also to coal. In the digging of coal and base ores other than copper, the Germans had no such dominance as in the digging of ores rich in silver or gold. Even in copper mining by the beginning of the fourteenth century, the mines of Stora Kopparberg in Sweden, developed under German influence, had come to rival those of the Rammelsberg. The English mines of lead ore—in Somerset, Durham, Cumberland, Shropshire, Flintshire, and above all in Derbyshire—grew increasingly prosperous during the thirteenth century, and a flourishing export trade in lead developed. Lead production in England rivaled that in Central Europe. The Continent was as dependent on Devon and Cornwall for its tin as it was on Saxony and Bohemia for its silver and gold. During the last half of the twelfth century the annual output of tin in southwestern England, mostly from Devon, apparently increased nearly fivefold. The early fourteenth century was another time of rapid progress, especially in Cornwall, where the output in 1338 was more than double that in 1301. In the 1330's production in the two counties together apparently reached seven hundred tons in good years. Since the middle of the twelfth century it had increased approximately tenfold. The figures of output for the 1330's were not regularly surpassed until the last half of the seventeenth century.[14]

As the supplies of iron ore were not localized like the supplies of scarcer minerals, there was no such concentration of population about the iron mines as about some mines of argentiferous lead ores, copper ores, and tin. But the medieval people wanted iron in much larger quantities during the great age of gothic building, which lasted from the early twelfth to the early fourteenth century. More iron was needed than before for plowshares and other farm implements, for tools, axles, cauldrons, and other accessories in the expanding industries, for anchors, keels, and nails in shipbuilding, for horseshoes, bits, and stirrups, and for armor, spears, swords, and daggers, which were used ferociously by our ancestors in their fighting in those times of often ruthless physical violence. Ironmaking prospered all over Europe. An international traffic in iron developed. Styria, Carinthia, the Basque provinces of Biscay, and Guipuzcoa in Spain, and, to a lesser extent, Hungary, Sweden, and Westphalia were the principal exporting countries. Iron was carried thence on packhorses and in carts, in river barges and in ships, especially to the most populous and civilized parts of Europe—to Italy, northern France, and the Low Countries.

All these regions had iron ore; so the imports of iron served only to supplement the local supplies. Italy produced much of its own iron, and additional supplies came from the island of Elba across the water to the rich and populous Tuscany, where at the turn of the thirteenth and fourteenth centuries building and manufacturing were pushed further perhaps than anywhere else in Europe. Both in England and in the provinces which were to form modern France small forges multiplied, especially in the

[14] G. R. Lewis, *The Stannaries* (Cambridge, Mass., 1907), pp. 252–55.

wooded uplands, to supply the needs of the neighboring towns and villages. These tiny mills required very little capital. It was not difficult for the iron-makers to pick up their equipment when they had thinned out the immediately surrounding woods for charcoal and move on to new clusters of trees. There were, in addition, some more important centers of production, with rather larger forges—Piedmont, the Forest of Dean, upper Champagne, Lorraine, and Dauphiné. Wrought iron was carried thence for longer distances to serve multitudes of smiths and artistic craftsmen.

In spite of the growing prosperity of the ironmaking industry, iron was produced even at the beginning of the fourteenth century in quantities which seem to us, in the present great age of iron and steel, almost negligible. The annual output of all the forges in Styria, a leading ironmaking center in Europe, probably seldom exceeded two thousand tons.[15] At the beginning of the twentieth century a single furnace produced more in a few hours. Iron remained a valuable commodity in the Middle Ages. It was hardly less scarce than in the early Roman Empire. At a time when ever larger multitudes of town craftsmen were learning to make use in new ways of every available material which could serve in fashioning religious images and other works of art, it was natural that so rare a substance as iron, which, in its finer varieties, as prepared in charcoal fires, was not only durable but lustrous, should have been in demand hardly less for aesthetic than for utilitarian purposes. Fine iron was wanted for grills and other decorative work, especially in connection with the cathedrals, churches, abbeys, and priories which were going up everywhere in the rising cities and towns, in old villages, and in hosts of new settlements. Skilful craftsmen also used iron to fashion for laymen fine window grills, entrance keys and locks, knockers, and decorations for strong boxes. As Roger Bacon explained, iron was made into charms designed to drive away evil spirits.

For the generation brought up in the early twentieth century, and accustomed to an annual output in Europe of several hundred million tons, the use of coal in the thirteenth century will seem as insignificant as the use of iron. But the generations who lived in the lands surrounding the Mediterranean during the first three centuries of the Christian era might have found the use of coal, unlike the use of iron, almost entirely novel. While its burning properties were not unknown in classical times, no systematic attempt was made to dig coal out of the earth except perhaps in Roman Britain. Authentic records of its use in Europe before the last decade of the twelfth century have not been discovered, though extensive recourse had been had to this black mineral in parts of China during the tenth and eleventh centuries. Beginning in Europe in the thirteenth century records of the use of coal abound. They provide further evidence of the mounting

---

[15] The output could hardly have been greater than it was a hundred and fifty years later, in the sixties of the fifteenth century (see below, n. 62).

prosperity which was bringing larger quantities of metal into circulation and use. The burning of coal followed the great expansion in building and in ironworking and was in large measure caused by it. In spite of protests against the dirt and the noxious smells generated by coal fires, when wood and charcoal grew dear the limeburner and those smiths who made the cruder ironwares turned to coal when it could be had nearby from out-cropping seams. These were found at a great many places. During the thirteenth century the local inhabitants began to dig shallow pits in nearly all the coalfields of England, Scotland, and the Low Countries, as well as in the neighborhood of Aix-la-Chapelle, in Franche-Comté, Lyonnais, Forez, Alais, and Anjou.

The chief centers for coal mining were in the Low Countries at Liège and Mons, and in the north of England. The traditional reputation of New-castle as the inexhaustible source of supplies dates from this age. Coal be-gan to be loaded into ships leaving the Tyne. It served as ballast in place of the bags of sand usually carried by medieval vessels. It found a small market among smiths and limeburners at London and, in smaller quantities, at other ports along the eastern and southern coasts of England and the northern coasts of the Continent, particularly in the Low Countries. There industry throve at the end of the thirteenth century hardly less than in Tuscany and northern Italy in the times of Dante and Giotto.

LAWS AND CUSTOMS OF MEDIEVAL MINING

As the situation of mines and metallurgical works was determined by the whereabouts of accessible ores and, to a lesser extent, by the whereabouts of woodlands and swiftly moving streams, the organization of mining and metallurgy from the twelfth to the early fourteenth centuries presents fea-tures which mark these industries off from the other rising medieval crafts. While clothmaking and the making of leather wares were usually the direct concern only of the towns, mining and metallurgy affected every political authority and every kind of country landholder from the emperor to the meanest serf.

The increasing need for revenue felt by almost all overlords, lay and ecclesiastical, provided them with a motive for throwing open the mines in their territories to all comers and for claiming as large a share as possible of the output. By establishing mints to coin silver and later gold, and by ordering the mining communities in the interest of their treasuries, some princes added greatly to their wealth and political power.

In feudal times, emperors, kings, popes, bishops, and numerous other lesser overlords exercised political authority in varying degrees. The origin of their claims to dispose of mines under private lands subject to their authority (the Bergregal) is obscure. It was certainly not Roman but feudal.

Regalian rights to mines, like regalian rights to coin silver money, were not recognized in western Europe before the tenth or even the eleventh century. The new claims probably had much to do with the remarkable growth in mining, particularly in the mining of silver-bearing ores which were needed for coinage. As claims to the *regale* were frequently limited, especially until after the thirteenth century, to ores containing gold or silver, there is a temptation to assume that one source of the regalian rights may have been the idea, later set forth in favor of these rights in the English "case of mines", in 1566, that the overlord had a special title as the most excellent person to the most excellent things within his territorial dominions.[16] As will be seen in a moment, there is solider ground for suggesting that the mining *regale* grew at least partly out of the claims of feudal overlords to dispose of waste land and "treasure trove" or hidden treasure.[17]

During the twelfth and thirteenth centuries European overlords were claiming with much success the right to dispose of ores containing gold or silver (then won mainly from seams of argentiferous lead ore), and in some cases of tin and copper ore as well, both in their own lands and in those of their subjects. When the mines were worked, they claimed a share in the produce. This share generally included a settled portion of the ore or metal, frequently a tenth. In addition the overlords usually received coinage duties; they often had the right of pre-emption over the entire output of the best metal, i.e., a right to buy all of it at a lower price than that which it might have commanded if sold on the open market. But as their interest was to have the mines worked, and as they seldom cared to bear the risks of operating them, there were practical limits to their demands. They could not afford to be exorbitant. Their claims to revenue were frequently reduced to meet the increased costs which the miners had to undergo in sinking, draining, and ventilating the pits.

During the last half of the twelfth century, and possibly even earlier, when the political authority of the German emperor was theoretically very great, the emperors pressed their claims to share throughout the Empire in the revenue of all mines producing silver or gold. At Roncaglia, Frederick Barbarossa (1155–89) claimed the *regale* as an attribute of imperial sovereignty.[18] The revival of Roman law was used as a basis for applying attributes of the Roman imperial authority to feudal conditions, for asserting that feudal overlordship everywhere belonged to the emperor. The em-

---

[16] Edmund Plowden, *The Commentaries or Reports* (1818 ed.), pp. 310 ff.; cf. Sir John Pettus, *Fodinae Regales* (1670), pp. 28–29.

[17] Cf. Adam Smith, *Wealth of Nations*, Bk. II, chap. i.

[18] P. W. Finsterwalder, "Die Gesetze des Reichstags von Roncalia von 11 November 1158," *Zeitschrift der Savigny Stiftung für Rechtsgeschichte*, Germanistische Abteilung, XLI (1931), 43–45, 62–69, a reference called to my attention by Professor Kantorowicz. I am indebted to him and to Professor McIlwain for helping me to understand the origin of the mining *regale*. If I have not got matters right, the fault is mine.

perors sought, not without opposition, to make the *Bergregal* a sovereign *regale*, as they tried unsuccessfully to make the *Münzregal,* or right of coinage.[19] They tried to establish the principle that the power to grant concessions for mining ores containing precious metals was exclusively imperial. As it was usually interpreted, that principle put the emperors under an obligation to set up an imperial administration for regulating the labor and the community life of the free men who came to try their luck with their picks and shovels. The emperors treated this participation in the administration of mining, along with their claim to a revenue from the mines, as attributes of sovereign authority, distinguished from those rights which went with the tenure of landed estates. According to this doctrine, no lord of the soil could have valuable minerals dug within his lands without the permission of the emperor. In case the emperor had delegated his authority to an overlord, the overlord's permission was required.

After the death of Barbarossa, the political powers of the emperors diminished throughout the Holy Roman Empire and especially in Germany. Territorial sovereign rights were increasingly split up among their chief vassals. As Charles IV made clear in his famous Golden Bull of 1356, the emperors relinquished their regalian rights to mines whenever they relinquished their sovereign authority. Regalian rights went with lordship of territories. This did not prevent a territorial prince, if he chose, from investing certain of his vassals, or even his rear vassals, with his regalian rights. He could do so while he retained the general authority which went with territorial lordship. In this way, he could rid himself of the obligation to oversee mines in many regions, at a time when mining enterprises were multiplying very rapidly. The emperors, the kings of Bohemia, the dukes of Silesia, and other princes of the Empire all took advantage of this opportunity to delegate their mining responsibilities. In consequence the number of overlords exercising regalian (or even sovereign) rights in Central Europe was continually growing. On the eve of the Reformation, the bishops, dukes, margraves, counts, and independent towns possessing these rights could be counted by dozens.

The unwary are likely to assume that the regalian authority of the territorial princes in the Empire was more extensive than was actually the case. In the fourteenth century few holders of the *regale* had successfully put forward a claim to base ores in the lands of private owners (*Grundherren*) within their territorial dominions. Someone, however, had to assume responsibility for orderly mining and for settling disputes between groups of miners, at a time when mining was still carried on largely by small bands of workpeople who claimed a share in the ownership of the ores by virtue of the technical ingenuity they exercised and the manual labor they per-

[19] F. von Schrötter, *Wörterbüch der Munzkunde* (Berlin, 1930), pp. 430–32.

formed. Where base ores were dug in considerable quantities in privately owned lands, the lord of the soil frequently took the place of the territorial lord. Like the territorial lord, he set up a mining administration and shared in the produce of the mines or the revenue from them.

Coal invariably and iron ore generally were treated as the property of the landlord. In the margravate of Meissen, which included the rich mines of Freiberg, the lords of the soil also retained the authority to work tin, lead, and copper ore without the permission of the margrave. In Bohemia the kings generally limited their claims to ores containing substantial quantities of gold or silver. Consequently much mining was carried on during the twelfth and thirteenth centuries outside the *regale*.

We are here frequently in the presence of a valid distinction which masks the reality. The territorial lord was always a private landlord as well. Within the territorial jurisdiction over which he ruled were estates that belonged to him directly. As it happened, a large part of the ores dug in Central Europe during the thirteenth century were in mountainous country, and so in wasteland, in no-man's land. Territorial princes claimed such land as part of their demesne. This gave them adequate authority as private landlords to dispose of many base ores in the same way as they disposed, by virtue of their sovereign rights, of ores containing precious metal.

What was the position of a private landlord, who was not a territorial prince, when mines were worked in his soil under the authority of his overlord? His obligations were heavy, but he often had in return certain advantages. Such a landlord was obliged to allow the miners and smelters who obtained concessions from the overlord access to the ore. He was obliged, when necessary, to provide these workpeople with land for their cottages, their mills, and their forges. In addition, the miners and smelters were frequently given parts of his land for farming and for pasture. They were allowed to use the streams for washing their ore and driving their mills. They were generally entitled to take from his manor or lordship at least a part of the lumber that they needed for building, together with fuel for their kilns and furnaces.

The miners and smelters had to pay for these privileges. The landlords received compensation for the use of their lands and for any damage done to them. Sometimes they shared with the regalian lord in the royalty on the produce of the mines containing precious metal. There were cases, for example in Bohemia, where the landlords appointed mining officials of their own to care for their interests. Two mining administrations, those of the territorial lord and of the lord of the soil, operated concurrently.

The problems arising out of mining operations, which called for settlement by administrative, legislative, and judicial procedures, were in fact almost endless. Much of the work of mining and producing metal was carried on in soil held by tenants of the landlord. These tenants were entitled to compensation when mining and metallurgical operations touched their actual holdings of arable and pasture land. There was no aspect of medieval life—economic, political, cultural, or religious—which was not affected by these expanding industries.

In the other countries of Continental Europe, and in Great Britain and Scandinavia, the medieval laws and customs concerning the ownership and the working of mines resembled those in the Empire. But the division of the sovereign authority after the twelfth century, characteristic of Central Europe, was by no means the rule during the later Middle Ages.

In France the process was reversed, in the sense that the supreme political authority—the French crown—was continually gaining in actual power throughout the realm. With the revival of Roman law, the legitimatization of illegitimate children was treated as a sovereign, i.e., an imperial, right. In 1205, a decretal of Pope Innocent III declared that this power of legitimatization belonged to the French king, Philip Augustus (1180–1223), within his dominions. Not long afterwards lawyers began to interpret the decretal as evidence that the French king was emperor in his realm—"Rex est imperator in regno suo." [20]

During and after the reign of Philip Augustus the French kings steadily encroached upon the independent governing authorities, the principal feudal overlords. When it came to contesting the rights of such lords to dispose of minerals within their ancient jurisdictions, the French kings generally proceeded warily. Compared with the emperors, the great German princes, and the English kings, they were slow in claiming regalian rights over mines in the lands of their vassals. They were slow about insisting upon a royalty from mining operations outside the territories that formed part of their royal demesne.

Their caution resulted partly from the strength possessed by some of the greater noblemen, foremost among whom were the Dukes of Burgundy, who had already begun to exercise regalian rights over mines. [21] To take the *regale* in France from feudal overlords, who had long exercised it, involved many difficulties. It may be questioned whether such a policy could have been embarked upon as soon as it was, had silver-bearing ores been as plentiful in France as they were in Central Europe. It might even have been necessary for the French kings to decentralize the *regale* as the emperors did. In so large a kingdom as France the administrative machinery required in the form of clerks, technical experts, and judges for regulating mining in many districts would have been beyond the capacity of a medieval ruler to staff. As things were, the French kings seem to have waited until

[20] J. Rivière, *Le Problème de l'église et de l'état* (Louvain, 1926), pp. 424–30, another reference for which I thank Professor Kantorowicz.

[21] Henri Beaune, "Note sur le régime des mines dans le duché de Bourgogne," *Mém. de la société des antiquaires de France*, XXXI (1869), 114–15; *Inventaire sommaire des archives départementales de l'Hérault*, C. Vol. III (1887), 258.

the great expansion in mining and metallurgy of the gothic age was over before acting vigorously. During the early fifteenth century, they set about to deprive French overlords of their mining authority. In 1413 a royal edict was passed making it illegal for any lord but the king to collect the royalty (*dixième*) on the produce of mines.[22] As the strength of the monarchy grew in France, and as administrative, legal, and judicial authority was more and more centralized at the end of the Middle Ages and in early modern times, the crown was able to centralize bit by bit the mining *regale*.

In England, government was centralized earlier than in any continental country, during the two centuries following the Norman conquest of 1066. Except in a few areas, like the Palatinate of Durham, the crown became the undisputed sovereign. In the thirteenth century the regalian rights which the English kings exercised in connection with mines seem hardly to have fallen short of those possessed by the emperor, or by leading princes of the Empire to whom the emperor delegated his sovereign authority. While the English kings showed no disposition to codify the customary laws of the mining communities, as some Central European princes were doing, they successfully claimed the authority to dispose of all gold- and silver-bearing ores in the lands of their subjects and to collect a royalty on the produce of gold and silver mines. While their attempts to extend their regalian rights to include base ores were sporadic and ultimately unsuccessful, they controlled the prosperous stannaries of Devon and Cornwall. In the thirteenth century the authority of the crown over the stannaries hardly fell short of that exercised over mines of silver-bearing ores by the territorial princes in Central Europe, Tuscany, and Sardinia. The privileges of prospectors for, and finders of, ore were at least as great as those usually allowed them on the Continent. Either directly, or through the Prince of Wales as Earl and later as Duke of Cornwall, the crown had the sole power to grant finders of ore and other miners concessions to tin mines in the unenclosed lands of private landlords in Cornwall and, in Devon, in the enclosed lands as well. Miners were free to search for tin in these lands without permission from the landlords.[23] The crown derived a considerable revenue from the coinage duties and from the purchase and sale of tin, which it could buy at an advantageous price by virtue of its right of pre-emption. As lord of the soil, not apparently as sovereign, the king possessed a similar control over some of the richest mines of lead ore in Derbyshire,[24] the leading center for lead mining in the country.

In the thirteenth century the most productive mines of iron ore were

---

[22] *Recueil général des anciennes lois françaises* (Paris, 1825), VII, 386–90.

[23] Cf. Lewis, *The Stannaries*, pp. 158–60; A. K. H. Jenkin, *The Cornish Miner* (London, 1927), p. 32.

[24] Cf. *Victoria County History, Derbyshire*. II, 325–27.

probably those in the Forest of Dean.[25] The crown seems to have claimed successfully a part in the produce of all iron ore and coal mines there, apparently because much of the land belonged to the royal demesne. In other parts of England iron ore and coal were dug independently of the crown in many private lands. Coal and iron ore were then of relatively small importance.

The chief mines in England in the thirteenth century were worked mostly under royal authority. From them the king derived a revenue, either by virtue of his sovereignty or by virtue of his direct possession of soil which formed part of the royal demesne. It was not until the end of the Middle Ages, after the Hundred Years' War, that important differences arose between the mineral rights attaching to overlordship on the Continent and in England. In the thirteenth century the situation respecting the *regale* was much the same in all European countries. The actual authority of the English king over mineral property in his dominion was hardly inferior to that of any prince in Christendom.

While there was an extraordinary diversity in such matters as weights and measures, European societies in the late twelfth and thirteenth centuries had a common unity. Everywhere there was a basic similarity in the manner in which men lived and worked, as well as in the manner in which they worshiped. Conditions in mining and metallurgy were no exception. Whether the minerals were at the disposal of the emperor, a king, a prince or lord, a bishop, or a city council, by virtue of delegated as well as usurped sovereign authority, or at the disposal of the lay or ecclesiastical lord of some manor or vill, by virtue of his property in the land,[26] mining concessions all over Europe resembled one another. When it came to fundamentals, the relations between the miners or smelters and the officials representing the lords were everywhere much the same.

The finder of ore staked out a claim to mine by applying for a concession to the lord's principal officer, generally known in the German mining

[25] Rhys Jenkins, "Iron-making in the Forest of Dean," *Transactions of the Newcomen Society*, VI (1925–26), 46.

[26] There were districts where the power to grant concessions and to order mining operations was vested neither in a sovereign prince nor in a single lord of the soil. In the lead mines of Mendip, in Somerset, the control was in the hands of four prominent local lords, each of whom controlled an area with its own separate officers, its mining code, and its mineral courts (*Mendip Mining Laws and Forest Bounds*, ed. J. W. Gough, "Somerset Record Society Publications," Vol. XLV [London, 1931]). In the coalfield west of Mons, in Hainault, where, as in the silver-mining districts, property in mines was separated from property in the soil, concessions were granted by the local officials charged with the administration of justice—the *seigneurs haut-justiciers* (G. Arnould, *Le bassin houiller du couchant de Mons* [Mons, 1877], p. 22; G. Decamps, *Mémoire historique sur l'origine et les développements de l'industrie houillère . . . de Mons,* Société des Sciences des Arts et des Lettres du Hainaut, Publications, 4th series, V [1880], 58 ff.).

districts of Central Europe as the *Bergmeister*. This officer, or his representative, invested the miner for an indefinite term with the right to exploit a section of the seam or to extract the minerals under a given plot of land. In many districts, especially in Central Europe, it was the custom to divide up the accessible portion of the seam near the surface into a number of small sections (meers), often square and of a size prescribed by local customs. The lord's officers then granted the finder the section that he had discovered and sometimes an additional section. One or more of the other sections was usually reserved for the lord, to be worked for him directly or leased out (a practice analogous to that of treating sections of agricultural land held by tenants in common as part of their lord's demesne). Each of the remaining sections of the seam was granted to a miner, ordinarily to the first applicant. In return for promises to mine continuously, to pay the customary royalties, and to abide by the mining customs of the district as enforced by the lord's officers, the miners had full power to work their concessions.

Wherever the digging and the working of ores were sufficiently important to employ several scores of miners and smelters, little mining communities were formed. These communities were separate from those of the local peasants engaged in tillage and pasture farming. They had their own laws and customs. Such special communities multiplied rapidly in number especially in Central Europe during the late twelfth and thirteenth centuries. They were everywhere the rule in the digging and smelting of silver, gold, copper, tin, and lead ores. In the making of iron they were rather less common. In the mining of coal they were found only in the Low Countries and the Forest of Dean. As coal and iron ore mining were less localized than the mining of more valuable ores, there were only a few places, such as Liège and the Erzberg in Styria, where considerable numbers of persons were engaged in either the coal-mining or the ironmaking industries. Elsewhere the digging of coal for the most part, and in many cases the digging and smelting of iron ore, were undertaken more informally by a few local peasants, working either for themselves or for some lord of the soil, frequently on days when they were not engaged in husbandry. They were subject to the ordinary local laws and customs concerning labor in the fields and forests.

In Central Europe as far as the Balkans, the principal regions of German colonization, the overlords generally threw open to all comers the rights to search for minerals, to mine, and to convert ores to metals. Elsewhere, in western Europe generally, there were many districts in which such rights were restricted to certain local persons who formed a closed body similar to a town gild. Such exclusive groups were obviously better suited to peoples who remained in their native provinces than to colonizers who came from many different regions and settled far from the countries of their origin. Exclusive communities were fairly common in the iron-making industry, especially in France, where they were also formed in other industries dependent on abundant woods for fuel, like the making of crude glass vessels. In the wooded, hilly country about Alençon, in Perche, and upper Normandy, a group of local lords, lay and ecclesiastical, known as *barons fossiers,* were alone entitled to open mines of iron ore or to build iron forges. The actual manual labor of making the charcoal fuel and the iron was in the hands of a corporation of *férons.* Admission was limited to the sons and sons-in-law of members.[27]

There were other cases in which the right to work (and indeed to own) mines was restricted to people living in a certain area. In the eastern Pyrenees no one could search for or exploit iron ore on the mountain of Rancié unless he was an inhabitant of the valley of Vicdessos.[28] Similar restrictions existed in at least one English mining district. Only persons born in the hundred of St. Briavels, who had worked with their picks for a year and a day, were eligible to obtain concessions from the king's gaveller to parts in the seams of iron ore or coal within the Forest of Dean.[29]

Whether or not the communities were exclusive, the social status of the miners and metallurgical workers was generally as high as that of the citizens in the rising towns. In the twelfth and thirteenth centuries settlement in the towns offered a means of escape from serfdom. During this age of growing population, peasants became free by taking up the profession of mining much as by taking up work as craftsmen or traders. In fact the formation of mining communities and towns may be considered as two parts of a single great movement of industrial and commercial expansion. There were cases in which these two parts converged. At Liège in the thirteenth century the coal miners were organized into a leading municipal gild. An accident of nature at this bend in the river Meuse had placed rich coal seams under one of the most thickly settled spots in the Low Countries, so that coal mining there was actually a municipal industry. There were other cases in connection with the discovery of ores rich in precious metals where the new mining communities were large enough to form actual towns. That happened, for example, at Freiberg, at Iglau, and at Schemnitz in Hungary. In these places municipal and mining law developed concurrently.[30]

Whether the mining community formed part of a town or not, it was

[27] H. de Formeville, *Les barons fossiers et les férons de Normandie* (Caen, 1852), pp. 1–7, and *passim.*
[28] Henri Rouzaud, *Histoire d'une mine au mineur* (Toulouse, 1908), pp. 11–12, 23–30.
[29] *Laws and Customs of the Miners in the Forest of Dean,* ed. T. Houghton (1687); H. G. Nichols, *Iron Making in . . . the Forest of Dean* (1866), pp. 71–82; Exchequer Depositions by Commission (Public Record Office, London), 13 Charles I, Mich. 42.
[30] Cf., for Iglau, Adolf Zycha, *Das böhmische Bergrecht des Mittelalters auf Grundlage des Bergrechts von Iglau* (Berlin, 1900), I, 43–44.

generally a sort of state within a state, with laws and regulations of its own, suited at least to some extent to the special needs and conditions of its members.[31] In such a community the actual workers possessed, to begin with, special privileges and a considerable amount of self-government. Wherever the miners or makers of metal contributed to the wealth of a sovereign prince, they were exempted from the obligation of paying the ordinary taxes. They generally had a voice in ordering their own labor. The regulations governing the manner of sinking and supporting pits, the manner of raising ore, the hours of work, and the division of profits and losses were determined by the lord's officials in company with representatives of the miners and metallurgical workers (jurés, geschwornen, jurors). Cases concerning the working of the mines and forges were tried in special courts, in which the workpeople were always represented and in which they often formed the majority.

The people in these mining communities were bound to conform to the worship of the Roman Church, whose priests followed the settlers everywhere. They were subject to the general political laws and regulations of the sovereign authority within whose jurisdiction they lived. But to such authority there were invariably limits defined by traditions and customs. The customs that developed in mining, in the formation of which working miners had a share, were actually helping to circumscribe the authority of the political sovereign. When the units of labor were very small, as they were in the beginning in mining and metallurgy, the participation of workpeople in political authority had a concrete and immediate reality which is less easy for workers to feel in the large industries of modern times, even when these industries are in the hands of a government which the workpeople have a share in choosing. The twelfth- and thirteenth-century miners were powerless to change the overlord, but they were frequently in a strong position to influence the decisions of the local leaders he appointed to supervise and regulate the mining communities.

THE ORIGIN OF MEDIEVAL MINING LAWS AND CUSTOMS

In many mining communities, especially in Central Europe, the laws and customs were eventually embodied in codes written in longhand. Codes were issued by the territorial lords holding regalian rights, or by the lords of the soil when the property in the minerals went with the property in land. The first code of which we have direct evidence is for Trent in the southern Tyrol. It was issued in 1185 by the Bishop of Trent. From that time the codification of laws and customs spread. In Central Europe and Scandinavia some codes, originally promulgated for one community, served

---

[31] Cf. *Victoria County History, Cornwall*, I (1906), 523.

as models for many others. The most influential codes were apparently those enacted by the king of Bohemia for the miners of Iglau, the first of which dated from about 1249.[32] The Iglau regulations formed the basis for all the written Bohemian laws relating to the mining of silver-bearing ores during the late thirteenth and fourteenth centuries. These Iglau codes left their trace on those of several mining communities in Germany, Hungary, Transylvania, and the Venetian Republic.[33]

It would be a mistake to conclude that all medieval mining laws and customs had a common origin. The most universal customs were the product not of a single lawgiver or even of a single tradition. They were the product of conditions which affected the whole of Europe, in times of remarkable political, social, cultural, and economic development.

Precedents can be found for them in earlier history. In Attica in the fifth and fourth centuries B.C. the principle that the right to dispose of valuable ores under private lands is an attribute of sovereignty, was apparently established in connection with the silver mines of Laurion.[34] While there is no evidence that this principle ever became a part of imperial Roman law, in the late Roman Empire most mines seem to have belonged to the imperial treasury or to the emperor. The emperor also levied a tax of a tenth on the produce of privately owned mines. References to this tax in the Roman codes studied by jurists in the twelfth and thirteenth centuries may possibly have encouraged medieval princes to claim a similar tax, in somewhat the same way that the emperors and later the French kings apparently used revivals of Roman law as a basis for putting forward exclusive claims to the mining *regale* as a whole.

The work of modern archaeologists has provided us with a knowledge of classical history inaccessible to medieval people. Among other things, it has proved that in the second century A.D. the Roman imperial administration issued written regulations for mining in certain imperial lands at and near Vispasca, in what is now Portugal. These regulations, set forth in the tables of Aljustrel, resemble very strikingly those embodying the customs of the medieval mining communities in the late twelfth and thirteenth centuries. There was the same division of interests between the lord and the occupiers of pits, the same kind of administrative control by the lord's officers over mining operations. There were the same little companies with transferable shares, formed by miners working together at a seam, the same special jurisdictions outside the ordinary courts for settling mining disputes. Regulations of the sort found in second-century Portugal apparently existed even

[32] Zycha, *op. cit.*, I, 49.
[33] Cf. J. A. Tomaschek, *Das alte Bergrecht von Iglau* (Innsbruck, 1897), pp. viii–ix.
[34] We must still regard the thesis of Henri Francotte (*L'industrie dans la Grèce ancienne* [Brussels, 1900], II, 183–91) that there were privately owned mines in Attica as unproved (G. M. Calhoun, "Ancient Athenian Mining," *Journal of Economic and Business History*, III [1931], 341–44).

earlier, as far back at least as Hellenistic times, in the countries of the eastern Mediterranean.

A knowledge of such a mining administration could hardly have been brought to medieval Europe by the revival of Roman law in the twelfth century, for there is no trace of such regulations in the code of Justinian, in earlier compilations of imperial legislation, or in classical legal treatises. But it is possible that remnants of the system may have been preserved across many centuries in the customs of a few districts where the working of ores was never entirely abandoned. This would help to explain why in medieval England this system of mining administration is found almost exclusively in connection with lead and tin mining, where there seems to have been no complete break in continuity during the early Middle Ages. These were the only kinds of mining which have left conspicuous traces during the Saxon period. Such laws and customs appear, moreover, at just those places where the Romans are known to have encouraged mining during their occupation of Britain.

At first sight it is more difficult to understand how these mining regulations of imperial Rome could have had any influence in Saxony and Bohemia, which were the chief centers of medieval mining laws and customs. The Romans probably had not worked mines in these countries as they had in Britain. Rome may have had an indirect influence for all that. The remarkable development of mining in Bohemia at the end of the twelfth and during the thirteenth century was brought about by the immigration of German miners who are said to have come from the south German lands, especially from Tyrol and other regions of the eastern Alps.[35] In the eastern Alps there is more evidence of continuity between Roman and medieval mining than in any other part of Europe.[36]

We have, then, strong circumstantial evidence of a connection between a mining administration of the kind that is known to have existed in second-century Portugal and the laws and customs very widely adopted in the medieval mining communities. But why should the western Europeans have adopted this particular form of ancient mining administration rather than another? While Montesquieu and various modern writers were wrong in thinking that classical mining was invariably the labor of slaves, slaves were perhaps the most common laborers in the mines.

For certain limited periods in classical history slave labor may have been almost universal. Somewhat less frequently mining was done by wage-earners who had no more share in ordering their work or governing themselves than the wage-earners in the European mines and factories of the

[35] It was once supposed that the first German miners in Bohemia came from western Germany, from the Harz and the Rhineland. But Zycha gives impressive evidence in favor of their Alpine origin. (Zycha, *op. cit.*, I, 17–33.)

[36] Cf. Clamor Neuburg, "Der Zusammenhang zwischen römischem und deutschem Bergbau," in *Festgaben für Wilhelm Lexis* (Jena, 1907), pp. 278, 298–99.

eighteenth and early nineteenth centuries. The wage-earning miners of classical times were in the employ sometimes of private capitalists, sometimes of the state, sometimes of contractors acting for the state, sometimes of farmers of the public revenues. There is no reason for supposing that the different system which existed in ancient Portugal in the second century A.D. gained ground in the later Roman Empire. Professor Rostovtzeff has taught that the emperors interfered more and more with the conduct of economic enterprises of all kinds—commercial, financial, and industrial. As part of this policy, the Roman imperial administration took over many mines formerly let out in various ways to private persons. It worked them directly, sometimes employing convicts as miners, a practice for which there were a great many precedents in classical history. Nothing could be further from the spirit of medieval mining than this treatment of the work as a kind of punishment. Mining by independent associations of workmen, whose right to dig for ore rested on a grant by a superior authority representing the imperial fiscal administration, is believed to have decreased in importance after the second century. It is impossible to say whether there was a revival of it on the eve of the barbarian conquests when the imperial enterprises were apparently replaced by small mining ventures under local lords.[37] In any event the tendency of later Roman history was not in the direction of the free mining communities. These appear to have been most exceptional during the thousand years or more when mining operations were of considerable importance in the economy of classical civilization.

Inventiveness has been characteristic of the people of western Europe at least as far back as the eighth century. It is a fundamental part of the process of invention to know what and how to borrow. To a greater degree than in any other age in Western history, perhaps to a greater degree than in any other age in all history, the eleventh and still more the twelfth and early thirteenth centuries awoke among the humble the talent, the desire, the knowledge, and the skill indispensable for co-operating in works of genius. In late romanesque and gothic Europe the same gifts for absorbing, reconciling, and unifying divers materials were manifested in the architecture, in which many participated, as in the creative learning on which a very small proportion of the population left a visible trace.

Princes and lords, lay and ecclesiastical, were granting charters to growing towns and freedom to serfs and the sons of serfs in the country. When valuable mines were discovered, the princes and lords who claimed the authority to dispose of them had to attract hands to get them worked. In order to do this they had to offer advantages equivalent to those granted to settlers in the towns.

Workpeople in the mining communities derived their privileges and their

[37] We have no evidence concerning the form of these ventures (cf. Neuburg, op. cit., p. 297).

independence from other circumstances besides their bargaining power. Mining made a positive contribution of its own to the new freedom and also, though this may seem paradoxical, to the new authority exercised during and after the thirteenth century by lesser political rulers, who nominally owed allegiance to the emperor.

The conditions under which mining was generally carried on added to the prestige attaching in a small degree to many kinds of manual labor, and especially to the artistic work in building and decorating churches and monasteries. The early miners and smelters, particularly in Saxony, and other regions of Central Europe, were explorers and even climbers cutting through forests, venturing into high valleys, and scrambling up the sides of mountains. Serfdom was almost unknown among the Germans colonizing these regions; so freedom was the virtually inevitable status for the miner.[38] The magic of the surroundings in which he often worked helped to class him in the hearts of men not with the slave but with the pioneer.

At the same time this connection of medieval mining and metallurgy with the highlands and woodlands helped to bring mining under the control of princes, lay and ecclesiastical, instead of under the control of private landlords. New seams were found very often in places where there had been little or no tillage and relatively few settlers before the twelfth and thirteenth centuries. In such areas the claims of strong private persons to the possession of the soil were weaker than in some thickly settled regions, where the land had been systematically exploited with little or no interruption since Roman times. The Alpine character of medieval mining, which marked it off from modern and from classical mining, facilitated the divorce, characteristic of medieval mining law, between the use of the surface and the possession of mines. As lordship of the soil was inclined to remain rather indefinite in the forests and Alpine regions, the minerals underneath could be more readily claimed by the overlords than would have been possible where the surface landlords were generally men of greater substance with traditional power over their estates.[39] Peasants who drove flocks to pasture in the Alpine regions were always moving about. They generally left during the winter. So the rights of the owners of cattle were rarely identified with any particular plots of land. If, as frequently happened, some of their animals tumbled into the miners' pits, the herdsmen were outraged. They demanded compensation. But it did not occur to them to claim a share in the mines. That left the territorial princes, lay and ecclesiastical, an excellent opportunity to stake out claims to take the miners and metallurgical workers under their tutelage, at a time when they granted

---

[38] Cf. Gustav Schmoller, "Die geschichtliche Entwickelung der Unternehmung," *Jahrbuch für Gesetzgebung, Verwaltung und Volkswirtschaft im deutschen Reich,* XV (1891), 677.

[39] Cf. *ibid.,* pp. 676, 679.

such working people much independence and welcomed their participation in local government.

An astonishing feature of early Western history in the Pyrenees, Normandy, England, Wales, the southern Low Countries, the Rhineland, as well as in the Alps and the Erzgebirge, was the disposition of overlords and lords of the soil to grant similar privileges and adopt similar regulations and similar administrative arrangements in hundreds of communities formed to exploit ores and metals. It was almost as if an invisible lawgiver inspired miners, landlords, and territorial rulers from one end of Europe to the other with a single conception of right and wrong, which could be translated into custom and positive law. For a brief spell, which in some regions hardly lasted through the thirteenth century, the western Europeans almost managed to universalize among the miners freedom and partial self-government. The conditions of industrial work in the country as well as in the town were helping to strengthen in western Europe an allegiance, that was largely new, to the small semi-independent unit of enterprise which came with other units to form part of a local community. This allegiance came to exist concurrently with the allegiances to the authority of a centralized state and a universal church, which the Europeans had inherited from the more distant past.

Like the gothic arch and the great cathedral spires, the community of free miners was a creation of western Europe. Like the philosophical *Summae* of Thomas Aquinas and Duns Scotus, it was indicative of a genius extensively awakened among the Europeans of the twelfth and thirteenth centuries. This genius consisted in the desire and the capacity to exploit for fresh purposes ideas, forms, and principles, including forms of industrial organization, suggested by the experience of earlier societies, to absorb and to generalize these ideas, forms, and principles in new ways that made them accessible to all. The power to universalize through small units for the benefit of western Christendom as a whole gave the age its special unity. To a degree apparently unknown in the past, the many and the one complemented and fortified without absorbing each other.

THE COLLAPSE OF PROSPERITY IN THE FOURTEENTH CENTURY

The balance was a delicate one. So far as mining and metallurgy are concerned, it became increasingly imperfect as the Middle Ages waned. The conditions of enterprise which prevailed during the period of expanding output at the end of the twelfth and in the thirteenth century were partly dependent upon the fortunes of nature which spread rich mineral resources out near the surface along the upland valleys and the sides of hills and mountains, readily accessible to adventurers with little capital. These surface resources obviously had limits.

During the fourteenth century the rapid progress in the output of minerals and metals, characteristic of most of Europe for several previous generations, came to an end. Except in a few districts, notably in eastern Franconia and perhaps in Bohemia, the miners began to encounter hard times early in the century or at least before the middle of it, when the bubonic plague swept away a substantial part of the European population. Both Franconia and Bohemia suffered relatively little from the Black Death. Their escape may have had something to do with the revival of the prosperity of the mines of silver-bearing ore in Bohemia during the third quarter of the fourteenth century. Progress was made also in the output of gold in Bohemia, Silesia, and Hungary.[40] But mining in Central Europe generally was not in a flourishing state during the fourteenth and early fifteenth centuries. The production of gold and silver in Europe as a whole actually declined. To judge from conditions at the famous copper mines on the Rammelsberg and at the equally famous tin mines in Devon and Cornwall, the production of copper and tin also diminished somewhat. In spite of frequent warfare, which kept up the demand for iron, the forges in the chief ironmaking districts were seldom prosperous. In many districts their number dwindled. The traffic in "seacoal" from England to the Continent was apparently not increasing.

What were the causes for this long slump which lasted for several generations? The prosperity of the mining and metallurgical industries was bound up with general prosperity. The depression in mining was partly a reflection of the economic and political troubles which beset most of Europe. After at least two hundred years of exceptionally rapid increase, the population was growing slowly, if at all. The peasants, who formed the great majority in every country, found it much more difficult to improve either their social status or their material welfare. In most towns there was no marked increase in the number of craftsmen or in industrial production. Except perhaps in the Low Countries under the Burgundian duke, Philip the Good (1419–67), there was nowhere any sustained economic boom until the last decades of the fifteenth century. Consequently there were few places where the demand for metal grew. Wars and political disputes between various European princes and between the rising national states of France and England were more frequent and more destructive than in

[40] Cf. Kaspar Sternberg, *Umrisse einer Geschichte der böhmischen Bergwerke* (Prague, 1838), I, ii, 32–34; E. J. Hamilton, *Money, Prices and Wages in Valencia, Aragon, and Navarre, 1351–1500* (Cambridge, Mass., 1936), p. 195. But the Silesian mines generally were in a depressed state throughout the fourteenth and fifteenth centuries (Konrad Wutke, "Die Salzerchliessungsversuche in Schlesien in vorpreussischer Zeit," *Zeitschrift des Vereins für Geschichte und Altertum Schlesiens*, XXVIII [1894], 107). Some of the gold used for the development of coinage in late fourteenth-century Europe came from the Sudan, a source of supplies since at least the twelfth century (Fernand Braudel, "Monnaies et Civilisations," *Annales: Economies, Sociétés, Civilisations*, I, No. 1 [1946], 11).

the thirteenth century. They interfered with the growth of trade in all products, including metals. In some cases the armies attacked mines and forges, filled the pits with earth and rubbish, smashed furnaces and bellows, and massacred miners and smelters. The Hussite wars of the early fifteenth century (1415–36) left the celebrated Bohemian mining towns of Kuttenberg, Eyle, and Deutsch-Brod in ruins.

A renewal of prosperity in mining depended upon general improvement in economic and political conditions. In turn, economic progress as a whole depended on a renewal of prosperity in mining. In addition to their other ills, most of the states of Europe suffered from a shortage of gold and silver during the fourteenth and most of the fifteenth centuries, especially after about 1375. Except in those states where princes resorted to the expedient of reducing the gold or silver content of their coins, this was a period of stable or slightly falling prices. Industry and trade were stagnant partly because of the difficulties encountered in trying to sell commodities at a profit. The markets provided by the territorial princes, lay and ecclesiastical, were clogged. One of the reasons for the sluggish demand was the unsatisfactory yield of the mines and the mints from which these princes often derived a portion of their revenues. To a degree that is difficult for modern men to grasp, orders for industrial products came from the great princes and still more from the church—from the pope and from the innumerable ecclesiastical foundations (large and small) spread through the whole of Europe.

In Saxony and the Harz, in Bohemia and Hungary, in Sweden, Alsace, and Devon, some of the most productive mines of silver-bearing ores were exhausted in the fourteenth century. Others were worked so deep that many miners were forced to flee before the onrush of water breaking through into the workings, if they had escaped being buried alive when the badly supported walls of underground passages caved in. Progress depended upon the discovery of new seams and better methods of draining the mines and supporting the walls. It also depended upon the invention of new and cheaper processes for extracting precious metals from the ores and for combining ores and metals.

THE PROGRESS OF INDUSTRIAL TECHNOLOGY

Heavier capital expenditures were necessary if deeper shafts were to be dug and more machinery installed. During the earlier medieval silver rushes, mining had been generally carried on by rather primitive methods. Much has been written recently about the backwardness of the peoples of the Roman Empire in engineering skill. But archaeologists have now shown that the Romans had actually used more costly methods in mining than the Europeans adopted at all extensively during the twelfth and thirteenth centuries. If miners in the gothic age had learned of the shafts that had been sunk in Roman times to depths of some six hundred feet in Spain, if they had learned of the adits that had been driven for more than a mile to drain the workings, or of the costly drainage devices in the forms of waterwheels and cochlea, moved apparently by human labor, their admiration for the technical skill of the ancients might have approached that felt by the schoolmen for the thought of the greatest classical philosophers. No such deep mines were to be found in medieval Europe until almost the end of the thirteenth century; nor were the attempts to rid the pits of water yet as enterprising as those sometimes made by ancient peoples.

Most of the coal and base ore was got either by quarrying or by digging a sort of cave, widening out at the bottom like a bell or cone, with its base a few feet below the surface. It was only in the digging of rich silver-bearing ores in Central Europe that shaft mining had become at all general in the late thirteenth century. Even in silver mining the shafts seldom penetrated deeply below the surface. The normal procedure in attacking silver-bearing ores was to puncture a sloping field with dozens of very shallow pits. As soon as water interfered with the hewers' work, a pit was usually abandoned. In this way hundreds of pits were sometimes sunk in a small area in the space of a few years. Some were so close together that a man could often leap the distance from one to another.[41]

The first attempts at drainage were of two kinds. Trenches open to the sky were dug for short distances from the bottom of the shafts down into the valley. Again, leather buckets filled with water were wound up a pit by a hand-turned windlass or passed along a chain of men stationed in an inclined shaft. In a few districts such methods of drainage went back to the beginning of the thirteenth century and probably much earlier. They seldom proved adequate for any long stretch of years, if the demand for ore grew at all rapidly. Long before medieval mining reached the depths that had been attained in the Roman Empire, such primitive drainage devices were unable to cope with the floods. The soil of the Alps and the countries to the north is much damper than that of most Mediterranean lands. At depths of from sixty to a hundred feet, flooding was likely to become a far more serious danger than it had been commonly in the mines of the Hellenistic age or of the Roman Empire.

The only way to meet the difficulties was to drain off the water continuously in fairly large quantities. This called for heavy expenditures in digging drainage tunnels or installing machines. At the end of the thirteenth century or at the beginning of the fourteenth, the first experiments were apparently made with long adits in Bohemia. Some had to be driven more than a mile underground before they reached an opening in the valley below the level of the shaft bottom or sump, in which the water that had seeped

[41] Schmoller, op. cit., p. 664.

into the workings was collected. But as the adits were seldom kept in repair, they were soon clogged up. Water worked its way back into the pits.

In Bohemia at the end of the thirteenth century, and a little later in Saxony, the Harz, and southern Bavaria, water- and horse-driven machines were tried for drawing water from the pits and also for raising brine water from deep salt springs. The mechanical use of water and horse power was not new. For generations water power and occasionally horse power had been employed in metallurgy and some other surface industries. But, if water and horse power were to be effective in draining deep mines, more substantial wheels, axles, and gears than those hitherto in use were indispensable. The early machines for fulling cloth, pounding rags to pulp, even those for driving the bellows and the hammers in metallurgy, were not equipped with the powerful wheels needed to raise enough water out of mines to staunch a flood underground. Apparently some thirteenth-century Europeans saw what was wanted better than the Romans. But the idea hardly brought important results in powerful, costly drainage engines driven by horse and water power for another two hundred years.

In the preparation and the smelting of ores and the refining of metals during the thirteenth century the methods for the most part were mechanically little more efficient than those used in mining. Washing, breaking, and crushing were usually done out-of-doors by hand labor. Smelters showed much resourcefulness and imagination in devising a variety of hearths, trenches, pots, ovens, and furnaces, suited to the species and the quality of the ore they had to treat. But however artful these forges and mills might be, they were not large or expensive to build and equip. Sometimes, as in the making of lead, smelting was undertaken in open-air hearths on the side of some hill where the fires were fanned by the wind. More often, as in the treatment of iron ore, the metal was produced at tiny forges equipped with hand- or foot-driven bellows. The capital invested in such forges seldom exceeded that required to set up the workshop of a smith. In the woodlands near the seams forges and hammers were almost as numerous as the pits and open works dug down to the ore. They were abandoned almost as lightly.

In metallurgy, as in mining, the first heavy capital expenditures were made in connection with silver. The extraction of this beautiful metal from argentiferous lead ore was a more complicated and expensive task than the preparation of gold or of base metals. After the ore had been raised from the shafts, it was washed, then broken and crushed, then smelted. The resulting argentiferous lead was next subjected to oxidation in a cupelling hearth to remove the lead or litharge, and the residual silver was finally refined in a separate "test" with bellows. During the twelfth century, the hammers and stamps for breaking and crushing the ore, and the bellows used in heating it, were probably mostly driven by hand or foot labor, as had been the practice at Laurion in the halcyon days of Attic mining in the fifth and fourth centuries B.C. But primitive power-driven machinery could be more effective in metallurgical operations than in draining mines. European societies were developing in many places where nature invited the use of water power. Streams poured down the slopes and ran through the mountain valleys of Central Europe in a profusion unknown in the drier lands of Greece and in most of the Mediterranean basin. By the first decade of the thirteenth century, if not earlier, water-driven wheels were set up at the silver mines of Trent, in the southern Tyrol, both for driving the hammers and the bellows. A hundred years later, in the principal silver-mining districts, water-driven machinery was frequently employed for breaking and crushing the ores as well as for blowing.

Similar water-driven wheels were introduced for operating the bellows and the hammers in the chief ironmaking regions—in Styria, Carinthia, Bohemia, Lorraine, and Dauphiné. Some bellows were already more skilfully constructed than seems to have been common in classical smelting. The modern type of heart-shaped bellows with a flap-valve, never extensively used in Hellenistic or in Roman times, is said to have appeared even before the twelfth century. In the early fourteenth century there were double and fairly sophisticated bellows producing a constant, instead of a panting, blast.[42] The hotter flame from the new and longer water-driven bellows produced bigger salamanders, or masses of metal, than had been made by the older methods. Consequently larger furnaces had to be devised to hold the ore and the fuel, while power-driven tilt hammers were needed to reduce the salamanders to blooms of wrought iron at nearby mills.

Three types of furnace had begun to replace the older bloomery forges in the fourteenth century: the Catalan forge, which had an ancient origin and was adopted mainly in the Pyrenees and the adjoining parts of Spain and France, the Osmund furnace, introduced in Scandinavia, and what was called in German the *Stückofen.* The *Stückofen,* the highest and most effective of the three, was found mainly in Central Europe, eastern France, and the Alpine districts between. Unlike the tiny woodland bloomery forges, which rose only three or four feet from the ground, the *Stückofen* was a fairly substantial structure of brick or stone, usually built close to the streams to make possible the use of water power. It was some 10 feet high, and consisted of a circular or quadrangular shaft, about 2 feet across at the top and bottom and widening out to 5 feet or so in the middle. Such a furnace could turn out 40 or 50 tons of iron in a year, something like three times the quantity ordinarily produced at the more primitive bloomery forges.

Like the long adits and the water-driven machinery for draining the

[42] Karl Sudhoff, *Beiträge zur Geschichte der Chirurgie im Mittelalter* (Leipzig, 1914), plate 31, a reference which I owe to Dr. White.

silver mines, the improved methods for manufacturing iron were not widely adopted in Europe for more than a hundred years after their introduction. While more progress was made during the fourteenth and early fifteenth centuries with water-driven bellows and hammers than with water-driven drainage engines or even with adits, the less powerful methods of making iron at small bloomery forges remained the rule in all except the leading centers.

In most of Europe the miners, smelters, and refiners of metal went on digging and treating ores in the fashion to which their ancestors had become accustomed. Neither the material condition of the European peoples nor the state of learning during the fourteenth and early fifteenth centuries were as favorable to exploration and discovery as in the gothic age. In the universities, students of natural science worked the views of the schoolmen and of the classical philosophers into dogmatic systems that left little room for the kind of re-examination which some of the great men themselves would have welcomed. Scholars, whose experiences led them to distrust authority, kept their own counsel for fear of trouble with their colleagues or with the church.

A new period of widespread prospecting for fresh seams of ore, and of remarkable technical progress in mining and metallurgy, began in the second half of the fifteenth century. It was an expression of the same forces that led to the discovery of new lands beyond the seas and to advances in natural science. The larger mines and metallurgical establishments of Central Europe became laboratories. The occasional association with them of learned men, such as Paracelsus (1493–1541) and Agricola (1494–1555), and of Biringuccio (d. 1540), a master craftsman in metal work, all of whom devoted a considerable part of their lives to science and engineering, helped to prepare the way for the destruction of the barrier which had existed during the Middle Ages between the work of the industrial craftsman and that of the speculative thinker. In the medieval hierarchy the separation of the liberal from the servile arts was perhaps as complete as the separation between two departments in some large modern university. It would be a mistake to suppose that the "servility" of handling matter in the Middle Ages was the same sort of servility that came later to attach to the wage-earning manual laborer in mines and factories. But it was the accepted medieval convention that the manipulation of material substances was a servile art and that the more abstract labor of the intelligence belonged to a separate category. For material progress and the rise of modern science the decay of this convention was of great advantage. It persisted through the sixteenth century, but the progress of mining and metallurgy helped to weaken it by providing a meeting ground for technical experts and some learned men.

The efforts of miners and metallurgical workers bore much fruit during the last half of the fifteenth century and the early decades of the sixteenth. New seams of rich ore were found in many districts, especially in those parts of Central Europe that had been famous for their mines already in the thirteenth century. Prospectors also came upon valuable supplies of cinnabar, the ore of mercury, and of alum stones. True brass, as distinguished from bronze, is an alloy of calamine and copper. Its production became common after centuries of neglect. The discovery of abundant calamine in the Tyrol and Carinthia and especially at Moresnet, near Aachen, led to an extensive manufacture of brass in Germany and the Low Countries. This increased notably the demand for copper.

An invention of the mid-fifteenth century, made perhaps much earlier in China, was of even greater importance than the working of calamine in the development of the copper mines. It was discovered that the separation of silver from the argentiferous copper ores, which abounded in Central Europe, could be effectively accomplished with the help of lead. The new method was apparently introduced in Saxony about 1451 by a certain Johannsen Funcken. The rich copper ores had been little exploited before this time because of the difficulty of extracting silver from them or of using them to produce brass. No other invention had so stimulating an effect as the new treatment of copper ore upon the development of the mining and metallurgical industries in Central Europe on the eve of the Reformation.

Just as this invention was helping to make profitable the workings of deeper seams of copper ore, the invention of more powerful drainage engines combined with the digging of more skilfully constructed adits to make it possible to cope with the water at greater depths. Better methods of ventilating the underground passages made it possible to blow away some of the noxious and explosive gases.

The most ingenious of the new machines were apparently constructed in Hungary and Saxony. The most curious of all was at Schemnitz in the Carpathian mountains. There the water from the bottom of the deepest pit was pumped up in three flights before it reached a sufficient height to be carried off down an adit. Each pump was set in motion by the rotation of a large horse-driven wheel. The animals to turn these wheels were led down to their labor along inclined shafts which sloped and twisted like screws. In construction these shafts apparently resembled the ramps that enable modern automobile owners to park their cars in congested city areas. The work required ninety-six horses. They were employed in relays at each of the three wheels.[43] The peoples of antiquity had apparently never devised so powerful a drainage engine. They seem never to have contemplated such a prodigious saving in human labor as the new engine effected.

Less important than improvements in drainage for the progress of mining and metallurgy at the end of the Middle Ages, but far more important in

[43] Cf. Georgius Agricola. *De re metallica* (Hoover ed.; London, 1912), pp. 194–95.

its eventual consequences for the rise of modern industrial civilization, was the invention of the blast furnace. The heavy manual labor and the great waste of metal involved in producing iron had restrained its use both in war and peace among earlier peoples than the western Europeans. Once iron ore could be made into metal cheaply, masses of men could be outfitted with weapons based on gunpowder and other explosives and with carriages, cars, and aeroplanes on which the weapons could be mounted. Machines and conveyances of all kinds to supply commodities intended for peaceful use and new structural materials of iron and steel for building could be produced in an equally bewildering profusion. The blast furnace was not by any means the only invention needed to bring the modern age of metal, but it was an essential one.

We now know that the Chinese had used blast furnaces extensively during the tenth and eleventh centuries to produce cast-iron commodities. In medieval Europe there had been perhaps no equivalent for these furnaces. We do not know yet for sure that the earlier Chinese discoveries in iron-making had any direct influence upon their progress in Europe. There were other ways in which the Europeans could have evolved the roundabout process of making cast or pig iron and converting the pig to bar iron, a process destined in their hands to contribute mightily to the coming of the age of metal.

Bronze, a compound of copper and tin, melts more readily than iron ore. In the later Middle Ages, in the early twelfth century or perhaps before, a liquefied mixture of copper and tin, produced by a strong heat, was run into holes prepared in the earth where the liquid solidified in such shapes as were desired. In this way bronze was cast into the marvelous church bells of medieval Europe, as well as into statues and domestic utensils. During the great age of gothic cathedral building bells of cast bronze were hoisted into the towers of churches, where they tolled their message, summoning the faithful, across a continent. The first guns were made of bronze by a process learned from bell and statue makers. The early bronze founders contributed unintentionally to the discovery of one of man's most awful weapons.[44]

The more powerful water-driven bellows, introduced in ironmaking during the thirteenth century, if not sooner, sometimes generated so fierce a flame in smelting that even the intractable ore of iron ran before the eyes of the astonished ironmasters. As the casting of bronze was already known, it was natural that the new discovery should be exploited in the same way for casting iron. It is not certain when the first cast-iron objects were made, but clearly they were made by the beginning of the fifteenth century and probably somewhat earlier. Cannon of cast iron appeared before the middle of the fifteenth century in the dominion of the powerful and enterprising

[44] Charles Ffoulkes, *The Gun-Founders of England* (Cambridge, 1937), p. 2.

dukes of Burgundy and somewhat later in Italy. These cannon were clumsy, ineffective pieces. It was not until after the Reformation that cast-iron cannon did effective execution or were turned out in any number, and then they were manufactured not on the Continent but in southeastern England. Meanwhile it was mainly cannon of wrought iron that helped to revolutionize the art of war at the turn of the fifteenth and sixteenth centuries.[45]

By this time, and possibly earlier, genuine blast furnaces, with auxiliary forges, were built in northeastern France and northern Italy.[46] There were few of them at the end of the Middle Ages however. An extensive development of the new process of making iron came only later in the sixteenth and during the early seventeenth century in the Low Countries and Great Britain and then in Sweden.

In the few instances where larger furnaces were introduced, cast iron replaced wrought iron as the primary product. In large fires the ore was maintained for long periods in contact with carbon at high temperatures, and the carbon was absorbed by the reduced iron forming an alloy, cast iron, of much lower melting point than the pure metal. The molten metal was allowed to collect in the hearth and was run periodically through a tap hole into an open oblong mould where it solidified into pieces called "sows." As larger amounts were cast at one time, bars branching from the sow were added, called "pigs"—a name suggested by their relationship to the maternal sow. The melting of the product permitted efficient recovery of the iron present in the ore and the cast iron produced was of great use in making a whole range of new products at the foundry—such as guns, shot, firebacks, andirons, and grave slabs—but it was not in a form fit to use for wrought products, such as tools, weapons, and armor. The cast iron therefore had to be given subsequent treatment to decarbonize it. This consisted of reheating under oxidizing conditions, producing an unlimited, spongy mass, that by continued forging became equivalent, and for modern industrial purposes even superior, to the old directly reduced iron. The new roundabout process not only facilitated the production of larger quantities of iron with less labor; it reduced the amount lost in the manufacture. Blast furnaces with their dependent forges were often larger than the *Stückofen* of Styria, Carinthia, and other regions of Central Europe. They were usually equipped with more powerful bellows and hammers. Their establishment, therefore, frequently involved a heavier investment in land, buildings, machinery, and other equipment.

[45] Rhys Jenkins, "The Rise and Fall of the Sussex Iron Industry," *Transactions of the Newcomen Society*, 5th ser., I (1920–21), 17; Ernest Straker, *Wealden Iron* (London, 1931), pp. 38–40, 141 ff.; V. Biringuccio, *Pirotechnia*, ed. Cyril S. Smith (New York, 1942), p. 226; Nef, *Western Civilization since the Renaissance* (New York, 1963), pp. 34, 37–38, and *passim*.

[46] Straker, *op. cit.*, pp. 40–43; Biringuccio, *op. cit.*, pp. 146–48.

These inventions were only the most spectacular technical achievements of the miners and metallurgical workers in the fifteenth century and at the beginning of the sixteenth. Few years passed without some important mechanical discovery, such as mills for flattening metal or for drawing wire. Machines driven by the rush of streams came into more widespread use in some metallurgical districts. Dams were built to store the water used to turn the larger and more powerful overshot wheels.

All the peoples of Europe made contributions to these technical discoveries. There was a good deal of interchange of mechanical knowledge between countries. In ironmaking it was the Italians and the French, not the Germans, who led the way on the eve of the Reformation toward larger and more powerful enterprises. It is not uncommon to think of the English as backward in labor-saving technique at the beginning of the sixteenth century. They were backward, but not unqualifiedly backward. Earlier in the Middle Ages they had had inventive ideas to give as well as to receive from foreigners. Even in the fifteenth century they were not without their influence on Continental mining. A celebrated English master miner was brought to Saxony in 1444 by Kurfürst Friedrich II to help search for fresh seams of ore. But the stream of fresh mechanical knowledge flowed in the opposite direction, with Central Europe as its source.

It was generally experts from Hungary, Bohemia, the Low Countries, the Tyrol, and Saxony who excelled in the technical development of mining and metallurgy. Miners and mechanics of German origin were the leaders in the discovery and the dissemination of new methods, particularly in the mining and working of ores containing silver, copper, zinc, and quicksilver, and in the manufacture of brass. New methods discovered in Central Europe spread to Scandinavia, Spain, France, and England. "In no place of the world shalt thou finde more witty engins and excellent peeces of workemanship than in Germany," wrote Thomas Coryat, the parson's son from Somerset, after he had traveled through much of Europe at the beginning of the seventeenth century. By this time Germany was on the point of losing this pre-eminence. She owed it mainly to the ingenuity of Germans and of some Slavs during the late fifteenth and early sixteenth centuries.

Inventions were essential to the great progress made in mining and metallurgy at the close of the Middle Ages. In the coalfields of the Low Countries and to some extent in those of the north of England shaft mining was becoming common; depths of 150 feet or so were reached. Still deeper shafts, descending some 400 feet or so below the surface, were sunk for mining cinnabar at Idria in Carniola and at Almadén in Spain.[47] The greatest depths of all were reached in working argentiferous copper ores in

[47] P. Hitzinger, *Das Quecksilber-Bergwerk Idria* (Ljubljana, 1860), p. 16; K. Häbler, *Die Geschichte der Fugger'schen Handlung in Spanien* (Weimar, 1897), p. 98.

Saxony, Bohemia, and Hungary, where a few pits went down 600 feet or more. At such depths the problem of drainage could be met only by driving long adits and pumping up water with powerful engines.

Remarkable though the inventions of the later Middle Ages were, they hardly revolutionized mining. Without them there would have been considerable, though less remarkable, progress in output, for new seams were still turning up at shallow depths. Only where the surface minerals were exhausted was recourse had to new methods. Horse- and water-driven drainage engines were installed almost exclusively at argentiferous copper ore mines. For the most part, the older ways of the thirteenth century prevailed. Though shaft mining was introduced for getting tin and lead ore, at the time of the Reformation most of these ores were still obtained at shallow depths of less than 50 feet, simply by surface workings. In Central Europe coal and iron ore were dug entirely from the outcropping seams, by means of open works or caves. The use of even a hand windlass was exceptional in the working of iron ore.

Mining deep below the surface was actually rare even in connection with silver-bearing ores in the most advanced districts. Except perhaps on the Schneeberg in Saxony, where shafts reaching down 200 feet and more seem to have been common,[48] the usual depth in the principal copper mines in Central Europe was about 75 or 80 feet. Many productive argentiferous copper mines were worked without horse- or water-driven engines or even long adits. In the valley of the Inn, at Schwaz, the leading mining center in Tyrol and one of the most productive in Europe of silver and copper, men were still engaged in 1537 to pass buckets full of water up an inclined shaft. That had been the universal method at Schwaz until about 1522, when the first attempt was made to introduce an expensive water-driven pumping machine. It is not certain that the attempt succeeded, although some sort of water pump was then installed.[49]

Folklore and superstition concerning their craft were still rife among the miners.[50] Special sight was attributed to a few experts who roamed over the hills, holding the ancient divining rod—a forked twig—straight out in front of them, until it turned and twisted as they passed over a hidden seam of ore. The mining communities still depended upon these mystery men for guidance, except when accidents of nature put them directly on the scent of new veins.

In metallurgy, as in mining, the important changes in methods were largely confined to silver and copper. At the time of the Reformation, water power had hardly begun to replace hand and foot power in the crushing,

---

[48] Oswald Hoppe, *Der Silberbergbau zu Schneeberg bis zum Jahre 1500* (Freiberg, 1908), pp. 158–59; cf. pp. 92–93.

[49] M. R. von Wolfstrigl-Wolfskron, *Die Tiroler Erzbergbaue, 1301–1665* (Innsbruck, 1903), pp. 39–41.

[50] Cf. Agricola, *op. cit.*, pp. 37–41.

smelting, and hammering of tin or lead ore, except perhaps at a few places in Germany. Even when water power was used for driving the bellows, the forges were generally small. The making of lead and tin did not require as fierce a flame as the making of iron. While blast furnaces had been built in northeastern France,[51] in Piedmont, along the valleys of the Rhine and the lower Meuse, and in Sussex, most iron was still made directly from the ore even in these regions. In southern Germany and the eastern Alps, while the blast furnace was apparently unknown, water power had become the common force both for driving the bellows and the hammers in the leading ironmaking districts, such as Styria and Carinthia, where the *Stückofen* had come into widespread use. But hand- or foot-driven bellows remained the rule at the pervasive bloomery forges in less advanced districts.

It is by no means certain that the European peoples had attained in the early sixteenth century a much higher level of technical proficiency in mining and metallurgy than the classical peoples of the early Roman Empire. But they had made discoveries never exploited by the ancients, of which the blast furnace and the *Saigerhütte*[52] are outstanding examples. They were using water power for turning machinery much more extensively than the Greeks or Romans had ever used it. The respect for the miners as pioneers, the freedom and dignity which their calling had come to possess during the twelfth and thirteenth centuries, had relieved the processes of mining and metallurgy from some of the stigma frequently associated with them in earlier civilizations. Was it not partly on that account that the western Europeans already in the later Middle Ages seem to have been less reluctant than the ancient Romans had been to exploit relentlessly the mineral riches of the earth, to devote their intellectual energies wholeheartedly to methods of cheapening the costs of mining and metallurgy?

By the period of the Reformation the study of engineering was beginning to claim greater attention than in classical times. Two books out of thirty-seven in Pliny's *Natural History,* written in the first century, are concerned with metals. Other Graeco-Roman works, mostly known to the moderns only at second hand, also treated the subject. But mining and metallurgy apparently never engaged the undivided attention of any classical writer[53] to the extent that they engaged men early in the sixteenth century, especially two men, a German and an Italian, Georgius Agricola and Vannoccio Biringuccio. The former devoted several treatises to it, the best known being a large book *De re metallica.* The latter was concerned with nothing else in his one long piece of writing, the *Pirotechnia.* Both treatises, and especially the *Pirotechnia,* are largely free from superstition. Neither

[51] Marcel Bulard, "L'industrie du fer dans la Haute-Marne," *Ann. de géog.,* XIII (1904), 232.

[52] For a description see p. 51, below.

[53] Cf. Rostovtzeff, *The Social and Economic History of the Hellenistic World,* II. 1212.

Agricola nor Biringuccio took the divining rod seriously, and the Italian scorned the pseudo-magic of the alchemists.[54] Several of their contemporaries composed works on the same subjects, but the books have been forgotten. This novel disposition to give undivided and more accurate attention to mining and metallurgy was indicative of the respect felt by western Europeans for the occupation of the miner, which had been so distasteful to classical men that they had felt little inclination to explore even with their minds the world underground, shunned as it was by all who could avoid the labor of mining.

THE BOOM IN MINING AND METALLURGY, 1460–1530

The wonderful artistic achievements of the late fifteenth and early sixteenth centuries, when much of Continental Europe was built or rebuilt in the new Renaissance style of architecture, were accompanied by a remarkable industrial development, especially striking in northern Italy, parts of Spain, the southern Low Countries, and in eastern and southern Germany. The progress of mining and metallurgy played an important part in this industrial development, above all in Central Europe. At some of the leading mines, as at Schneeberg in Saxony, the production of silver reached its zenith by the eighties of the fifteenth century. At others, as at Freiberg, the zenith was not reached until after the middle of the sixteenth century. For most mines the time of greatest prosperity was from about 1515 to 1540, when Agricola and Paracelsus reached maturity, when Dürer (1471–1528) and Holbein (1497–1543) painted many of their incomparable masterpieces, and when the doctrines of Luther (1483–1546), Zwingli (1484–1531), and other reformers fired the German people with a new religious enthusiasm. Between 1460 and 1530 the annual output of silver in Central Europe increased several times over, perhaps more than fivefold. It probably reached a maximum during the decade 1526–35. Nearly three million ounces were then produced each year, a figure not again attained until the fifties of the nineteenth century.[55] The output of copper probably grew at least as rapidly as the output of silver. By the thirties of the sixteenth century, it amounted to several thousands of tons annually.

The wealth of the Germans in silver, copper, and brass had become a marvel for the rest of Europe. The most productive mines were in the Erzgebirge (at Schneeberg, Annaberg, and Joachimstal), at Schwaz, at Neusohl in Hungary, and at Mansfeld, where Luther spent part of his childhood in the mountain air after his father had moved there to earn his bread as

---

[54] Cyril S. Smith's introduction to Biringuccio's, *Pirotechnia,* p. xv. His admirable piece of editing has added substantially to knowledge of industrial history.

[55] Nef, "Silver Production in Central Europe," *Journal of Political Economy,* XLIX, No. 4 (1941), 584–86.

a miner. Several thousand men were drawn to each place to work underground, in carrying materials, in preparing charcoal, and in smelting, separating, and refining the ores and metals.[56] With their families, they formed some settlements nearly as large as Leipzig and the other chief towns of southern and eastern Germany, which were growing rich and prosperous partly through the prosperity of the mines.[57] Emperor Charles V was possibly not exaggerating in 1525 when he placed at a hundred thousand the number of persons employed in mining and metallurgy in all the countries of the Empire.[58]

The rapid growth in the output from mines was not limited to Central Europe. In Sweden and Alsace, the production of silver, while inferior in volume to that of Saxony, Bohemia, Hungary, the Tyrol, or even Silesia, increased at nearly as rapid a rate as in those countries. During the first half of the sixteenth century the cinnabar mines at Almadén in Spain were almost if not quite as productive as those at Idria in Carniola.[59] Italy led in the new alum-making industry. The principal enterprise was at Tolfa, near Civita Vecchia, in the Papal States.[60] Rich deposits of alum stones were discovered there in 1462, by John de Castro, the general "commissar" of the revenue for the Papal Chamber. He predicted that the vast works set up under his direction for the popes would assure the defeat of the infidel by freeing Europe from its long dependence upon the Near East for alum. This was an essential element in the dyeing of fine cloth, at a time when textiles employed a great many more hands than any other industry. In the early sixteenth century alum-making on a considerable scale spread to other parts of Europe.

All over the Continent the manufacture of iron and steel grew rapidly to meet the demands of a large number of expanding industries. Cannon, mainly of wrought iron, were coming into widespread use for the first time, as kings and princes stored up ordnance in anticipation of a coming struggle for authority and dominion and tried out their artillery especially in Italy, where the fields were stained with the blood from frequent battles. At many places on the Continent the manufacture of salt was expanding. Pumping machinery with iron parts, and iron pans the length and breadth of a fair-sized room, were installed to raise and to hold the water from the rich brine springs in Franche-Comté and Lorraine.[61] Tools, gears, and machine parts, and various other iron wares, were wanted in larger quan-

[56] Cf. Zycha, *Das böhmische Bergrecht des Mittlalters,* II, 299; Wolfstrigl-Wolfskron, *op. cit.,* pp. 45, 66–67.

[57] Cf. Ernst Kroker, "Leipzig und die sächsischen Bergwerke," *Schriften des Vereins für die Geschichte Leipzigs,* IX (1909), 26–27, 32–33.

[58] Jakob Strieder, *Studien zur Geschichte kapitalistischer Organisationsformen* (2d ed.; Munich, 1925), pp. 3–4, 376–77.

[59] Häbler, *op. cit.,* p. 102; Hitzinger, *op. cit., passim.*

[60] Jean Delumeau, *L'Alun de Rome XVᵉ–XIXᵉ siècle* (Paris, 1962).

[61] See below, pp. 104–5.

tities than before in mining and metallurgy, in shipbuilding, and in construction work of all kinds. In Styria the output of iron seems to have quadrupled between the sixties of the fifteenth century and the thirties of the sixteenth, when it amounted to some eight thousand tons or more a year.[62]

As the German countries were not the leaders at this time in the technical development of ironmaking, it is reasonable to suppose that such an expansion in iron production was by no means exceptional. Scattered figures concerning the iron mills in the Ardennes forest and the Meuse Valley indicate that the growth of the industry there at the beginning of the sixteenth century was at least as rapid as in Styria. In Carinthia, Carniola, Westphalia, and the Harz, in Lorraine, Champagne, Dauphiné, and Nivernais, in Tuscany and Piedmont, in the eastern Pyrenees and the Basque provinces of Spain, the development characteristic of Styria and the Low Countries was repeated. The ironmasters deserted the highlands, with their woods, for the streams and rivers with their water power. They built larger mills and stayed much longer in one spot than they had done when the location of forges had been more dependent upon clusters of trees, which were soon hewed down to serve the charcoal burners. The new labor-saving machinery made it economical sometimes to bring wood and charcoal from considerable distances on packhorses and in carts. Thus the area serving a single metallurgical enterprise was extended.

Old peasants in the valleys complained that the new furnaces, forges, and mills were converting once quiet villages into noisy bedlams. The machinery swished and creaked as the large wooden wheels, for transmitting the power, rotated in the streams or under the force of water poured from the end of an elevated wooden trough running from a newly built reservoir. The blows of great power-driven hammers, sometimes weighing two hundred pounds and more, echoed through the forests and hills. As larger ironworks were installed, as stronger bellows were introduced, the air was often filled with such a stench and smoke as to trouble travelers as well as old inhabitants. In some places, according to the villagers, the waste products from the forges and furnaces so polluted the streams as to frighten the fish.[63]

The growth and multiplication of considerable enterprises for mining and making metals put strains upon the forests in many parts of Europe. Lumber of various kinds was used for pit props, in making machinery, in build-

[62] L. Bittner, "Das Eisenwesen in Innerberg-Eisenerz," pp. 628–29. These statistics of output are for Innerberg-Eisenerz only. There production increased from about 1,300 tons in 1466 to about 5,000 tons in 1536. At Vordernberg, the other iron-producing district of Styria, the annual output is said to have averaged more than 3,000 tons between 1535 and 1537 (ibid., p. 490, n.). I have assumed that in 1466 the output at Vordernberg was more than half that at Innerberg-Eisenerz, as in 1536.

[63] A. Meister, "Die Anfänge des Eisenindustrie in der Grafschaft Mark," Beiträge zur Geschichte Dortmunds und der Grafschaft Mark, XVII (1909), 140.

ing houses, shops, dams, and small factories needed for manufacturing metal. The demand for logs and charcoal grew almost as rapidly as the output of metal, for even the new furnaces and mills effected little saving in fuel. They caused the destruction every year of the trees and shrubbery on thousands of acres.

Increasing pressure on timber supplies aroused a fresh interest in the coal seams. In several provinces of southern and central France, notably in Lyonnais and Forez, where coal outcropped, and also in Germany—in Westphalia, Saxony, and Silesia—the digging of coal early in the sixteenth century began to employ larger numbers of local peasants than in the past. Some of them loaded the black stones and gravel into sacks and carried the stuff to nearby towns on packhorses, or, if river traffic was possible, in flat-bottomed boats. The dirty fuel was beginning to command a price at some distances from the pits among limeburners and those smiths who specialized in the rougher kinds of ironwork. But most of the peasants who dug and carried coal had other labor, usually in husbandry. They handled the mineral as a by-occupation.

It was only in the principality of Liège that coal mining actually became an industry of some importance, employing considerable numbers of trained miners. The wide gently flowing Meuse, so convenient for the transport of cheap, bulky commodities, veers at almost a right angle from east to north. At Liège the production of coal had been more noteworthy during the fourteenth and fifteenth centuries than at any other place on the Continent. Charles the Bold, the fiery Duke of Burgundy, had ordered his soldiers to erase the city from the map and had vowed that even its name should not be revived. Yet in the decades that followed his death in 1477, it became one of the great armories for the European princes who followed him. The output of coal tripled or quadrupled to help feed with fuel the growing metal and armament manufactures in the town itself and at many places up and down the river. Liège coals were not quite carried to Newcastle! But fuel from the land of "Luick" actually competed at Calais and other channel ports with "seacoals" from the Tyne. At Liège the long adits which drained the coal pits were driven and interconnected in such a way as to provide the main city water supply. The mounds of black earth thrown up beside the pits were hardly less prominent a sight than the spires of the churches. They were more portentous of the future that awaited the Western peoples than the city halls, the courts of justice, and the merchant palaces that were rising in profusion in a host of European towns.

THE CLEAVAGE BETWEEN CAPITAL AND LABOR

The long adits and the drainage engines, the largest of the new furnaces and mills with their horse- and water-driven machinery, were costly to construct, to maintain, and to operate. They added greatly to the capital re-quired in mining and in extracting metals from the ores. Even when it was possible to supply the increased demand for ores and metals without funda-mental changes of industrial technique, the increase in the demand often made it profitable to increase the scale of enterprise. Under the spur of technical changes and of expanding markets, a striking cleavage was taking place between capital and labor in many of the mining districts on the Continent, especially in southern and eastern Germany, Bohemia, Hungary, and the eastern Alps.

While mining and metallurgy had always required capital and had lent themselves to enterprise on a considerable scale more readily than other important medieval industries except building, it would be a mistake to suppose that from the beginning the organization of the workmen resembled in miniature that in a modern mine or factory. During the late twelfth and early thirteenth centuries it was common for the finders of the ore and their fellows who held adjoining meers in the same seam to band together in associations. They worked many concessions as a single undertaking much as the peasants plowed and sowed their holdings in common. Thus com-panies of working miners were formed with a number of parts, in some cases as many as thirty-two. These parts could be passed from father to son. They could be sold or exchanged. In some cases they could be leased.

Working partnerships of this kind were not unknown during the thir-teenth century in the preparation, the smelting, separating, and refining of ores and metals; but they were rare. Sometimes forges and hammers were provided by the miners themselves. Sometimes, especially in the production of silver, the metallurgical establishments belonged to the princes who coined money and granted mining concessions. In fourteenth-century Ger-many, furnaces for separating silver from lead ore and for making silver, lead, and copper were frequently farmed out to a working master, generally under short-term leases with a year or so to run. In the production of iron, as we have seen, the works were frequently owned by the local lords of the soil. The iron forges themselves, or the sites on which to build them, were often leased out by these lords either to some of their chief tenants or to traders in metal from the nearby towns. In many cases the early iron forges, hammers, and mills were manorial ventures like corn mills or wine presses. The work was done for wages or under contract by local villagers, many of whom held small plots of land and were occupied in husbandry a part of their time. As it was rare before the late thirteenth century for more than four or five persons to work in one pit at a time, it was probably also rare in metallurgy for more than four or five persons to work at a single forge or stamping mill.

In many parts of Europe little manorial enterprises employing less than a dozen local villagers remained the normal type in mining and metallurgy even at the time of the Reformation. That was the case in the digging of coal except in the Low Countries, along the Tyne in Durham, and in southern Nottinghamshire. It was the case with the mining of iron ore and its conversion to metal in the numerous ironmaking districts where tiny bloomery forges still prevailed. It was frequently the case in tin mining and lead mining, except in those districts of Central Europe where silver was won in substantial quantities from argentiferous lead ores.

Wherever the demand for minerals and metals grew rapidly, independent partnerships of working miners or smelters were placed in the defensive. As the expenses of mining and smelting increased, the miners and smelters were obliged to borrow money. They often borrowed from the traders with whom they had been accustomed to enter into contracts for the sale of their coal, ore, or metal. It is an almost universal rule in economic history that such loans give the creditor the upper hand. During the late Middle Ages, they put him in a position to take over the enterprise when the workers were unable at a specified time to pay off the loans or the interest due on them. Creditors who foreclosed might then work the mine on their own account. More frequently they either employed an expert to operate it for them or, if they could find someone with funds willing to assume the risks, they leased it. In any case the workpeople, once independent adventurers in a small way, were turned into wage-earning employees.

In the principality of Liège, by 1520 or so, the independent working partnerships of coal miners had given way almost entirely before small capitalistic enterprises, usually owned and managed by partnerships of town traders. Farther west in the neighborhood of Mons, where coal had also been dug and sold for centuries, the disintegration of the working partnership under the impact of similar financial forces was already well under way. In England there were a few new capitalistically organized collieries on the south bank of the Tyne opposite Newcastle, and north of the Trent near Nottingham.

On the Continent in the principal ironmaking districts the chief ventures were staffed by scores of wage-earners, engaged in digging and carrying the ore, in preparing charcoal, and in tending the furnaces, forges, and hammers. The introduction of the roundabout process for producing iron increased the number of operations that had to be co-ordinated and, at the same time, added to the capital equipment required in each process. The landlords generally seem to have maintained their share in the ownership of the ironworks. But they frequently leased the establishments for short terms to merchants from the nearby towns. Such merchants might form small smelting companies with transferable shares, as in the Schmalkalden district in south Hesse.

In the mining of quicksilver, copper, and all other silver-bearing ores, in the making of silver, copper, brass, and alum, the partnerships of working miners and the small manorial ventures, characteristic of mining and metal-lurgy in the thirteenth century, gave way almost entirely (especially in the industrial regions of Central Europe) before new forms of enterprise re-quiring greater resources in capital. Argentiferous copper ore mining in-volved especially heavy expenditures. It was almost inevitable, therefore, that the great expansion in the mining of silver-bearing copper ore at the close of the Middle Ages should help to destroy the type of mining enter-prise characteristic of the thirteenth century. Under the pressure of expand-ing production, larger concessions were granted. It was out of the question for a single miner to work one of these alone.[64] In any case several conces-sions were often combined in the interest of a more efficient administration.

As a consequence of the growing need for capital the old companies of working miners, common in the late twelfth and thirteenth centuries, were replaced by new companies of absentee shareholders. Parts grew more numerous. They were sold to local noblemen and landed gentry, to monas-teries, merchants, sometimes to municipal governments and even to uni-versities. By the beginning of the sixteenth century a division of mining companies into 128 parts (*Kuxen*) was usual in silver and copper mining in Saxony and Bohemia. There were companies with as many as 256, with 384, and (in at least one case) 640 parts.[65] Even these numerous parts were sometimes subdivided.

After the original capital had been raised, all the partners could be called on to meet their share in any additional expenditures. Dividends were some-times paid in ore, the ore being separated near the mines into a number of piles of various sizes, one for each partner. When the company sold the ore, or smelted it and sold the metal, dividends were paid in cash. The actual direction of the enterprise was left increasingly to managers and foremen. They hired the hewers, barrowmen, and winders to work in the pits, paid them, and supervised their labor. As the number of partners and the part-ners living at some distance from the mine multiplied, it became difficult, if not impossible, for the shareholders to meet frequently to settle matters of policy. In the late fifteenth and early sixteenth centuries the weekly meet-ing gave way to the biweekly, the monthly, the quarterly, and the semian-nual meeting. There were partners who never appeared even at these infre-quent meetings. They appointed local agents to manage their interests and to represent them in dealing with the managers.

In spite of such absentee proprietorship and of the wide distribution of mining shares, the enterprises were seldom large even in the chief silver-mining districts. In each district there were commonly a number of sep-arate competing units. At Joachimstal the chief companies had normally

---

[64] Cf. E. Gothein, "Beiträge zur Geschichte des Bergbaus im Schwarzwald," *Zeit-schrift für die Geschichte des Oberrheins*, N.S., II (1887), 435–36.
[65] Cf. Hoppe, *Der Silberbergbau zu Schneeberg*, pp. 149–56.

only from sixteen to thirty-two workpeople on their payrolls. There were actually small ventures with only four or five employees.

As a result of the cleavage between capital and labor, the miners of argentiferous copper ores, together with some of the miners of tin and lead ores, lost most of the special privileges granted by the princes and overlords who had claimed regalian rights during the twelfth and thirteenth centuries. It was the owners of parts in the mining companies and the experts in the new mining technique who fell heir to such privileges, in so far as they persisted, and in so far as fresh privileges had been granted in connection with newly developed mines. The exclusion of craftsmen from access to the mastership in some towns led to the organization of journeymen's gilds. In a somewhat similar way the creation of large groups of wage-earning miners led to the formation of pitmen's associations for keeping up wages and maintaining decent working conditions. Such associations appeared at Freiberg early in the fifteenth century and at the principal mining districts in the Erzgebirge early in the sixteenth. At Joachimstal and Schneeberg dissatisfied miners struck work. The new associations and the strikes indicate how little was left of the community which the European peoples had sometimes achieved in connection with industrial labor during the first great wave of economic progress and prosperity in the twelfth and early thirteenth centuries.

To reach Strieder's conclusion that the modern struggle between capital and labor originated at the juncture of the fifteenth and sixteenth centuries would be too simple. The mining communities were split at this time not in two ways but in three. In addition to the working wage-earners and their capitalist employers, there were the holders of regalian rights. As we shall see in a moment, this third group was gaining tremendously in strength and assertiveness on the eve of the Reformation. It held the balance of power. While it can hardly be represented as a defender of the wage-earning miners against their employers, it was unwilling to have the private companies gain an ascendancy in the mining communities. That ascendancy it reserved for itself.

The regalian lords were obliged to call on wealthy merchants or financiers for help. The problems of draining pits and of ridding underground passages of noxious and explosive gases concerned these lords. They found it desirable not to leave such matters to the numerous groups of concessionaires, to be dealt with piecemeal by each group. It was recognized that the drainage of a mining field was actually a single task, which could be met most effectively by a single drainage system. Some of the greatest merchant-financiers of the Renaissance helped the regalian lords in meeting the costs. These wealthy men, who patronized the leading artists and lent money to kings, popes, and emperors, furnished much of the capital needed to drive long adits and to set up expensive drainage machinery. The Fuggers and

Welsers and other leading mercantile families of Augsburg, Nuremberg, Leipzig, and other flourishing German towns participated in many ventures of the kind throughout Central Europe. They extended their investments into Spain and Sweden. In return they received shares in the mining companies whose pits they helped to drain.

In spite of their loss of economic independence, the working miners in Germany retained something of the dignified social status that had attached to their profession earlier in the Middle Ages. In his best-known treatise, which appeared first in 1556, when the labor struggles at the ore mines of Central Europe had been going on for two generations, Agricola wrote that "not even the common worker in the mines is vile and abject." He knew at first hand conditions in the most populous and highly developed mining settlements of Saxony and western Bohemia. He had spent some years of his life as a physician at Joachimstal, where the cleavage between the miners and their employers was perhaps as wide as anywhere in Europe.

Carried on even more than during the thirteenth century in the mountains and high valleys, amid some of the most charming scenery in the world, mining retained a romance and even a certain magic which accompanies the conquest of nature. The work of the mountain men, as the miners were called in German, also encouraged the kind of courage and resourcefulness that proved invaluable in the army and that so warlike a people held in particular esteem. With the help of their experience in driving subterranean passages, miners brought from the silver-mining districts of the eastern Alps in 1529 to defend Vienna are said to have met and outwitted the Turks, who were trying to tunnel their way under and into the city.[66]

Later, in seventeenth-century England, a customs officer, engaged in pressing men into the navy for war with the Dutch, spurned the keelmen who loaded coal into ships from the mines near Newcastle, saying it "would do more harm than good . . . to have such nasty creatures on board" the men-of-war.[67] Such an attitude toward members of the German mining settlements would have been hardly conceivable at the time of the Reformation. In recruiting their units the German army officers preferred miners to townsmen and even to peasants. The search for silver-bearing ores in medieval Europe had not stained the bodies of the workmen or made them social outcasts as coal mining later was to do. Many miners had their Saturday night baths with the efficient regularity that we associate with the Germans. Silver was thought of as an excellent thing in itself. Digging for it was widely regarded as a more honorable way of earning a living than accumulating it in strong boxes by sharp financial practices. The calling of

---

[66] Wolfstrigl-Wolfskron, *Die Tiroler Erzbergbaue*, p. 393; Leopold Ranke, *History of the Reformation in Germany*, trans. Sarah Austin (London, 1905), pp. 582–83.

[67] Nef, *Rise of the British Coal Industry* (London, 1932), II, 151.

the miner, Agricola remarked, "excels in honour and dignity that of the merchant trading for lucre." [68]

In France, as well as in Germany, princes frequently treated the miners with a consideration that they did not always accord the greatest merchants of the age. After confiscating mines of silver-bearing lead and copper ores in Lyonnais and Beaujolais belonging to Jacques Coeur, perhaps the richest French merchant of the time, Charles VII was faced with the task of reviving these enterprises. In 1454 the royal officials engaged for this purpose a large number of miners, some of the most skilful of them Germans. These workpeople were sumptuously housed and lavishly nourished with varied meats, wines, and fruits, such as might arouse the envy of an ambitious twentieth-century trade-union leader if he had the taste for excellent dining common among the wealthy in nineteenth-century Europe.[69]

Large-scale private enterprise seems to have made its most striking progress in some branches of metallurgy, rather than in mining. The principal establishments for producing silver and copper represented a heavier concentration of capital and labor than was apparently to be found in any single mining company. It was the discovery of the new method of separating copper and silver that led to the erection of the most impressive metallurgical works. These *Saigerhütten* were built in Saxony, Thuringia, the Tyrol, and Carinthia. Agricola described one of them in *De re metallica*. It consisted of four parallel walls, the longest more than a hundred meters long, broken by transverse walls into a series of rooms of various sizes and with diverse costly equipment. This included a great many hearths and furnaces, bellows, hammers, and stamping machinery—mostly driven by water power—and a variety of tools and crucibles, all for treating the metals in different stages of manufacture.[70] At Hohenkirchen near Georgenthal in Thuringia, where the Fuggers built such a factory, scores of workmen were employed.[71] The same family had another equally impressive factory near Villach, at Arnoldstein.[72] Supplies of argentiferous ore were brought to both these establishments from mines at Neusohl in Hungary, hundreds of miles away.

Nowhere else in Europe, perhaps, was there a greater concentration of capital and labor in a single plant than in these *Saigerhütten,* except at the

---

[68] Agricola, *De re metallica*, p. 24. Biringuccio took the same view of the moral superiority of the miner to the merchant.

[69] S. Luce, "De l'exploitation des mines et de la condition des ouvriers mineurs en France au XVᵉ siècle," *Revue des questions historiques,* XXI (1877), 192–95.

[70] *De re metallica*, pp. 491–535.

[71] Ernst Koch, "Das Hütten- und Hammerwerk der Fugger zu Hohenkirchen bei Georgenthal in Thüringen, 1495–1549," *Zeitschrift des Vereins für Thüringische Geschichte,* N.S., XXVI (1926), 296–306.

[72] F. Dobel, "Ueber den Bergbau und Handel des Jacob und Anton Fugger in Kärnten und Tirol, 1495–1560," *Zeitschrift des historischen Vereins für Schwaben und Neuburg,* IX (1882), 194–96.

alumworks of the pope at Tolfa, at a few salt springs like those at Salins in Franche-Comté, where the houses and pans were huddled into an enclosure as large as a fair-sized medieval village,[73] and at a few shipbuilding yards such as the famous arsenal at Venice.[74] Unlike the alum- and saltworks and the largest shipyards, the chief *Saigerhütten* were owned and operated by private capitalists, not by the sovereign rulers or under their direction. The assertion of regalian authority in connection with ores was rarely possible so far away from the mines.

THE GROWTH IN THE AUTHORITY OF THE PRINCE

Nothing limited so much the power of private capitalists in the principal mining districts as the growing authority of the regalian lords. In the later Middle Ages medieval constitutionalism was breaking down. The time of Machiavelli was an age of growing despotism. The kings of France and Spain and the emperors, who were Machiavelli's contemporaries, together with scores of other princes, lay and ecclesiastical, in Italy and Central Europe, set about increasing their power at the expense of all independent authority. Mining communities were governed more and more paternally and even despotically. The capitalists, as well as the workers, were expected to obey the laws and orders of the prince and his officers.

The independence of the mining companies, and of the metallurgical enterprises which were closely dependent on the mines, was curtailed by the enactment of regulations far more comprehensive and rigid than those of the thirteenth and fourteenth centuries. During the first forty years of the sixteenth century the issue of mining laws reached a high point.[75] More mining officials were always being appointed and their authority was always being extended. Saxon mining law, as embodied in a code of 1509 issued by the Duke of Saxony for his newly developed mines of Annaberg, became the basis for mining law throughout northern and eastern Germany. In southern Germany and Central Europe generally, the regulations were somewhat less comprehensive. But everywhere the new codes, notable among which were the Austrian regulations of 1517, curbed the initiative of private investors in the mines, forges, and mills.

Problems connected with the digging of long adits, which the princes often helped to finance, provided them with an excuse for increasing their supervision over all kinds of mining operations.[76] Any small scheme for draining or ventilating the pits, or for using fire to shatter the rock that was encountered in sinking shafts, had to be approved by the prince's mining

[73] See below, pp. 104–6.
[74] See below, pp. 89–90.
[75] Cf. Schmoller, "Die geschichtliche Entwickelung der Unternehmung," pp. 979–82.
[76] Cf. *ibid.,* pp. 972, 976.

officials. An *Oberberghauptmann* was given general authority by the regalian lord over the entire administration. At periodic intervals of thirteen days or so, one of the chief officers, the *Bergmeister,* accompanied by a group of technical experts, visited each mining enterprise to see that the regulations contained in the codes and in the supplementary orders issued by the central mining administration were enforced. The wage rates and the hours of labor for the miners and the metallurgical workers were settled by this administration. Managers and foremen who worked for the mining companies and for the masters of forges could be appointed only with the approval of the prince's officials. They could be discharged without the consent of their employers, but the shareholders in the mining companies could not discharge their own managers and foremen without the approval of the prince's officers.

Officers appointed by the regalian lords had frequently participated in the working partnerships of the thirteenth and fourteenth centuries. But the new regulations forbade such officials to hold parts in the mining companies, in order to insure their loyalty to the prince. The number of these officials was continually increasing, as the work of the prince's administration was amplified. In some cases, as at Kuttenberg in Bohemia, the officials were almost as numerous as the hewers in the mines.[77] Many princes took advantage of the dissatisfaction felt by the mining companies and the buyers of ore with the private masters of the local smelting works to engross those enterprises into their own hands.[78] They provided chapels for the miners and smelters, and looked after the health as well as the religious instruction of all the workmen. Rules were passed forbidding the introduction of prostitutes into the industrial communities. Swearing was prohibited, probably because of the superstitious dread of its consequences.

In every direction the princes and other regalian lords tightened their grip on the communities of miners and smelters. The real directing unit ceased to be the individual enterprise and became the ruler's administration. By the Reformation many of the rulers were coming to treat as their property, not only the minerals which contained precious metal but the mines.[79] Some, like those at Mansfeld and Goslar, actually became state enterprises.

This movement toward an administrative control of mining by political rulers was not confined to the German countries. It was general on the Continent. The abundance of silver-bearing ores in Central Europe made the movement especially prominent there. But the French kings were proceeding in the same direction. In the late fifteenth and early sixteenth centuries they set out to gain control of mining enterprises throughout the

[77] *Ibid.,* p. 973.
[78] Cf. *ibid.,* pp. 692–93.
[79] Cf. A. Zycha, *Das Recht des ältesten deutschen Bergbaues bis ins* 13. *Jahrhundert* (Berlin, 1899), p. 157; Schmoller, *op. cit.,* p. 1018.

realm. The problem of control was in some ways more difficult than in the small principalities of Central Europe. Size was a considerable handicap to effective government. Furthermore the French kings had the problem of absorbing and making their own the regalian authority exercised by territorial lords, whilst in Germany, as we have seen, it was the territorial lords who absorbed the regalian authority.

A royal mining administration was eventually created for the entire French kingdom. In general character it resembled the smaller territorial mining administrations of Central Europe. While private landlords were allowed to dig for ore in their own lands and those of their tenants, Louis XI issued an edict in 1471 requiring them to report within forty days the discovery of any minerals and to signify their intention of working them. If they failed to comply, or if they did not wish to finance an enterprise of their own, the royal mining administration was instructed either to lease the mine or to work it directly. All mining, even that carried on by private landlords in their own lands, was placed under the supervision of the royal mining administration. The crown could send experts to search for ore in privately owned lands without the consent of the owner. All mines which they found were at the disposal of the royal mining administration. If, in accordance with the edict, the crown worked or leased mines in privately owned lands, the landlords were to receive compensation for damage to the soil. They were to receive also a portion of the returns, beyond the "tenth" due to the sovereign. The holders of royal concessions and their workmen were exempted from the payment of ordinary taxes. All mining disputes, except those touching the property of the landlords, were to be settled, not by the ordinary courts, but by the king's principal mining official, the *maistre général,* or his lieutenants.[80]

While the *parlement de Paris* modified the edict of 1471 in minor respects before registering it, its main provisions were apparently upheld. During the next seventy years, the royal mining administration occasionally organized enterprises under its direct control for working silver-bearing ores. More often concessions were leased to royal favorites or capital was raised for mining by selling to merchants and traders parts in companies organized in much the same way as those in Germany.[81] Results were meager, mainly no doubt because France was poor compared with Central Europe in silver-bearing ores, partly because of the administrative difficulties of supervising activity in remote parts of what was for the medieval European a vast realm. But practical disappointments interfered little with the assertion of the principle that the king had a title to all valuable mines within his dominion.

[80] *Recueil général des anciennes lois françaises,* X, 626–27.
[81] Archives nationales, Paris, Minutier central, fonds XIX, liasse 152 (documents concerning André de Rozembourch of Bohemia and Nicholas Hermans of Brussels, masters of the French king's mines and forges of gold and silver, 1539).

By the middle of the sixteenth century the regalian claims of the French crown covered most of the country north and east of the Pyrenees and west of the Spanish Netherlands, Lorraine, Franche-Comté, and the Alps. Concessions were granted by royal patent to mine in almost every part of the kingdom, though not all the French nobles willingly permitted the royal concessionaires access to ores in their lands.[82] In Lorraine and Franche-Comté, which were not yet a part of France, the local rulers regulated and supervised the operations of their mining concessionaires, as in France. In Lorraine the dukes apparently threw open the mines to all comers, as had been the general practice of medieval rulers in Central Europe.[83]

With the growth of sovereign political power on the Continent, efforts were made to extend regalian rights to cover base ores. In Central Europe several territorial rulers successfully brought seams of iron ore, as well as of lead and tin, into the same category with ores containing silver or gold. Ironmaking enterprises in Styria, Austria, and the upper Harz were subjected by the duke of Styria, the emperor, and the duke of Brunswick to taxes, regulations, and inspections similar to those which had become the rule in the silver-mining communities. The French king, François I (1515–47), also interested himself in iron production. In 1542 he levied a tax on all forges and furnaces throughout the kingdom. Its collection was confided to the royal mining administration.

The reception of Roman law in France and other Continental countries in the late fifteenth and early sixteenth centuries helped rulers to stretch their regalian claims, both because a very large proportion of all mines had belonged to the state in the late Roman Empire, and because the imperial tax of a tenth on the produce of mines in privately owned lands had been levied indiscriminately on all ores or metals,[84] at a time when all metals were scarce. Here we have an illustration of the differences between the classical revival of the twelfth century and that of the later Middle Ages.

[82] Archives nationales, $X^{IA}8624$, ff. 271–74 (Ordonnance sur les mines et leur exploitation, 1560).

[83] Archives nationales, K. 876, no. 14 (Des mines de Lorraine, 1520).

[84] As we now know that Roman law did not deprive the private landlord of the ownership of mines under his land (see above, p. 25), it seems inconsistent, at first sight, to argue that the revival of Roman law helped the European princes to extend their regalian rights at the end of the Middle Ages to cover base ores. It is true nevertheless. The use to which Roman law was put rested, to some extent, on a misinterpretation. Until the work of Achenbach was published in 1869, European jurists quite generally assumed that property in mines had been divorced from property in land under the Roman Empire. In the Middle Ages such a view was probably widely held by men learned in the law. It was encouraged by a misconstruction by Lombard commentators of passages in the Theodosian code and the code of Justinian (cf. Lewis, *The Stannaries,* pp. 66–68). Roman law, moreover, could be legitimately invoked in favor of putting base in the same category with precious metals, for the tax that had been levied by the Roman emperors on the produce of mines had fallen on both indiscriminately (cf. Müllner, *Geschichte des Eisens in Krain, Görz und Istrien,* pp. 195–96).

One side of ancient experience—the administrative practices of a few districts as these practices were handed across the centuries by custom and tradition—helped the Europeans in the gothic age almost to universalize the essentially democratic community of free miners. Another side of classical experience—formal Roman law, as recorded in the codes and digests of the Empire—helped the European rulers in a later age of waxing political authority almost to universalize the claim of the state to a revenue from all mining operations.

With the increasing need for capital in mining and metallurgy in the age of the Renaissance, a point had been reached, especially in the production of silver and copper, where the costs could be met only by the richest merchants, whose power came from their skill in trade and in managing money and credit, or by kings, princes, and overlords, whose power rested on their inherited position and their political rights. In mining and metallurgy, earlier than in other great industries, Europe faced a choice between the dominance of independent capitalists and the dominance of sovereign authorities. On the Continent the sovereign authorities generally prevailed.

This fact has been obscured by the conspicuous place occupied by certain enormously rich merchants, among whom the Fuggers of Augsburg have received the most attention from historical writers, at least since the time, a century ago, when Michelet wrote his chapters on "la banque." The cost of maintaining an elaborate mining administration strained the resources of sovereign political authorities at the end of the Middle Ages. They had recourse in this connection, as in so many others, to the money of merchants of great wealth—among whom these same Fuggers occupied a place of the greatest prominence. Territorial princes, who borrowed money in large doses, sometimes repaid the loan by granting their creditors, for a term of years, a portion of the revenue which they derived from their regalian rights. In extreme cases they even put the merchants in possession for a time of their entire mining administration, with all its duties and privileges, including the authority to grant mining concessions. This happened at Reichenstein, in Silesia, where the *regale* belonged to the Dukes of Münsterberg-Oels.[85] Again, the important quicksilver mines of Almadén, which had once played a considerable role in the economy of the Romans, were leased for four-year periods to the Fuggers.[86]

For all this, the ultimate authority of the political rulers to control the mines was hardly questioned. If the merchant fell out of favor, it was always possible for the prince to confiscate his property. In 1453 the French king, Charles VII, acting in what nineteenth-century Europeans almost universally would have condemned as an arbitrary and despotic manner, confiscated

---

[85] E. Fink, "Die Bergwerksunternehmungen der Fugger in Schlesien," *Zeitschrift des Vereins für Geschichte und Altertum Schlesiens*, XXVIII (1894), 308.

[86] Häbler, *Die Geschichte der Fugger'schen Handlung in Spanien*, pp. 93–95.

the three mining enterprises in Lyonnais and Beaujolais belonging to Jacques Cœur of Bourges, the most glamorous merchant of the fifteenth century.[87]

Princes, lay and ecclesiastical, welcomed the participation of merchants in mining. They borrowed from them freely to get money to exercise their rights of pre-emption. They even shared control of the mining administration with them. But in Continental Europe the course of history was not running in favor of mercantile domination, as it was destined to run for a time in the late eighteenth and nineteenth centuries. When it came to a showdown, the prince held the brute force that was decisive. In a cruel age, which was not to be the last, he was capable of exercising this force in the most ferocious ways. *In the sphere of art alone was the subject left any real independence.* In the last analysis, everything material was claimed by the prince, at a time when the material aspects of existence were coming into the foreground of thought, worship, and conduct to a greater extent than ever before in Western history. The absolute authority that the prince exercised over the bodies as well as the economic existence of his subjects has been described in unforgettable detail by Ranke, in his chapter on Ferrara under Alphonso II. The duke had concentrated every scrap of prosperity in the court itself. The country was poverty-stricken. His control over industry extended to food, including the prime necessities of flour and bread. Even nobles were limited in their right to hunt, and one day the bodies of six men were left hanging in the market place, with dead pheasants tied to their feet, to show, it was said, that the culprits had been shot while poaching on the duke's preserves.[88] On the Continent the growing strength of despots made fleeting the control exercised by mercantile capital in the mining administrations of the political rulers. At the close of the Middle Ages in most European states it was the political ruler who held the reins which guided large-scale industry.

In England and Scotland no such bulwarks against the independent power of private capital in mining were built up during the later Middle Ages. Henry VIII retained the regalian rights that his predecessors had exercised during the twelfth and thirteenth centuries. He collected a revenue from mines royal and he continued to appoint officials to oversee and protect the royal rights over mineral property. But the share of the crown in the direction of mining had not been extended. No national mining administration, like that introduced in France by the Valois kings, had been established. No legislation had been passed like the French edict of 1413, making it lawful for the crown, and the crown alone, to collect a royalty on the produce of all mines worked throughout the realm. No legislation had been

---

[87] See below, p. 108.
[88] Leopold Ranke, *The Ecclesiastical and Political History of the Popes of Rome,* trans. Sarah Austin (London, 1841), Bk. VI, chap. vii.

passed like the French edict of 1471, permitting the crown to send experts to search for ore in privately owned land. No new codes governing mining were issued, at a time when mining legislation in Central Europe reached a peak. No apparent effort was made to regulate more minutely operations of private mining companies holding concessions from the royal authority. While the crown maintained its control over mines containing precious metals and mines under the royal demesne, while it maintained the rights of the royal family in the stannaries, elsewhere all base ores and minerals were left at the disposal of private landlords.

The resources of Great Britain in gold- and silver-bearing ores proved to be negligible. The crown was to sell a great part of the royal demesne in the late sixteenth and seventeenth centuries. The English tin mines were not again to occupy as prominent a place in European mining history as in the Middle Ages. For all three reasons the power of the sovereign in mineral matters was on the point of contracting in England, at the very time when it was expanding strikingly on the Continent. Stronger than the French crown in its control over mining in the twelfth and thirteenth centuries, the English crown was potentially much weaker at the time of Henry VIII's break with Rome.

These differences between English and Continental mining history in the later Middle Ages had an influence upon industrial development in modern times. They facilitated the regime of free economic enterprise which then thrived especially in the English-speaking countries. What are the explanations for the failure of the English kings during the late fifteenth and early sixteenth centuries to follow the course taken by so many Continental rulers and to add to their authority over mines? [89]

The lack in Great Britain of ores which contained large quantities of precious metals and which were generally acknowledged as royal property was undoubtedly something of a stumbling block. The great abundance of such ores in Central Europe enabled the princes to establish a control over mines in many districts. When an opportunity presented itself to extend regalian rights to mines of base ores, the form of administration was ready to hand. Again England's size proved a disadvantage. While it is common today to think of Great Britain as a small island, in the sixteenth and seventeenth centuries the area covered by England and Wales was much larger than that of most of the principalities of Central Europe. The division of sovereignty within the Empire during the later Middle Ages made it easier than in England to strengthen the regalian rights which went with sovereignty. In an age when the slowness of travel and communication added to the difficulties of governing distant regions, this division often reduced to manageable dimensions the territory within which a single ruler exercised

---

[89] For a development of this subject, see Nef, *Industry and Government in France and England, 1540–1640* (Ithaca, N.Y., 1957), pp. 5–12.

his authority over mines, and made it comparatively easy for him to maintain a staff of obedient officers sufficient to enforce his authority.

But such explanations of the divergence between the history of the mining *regale* in England and on the Continent are inadequate. Neither the size of France, considerably larger than England, nor the lack of abundant supplies of ores rich in precious metals, prevented the French kings from strengthening their regalian rights. More adequate explanations of the special position occupied by England in the development of mining law in the later Middle Ages are to be found in two legal conditions. Sovereign authority was centralized earlier than in any Continental country, and property claimed by the subjects, over which the crown had failed to establish its control, possessed greater immunity through the greater effectiveness of the English Parliament compared with any restraining bodies on the Continent.

Sovereign authority was centralized in England during the late eleventh and twelfth centuries, at a time when medieval constitutionalism was strong. This made the medieval estates, in which mercantile interests were represented, a more essential part of the machinery of government in England than in other countries. Early centralization also made it necessary to create a system of legal principles common to the whole realm, before imperial Roman law had been sufficiently recovered by medieval jurists to permit it to take its place as that system.[90] In imperial Roman law the sovereign political authority was much more pre-eminent than in the European practice of the eleventh and twelfth centuries.

The early authority of the English crown, which was a limited authority, fixed limits to the exercise of regalian rights. They proved less elastic than the regalian rights of most Continental rulers. Partly as a result of the development of common law, the English kings were unable to use the revival of Roman law in the late fifteenth and early sixteenth centuries, as so many Continental rulers were doing, to help them claim a royalty on the produce of mines of every description. In Europe generally the authority of great vassal landlords had been stronger in feudal times than in the later Middle Ages. The early strength of the English Parliament and of the English common law helped landlords to conserve their property rights.

The first Tudor monarchs, Henry VII and Henry VIII, might nevertheless have made an energetic bid to extend their authority over mines, as the French kings were doing, if mining and metallurgy had been growing in importance as rapidly in England as on the Continent, and if they had not been confronted by a Parliament composed of lawyers and propertied men determined to resist encroachments upon the property rights they represented. The early Tudors showed great skill in exercising their political

[90] See C. H. McIlwain, "Medieval Estates," in *The Cambridge Medieval History.* VII (Cambridge, 1932), 709–14.

powers, at a time when the will of the king was still regarded by nearly all Englishmen as supreme in matters of government. According to the Spanish ambassador, Henry VII expressed the desire "to keep his subjects low, because riches would make them haughty." [91] It is improbable that he would have been more disposed than Continental rulers to give merchants a free hand to dominate the mines if their value had been as obvious in England as it was in Central Europe. His son, Henry VIII, was out to raise all the money he could. If he bothered little with the mines it was very likely because his advisers regarded them as of trifling importance. He had a hard time, moreover, in getting his way with Parliament in matters of property, as is shown by its not ineffective opposition to the dissolution of the lesser monasteries in 1536, and by its emasculation in 1539 of the king's proposed Statute of Proclamations as finally passed.

Scarce metals were still the principal objectives for which mining and metallurgical operations were carried on in Europe before the mid-sixteenth century. Great Britain was poor in the ores providing those metals, rich in *base* minerals. Partly perhaps on that account the development of mining in England during the late fifteenth and early sixteenth centuries was much slower than in Central Europe. The searches for silver-bearing ores, conducted on the eve of the Reformation with the help of miners from Germany, gave disappointing results. The production of tin increased only some 60 or 70 per cent between 1470 and 1540,[92] as compared with an increase of four- or fivefold in the production of metals in Central Europe. The increase little more than offset the slump in output that had occurred in England during the first half of the fifteenth century. The supremacy gained during the Middle Ages by the tin of Devon and Cornwall in Continental markets was threatened by the progress of tin mining in Spain, Saxony, Bavaria, and Bohemia. English lead was also finding more competition abroad than in the past. In 1539 one of Thomas Cromwell's correspondents described the lead mines of England as "dead." [93] Until after the dissolution of the monasteries, mining and metallurgy were carried on in Great Britain mainly by small enterprises, which used the methods prevalent on the Continent before the boom of 1460–1530. The sluggish growth of English mining at that time helped to keep the field open to private enterprise, unfettered by government control, at a time when the crown was strong. Later, after the dissolution of the English monasteries and especially after about 1580, a remarkable industrial expansion occurred in England and spread to Scotland. But, by that time, royal authority had grown so weak that the kinds of state control over economic development

[91] *Calendar of State Papers, Spanish,* 1485–1509, p. 177.
[92] Lewis, *The Stannaries,* p. 253.
[93] J. W. Gough, *The Mines of Mendip* (Oxford, 1930), p. 65.

which had been effectively set up in many Continental countries, proved impracticable.[94]

The English crown retained the very considerable mineral rights which it inherited from an earlier age. But a variety of conditions blocked it from extending these rights at the very time when such an extension had become the price of effective political authority in mineral matters even more in England than on the Continent.[95] Such resources as the English crown held by virtue of medieval law crumbled to dust in its hands when coal and iron ore replaced silver and gold as the main treasure of the subsoil.

THE TRANSITION TO MODERN TIMES

At the end of the Middle Ages the rapid development of Continental mining and metallurgy showed signs of waning. The discovery of ores extraordinarily rich in silver in South and Central America, and particularly the opening about 1546 of the famous mines of Potosí in Bolivia, dealt a heavy blow to the European silver-mining industry. Treasure from the New World could be delivered in Europe, even by the unwieldy Spanish galleons, more cheaply than the trained miners of Saxony, Bohemia, Tyrol, Hungary, and Silesia could dig and smelt their ores and ship their metal, with the help of the most skilful German, Hungarian, and Bohemian engineers and technical experts. While a few mining communities in Silesia, and at Freiberg and Goslar in Germany, continued to prosper after the middle of the sixteenth century, a slump had begun by that time in the output of silver and gold in most parts of Central Europe, and also in Alsace and Sweden.

Fifty years later this slump in the production of precious metals had gone very far. On the eve of the Thirty Years' War (1618–48), which was to bring mining in Central Europe temporarily almost to a standstill, the annual output of silver was perhaps less than a third as great as it had been in the twenties and thirties of the sixteenth century.[96] Even in Sweden, which unlike most of Central Europe prospered industrially during the hundred years following the Reformation, the production of silver in the best years of the mid-seventeenth century was hardly half what it had been in the 1540's.[97]

At the close of the Middle Ages the progress of Continental mining was bound up, almost as much as in the twelfth and thirteenth centuries, with the prosperity of the silver mines. The collapse of the market for European silver brought a reduction in the value of argentiferous copper and lead ores.

[94] Nef, *Industry and Government in France and England*, pp. 149 ff.
[95] See also the discussion in Nef, *Rise of the British Coal Industry*, I, 267–85.
[96] Nef, "Silver Production in Central Europe, 1450–1618," p. 589 and *passim*.
[97] Eli F. Heckscher, *Sveriges Ekonomiska Historia* (Stockholm, 1936), II, 439.

Conditions proved almost equally unfavorable to other kinds of mining. Before the end of the sixteenth century, the rapid expansion in iron smelting[98] and coal mining on the Continent came to an end. Thus the signs of an industrial revolution at the end of the Middle Ages proved deceptive. The boom in production from about 1460 to about 1530 petered out. It lasted only during the interval between the Hundred Years' War and the beginning of the religious wars in the mid-sixteenth century. It was not until the eighteenth century that the rate of growth in industrial output again seems to have become as rapid on the Continent generally as it had been during the late fifteenth and the early sixteenth centuries.

What was lacking to bring about a development of mining and metallurgy that would lead directly to the wealthy industrial civilization destined to dominate the whole of western Europe in the nineteenth century? Why was the new machinery for draining and ventilating mines at considerable depths, which had been devised in connection with the mining of argentiferous copper ores, not taken over extensively in the mining of tin, lead, and above all coal on the Continent, as it was in Great Britain in the late sixteenth and seventeenth centuries? [99]

After the Reformation, warfare on the Continent again became destructive and damaging to heavy industry.[100] The dissolution of the monasteries and other ecclesiastical foundations played into the hands of private landlords and merchants in Great Britain, eager to exploit mineral wealth. But in Continental mining districts, the course taken by the religious struggle was different and the church retained a greater portion of the landed property. Some churchmen possessed regalian rights by virtue of their political authority. Ecclesiastical foundations were less ready than lay landlords to invest large capitals in mines and metallurgical plant. They were unwilling to lease their mines on as favorable terms as lay landlords.[101] Again, the natural difficulties of carriage through mountainous country and the numerous tolls and taxes, which stood in the way of transporting heavy ores and coal for considerable distances, imposed handicaps upon the progress of mining on the Continent. The great authority over the mines and the mining and metallurgical ventures, established at the end of the Middle Ages by so many Continental rulers, discouraged private enterprise.

---

[98] In Styria the output of iron reached a high point during the middle decades of the sixteenth century. From 1601 to 1625 the annual production at Innerberg-Eisenerz was considerably less than from 1536 to 1560 (Bittner, "Das Eisenwesen in Innerberg-Eisenerz," pp. 490, 628–29). In Siegerland the number of forges was reduced by half in the late sixteenth century (Richard Utsch, *Die Entwicklung und volkswirtschaftliche Bedeutung des Eisenerzbergbaues und der Eisenindustrie im Siegerland* [Gorlitz, 1913], p. 34).

[99] See below, chaps. iii and iv.

[100] Nef, *Western Civilization since the Renaissance*, pp. 19, 113, and Part I generally.

[101] See below, p. 234; Nef, *Rise of the British Coal Industry*, I, 142–56.

At the time of the Reformation political considerations frequently out-weighed economic in the guidance of mining and metallurgy. While this helped European rulers to strengthen their authority, it was on the whole unfavorable to the growth of industrial output, at least to the growth in the output of products like iron and coal, upon whose abundance the progress of modern industrial civilization has been so largely based.[102] It was only in the eighteenth and nineteenth centuries, after changes in the mining laws first of France and later of Germany made conditions more favorable to the initiative of private capitalists,[103] that the output of mines again grew rapidly in either country.

In exploiting their silver resources, the western European peoples were only following in the footsteps of their classical predecessors, who had ransacked the surface supplies of argentiferous ores in Spain and all along the shores of the Mediterranean. If the western Europeans had turned aside from the supplies of iron and coal, as the classical peoples had done, they could hardly have created the industrial world of late nineteenth-century Europe and the United States, which seemed to offer a foretaste of the millennium for those who measure happiness primarily in material terms.

It is, perhaps, beyond the scope of history to inquire what would have happened if there had been no America and no regions in the north of Europe rich in mineral resources and rich also in industrious workpeople.[104] But it is certain that the most notable progress of mining and metallurgy during the late sixteenth and seventeenth centuries was not in those Euro-pean countries which had been in the vanguard of economic development during the Middle Ages. The progress occurred in Sweden, to some extent in parts of the Low Countries, and above all in Great Britain. All of these countries were protected for various reasons from the full force of the re-

---

[102] The late Professor Strieder made much of the collaboration between the German princes and the merchants as an element in the great expansion of mining and metal-lurgy in Germany and Central Europe in the late fifteenth and early sixteenth centuries (*Studien zur Geschichte kapitalistischer Organisationsformen*, pp. 362–63). To some extent, he seems to have put the cart before the horse. As Inama-Sternegg has pointed out, in connection with the progress of the German saltmaking industry at an earlier period, it was less that the princes' control caused the expansion, than that the ex-pansion enabled the princes to strengthen their control. "So ist schliesslich mehr von einer Beförderung des Regalitätsgedanken durch die Entwicklung der Salinen, als von einer Beförderung des Salinenwesens durch die Entwicklung der Regalität zu sprechen" (K. T. von Inama-Sternegg, "Zur Verfassungsgeschichte der deutschen Salinen im Mittelalter," *Sitzungsberichte der kaiserlichen Akademie der Wissenschaft*, CXI [1866], 578). Otto Hue found these remarks applicable to German mining. "Dieselbe Wechselwirkung vollzog sich auch zwischen der Bergbauentwicklung und der Ausdehnung der Bergregal ansprüche" (*Die Bergarbeiter* [Stuttgart, 1910], I, 93).

[103] Marcel Rouff, *Les mines de charbon en France* (Paris, 1922), esp. Part 1, chaps. ii, iv, and pp. 63–64; Schmoller, "Die Geschichtliche Entwicklung der Unterneh-mung," pp. 1027–28.

[104] For a consideration of the subject see Nef, *La Naissance de la civilisation in-dustrielle et le monde contemporain*, chaps. iv and v.

ligious struggle and its actual battles.[105] All established, partly with the help of these favors, traditions of constitutional government which facilitated private initiative in the exploitation of natural resources.[106]

Many novel inventions and discoveries, which diminished the cost of manual labor and were indispensable for the eventual triumph of industrial civilization, had been made by the Western peoples during the Middle Ages, from the eighth to the early sixteenth century.[107] If these inventions actually were to produce such a triumph, they had to be exploited relentlessly. Their development had to take a position of precedence in the minds of men. At the end of the Middle Ages conditions in Continental Europe, where most of the inventions had been made, were not favorable to such precedence or to such relentless exploitation. Would the triumph of industrialism have occurred without a change of scene? The answer is most probably "yes," but it seems certain that the change of scene contributed to the triumph.

[105] The effects of war on industrial development are discussed at some length in Nef, *Western Civilization since the Renaissance.* For the period 1540 to 1640, see esp. chap. iv; for the period 1640 to 1740 see esp. chap. xii.

[106] See Nef, *Industry and Government in France and England,* esp. chap. v.

[107] Cf. Lynn White, *Medieval Technology and Social Change* (Oxford, 1962).

PART 1

The European Scene during the First Age
of Overseas Expansion

2

Industrial Europe at the Time
of the Reformation, c.1515–c.1540

Il y a . . . un lien étroit et un rapport nécessaire entre ces deux choses: liberté et industrie.—ALEXIS DE TOCQUEVILLE

During the last four hundred years the Western peoples have concerned themselves, to a greater degree than any other peoples before them, with the conquest of the material world. In the twelfth and thirteenth centuries Europeans generally agreed that the highest ideal in human conduct was the renunciation of earthly pleasures, even though the pleasures themselves might be legitimate in the sight of God. They subordinated actual life to certain absolute values, derived, as they believed, from God. These values could be discovered by the human mind, without revelation, in so far as

From *Journal of Political Economy*, XLIX, Nos. 1–2 (February and April 1941), 1–40, 183–224.

This essay is based upon some of the research, done during the last century and a half, bearing on the industrial history of Germany, France, and Great Britain at the end of the Middle Ages. The conditions portrayed are those which existed in Europe from about 1515, when Francis I became king of France, until the dissolution of the English monasteries in 1536 and 1539. It would be inappropriate to burden the reader with an exhaustive list of references in support of each statement, as the secondary works which I have used are to be found in the standard historical bibliographies. Years ago I made a select bibliography of works on the mining and metallurgical industries, in connection with the essay which is reprinted as chapter i of this present book. It will be found in *The Cambridge Economic History of Europe*, Vol. II (Cambridge, 1952), pp. 561–67.

Footnotes have been used mainly when the statements in the text seem to be subject to controversy or when I have drawn on special material that I have been collecting for a history of industry and civilization in France and England since 1540. Parts of this history, in tentative form, are already in print. See below, chapters iii–viii. See also Nef, *Industry and Government in France and England* (Ithaca, N.Y., 1957); Nef, *Western Civilization since the Renaissance* (New York, 1963); Nef, *Naissance de la civilisation industrielle et le monde contemporain* (Paris, 1954); Nef, *Cultural Foundations of Industrial Civilization* (New York, 1960). The present essay forms an

men could rise above their imperfections. After the thirteenth century, and especially after the Reformation, the ancient Christian ideal of renunciation lost its hold. With the Renaissance, and especially after the sixteenth century, it was gradually replaced by the ideal of obtaining material happiness in this world for the largest possible number of individuals.[1] Until the last half of the nineteenth century the countries of northern Europe—the Netherlands, Great Britain, Sweden, northeastern France, and Belgium—took the lead in the efforts to multiply commodities, lighten manual labor, and prolong human life. In regions where the climate is harsh and the problem of wringing a living from the soil challenging, the Europeans aimed to secure comfort and ease never enjoyed by the inhabitants of those parts of the earth where nature is kinder to man.

As the fruits of man's conquest of nature multiplied during the decades preceding 1914 and extended from nation to nation and from continent to continent, men became disillusioned with the results. They quarreled over the unequal distribution of wealth within each nation. They quarreled over its unequal distribution among the nations. The yield from the earth, though increased beyond the most dazzling dreams of Francis Bacon and Descartes, acquired a bitter taste. In recent times its very abundance has taken away, to some extent, in many countries the incentive for effort and sacrifice which gives a purpose to life. The multiplication of material commodities has not brought with it the peace and security necessary ultimately even to the maintenance of the high material standard of living which prevails in parts of Europe, the British Commonwealth, and the United States. The technical skill that men have acquired in the conquest of nature has made possible the destruction of life and property on a scale never known before in history. The objective of material progress has hardly provided protection against this destruction, or against the hatred that is responsible for it.

As the central guiding principle for conduct among the Western peoples, that objective seems to be nearing exhaustion. No other human force has done so much in the last four centuries to alter conditions in our world. The successful pursuit of wealth and health has been accompanied by a revolution in the ways of living, the ways of thinking, and the ways of working. It is fashionable to say that human nature does not change. There is an element of truth in this statement when it is rightly understood. But the objectives of human existence are numerous.[2] Some of them are rational, some irrational. The emphasis laid on the various objectives has differed

---

introduction to these studies. While it sometimes touches on conditions in Italy, Spain, and Scandinavia, it makes no pretense at dealing at all adequately with these countries. It is not based on a knowledge of works published in languages other than English, French, or German.

[1] Cf. T. E. Hulme, *Speculations* (London, 1924), pp. 9, 12; J. Huizinga, *The Waning of the Middle Ages* (London, 1927), p. 28.

[2] See Nef, *A Search for Civilization* (Chicago, 1962).

in different countries, among different races, and among different societies. These differences are an important part of the stuff of history.

As salvation has been sought during the last four hundred years, as never before, in the increased output of material commodities, the methods of manufacturing, the forms of industrial organization, and the purposes for which the commodities are made have changed profoundly. The changes have presented us with an industrial structure unique in human experience. How has the course of European history since the Reformation, how have the ways of working, living, and thinking, inherited from the Middle Ages and developed in the harsh climate and in the midst of the rich natural resources of northern Europe, made possible this industrial structure? How has its growth influenced the ways of working, the ways of living, and the ways of thinking, writing, and speaking which have gained ascendancy in both the popular and the scholarly organs of communication in the twentieth century?

THE RENAISSANCE: AN ERA OF INDUSTRIAL EXPANSION

In the early sixteenth century industrial workpeople formed a small but considerable minority of the inhabitants of Europe. They gained their living by mining, quarrying, building, clothmaking, and by many other kinds of manual work, including the various industrial arts such as printing and painting. It is often difficult to distinguish between industrial workers and farmers and shopkeepers. Some labor that we now think of as industrial— like the making of salt—was carried on in much the same manner as husbandry.[3] A great many families divided their time among a variety of occupations—some industrial, some mercantile, some agrarian. Out of perhaps sixty to seventy million people living in western Europe,[4] the persons engaged during most of their working days in industry may have numbered some two or three millions or even more.

For Europe generally the late fourteenth and early fifteenth centuries had not been times of industrial prosperity. With the use of gunpowder for driving projectiles, which began apparently in the second or third decade of the fourteenth century, the advantage in war tended to pass from the defenders to the attackers.[5] This invited conquest and counterconquest, which

---

[3] See below, pp. 102–3.

[4] The best estimate that we have puts the population of western Europe round about the year 1600 at 73,500,000 (Julius Beloch, "Die Bevölkerung Europas zur Zeit der Renaissance," *Zeitschrift für Sozialwissenschaft*, III [1900], 783; cf. 765–86). At that time the population of England and Wales was considerably larger than in 1540, while the population of Spain, Italy, and possibly other countries was somewhat larger. On the other hand, the population of France and the southern Low Countries was probably somewhat smaller than in 1540.

[5] Nef, *Western Civilization since the Renaissance*, pp. 24–32.

increased the instability inherent in political institutions. The wars interfered with trade and led to the destruction of industrial plant.[6]

In contrast to the late fourteenth and early fifteenth centuries, the late fifteenth and early sixteenth centuries were a period of renewed prosperity. The Middle Ages drew to a close in the midst of great movements of discovery, colonization, invention, and economic growth, in some respects even more striking than those of the Gothic period. The generation of Leonardo da Vinci (1452–1519) and the generation of Luther (1483–1546) participated in a remarkable industrial expansion. In some parts of Europe this expansion culminated in the 1520's and 1530's,[7] at the time when the doctrines of the Reformation were spreading from town to town and were making hosts of converts among the industrial workers and the small traders in the countries north and west of the Alps.

While Vasco da Gama, Columbus, and other explorers were finding new sea routes and a new continent, while Copernicus was discovering a new celestial world, the Western peoples were again on the lookout for minerals, as they had been in the late twelfth and thirteenth centuries. Miners and smelters were searching for new supplies of ore all over the Continent.[8] This busy interest in mining and metallurgy, which has already engaged our attention in chapter i, was partly a reflection of the growing need for metal tools and accessories in a vast number of trades that were making Renaissance Europe an increasingly active hive of craftsmanship and manufacturing. The incantations of the alchemists were not actually turning stones to gold. Their methods were already distrusted by more scientifically minded men like the great south German physicians Paracelsus and Agricola, both of whom spent part of their lives in the mining communities[9] and learned about the new mineralogy and the new mechanics at first hand. But science was only beginning to take the place of superstition.[10] So it may well have seemed to many that the alchemists had set great numbers of persons to work by mixing various ingredients in mysterious new combinations.

It was not magic but the improvement and the spread of old industrial processes, the introduction of new or virtually new processes into Europe, and the increase in the demand for manufactured products of all kinds—from the salt needed to preserve meat and fish to the table linen of the very wealthy—which accounted for the growth of industry. The markets for luxuries and artistic wares grew rapidly among rulers, nobles, and rich churchmen, and above all among the rising merchant princes who engaged in trade and moneylending on a large scale and to some extent in the financing of mining and manufacturing. This class of rich merchants was gaining

[6] See above, p. 31.
[7] See above, p. 42.
[8] See above, pp. 42 ff.
[9] See above, pp. 41–42.
[10] Cf. below, chap. vii.

in wealth and in numbers all over Europe, particularly in the towns in the east and south of the old Holy Roman Empire, as well as in Italy, Spain, and Portugal.[11] Unlike the town merchants in the twelfth and thirteenth centuries, they seldom turned over the bulk of their increasingly large fortunes to cathedral chapters and other ecclesiastical foundations to atone for their sins. They often confined their contributions to adding vestries and chapels, bearing their names, to the great gothic churches. A far larger part of private fortunes much greater than those accumulated in the Gothic age was spent, not to glorify God, but to satisfy the taste of men and women full of worldly ambitions. They delighted in works of art and decoration, many of which the church had condemned as sensuous.

In the ancient, compact, entrancing town of Bourges, the contrast between the buildings of the Gothic age and those of the Renaissance can be seen very sharply. In a sort of saucer in the lower part of the city, set off from the other buildings, rises one of the most beautiful of medieval cathedrals. Not far off, up the hill flush against a narrow, curving street, is the great palace of Jacques Cœur—one of the richest and most glamorous merchants in the age of the Renaissance. It was built in the 1440's before the industrial expansion of the Renaissance had really begun, but two or three hundred years later than the cathedral. The interior walls are covered with Cœur's celebrated motto, with its play upon his name, "A vaillans cœurs, riens impossible." [12]

The cathedral is a world in itself. It has come down to us much as it was in the thirteenth century, with statues in stone and incomparable stained-glass windows, cut and fashioned to instruct the people in morality and beauty, to strengthen and console them in their faith. By comparison, the palace of Jacques Cœur for all its harmony and symmetry is obsolete and barren. Erected for the purposes of one man rather than for all the faithful, its raison d'être, unlike that of the cathedral, disappeared ages ago. It was once full of rich chests and beds, exquisite ornamental iron, gold, and silver work, and painted-glass windows, wonderful hangings and bedding and tapestries, and curious pieces of sculpture sometimes hidden in closets reached only by a concealed staircase. The dining tables were set with the finest pewter service. Among the most perfect of all French fifteenth-century buildings, the palace was for a few brief years full of the luxurious, exciting life led by Cœur and his friends and associates, including many of the most powerful officials in France. After Cœur's disgrace and imprisonment,[13] his palace was confiscated by the crown in 1453. It has since passed through

[11] Cf. Jakob Strieder, *Zur Genesis der modernen Kapitalismus* (Leipzig, 1904); Richard Ehrenberg, *Capital and Finance in the Age of the Renaissance,* trans. H. M. Lucas (London, 1928); J. A. Goris, *Etude sur les colonies marchandes méridionales à Anvers de 1488 à 1567* (Louvain, 1925); etc.
[12] "For valiant hearts, nothing is impossible."
[13] See below, p. 109.

the hands of many persons, including (two hundred years afterward) the great Colbert, whose rise from a humble origin to the highest offices in the state resembled in some respects the rise of Cœur himself. Eventually the palace was taken over by the municipal government. In the course of time it was stripped of many of its interior decorations and of all its original purpose.[14] Now it is a museum.

The palaces of merchants and the town halls and municipal law courts, representing a mercantile society, were rising in profusion in towns all over Europe.[15] In Italy, where such buildings first appeared in large numbers, a new style of architecture—the Renaissance—had begun to replace the flamboyant gothic as early as the middle of the fifteenth century. During the next hundred years, the new Italian architecture spread north of the Alps to many towns, such as Nuremberg, Augsburg, Leipzig, Antwerp, Lyons, Paris, Rouen, and Caen. In the German cities care was extended to the construction and the upkeep of the streets, the bridges, and the quays. In Italy the palaces with their wonderful exteriors and their lavish interior decorations and embellishments were surrounded by dirt and squalor. Here in the warm south was what the French call a *beau désordre*. It was the disorder of the artist who concentrates upon his masterpiece and leaves the rest of his studio to accumulate dust. Unlike the modern business executive or social science professor, he cannot afford the time to put away his materials or trust secretaries to do it for him. Travelers crossing the Brenner, passing from the areas of German settlement into Italy, seldom failed to comment on the change in the aspect of the cities and small towns. They passed from general neatness and order, from roomy streets and ample public squares, from a society in which miners had their Saturday night baths with a methodical regularity,[16] to great beauty in a setting of many unkempt, poor houses, without windowpanes or other amenities, built along narrow, winding passageways which had served as paths for cattle centuries before.

Whether the new buildings went up under the direction of south German discipline or under the influence of the seemingly more easygoing Italian artistry, it was largely the requirements of the social orders who built them, either for their own purposes or the purposes of their cities, bourgs, and states, which brought about the expansion of European industry in the decades preceding the Reformation. Great also was the role played in these demands by the rulers of the small principalities into which Central Europe

[14] Cf. Pierre Clément, *Jacques Cœur et Charles VII* (Paris, 1866), pp. 147 ff., 342–44, 420–26.

[15] Even in some of the provincial towns of England, which remained in something of an industrial backwater compared with most Continental countries (E. M. Carus-Wilson, "The Overseas Trade of Bristol," in E. Power and M. Postan, *Studies in English Trade in the Fifteenth Century* [London, 1933], p. 231).

[16] Cf. above, p. 50.

and Italy were divided. Political authority increasingly dominated authority derived from mercantile pursuits; and even the merchants, as Jacques Cœur's device suggests, thought less of comfort and material security than of daring and splendor. It would be incongruous to confuse his motto with that of a modern beer baron or steel magnate. The bodily risks run by rich men were then far greater than they became in nineteenth-century Europe, with its police and its greater social order, for at the Reformation trade and piracy were still first cousins.

To the demand for articles to satisfy the need for splendor and decoration in the age of the Renaissance was joined the demand for weapons of war. The technique of warfare was changing with what contemporaries regarded as revolutionary speed, so that the older methods of defense were out of date. Kings and princes stored up ordnance and ammunition during a lull between wars, in anticipation of a coming struggle for authority and dominion.[17] To the demands of war and decoration was joined the demand for conveyances, above all for ships, to move raw materials and finished products from one part of Europe to another, in an age when the trade in light luxury articles of all kinds and some heavier products—such as copper, alum, tin, and steel—was international.

Various stimuli brought about an increase in the production of fine silk and woolen cloth, tapestries, sails, and ropes. In all probability the growth in the output of these goods was hardly less rapid than the growth in the output of metal. As shipping increased and markets widened, the demand for salt expanded. At scores of centers in Continental Europe—from the rock-salt mines at Wieliczka in Poland to the marshes along the coasts of Provence and Languedoc—there were fresh calls for labor to help in heating brine and rock-salt solutions or in evaporating seawater.[18] The growth in the cloth and the salt manufactures was accompanied by a remarkable development of industries like printing, which were entirely novel; of others like the making of paper, soap, glass, and gunpowder, for which the demand had been slight; and of still others, like the making of alum and sugar,[19] for which Europe had been mainly dependent upon the older societies of the Near and the Far East.

The progress of the manufacture of alum brought with it an exceptionally large concentration of capital and labor in a single enterprise. Nothing in

---

[17] Nef, *Western Civilization since the Renaissance*, pp. 24 ff. On the growth of centralized political authority in industrial matters, see above, pp. 52 ff., and below, pp. 101 ff.

[18] Konrad Wutke, "Die Versorgung Schlesiens mit Salz während des Mittelalters," *Zeitschrift des Vereins für Geschichte und Altertum Schlesiens*, XXVII (1893), 283. For Provence I have consulted various manuscripts in the Archives départementales des Bouches-du-Rhône.

[19] For the introduction of sugar refining into Europe toward the end of the Middle Ages, see Edmund O. von Lippmann, *Geschichte des Zuckers* (Berlin, 1929), esp. pp. 324, 326–31, 337, 339, 357, 428–29.

Renaissance Italy was more expressive of the new joy in life and in the luster man can give to life by art than the love of color. That love of color achieved its greatest harmony and perfection in the paintings of the Venetians, Giorgione and Titian. It was also revealed in the creations of the textile workers who prepared clothing, bedding, table coverings, and hangings for the wealthy and the powerful throughout Europe. In order to dye cloth successfully and to bring out the qualities that inspired some of Titian's wonderful interiors, adequate supplies of the very best alum were indispensable.

A little alum, inferior in quality to that of the Near East, had been made in Europe before the fifteenth century. But the European supply had never been fine enough or nearly large enough to meet the needs of the medieval textile workers. Even Italy remained almost totally dependent upon imports from the Levant until 1462. In that year John de Castro, the widely traveled son of a famous jurist of Padua, was rewarded for a long search by the discovery, in the papal estates at Tolfa, of stones which, from his earlier visits to Constantinople and Asia Minor, he knew to contain alum of the highest quality.[20] The proximity of the deposits to Civita Vecchia made the shipment of the dyeing matter easy. Castro, whom the pope had appointed commissary general for the revenues of the papal chamber, told his holy master that the discovery assured the defeat of the infidel, as it promised to make Europe independent of the Near East for its costly supplies of alum. A decade later, in 1471, the yearly output at Tolfa amounted to over a thousand tons—almost twice the quantity annually imported at Genoa on the eve of Castro's discovery, when Genoa had been the chief receiving center in Europe.[21]

The vast works at Tolfa were under the control of the pope. They produced so much alum that the papacy set about, with a measure of success, to monopolize the supply for all Europe. The pope threatened to excommunicate not only the traders who sold alum from the Levant but also the civil and religious authorities who tolerated such a trade. By the beginning of the sixteenth century newly found deposits of alum stones in southern Spain, near Cartagena, and in Central Europe were also being exploited. Reports of further supplies came from many districts on the Continent. Though these reports frequently proved inaccurate, enough alum was made outside Italy to interfere seriously with the efforts of the pope to monopolize

[20] According to John Beckmann, alumworks were built somewhat earlier, in 1458, near Pisa (*A History of Inventions* [4th English ed.; London, 1881], I, 193). The definitive work on the alum-making industry at Tolfa has just appeared: Jean Delumeau, *L'Alun de Rome XVᵉ–XIXᵉ siècle* (Paris, 1962), pp. 20 ff.

[21] Delumeau, *op. cit.*, p. 124; Goswin van der Ropp, "Zur Geschichte des Alaunhandels im 15. Jahrhundert," *Hansische Geschichtsblätter*, X (1900), 123–26, 129; cf. Jakob Strieder, *Studien zur Geschichte kapitalistischer Organisationsformen* (2d ed.; Munich, 1925), pp. 170–71.

its manufacture.[22] The ascendancy of papal alum diminished. In 1549 the alumworks in Bohemia were regarded by the king as sufficiently productive to supply all the needs of that country.[23] Before this time, as Castro had foreseen, the Europeans, with the help of the Roman supplies, had become virtually self-sufficient for their alum.

The multiplication of building enterprises, together with the growth of metallurgy, alum-making, and many other fuel-consuming industries, put a strain upon the supplies of wood in a number of districts. In Central Europe and central and northern France the thick forests generally stood the strain, in spite of local shortages of firewood and charcoal. Along the Mediterranean, in those parts of southern Europe sparsely stocked with timber, like Languedoc and the districts around Venice, industries spendthrift of fuel or lumber languished.

The rapid increase in the demand for fuel combined with the increasing pressure on the supplies of wood to arouse a fresh interest in outcropping coal seams. At many places coal had provided firing ever since the thirteenth century for those smiths and limeburners who lived within a few miles of supplies.[24] In a number of districts in southern and central France (especially in Lyonnais, Forez, Nivernais, and Alais), in Silesia, Saxony, Westphalia, and the Wurmrevier, coal digging began to employ a larger number of local peasants during the fifty years preceding the Reformation than earlier in the Middle Ages. Other peasants loaded the dirty black stones and gravel into sacks and carried them on packhorses or in river boats to nearby towns, where the smiths and limeburners had got along in the past with wood and charcoal. But nowhere on the Continent, except in the southern Low Countries, had coal mining become an industry of real importance at the time of the Reformation. In what we now call Belgium, after 1500, the progress of building and metalworking, gunpowder-making, and the manufacture of firearms was as striking as in Saxony and southern Germany. The woods were leaner north of the Ardennes than in most parts of Central Europe or France. Consequently the output of coal, already more noteworthy in the fifteenth century in what we now call Belgium than in any other Continental country, increased notably at the time of the Reformation.[25]

The growing output of all kinds of minerals was part of a general expansion in the volume of commodities and trade. How did this expansion alter the economic conditions among the workpeople of Europe?

[22] Jules Finot, "Le Commerce d'alun dans les Pays-Bas," *Bulletin historique et philologique du comité des travaux historiques et scientifiques,* 1902, pp. 419–27; Strieder, *op. cit.,* pp. 180–81.

[23] Kaspar Sternberg, *Umrisse einer Geschichte der böhmischen Bergwerke* (Prague, 1836), I, Part II, 83–84.

[24] See above, pp. 14–15.

[25] See above, p. 45.

INDUSTRIAL ORGANIZATION IN AND AROUND THE ANCIENT TOWNS

At the beginning of the twentieth century the most characteristic venture in mining and manufacturing in Europe was a plant especially built for industrial purposes, owned and operated for the profit of a capitalist or a group of capitalists who took no part in the manual labor, and staffed by wage-earners hired in a free market who left their homes every day to go to their work. The policy of the enterprise was settled by the owners and the administrative officers they appointed or by those among the owners who secured by their financial connections a controlling voice in the management. As long as the enterprise broke no general political laws, as long as it did not lay itself open to prosecution in the courts, the state had no authority to interfere with it.

While enterprises of this type have existed in most, if not all, advanced societies, for example in the Roman Empire and in China, notably during the Sung dynasty, it is among the western European peoples that they first became dominant in the sense that a majority of all industrial workers came to be employed in them. Their rise to dominance accompanied the conquest of the material world during the four centuries that have followed the Reformation. It is connected in a variety of ways with that conquest.

In the late twelfth and thirteenth centuries, in the age of Albertus Magnus and Thomas Aquinas, the main industrial pursuits—other than mining, metallurgy, and saltmaking—had been concentrated in the rising towns. Except in a few clothmaking centers, most of the master craftsmen owned not only their tools and industrial utensils and the hearths and ovens for heating their materials, but also the raw materials they needed in their work. Most of them sold their products either indirectly to local tradesmen or directly to the municipal governments and cathedral chapters, and to townspeople, churchmen, landlords from the neighboring country, and passing travelers.

Two hundred years later, at the time of the Reformation, the proportion of all industrial pursuits carried on in those ancient towns had diminished. The old towns, together with such suburbs as had grown up outside their medieval walls, remained, nevertheless, the chief foci of industrial life except in parts of Central Europe, the Low Countries, and the west of England, where the expansion of mining, metallurgy, and textiles had been particularly rapid.

On the Continent there were thousands of places that had existed as municipalities, with a governing administration and laws of their own, at least as far back as the time of Dante (1265–1321). What was the size of these towns two centuries after his death? How far did their growth reflect the industrial expansion of the Renaissance?

It was the fashion for writers of the time to exaggerate the number of urban inhabitants, sometimes out of civic pride.[26] They might be surprised to find how seriously their figures have been taken by some unwary recent scholars who have not realized how uninterested their distant ancestors were about precision in such matters. Recent historical research provides much more reliable estimates of urban population after the twelfth century, and enables us to determine with some confidence how populous towns were at the time of the Reformation.

How can this be? The explanation seems clear. Medieval officials collected pretty accurate data when they levied municipal taxes. A considerable proportion of this data has survived filed away in archives, which have provided a hunting ground for increasingly numerous historical researchers ever since the nineteenth century. These modern scholars are quantitatively minded to a far greater degree than their ancient predecessors. When they see this data, they pounce on them, add them up, consider them scientifically and provide us with figures which as estimates are almost always superior to those provided by early historical chroniclers. As a result we can now learn a lot more accurately how many people there were in European towns in the early sixteenth century than the servants of Charles V, Francis I, and Henry VIII could have told those princes, who were in any case less concerned with accuracy in such matters than a modern ruler.[27]

So we can now say with some confidence that there were in 1540 a few fairly large cities in the Mediterranian countries. Palermo, Naples, Rome, Venice, Florence, Seville, perhaps Barcelona, each had in the neighborhood of a hundred thousand or more inhabitants. North of the Alps and the Pyrenees, Paris was even larger. But it was the only city in that class around 1530. In the north there had been, nevertheless, during the decades preceding the Reformation, a remarkable growth in many smaller places. In Germany and the Spanish Netherlands, in particular, several towns had increased rapidly in population with the expansion of industry and trade. Nuremberg more than doubled, Leipzig tripled, and Antwerp probably

---

[26] Cf. Heinrich Kretschmahr, *Geschichte von Venedig* (Gotha, 1920), II, 302. The work of historians during the past century has shown that the figures given by medieval writers for the population of towns or for the death rate or the birth rate usually bear little resemblance to statistical truth. These medieval writers were capable of assigning a town a population of from double to five times the actual figure. For example, modern research into medieval documents has shown that in 1449 Nuremberg had about twenty thousand inhabitants. Yet we are told that in the plague of 1437 some thirteen thousand citizens perished! (Karl Bücher, *Die Bevölkerung von Frankfurt am Main* [Tübingen, 1886], I, 9–10). Examples could be multiplied. (Cf. Henri Pirenne, "Les Dénombrements de la population d'Ypres au XV⁰ siècle," *Vierteljahrsschrift für Social- und Wirtschaftsgeschichte*, I [1903], 5–6, 10–11.)

[27] See Nef, *La Naissance de la civilisation industrielle et le monde contemporain*, pp. 23–24. Also Nef, *Cultural Foundations of Industrial Civilization*, pp. 6 ff.

quadrupled during the late fifteenth and early sixteenth centuries.[28] By 1540 Nuremberg, Augsburg, Breslau, Danzig, Strasbourg, Bourges, Lyons, Lille, Rouen, and London each had from twenty-five to fifty thousand inhabitants. There were other places in the same class, and Antwerp was larger, with upward of fifty thousand people.

Yet the great majority of towns were still very small, hardly towns at all in point of numbers according to our twentieth-century notions. Many of them had a population of between one or two and fifteen or twenty thousand inhabitants. England had only a few places of more than five thousand, while London, which was already swelling in Henry VIII's reign, was apparently the sole city which had more than fifteen thousand people.

With the growth in urban population in the age of the Reformation, especially on the Continent, the size of some workshops and studios in and about the towns increased. At the same time the proportion of the municipal craftsmen who were independent of capitalist traders either for their materials or for their markets or for both diminished, especially in the chief industrial regions of Italy, Central Europe, and the Low Countries. Yet, in spite of the increase in the scale of production, the home generally remained the place of work. Labor was done either in the actual living quarters or in a studio or shop opening off from them. Some of the wealthier craftsmen, especially those engaged in the numerous decorative arts, had little houses of their own. Others lived in rented rooms, garrets, or cellars. Unlike the modern industrial workman, businessman, doctor, lawyer, or professor in the United States, most town craftsmen on the eve of the Reformation had everything they needed to earn their livelihood ready to hand where they slept and ate and conversed with their family, their apprentices, and their journeymen. No time was lost going to work, going to lunch, going to a club. In a fraction of the time needed by a city dweller today to reach his place of business in his automobile or in a fast train, most craftsmen could make their way on foot along the narrow, sinuous streets to the fields beyond the town walls. A weekly or perhaps a monthly visit to the town market place or to the warehouse of some local merchant supplied them with the materials they needed, if, indeed, these materials were not brought to them by the merchants or their agents. The craftsmen often depended for their sales upon citizens who came to the shops to buy and who often looked on while the labor was being done. The wives of the cutlers and other workers in some towns on the main-traveled roads called at the inns or loitered about the town gates to ensnare the patronage of passing travelers.

---

[28] J. Jastrow, *Die Volkszahl deutscher Städte zu Ende des Mittelalters* (Berlin, 1886), pp. 157–58; Ernest Kroker, "Leipzig und die sächsischen Bergwerke," *Schriften des Vereins für die Geschichte Leipzigs,* IX (1909), pp. 26–27; Henri Pirenne, *Histoire de Belgique* (3d ed.; Brussels, 1923), III, 274–75.

Smiths of most kinds, cutlers, coopers, hatmakers, glovemakers, and other makers of wearing apparel remained almost everywhere independent workmen. They sold their wares, or contracted in advance for the sale, at prices which were generally regulated by their gilds or by the town governments when they were not organized into formal gilds. Further rules governed the quality and the size of the products. Similar conditions prevailed in the baking of bread for public sale, which had become fairly common, at least in the larger towns. Art had hardly begun to be separated from ordinary craftsmanship, except to some extent in the great Italian centers— Rome, Florence, Venice, and Milan. For the most part the organization of pewterers, wood-carvers, goldsmiths and silversmiths, sculptors, painters, glaziers, etchers, and makers of ornamental ironwares resembled that of ordinary smiths. Orders came to them from the cathedral chapters and other ecclesiastical foundations, as the stalls and the choirs and the interior walls of cathedrals and churches were decorated anew. Orders also came from the town governments for the embellishment of municipal buildings, from the wealthy merchants who were putting up great new houses and palaces with elaborate courtyards, and from princes, nobles, and other powerful landlords who wanted statues and all kinds of ornaments and furniture for their castles and manor houses. The orders were frequently precise. The cathedral chapter, for example, specified the size of the object to be supplied, the subject, and the design, often down to most minute details, such as the disposition of the draperies of the Virgin's dress.

Craftsmen were called on for labor both in their own shops and in the buildings they were asked to decorate. The main object often was to create beautiful and lastingly satisfactory artistic effects, as is evident from the methods of making the painted-glass windows for churches in northern France and in England. In both countries and in Flanders, according to Vasari, by a happy choice of glass the makers got even more perfect results than in Venice.[29] Glass-painting was ceasing to be an independent art and was becoming the handmaid of painting proper.[30] In Brittany all the operations were done by one person or by a master with an apprentice or two and a journeyman. The same craftsman who prepared the white plates or panes of glass in his little furnace painted them with a composition of brilliant colors. These were then burned into the plate as it was baked again and again and finally riveted together with other plates into a single window. In glassmaking of this kind it was impossible to separate industry from art. If quantity suffered as a result of this combination of functions, the artist gained in unity of purpose and composition. He did not have the material

[29] Georgio Vasari, De la peinture (1551), French trans. by Charles Weiss (Paris, n.d.), chap. xviii.
[30] Eugène Müntz, Les Arts à la cour des papes (1878), p. 76; as cited by G. G. Coulton, Art and the Reformation (Oxford, 1928), p. 430.

objective of making a large profit, which pushes the owners of a modern factory or electrical power plant to run their enterprise.[31] It was essentially the same in pewter work and goldsmith's work, in cutlery, in wood-carving. It was essentially the same in the many kinds of ironwork which belonged among the decorative crafts. The Middle Ages were the most brilliant period in the history of artistic ironware, partly because the metal was scarce and dear, partly because the labor of manipulating it was done without machinery and almost always with the object of obtaining a beautiful appearance. "Every good smith," according to a student of the ironmaking industry in Lorraine, "had to be a veritable artist." [32]

The labor of a great many of the craftsmen who worked with glass, wood, or metal resembled that of a painter or etcher; and unlike the work of some modern painters or etchers, it involved the preparation as well as the use of the materials. It was also work that had a definite and immediate purpose which the craftsman understood. What he did was destined often to fit into a particular part of a building or monument which he knew intimately. Such work called not only for a detailed knowledge of materials, of color combinations, of designs, and of plastic effects; on account of the prescribed subject matter, it also called frequently for some knowledge of theology and history.

Most craftsmen lived on a far lower material standard—insofar as the quantity of amenities and comforts was concerned—than the one now prevailing among manual workmen in most of Europe. As disease was more deadly, their lives were generally much shorter. For a variety of reasons they had to endure greater bodily pain. Sanitation and medical and surgical treatment were crude, and anesthetics were lacking to diminish suffering. In the give and take of ordinary life physical cruelty was much more taken for granted than it is today.

In spite of material want and the prevalence of physical pain, many craftsmen in their small shops created with their hands and their minds a richer and more varied world than is now accessible to most mechanics and clerks. The work was generally more absorbing.[33] It required a special

[31] Cf. Auguste André, "De la verrerie et des vitraux peints dans l'ancienne province de Bretagne," *Bulletin et mémoire de la société archéologique du département d'Ille et Villaine*, XII (1878), 119–20.

[32] E. Gréau, *Le Fer en Lorraine* (Nancy, 1908), p. vii.

[33] The views expressed here and later in this essay, concerning the nature of Renaissance craftsmanship, may seem to the casual reader to be sharply at variance with those of Dr. G. G. Coulton and some other writers (see especially his *Art and the Reformation*). In essential respects, the differences are more apparent than real.

For one thing, Dr. Coulton is concerned mainly with masons, carpenters, and other building workmen. He gives less attention to the numerous town craftsmen who provided the furniture, the ornaments, and the other decorations for the buildings and the rooms within them. Generally speaking, the labor of the Renaissance craftsmen who made such articles in their domestic workshops, and even in studios specially constructed for the purpose, had more variety than the labor of the rank and file of build-

training. Throughout the Middle Ages the crafts had been the places where persons who labored with matter got their education. Universities were reserved for those who pursued the liberal arts, who were concerned with speculations and constructions of the mind. In the shops the master craftsman was the teacher. He employed apprentices, whom he was bound to feed and clothe, to lodge, and to instruct. He also employed journeymen, though the number of assistants he could keep at a time was usually limited to a very few by the rules of his gild or of the town government. Since the early thirteenth century there had been a growing tendency, especially in the crafts where the equipment was costly, for the mastership to become exclusive. Not all journeymen could look forward to becoming masters; the proportion who ended their careers as wage-earning employees of some master was increasing. By the beginning of the sixteenth century in all the chief towns many were obliged to serve their whole lives as journeymen. Even in those crafts where the workshops were small—and few masters kept more than two assistants—their relations with their employers were often unsatisfactory. Journeymen frequently objected to the long hours of

---

ing workmen. It called for more artistic initiative. The contrasts between the nature of work of this kind in Continental Europe in the early sixteenth century and in the Anglo-Saxon countries today are more striking than those between the nature of building work in the two periods.

In the second place, Dr. Coulton has never denied that very great changes have taken place in the occupations of the common workman. While he remarks that the generality of men were no more artistic in the Middle Ages than they are now (*op. cit.*, pp. 429, 479, 484 ff.), he recognizes that the conditions of ordinary industrial work provided more scope for the exercise of artistic impulses (*ibid.*, pp. 480, 487–88). If I understand him correctly, in questioning as vigorously as he does the validity of the idyllic pictures of the life of the medieval craftsmen that have been sometimes painted, his chief purposes are two. He is challenging the view that *modern* society would be better off than it is if we abandoned machinery for handicraft and tried to return to the working conditions prevalent in the Middle Ages (*ibid.*, pp. 480, 482). He is also challenging the view that medieval art was the product, in any exclusive (or even predominant) sense, of the church or of the religious outlook fostered by Catholicism. I need hardly say that, as a historian, I am not writing to advocate the restoration of the working conditions or even the religion of medieval Europe! As a historian, I am trying to show, however imperfectly, what working conditions were like in the early sixteenth century.

If, in what I have written, there is any fundamental disagreement with Dr. Coulton, it is over the extent to which artistic craftsmanship persisted in Continental Europe in the age of the Renaissance. My suggestion is that the industrial development of the Continental countries from about 1460 to about 1540 provided more scope for artistic craftsmanship than did the later very rapid industrial expansion which began in Great Britain after about 1540 and particularly after about 1580 (cf. Nef, *Industry and Government in France and England, 1540–1640*, pp. 139–40). That is not to exalt the former and belittle the latter. Artistic craftsmanship is an important value, but it is not the only one worth striving for. Nor is there anything novel in my position. It is more or less a commonplace among Americans who have understood the Latin and particularly the French contribution to civilization (see, e.g., Edith Wharton, *French Ways and Their Meaning* [New York, 1919]).

On the role played by artistic taste in preparing the way for industrialism, see Nef, *Cultural Foundations of Industrial Civilization*, pp. 111–23, 132–38.

their labor, to the low wages they were paid, or to the kind of tasks they were asked to perform. When masters were organized into gilds, journey-men sometimes formed associations of their own to advance their interests. But the trouble between masters and journeymen was more like that which arises between housewives and domestic servants, than that between modern industrial wage-earners and factory directors.

Master and journeyman often had in common one experience seldom shared by a housewife and a domestic servant and never shared by the owners of a modern industrial plant and their employees. Both were en-gaged directly and continuously on a common piece of work. If the master rose from his bed in the early morning to peer with the help of a candle, or of the dim light that came through a slit in the wall, at the glass he had been preparing or the ornamental balustrade he had been fashioning the day before, he may have cursed his journeyman for the stupid way he had bungled a part of the job, or he may have remembered with pleasure some skilful turn of the hand. In any case he thought of the journeyman, and the journeyman thought of him, as an associate in an enterprise that was often artistic.

Not all the domestic workshops were autonomous, in the sense that the master bought his own raw materials and sold the product of his labor at a profit or loss depending on his manual skill, his location, and his success as a manager of his small venture. In most towns which specialized in the manufacture of fine cloth, not even a majority of the domestic workshops were autonomous in that sense. Ever since the thirteenth century, textile manufacturing had lent itself to the formation of larger enterprises, requir-ing capital running into the modern equivalent of many thousands and in a few cases tens of thousands of dollars.[34] Such enterprises were especially common at the time of the Reformation in the towns of northern Italy, Flanders, and Brabant, where beautiful silk and woolen cloth and brilliant tapestries were produced for markets throughout Europe and even to some extent for markets in the Near East. As clothmaking, with its endless rami-fications, perhaps employed something like half as many workpeople as all the other medieval industries combined, the forms of industrial organization which predominated in it are of special interest.

Three conditions provided favorable openings for wealthy merchants with substantial savings to invest. One was the need for bringing the stuffs and the dyeing materials, particularly alum, from distant places. In making nearly any kind of woolen cloth a great variety of wools, sometimes thirty or more, had to be skilfully mixed. They were often obtained from the sheep of several districts. A second condition that provided an opening

[34] Cf. Georges Espinas, *Sire Jehan Boinebroke* (Lille, 1933), pp. 92, 95–142, and authorities there cited; Frances Consitt, *The London Weavers' Company* (Oxford, 1933), pp. 6 ff., 30–31.

for the capitalist trader was the number of separate stages through which the material had to pass before it was ready for the market. The making of fine woolens or silks involved a score or more operations, each undertaken by a different workman in a different workplace. Without some central administration to arrange and co-ordinate the operations, to provide carts, mules, and packhorses to carry the wool to the women who spun in the suburbs and surrounding villages, and to instal warehouses at convenient places where the weavers could come for yarn, the manufacture would have been in hopeless confusion. Finally, the international character of the markets for the finer cloth and tapestries, produced in the chief centers of the manufacture in Italy and the Low Countries, made it necessary to have trading connections in distant countries, in order to decide what quantities of the various types of cloth should be made and to dispose of them where they were wanted.

In response to these conditions, the greater part of all the best kinds of cloth manufactured in Europe in the early sixteenth century was made under the direction of traders or financiers with capital, whose investments in the larger of these commercial enterprises might run into the modern equivalent of hundreds of thousands and even millions of dollars. The textile business attracted many of the richest merchants in Christendom, the Medicis of Florence and the Fuggers of Augsburg, whose faces and bearing have been immortalized in some of the best-known paintings of the Renaissance. One of the most striking hangs at Munich in the Alte Pinokothek. It is the great likeness made by Dürer of Jacob Fugger, the founder of the house, with a wrap made of the choicest fur thrown round his shoulders.

These rich and powerful merchants were nearly always engaged in many other kinds of business besides the manufacture and sale of cloth. They had a finger in most financial pies. So they generally left the administration of their textile enterprises in the hands of managers, who were frequently taken into partnership without having, like the other partners, to invest much, if any, capital. Both in Italy and southern Germany it was common for less wealthy merchants, as well as for these great lords of finance, to form partnerships for the manufacture of cloth, generally for a short term of three or four years. In the Low Countries almost all the actual manufacture was in the hands of these lesser merchants, who generally had at least indirect connections with the great financial dynasties of the south, many of whom maintained commercial houses at Antwerp. The partnerships and the independent merchants dealt with the craftsmen sometimes directly and sometimes through salaried officials and agents working for commissions.

Many cloth merchants kept carders and combers and, less frequently, weavers, dyers, and pressers at work in the shops, which were often at-

tached to their warehouses.[35] Some Italian textile firms had large warehouses of several stories, and sometimes one or more of the rooms were
given over to clothworkers who labored for wages. But even those textile
partnerships in which the Medici participated at Florence ordinarily had
only about a dozen wageworkers in their establishments.[36] In a few exceptional cases a score or more looms were installed, all in a row, under a
single roof—as at Ferrara and Venice and at Newbury in the south of
England, where the famous English cloth merchant, John Winchcombe,
said to have been one of Henry VIII's hosts, employed many weavers in
one building. Yet, on the eve of the dissolution of the English monasteries,
the proportion of all the European textile workers who labored under semifactory conditions of this kind, alongside twenty or more of their fellows,
was still small.

Most of the actual labor connected with the making of all kinds of
cloth was done in the homes of the craftsmen, often by masters with journeymen and apprentices. Sometimes, as was frequently the case with the
spinners and carders of wool, the material was brought to the cottages,
cellars, or garrets of the workers, and the labor was performed for a piecework wage. The partly finished goods were placed on a shelf until a trader
or a factor or agent of a trading partnership came to collect them and to
chat with the maker about the problems of the trade or about their common
domestic trials. Again, as was frequently the case with the weavers and
the sorters of wool, the craftsman came to the warehouse for his materials.
He was expected to turn in his work there before he was paid, though the
merchants sometimes advanced money to weavers, who pledged their looms
as security for the loans. Finally, as was frequently the case with the fullers
and dyers, the craftsmen purchased the stuffs either outright or on credit
and worked them up to sell to merchants with whom they had entered into
contracts for delivery. Sometimes these were a different set of merchants
from those who had furnished the stuffs.

Masters with some degree of independence from the textile firms existed
in practically every branch of clothmaking, even in the chief manufacturing
centers. It is not certain that the majority of the master craftsmen in the
town textile industries were employed for wages, though the proportion so
employed was certainly large.[37] Even the wageworkers under this putting-
out system possessed an independence that is denied the employee in a
modern mine or factory. While the textile firms, which co-ordinated the

[35] Heinrich Sieveking, "Die genueser Seidenindustrie im 15. und 16. Jahrhundert,"
Jahrbuch für Gesetzgebung, Verwaltung und Volkswirtschaft, XXI (1897), 132.
[36] *Ibid.,* pp. 129–30.
[37] For the conditions in making silk cloth in Italy, see R. Broglio d'Ajano, *Die
venetianische Seidenindustrie . . . bis zum Ausgang des Mittelalters* (Stuttgart, 1893),
pp. 33–34, 47, 49; Sieveking, *op. cit.,* pp. 103, 106–12, 128. For the conditions in the
woolen industry see, *inter alia,* Consitt, *op. cit.,* p. 104.

various processes of manufacture, sometimes tried to supervise labor on the looms in the workers' homes, the methods used and the hours worked were generally left to the discretion of the workmen. Wage rates were sometimes fixed by the gilds, more often by the governing authorities.[38] The domestic wageworkers had, of course, to deliver a product which suited the merchants or other employers for whom they worked and a product which conformed to the specifications laid down by the gild and the municipal government. They had also to work hard in order to keep from starving.

In and about the chief textile towns the most independent units in the manufacture of cloth were, generally speaking, in the finishing branches— stretching, pressing, dyeing, and fulling. These operations ordinarily required much more capital than spinning, carding, or even weaving. In an age when all metal was scarce and dear according to our modern notions, the cost of providing the rollers for pressing cloth, or the vats in which the ingredients used in dyeing it were stewed, exceeded the costs of the most expensive looms. The materials needed in dyeing—the alum and other drugs—were also expensive. The largest dyeing establishments at Florence had from five to eight or more apprentices and journeymen. A number of dyeing vats were sometimes installed in substantial houses, a few of which were actually built as dyeing establishments. Some such enterprises were operated by partnerships, and these occasionally included some of the richest merchants of the day. It was a common practice to take the master dyer into the partnership and to give him a share in the profits for managing the venture. In Brussels, as in Florence, the capital invested in the largest dyeing shops amounted, in terms of modern money, to tens of thousands of dollars.[39]

But there were still plenty of small dyeing enterprises in the chief cloth-making towns even at the end of the sixteenth century. By that time Nîmes, in southern France, had become a leading center for the silk manufacture. A journeyman employed by a silk dyer there unwittingly left behind him a view of what was perhaps still the most common type of dyeing venture, when he sent for the local notary to make his will. The notary recorded in his book the circumstances that had led the journeyman to despair of his life. One day he was alone in the shop and dyeing room that formed part

---

[38] Cf. Consitt, *op. cit.*, pp. 83–84.

[39] G. des Marez, *L'Organisation du travail à Bruxelles au XVᵉ siècle* (Brussels, 1904), pp. 180, 202–5, and *passim*. On dyeing and other aspects of the woolen textile manufacture at Florence I have made considerable use of an unpublished essay by Raymond de Roover, "A Florentine Firm of Cloth Manufacture." He deals especially with a clothmaking partnership of 1531–34, in which two members of the Medici family participated. (It is my impression that this essay has since appeared in *Speculum*.) According to de Roover, Doren exaggerated the scale of enterprise in the Florentine textile industry in his *Die florentiner Wollentuchindustrie vom XIV. bis zum XVI. Jahrhundert* (Stuttgart, 1901).

of the master's house. He had seated himself on the edge of a vat in which silks were immersed in a properly prepared bath of boiling water. While the journeyman was awaiting the right moment to remove the silks, he fell unwittingly into what he described as "a slight nap" and soon tumbled head over heels into the cooking mixture. As there was no one to hear his screams, it took him a long time to extricate himself. It is evident that the metal vats of such dyeing houses were fairly large. It is equally evident that they could be tended with little labor.[40]

Fulling—the process of thickening the cloth after it had been woven— was done originally in medieval Europe without any machinery. The pieces were laid on the floor of the worker's room, where he and his wife and children could tramp them out with their feet. That was still a common method in the early sixteenth century, except in the leading textile districts of Italy and the Low Countries. As it was necessary to eat and sleep in the same or in an adjoining room, the stench of the dung used in the fulling process must have been offensive even in an age when noses generally were less delicate to the smells of waste products than are ours.

Fulling was ceasing to be strictly speaking a domestic industry in many districts even before the Renaissance. Waterwheels rotating in the moving streams had been installed for milling corn all over the Continent and in England at least as early as the eleventh century. They were gradually adopted in various industrial processes, fulling among them, in the thirteenth century if not before.[41] On the eve of the Reformation fulling mills, "where hammers, rising and descending, learn to imitate the industry of man," [42] were a common sight along the streams running into and out from the leading textile towns like Florence. More costly to make than several looms, they were generally managed, nevertheless, with the labor of one or two men. They were sometimes family enterprises with living quarters attached to the mill.

Mills of a similar sort were also common in the tanning of leather, carried on in a small way all over Europe. Both in the tanning and in the fulling industries the waterwheels were often the property, not of the laborers who worked at them, but of local landlords or monasteries or of merchants who were buying up land in the neighborhood of the towns. Much less frequently the mills were owned by a town gild. They were leased out, generally for a short period of a year or three years at the most, sometimes to firms of merchants, but more often to master craftsmen who organized the

[40] *Inventaire sommaire des archives départementales du Gard*, E, 11, 146. There were, however, larger dyeing enterprises than this in sixteenth-century Nîmes (Archives départementales du Gard, E, 557, fols. 172–73).

[41] Consitt, *op. cit.*, p. xi.

[42] J. Dyer, *The Fleece* (1757), Bk. II, 570; as quoted by Herbert Heaton, *The Yorkshire Woollen and Worsted Industries* (Oxford, 1920), p. 342.

work. These craftsmen entered into contracts with various traders for the delivery of the products at specified prices.

As industrial enterprises requiring more space than could be provided by a fair-sized room or two were introduced in the leading industrial towns, a good many houses were remodeled to suit the needs of manufacturers, and a few houses were especially built for industrial purposes. The older type of town workshop or studio was inappropriate for such industries as the making of soap and the refining of sugar, wherever these manufactures came to be carried on at all extensively. At Marseille in 1431 an orchard held by a local monastery was acquired for the purpose of putting up a soaphouse. Fourteen years later the owner of the enterprise supplied two coppersmiths of Draguignan with bronze to make a kettle weighing more than one hundred and fifty pounds. It was eventually brought along paths winding for some seventy-five miles through the wooded hills and valleys to Marseille. There it was installed in the soaphouse.[43]

Antwerp had apparently become the leading center in Europe for sugar manufacturing by the middle of the sixteenth century. Some of the sugar refineries were new buildings built to accommodate the iron rollers and other equipment required in the process. More often the manufacturers made use of old buildings which they were able to renovate and rearrange.[44]

The old domestic workshops were especially ill-suited to printing and to the manufacture (begun in the fifteenth century in Italy, at Venice[45] and Altare, near Genoa) of a new kind of glass which was called "crystal" because of its exceptional transparency. Furnaces for making crystal glass were apparently invented at Venice in 1463.[46] The glass was fashioned into the goblets, decanters, jugs, vases, and mirrors that ornamented the rooms and the tables of the rich citizens of the Renaissance and added almost as much to the charm of their life as the oil paintings on the walls. The equipment needed in these new industries of printing and crystal glassmaking was more expensive to provide, and it frequently required more room than that required for ordinary weaving or even dyeing. More space was also needed for storing materials. The light which came through the narrow slits of the old medieval buildings was insufficient for typesetting, and this gave an advantage to those printers who were able to design special rooms or even buildings for their craft.

As a result of the progress of these new manufactures, a few industrial ventures in European towns at the time of the Reformation were carried on in what might be described as tiny factories, mostly without power-

[43] L. Barthélemy, *La Savonnerie marseillais* (Marseille, 1883), pp. 9–10.
[44] Goris, *Etude sur les colonies marchandes méridionales à Anvers,* pp. 437–38.
[45] Cf. Kretschmahr, *Geschichte von Venedig,* II, 454; III, 171.
[46] H. Schuermans, *Verres "façon de Venise" ou d'Altare fabriqués aux Pays-Bas,* letters published 1884–93 (Paris: Bibliothèque nationale, 8° V. 40792), pp. 723–24.

driven machines. Such enterprises seldom seem to have occupied more than a score of workers; they usually occupied less than a dozen. Sometimes an establishment, like a fulling or a tanning mill, was leased out to a master craftsman for a short term or operated by a partnership which included the master craftsman as the managing partner. More frequently, especially in crystal glassmaking and in printing, the owner managed the enterprise himself, which was attached to his home.

As conducted at the time of the Renaissance, crystal glassmaking always and printing very frequently were artistic industries. The owners of the Venetian glasshouses took almost as much pride in the beauty of their wares as their fellow citizens—Carpaccio and the Bellinis—took in that of their oil paintings. The Estiennes, who formed a dynasty of printers at Lyons in the early sixteenth century, spent no less time on the appearance of the books designed in their shops than on the erudite translations of ancient Greek and Latin authors which they made to instruct their contemporaries. The crystal glassware and sometimes the books were works of art. The best of them have a beauty that no modern glassmakers or printers have been quite able to equal.

It is true that many of the masters kept their employees at a distance and often treated them with what a sensitive contemporary would regard as inhuman violence. There was less comradeship, less artistic co-operation between the masters and their wage-earning associates and assistants, particularly in the printing shops, than in the smaller domestic workshops common in the more ancient decorative crafts. In the illumination of books for religious services, the head of the workshop alone was a real artist. Sometimes, in printing, the workers grew so bitter over the wages they were offered and the long hours they were asked to labor at hard tasks, that in Lyons and Paris the journeymen printers began a series of strikes against their employers.[47]

Yet in the management of the enterprises profit-making was generally a less predominant consideration than it was destined to become in more recent times. The masters gave it little thought during the hours that they worked with their hands alongside their journeymen wage-earners. Their outlook was different from that of the factory manager of the nineteenth century, whose primary object was to satisfy the demands of his employers for a return on their capital. Their outlook also bore little resemblance to that of a stockholder in a modern industrial corporation, whose interest is usually limited to the market price of the shares he owns and the dividends he receives from them.

Large numbers of industrial workpeople—more than fifty—were almost never assembled together in a single establishment in any town of Renaissance Europe except in the construction of ships and in various kinds of

[47] Cf. H. Hauser, *Ouvriers du temps passé* (5th ed.; Paris, 1927), pp. 177 ff.

building enterprises. In the late fifteenth and early sixteenth centuries new types of vessels were introduced, especially for the Atlantic voyages. The practical mariner's compass with a pivoted needle and compass card, adopted before the fourteenth century, was coming into widespread use. At the same time big three-masted sailing ships, more adaptable to gales than the older, single-masted vessels which had hoisted square sails, were replacing the latter.[48] With their high pointed bows they could resist the buffetings of a strong head sea.[49] In the trade of Spain and Portugal, galleys were being replaced by caravels, better built to hold commodities in large quantities. The voyages of discovery, and the growth in sea commerce which accompanied and followed them, provided a vastly increased business for shipyards and arsenals suited to turn out new boats and to repair old ones. The changes in the types of ships wanted both for commerce and for sea warfare led to the establishment of new yards and to an extension of old ones. At the time of the Reformation the chief yards, with their stocks for launching the vessels and their cranes for lifting the lumber into place, together with the workshops sometimes attached to them for making sails, ropes, anchors, and glutinous material to calk the seams, employed scores and in a few cases hundreds of workpeople.

The most famous of all such establishments was the arsenal at Venice. To Dante it had seemed so dark, so noisy, and so filthy that he compared it to the fifth chasm of the Inferno, where the barterers in public offices and authority lay expiating their sins in a bath of the foulest pitch.[50] During Dante's later life the arsenal was growing rapidly in size and importance. Between 1303 and 1325 the space occupied by the wharves, launching yards, workshops, and storage houses increased some fourfold, until it covered several large modern city blocks. The seventy years from 1470 to 1540 was the other period of rapid growth. Covered docks were introduced and also long buildings of brick and stone, with carefully timbered roofs, for storing construction materials, ordnance, and ammunition. The inclosed area was almost doubled. In 1540 the arsenal occupied about sixty acres of land and water.[51] It had become as large and as populous as many a medieval town, and was almost certainly a vaster enterprise than any other establishment, even the papal alumworks.[52] According to a sixteenth-century visitor, the ropemaking house, which flanked one side of the inclosure, was so commodious that a fiery charger could have taken his daily

[48] B. Hagedorn, *Entwicklung der wichtigsten Schiffstypen* (Berlin, 1914), pp. 61–64.
[49] E. M. Carus-Wilson, "The Iceland Trade," in Power and Postan, *Studies in English Trade in the Fifteenth Century*, pp. 159–60; cf. F. C. Lane, "Venetian Shipping during the Commercial Revolution," *American Historical Review*, XXXVIII (1933), 231.
[50] *Inferno*, Canto XXI, 11. 1–18.
[51] F. C. Lane, *Venetian Ships and Shipbuilders of the Renaissance* (Baltimore, 1934), pp. 129–30, 137–40, 146.
[52] Delumeau, *L'Alun de Rome*, pp. 76–77.

workout within it.[53] The accounting books kept by the officials show that the annual expenditure on materials and labor amounted to two hundred thousand ducats or more—that is, millions of dollars in terms of modern money. Between one and two thousand men were employed. The arsenal probably formed the largest single industrial unit in Europe.

This great establishment, maintained to give the Republic of Venice its powerful war fleet, had never been in private hands. It belonged to the doge and senate. It was managed by the chief admiral and other state officials. It was financed out of the public revenues. All the workpeople who labored in it—the shipwrights, ship and house carpenters, calkers, sawyers, ropemakers, the nail and anchor smiths—were on the government payrolls. They were usually paid day wages, and some of them had shops in the city. They worked on their own account in these shops and in private shipyards, when they were not engaged at the arsenal.[54]

The design of each vessel was generally determined by the shipwrights in charge of its construction. In only one case was an effort made to turn the work of architectural planning into a specialized technique for experts —an occupation separate from actual manual labor in the shops and yards. That was the case of a learned and traveled son of obscure Venetian parents, one Vettor Fausto. In 1525 and 1526 he set about to reform the naval architecture of his city's ships, with the help of mathematical science and the mechanical principles of Aristotle and other sages of antiquity. The distinction drawn in Fausto's case between the work of architect and that of ship carpenter did not prove permanent.[55] The age of the naval architect lay in the future. At the time of the Reformation architectural skill and manual labor in shipbuilding were still usually combined.

The construction of merchantmen at Venice was in the main apparently independent of the arsenal. But it had not become the business of special capitalist entrepreneurs. A majority of all boats launched for trading purposes at Venice and at other Mediterranean ports seem to have been tiny craft, some of them no larger than a small motor launch or a big modern rowboat. Such craft were generally built in little private yards, owned or rented by a shipwright or a carpenter who took part in the manual labor himself, like a master dyer or a master printer, and who was assisted by only a few apprentices and journeymen. The construction of more substantial merchantmen required much more capital and much more labor than

---

[53] Sieveking, "Die genueser Seidenindustrie im 15. und 16. Jahrhundert," pp. 131–32. The description is from Andreas Ryff's diary, written at the end of the sixteenth century, but it is improbable that the ropemaking house was less commodious two generations before, because shipbuilding at Venice had declined in importance in the interval and the arsenal as a whole had probably not increased in size (Lane, "Venetian Shipping during the Commercial Revolution," pp. 231–35).

[54] Lane, *Venetian Ships and Shipbuilders, passim.*

[55] *Ibid.,* pp. 64–70.

the richest of these shipwrights or carpenters could provide. Sometimes such ships were built in the arsenal by the government; sometimes they were built at large private shipyards in Venice and the neighborhood. At these private shipyards the capital was almost never provided by persons who made building ships for profit their major business. It almost always came from merchants who formed commercial partnerships and ordered the vessels which they needed in their trade. Thus the large merchant ships were made to order for trading ventures. The traders or their agents leased the space for yards and hired the craftsmen whom they needed.[56] Private shipbuilding was not yet an industry in the hands of capitalists who bid for orders. In many cases the preparatory processes—the making of the sails, ropes, and anchors—was done not at the shipyards but in the domestic shops of small working masters who labored to supply the yards, much after the fashion of independent pewterers, coopers, or ordinary smiths. They were in no sense factory hands.

During the seventy years from 1470 to 1540 the proportion of all Venetian vessels—men-of-war and merchantmen combined—built by the government at the arsenal and outside it was increasing.[57] Public control over the shipbuilding industry had become more widespread at the Reformation than it had been two generations earlier. With industrial concentration and the growth in the need for large capitals during the age of the Italian Renaissance, kings, princes, and municipal governments all over Europe stepped in to supply the funds and to order the work of large enterprises. Where the labor of shipbuilding craftsmen became subject to discipline from above, as at the arsenal, the discipline was much more often exercised by the officials of a political ruler than by private capitalists or their agents.

There was perhaps no European industry, except textiles, which engaged a larger number of workpeople during the first three or four decades of the sixteenth century than building. New town bridges and walls were wanted wherever population was growing and industry expanding rapidly, as in Italy, southern and eastern Germany, and in the Low Countries. In Germany whole cities were built or largely rebuilt on a new plan with an elaborate system of waterworks, invented by skilful mechanics, for supplying the townspeople and the public fountains with water. Three of the most costly German cities were Leipzig, Nuremberg, and Augsburg. Augsburg had elaborate pumps for raising water from the river, which Montaigne much admired when he visited the place forty years or so after they had been installed. He found the houses much more handsome, much larger and taller, than in any French town. He found the streets much wider.[58]

[56] *Ibid.*, pp. 112–18 and *passim*.
[57] *Ibid.*, p. 110.
[58] Michel de Montaigne, *Journal du voyage* (Paris, 1774), I, 119–21.

Everywhere in Europe the construction of town bridges, walls, and fortifications was undertaken by the municipal administration or by the sovereign authority or by both together. Local princes, nobles, and ecclesiastical foundations were perhaps even more active than town governments in carrying out other building projects. The workmen who participated in some of the largest enterprises numbered many hundreds. In other cases, as in the upkeep, the rebuilding, or the enlargement of churches, cathedrals, or town bridges, a regular force of a few score craftsmen and laborers—masons, carpenters, tilers, bricklayers, smiths, etc.—might be employed continuously over a long period of years.

When the enterprise was undertaken by a prince, a town, or an ecclesiastical foundation, the administration was generally confided to royal, municipal, or church officials. As these officials rarely had the knowledge and the skill required to carry through the construction of artistic architecture, they generally called in an expert, frequently a master mason, to direct and co-ordinate the work. His position resembled that of the chief master carpenter in the building of a large ship. Sometimes a portion or even the whole of the construction was granted out to private persons under contract; and the contractors were left to assemble the materials, the craftsmen, and the unskilled laborers and to pay the wages. Such an arrangement was especially common in Italy, where the construction of the palace and church of San Marco at Rome was confided by the pope to a partnership of four contractors. They were paid at an established rate for each yard of masonry.[59] More frequently, perhaps, especially in the north of Europe, the management of the work was left to a number of expert craftsmen who were paid salaries. In that case the administration of the funds appropriated for the building as a whole was kept under the thumbs of public officials.

Private building for rich noblemen and merchants was probably carried on more frequently than public or ecclesiastical building by contractors operating on a fairly large scale; but there were many cases in which private persons, in putting up their town houses and their country castles, employed salaried stewards to manage the work for them, in much the same manner that officials managed public building projects. There were even cases in which the private builders directed all the work themselves.

Like the textile workers under the putting-out system, the building craftsmen generally had a measure of independence. Many of them led a nomadic life.[60] They labored, now for one employer, now for another. When they were assembled by the score or the hundred, it was generally necessary to provide the masons, the carpenters, and some of the other skilled artisans with wooden houses or sheds as workshops. Often, especially in the coun-

[59] Cf. Coulton, *Art and the Reformation*, pp. 464 ff.
[60] *Ibid.*, pp. 165, 200–1, 429.

try, it was also necessary to provide them with living quarters while the work was in progress, occasionally for many years.

Of course the majority of these craftsmen performed stereotyped work, often requiring more strength than art. Comparatively few masons were stone-carvers as well as stone-dressers. But the proportion of the building workers who needed to exercise artistic initiative was much larger than in modern times. Some master masons were as autonomous as master pewterers, master goldsmiths, or master sculptors.

Ordinarily, the building workmen were employed for day wages, generally supplemented by various payments in kind. But there was a good deal of contracting by expert masons and carpenters, who themselves employed small groups of workmen to perform particular tasks within the general scheme of building, as this was outlined by the principal mason and the officials in charge of the whole venture.[61] In Flanders, as in England,[62] some quarrying enterprises employed a score or more workmen, like the mines of silver-bearing ore in Central Europe, but the carriage of freestone was undertaken by poor peasants. Until the end of the sixteenth century there is no trace in the region of Tournai of a large venture for the transport of freestone.[63]

As Werner Sombart has brought out, building work was coming to be more standardized than it had been in the late twelfth and thirteenth centuries, during the great age of the gothic cathedrals. In the palace of the popes at Avignon, built in the fourteenth century, the principal blocks of stone were cut to one prescribed size.[64] That practice had become fairly common by the time of the Reformation. Yet the careful student of Renaissance architecture is bound to reject the view that utilitarian dominated artistic considerations in the construction of the rooms or of the whole edifice, as they came to do in the nineteenth century. Nor were the chief builders of the Renaissance merely imitating an older style of architecture, like the exponents of modern "Gothic." Their general design tried to fulfil an ideal conception of the world, fashioned to artistic principles of their own, partly based, it is true, on a tradition derived from the antiquity then much admired.[65] The mason-architects were usually much closer to the building work itself than the architects of recent times.

It is a mistake to regard standardization and the contract system as novel characteristics of the industrialized civilization which came to dominate the

[61] Cf. D. Knoop and G. P. Jones, *The Mediaeval Mason* (Manchester, 1933), pp. 16–43, 56 ff.

[62] *Ibid.*, p. 46.

[63] Marc Bloch, "Une Matière première au moyen âge: la pierre de taille," *Annales d'histoire économique et sociale,* XXVI (1934), 190.

[64] Cf. Coulton, *op. cit.,* pp. 470–76.

[65] Cf. Geoffrey Scott, *The Architecture of Humanism* (London, 1914).

Western world in the late nineteenth century. Standardization was the order of the day in the Roman Empire. The plans of ancient Roman towns, with streets arranged to form a checkerboard, remind one of a real estate sub-division in the latest American city. The contract system was common in a number of classical industries. Neither standardization nor the contract system in classical times produced a world of steel, steam, and electricity. Neither led to the domination of large-scale, privately owned enterprises in industry.

It is misleading to say that the multitudes of craftsmen, who occasionally assembled to carry out the plans of Renaissance masons and architects, of whom Michelangelo was one, were employed under conditions of industrial capitalism. At least two important features peculiar to the building trades of the late nineteenth and twentieth centuries were lacking in the early sixteenth century. One is the widespread use of power-driven machinery and metal materials, which have made manual work in building, as in other industries, more routine and stereotyped than ever before in Western history. The other is the predominance of the motive of private profit divorced from both art and craftsmanship. While building operations at the time of the Reformation frequently required a great amount of capital, which ran into the modern equivalent of hundreds of thousands and even millions of dollars,[66] unlike modern building ventures, they were not car-ried on primarily for the returns they would bring to financial corporations and real estate firms, but to satisfy the needs and the tastes of princes, lords, churchmen, and municipal authorities or the needs and tastes of merchants in their capacity not of businessmen but of private citizens. The architects and other masons were freer then than now to appeal to their clients on genuine aesthetic grounds. Their competence was widely recog-nized, for the new style of architecture involved artistic conceptions hardly less generally accepted by persons who, like Vasari, felt themselves en-titled to judge than the conceptions which had prevailed in gothic building. However much the building craftsmen of the Renaissance were out for their bread and butter, artistic decisions were usually more powerful directing forces behind their labor than the desire of individual businessmen to make money by that labor.

INDUSTRIAL ORGANIZATION OUTSIDE THE ANCIENT TOWNS

Much building was done in the country. In France under Francis I (1515–47) the king himself was probably the greatest builder. The cele-brated châteaux constructed along the Loire, in Berry, and in Normandy, at a tremendous cost in labor, craftsmanship, and art, were placed to domi-nate bourgs and villages more frequently than ancient towns.

[66] Cf. Goris, *Etude sur les colonies marchandes méridionales à Anvers*, p. 440.

During the late fifteenth and early sixteenth centuries industry was spill-
ing out beyond the municipal walls, along the paths and roads leading away
from them. It was also carried in some regions far into the country, even
into forests and mountains. Industrial centers grew up upon the nuclei
of villages whose inhabitants had hitherto devoted themselves almost entirely to arable or pasture farming. This movement of industry away from
the ancient independent or semi-independent towns became especially
strong with the rapid growth of industrial output on the eve of the Reformation. It was most pronounced in those parts of the Low Countries that
formed modern Belgium, in the west of England, and in the rich mining
regions of the Erz Gebirge, the Sudetic Mountains, the Eastern Alps, and
the Carpathians. In those parts of Europe the industrial laborers and
craftsmen in recently formed settlements were perhaps almost as numerous
as in those ancient towns whose charters had been granted during the
Gothic age.

In point of the numbers employed, clothmaking of various kinds was
probably the most important industry outside those towns as well as in
them. The opportunities seized upon by merchants and their factors and by
the richest craftsmen to engage cheaply the wives and daughters of husbandmen, in labor at the distaff or the spinning wheel in their cottages and
hovels, had carried spinning into scores of rural villages in the immediate
neighborhood of the older textile centers. Other branches of clothmaking
had followed spinning to certain favorably placed sites many miles away
—particularly in Flanders, Brabant, the principality of Liège, and the west
of England. Numerous villages at the foot of the Cotswolds and the
Mendips and along the valleys of the Somerset Avon and its tributaries had
organized groups of weavers, dyers, and tuckers. The fullers made ample
use of the water power from the hills to drive their mills.[67]

In the country the owners of raw materials and of cloth in various stages
of manufacture were not hampered, as much as in the old textile towns, by
ancient industrial regulations which interfered with the introduction of new
methods of manufacturing and with the growth in output.[68] As a result,
weavers as well as fullers, dyers, and finishers had been encouraged to move
into the areas surrounding old villages, where they were generally able to
get small plots of land on some sort of tenure from the local landlords.
These new textile settlements were strung out in every direction, "like the
rays of a star" at night, from the village square with its church and steeple,
along pathways lined with little cottages and workshops and occasional
warehouses.[69] Some of the largest (Hondschoote, for example, a few miles
from Dunkirk on the English Channel) already had six or seven thousand

[67] Carus-Wilson, "The Overseas Trade of Bristol," p. 188.
[68] Cf. Pirenne, *Histoire de Belgique,* III, 233 ff.
[69] *Ibid.,* pp. 236–37.

inhabitants. Almost all the able bodied adults were employed in clothmaking. Hondschoote had been transformed since the thirteenth century, when
it was a village of a few hundred manorial tenants who had earned their
living by farming. Growth was apparently most rapid during the two generations preceding the Reformation. Between 1469 and 1540, the place at
least tripled in population, as a result of the progress of its serge draperies.[70]

The forms of industrial organization in the new clothmaking settlements
did not differ fundamentally from those among the textile craftsmen in the
old towns. In both most of the labor was done in homes, where men and
women lived and died and brought up their children. The established
municipal governments of the old towns attempted, usually without much
success, to extend their regulations to cover work in the rising clothmaking
villages of the neighborhood. The absence of such regulations and of formal
gilds in the growing settlements facilitated the concentration of capital.
There was less effective opposition than in the ancient industrial centers to
the multiplication of looms under a single roof and to the carrying on of
several clothmaking operations within one house. The opportunities for
building more efficient fulling mills and more commodious shops for dyeing,
stretching, and pressing cloth were greater in rural areas, for there was
much more space than in the old, compact towns, where the houses were
crowded within medieval walls that had served their turn. It was easier to
enlarge the warehouses of the merchants and thus provide room for dyers,
finishers, and sometimes for weavers, as well as to provide land for hanging
out cloth to dry. The industry had no longer to conform, as in ancient
towns, to a framework sometimes inherited from an age before clothmaking
had been the main business of municipal life. To a considerable extent, the
disposition of houses in the rising textile settlements could be made to conform to the needs of the industry.

The greater freedom of enterprise and of movement did not lead to
establishments with machinery, such as were being built sometimes in
metallurgy and, as we shall see, in the manufacture of salt from the brine
of natural springs. In the Low Countries the nearest approach to a large
unit, employing scores of craftsmen under a unified discipline, occurred in
one of the most artistic branches of the textile trades—the making of
tapestries. Where enough land could be had, the workmen's cottages were
sometimes built in groups of from thirty to sixty. All were placed under the
supervision of a director, skilled in an art for which Flanders had become

[70] The population increased from about twenty-five hundred in 1469 to at least
twelve thousand at the height of its development a hundred years later. (E. Coornaert,
La Draperie-sayetterie d'Hondschoote [Paris, 1930], pp. 15, 30–31.) The population
in the 1530's is uncertain; but, if the statistics of the production of cloth can serve as
a rough guide (ibid., pp. 16–17, 493), it was probably more than three times as large
as at the time of the great fire of 1469.

famous.[71] The director represented the owners of the materials, and, like the craftsmen, he was paid by them. This was a system that the French crown was destined to foster in clothmaking during the seventeenth century. Under Louis XIV such enterprises were almost always under the control of the crown.

In other branches of the textile industry than tapestry-making, the principal developments which accompanied the movement into the country were an increase in the proportion of the manual workers who labored for wages and a decrease in the proportion who were masters. These developments apparently took two main forms. They are exemplified by conditions in southwestern England and in Flanders.

In southwestern England, particularly in the Cotswolds to the east and north of Bristol, the number of workpeople in clothmaking to whom materials were put out by a single merchant clothier or partnership of clothiers was often larger than in the ancient textile centers, even in the Italian cities. The very rapid growth in the demand for cloth that followed the accession of Henry VII in 1485 was, above all, a growth in the demand for unfinished cloth to be carried to the Continent, and particularly to the Low Countries, to be dyed and dressed. Thus the new demand was part of the industrial expansion which England had hardly begun to share. It led to a great increase in the number of English spinners, carders, combers, and weavers. It did not lead to any marked increase in the number of English dyers, stretchers, and pressers. It was branches of the manufacture in which the workers' equipment was light and cheap that needed hands. Distaffs or spinning wheels and looms, cards or combs with little stoves for warming them to make them ready for use, could be bought or rented even by families in very modest circumstances. Most of the equipment could be installed in the tiniest village cottage. The opportunities afforded the rising merchant clothiers for profitable investment in workshops and equipment were small compared with the opportunities for profitable investment in the fine raw wool for which the Cotswold sheep were so justly famous. Local clothiers bought up wool in large quantities, either directly or through middlemen, and put it out to be spun, scoured, carded, or combed. The same clothiers put out the yarn to be woven by domestic workpeople living in villages scattered through the hills or bunched in settlements like Burford, Fairford, Stow-on-the-Wold, Northleach, and Stroud. These places were expanding into the picturesque towns, grouped about a central spacious High Street, which are now so familiar to visiting tourists.

Many hundreds of workers were sometimes employed by a single rich clothier or by a partnership of clothiers. These merchants were always putting out their materials, either directly or through their agents and factors, to new craftsmen. At the same time many craftsmen who had worked for

[71] Pirenne, *op. cit.*, III, 249–50.

them at one time or another were treating with other employers. A large proportion of the textile laborers in southwestern England got their material now from one clothier or firm of clothiers, now from another. They worked it up for so much a piece, at wages regulated by the clothiers and the local justices of the peace, who were frequently the same persons.

To the villagers and townspeople, some of these English clothiers seemed very rich. They had enough money to build handsome houses and churches and to decorate them with beautiful painted-glass windows. Their fortunes were small, nevertheless, compared to those of the Fuggers, the Medicis, or other leading financial families on the Continent. Unlike these Continental financiers, the English clothiers put most of their financial eggs into a single basket—the only very lucrative one which English industrial life provided on the eve of the Reformation. That enabled some of them to operate on an even larger scale *in clothmaking* than the largest textile firms of Augsburg or Florence. Wagework under the putting-out system by laborers who did not aspire to be masters was becoming much more common than in the ancient textile towns.

The other line of development leading to an increase of wagework was taking place especially in the new textile settlements in Flanders, and also on a smaller scale in Yorkshire.[72] The key positions in the manufacture of cloth were occupied by drapers or clothiers. Unlike the clothiers of southwestern England or the merchants of the Italian towns, they were often master workmen with shops in their homes. They were more numerous and generally less rich than the Cotswold clothiers. They had under their control a smaller number of workpeople. They depended for most of their raw materials, for their markets, and often for credit upon financiers, some of whom came or sent their representatives from the south of Europe to establish themselves at Antwerp, which was becoming a great financial clearing house for the European economic world. In their workshops, the drapers in the rising industrial settlements commonly employed for wages several workers, often as many as six and sometimes a dozen. These workers were usually either weavers, dyers, or fullers. Occasionally several clothmaking operations were carried on together in the draper's shop and at adjacent mills along a nearby stream. Some of the workmen lived in the draper's house; others lived in hovels of their own nearby and came for the day. Still others worked up materials in their cottages or rooms for the drapers who paid them wages, generally by the piece. These domestic workmen formed the majority. The number on the payroll of a single enterprise was generally smaller in the Flemish textile settlements than in the great Italian cities, but there were fewer independent master craftsmen. About

[72] Heaton, *The Yorkshire Woollen and Worsted Industries,* pp. 9–92; E. Lipson, *The Economic History of England* (London, 1931), II, 14, 69–71.

three-fourths of all the manual workers in the textile industry of Hond-schoote were wage-earners, and only about a fourth were masters.[73]

Wagework for private employers, carried on, for the most part, in the homes of the workmen, was becoming the rule in the growing country settlements which specialized in the manufacture of all kinds of woolen cloth, though such a high proportion of wageworkers to masters as prevailed at Hondschoote was probably exceptional even in the Low Countries. Similar forms of enterprise were beginning to appear in a few villages, which were becoming new centers of the expanding metallurgical finishing trades.

In rural industries, other than clothmaking and metal finishing, the forms of enterprise were generally different. In most of them there was much variety in the matter of industrial organization. They may be divided, nevertheless, into two groups. There was, first of all, the group in which tiny ventures were almost universal. There was, second, the group in which the tendency toward a considerable concentration of capital and labor was beginning to be pronounced. The first of these groups of industries was less prominent than the second. It included crude glassmaking and papermaking. The second group included the three rural industries which, after textiles, employed the largest number of hands—the saltmaking, the mining, and the metallurgical industries.

Ever since the end of the thirteenth century the making of what the French called *verre de fougère*—small bottles and crude glass vessels—had been spreading into the woodlands all over the Continent.[74] Papermaking, brought by the Arabs to Spain, whence it spread to other countries, made even more rapid progress along the streams than crude glassmaking did in the forests. The introduction of printing greatly stimulated the demand for paper during the late fifteenth and early sixteenth centuries.

Unlike clothmaking, glassmaking had seldom created considerable industrial settlements at the time of the Reformation. Rural glassmaking, at least in France, was a scattered craft, practiced at dozens of places in most provinces. The huts, with their little furnaces, were hastily built. They were generally set up where the trees and shrubberies were thick enough to provide abundant fuel. They seldom employed more than a handful of craftsmen. When the local supplies of wood began to give out, the glassmakers moved on to another site, as many ironmakers had done until the fifteenth century

[73] Coornaert, *op. cit.*, pp. 354, 397. Coornaert found the proportion of wageworkers to masters even larger, but he is speaking presumably of conditions a generation later than the period I am treating here, when the sergecloth manufacture at Hondschoote reached its zenith.

[74] E.g., Saint-Quirin, "Les Verriers du Languedoc," *Bulletin de la société langue-docienne de géographie*, XXIX (1906), 56–57, and cf. also pp. 149–52; also XXVIII (1905), 340; and cf. A. Milet, *Histoire d'un four à verre de l'ancienne Normandie* (Paris, 1871), pp. 8–9. Time has not permitted me to investigate the glassmaking industry in Bohemia and Lorraine, where it was more important than in France.

and as some continued to do at the beginning of the sixteenth, in districts where the iron industry was backward.

It is sometimes possible to follow the movements of the glassmakers, in regions like Provence or Languedoc, by the large number of tiny villages and hamlets that have retained the name of La Verrerie. On some of the winding mountain roads of the Massif des Maures, motorists can pass half a dozen of these places in an hour.[75] The master craftsmen, who were known in France as *gentilshommes verriers*, performed manual labor in the huts and supervised the work of a few assistants, in much the same manner as the master weavers, pewterers, or coopers in the towns. These gentlemen glassmakers had obtained from the French crown special privileges, which enabled them to claim a higher social status than the ordinary town craftsmen. Glassmaking was almost the only medieval industry that a Frenchman of noble family could enter without losing his rank.[76]

In papermaking the ordinary procedure was to set up tiny mills resembling the mills for grinding grain or fulling cloth. At a number of places old flour mills along the streams were remodeled to serve a new purpose.[76a] Like the fulling and the tanning mills, the paper mills could generally be tended by two or three workmen. Unlike the small furnaces for making cheap glass, they were frequently built in the neighborhood of towns and in some cases along the banks of the rivers where they flowed through the towns.

At the time of the Reformation most paper mills in France, Italy, and Germany were apparently owned, not by master craftsmen, but by landlords. Sometimes the land belonged to an ecclesiastical foundation—an abbey or a priory; sometimes the landlord was a merchant in a nearby town; sometimes he was a descendant of the ancient nobility or the country gentry. The landlords leased out their mills for short periods on various terms, which included, on occasions, the right to a share in the profits from the sale of the paper. At Troyes, Corbeil, and Essonnes—leading papermaking centers in the north of France—the master papermakers had ceased

[75] I remember with appreciation that the U. S. Navy asked me to supply them with information to help with the landings along the Riviera in 1944.

[76] The privileges granted to a group of local lords—lay and ecclesiastical—in connection with the making of iron in the neighborhood of Alençon were hardly comparable, for these lords do not appear to have taken part in the manual labor of mining or smelting (H. de Formeville, *Les Barons fossiers et les férons de Normandie* [Caen, 1852], pp. 1–7 and *passim*). French noblemen were also granted permission, as early as the beginning of the seventeenth century at any rate, to participate in new mining companies (Archives nationales, $X^{IA}8644$, fols. 390–95). But these concessionaires, like the *barons fossiers* of Normandy, took no part in manual labor.

[76a] Henri Stein, "La Papererie d'Essonnes," in *Annales de la société historique et archéologique du Gâtinais*, XII (1894), 338, 349 n., 356; Jules Gauthier, "L'Industrie du papier dans les hautes vallées franc-comptoise," *Mémoirs de la société d'émulation de Montbéliard*, XXVI (1897), 20.

for the most part to work at the mills.[77] Some of them had become traders of substance, who disposed of the production of a number of mills. But in many other places in France most master papermakers were craftsmen who took part in manual labor.

In Lombardy and in southern Germany a few mills had been built more powerful than any of which I have found a record in early sixteenth-century France. The overshot wheels to drive the machinery, with dams constructed to hold the water to turn them, resembled those of the great new iron-smelting furnaces.[77a] The machinery at the iron mills probably often served as a model. With houses and barns for storing and preparing the materials, the largest paper mills occupied an acre or more ground and employed a score or more workers. Such enterprises may be properly regarded as antecedents of the modern factory. But they were probably the exception in papermaking, even in Central Europe. The number of wageworkers employed in all of them could hardly have exceeded a few hundreds.

THE GROWTH OF ECONOMIC DESPOTISM IN COUNTRY INDUSTRY

The movement of industry away from the ancient towns at the end of the Middle Ages has been represented sometimes as a successful effort on the part of private persons—traders, money-lenders, and progressive craftsmen—to escape from the increasingly thorough regulations of the gilds and municipal governments. That explanation fits the woolen textile industry in England and the Low Countries. The prominence given the explanation arises, in fact, from the habit economic historians have had of generalizing from conditions in clothmaking. As a generalization concerning the growth of other country industries in the age of the Renaissance, this explanation leaves much to be desired. It is not only inadequate; it is misleading.

Saltmaking and mining (and metallurgy in so far as it was associated with mining) grew up, obviously enough, outside the old towns because, for the most part, Nature had distributed the natural resources—the salt water, the brine springs, and the ores and minerals—about the country, along the coasts, in the forests, the hills, and the mountain valleys. Students of economic history have not failed to observe that this dispersion of the sources of raw materials was an important factor drawing industry away from its old centers at the time of the Renaissance. What they have seldom recognized is that this progress of country industry was by no means generally a movement in the direction of economic freedom. In saltmaking, as in mining, it was rather a movement in the direction of economic despotism. Kings and princes, lay and ecclesiastical, were generally less inclined to

[77] Stein, *op. cit.*, p. 347.
[77a] See above, p. 38.

meet the wishes of private capitalists than were the municipal governments. To some extent, such autonomy from the local political rulers as the medieval towns possessed served to protect the economic privileges of traders and moneylenders, because the municipal governments, unlike the governments of most sovereign states, represented to a considerable and often to a predominant extent the local mercantile interests. When the power over economic life was acquired by sovereign rulers in this age of increasing despotism, they used it mainly to serve political purposes.

Their power over industry was not only less easily bent to suit mercantile interests than the power of town mayors and boards of aldermen; it was more comprehensive. The growth of country industries in Continental Europe on the eve of the Reformation has been imperfectly understood, because its relation to the spread of authoritarianism has not been sufficiently emphasized. In the early sixteenth century the regulation of industry in most European countries was becoming more extensive and effective than it had been in medieval times.

I have described already the increasing control exercised by political authorities on the Continent over the expanding mining and metallurgical industries. At the time of the Reformation, sovereign rulers on the Continent had obtained the power to dispose of much of the mineral wealth then exploited within their dominions, even when it was found under private lands. Their regalian rights had helped them exercise an authority over industrial enterprises greater than that of most municipal governments. They did not always confine themselves to enacting and enforcing industrial regulations; in some cases they took industrial plant into their own hands and operated it as what many today would call a state enterprise.[78]

Saltmaking, like mining, had not the same protection from the authority of kings and sovereign princes as had the industries carried on within the ancient municipal walls. In France, Italy, and Spain the production of salt was accomplished mainly by the evaporation of seawater in the bright summer sun along the coasts of the Mediterranean and the Bay of Biscay. In the Alps and north of them it was accomplished mainly by heating the brine from springs, found in abundance in Franche-Comté, Lorraine, Germany, and Central Europe generally. In both branches of salt production there were large ventures employing scores and sometimes hundreds of workpeople. But the evaporation of seawater in shallow rectangular troughs hollowed out of the earth was hardly an industrial occupation. It was carried on in the late summers and early autumns by peasants, nearly all of whom also cultivated plots of land nearby. Their labor as salters required little capital and no machinery. Their relation to the owners of the marshes

---

[78] See above, pp. 52–57.

was like the relation of a tenant to the lord of his manor, rather than like the relation of an industrial wagehand to the owners of a factory.[79]

Saltmaking at the chief brine springs and at the famous old rock-salt mines at Hall in the Tyrol and at Wieliczka in Poland, had become a much more industrial occupation than saltmaking along the sunny seacoasts. The evaporation of a thick salt solution in metal receptacles over fires of wood was one of the oldest manufactures of Central Europe. There are reliable records of it at some fifty separate places in the Holy Roman Empire before the end of the twelfth century.[80] At each place the brine was carried from the springs to a number of small wooden houses, where it was heated in little pans often no larger than a washerwoman's tub. Almost everywhere, for many generations, the work at the houses had been in the hands of local peasants who labored in tiny units of four or five at the most. These peasants worked for their landlords as serfs and, with the improvement of the status of the peasantry, as free men.

During the thirteenth and fourteenth centuries, if not earlier, many salt-making units lost some of their independence. A movement gained ground to bring those which drew their brine from the same group of springs under a single control. On the initiative often of the local traders in salt, a kind of cartel was established. It undertook to provide the iron and other metal, the wood for fuel, and sometimes also a portion of the money needed to instal larger pans. It allotted quotas of production to the units and sold the bulk of the salt manufactured. Usually the owners of each house entered into a contract with the cartel or company for the delivery of a stipulated quantity of the product. At the same time they entered into a contract with the working salters for the production of salt at the pans. Sometimes the salters were paid in money; much more often they retained, instead, a portion of the salt they had made and disposed of it locally. The demand was generally considerable, especially to provide for the cattle and other livestock pastured in the neighborhood. Salt was used to preserve and season their fodder. It was also used as fertilizer.

Another movement, destined to interfere with the independent control of local landlords and peasant salters over saltmaking, accompanied the growth of mercantile interests. Sovereign princes—lay and ecclesiastical—at least as far back as the twelfth and thirteenth centuries, had begun to claim regalian rights to brine springs and rock-salt deposits in their dominions, even when these resources were in the lands of local lords of the soil. As in mining, these regalian rights were many sided and elastic. Ulti-

---

[79] Archives départementales de la Loire Inférieure, B. 682 (1415); B. 6, fol. 131 (1468).
[80] K. T. von Inama-Sternegg, "Zur Verfassungsgeschichte der deutschen Salinen im Mittelalter," Sitzungsberichte der kaiserlichen Akademie der Wissenschaft, CXI (1886), 573.

mately they might give the prince the power to dispose of the salt resources within his dominions as he saw fit and to regulate production through his own officials, as well as to levy a tax on salt.

At the time of the Reformation the two movements—to unite the little independent enterprises in each district and to extend the power of the political rulers over the saltmaking industry—were growing in strength. The revival of Roman law provided sovereigns with a precedent for taxing salt and even for declaring its sale a state monopoly, as the Roman Republic apparently had done even before the Punic Wars.[81] The French crown is also said to have derived precedents for the salt *gabelle* from Chinese experience during the Sung dynasty in the eleventh century.[82]

Princes of the Renaissance needed more income, both to maintain their military power in an age of new and more deadly weapons, and to extend their administrative authority with the help of efficient civil servants. Its great bulk made salt the easiest of all necessary commodities to tax. French experience was to show that no other product could be made to yield so large a revenue. By successfully claiming the disposal of the sources of salt as a sovereign right, kings and princes placed themselves in a position to appoint officials of their own to supervise the management of the companies which apportioned output among the pans. Some rulers were beginning to make the sale of salt a state enterprise, as it seems to have been to a large extent in the Roman Empire.[83] They could then add a heavy tax to the selling price and force their subjects to buy large quantities of the commodity whether they needed it or not—an abuse destined to become especially flagrant in the French kingdom.[84]

The success of these plans depended partly upon the elimination of alternative sources of supply. It was difficult for the prince's officials to force shepherds to take salt at an inflated price when they could buy it more cheaply from private saltmakers or traders. So the movement toward the concentration of production in large establishments and the movement toward princely ownership went hand in hand. The one complemented the other.

West of the Rhine, in Franche-Comté and Lorraine, both movements were on the verge of completion by the third and fourth decades of the sixteenth century. At this time the celebrated saltwork called the *grande saunerie,* in the upper part of the town of Salins in Franche-Comté, was

---

[81] Cf. Alfred Schmidt, *Das Salz* (Leipzig, 1874), pp. 55–56.

[82] So Robert Hartwell informs me.

[83] The meager knowledge we have of the extraction of salt in the Roman Empire is insufficient to permit of a general characterization (M. Rostovtzeff, *The Social and Economic History of the Roman Empire* [Oxford, 1926], p. 294).

[84] On the development of the *gabelle* in France during the sixteenth and seventeenth centuries see Nef, *Industry and Government in France and England,* pp. 76–83, 123–24.

among the largest and most sumptuously appointed industrial enterprises in Europe. The works had an old history running back at least to the beginning of the eleventh century.[85] On the eve of the Reformation they had been modernized and greatly extended to compete with the other less important saltworks of Franche-Comté for the rapidly expanding salt market. Smiths had installed large pans made of scores of pieces of iron riveted together to form round vessels, as large as a good-sized, flat-bottomed boat some twenty-five feet across.[86] Nearly two feet deep, each of these vessels held a wading pool of brine. The pan was built upon a stone furnace. The heat of the furnace kept the pool evaporating until a massive cargo of salt had formed in the pan ready for shipment.

At the *grande saunerie* there were at least eight of these pans, each forming part of a covered house. Subterranean canals had been artfully constructed to help separate the brine from the fresh water at the springs and to bring the brine to two wells. At one of them it was drawn to the surface in buckets attached to an endless chain, set in motion by a newly installed horse-driven engine, similar to the engines which drained some of the deep mines in Central Europe. Afterward the brine was distributed through a series of wooden troughs to the pans. It was made to trickle into them through lead pipes as the occasion demanded. The yield of salt was largest when the pans were new or freshly repaired.

Four forges were in continual operation to provide the metal parts for the pans, the engines, and the pipes. With the numerous chambers where the workpeople and their families were lodged, and with the ample buildings for the foremen, the accountants, and the chief administrative officers, the *grande saunerie* formed a self-contained village. Fountains played in the squares. In the center was a handsome edifice with a fine court and chapel —a good example of Renaissance architecture. It served for worship, it housed some of the workers, and it provided a meeting place for the directors of the enterprise. A sort of citadel, with night watchmen to keep marauders from pilfering salt or firewood, the *grande saunerie* occupied at Salins an irregular strip of land running nearly three hundred yards along the fast-moving stream, appropriately named the Furieuse. At its widest point the enclosure reached a hundred yards back from the bank.[87] With its towers and arcades and Doric columns, the saltworks was an imposing sight for the traveler as well as for the villagers of Salins, many of whom had watched it being built, and for the local peasants who drove carts loaded with logs and kindling down winding paths from the thick forests of the neighborhood to feed the fires lit under the pans. To Gollut, the six-

---

[85] Max Prinet, *L'Industrie du sel en Franche-Comté avant la conquête française* (Besançon, 1900), p. 52.

[86] At Dieuze, in Lorraine, the pans were square or rectangular and apparently even larger than at Salins (Bernard Palissy, *Œuvres*, ed. B. Fillon [Niort, 1888], II, 145).

[87] Prinet, *op. cit.*, pp. 80, 156–58, 168–70.

teenth-century historian of Franche-Comté, this enterprise provided one of the architectural wonders of the country.[88]

Like the arsenal at Venice and the saltworks at Dieuze in Lorraine,[89] the establishment at Salins was owned and operated by a sovereign political authority. Most of the small pans in the upper town had been united to form a single enterprise in the late thirteenth century. During the fifteenth century the dukes of Burgundy, who governed Franche-Comté, increased their shares in the company.[90] In 1477, at the death of Charles the Bold in battle, the county passed to the Hapsburgs through the marriage of Maximilian I to Mary of Burgundy, the daughter and heiress of that fiery duke. By this time the *grande saunerie* already belonged to the princess. When the child of this marriage, the Archduchess Margaret, was made sovereign governess of Franche-Comté in 1507, her administration appointed the officials for the *grande saunerie*—the *pardessus*, the *lieutenant du pardessus*, and their subordinates. These officials managed the works as a unit.[91]

The rulers were trying to bring the salt pans of the lower town under the same administration as the *grande saunerie*, and to concentrate salt production, formerly scattered about the country, at Salins. While neither of these projects were consummated until after the Reformation, the dukes of Burgundy and their Hapsburg successors had made much progress with both,[92] as had the dukes of Lorraine, who were pursuing the same policy of monopoly in the duchy in favor of their pans at Dieuze.[93]

At several places in Germany—such as Hall on the Inn just below Innsbruck, Reichenhall near Berchtesgaden, Halle in the Duchy of Magdeburg, and Lüneburg southeast of Hamburg—the output of salt rivaled that at Salins.[94] But nowhere east of the Rhine does the manufacture appear to have been concentrated in so sumptuous a public enterprise with as big pans and as powerful machinery until after the Reformation.[95] In many

[88] L. Gollut, *Les Mémoires historiques de la République Séquanoise* (Arbois, 1846), Bk. II, chaps. xxvi and xxvii. While these memoirs were written in 1592, the description of the *grande saunerie* contained in them is applicable to conditions two generations earlier, at the time of the Reformation, because the structure of the saltworks hardly changed between the beginning of the sixteenth century and the beginning of the nineteenth (Prinet, *op. cit.*, p. 158).

[89] Cf. Ernst Koch, "Geschichtliche Entwickelung des Bergbaues und Salinenbetriebes in Elsass-Lothringen," *Zeitschrift für Bergrecht*, 1874, pp. 162–63.

[90] Prinet, *op. cit.*, pp. 81, 89, 113.

[91] Cf. Prinet, *op. cit.*, pp. 128–39; *Inventaire sommaire des archives départementales du Nord*, B., I, Part II, 20.

[92] Prinet, *op. cit.*, pp. 90–101, 118–20, 154–55.

[93] Koch, *op. cit.*, p. 162.

[94] Montaigne, *Journal du voyage*, I, 150–51; J. E. R. von Koch-Sternfeld, *Die deutschen Salzwerke zunächst im Mittelalter* (Munich, 1836), II, 141; G. Schmoller, "Die wirtschaftlichen Zustände im Herzogthum Magdeburg," *Jahrbuch für Gesetzgebung, Verwaltung und Volkswirtschaft im deutschen Reich*, XI (1887), 840.

[95] When Montaigne visited Hall late in the sixteenth century, the pans there were apparently almost as large as those at Salins (Montaigne, *loc. cit.*), but at Halle and

places in Germany the ownership of the pans was still divided among many independent producers. Few important changes in the technique of the salt manufacture were introduced before the third decade of the sixteenth century. In some places, for example at Halle, the widespread division of ownership and management persisted until the eighteenth century.[96]

Yet everywhere in Germany and in the regions to the east, the authority of political rulers over the saltmaking industry was growing in the age of the Renaissance. In many districts the territorial lords were extending their regalian rights. They not only claimed a share in the produce of brine springs and rock-salt deposits within their dominions: they also claimed the right to dispose of the springs and the mines.[97] In addition, a few princes were successfully bringing salt production under the control of their fiscal administration and were even taking over the management of the pans. Sometimes, as in the Salzburg region, they accomplished this indirectly and slowly by buying up piecemeal the shares of private persons in the furnaces and pans and in the companies which monopolized the sale of salt. Again, when the companies were bankrupt, as at Liebenhall in Brunswick and at Allendorf in Hesse, the territorial lords bought them out altogether or leased their rights.[98]

As in Franche-Comté and Lorraine, the establishment of enterprises managed by the sovereign authority generally went hand in hand with the introduction of larger pans, more powerful machinery, and other improvements. At Sooden near Allendorf, about 1560, lignite from the Meissner was substituted for wood fuel.[99] Thus a step was taken, foreshadowed centuries before in China during the Sung dynasty, toward the general use of coal as fuel in the manufacture of salt.

Under government management, independent salters were encouraged, if they were not forced, to give up their small businesses. In some cases the concentration of production in an improved plant halved the labor costs. At a time when Continental princes were increasing their authority over all the activities of their subjects, including their economic activities, government management seems to have provided the principal key to increased efficiency in saltmaking.[100]

Lüneburg they were still very much smaller even in the eighteenth century (G. Jars, *Voyages métallurgiques* [Paris, 1781], III, 347–48, 351–54).

[96] Schmoller, *op. cit.*, p. 848.

[97] See, e.g., Konrad Wutke, "Die Salzerschliessungsversuche in Schlesien in vorpreussischer Zeit," *Zeitschrift des Vereins für Geschichte und Altertum Schlesiens,* XXVIII (1894), 99.

[98] Cf. Schmoller, "Die geschichtliche Entwickelung der Unternehmung," *Jahrbuch für Gesetzgebung, Verwaltung und Volkswirtschaft im deutschen Reich,* XV (1891), 659–60; Koch-Sternfeld, *op. cit.*, II, 76.

[99] Schmoller, *Jahrbuch für Gesetzgebung,* XI, 851.

[100] Schmoller, "Die geschichtliche Entwickelung der Unternehmung," p. 660; cf. Koch-Sternfeld, *op. cit.*, II, 77.

It would be hasty to conclude that a general system of government participation in economic enterprise, such as many Continental rulers were trying to establish at the time of the Reformation, was bound, in the long run, to increase the output of the heavy industries more than the conditions of free enterprise developed later in seventeenth-century England. It would be hasty to conclude that, in the long run, a system of government control promoted the most economical methods of production. If the relation of the subject to the sovereign and the nature of industrial development in the principalities of the Holy Roman Empire had been such as to make it possible for private capitalists to defy the prince successfully, as they were destined to do in England under the early Stuarts,[101] they might have reduced costs in saltmaking as much as, or even more than, the political rulers and their officials. The building of Doric pillars and ornamental fountains, after all, could hardly be justified as a device for cheapening the costs of producing salt. It had not occurred to anyone that these embellishments might be used to advertise the product! In terms of costs of production they were sheer waste. Like the artistic craftsman in the Italian towns, the prince who sponsored them had his mind fixed on art rather than on profits. This is another important distinction between industrial development in Renaissance Europe, which emphasized style and beauty, and industrial development in late Elizabethan and Stuart Great Britain,[102] which emphasized efficiency. Both government ownership and a concern with art imposed brakes upon rapid progress toward industrialism.

As a well-known German historian has written in his study of saltmaking in Central Europe at a still earlier period, "it is more proper to speak of the promotion of regalian rights through the development of the saltworks, than of the promotion of saltmaking enterprise through the development of regalian rights." The rapid growth in the demand for salt on the eve of the Reformation was caused especially by the increasing need for it in preserving fish and meat, as markets grew and sea voyages became longer and more frequent. The princes took advantage of an industrial expansion for which their authoritarian economic policies were hardly responsible.

During the Renaissance the power of the political authorities over economic enterprise increased notably in many regions of Continental Europe. While a few merchants, foremost among whom was Jacob Fugger, might seem for a time to hold the greatest sovereigns in the hollow of their financial hands, their power to collect interest on their loans, and even to exact repayment of the principal, rested ultimately on the good will of rulers who were seldom subject to any effective control by representative assemblies and some of whom were ceasing to feel bound even by natural law.

---

[101] Nef, *Industry and Government in France and England*, pp. 149 ff.

[102] Nef, *Western Civilization since the Renaissance*, pp. 244–49 and *passim*. Inama-Sternegg, "Zur Verfassungsgeschichte der deutschen Salinen im Mittelalter," p. 578.

Princes borrowed freely from the merchants. They did not allow the financial obligations which they had assumed to interfere with their policies of strengthening their mining administrations and extending the scope of their regalian rights. When a rich merchant grew too powerful to suit his sovereign creditors, ways could be found to confiscate his property or even to get rid of him altogether.

Charles VII was king of France when the wealth and influence of Jacques Cœur reached its zenith in 1451. In that very year, and only a few days after the king had accorded this great merchant a new mark of his favor, he signed an order for his arrest on the flimsiest of pretexts. A year and a half earlier the king's mistress, Agnès Sorel, had died of an illness which came on suddenly following childbirth. The fame of her beauty was so great that it became a part of French popular tradition. Yet the king consoled himself with others, even before the question of poison was raised in connection with Agnès Sorel's death. Suspicion had first centered on the dauphin, the future Louis XI. But now Jacques Cœur was charged with the murder and was imprisoned on that ground. The charge was preposterous and it was eventually dropped. In the meantime charges of various financial machinations were brought against him. The real trouble seems to have been that the court was too heavily in his debt, that his good fortune had made him enemies. He was the creditor of many courtiers and of the king himself, whom he had supplied with money to buy back the crown jewels that the royal lover had lavished on Agnès Sorel. The powerful had little interest in Cœur's acquittal. In 1453 the king seized his vast properties, including his mines of copper, silver, and lead in Lyonnais and Beaujolais. Most of Cœur's other property was sold at public auction, and he was forced to flee the country, only to die in 1456 on the famous old Greek island of Chios. Wealth did not always embody a claim even to justice, when its possessor incurred the displeasure of his sovereign.[103]

In Germany, where sovereign authority was divided among a large number of independent princes, as well as in France, where it was coming to be centralized in the crown, opportunities were increasing for local industrial monopolies. In the case of products like alum and quicksilver, found in only a very few places, there were opportunities even for European monopolies. The only monopolies that were recognized as legitimate by such public opinion as existed and made itself articulate were those exercised by the political ruler to further the general welfare.[104] So the stage was set for public ownership and control, and most Continental rulers were able to take advantage of their opportunities. Unlike the Stuart kings in England a century later, the sovereigns of Continental Europe at

---

[103] Cf. Clément, *Jacques Cœur et Charles VII*, pp. 345–46, and *passim*.
[104] Cf. Jakob Strieder, *Studien zur Geschichte kapitalisticher Organisationsformen*, p. 90; cf. also Archives départementales du Nord, B. 1834, fols. 48–51.

the time of the Reformation seldom brought the monopolistic principle into discredit by allowing rich merchants, even when they were favorites, to manage the monopolies in the interest of their private fortunes. The Continental rulers succeeded, as the Stuarts were unable to do, in building up and maintaining effective bureaucracies.[105] As long as private merchants co-operated with these officials in the interest of their sovereign, they might be tolerated, but when it came to a showdown the prince was generally in a position to break them. In most European states at the end of the Middle Ages it was the political ruler and not the private capitalist who held the reins which guided large-scale enterprise.

CONCLUSION

No single form of industrial organization was predominant in the Europe of the Renaissance. A great deal of rough industrial work was not done for a market. The products were not sold. Throughout Europe, and especially in areas economically backward, the husbandmen, who tilled and plowed and pastured animals, still depended largely on their own labor and that of their wives and children to repair and furnish and even to build their hovels and cottages. They repaired all and made most of their own clothing and bedding, though the production of the cloth and the leather that they used was mainly in the hands of industrial specialists. Nearly every peasant was a jack of most of the crude trades necessary for his rude existence. As the husbandmen, with their families, together with the village smiths, probably formed something like four-fifths or more of the entire population of Europe, the amount of household industry must have been extensive. Even in the towns and the rising industrial settlements, there were still many poor craftsmen who depended on themselves and their wives and children for most of the industrial products which they needed. The requirements of the masses had hardly begun to play an important role in determining the character of industry.

The organization of industrial labor for a market, which presumably occupied some two or three million workpeople in Europe the major part of their time, was of many kinds. Almost every form of enterprise known to historians existed. The independent master craftsman who worked in his own home or in living quarters that he rented, with an apprentice or two and one or two journeymen, was still a very common figure, particularly in the ancient towns. But it is not certain that independent craftsmen greatly outnumbered their fellows who, while they also worked at home, had become dependent, either directly or indirectly, for their raw materials and their markets upon rich masters or merchants, who supplied them with materials and paid their wages by the piece. In many towns, particularly

[105] Nef, *Industry and Government in France and England*, pp. 21–24, 35–57.

in economically backward regions, independent master craftsmen were in the majority, often in the great majority. But in the leading textile towns, particularly in Flanders, Brabant, and the English west country, where cloth was produced in large quantities for the whole European market, they were often in the minority. Sometimes in new industrial settlements beyond the ancient towns, as at Hondschoote in Flanders, they formed only a small minority.

Work in the home, done either by independent master craftsmen and their apprentices and journeymen or by wageworkers under the putting-out system, was probably the lot of something like two-thirds of all the industrial workpeople who labored for the market. The remainder found work mainly outside their actual living quarters, in building operations of various kinds, at mills, forges, and furnaces, in mines, especially constructed workshops, and factories. There was a great deal of variety both in the scale and in the form of enterprise.

Much the greater proportion of the nondomestic workers—for example, many country glassmakers, many diggers of coal and iron ore, and many smelters—worked in groups of less than a dozen, generally less than half a dozen. A few of these groups were as independent of outside capital as the autonomous master craftsmen in the towns. The numerous tanning, fulling, and small paper mills were generally operated by from two to five craftsmen. Like the working partnerships of miners in regions where mining was developing rapidly, many were coming under the financial control of traders who advanced them money in return for a promise to deliver a stipulated quantity of the product at a specified price.

The building craftsmen, who often labored in very much larger units, probably formed an even more numerous element among the nondomestic workpeople than the craftsmen and laborers at all the small mines, forges, mills, and shops. Among the building craftsmen, wagework seems to have been the rule. Some craftsmen worked alternately in their little shops, preparing materials, and at the edifices they were putting up.

There was, finally, the section of the nondomestic workers who labored for wages in establishments—at mines, in extensively remodeled old buildings, and in structures specially built for manufacturing. Not all by any means worked in enterprises with over a dozen employees. Those who did were probably in the minority, but, if so, they formed a considerable minority. A great many thousands were employed in mining or in metallurgy, especially in Central Europe, that is to say in the Holy Roman Empire as it stood in Charles V's time. Thousands were employed for wages in the principal shipyards; others in large salt- and alumworks. Large-scale enterprise had made an appearance in the printing, papermaking, glassmaking, and soapmaking industries, in the refining of sugar, and in a few exceptional cases in clothmaking. Units of more than twelve were rare in these industries; but all told the number of laborers employed in such units probably ran to a great many hundreds.

There were in the whole of Europe only a few large establishments that might perhaps be classed as big factories because they employed upward of a hundred workpeople. Perhaps the largest two were the arsenal at Venice, with somewhere between one and two thousand workpeople, and the papal alumworks at Tolfa, which had 711 on its payroll in 1557.[106]

The mines and workshops which employed from a dozen to a hundred workers already formed a quite respectable array at the Reformation. If all the persons who worked in them and in still larger industrial establishments had been mustered out and assembled in one place, they would have provided as big an army of ragged soldiers as any European sovereign in the time of Charles V could have put in the field, which is to say upward of fifty thousand.

These enterprises were also of many kinds. In some, such as the chief printing and crystal glassmaking shops, the owner usually lived in and participated, at least to some extent, in the manual labor alongside his employees. In the larger establishments, like the saltworks at Salins or the metallurgical factory at Hohenkirchen, living quarters and a place of worship for some or all the workpeople and their families were built as part of the plant or immediately adjoining it. The factories and quasi-factories of the Renaissance did not separate domestic and religious from working life as do the factories of more recent times. Homework was the traditional form of industry which Europe had inherited from the Middle Ages. It had a tenacious hold on the minds and habits of workmen and their employers. When technical conditions made it impossible to carry work into the home, an attempt was usually made to carry the home to the workshop. The attempt was at least partly successful. The German miners and smelters who migrated to England early in Elizabeth's reign to develop the copper mines near Keswick seem sometimes to have installed their sleeping quarters in the metallurgical plants. They put a bed in the small chamber above the assay-room.[107] In this way the line between factory and domestic work was blurred. Industrial workpeople almost always lived and worshiped close to their place of labor.

The largest establishments were nearly all owned or rigorously controlled by some public authority—the pope, a king, a prince, a bishop, a duke, or a town council. An increasing proportion of those mines and quasi-factories which employed from a dozen to fifty workers were coming under the direct supervision of such authorities. Large-scale private enter-

---

[106] See above, p. 90; Delumeau, *L'Alun de Rome*, pp. 76–77.
[107] W. G. Collingwood, *Elizabethan Keswick* ("Cumberland and Westmorland Antiquarian and Archaeological Transactions," Tract No. VIII [Kendal, 1912]), pp. 36–37, 48–49.

prise, in which the owners took no part in the manual labor and which they managed independently of the administrative officers of political rulers, was the exception. Only a negligible portion of the industrial workpeople labored under private industrial capitalism of the type which came to dominate European industry in the late nineteenth century, and toward which the economy of Great Britain was destined to move more rapidly after the Reformation.

For an understanding of the industrial conditions of the past, ready-made categories are more of a handicap than a help. Our age has been inclined to make a fetish of categories and statistics. What is more important than either, if we are to grasp the meaning of industrial organization at the time of the Reformation, is the spirit in which the work was done and in which the capital was supplied. Labor for wages was already common; but wagework generally meant something different from what we mean by it. Wages were almost always earned either in the home itself or close beside it. A great many industrial wageworkers had also plots of land which they cultivated with the help of their families. Few families were without by-occupations which added to the income they received from wages, and some workers in industry were mainly dependent for their livelihood upon husbandry. Many persons who worked for wages were master craftsmen with apprentices and even journeymen. That makes it impossible to draw the sharp line between masters and wageworkers that students of modern industrial organization have found so convenient for statistical purposes. Moreover, the distinctions between labor for wages and labor to fulfil a contract or to supply an order for a work of art were not as sharp as they are today. Piecework wages and contracts to deliver commodities at a stipulated price per unit shaded into each other.

The objective of much industrial work was to raise monuments, to weave tapestries, and fashion decorations of every kind for the sake of their beauty and for the sake of sumptuous effects that would enhance the luxury and splendor of churches, public buildings, and of private houses of the very rich. The objective was not primarily, as in recent times, the manufacture of cheap goods in large quantities for profit. People shared in the products of industry mainly through their participation in the life of the church, the life of the sovereign, the life of a powerful landlord, or the life of a municipality. A large proportion of the persons engaged in industrial labor had a direct part in the actual fashioning of some object, designed generally to fit into churches, castles, palaces, or municipal halls and monuments with which they were familiar. Today a large proportion of so-called industrial work—such as advertising and sales promotion—has no direct relation to the production of a concrete object. Nor has the workman engaged in some particular task in a factory any part in conceiving the object as a whole to which his tiny increment of labor contributes. In the early sixteenth century a great many manual workmen were free to conceive of an entire piece of workmanship, such as a statue or an ornamental balustrade, and to solve by the thoughtful improvisation, which is a part of art, the aesthetic problems connected with its making. Quality still took precedence over quantity.

In contrast to the four hundred years since the Reformation which became increasingly, especially in the north of Europe, an age of coal and iron, the Renaissance was an age of silver. The output of silver in Europe—more than three million ounces a year in the 1520's and 1530's[108]—was little inferior to what it is today. But even at the height of the industrial expansion of the Renaissance, the production of iron and coal was negligible compared with what it is today. The annual output of iron and steel in Europe around 1525 was possibly about a hundred thousand tons.[109] On the eve of the last World War, in the 1930's, more than seventy-five million tons were produced annually, something like seven hundred times as much. The annual output of coal in Europe at the Reformation perhaps amounted to some three or four hundred thousand tons at the most.[110] In the 1930's it amounted to some six hundred million tons, fifteen hundred times as much. In the age of the Renaissance the extractive industries were pursued, in the main, to provide precious metal and other substances for artistic craftsmanship, rather than to provide, as in modern times, the massive materials for heavy mechanized industries.

[108] Nef, "Silver Production in Central Europe, 1450–1618," *Journal of Political Economy*, XLIX, No. 4 (1941), 585, 590.

[109] Any estimate of the output of iron in Europe has to be based largely on guesswork. But, from the scattered information available, it is clear that production should be counted in tens rather than in hundreds of thousands of tons. There was probably no single center where the output was greater than in Styria, with its eight thousand or nine thousand tons (see p. 44). In Spain, which had been famous for its iron throughout the Middle Ages, the output of the two most productive provinces—Biscay and Guipúzcoa together—according to a contemporary Spaniard, amounted to about fifteen thousand tons annually toward the end of the sixteenth century (James M. Swank, *History of the Manufacture of Iron in All Ages* [Philadelphia, 1892], pp. 22–23). By that time the provinces were probably turning out rather more iron than in the thirties. The output of the Low Countries—another leading ironmaking region —was probably somewhat below that of Styria or the Spanish Basque provinces. The chief ironworks were in Namurois, in the neighborhood of Charleroi, and in the dominion of the prince-bishop of Liège. According to an estimate made in 1562, when the Belgian iron industry was apparently less prosperous than it had been in the twenties and thirties, the average annual output in the Liège district amounted to some eight hundred tons. Namurois and perhaps Charleroi were somewhat more productive (Goris, *Etude sur les colonies marchandes méridionales à Anvers,* pp. 477–79, 486). The output of all the ironworks in England and Wales on the eve of the dissolution of the monasteries, in 1536 and 1539, did not perhaps exceed six thousand or seven thousand tons a year on the average (Nef, "Note on the Progress of Iron Production in England, 1540–1640," *Journal of Political Economy,* XLIV [1936], 402).

[110] Probably not more than 200,000 in Great Britain (see below, p. 169), and hardly as much again in the rest of Europe.

The volume of industrial output in the early sixteenth century can be counted in units of thousands, instead of in the units of millions to which the Western peoples are now accustomed. But industrial labor was by no means primitive when the lives of three of the greatest figures of the Renaissance—Leonardo da Vinci (1452–1519), Dürer (1471–1528), and Erasmus (1467–1536)—came to an end. The time spent upon a single unit was often many times as great as today, and the results should be judged in terms of quality rather than quantity. The labor of industrial workmen was generally more complicated than it now is. In the most highly civilized regions—Italy, southern and eastern Germany, the Rhineland, parts of the Low Countries, Spain, and France—building and the fashioning of commodities for the market usually called for more taste and resourcefulness than today. In Italy and in those countries north of the Alps to which Italian architecture and Italian art were spreading, society was more sophisticated in its knowledge and its understanding of beauty than any society of our own time. With its elaborate castles and palaces, furnished with exquisitely woven tapestries, with its handsome beds, chests, and musical instruments, with its paintings, its books, its gold saltcellars, and its embellished glass mirrors, the society of the Renaissance was nourished on objects fashioned to delight the senses and the imagination to a degree that is seldom true of objects turned out by machinery and mass production.

All the countries of Europe shared to some degree in the remarkable industrial development at the end of the fifteenth and the beginning of the sixteenth centuries. This development was most striking in Italy (where it continued during the second half of the sixteenth century), in southern and eastern Germany and the adjacent countries to the south and east, in the Rhineland, Lorraine, Franche-Comté, and in those parts of the Low Countries which were coming under Spanish domination—the parts that form modern Belgium. Almost all the large industrial establishments were started in these countries. Elsewhere development was slower, though the late fifteenth and early sixteenth centuries were a period of much prosperity in every Continental nation. The industrial expansion of the Renaissance was a movement which centered in those countries that took the lead between 1914 and 1944, as they took the lead in the early sixteenth century, in fostering despotic government.

Great Britain occupied a place apart. There, after the Black Death, output increased very slowly until the end of the Wars of the Roses in 1485. Until about 1540 rapid industrial development was mainly confined to one area—the southwest—and to one industry—the manufacture of woolen cloth.[111]

[111] Cf. above, p. 97.

The industrial expansion on the Continent seems to have come to an end in Hungary with the Turkish invasions of the 1520's but not until later in Saxony and Bavaria. It culminated there in the thirties and forties,[112] earlier than in Franche-Comté and the Spanish Netherlands, where it continued almost until the first sack of Antwerp in 1576. In Italy, and probably also in southern France and in Spain, growth in output ceased only after the seventeenth century had begun.

In some countries, such as Saxony and Bavaria, a measure of industrial prosperity was maintained for many years after the high point had been reached. In others, as in the Spanish Netherlands, there was an abrupt, though probably brief, collapse. Eventually the industrial expansion of the Renaissance was followed in many Continental countries by a long period of industrial stagnation and even retrogression. During much of the seventeenth century, the volume of production actually fell in Spain, in the states of Central Europe, and probably also in Italy. The torch of industrial leadership passed to some extent to France; it passed mainly to the United Provinces, to Sweden, and, above all, to Great Britain.

The new industrial development that followed the Reformation in the north of Europe, in countries backward industrially at the beginning of the sixteenth century, differed from that of the Renaissance in ways that led more directly toward industrialism. In the north men turned away from quality in the direction of quantity, away from splendor and beauty in the direction of plenty and comfort. In mining they turned from silver-bearing ore to coal and iron ore. Especially in Great Britain, they turned increasingly for a long time from warfare and preparation for warfare to peaceful occupations. In the creation of the new world, with its great emphasis on material values, the motives of private profit and of individualism played a role with which despotic government was bound to interfere.

In the form in which they were nourished in the north of Europe from the end of the sixteenth to the early twentieth century, the conceptions of individualism and free enterprise were novel in the history of civilized societies. In many ways such conceptions were more in keeping with the spirit of the Renaissance—the enhancement of the value of man—than were the growing despotism and regulation in political and economic life fostered in the countries which first assumed the leadership in industry at the end of the Middle Ages. At a time when the ideal of renunciation to the divine will was losing its hold over men, princes and their advisers in these states were asking for a new kind of renunciation. They were asking the individual to accept the dominion of civil authority without the restraint of natural

[112] Nef, "Silver Production in Central Europe, 1450–1618," pp. 577–91. (This article is of some value concerning the progress and decline of industrial prosperity in Germany and Austria. It was my intention to include it in this volume, but my publishers, for reasons of space, were unwilling to do so.)

law, without the restraint of the divine will—to accept the lordship of a man over men. Such submission did not accord with the aspirations, born of the Renaissance, to substitute for renunciation the glorification of life in this world and the right of men to express themselves more freely and personally in thought, in art, and in science than had been possible in the Middle Ages. The faith in material progress, expounded as a part of philosophy in the early seventeenth century by Bacon, Hobbes, and Descartes, seemed to accord better with the aspirations of humanism.

In England and in the Netherlands, where the philosophy of material progress first made striking headway, the traditions of absolute government were less firmly established than in Italy and Germany. While despotism grew in strength in those countries during the industrial expansion of the Renaissance, it gave way in England before the even more rapid industrial growth of the late sixteenth and early seventeenth centuries.[113]

As time went on, the spirit of individual freedom in the pursuit of economic advantage was cultivated in northern Europe largely without those values of beauty and splendor in workmanship which were an integral part of the Renaissance spirit no less than individualism. Utility replaced quality as the mainspring of industrial progress. For more than two centuries France managed to maintain a balance between the individualism bred in northern Europe and the authoritarianism bred in southern and Central Europe. While England became the focus of rapid industrial growth at the juncture of the sixteenth and seventeenth centuries, France preserved the traditions of aesthetic workmanship inherited both from the Gothic age and from the Renaissance. France also provided, however imperfectly, the most congenial setting for the cultivation of the gentler virtues indispensable to the civilized manners which were new and which proved also an essential foundation for the triumph of industrialism.[114] From the late sixteenth century until well into the nineteenth the two great contrasting societies which nourished most of the European peoples, in the New World as well as in the Old, were the English and the French. The similarities, and still more the contrasts, between French and English development help to reveal some of the principal forces which have determined the history of Western civilization during the last four hundred years.

[113] Nef, *Industry and Government*, chap. vi, and *passim*.
[114] Nef, *Cultural Foundations of Industrial Civilization*, esp. chaps. iv, v, and vi.

PART 2

Industrial History in the Late Sixteenth and Seventeenth Centuries

3

The Progress of Technology
and the Growth of Large-Scale Industry
in Great Britain, 1540–1640

Since Arnold Toynbee, the elder, gave his famous lectures at Oxford, eighty years ago, closer study has taken from the concept of the "industrial revolution" much of its revolutionary character.[1] Nowhere, perhaps, has the revision of earlier notions concerning the period from 1760 to 1832 been more drastic than with respect to the nature and magnitude of the changes in industrial technique and organization. The industrial plant staffed by dozens and sometimes scores or even hundreds of workmen was not the novelty it was once believed to be. Large-scale industry, in this sense, had developed extensively in Europe during the later Middle Ages and particularly at the time of the Renaissance.[2] Evidence has been piling up to prove that in Great Britain similarly large enterprises, controlled to a much greater degree than those of the Continent by private capitalists, became common in mining and many branches of manufacture long before the middle of the eighteenth century. At the same time, more detailed studies of nineteenth-century economic history, especially the quantitative survey of Professor Clapham, have shown that earlier writers, with their eyes focused upon cotton and iron and upon the most advanced industrial areas, have exaggerated the place of the steam engine and of large-scale industry in the economy of the 1830's.

But it is still common to regard the 1760's and 1770's as an important historical boundary, in the sense that there began at this time the first great speeding up of industrial development. If Toynbee had lived to reply to some of the criticisms of the phrase "industrial revolution," he might have defended his position by referring to the passage in Macaulay's celebrated

From *Economic History Review*, V, No. 1 (October, 1934), 3–24.
[1] Cf. H. L. Beales, "Historical Revisions: The Industrial Revolution," *History*, XIV (1929), 126–28.
[2] See above, chaps. i and ii.

third chapter—which may possibly have influenced him during his short life—where Macaulay says that about the middle of the eighteenth century economic progress became for the first time "portentously rapid." [3]

Was this the first period of English history during which a remarkable speeding up of industrial development occurred? The opinion is gaining strength that there was at least one earlier period during which the rate of change was scarcely less striking. This period begins at about the time of the dissolution of the monasteries, and the industrial development becomes most rapid during Shakespeare's lifetime, during the latter half of Elizabeth's reign and the reign of James I. The forces of rapid change then set in motion continued throughout the seventeenth and early eighteenth centuries, but it was not until the 1780's,[4] on the eve of the French Revolution and at the time when the Constitution of the United States[5] was drafted, that an even greater speeding up in the rate of economic growth announced itself in Great Britain, preparing the way directly for the atomic age.

Support for this view is to be found in the excellent book of Mr. Wadsworth and Miss Mann on the cotton textile industry. It is there suggested that the growth of an elaborate network of middlemen, who supplied the materials upon which thousands of domestic workpeople labored at their spinning wheels and looms, was so remarkable in the late sixteenth and early seventeenth centuries that the changes in the face of industrial Lancashire were scarcely less important than between 1760 and 1832, when the county was the classic home of the "revolution" in cotton manufacture.[6] Evidence of an equally remarkable expansion, beginning about the middle of the sixteenth century and becoming decisive in the 1580's, the decade of the Armada, in the output of coal, salt, glass, and ships, and in the production of many other industrial commodities, such as alum, soap, gunpowder, metal goods and accessories, will be found in my book on the coal industry[7] and in the chapter which follows this one. The rate of growth per decade in the production of mines and manufactures was, it seems probable, no less from about 1540 to 1640 than from about 1735 to 1785, the period when, according to Macaulay, economic progress first became "portentously rapid." Recent research[8] seems to indicate that the rapid growth of

---

[3] T. B. Macaulay, *History of England* (1866 ed.), I, 220. According to the late Professor Ashley, Toynbee used the term "revolution" in the sense of a speeding up of evolution (Henry Hamilton, *The English Brass and Copper Industries to 1800* [London, 1926], p. ix). See Nef, *Western Civilization since the Renaissance* (New York, 1963), pp. 273–76 and ff. for a fuller and later treatment of this matter.

[4] *Ibid.*, chap. xiv.

[5] See below, chap. viii.

[6] A. P. Wadsworth and J. de L. Mann, *The Cotton Trade and Industrial Lancashire* (Manchester, 1931), p. 11.

[7] Nef. *Rise of the British Coal Industry* (London, 1932), I, 19 ff. 123–24, 165–89.

[8] For books and articles dealing with the industrial history of the sixteenth and seventeenth centuries, the reader is referred to Professor R. H. Tawney's "Studies in

industry and the striking increase in the importance and complexity of the domestic system, which began in the Elizabethan Age, were accompanied in England by a remarkable expansion in the use of machinery driven by water and horse power and by a concentration (unprecedented in previous history) on inventive objectives primarily aimed at the reduction of labor *costs* in the interest of quantitative production.

Three kinds of technical development helped the growth of large-scale, privately controlled enterprise between 1540 and 1640. The first was the introduction of a series of industries which had appeared somewhat earlier on the Continent, but which hardly gained a foothold in Great Britain until after the Reformation. The second was the application to old industries of various technical processes known before, especially in some districts on the Continent, but hitherto very little used in Great Britain. The third was the discovery and application of new technical methods, little known in Europe at the Reformation.

THE INTRODUCTION OF "NEW" INDUSTRIES

During the last sixty years of the sixteenth century the first paper and gunpowder mills,[9] the first cannon foundries, the first alum and copperas

Bibliography: Modern Capitalism," *Economic History Review*, IV (1944), 336–53; and to the economic history section of Professor Conyers Read's *Bibliography of British History, Tudor Period, 1485–1603* (1933). A knowledge of the following books is indispensable for an understanding of industrial development during the two centuries preceding the "industrial revolution": T. S. Ashton and J. Sykes, *The Coal Industry of the Eighteenth Century* (1929); T. S. Ashton, *Iron and Steel in the Industrial Revolution* (1924); J. W. Gough, *The Mines of Mendip* (Oxford, 1930); Hamilton, *op. cit.;* Herbert Heaton, *The Yorkshire Woollen and Worsted Industries* (Oxford, 1920); A. K. H. Jenkin, *The Cornish Miner* (London, 1927); G. R. Lewis, *The Stannaries* (Cambridge, Mass., 1907); E. Lipson, *The Economic History of England* (London, 1931), Vols. II and III; G. I. H. Lloyd, *The Cutlery Trades* (London, 1913); W. H. Price, *The English Patents of Monopoly* (Cambridge, Mass., 1906); W. R. Scott, *The Constitution and Finance of Joint Stock Companies* (3 vols.; Cambridge, 1910–12); Ernest Straker, *Wealden Iron* (London, 1931); George Unwin, *Industrial Organization in the Sixteenth and Seventeenth Centuries* (New York, 1904); Wadsworth and Mann, *op. cit.* In the present article, I have made free use of these works, without specific acknowledgment. Where I have drawn on other material for important statements of fact, I have generally given references.

For the relation of the inventive ingenuity, aroused intensively for the first time at the juncture of the sixteenth and seventeenth centuries, to the later development of the iron and steel industries, steam-driven machinery, steam-driven locomotives and ships, see Nef, "Coal Mining and Utilization," in C. Singer, E. J. Holmyard, and A. R. Hall (eds.), *A History of Technology,* III (Oxford, 1957), 72–88.

[9] A paper mill of the type successfully introduced into England in Elizabeth's reign had been set up at Hertford, probably about 1500, but it had a short life of not more than ten years. Apparently no further attempt was made to erect a large paper mill until 1557. This, too, was a failure; but papermaking by water-driven mills was established before the end of the sixteenth century (Rhys Jenkins, "Early Attempts at Paper-making in England, 1495–1680," *Library Association Record,* II, Part II (1900), 481–85; G. H. Overend, "Notes upon the Earlier History of the Manufacture

factories, the first sugar refineries, and the first considerable saltpeter works were all introduced into the country from abroad. The discovery of calamine, the ore of zinc, in Somerset and elsewhere, together with the first really effective attempts to mine copper ore, made possible the establishment of brassmaking and battery works for hammering brass and copper ingots into plates.

Not all the commodities turned out by these manufactures were being produced in England for the first time. If English-made sugar and brass were new, some paper and alum, probably some saltpeter and gunpowder, and perhaps some copperas had been obtained from native workshops before the sixteenth century. But the quantities had been insignificant. The important thing about the "new" Elizabethan industries, for the spread of capitalistic ventures, was that in all of them plant was set up involving investments far beyond the sums which groups of master craftsmen could muster, even if these artisans were men of some small substance. While in London, Sheffield, or any provincial town, the typical workshop of the smith, the cutler, or the weaver could be equipped with its forge or grinding wheel or loom and other necessary tools for a few pounds, the establishments erected in these new industries cost hundreds, and in many cases thousands, of pounds, at a time when a wage earner did well if he earned more than five pounds a year. A further heavy outlay had to be made on materials and labor, because the process of production frequently required a long time, and it was many months before any return could be expected from sales.

In the reign of James I, the alum houses erected near Whitby, on the Yorkshire coast, were great wooden structures. Each contained large brick furnaces and cisterns, piles of alumstone, coal, and wood fuel and about ten metal pans for heating the ingredients. Many thousands of pounds were spent on each of these houses, and the annual expense of the materials consumed in the manufacture exceeded £1,000, at a time when that sum was equivalent to more than $60,000 in terms of modern money. One of the farmers of these houses wrote in 1619 that alum-making was "a distracted worke in severall places and of sundry partes not possible to bee performed by anie one man nor by a fewe. But by a multitude of the baser sort, of whom the most part are idle, careless and false in their labour." [10] Actually about sixty workmen were regularly employed at a single house, and, in addition, there was the casual labor of coopers, smiths, and carpenters to keep the building and equipment in repair. Eighteen drivers with their carts were needed for each house, to bring alumstone, coal, and

---

of Paper in England," *Proceedings of the Huguenot Society of London,* VIII (1909), 177–80. For the introduction of gunpowder-making in the fifties, see *Victoria County History, Surrey,* II, 246.

[10] British Museum, Lansdowne MSS., 152, f. 57.

wood, and to carry away the finished product.[11] The total sum invested in the Yorkshire alumworks by the 1630's probably amounted to the modern equivalent of millions of dollars.

In the reign of Charles I, the copperas house at Queenborough in Kent, with its great wooden troughs, leaden pipes, and cisterns, was built on a similar scale to an alum house.[12] In 1613 John Browne, later crown commissioner for making ordnance and shot and official gunmaker to the Parliament in the Civil War, employed some 200 men in his cannon foundry at Brenchley in Kent.[13] At Dartford, in the same county, a paper mill had been set up by John Spilman, a naturalized German, about the middle of Elizabeth's reign. According to Thomas Churchyard, who wrote a long poem about it:

> The mill itself is sure right rare to see,
> The framing is so queint and finely done,
> Built all of wood, and hollowe trunkes of tree
> That makes the streames at point device to runne,
> Nowe up, nowe downe, nowe sideward by a sleight,
> Nowe forward fast, then spouting up on heights,
>
> .   .   .   .
>
> The hammers thump and make as lowde a noyse,
> As fuller doth that beates his wollen cloth.

The building in which the paper was produced seemed to Churchyard "a house of some estate." The enterprise may have employed scores of hands, though the poet certainly exaggerated when he spoke of 600 workmen.[14] One of the two great waterwheels which drove the hammers for beating the cloth and the stamping machinery had formerly been used to drive the bellows of a blast furnace on the same site, and the cost of converting it to its new purpose is said to have been between £1,400 and £1,500 in money of that time, which should be multiplied by more than twenty to get its equivalent in terms of today. Powder mills, introduced into Surrey just after the middle of the sixteenth century, were also driven by water power, and the machinery was perhaps no less costly than at the paper mills. In addition, there were at least two other elaborately equipped buildings at a gunpowder factory—the corning house and the stove (a separate establishment about twenty feet square in which the powder was dried by the heat from an iron fireplace). The battery works introduced from Germany in

[11] Ibid., 152, no. 6; State Papers, Domestic, James I, Vol. LXXIV, No. 20.

[12] Sir William Brereton, Travels in Holland, the United Provinces, England, Scotland and Ireland ("Chetham Society Publications," Vol. I [London, 1844], pp. 2–3).

[13] State Papers, Domestic, James I, Vol. CV, No. 92 (as cited in Straker, op. cit., p. 163).

[14] Thomas Churchyard, A Description and Playne Discourse of Paper, 1588 (reprinted in John Nichols, The Progresses of Queen Elizabeth [1788], Vol. II).

Elizabeth's reign, with their furnaces and numerous great hammers, some of which weighed five hundred pounds, probably cost as much to build as the larger powder and paper mills. The hammers were driven by water power at a heavy cost. As in all the rising English industries the overshot wheel was generally used rather than the less expensive undershot wheel. To turn the former a stream had to be diverted from its course, and a dam built to store up the water against a drought.

There was nothing new about the use of the overshot wheel in industry, but its adoption during the late sixteenth and early seventeenth centuries in England appears to have been unprecedentedly rapid, and large water-driven wheels had probably come into more widespread use by 1640, on the eve of the Civil War, than in other countries.

Among other industries introduced into England during the last sixty years of the sixteenth century, sugar-refining and brassmaking by the process of cementation also required an extensive outlay in buildings, furnaces, boilers, machinery, tools, and materials. Sugarmakers had to invest scores and sometimes hundreds of pounds in lead pipes, cisterns, copper kettles, and iron rollers for grinding the cane. Brassmakers had to provide expensive metal pots, in which the copper was mixed with prepared calamine, and one or more large ovens in which eight or more of the pots were placed for heating.

In many parts of Great Britain the introduction of these manufactures during the last sixty years of the sixteenth century opened fresh fields for the development of industrial plant requiring considerable blocks of capital. It is important to form a rough impression of the number of enterprises and of the influence upon industrial organization of the "new" manufactures. While all of them gained a firm foothold in England before the Civil War, they had an earlier history in Europe, and some of them were carried on much more extensively abroad than in England. This was the case with papermaking and sugar-refining. Although ten or more paper mills are known to have been at work in England in the thirties of the seventeenth century, the great new demand for paper, brought about by the growing importance of the printing press, continued to be met largely by imports, especially from France.[15] Most of the sugar consumed in Great Britain was brought in refined from the West Indies.

The other manufactures with which we have been dealing made more headway in capturing the domestic market. England was becoming much less dependent upon imports for its supplies of alum, copperas, brass, and copper than for its supplies of paper and sugar. The output of saltpeter and gunpowder was becoming sufficient to meet native needs, which were modest because the English and the Scots managed to stay aloof from most of the

---

[15] Jenkins, "Early Attempts at Papermaking in England," pp. 581–86; Edward Heawood, "Paper Used in England after 1600," in *Library,* 4th ser., XI, 292 ff.

European warfare between 1560 and 1625. English-made cannons proved so excellent in quality and so cheap in price that, before the end of Elizabeth's reign, they were in demand all over the Continent.

In each of these manufactures, the market could be supplied by a rather small number of enterprises. Sussex, perhaps the principal seat of the cannon manufacture, apparently had only four foundries for casting cannons in 1613.[16] Wars were still won with what seems to us an infinitesimal expenditure of metal and gunpowder.[17]

It is probable, nevertheless, that the number of considerable establishments at work in all these "new" manufactures, taken together, had reached several scores before the Civil War. And the introduction of such establishments, with their elaborate water-driven machinery, their large furnaces and accessories, must have had an influence upon the growth of industrial capitalism in England beyond that which can be measured in terms of the output or the number of workpeople engaged in them. Mechanics and inventors could study the new machinery, furnaces, and boilers with a view to adapting them to suit other processes of manufacture. Landlords and merchants, with capital to invest in other industries, were stimulated by example to set up works on a larger scale than they might otherwise have done. For a variety of reasons, they were able as time went on to develop their enterprises free from government participation and even government regulation to a degree that had not been common hitherto in Europe, if indeed anywhere in the world. While the period preceding the Reformation had been, on the Continent especially, a time of increasing political control over industry,[18] the late sixteenth and seventeenth centuries were in Great Britain a time when private enterprise increasingly escaped effective government interference.[19]

THE PROGRESS OF ADVANCED TECHNICAL METHODS IN OLD INDUSTRIES

A larger number of workpeople and a greater amount of capital were drawn into such capitalistic enterprises by the extensive changes in old industries than by the introduction of these "new" manufactures. The very rapid growth of markets for coal and ore[20] was making it imperative to adopt less primitive methods in mining and the production of metals. As a result of the application of improved methods known before the middle of the sixteenth century, at least on the Continent, conditions in these in-

[16] Straker, *Wealden Iron,* p. 163.
[17] On the whole subject, see Nef, *Western Civilization since the Renaissance.* Part I, *passim.*
[18] See above, pp. 52 ff., 102 ff.
[19] See Nef, *Industry and Government in France and England, 1540–1640* (Ithaca, N. Y., 1957) where the subject is treated much more fully.
[20] See below, chap. iv.

dustries were largely transformed during the century following the dissolution of the monasteries.

Before the sixteenth century, in Great Britain, the expensive adit or long tunnel for draining mines was rare,[21] machinery driven by water or horse power for pumping out water or raising minerals was perhaps still rarer. The problems of prospecting for coal and ore, of sinking through rocky strata, and of ventilating the pits to force out noxious gases, hardly tried the ingenuity of the miner, for the depths of the workings seldom exceeded a few fathoms. Except at silver mines,[22] which were scarce in Great Britain, and at a very few tin and coal mines, mining seldom required the investment of much capital. Ore and coal were normally dug by independent partnerships of working miners.

Great changes occurred in the importance of mining and metallurgy as a result of the very rapid expansion in the demand for copper, lead, iron, and above all coal. Seams of that base mineral abounded, and the rate of growth in the output of coal was more rapid than the rate of growth in the output of silver had been during the previous hundred years in Central Europe.[23] Production of coal in Great Britain increased some seven- or eightfold or even more between the 1530's and the 1630's.[24] In order to meet the demand it became necessary to sink to depths of twenty, thirty, and even forty or fifty fathoms. In many parts of England, Scotland, and Wales miners were threatened by water which drowned out their workings and by gas explosions which killed scores. Never before in any country had mining and the transport of coal engaged as workers so large a proportion of the population as in Great Britain on the eve of the Civil War, which is to say in the 1630's.

During the reigns of Elizabeth and her two Stuart successors, money was poured out lavishly in the construction of hundreds of adits, ventilation shafts, and drainage engines, driven by water or more often by horse power, at tin, copper, and lead mines and, above all, at collieries.[25] As the digging and lining of an adit often cost thousands of pounds (the equivalent of hundreds of thousands of dollars in today's money), and as the expense of operating a horse-driven pump sometimes amounted to about £2,000 a year, the new mining enterprises had to be conducted on a scale which

---

[21] I am aware, of course, that we find references to adits comparatively early in the Middle Ages (Jenkin, *The Cornish Miner*, pp. 83–84; L. F. Salzman, *English Industries of the Middle Ages* [2d ed.; Oxford, 1923], pp. 53–54); cf. Nef, *Rise of the British Coal Industry*, I, 354, esp. n. 2.

[22] Stephen Atkinson, *The Discoverie and Historie of the Gold Mynes in Scotland, 1619* (Edinburgh: Bannatyne Club, 1825), p. 51; cf. Lewis, *The Stannaries*, p. 194.

[23] Nef, "Silver Production in Central Europe, 1450–1618," *Journal of Political Economy*, XLIX, No. 4 (1941), 585–86.

[24] See below, chap. iv, p. 169.

[25] For a fuller treatment of the subject see Nef, *Rise of the British Coal Industry*, I, 350 ff., and *passim*.

would have seemed almost incredible to an untraveled Englishman of the time of Henry VIII and Sir Thomas More. What he would have considered large-scale industry was becoming, except in backward shires, the normal form of enterprise both in mining and metallurgy.

While the annual output of a coal mine before the middle of the sixteenth century had rarely exceeded a few hundred tons, and much of the mining had been done casually by manorial tenants who worked part of the year as husbandmen, collieries producing from ten to twenty-five thousand tons of coal, representing an investment of many thousands of pounds in money of that time, and employing scores and sometimes hundreds of miners, became common before 1640. They were to be found not only in the north of England but also in Scotland, and even in the Midlands which had no direct access to the mounting trade in seaborne coal. Large enterprises were the rule in the mining of copper, as well as in the much less extensive mining of silver; considerable investments of capital were common in the mining of tin and were not unknown in the mining of lead.[26]

In the conversion of metallic ores into metals, and the preparation of these metals for the smiths, nailers, and other craftsmen who fashioned them into finished articles, the scale of enterprise grew also strikingly. The blast furnace for producing cast iron was probably introduced from the Continent toward the end of the fifteenth century.[27] But it was little used at that time even in Sussex, the center of the English iron industry, and apparently not at all elsewhere, until after 1540.[28] Before the sixteenth century, most English wrought iron had been obtained directly from the ore, by the so-called "bloomery" process, at small forges, which cost little to build, rarely produced more than twenty tons a year, required few tools and appliances, no buildings beyond the forge itself, and seldom employed more than half a dozen or so manorial tenants. Between 1540 and 1640, the process of ironmaking assumed a more capitalistic form, and the changes were second in importance only to those which revolutionized the industry during and after the eighties of the eighteenth century. The ore came to be smelted generally in blast furnaces,[29] first in Sussex, then in Glamorganshire, Monmouthshire, the Midlands, the Forest of Dean, and Scotland.[30] These furnaces were considerable structures compared with

[26] Cf. *Victoria County History, Derbyshire*, II, 332.

[27] Water power was occasionally used for driving the bellows or the hammers at more primitive ironworks in the Middle Ages.

[28] Beck believed that, even on the Continent, the use of large furnaces and water power in the manufacture of iron did not become extensive until the middle of the sixteenth century (Ludwig Beck, *Die Geschichte des Eisens* [2d ed.; Brunswick, 1891], I, 781).

[29] I do not mean, of course, that all the primitive bloomery forges had disappeared by the time of the Civil War or even by the beginning of the eighteenth century.

[30] Straker, *Wealden Iron*; W. Llewellin, "Sussex Ironmasters in Glamorganshire," *Archaeologia Cambrensis*, 3d ser., IX, 83–111; *Victoria County History, Derbyshire*, II, 358–59; Rhys Jenkins, "Iron-making in the Forest of Dean," *Transactions of the*

the earlier English forges, though even more extensive metallurgical plant had been set up for treating argentiferous copper ores in Central Europe during the great expansion of industry on the Continent which preceded the Reformation.[31] The new English blast furnaces often rose to a height of thirty feet and were usually more than twenty feet square at the bottom, with walls five or six feet thick of brick and stone to withstand the great heat necessary to obtain molten iron. That heat itself was generated with the help of a large leathern bellows about twenty feet long, usually driven by an overshot wheel almost as high as the furnace itself. To obtain the power, the water from a dam was carried high above the ground along a wooden trough, often seventy-five yards or more in length, to a point above the wheel. A large additional outlay in buildings was required—a furnace house of stone and timber, a bridge house to protect the waterwheel, several smaller houses and cabins for the workmen, stables for the horses used in hauling ore, timber, and coal, and dry storage space for the ore and the charcoal which had to be obtained in greater quantities as the scale of enterprise increased, and at higher prices as the cost of wood rose more rapidly than that of other commodities.[32]

These new ironworks involved an original outlay which normally exceeded a thousand pounds, equivalent in modern money to more than twenty times that sum; they often employed scores of workmen to bring the materials, to convert wood to charcoal, to operate the machinery, and to handle the cast iron, and they were capable of producing from 100 to 500 tons and even more in a year. They were sometimes combined with, sometimes separate from, the finery and chafery, at which cast iron was made into wrought iron. The latter processes were, in any case, scarcely less capitalistic than the former, for before the Civil War water power came to be generally employed both to fan the flames at the hearths and to drive the hammers which forged the metal into bars. As early as 1607, Camden commented upon the water-driven hammers in Sussex, which filled "the neighbourhood . . . night and day with continual noise." [33] Whether the forges were situated near the furnace or at a distance, they were often owned by the same entrepreneur or partnership, so that many ironmasters in calculating their outlay had to add the cost of their forges to that of the furnace.

Other branches of the metallurgical industry, besides the making of iron, were changing their form under the stimulus of technical improvements introduced from abroad. With the help of skilled workmen from Germany,

---

Newcomen Society, VI, 42–65; Ivison MacAdam, "Notes on the Ancient Iron Industry of Scotland," Proceedings of the Society of Antiquarians, Scotland, XXI, 89, 109, 112–113.

[31] See above, p. 51.
[32] See below, chap. vi, pp. 261–64.
[33] William Camden, Britannia, ed. Gough (1753), I, 195.

copper smelting was combined with copper mining in the large financial enterprise known as the Society of Mines Royal. According to a writer familiar with the works of the Society at Keswick before the Civil War practically put a stop to their operations, "the smelting houses were so many that they looked like a little town." [34]

Metals other than iron and copper were usually produced in less elaborate plants and sometimes without the aid of machinery. But mills driven by water power came to be extensively used in the last half of the sixteenth century for breaking lead ore[35] and for smelting and stamping tin. As a result, the process of smelting tin ore passed from the hands of small craftsmen to those of capitalist employers.

These changes of industrial organization in connection with the conversion of ores into metals were accompanied by similar changes in the processes which supplied the craftsmen with standardized metal goods, in the form of ingots, sheets, rods, and wire. Steel had been made in England in small quantities throughout the Middle Ages, but the country had been mainly dependent for its supplies upon Germany. Attempts to introduce a considerable manufacture occurred early in Elizabeth's reign in Sussex, Kent, and Glamorganshire, with the help of skilled Dutch technicians. Thirty foreign workmen were employed in a steelwork at Robertsbridge in Sussex, started in 1565,[36] and the buildings included two large coal houses and a dwelling house, besides the workhouse and several forges. A partnership, which included Sir Henry Sidney and Jone Knight, the widow of an important London merchant, spent £1,960 in 1565–66 in setting up a steelmaking plant in Kent.[37] From that time on, the industry was undertaken increasingly in establishments requiring a greater concentration of capital than had been at all common in English manufacturing during the Middle Ages. In James I's reign, cutting mills were set up in or near London for producing iron rods to be used by nailers, smiths, and shipwrights.[38] The drawing of metal wire, which is said to have been carried on exclusively by hand labor until the 1560's, changed its character during the next few decades. Water-driven machinery was adopted both for hammering the metal bars into the proper form and for the actual drawing of the wire from the metal. The new processes involved an extensive outlay in buildings and machinery, for there were two mills, one for the small and another for the large wire, besides the furnaces in which the metal was annealed. The celebrated wireworks at Tintern apparently employed about a

---

[34] Hamilton, *The English Brass and Copper Industries,* p. 55.
[35] Salzman, *English Industries of the Middle Ages,* pp. 55–56.
[36] Rhys Jenkins, "Notes on the Early History of Steel Making in England," *Transactions of the Newcomen Society,* III, 17–18, 33–40.
[37] Straker, *op. cit.,* pp. 313–14.
[38] John Nicholl, *Some Account of the Company of Ironmongers* (2d ed.; 1866), pp. 164–69.

hundred workers as early as 1581. So, except in the finishing processes, the considerable plant, consisting usually of a group of small buildings and based on water-driven machinery and furnaces much larger than those common in medieval England, made its way into one branch of the metallurgical industry after another. Before the Civil War it had firmly established itself.

The adoption of new machinery and large furnaces was accompanied, as I have just said, by a remarkable expansion in the output of coal, and a notable growth in the output of metal. The demand for workpeople was increasing nearly as rapidly as the output; for while the introduction of machinery reduced the labor costs of producing metal from the ore,[39] the advantages provided by labor-saving devices in mining were partly offset by the increasing difficulties of extracting coal and ore from greater depths, and of transporting both for greater distances. During the century preceding the English Civil War of the 1640's, many thousands of men and some women, whose ancestors had labored on the land or as small craftsmen in their own homes in medieval towns and villages, were drawn into substantial enterprises in mining and in converting ore into anchors, and into various forms of metal suitable for workmen to fashion into tools, machine parts, wool combs and cards, axletrees, bits, stirrups, spurs, grates, nails, locks, and keys, plowshares, kettles, pots, pans and other cheap wares, which were wanted in much greater quantities than ever before as a result of the increase in population, the general expansion of industry, and the spread of homely comforts among the upper and middle classes.

The concentration of capital in mining and metallurgy from 1540 to 1640 was stimulated by the application of technical processes introduced with the help of skilled foreign artisans. But the English and even the Scots were experimenting more seriously than the Europeans had done heretofore with a view to draining mines by steam power, transporting coal by railways, and smelting iron ore with mineral fuel.[40] Great Britain was not only catching up with Continental countries in the early seventeenth century in mining and metallurgy, she was beginning to forge ahead of them, partly because of the shrinkage in the output of silver-bearing ores in Central Europe. There was no growth in the output of coal abroad at all comparable to that in Great Britain, and, on the eve of the Civil War, three or four times as much was probably produced in Great Britain as in the whole of Continental Europe. Britain had gained no comparable lead in the extraction of ores, but as coal mining already required the investment of more capital and the employment of more labor than all other kinds of British mining combined, it may be presumed that mining already occupied a more prominent place in the national economy than in any foreign country.[41]

[39] Cf. below, chap. vi, p. 267.
[40] Nef, "Coal Mining and Utilization," in *A History of Technology,* III, pp. 72–88.
[41] See below, chap. iv, *passim.*

Only the failure to solve the problem of smelting ores with coal had prevented Great Britain from capturing a place of pre-eminence in metallurgy.

With the critical shortage of timber that accompanied the industrial expansion of the Elizabethan Age,[42] manufacturers were heavily handicapped unless they could substitute coal, which was abundant and cheap, for firewood and charcoal. Nowhere were the effects of the shortage of wood felt more keenly than in smelting. The high cost of fuel began to check the expansion in the output of iron before the end of Elizabeth's reign; it brought this expansion to a standstill before the Civil War,[43] and had begun to interfere with the production of lead, copper, and tin, the ores of which could be smelted with less fuel than iron ore. But the effects of the failure to solve the technical problem of substituting coal for wood in the process of converting ores to metals were somewhat less serious for the metallurgical industry as a whole than has been sometimes assumed. During the reigns of Elizabeth I, James I, and Charles I, coal was successfully substituted for wood fuel in calcining ores prior to their smelting, in remelting lead after it had been smelted, in extracting silver from lead, in converting iron into steel, in battery and wirework, and in nearly all the finishing processes. While Great Britain may have stood at some disadvantage in smelting ores as compared with Continental countries,[44] in most parts of which the timber shortage became critical somewhat later, she had already obtained an advantage in many other metallurgical processes through the greater abundance and accessibility of her coal supplies. She had begun to supplement her domestic stock of metals by more substantial imports of iron from Flanders and of iron and copper from Sweden.[45] And, as time went on, the growing use of coal relieved the pressure on the English wood supplies.

THE DISCOVERY AND APPLICATION OF NEW TECHNICAL METHODS

The substitution of coal for wood frequently involved technical problems of considerable magnitude in other processes than smelting and in other industries than metallurgy. By the successful solution of some of these problems early in the seventeenth century, the British were already making a positive contribution of their own to industrial technology. Fuel economy

[42] See Nef, Rise of the British Coal Industry, I, 156 ff.
[43] See Nef, "Note on the Progress of Iron Production in England, 1540–1640," Journal of Political Economy, XLIV (June, 1936), 398–403.
[44] It is a mistake to suppose that in the ordinary process of producing wrought iron, no coal at all was used prior to the successful introduction of coke in the blast furnace by the elder Derby about 1709. Some coal was commonly employed along with charcoal during the seventeenth century, at least in the Forest of Dean and the Midlands, at the forges where pig iron was made into bars. Such a use was not limited to the finery, as my book suggests (Nef, Rise of the British Coal Industry, I, 250), but extended to the chafery (Jenkins, "Iron-making in the Forest of Dean," p. 60).
[45] Nef, Western Civilization since the Renaissance, p. 11.

became a much more vital matter in the Elizabethan Age in England than on the Continent, and English "inventors" spent much of their time experimenting with new kinds of heating apparatus, which, it was hoped, would either reduce the consumption of wood[46] or make possible the use of coal. As a coal fire often damaged the quality of the raw materials with which it came in contact, it was necessary either to devise more elaborate and expensive furnaces than had hitherto been used, in order to separate the materials from the sulphurous flames and fumes of the new fuel, or to attempt to purify the coal itself. About the middle of the seventeenth century, the second kind of attack on the problem led to the discovery of coke, which was first used in drying malt.[47] Already during the reigns of James I and Charles I, the introduction of new kinds of furnaces, suited to the use of raw coal, had begun to increase the capitals and alter the nature of the work in a number of manufactures.

The calcining of iron ore prior to smelting had been accomplished in an open-air fire before the seventeenth century. It was probably in order to make possible the substitution of coal for charcoal that the process came to be carried on in brick kilns in the Midlands and the Forest of Dean before the Civil War. Bricks had occasionally been baked in coal fires on the Continent in the sixteenth century, but the adoption of a more elaborate kiln heated by several small furnaces was apparently a device worked out in England in the reign of James I. This facilitated the use of coal and greatly increased the importance of the production of bricks, which were coming into general use for the first time in building, paving, and in the construction of cisterns, furnaces, and kilns of all kinds. Shortly before 1612, glassmaking was transformed by the discovery of the method of closing the clay crucibles in which the potash and sand were melted down, in order to make possible the substitution of a coal for a wood fire.[48] It has been suggested [49] that the invention of the closed crucibles for making glass may have given William Ellyott and Mathias Meysey ideas for their important invention of the cementation process for steel manufacture in 1614. The enclosing of bar iron and charcoal in crucibles, similar to those invented for melting glass, was an essential feature of the process.

The newly awakened interest in mechanical improvements, which spread

[46] Cf. Lansdowne MSS. 105, no. 44.

[47] The discovery of coke had been made already by the Chinese in the eleventh century, but the process apparently never penetrated to Europe and was forgotten in China. From a thesis written by Robert Hartwell for the Committee on Social Thought of the University of Chicago, "Iron and Early Industrialism in Eleventh Century China" (1963).

[48] There can be little doubt that this was a *British* invention, for it was introduced *later* at various places on the Continent. Cf. F. Pholien, *La verrerie et ses artistes au pays de Liége* (1899), pp. 57, 77.

[49] By E. W. Hulme. See Jenkins, "Notes on the Early History of Steel Making," pp. 28–29.

among all classes in England from the nobility to the humble artisan, and sent those who could afford it traveling in foreign countries for instruction, was not limited to the problem of saving firewood. In an age that Jevons and other nineteenth-century writers believed to be virtually barren of practical inventive achievement, England was actually becoming a busy hive of experiments designed to reduce labor. Shortly before the end of Elizabeth's reign, boring rods for finding out the nature of underground strata and railed ways with large horse-drawn wagons for carrying coal were devised by the ingenuity of some inventors who remain anonymous. In southern Nottinghamshire, at about the same time, in 1589, William Lee gave the world his stocking-knitting frame.

It is impossible to determine to what extent workmen were drawn into capitalistic plants before 1640 as a result of such English inventions. In some cases, the technical discoveries had little, if any, effect upon the form of industrial enterprise. In most of the metallurgical finishing trades and in many branches of the textile industry, small domestic enterprises were still the rule even after the widespread adoption of coal in place of wood fuel. Framework knitting remained domestic until the nineteenth century, for Lee's invention did not cause a sufficiently great increase in the capital required to draw the industry into the factory.[50] Boring rods added something, but not much, to the costs of mining. Railed ways involved a far heavier outlay, especially where collieries were worked at some distance from navigable water and where the terrain between was full of hills and ravines. Their installation eliminated the independent local carter, who plied his horse and cart for hire, and changed the transportation of coal into a capitalistic industry. But neither railed ways nor boring rods made much headway in connection with mining until the end of the seventeenth century.

The introduction of new furnaces, to permit the burning of coal, was of greater immediate importance. Calcining kilns added to the cost of ironworks. Before the invention of the closed pots, glass had been made by the foreign artisans, who had introduced extensive commercial glasswork into England after the middle of the sixteenth century, in specially built houses, with oblong furnaces about six feet long;[51] so it would be inaccurate to say that this invention converted a domestic into a factory industry. But it furthered the concentration of capital, and had far-reaching consequences for the progress of the British glass manufacture. The labor done at the new houses for producing sheet glass was of a different nature from that for producing fine goblets and mirrors. Glassmaking as carried on at Altare and

[50] See Jonathan David Chambers, *Nottinghamshire in the Eighteenth Century* (London, 1932) chap. v.
[51] For the description of a glasshouse erected by some Frenchmen at Buckholt, near Salisbury, probably about 1576, see E. W. Hulme, "English Glass-Making in the Sixteenth and Seventeenth Centuries," *Antiquary*, XXX, 214.

Venice in the late fifteenth and sixteenth centuries, and as taught by the Italians to the French, the Dutch, and the English, was an art. The persons who practiced it in Italy enjoyed a prestige and dignity similar to that attaching to the goldsmith, or even the sculptor or painter. An Italian glass goblet of the early sixteenth century can be appropriately set beside Benvenuto Cellini's saltcellar or a fine canvas by Carpaccio. But the new glass furnaces in seventeenth-century England were staffed largely with stokers and other unskilled laborers. It was the coarsest glass which consumed the largest quantities of coal, and the English especially excelled in the manufacture of this cheap glass.[52] The use of glass for windows and bottles was becoming common, and such modest luxuries were spreading from the highest to the middle orders.[53] Brickmaking, like commercial glassmaking, owed its rapid progress during the decades preceding the Civil War in no small measure to the adoption of coal fuel.

Wherever coal was substituted for wood in manufactures, it tended not only to increase the costs of the installation, but also to cheapen the quality of the product and reduce the prestige attaching to manual work. By cheapening the quality of the product it widened the market for it, and thus increased the potential advantages of large-scale production. Quite apart from the direct influence of the substitution of coal for wood in encouraging large-scale manufacture, it is clear that the inventions making this substitution possible enabled several capitalistic industries, which would otherwise have withered, to flourish as they could not in foreign countries lacking cheap and easily accessible coal supplies.

The "early English industrial revolution" was a many-sided matter. Its significance will not be grasped if we look only for increases in the *scale* of industrial enterprise, for increases in the *size* of the capital invested. We have also to consider the *conditions* under which capital was invested and the *purposes* for which it was employed. In Great Britain during the late sixteenth and seventeenth centuries there was a novel shift not only toward freedom for private enterprise,[54] but also toward the investment of considerable capital in industrial enterprises which, as above all with coal, served in the manufacture of more homely wares, designed primarily for daily comfort. Capital investment, along with technical inventive ingenuity,[55] was being oriented as never before in the direction of production for the sake of *quantity*.[56] This new orientation helped to precipitate the industrial revolutions of the nineteenth and twentieth centuries.

[52] Cf. *The Mischief of the Five Shillings Tax Upon Coal* (1699), p. 22.
[53] See below, chap. iv.
[54] See below, p. 211.
[55] *Ibid.*
[56] For further details see Nef, *La Naissance de la civilisation industrielle et le monde contemporain* (Paris, 1954), chap. i, esp. pp. 28–32; and Nef, *Cultural Foundations of Industrial Civilization* (Cambridge, 1958), pp. 50 ff. and *passim*.

OTHER FACTORS CAUSING THE CONCENTRATION OF INDUSTRIAL CAPITAL

The adoption of mechanical methods, little used in Great Britain before the Reformation or invented during the hundred years which followed, clearly played an important role in the "early industrial revolution." But there were manufactures in which a notable concentration of capitals occurred without any fundamental change in the technique of production. Two principal factors were making larger industrial ventures more economical, even without the introduction of labor-saving machinery or new types of furnaces. One was the growth in the size of markets; the other was the shift from wood to coal fuel in a great many branches of industry, where the substitution involved no technical problem. As coal supplies were localized and the costs of transporting so bulky a commodity extremely high,[57] the substitution encouraged industrial concentration.

In no industry perhaps was the increase in the scale of manufacture more impressive than in the making of salt by the evaporation of seawater. Although the manufacture of salt at the brine springs in Cheshire had been carried on at least as early as the thirteenth century in small salt houses, normally furnished with from six to twelve tiny lead pans,[58] sea salt had been generally produced on a smaller scale without special houses at points scattered all along the coasts of Great Britain. The growth of population in London and other towns during and after Elizabeth's reign caused a great increase in the demand for salt to be used in preserving fish and meat; and the advantages offered by abundant supplies of an inferior grade of coal, which would have gone to waste at the mine but for the saltworks,[59] drew the growing industry to the colliery districts. During the last two decades of the sixteenth century and the first four of the seventeenth, most of the sea-salt manufacture in Great Britain came to be concentrated at the mouth of the Tyne and Wear and along the coasts of the Firth of Forth. The old casual workings of local peasants were superseded by iron pans twenty feet or more square, and five or six feet deep, in which seawater was evaporated by the heat from a furnace underneath. This structure was covered by a wooden roof, so the salt house also served as a storing place for the supplies of coal and often as a dwelling place for the workmen recruited for this labor. Such a plant required a substantial investment. Although only four workmen were needed to keep a single pan in opera-

---

[57] Cf. Nef, *Rise of the British Coal Industry*, I, 78 ff., 380 ff.

[58] H. J. Hewitt, *Mediæval Cheshire* (1929), pp. 109 ff.

[59] Nef, *loc. cit.*, I, 95, 112; II, 117, 249. This "pan-coal" was also used in the manufacture of alum and copperas (*ibid.*, I, 210). The expansion of the salt, alum, and copperas manufacture during the two decades preceding the Civil War provided substantial markets for this coal, which had hitherto been mixed with "ship-coal" to the despair of the London domestic consumers.

tion, the principal saltworks were composed of many small houses clustered together. As early as 1589, one capitalist claimed to employ three hundred men at saltworks on the Wear in which he had invested the equivalent in today's money of some $200,000 or more. The works at South Shields, which came temporarily under the control of the state at the time of the Civil War, employed about a thousand men, and represented an investment equivalent to perhaps a million dollars today.[60]

Changes in the supplies of fuel and raw materials and a growth in the market for the products also combined to bring about a similar increase in the scale of enterprise in soap-boiling and a slower increase in the scale of enterprise in limeburning and brewing. Before the dissolution of the monasteries, all three had been almost entirely household manufactures;[61] limeburning and brewing perhaps remained predominantly so at the time of the Civil War. But in the meantime a number of considerable enterprises had crept in. From the large orders that some London brewers placed with coal dealers about the middle of the seventeenth century, it appears in a few cases that the small domestic manufacturer, with a brewing equipment worth £25 or so installed in a part of his house,[62] was being superseded by brewers in a substantial way of business. One London brewery in the reign of James I had a capital of £10,000, which must be multiplied by perhaps twenty or more to get its equivalent in money of the 1960's.[63] Limekilns made of brick, in which the fire was not extinguished from one end of the year to the other,[64] were appearing not only in and near the capital, but in provincial towns like Newcastle-on-Tyne, where large supplies of lime were needed by builders, who purchased it from the owners of the kilns.[65] Before the end of Elizabeth's reign, the soap-boiling industry of London, which supplied most of the kingdom, was already being carried on mainly in sizable buildings, with an outlay in vats of brick and boilers of metal which was in some cases perhaps almost as extensive as the equipment at the Yorkshire alum houses built in James I's reign.

Two other important industries remain to be considered: shipbuilding and textiles. The former had long been organized in some cases in large enterprises, for while smiths and carpenters, sail- and rope-makers might prepare the materials in their own households, the shipyards where these materials were assembled were often costly establishments in which many workers labored for wages.[66] Those in seventeenth-century Holland were

---

[60] Lansdowne MSS., 59, no. 69; *Calendar of State Papers, Domestic*, 1655, p. 36.

[61] Although special limekilns were erected to supply solder for the great medieval buildings, these works were abandoned as soon as the building had been completed.

[62] "Inventory of Goods Found in the Tenements and Ale-brewhouse of James Barre," 1598 (British Museum, Sloane MSS., 2177, ff. 23–24).

[63] For this information I am indebted to F. J. Fisher.

[64] Cf. Brereton, *Travels*, pp. 1–2.

[65] Cf. Sir Balthazar Gerbier, *Counsel and Advice to All Builders* (1663), p. 55.

[66] Cf. above, chap. ii, pp. 88 ff.

fitted with wind-driven sawmills and large cranes for moving heavy timbers;[67] and it seems probable that similar machinery was set up in some English yards before the Civil War.

In the century following the dissolution of the monasteries, the importance of English shipping increased greatly, as a result of the rapid growth of the Royal Navy, the progress in all branches of foreign trade and in the fishing trade, and the phenomenal expansion in the coastal trade, especially in coal, which increased perhaps from not more than fifty thousand tons per annum to upward of five hundred thousand tons.[68] During the seventeenth century the bulk of the English fishing trade and of foreign commerce was in the hands of Dutch shipowners and a good many mercantile vessels which flew the English flag were built in Dutch shipyards, where they could be produced more cheaply.[69] But shipbuilding in England became a very much more important industry than it had ever been before, both in state-owned and in private yards, like those at the principal ports of East Anglia and at London, Bristol, and Newcastle-on-Tyne.[70] It is probable that the number of persons employed in shipyards owned by private individuals, or by partnerships of such individuals, multiplied several times over. As the size of the ships was increasing, there was doubtless a corresponding increase in the cost of the materials and of the yards in which they were built.

In the textile industry, with its endless ramifications, the domestic workshop remained the rule. But semifactory conditions in connection with the finishing processes—dyeing, fulling, and calendering—were much less exceptional even in medieval times than was once believed. It is not possible to estimate the extent to which such conditions existed in England before the Reformation. But a number of developments during the next century encouraged their spread. The growth in the demand for cloth of all kinds, and especially for worsteds, cottons, and linens, which were being extensively produced in England for the first time, was accompanied by a notable increase in the proportion of all cloth dyed and dressed at home. It was the finishing processes, most readily suited to semifactory conditions, that expanded most rapidly in importance. With the great increase in the market for cloth in London, as a result of both the rapid growth in population

[67] Violet Barbour, "Dutch and English Shipping in the Seventeenth Century," *Economic History Review*, II, 274.
[68] See below, chap. iv; Nef, *Rise of the British Coal Industry*, I, 390–95.
[69] Barbour, *op. cit.*, pp. 265–66, 274–77, 288–90; *The Mischief of the Five Shillings Tax on Coal*, p. 18. The proportion of English mercantile tonnage which was foreign-built is quite uncertain, but Professor Barbour does not think that it exceeded one-third or one-fourth after the three Dutch wars, and, as these wars brought the English many captured Dutch ships, the proportion before the Civil War may have been even smaller. England was building her own warships.
[70] Cf. Defoe, *Tour*, ed. Cole (London, 1927), I, 40, 42; Nef, *Rise of the British Coal Industry*, I, 174; II, 25–28.

and the increase in the quantity of clothing, bedding, and hangings used by the rising middle class and by domestic servants, the advantages of concentration in the finishing processes grew. Before the middle of the seventeenth century, some London dyers were buying coal in as large quantities as the chief brewers and soap boilers.[71] This suggests that their equipment in furnaces and metal boilers may have been equally extensive. Hatmakers, too, were sometimes large buyers of coal, and this suggests that the introduction of the felt hat in the Elizabethan Age may also have furthered the growth of a semifactory form of enterprise.[72]

CONCLUSION

Without a thorough investigation of many industries hitherto neglected by economic historians, no quantitative estimate can be made of the total number of laborers employed in capitalistically owned mines and manufacturing establishments in the 1530's, on the eve of the Civil War. No doubt the great majority of all the workpeople engaged in industry labored in their homes, in town cellars or garrets or in village cottages. But that majority was by no means so overwhelming as was supposed in Toynbee the elder's time. During the hundred years from 1540 to 1640 the proportion so employed had been notably reduced. Tens of thousands of workpeople had been swept from the country dwellings and town shops of their forefathers or from a ragged existence of vagabondage into hundreds of new, capitalistically owned enterprises. The introduction of new industries and of new machinery, tools, and furnaces in old industries, had brought about technical changes in the methods of mining and manufacturing only less momentous than those associated with the great inventions of the late eighteenth and early nineteenth centuries. The expansion of mining and metallurgy after about 1580 also raised in more acute forms than ever before three technical problems which remained partly unsolved in 1640, in spite of all the busy work that had been done on them during the previous sixty years: the substitution of steam for water, wind, and horse power for driving machinery; the laying of railed ways for the transport of bulky goods; the substitution of coal for wood fuel in the production of metals, particularly iron. It was further work which led to the solution of all these problems in Great Britain at the juncture of the eighteenth and nineteenth centuries.[73] These discoveries precipitated the still greater speeding up in the rate of industrial development which began in the 1780's[74] and led to the conquest of the material world. The concentration of

[71] Nef, *op. cit.,* I, 213–15 and *passim.*
[72] The subject requires further investigation.
[73] Nef, *Civilization, Industrial Society, and Love,* Center for the Study of Democratic Institutions, Santa Barbara, Calif., 1961. Occasional Paper No. 118.
[74] Nef, *Western Civilization since the Renaissance,* chap. xv, pp. 290–92.

inventive skill on these three problems at the juncture of the sixteenth and seventeenth centuries was novel. It is another aspect of the "early English industrial revolution."

It must not be supposed that the developments we have attempted to sketch came to an end in the mid-seventeenth century. While workpeople were perhaps drawn into large-scale industry at a somewhat less rapid *rate* in the hundred years following than in those preceding 1640, the striking changes in technique and the greatly increasing concentration of capital which began in the Elizabethan Age led directly to the rapid industrial progress which we associate with the nineteenth and twentieth centuries. It follows that if we are concerned with the relations of other historical developments to the *origins* of industrial civilization, these must perhaps be sought more in the late sixteenth and seventeenth centuries[75] than at the time of the "industrial revolution" as described by Toynbee the elder and his followers.

The rise of industrialism in Great Britain can be more properly regarded as a long process stretching back to the middle of the sixteenth century and coming down to the final triumph of the industrial state toward the end of the nineteenth, than as a sudden phenomenon associated with the late eighteenth and early nineteenth centuries. It is no longer possible to find a full explanation of "the great inventions" and the new factories of the late eighteenth century in a preceding commercial revolution which increased the size of markets. The commercial revolution, if that is the proper term to apply to a rapid growth in foreign and domestic trade during a period of two centuries, had a continuous influence reaching back beyond the Reformation upon industrial technology and the scale of mining and manufacturing. But the progress of industry, in turn, had continually stimulated in a variety of ways the progress of commerce.[76] The former progress was quite as "revolutionary" as the latter, and quite as directly responsible for the speeding up of industrial growth in Great Britain at the juncture of the eighteenth and nineteenth centuries which led to the triumph of industrialism.

There are reasons for believing that the progress toward modern technology and the concentration of industrial capital were more rapid in Great Britain than in any foreign country between the middle of the sixteenth and the early eighteenth centuries. Before the dissolution of the monasteries, Great Britain was, industrially, in something of a backwater compared with Italy, Spain, the Low Countries, the south German states, and France. Englishmen had little to teach foreigners in the way of practical mechanical knowledge, except in connection with the production of tin and the manufacture of pewter. By the end of the seventeenth century, the position was reversed, not indeed in the artistic and luxury industries, but in the manufacture of such commodities as sharp cutting knives, playing cards, plain window glass, and fire grates. "Our artisans," wrote a certain James Puckle in 1697, are "universally allow'd the best upon Earth for Improvements." [77] His remark is typical of the opinion of most Englishmen of his age. It was more than a patriotic boast insofar as improvements leading to production mainly for the sake of *quantity* and *practical efficiency* were concerned. Foreigners spoke soon after no less emphatically in the same sense. In the letters which he wrote during the 1730's and 1740's, Voltaire's admiration for the skill of the English mechanics and the solidity of the products of English manufactures was second only to his admiration for the minds of Newton and other English scientists, whose exploits reflected to some extent the need to solve the mechanical problems raised by the rapid growth of mining and manufacturing.[78] If in the early eighteenth century, as seems probable, the English were as far ahead of foreigners in technological skill for quantitative purposes as they had been behind before the middle of the sixteenth, it is plain that during the intervening period progress toward mechanical efficiency was more rapid in England than in any foreign country.

The concentration of industrial capital in Great Britain during the period from 1540 to 1640 and after was caused to a considerable extent, as we have seen, by the progress of practical technology. If this progress was more rapid in England than elsewhere, that in itself suggests that heavy industry made more headway in England than on the Continent between the Reformation and the eighteenth century. Other considerations point to the same conclusion. Another very important cause for the concentration of industrial capital in Great Britain was the general change from a wood-burning to a coal-burning economy. Except in the Catholic Low Countries and perhaps in Lyonnais and Forez, there was no European area besides Great Britain where an extensive use was made of coal before the eighteenth century, and the development of the coal industry in the Low Countries and in central France between 1540 and 1720 was very much slower than in Great Britain. The growth in the size of markets, which also promoted industrial concentration, was encouraged by the facilities for cheap water transport which Great Britain, by virtue of her insular position and good harbors, enjoyed to a greater degree than any foreign country except Holland. The cost of the plant in many British industries was increased by

[77] *A New Dialogue between a Burgermaster and an English Gentleman* (1697), p. 20.

[78] Cf. B. Hessen, "The Social and Economic Roots of Newton's 'Principia,'" in *Science at the Cross Roads* (papers presented to the International Congress of the History of Science and Technology, London, by the delegates of the U.S.S.R., 1931), pp. 151–212. Cf. Nef, *Rise of the British Coal Industry*, I, 240–56. (But I now accept this position with more reservations than when, as a young man, I wrote my coal book [see below, chap. vii, pp. 318 ff.])

the growing use of water-driven machines. England had plenty of water, but, as she possessed fewer dependable rapid-flowing streams than did most Continental countries, it was necessary to resort more frequently to the overshot wheel. It followed that the use of water-driven machinery was especially costly in England and that the discovery of an alternative to water power was a more urgent necessity there than in most other European countries. The British climate[79] was also partly responsible for the heavy investment in saltworks. Along the Mediterranean and the Bay of Biscay it was possible to produce salt without artificial heat. Sea-salt manufacture in Great Britain became capitalistic while this equally productive manufacture in France remained the work of peasants.[80]

It was probably not, as has been supposed, during the half century preceding the French Revolution (1735–85) that the contrasts between industrial progress in England and in Continental countries were most striking,[81] but during the period which began with the English Reformation of the 1530's and 1540's, and lasted through the times of Louis XIV, who died in 1715. As rapid progress toward industrial capitalism free from government control and toward invention and investment for the sake of quantity production appears to cover the longest period of time in England, the concept of an "industrial revolution," as put forward by Toynbee the elder and his followers, would seem to be an especially inappropriate explanation of the triumph of industrialism. It gives the impression that the process was especially sudden in Great Britain, when it was in all probability more continuous than in any other country.

[79] For influences of the geographical setting upon British industrial development during the sixteenth and seventeenth centuries, see Nef, *La Naissance de la civilisation industrielle et le monde contemporain,* chap. iv.

[80] See below, chap. iv, pp. 151–52.

[81] Nef, *War and Human Progress,* pp. 276 ff.

4

A Comparison of Industrial Growth
in France and England from 1540 to 1640

In seeking to understand better the origins of the industrial civilization which has swept over the globe since the 1780's it is important to contrast industrial development after the Reformation in England with that in other countries. The genesis of the atomic age was primarily a European phenomenon. Industrial history was related to all sides of European history. As a basis for probing these relationships we need to recognize what differences there were between the progress of various industries in the different European countries. The previous chapter suggests that technological development and the concentration of capital for the sake of quantity and economy of manual labor was startlingly rapid in England between the Reformation and the Civil War, as compared with previous centuries.

How far is this "early revolution" to be understood in terms of other developments such as the rise of new religious practices and the rapid increase in prices resulting from the inflow of precious metal from America?[1] How far are other historical developments, such as the progress in the natural sciences and the movement to establish parliamentary government,[2] to be understood in terms of this "early revolution"? Comparisons between English history and the history of other countries can help us to arrive at partial and tentative answers to these questions. We should begin by trying to discover in what respects industrial development in various Continental countries resembled that in England during the century following the Reformation, and in what respects it differed. Then, as part of a larger study, we should try to find out how far the differences can be explained by other differences between English and Continental history. Such historical com-

From *Journal of Political Economy*, XLIV (1936), 289–317, 505–33, 643–66.
[1] See below, chaps. v and vi.
[2] See below, chap. viii, and Nef, *Industry and Government in France and England, 1540–1640* (Ithaca, N.Y., 1957).

parisons may most properly begin with France, the only country besides England which has had a continuous history since the Reformation as a great European power.

Was there an "early industrial revolution" in France at the same time as in England? The preliminary English "industrial revolution" had several aspects. One was a great expansion in the markets for industrial products, which encouraged the formation of new and larger enterprises. Another was the introduction of a series of technical changes in the processes of production, which greatly increased the amount of expensive machinery, equipment, and land required in mining and manufacturing to achieve quantity and efficiency. For a modern observer, who lives in a world where large-scale enterprise has become for the first time in history the rule in industry, the most arresting result of both developments was the rapid increase in many branches of mining and manufacturing of more expensive establishments, privately owned and controlled, and costing, with their buildings and raw materials, thousands and in some cases tens of thousands of pounds—figures which should be multiplied by more than twenty to get their equivalent in modern money. By 1640 the workpeople in England and Wales, who labored for wages in such establishments, numbered several tens of thousands.[3] While considerable enterprises had not been uncommon in the economy of Continental Europe at the time of the Reformation, such a concentration of labor in them in a small country with perhaps only six million people was more novel.

How can we compare the progress in France and in England of this new form of enterprise with other changes in industrial organization? As no exact statistics are ever likely to be obtained concerning the number of workmen employed under conditions of industrial capitalism in the sixteenth and seventeenth centuries, our attack on the problem has to be roundabout. A comparison of the growth of output, as well as of the introduction of new technical methods designed to reduce labor costs of production, can help us, because these were the principal factors *directly* responsible for the progress of more capitalistic enterprise.

How far did the growth in industrial production in France between 1540 and 1640 resemble that in England? Which country had the greater volume of output relative to its population at the end of these hundred years? [4]

By comparing the progress of a number of industries in the two nations, and the place which they occupied in the national economy of each about 1540 and about 1640, we can form an impression of the growth and the relative importance of the markets for various commodities. As some commodities lent themselves to production for the sake of efficient multiplica-

---

[3] Cf. above, p. 140.

[4] I am indebted to Professor F. J. Fisher, of the London School of Economics, and to A. Mirot, of the Archives Nationales in Paris, for help in obtaining copies of manuscripts which I have used to some extent in connection with this chapter.

tion more readily than others, a comparison of industrial growth provides us with one means for estimating in which country modern forms of industrial enterprise spread most rapidly, and in which they came to occupy the more important place.

FRENCH INDUSTRY AND THE RELIGIOUS WARS

In the last half of the sixteenth century the comments of many Frenchmen on economic conditions suggest that these fifty years of rapid growth in English industry were in France a period of retrogression, and that industrial production, far from increasing, actually declined sharply during the seventies and eighties, when the country was divided into rival camps by disputes connected with the religious wars. In 1596 some citizens of Tours addressed a *cahier de remonstrances* to Henri IV, the king whose accession in 1589 had helped to heal the wounds of three decades of recurring civil warfare. The town lives mainly, these citizens write, by the making of silk goods of all kinds. Before the wars there had been 800 master workmen in silk, 6,000 journeymen engaged in labor at silk looms, 300 persons who wound thread, and many others who dyed and dressed the material. Now, they complain, only 200 masters are left, and the amount of silk worked into cloth is about a tenth of what it once had been.[5] These figures in round numbers suggest that the calculations were made by persons tinged with medieval statistical fantasy. They suggest nevertheless that the silk manufacture of Tours had received a serious setback during the previous forty years.

Contemporary statements of a similar nature abound, concerning the collapse of the industry and trade of various French towns or districts during the religious wars.[6] While there can be no doubt that these wars had an unfavorable effect upon industrial development,[7] historians have been rather too ready to take such statements *au pied de la lettre*. The *cahier de remonstrances* of the citizens of Tours is an obvious example of special pleading, designed to persuade the crown that the town cannot afford to pay the royal levies imposed upon it. The authors had every interest in exaggerating both their past affluence and their present poverty. There is little difficulty in showing that the figures in the document are unreliable.[8]

[5] E. Giraudet, *Histoire de la ville de Tours* (Tours, 1873), II, 59–60.
[6] Cf. G. Fagniez, *L'économie sociale de la France sous Henri IV* (Paris, 1897), pp. 82–83.
[7] See Nef, *War and Human Progress* (Cambridge, Mass., 1950), chaps. iv and v.
[8] The *cahier* tells us that Tours has lost more than two-thirds of its inhabitants as a result of the religious wars (Giraudet, *op. cit.*, II, 58). But two years later, in 1598, the population of the town was estimated at 55,331. As the population of Tours seems never to have reached 60,000 in the sixteenth century (*ibid.*, pp. 97, 320), and does not amount to quite 75,000 today, this estimate for 1598, exaggerated though it undoubtedly is, makes the statement that the town had lost "more than two-thirds"

And the same thing is true of those in most contemporary statements concerning the disastrous decline of commerce and industry. The statements are good as evidence that French economic development was hindered by the religious wars, but they give an exaggerated impression of the extent and the permanence of the retrogression in production.

There were some places, devastated by fierce fighting and long occupied by troops who pilfered warehouses, ransacked trains of packhorses, and even set fire to buildings, where industry *was* brought temporarily to a virtual standstill by fighting.[9] But the area affected at any given time by warring armies was small when compared with the total area of the country. And there was generally a sharp recovery after the troops moved on.

After reading statements like those contained in the *cahier de remonstrances* from Tours, many historians have assumed that French industrial output as a whole was much greater in the late 1550's, before open hostilities had broken out, than in the late nineties, after peace had been almost completely restored. But that is by no means certain. In Poitou the production of cloth and leather goods grew substantially during the second half of the century.[10] While the silk manufacture at Tours may have lost ground, that at Lyons increased in importance. Actual records of workmen employed in the various branches of silkmaking in the latter town indicate that the growth which began early in the sixteenth century continued through

---

of its inhabitants look absurd, and throws discredit on all the figures in the *cahier*. Again, the document tells us that nearly 40,000 persons had once lived by the silk industry at Tours and its environs. Monsieur Godart has shown that at Lyons similar estimates of the number of silk workers cannot be taken seriously. They were sometimes represented as more numerous than the population of the town itself is known to have been (J. Godart, *L'ouvrier en soie* [Lyons, 1899], pp. 16–18).

[9] Cf. Fagniez, *op. cit.*, pp. 77–80. I am familiar with only one case in which actual records of production for all the years of the religious wars have been brought to light. These are for the output of cloth in the great woolen textile center of Hondschoote in Flanders, which was at the time outside the boundaries of France. Production fell from 91,878 pieces annually on the average during the sixties to less than 12,000 pieces from 1585 to 1589, when the place was sacked and occupied by troops, and though there was an important revival of the industry during the second and third decades of the seventeenth century, the manufacture never completely regained its old importance (E. Coornaert, *La draperie-sayetterie d'Hondschoote* [Paris, 1930], pp. 28, 42, 47, 50, 57). But it would be rash to assume that there were many French towns which did not recover from the wars more fully than Hondschoote. It was part of the Spanish Netherlands, where the textile industry was harder hit and more permanently dislocated than in France. It was more vulnerable to attack than most textile centers even in Flanders. And, finally, it might have recovered entirely, in spite of these disadvantages, had it not lost at the end of the sixteenth century the monopoly of a special technique on which the development of its textile industry before the religious wars had been based (*ibid.*, pp. 48–49).

[10] P. Raveau, *Essai sur la situation économique et l'état social en Poitou au XVIᵉ siècle* (Paris, 1931), pp. 18–21, 41, 43–45. The late M. Raveau, whose knowledge of the economic history of Poitou was rivaled only by that of the late Professor Boissonnade, made a close examination of conditions in the textile and the tanning industries.

the period of civil warfare, and that there were more than three times as many silkworkers in 1621 as in 1575.[11] While the exports of French salt to the Baltic in the years 1595–99 were little more than a third what they had been in the years 1562–66,[12] the transatlantic commerce from Havre and Honfleur, at the mouth of the Seine, was greater during the years of the religious wars than after Henri IV had established more peaceful conditions.[13] While the towns of Languedoc, especially Montpellier and Aigues Mortes, were apparently declining in commercial importance during the last half of the sixteenth century, Marseille had an expanding traffic at least well into the eighties, both up the Rhone valley and by sea with other Mediterranean ports.[14] If industrial output in the lower Seine and the lower Rhone valleys had declined seriously during the religious wars, we should expect to get some reflection of this in the trade of the principal ports.

Periods of warfare and civil strife always produce exaggerated utterances. During the French religious wars no readily accessible information was available to impose a curb on statistical extravagances, and men probably still spoke of "soixante mille," as they had done in the Middle Ages, meaning merely "a large number." [15] The statements of contemporary writers are valuable indications that French industry was developing much more slowly than English between 1560 and 1595. But if we are to reach an opinion about the actual course of French industrial output during the religious wars, and in the century from 1540 to 1640 as a whole, they cannot be relied upon. We must attempt, by piecing together such data concerning production as are available in scattered sources, to compare the progress of particular industries in France with their progress in England.

[11] Godart, *op. cit.*, pp. 17–19. Godart puts the number at 448 for 1575, and finds a record of 1,460 workers of all kinds in 1621.

[12] The shipments of salt entered in the records of the Danish Sound tolls as coming from French ports fell from 17,162 "laests" annually on the average for the years 1562–66 to 6,129 "laests" for the years 1595–99 (Nina Bang, *Tables de la navigation et du transport des marchandises passant par le Sund, 1497–1660* [Copenhagen, 1922], Vol. II, *passim*). Miss Astrid Friis has shown that the Sound toll accounts must be regarded in many respects as unreliable, at any rate insofar as cloth shipments are concerned (*Alderman Cockayne's Project and the Cloth Trade* [London, 1927], pp. 225–26). But I do not feel that the errors which she has revealed (I have not seen her article in the *Dansk Historisk Tideskrift*) are sufficiently grave to compel us to abandon the use of Miss Bang's work as a rough guide to the progress of various branches of Baltic commerce in the sixteenth and seventeenth centuries. I am grateful to my colleague, Mr. A. G. Hart, who did a paper in one of my courses some years ago on English trade with the Baltic, for help in interpreting the data printed by Miss Bang.

[13] P. Barrey, "Le Havre transatlantique, 1571–1610," in J. Hayem, *Mémoires et documents pour servir à l'histoire du commerce et de l'industrie,* 5th ser. (1917), pp. 68–70.

[14] *Encyclopédie départementale. Les Bouches-du-Rhône,* ed. Paul Masson (1920), III, 178–82.

[15] See Nef, *La Naissance de la civilisation industrielle et le monde contemporain* (Paris, 1954), pp. 23–24.

Before turning to the group of industries which, between them, probably employed a majority of the industrial workers in both countries—mining, metallurgy, textiles, and building—we shall consider three other industries —saltmaking, glassmaking, and shipbuilding—that have not received from historians the attention to which their importance entitles them.

The kingdom of France in the late sixteenth and early seventeenth centuries was much smaller in area than the French Republic as we now know it. Alsace, Lorraine, Franche-Comté, Artois, Hainault, Flanders, and Roussillon, to name only the principal provinces which were added before 1789, lay outside. Even without them, France was a much larger country than England and Wales, and in the reign of Louis XIII, from 1610 to 1643, it was very nearly if not quite three times as populous as the English kingdom of James I and Charles I.[16] For the purpose of comparing the place occupied by the various industries in the national economy of the two countries, it seems reasonable to consider the volume of production in relation to the size of the population. Judged on this basis, the industrial output of England, smaller in quantity at the time of the Reformation, appears to have overtaken and even to have surpassed that of France before 1640.

THE MANUFACTURE OF SALT

In his *Description de la France,* first published in 1663, Pierre Duval said the saltworks might well be regarded as mountains of gold to the French king. During the late summer and early autumn, foreign ships from the north of Europe came in scores and even in hundreds to the mouth of the Rhone, to Hyères and Aigues Mortes, and to ports along the Bay of Biscay between the Gironde and the Loire, to load cargoes of salt that had been scooped up by thousands of local peasants after the sun had done a long summer's work among the numerous *marais salants* of both regions.[17] The

[16] The best estimates of population prior to the nineteenth century involve a large amount of guesswork. But it is probable that there were more than fourteen million people in Louis XIII's kingdom, while the population of England and Wales at that time was probably not less than four and a half nor more than six millions (E. Levasseur, *La population française* [Paris, 1889], I, 191–92, 206; G. T. Griffith, *Population Problems of the Age of Malthus* [Cambridge, 1926], p. 12 n.; cf. J. Beloch, "Die Bevolkerung Europas zur Zeit der Renaissance," in *Zeitschrift für Sozialwissenschaft,* III [1900], 773–75).

[17] Pierre Duval, *Description de la France* (Paris, 1663), pp. 38–39; H. Hauser, "Le sel dans l'histoire" in *Les origines historiques des problèmes économiques actuels* (Paris, 1930), p. 60. Some salt was also produced by heating seawater along the northern coasts of France, especially in western Normandy near Avranches and Mont-Saint-Michel, and by heating brine from springs in Béarn. But the quantity was negligible compared with that made at the salt marshes along the Mediterranean and the

salt produced in England and Wales on the eve of the Civil War was still insufficient to supply the needs of the country. It had to be supplemented by imports, partly from Scotland, but mainly from Portugal and France.

The supremacy of the French in salt production was no new thing. Visits by fleets of ships from English, Dutch, German, and Baltic ports to the marshes along the Bay of Biscay had formed an important branch of medieval sea trade in the fifteenth century,[18] and doubtless much earlier. While England still lagged behind France in salt production in the 1630's, her position had improved greatly during the previous hundred years. There had been a rapid growth in the English demand for salt to preserve fish and other perishable foods, as a result of both the increase in population and the breakdown of the economic self-sufficiency of local areas, which were no longer able to feed themselves.[19] The new demand had been largely met by the progress of the domestic manufacture. At the mouth of the Tyne, where salt was obtained by heating seawater and where the work had once been almost entirely in the hands of the monks, annual production increased from some few score or at the most some few hundred tons, when Henry VIII ordered the dissolution of the monasteries,[20] to about 15,000 tons in the reign of Charles I, when the industry came under the control of a powerful group of merchants from Newcastle and East Anglia. Salt was also manufactured from seawater at many other places along the coast of England and Wales and inland at natural springs. While progress was nowhere as remarkable as at the mouth of the Tyne, there was a rapid increase in the quantity of salt made by heating brine water in Worcestershire and especially in Cheshire.[21] At the time of the dissolution of the monasteries, 1536–39, the annual output of salt in England and Wales was probably under 15,000 tons.[22] A century later it had probably reached at least 50,000 tons.[23]

Bay of Biscay (E. Lefebvre, *Le sel* [Paris, 1882], p. 93; P. Boyé, *Les salines et le sel en Lorraine* [Nancy, 1904], p. 5; C. Dartigue-Peyrou, *Le vicomté de Béarn, 1517–55* [Paris, 1934], pp. 362–64). The salt manufactured in the west of Normandy was apparently entirely for local consumption, for Rouen got its salt supplies in 1631 not from the Avranches region but from the Bay of Biscay (Eugène Sue, *Correspondance de Henri de Sourdis* [Paris, 1839], III, 213–14).

[18] M. M. Postan, "The Economic Relations of England and the Hanse 1400–1475," in *Studies in English Trade in the Fifteenth Century,* ed. E. Power and M. Postan (London, 1933), pp. 128, 142. Cf. E. Levasseur, *Histoire du commerce de la France* (Paris, 1911), I, 162.

[19] Cf. below, p. 159.

[20] For a possible relationship between the confiscation of ecclesiastical property by the crown and this growth in production, see below, pp. 231 ff.

[21] Nef, *Rise of the British Coal Industry* (London, 1932), I, 174–77.

[22] Edward Hughes, "The English Monopoly of Salt in the Years 1563–71," *English Historical Review,* XL (1925), 334.

[23] Between 15,000 and 20,000 tons were produced annually in the 1630's in Durham and Northumberland alone, and the output at the brine pits in Worcestershire and

As a result of the growth in domestic manufacture and the beginning of substantial imports from Scotland, where the salt industry grew almost as rapidly as on the Tyne, the proportion of English supplies obtained from the Continent fell from two-thirds or three-fourths[24] to perhaps a third.[25] Hence there was little room for the French to expand their exports to England. Their shipments to the Baltic actually declined slightly, to judge from the records of cargoes passing eastward through the Danish Sound.[26] The French export market for salt seems to have remained practically stationary between 1540 and 1640.

What about the French domestic market? It is improbable that it grew at as rapid a rate as the English market for the main factors which caused the great increase in the consumption of salt in England—the growth of population and the breakdown in the economic self-sufficiency of local areas—were not operating to anything like the same extent in France.[27] Until the statistical evidence which is available concerning salt production along the Bay of Biscay and the Mediterranean coasts has been sifted and presented,[28] there is no way of estimating the course of French output from 1540 to 1640. As the king of France was obtaining a rapidly mounting revenue from the *gabelle*,[29] which taxed all salt, and as pressure was brought by royal officials on consumers to take more salt than they needed, it would be rash to assume that production languished.

The principal contrast between the growth of the saltmaking industry between 1540 and 1640 in Great Britain and in France was in the methods by which salt was produced. In Cheshire and the north of England fires were lit in hundreds of new furnaces, underneath cauldrons of lead filled with brine and large pans of iron filled with seawater. The output of English salt increased three- or fourfold or even more between 1540 and 1640. In western and southern France the peasants continued to gather salt as their

Cheshire was probably even greater (Nef, *Rise of the British Coal Industry*, I, 177, 174–75).

[24] Hughes, *loc cit.*

[25] Mr. Hughes estimates the annual consumption of salt in England in Henry VIII's reign at about 40,000 tons (*loc. cit.*). A century later it may well have doubled (cf. Nef, *Rise of the British Coal Industry*, I, 179, esp. n. 1), but by that time England and Wales were probably producing at least 50,000 tons, and some of the imports were coming, not from the Continent, but from Scotland.

[26] The average annual shipments of salt eastward through the Sound amounted to 31,282 "laests" during the five-year period 1562–66; 29,000 during the five-year period 1605–9; and 26,883 during the five-year period 1635–39. It is difficult to determine the precise share of France in this trade, as there were many reshipments, but the annual average entered as coming from French ports fell from 17,162 to 15,358 and 14,694 "laests" in the three five-year periods (Bang, *op. cit., passim*); cf. above p. 148, n. 12.

[27] Cf. below, p. 164.

[28] I have in my possession considerable statistical material from the French Archives départementales, and I hope to have an opportunity to exploit this material.

[29] Nef, *Industry and Government in France and England*, pp. 76–83.

ancestors had done for centuries, encouraged by efforts made by the crown, especially along the Bay of Biscay, to facilitate the flow of seawater into the marshes, where it was dried by the heat of the sun.

THE MANUFACTURE OF GLASS

In order to compare the development of the French glassmaking industry with the English it is necessary to distinguish between the different kinds of glasswork done in Europe in the sixteenth and seventeenth centuries. First of all, there was the beautiful stained glass designed mainly for the windows of churches and cathedrals, and also to some extent for those of castles and public buildings. The glazed windows were an inheritance from the great age of gothic building in the twelfth and thirteenth centuries. But the methods employed in glazing had changed and also the artistic effects, as everyone knows who has visited cathedrals like those of Bourges and Sens, where the jeweled mosaics of the earlier period can be seen side by side with the much less complex painted glass of the Renaissance.

Accounts kept in connection with the building of English medieval churches show that much of the glass for their windows was imported.[30] But by the beginning of the sixteenth century the painted glass of native glaziers, which may still be seen in churches like that of Fairford in the Cotswolds, had come to rival in beauty any made in France. In both countries this kind of work lost its importance before the seventeenth century, when the production of stained glass windows had become negligible compared with that of glass fashioned for more worldly purposes into goblets, windowpanes, and mirrors, bottles, jugs, and drinking cups of all varieties, test tubes and lenses and, toward the end of the sixteenth century, microscopes and telescopes.

Ever since the beginning of the fourteenth century, if not earlier, glass had been produced in artistic forms for rich patrons in growing quantities all over Europe. But there were three countries where the glaziers had attained a special fame by the beginning of the sixteenth century for their artistic glassware. One was Italy, where the goblets, decanters, jugs, vases, and artistically framed mirrors made at Venice and Altare, near Genoa, enjoyed an unrivaled reputation for beauty and elegance of design. Italian glaziers were celebrated, above all, for the exceptional transparency of the white glass, widely known as "crystal," [31] in which much of their finest work was done. The other two countries were Bohemia and Lorraine. The *gentilshommes verriers* of Lorraine were especially noted for their colored glass, but they also made plain windowpanes and somewhat less perfect

---

[30] L. F. Salzman, *English Industries of the Middle Ages* (2d ed.; Oxford, 1923), p. 188.

[31] Some French glass was also called "crystal." See below, p. 154.

versions of most of the objects for which Italy was famous.[32] The technical processes by which the Italian glaziers attained the remarkable artistic effects, which gave their work a charm comparable to that achieved on a canvas by some of the greatest contemporary painters of the Venetian School, were a secret which countries farther north were anxious to acquire. The history of glassmaking in France during the century beginning about 1540 divides into artistic glassmaking in ovens set up and used by Italian glaziers, and the making of cruder glasswares by native craftsmen, occasionally with the help of artisans from Lorraine.[33]

The making of Italian crystal found much more congenial soil in France than in England. In spite of legislation condemning to death the glazier who carried the secrets of his art to other nations, and threats that the sentence would be carried out by spies sent to poison him in his adopted country, a number of Italian artisans started glassworks in various French provinces. There is some evidence that glaziers came across the Alps into Provence, Dauphiné, and Languedoc before the sixteenth century, and Venetian crystal was certainly produced at Lyons as early as 1511.[34] But, in northern and western France, it was only after 1550 that glass was blown for crystal goblets by Italians, or under their supervision. During the next sixty years various enterprises, which aimed to produce every kind of fine Italian glassware, with the exception of very large mirrors, were established at Saint-Germain-en-Laye, Nevers, Nantes, Rouen, at two villages in Brittany, at Mézières on the Meuse, and possibly in Paris at Saint-Germain-des-Prés, while Italian glassmaking at Lyons was promoted by the family of Sarode.[35]

[32] There is no doubt that the techniques employed in the two countries were quite distinct, for attempts were made in the seventeenth century to introduce Venetian glassmaking into Lorraine, long after Lorraine glass had established a great reputation throughout Europe. Moreover, there were attempts to introduce Lorraine glassmaking into Italy (H. Schuermans, *Verres "façon de Venise" ou d'Altare fabriqués aux Pays-Bas.* Letters published 1884–93 [Bibliothèque Nationale, Paris, 8° V. 40792], p. 731; Abbé Boutillier, *La verrerie et les gentilshommes verriers de Nevers* [Nevers, 1885], pp. 139–41). According to Symphorien Champier, glass mirrors were invented in Lorraine (*Les gestes ensemble de la vie du preux chevalier Bayard* [Paris, 1526], as cited in J. B. Giraud, *Documents pour l'histoire de l'armement au Moyen Age et à la Renaissance* [Lyons, 1904], II, 119–20 n.). On the early progress of the glass industry there, see M. Beaupré, *Les gentilshommes verriers . . . dans l'ancienne Lorraine* (2d ed.; Nancy, 1846–47), esp. pp. 7–38; H. Lepage, "Recherches sur l'industrie en Lorraine," *Mémoires de la Société des sciences, des lettres, et des arts de Nancy* (Nancy, 1849), esp. pp. 26–61.
[33] E.g., in Nivernais (Boutillier, *op. cit.,* p. 127).
[34] Schuermans, *op. cit.,* pp. 635–37, 693, 723–24, 739.
[35] *Ibid.,* pp. 103–4, 698–700 (Saint-Germain-en-Laye), 703–6 (Paris), 663–66 (Nantes), 673 (Mézières), 668–69 (Javardan and Laignelet in Brittany); Boutillier, *op. cit.,* pp. 10–45 (Nevers); A. de Girancourt, *Notice sur la verrerie de Rouen, 1598–1664* (Rouen, 1867), pp. 6 ff. I have included only those cases in which unassailable proof is given that enterprises producing Italian glassware were actually set up before 1640. There were probably other Italian glassworks, for example at Orléans and in Poitou (Benjamin Fillon, *L'art de terre chez les Poitevins* [Paris, 1864], pp. 208–9).

The concession for the enterprise at Rouen was granted in 1598 to two Italians from Altare,[36] but the plant was not actually erected until 1605 or 1606. Although it was then owned by a Frenchman, François de Garsonnet, from Aix-en-Provence,[37] there is little doubt that in it crystal was made after Italian methods. The shop at Saint-Germain-en-Laye was closed during the religious wars, and that at Mézières was burned down shortly before 1611.[38] The others survived. All of them appear to have been in operation in 1640.

The owners of these new establishments did not always limit themselves to blowing glass for the finest artistic wares, which were wanted mainly by the court and the very wealthiest classes. Most of them appear to have combined an increasing amount of common glasswork with their artistic production. Their influence in promoting fine glassmaking on the Italian model was by no means confined to these workshops. There were a number of native glaziers who were attempting, with their own methods, to fashion a product fine enough to rival Italian crystal,[39] which was simply a glass of singular translucence and refinement.[40] Italian example was making itself powerfully felt in France in glassmaking as in all the arts. "Of all European countries [except Italy]," writes the principal authority on the influence of the Italian glaziers, "France was the one where glasswork, 'façon d'Italie,' was best organized and practiced longest and most successfully." [41]

In England these methods had little success. Hardly any important enterprises for fashioning Venetian crystal were established there. An unsuccessful attempt by fugitive Venetians to start artistic glassmaking in England between 1549 and 1551 does not seem to have left much impress,[42] and it was mainly from the "gentlemen glaziers" of Lorraine that the English

[36] Girancourt, Nouvelle étude sur la verrerie de Rouen . . . au XVIe et XVIIe siècles (Rouen, 1886), pp. 63–65.
[37] Girancourt, Notice sur la verrerie de Rouen, pp. 7–8.
[38] Schuermans, op. cit., pp. 105, 673. It is possible that the furnace at Mézières was rebuilt.
[39] Cf. Jules Houdoy, Verreries à la façon de Venise (Paris, 1873), p. 5.
[40] It is not to be confused with the celebrated English crystal, made with lead oxide, which was first produced toward the end of the seventeenth century. Italian crystal was distinguished from native French "verre de fougères" by the fact that it was "mieux affiné et plus blanc" (cf. Girancourt, op. cit., p. 12; Houdoy, op. cit., p. 23). The better grades of French glass were also sometimes called "crystal" (cf. Saint-Quirin, "Les verriers du Languedoc," Bulletin de la Société languedocienne de géographie, XXVII [1904], 309–10).
[41] Schuermans, op. cit., p. 634. Although Schuermans' letters are devoted primarily to the influence of Italian glassmakers in the Low Countries, he made a thorough study of their influence in France. In the copy of his work in the Bibliothèque Nationale (see above, p. 153, n. 32) has been inserted a great deal of MSS correspondence which he carried on with French antiquarians, who were studying their local glass industry, and with archivists in the various departments of France.
[42] Albert Hartshorne, Old English Glasses (London, 1897), pp. 147 ff.; cf. Calendar of State Papers, Domestic, 1591–94, p. 179.

acquired such knowledge of foreign technique as they utilized in the industrial expansion of the late sixteenth and early seventeenth centuries.[43]

Owing to the restricted character of the market for artistic glassware,
and the remarkable craftsmanship required in fashioning it, the quantity
produced was bound to remain small. In volume, it was probably of little
importance around 1640 compared to the output of ordinary windowpanes
and bottles and crude glass objects of all kinds. The production of such
commodities had greatly increased in England, because of the growing
demand, following the Reformation,[44] for comforts and conveniences among
the merchants and their servants, as well as the nobility into which mercantile elements had infiltrated rapidly during the reign of Elizabeth I and
especially during that of James I.[45] Progress in the production of cheaper
kinds of glass in France between 1540 and 1640 was less striking than
progress in making those fine goblets, plates, vessels, and mirrors which
adorned the palaces of the king and the châteaux of noblemen, and which
have now fittingly found their place in the Musée de Cluny, beside the
Venetian glass after which they were sometimes modeled.

At the beginning of the sixteenth century common glass bottles, bowls,
lanterns, and drinking cups, together with some windowpanes, were being
manufactured at ovens or small furnaces in every French province.[46] This
was no new thing. These small glassmaking huts had a history reaching
back at least to the fourteenth century. They were usually set up in wooded
lands, which supplied fuel, and the products were extremely crude compared with those of modern manufacturers. What we should like to know
is how far the growing demand after 1540 for glass to be used for practical
purposes extended to other classes in French society besides the nobility
and the richer bourgeoisie, who could generally afford, and who naturally
preferred with the increasing elegance fostered by French society, to buy
artistic glassware on the Italian model. And we should like also to know

---

[43] The only evidence which Schuermans gives in support of his contention that
Italian glassmakers had a direct influence upon the industry in England relates to the
period after 1640 (*op. cit.*, pp. 121, 543–46).

[44] See below, pp. 229 ff.

[45] On the growing wealth of these classes in connection with coal mining, see Nef,
Rise of the British Coal Industry, II, 3–42.

[46] Apart from the evidence given below of glassmaking in Normandy, Nivernais,
Poitou, and Languedoc, we know that the industry was carried on in Provence,
Dauphiné, Limousin, Aubergne, Picardy, Burgundy, Forez, Béarn, Champagne,
Rouergue, Comté de Foix (L. Barthelemy, *La savonnerie marseillaise*, Marseille,
1883, p. 7; Schuermans, *op. cit.*, pp. 828 ff., 692–95, 824 ff., 727, 812, 822, 656;
L. J. Gras, *Notes historiques sur l'industrie de la verrerie en Forez et Jarez* [St.
Etienne, 1923], p. 156; P. Boissonnade, *Le socialisme d'état, 1453–1661* [Paris, 1927],
pp. 233–34), and Brittany (A. André, "De la verrerie et des vitraux peints dans
l'ancienne province de Bretagne," *Bulletin et Mémoire de la Société archéologique du
départemente d'Ille et Villaine*, XII [1878], 119 ff. See also *Revue des sociétés savantes*,
7th ser., II [1880], 83 ff.).

how far the poor man was able and willing to pay for the added comfort provided by glass windows, which had been installed hitherto only in the residences of the rich. It will help us to answer these questions if we can learn to what extent ordinary glass furnaces in France increased after 1540 in number and importance.

Several local studies made during the second half of the nineteenth century, but almost forgotten even by economic historians, provide us with a basis for estimating, very roughly, the progress of the manufacture. The most comprehensive deals with Normandy. It is the work of Le Vaillant de la Fieffe, a member of one of the four noble families which had, until the French Revolution, the exclusive right to make common, as distinguished from Italian, glass within the province. Le Vaillant scoured the local archives for evidence concerning seventy separate glassworks which existed at one time or another between 1302 and 1873. His survey shows that in 1540 there were certainly seventeen, and possibly as many as twenty-four in operation. By 1640 the number had increased to at least twenty-eight and possibly to as many as thirty-three.[47] We cannot take for granted, of course, that these figures provide a guide to the growth in output. The scale and nature of operations may have changed. But there is no evidence of any notable growth between 1540 and 1640 in the capital invested in particular enterprises, such as occurred in the same province in the late seventeenth and eighteenth centuries. The manufacture of common glass still showed no tendency to concentrate in considerable establishments, as it was already beginning to do in Great Britain.[48]

Normandy was the principal glassmaking province in the French kingdom. Norman windowpanes rivaled in fame those of Lorraine, and the methods of Norman glaziers had an influence throughout France, second to those of the Italians, but hardly inferior to those of the Lorrainers.[49] All kinds of Norman glass were sold in the Parisian market, and some Norman windowpanes were exported to the Low Countries and even to England.[50] No other province, with the possible exception of Nivernais,[51] had such important outlets for its glassware beyond provincial boundaries.

What we know about glassmaking in other French provinces does not suggest that production in the country as a whole was growing more rapidly than in Normandy. In the case of Nivernais, the century from 1540 to 1640 appears to have been one of considerably increased activity, but we cannot be sure that the enterprises of which we hear for the first time had

[47] O. Le Vaillant de la Fieffe, *Les verreries de la Normandie* (Rouen, 1873), *passim*.

[48] See below, pp. 157–58.

[49] Girancourt, *Nouvelle étude*, pp. 57–58; L. Roubet, "La verrerie d'Apremont," *Bulletin de la Société nivernaise des sciences, lettres et arts*, 3d ser., II (1886), 93.

[50] Le Vaillant, *op. cit.*, p. v; Girancourt, *op. cit.*, p. 57; J. E. Thorold Rogers, *A History of Agriculture and Prices in England* (Oxford, 1887), VI, 472.

[51] Cf. Boutillier, *op. cit.*, pp. 131, 133–36.

not an earlier history, because there has been no investigation of local glass-making comparable to that of Le Vaillant for Normandy.[52] The glass industry of Poitou, on the other hand, apparently began to decline in the reign of Henri IV, partly as a result of competition from the neighboring provinces, and this decline was not arrested in the seventeenth century.[53] In Languedoc, for which our information is again more complete, the early fifteenth century was the period during which the greatest number of new glassworks were established.[54] The late sixteenth and seventeenth centuries were not a propitious time for the glass industry, for most of the glaziers embraced the Protestant religion and suffered in the persecutions carried on in southern France.[55]

In France, the century from 1540 to 1640 saw the continuance of a growth in the production of common glassware, which had been long in progress. But the growth was not remarkably rapid. It is evident that the use of ordinary windowpanes, bottles, and other cheap glass vessels was extending only gradually to families whose ancestors had got along without them.

In England conditions were different. Before the Reformation the output of English ovens had been confined to small quantities of the crudest sort of urinals and little bottles.[56] The author of *A Discourse of the Common Weal,* whose knowledge of the articles commonly used in housekeeping was considerable, wrote at about the middle of the sixteenth century as if the English were still dependent entirely upon imports not only for their mirrors, but also for their drinking glasses and even their windowpanes.[57] The hundred years from 1540 to 1640 were marked by the first notable expansion in the native manufacture of window glass and every variety of plain glass. Furnaces for the manufacture of the cheap window glass known as broad glass were first set up in Sussex in the sixties of the sixteenth century. During the next two decades much progress was made in the production both of windowpanes and of other glassware wanted in ordinary housekeeping such as bottles, cups, jugs, lanterns, apothecaries' glasses,

---

[52] *Ibid.,* pp. 116–33. The Abbé Boutillier's monograph is devoted mainly to the history of the artistic glassworks at Nevers, started by Italians (see above, p. 153).

[53] Fillon, *op. cit.,* pp. 205, 211.

[54] Saint-Quirin, *op. cit.,* XXVIII (1905), 340. Glassmaking appears to have been considerably extended in other parts of France during the fifteenth century (cf. P. Marchegay, "Une verrerie dans las Forêt de Roche-sur-Yon en 1456," *Annuaire de la Société d'Emulation de la Vendée,* IV [1857], 220–23; *Encyclopédie Départementale, Les Bouches-du-Rhône,* III, 167).

[55] Saint-Quirin, *op. cit.,* XXIX (1906), 202.

[56] Cf. E. W. Hulme, "English Glass-Making in the 16th and 17th Centuries," *Antiquary,* XXX (1894), 210–11, 261. Some ordinary window glass had been made in England in the fifteenth century, but the manufacture had disappeared, perhaps for want of technical skill.

[57] *A Discourse of the Common Weal of This Realm of England,* ed. Eliz. Lamond (1893), pp. 16, 63–64, 126.

spectacles and other kinds of lenses. By the middle of Elizabeth's reign, Harrison, who felt that the introduction of too many comforts during his lifetime had undermined the Spartan virtues once possessed by the English people, commented upon the remarkable increase in the number of window-panes. He also spoke of the spread of cheap glassware for daily use among the less affluent. The new demands, he tells us, unlike the demand for artistic glass, are already being met by a native manufacture.[58] By the reign of James I, that manufacture had grown so prodigiously that glass windows were generally found in the houses of the yeoman, the small shopkeeper, and the craftsman, as well as in those of the nobleman, the gentleman, and the rich merchant. It appears that they had already become more common than in France. In 1608, Thomas Coryat, the parson's son from Somerset who left behind a detailed account of his Continental travels, was surprised to find in Lyons that many of the windows were covered entirely with white paper, and that in France generally panes were put only in the upper portion of the window.[59]

The discovery, before 1612, by some inventor whom the historian has not yet identified, of a method of separating the raw materials in covered crucibles from the flames, made possible the substitution of coal for wood in the glass furnaces.[60] This cheapened the product and greatly stimulated the production of glass during the decades preceding the Civil War.[61] Furnaces for the manufacture of broad glass spread in considerable numbers from Sussex to London, Wiltshire, Gloucestershire, Worcestershire, Staffordshire, Nottinghamshire, the Tyne valley, and Scotland.[62]

While furnaces for the manufacture of ordinary glassware were still more numerous in France than in England in the 1630's, they were generally smaller. The use of coal in place of wood had encouraged the concentration of capital in larger plants with a greater output.[63] English glassmaking, which had been of very slight importance compared with French before Shakespeare's time, had grown so rapidly that by 1640 the manufacture may have rivaled that of France in so far as the mere volume of output was concerned.[64] Before the end of the seventeenth century, if not earlier, England apparently led other countries in the production of windowpanes and bottles. According to an anonymous authority, who wrote in 1699 on eco-

---

[58] An Historical Description of the Island of Britain (1587 ed.), p. 167.

[59] Coryat's Crudities Hastily Gobled Up. . . . (new ed.; Glasgow, 1905), I, 197, 204.

[60] See above, p. 134.

[61] Cf. Nef, Rise of the British Coal Industry, I, 181–83, 218–19.

[62] Ibid., pp. 181–82; Hulme, op. cit., pp. 211, 214, 262.

[63] Cf. Saint-Quirin, op. cit., XXVIII (1905), 343. Furnaces making in the neighborhood of 100 tons of glass a year were common in England early in the seventeenth century (Nef, Rise of the British Coal Industry, I, 183).

[64] Cf. Hulme, op. cit., XXXI, 104, 134.

nomic conditions, the London glaziers "have Excelled all the World, and beat the Dutch Intirely and almost all our Neighbours, out of the Trade of Glass." [65]

THE BUILDING OF SHIPS

There was little in the natural resources and geographical features of the French kingdom to encourage the extensive building of ships for ocean trade.[66] The same anonymous authority who wrote about the superiority of the London glaziers, tells us that "the [Dutch] want of most things within themselves, creates a constant and never failing work for their Navigation. The French, that have every thing within themselves . . . have not the same occasion to raise and Support any considerable number of Ships and Sailors." [67]

Between the accession of Elizabeth in 1558 and the outbreak of the Civil War in 1642, England came to occupy an intermediate position between these two extremes. She lost to some degree the insularity which had made her economically hardly less self-contained than France in the Middle Ages. At the same time, local regions lost to a much greater degree the economic self-sufficiency that had hindered the growth of coastal commerce, to which the ragged English coastline, with its abundant harbors, offered an invitation. Colliers, hoys of all kinds to carry food and bulky goods from one English port to another, barks and larger ships for overseas trade were launched in growing numbers at many towns, and especially from the private shipyards in East Anglia, which was becoming the traditional home of seafaring men. After the reign of Elizabeth, many of the new ships, especially the colliers, were built after the model of the Dutch *flute,* in order to enlarge the hold space available for bulky cargoes, and to reduce the number of seamen required to sail each vessel.

In an age when many seagoing craft were manned by less than a dozen sailors, and when the average tonnage of ships engaged in many branches of ocean commerce was less than fifty,[68] a merchantman of more than 100 tons' burden was regarded as a great ship. There were many different methods of calculating a ship's tonnage, and these gave divergent

[65] *The Mischief of the Five Shillings Tax upon Coal* (London, 1699), p. 22.
[66] Cf. Nef, *La Naissance de la civilisation industrielle et le monde contemporain,* pp. 91–94.
[67] *The Mischief of the Five Shillings Tax,* p. 9.
[68] Except for the coal trade between Newcastle and London there were few, if any, branches of English commerce in which the ships averaged over 100 tons' burden before the middle of the seventeenth century. Hoys and barks employed in the coal trade of Sunderland and the west coast averaged less than 40 tons, and those employed in various branches of foreign trade appear to have averaged between 36 and 54 tons (Nef, *Rise of the British Coal Industry,* I, 390, 392; II, 387–88; V. Barbour, "Dutch and English Shipping in the Seventeenth Century," *Economic History Review,* II [1930], 262–63 n.).

results, differing sometimes as much as 25 per cent.[69] It would be rash, therefore, to claim that the tonnage figures in records of the period are more than rough approximations. But the range of variation was small enough to permit their use when we are simply attempting a rough estimate of the progress of shipping. The figures in contemporary documents suggest that the number of ships of more than 100 tons in the English merchant marine increased nearly fivefold between 1560 and 1629. A list for the earlier year, which is virtually complete save for the unimportant omission of the ships of Bristol,[70] enumerates 76 such merchantmen. Another, for the later year, somewhat less complete, includes 355.[71]

Meanwhile, smaller seagoing craft, which outnumbered these large merchantmen by something like ten to one, probably increased almost proportionately.[72] Keels and lighters of all kinds for loading and unloading cargoes in the harbors and rivers, and barges for carrying passengers across the Thames, became many times more numerous, as the population of London grew five- or sixfold and the coastal traffic in some commodities expanded at a still more rapid rate. A river traffic calling for "trows" and "frigates," sometimes larger than small ocean-going barks, sprang up on the Severn.[73] To protect the expanding trade by sea, always vulnerable to the harassing attacks of the Dunkirk pirates,[74] and exposed to the graver threat of a possible Spanish or Dutch armada, many of the larger merchantmen were armed with small cannons; and men-of-war, sometimes of more than 1,200 tons' burden, were built in the shipyards of the crown at Woolwich, Deptford, Chatham, and Portsmouth, where they could be easily outfitted with the largest culverins and cannons cast at the new iron furnaces. During the eighty years between the end of Henry VIII's reign and the beginning of Charles I's, the tonnage of the Royal Navy about doubled.[75]

We have not found any comprehensive lists of French merchantmen drawn up earlier than the 1630's which would enable us to compare directly the progress of the French merchant marine with the English. All

---

[69] M. Oppenheim, *A History of the Administration of the Royal Navy* (London, 1896), pp. 266–67.

[70] This omission is not serious, for Bristol apparently had only four 100-ton ships in 1572 and only eight in 1577 (E. Lipson, *Economic History of England* [London, 1931], II, 250; Oppenheim, *op. cit.*, p. 173).

[71] Oppenheim, *op. cit.*, pp. 172, 271. Cf. below, p. 164.

[72] In two lists, for 1582 and 1583, of English merchant ships of 20 tons' or more burden, about 10 per cent were larger than 100 tons (*ibid.*, p. 175). This figure considerably understates the proportion of small craft at the time, for boats of less than 20 tons' burden were sometimes used in the fishing and coasting trades during the sixteenth and seventeenth centuries. Beginning in the second decade of the later century, a relatively greater proportion of large ships were built, but it may be doubted whether by 1629 this had greatly altered the percentage of large to small craft.

[73] Cf. Nef, *Rise of the British Coal Industry*, I, 387–89, 393.

[74] *Ibid.*, II, 263 ff.

[75] Werner Sombart, *Der moderne Kapitalismus* (4th ed.; 1921), I, 762.

that can be done is to make use of the very meager data available concerning the growth of the main branches of commerce in the two countries. While these data are not complete enough, nor in all cases reliable enough, to permit even the roughest sort of quantitative statement concerning the value or the volume of the general trade of either country, they are sufficient to suggest that French trade was growing more slowly than English.

In the sixteenth and seventeenth centuries traders wanted seagoing craft for one of three purposes: for fishing expeditions, for foreign and for coastwise commerce. The English market for seafood probably grew more rapidly than the French, but, to the despair of English pamphleteers, anxious to have their nation strong at sea, Dutch busses and smaller craft manned by Hollanders brought the larger proportion of the herring and the salmon eaten in England. France was possibly somewhat less dependent than England on foreigners for seafood. While Dutch fishermen caught most of the herring for the French as well as for the English market, French fishermen, particularly the Basques and the Bretons, firmly established the important place in the Newfoundland cod fishery that the Bretons have retained ever since.[76] By the beginning of the seventeenth century every considerable port in western France had its *terre-neuviers*. Travelers who visited Saint-Malo saw them in the spring setting out to sea in scores with all the food and fresh water they could carry, or, in the autumn, watched them return to port, each with one or more sailors less on board. In Mediterranean waters the little French fishing boats, which put out early in the morning for a day's work at dragging the nets, had nothing to fear from foreign competition.

While the demand on shipbuilders for new fishing craft may have grown more rapidly in France than in England, in spite of a probable slower growth in the market for seafood,[77] the demand for new merchantmen to engage in foreign trade certainly increased more rapidly in England. The religious wars interrupted progress in French foreign commerce at a time when English foreign commerce was expanding rapidly, and caused a great, though temporary, reduction in the volume of French trade in certain commodities, such as salt. While English exports of coal to all countries[78] and of cloth to the Baltic[79] perhaps increased something like threefold between the 1560's and the 1590's, French exports of salt to the Baltic fell to

---

[76] Cf. Fagniez, *L'économie social de la France*, pp. 274–75, 324. The English share in the Newfoundland fishery was also considerable (W. R. Scott, *Joint-Stock Companies to 1720* [Cambridge, 1912], I, 203).

[77] Cf. below, p. 250.

[78] Nef, *Rise of the British Coal Industry*, I, 84.

[79] From 1562 to 1566 the annual shipments of cloth of all kinds, entered in the Sound toll accounts as coming from English ports, amounted to 9,793 pieces on the average; from 1595 to 1599 to 34,173 pieces (Bang, *Tables de la navigation et du transport*, II, *passim*); cf. Friis, *Alderman Cockayne's Project*, p. 227.

hardly a third of what they had been.[80] The religious wars undoubtedly held up new construction in France, at a time when there was a considerable increase in building at English shipyards, and the recovery under Henri IV hardly did more than restore French foreign trade to the position it had occupied before 1560. After Henri IV's assassination, in 1610, while the trade of England continued to expand, that of France suffered another serious setback. This was caused by the partial collapse of the important French commerce with the Levant. The annual value of this traffic apparently fell from about thirty million *livres tournois* in the decade from 1611 to 1620 to perhaps six or seven million from 1635 to 1648.[81] Meanwhile, the English seem to have increased their stake in the Levant trade.[82] English imports of tobacco from the colonies and of iron from Sweden grew many fold.[83] Expansion in English trade with the Baltic, with the coastal towns of northern Germany, and with Holland, which had begun under Elizabeth I, continued during the reign of James I and the 1630's.

English overseas commerce was evidently growing much more rapidly than French between 1540 and 1640. That by itself tells us little about the comparative progress of shipbuilding in the two countries, for throughout the century the native merchantmen engaged in the foreign trade of England were probably outnumbered by foreign, and a few of the foreign ships were French.[84] But the situation was not the same as in the fishing trade. There was apparently no branch of the foreign commerce of northern or western France in which French shipping retained its importance to the same extent as in the cod fishing on the Newfoundland banks. The

[80] According to Monsieur Charliat, French foreign trade was ruined, and "la marine marchande française . . . anéantie en pleine vitalité," as a result of the religious wars (P. Charliat, *Trois siècles d'économie maritime française* [Paris, 1931], pp. 14–15). He does not support this statement by any quantitative evidence, though he could have found some justification for it in the Danish Sound toll records. These show that shipments of salt to the Baltic from French ports fell from an annual average of 17,162 "laests" during the period from 1562 to 1566 to 3,805 from 1574 to 1578, to 5,864 from 1581 to 1585 and 6,129 from 1595 to 1599. But during the period from 1605 to 1609 the average was 15,358, so that the old position had been practically regained (Bang, *op. cit.*, II, *passim;* and compare above, p. 148). Nor can we assume that all branches of French commerce suffered nearly as much as the salt trade (see above, pp. 150–51).

[81] P. Masson, *Histoire du commerce française dans le Levant au XVIIe siècle* (Paris, 1896), pp. 118, 131. These figures should not be accepted without some reserve, for they are estimates based on the rents paid for farming the taxes on the Levant trade (*ibid.*, App. VI)

[82] *Ibid.*, pp. xxiv, 125.

[83] See below, pp. 181, 199.

[84] But not all the ships listed as "French" were built in France. We know that French merchants sometimes hired "Hamburgers and Flemings" to bring English coal to Normandy and Brittany (*State Papers, Domestic* [Public Record Office, London], Vol. CLVII, No. 32).

Dutch were becoming carriers for the French at least as much as for the English. Moreover the English also sometimes became carriers for the French, so that by the end of the sixteenth century the English ships which carried cargoes to and from France probably more than offset the French ships which took part in English foreign trade.[85] The proportion of all English exports and imports carried in native ships appears to have been increasing somewhat, and it is therefore certain that the expansion in foreign commerce, for which there was no equivalent in France, brought growing business to English shipyards.[86]

There is no difficulty in showing that a direct connection existed between the expansion in shipbuilding and the growth of coastwise trade in the two countries, for that was handled almost exclusively by native ships. And the contrast between French and English development was even more striking in the coastwise traffic than in foreign commerce. The growth in the volume of English foreign trade, though impressive, was not comparable to the growth in the volume of coastwise trade. This was particularly true of the traffic in coal, which required, because of its bulk, more ship's space than any other commodity. Exports of coal perhaps increased sixfold at the most between 1550 and 1640,[87] but coastwise shipments seem to have increased at least tenfold. In the two decades 1550–69, something like 45,000 tons may have been carried annually from Durham and Northumberland to ports in England.[88] By the decade 1631–40, the amount had increased to 470,000 tons or so.[89] A new and important coastwise traffic had sprung up in two other bulky commodities—glass and salt—as their manufacture came to be concentrated about the coal fields of the Tyne

[85] Cf. Fagniez, *op. cit.*, pp. 294–95, 323–24.

[86] For data showing the proportion of foreign to native ships in the English export trade in coal, see my *Rise of the British Coal Industry*, II, 23–25. The proportion of all cargoes carried in English ships increased greatly in some branches of foreign trade, for example in the export of tin. (G. R. Lewis, *The Stannaries* [Cambridge, Mass., 1907], pp. 63–64.) In the luxury trade with the Mediterranean, English ships were able to compete successfully with Dutch.

[87] Nef, *op. cit.*, I, 84 (Scottish exports are not included in my calculations); II, App. D (I) a.

[88] This estimate is derived from statistical data extracted from manuscripts almost forty years ago (*ibid.*, pp. 79–80, II, App. D (I) a). I have made corrections in my tonnage figures, as I find that a radical change was made in the content of the Newcastle chaldron in 1530 which escaped my notice when I published my book in 1932 and that I may have given inadequate importance then to a record I used of coastwise shipments from Newcastle in 1549–50 (London, Public Record Office: *Exch. K.R. Customs Accounts*, 110/3). I have Dr. J. R. Mott to thank for this information ("The London and Newcastle Chaldrons for Measuring Coal," *Archaeologia Aeliana*, 4th ser., XL, 227 ff.).

[89] Nef. *op. cit.*, II, App. D (I) a. I have only one actual record for coastwise shipments from Newcastle and Sunderland during the decade of the 1630's, that for the year 1633–34. It amounts to 470,582 tons. Small additional shipments probably came from Blyth and Cullincoates (App. D (I) f.).

valley. On the eve of the Civil War about three hundred tons of glass and many thousands of tons of salt left Newcastle every year to be carried to other Engish ports—above all to London.[90]

The capital was becoming more dependent than in the past upon the growing seaborne traffic for its supplies of food. While England's foreign trade in corn did not increase very much between 1540 and 1640, save in famine years,[91] the coastwise imports at London in non-famine years grew from less than twenty thousand quarters about the middle of Elizabeth's reign to more than sixty thousand quarters before the end of James I's reign.[92]

No comparable growth occurred in French coastwise traffic. The main cause of the English expansion was the growth of the London market; by the mid-seventeenth century something like half of all coal shipped coastwise from the north of England went to the capital; at the end of the century almost two-thirds.[93] Paris was not growing at nearly as rapid a rate in population as London, and while it was reaching out in the north of France and into the Loire valley for its supplies of grain, it continued to depend mainly on the basin of the Seine and the tributary rivers not only for its fuel but for its food. The French coasting trade in grain remained of slight importance.[94] While many English counties were coming to exchange food for the products of industry, or the products of industry for food, French provinces retained to a much greater degree their economic self-sufficiency.

At the time of the Reformation English coastwise commerce required only a small number of ships. The change brought about by the increase in this traffic was quite phenomenal. By the thirties of the seventeenth century between 300 and 400 colliers, a substantial proportion of more than 100 tons' burden, were employed in the coastwise coal trade from the north of England alone.[95] France had practically no coastwise traffic in coal. Apart from the extraordinary increase in the number of east coast English colliers, there was a large growth in the number of hoys carrying coal along the west coast and also in the craft engaged in other branches

[90] *Ibid.*, I, 176, 183.

[91] England was both an exporter and an importer of corn. Exports grew considerably down to the middle of Elizabeth's reign, but declined almost as considerably during the next half-century. Imports were negligible save in famine years, except in the case of London, and, if we leave out the year 1638, the records do not indicate any very striking increase in the London imports between 1540 and 1640. (N. S. B. Gras, *The Evolution of the English Corn Market* [Cambridge, Mass., 1915], pp. 111–12, 101–2, 275.)

[92] F. J. Fisher, "The Development of the London Food Market, 1540–1640," *Economic History Review*, V (1935), 47, 50; cf. Gras, *op. cit.*, p. 319.

[93] Nef, *Rise of the British Coal Industry*, II (compare Appendixes D [i] and D [iv]).

[94] Cf. A. P. Usher, *The History of the Grain Trade in France, 1400–1700* (Cambridge, 1913), pp. 33, 56–58, 61–63, 69–70, and frontispiece.

[95] Nef, *Rise of the British Coal Industry*, II, 95; cf. Oppenheim, *A History of the Administration of the Royal Navy*, p. 271.

of coastwise commerce, such as the traffic in salt, glass, corn, butter, and cheese. It is evident that by 1635 a large share of the entire English merchant marine—possibly a third or even a half—was employed in domestic commerce.

The growth of the English shipbuilding industry between 1560 and 1640 must have been due in large part to the expansion of coastwise trade. As there was no comparable growth in that branch of French commerce, it is reasonable to conclude that the number of workmen employed in various branches of shipbuilding, and the capital invested in shipyards, was increasing much more rapidly in England than in France.

Shortly after he became Louis XIV's *contrôleur-général,* Colbert got the admiralty officials to send him lists of all the privately owned, seagoing ships of over 10 tons' burden in the French kingdom. The results were tabulated in 1664, and they showed a total tonnage of 129,605. The tonnage of craft over 10 but under 100 tons was 73,765, and there were 2,039 ships in this category; the tonnage of the larger merchantmen whose burden exceeded 100 tons was 55,840, and they numbered 329.[96] We know from the lists which M. de Séguiran made in 1633 of the great ships, polaccas, and barks belonging to every port in Provence from Marseille to Antibes, that the number of Mediterranean merchantmen of 100 tons' burden had decreased. In 1633 there had been perhaps 60 to 75;[97] in 1664 there were 30. This decrease had undoubtedly been caused by the collapse of the Levant trade,[98] which scarcely affected shipping in northern and

---

[96] Masson, *op. cit.,* p. 134 n.

[97] Sue, *Correspondance de Henri de Sourdis,* III, 234–37, 254, 259, 264–65, 267, 274, 284–85, 289–90, 294, 299, 302, 309–11. Séguiran's figures are not in tons but in *quintaux.* It is reasonable to suppose that these were ordinary *quintaux,* not *quintaux métriques* as Monsieur Masson has apparently assumed in using Séguiran's lists (Masson, *Histoire du commerce,* p. 133). The ordinary *quintal* was a common measure in Languedoc and many other French provinces during the *ancien régime.* It frequently contained only 100 *livres* and never more than 134 *livres* (M. Rouff, *Les mines de Charbon en France* [Paris, 1922], p. lx; Larousse, *Grand dictionnaire universel*). In reaching the figure "perhaps 60 to 75," I have assumed that 2,000 *quintaux* were roughly equivalent to 100 tons.

Séguiran actually enumerated 49 vessels of 2,000 *quintaux* or more. In addition, he grouped some such vessels with a much larger number of smaller boats in his lists for Le Ciotat, Toulon, and Saint-Tropez, without specifying the burden of the individual ships (Sue, *op. cit.,* pp. 259, 274, 285). The number of ships of 2,000 *quintaux* or more included in those lists is quite uncertain, but it was not large, possibly from 10 to 20. An allowance should also be made for the large ships belonging to Marseille which were not in the port at the time of Séguiran's visit (Masson, *op. cit.,* p. 133 n.).

Séguiran's lists include in all about 650 ships, not counting the little fishing boats which had in some cases a burden of only from 15 to 30 *quintaux* (Sue, *op. cit.,* p. 265). From other lists of the period we should expect that the small vessels of from 10 to 100 tons' burden would outnumber the larger ships by at least 7, and possibly as much as 9 to 1 (cf. above, p. 160). The result (60–75 large ships out of about 650) which we have obtained by assuming that Séguiran's figures are in ordinary *quintaux* does not seem unreasonable.

[98] Masson, *op. cit.,* pp. 130–34.

western France. The tour of inspection carried out for Richelieu by M. d'In-freville, *commissaire-général de la marine,* to determine the number of trading vessels large enough to be effectively armed in case of war, indicates that at Atlantic and Channel ports there *were* more large ships in 1664 than in 1631.[99] Between the thirties and the sixties a gain in the north and west apparently offset the loss of shipping in the Mediterranean. It is not likely that the French merchant marine as a whole was smaller in the sixties than it had been in the thirties. But it was not much larger.

By the mid-seventeenth century England had apparently overtaken France, for she had at least 400 merchantmen of 100 tons,[100] and prob-ably more hoys and other smaller craft than belonged to French ports.[101] The navies of the two countries seem to have been fairly evenly matched, for the naval program of Richelieu had brought the French marine abreast of the British by 1631.[102] But this revival of the French navy, which had been neglected from 1559 until about 1625, was short-lived.[103] England's ship tonnage, therefore, was probably at least equal, and perhaps superior, to that of France in the thirties.[104] When account is taken of the difference between the population of the two countries at that time, it is evident that the shipping trade of England had become relatively much more impor-tant.

This of itself is not enough to prove that more ships—relative to popu-lation—were being *built* in England than in France. Partly as a result of the invention of the *flute,* the Dutch were able to turn out ships designed to carry heavy cargoes more cheaply, ton for ton, than either the French or English. So not all trading craft which flew the English flag had brought labor to English carpenters, joiners, mastmakers, calkers, sailcloth weav-ers, sailmakers, hemp dressers, twine spinners, ropemakers, shipwrights, compass makers, and anchorsmiths. The proportion of England's mercan-

[99] In the whole of Normandy and Brittany, Infreville found only about 150 trading vessels owned by subjects which he thought important enough to be used in a war. Most, but not necessarily all, of them were of more than 100 tons' burden (Sue, *op. cit.,* 206–7).

[100] An incomplete list of English ships of over 100 tons' burden, made in 1629, enumerates 355 vessels (see above, p. 160). It does not include ports in Yorkshire, Somerset, Cheshire, and Sussex, and it does not include all the ships from the port of Newcastle. By 1634, the number of ships of 100 tons had almost certainly increased, for 95 new vessels of that class had been added since 1629 (Oppenheim, *op. cit.,* p. 271).

[101] About 13 per cent of all French seagoing craft enumerated in the list of 1664 were of more than 100 tons' burden (see above, p. 165). In England before the Civil War the proportion was probably nearer 10 per cent (see above, p. 160, n. 72).

[102] Oppenheim, *op. cit.,* pp. 251–55, 264–65; Sue, *op. cit.,* III, 201–6; Charles de la Roncière, *Histoire de la marine française,* IV (Paris, 1910), 581 ff.

[103] J. B. T. de Boismêlé, *Histoire générale de la marine* (Amsterdam, 1746), pp. 371, 406.

[104] According to Fagniez, the English merchant marine was already superior to the French at the beginning of the reign of Henri IV (*L'économie sociale de la France,* p. 294).

tile tonnage that was of foreign build, after the three wars with Holland, has been estimated at from one-fourth to one-third.[105] These wars brought England a good many enemy ships as prizes, and before the middle of the seventeenth century therefore, the proportion of Dutch-built ships in the English service was probably smaller. Out of 380 new English merchant ships sent to London for ordnance between 1625 and 1638, only 37, hardly 10 per cent, came from foreign yards.[106] Notwithstanding the economic advantage held by the Dutch over the English shipbuilders, the great majority of English merchant ships on the eve of the Civil War had apparently been launched from domestic shipyards erected mainly with English capital. By this time the *largest* English naval vessels were generally regarded as superior to those of the Continent, and almost all English men-of-war were built at home. On the other hand, the French navy resurrected by Richelieu contained several vessels purchased in the Low Countries,[107] and the French merchant marine also included ships obtained abroad.[108] If we consider the navy and the merchant marine together, it is improbable that the percentage of foreign-built tonnage was smaller in France than in England. So it is reasonable to conclude that English shipbuilding tonnage had expanded much more notably between 1540 and 1640 than had the French, and that the demand for new (or for the enlargement of old) shipyards was greater in England.

This was, it seems, especially true on the eve of the English Civil War. During the five years from 1629 to 1633, ninety-five colliers and other craft of more than 100 tons' burden were launched from English shipyards,[109] almost one-third as many as there were in the whole French merchant marine in 1664. In France the decline in the Levant trade left the carpenters in the Mediterranean shipyards unemployed, and when M. d'Infreville visited Saint-Malo and the other ports of Brittany and Normandy in 1631, he was not impressed by the number of new keels he saw laid down. By this time England was almost certainly turning out a larger absolute quantity of shipping tonnage. The "revolution" which had put her common glass manufacture on the eve of the Civil War at least on a par with that of France, had made her shipbuilding industry *in terms of tonnage produced* about three times as important, relative to her population, as that of her neighbor.

The group of industries which has so far engaged our attention occupied an important place in the economy of both France and England. Salt-

---

[105] Barbour, "Dutch and English Shipping in the Seventeenth Century," pp. 289–90.
[106] Oppenheim, *op. cit.,* p. 269.
[107] Barbour, *op. cit.,* pp. 261, 263, 264. Oppenheim, *op. cit.,* p. 264.
[108] Cf. above, p. 166.
[109] Oppenheim, *op. cit.,* p. 271.

making and glassmaking each employed many hands in the mid-seventeenth century. The inhabitants of the town of Berre in Provence, where nearly all the grown men were salters, numbered more than three thousand in 1588.[110] Along the Atlantic coast, in Poitou, Aunis, and Saintonge, and especially in the Bay of Bourgneuf, there were thousands of peasants who combined work at the salt marshes with their husbandry. Nearly a thousand men found employment in Charles I's reign at the great saltworks at the mouth of the Tyne, and lived with their families in hovels near the furnaces, in the midst of "such a cloud of smoke as amongst these works you cannot see to walk." [111] In 1615 there were said to be about 2,500 *gentilshommes verriers* in the various provinces of the French kingdom,[112] without counting the common laborers, who performed all the rougher and more laborious tasks at the ovens and brought their masters food and wine which they ate sitting near their work, according to an ancient and well-established ritual.

Shipbuilding had numerous ramifications; for the sails and ropes, the nails and anchors, and even the masts and the planks for the hulls were frequently prepared in the scattered shops of various craftsmen before they were assembled in the shipyard, with its cranes for hoisting timbers into their places, and its launching ways down which the partly finished vessels could slide from their stocks into the water. By the mid-seventeenth century the laborers engaged in the various branches of shipbuilding almost certainly outnumbered the workers in glass.

All three industries—saltmaking, glassmaking, and shipbuilding—deserve a larger place in history than has been accorded them, and their growth in England between the Reformation and the Civil War formed part of the movement of rapid expansion in industrial production which began in the sixteenth century. The growth of each industry, and of all three taken together, helps to reveal contrasts between English and French economic history from 1540 to 1640.

Their place, nevertheless, was secondary to that of another group of industries. The majority—probably the great majority—of all the industrial workers of England and France earned their living in the mining and metallurgical industries, the textile manufactures, and the building trades. Any comparison between the growth in the volume of output in England and France from 1540 to 1640, must rest mainly upon a study of these industries.

[110] Sue, *op. cit.*, III, 311.

[111] Nef, *Rise of the British Coal Industry*, I, 176, 178 n. There were said to be 222 pans, 180–90 of which were usually in operation; and four men ordinarily worked at a pan.

[112] Boissonnade, *Le socialisme d'état*, p. 234.

THE MINING OF COAL

In England the output of all these heavy industries was growing fast during the late sixteenth and early seventeenth centuries. This growth was most remarkable in mining. It was caused primarily by the phenomenal expansion in the demand for coal fuel in heating, cooking, and manufacturing. Before the Reformation coal had not been used at all extensively in any European country for domestic fuel, except by poor people in places where the seams outcropped. Recourse was seldom had to it in connection with manufactures.[113] Even as late as 1563–64 the shipments recorded in the account book of the corporation of Newcastle, at that time the only coal port of any importance in the kingdom, amounted only to about 40,000 tons.[114] Seventy years later, in 1633–34, they had increased to about 450,000 tons. Sunderland, a port with a negligible trade in coal when Elizabeth I ascended the throne in 1558, shipped almost 70,000 additional tons in 1633–34. Coal shipments from the north of England had consequently multiplied at least tenfold and possibly much more.[115] The traffic from Chester and Liverpool grew perhaps from less than 1,000 to more than 12,000 tons during the same period.[116] Statistical materials for the ports of South Wales are inadequate for reaching an estimate, but they suggest a notable growth in the Welsh coal trade between 1580 and 1660.[117] In every country which had readily accessible mines there was a feverish interest in the discovery and the development of coal resources, and so great was the need for the new fuel, that coal-finders wasted their time boring for it in counties where it was not to be found. Many mining enterprises each with scores of laborers, and more than a dozen with over a hundred, were in operation on the eve of the Civil War. Adventurers poured their own capital and that of their creditors into pumping engines and adits to drain their new collieries, with an abandon which sometimes landed them in debtors' prisons.[118]

The annual output of coal in the whole of Great Britain, possibly less than 200,000 tons when the monasteries were dissolved, had probably reached 1,500,000 tons a century later.[119] The rate of increase in British

---

[113] See above, p. 45.

[114] Nef, *Rise of the British Coal Industry*, II, App. D (I). Content of the Newcastle chaldron corrected (see above, p. 163, n. 88).

[115] Nef, *op. cit.*, II, App. D (I). The figures suggest thirteenfold, but I leave a possible margin for error in case the Newcastle account book for 1563–64 provides an incomplete record.

[116] *Ibid.*, App. D (III).

[117] *Ibid.*, App. D (II), and I, 53.

[118] *Ibid., passim.* See esp. I, 76–77; II, 72, 140 n., 66 ff.

[119] No doubt the output in the 1530's was somewhat less than in the fifties, when I have estimated it at 210,000 tons (*ibid.*, I, 19–20). In the 1630's more than 500,000 tons were shipped from Durham and Northumberland in normal years for trade,

coal production was perhaps as rapid during the reigns of Elizabeth I and James I, between 1558 and 1625, as in the traditional period of the "industrial revolution" from 1760 to 1832.[120] By the reign of Charles I coal had been widely adopted as fuel by the saltmaker, the glassmaker, the shipbuilder, the steelmaker, the wire drawer, the saltpeter and gunpowder maker, the brewer, the sugar refiner, the soap boiler, the alum maker, the dyer, the hatmaker, the brickmaker, and almost every manufacturer except the smelter, who converted ore into metal. By the mid-seventeenth century a new industrial structure was being built in England on coal and this structure provided the basis for the industrialized Great Britain of the nineteenth century.

At the same time, between the Reformation and the Civil War, families in London and many parts of England replaced wood and charcoal by coal in their cooking and their laundry work. The iron grate with its coal-burning fire had become the center of domestic life, not only in the neighborhood of the coal fields, but in the capital and most provincial towns.

No domestic practice marked off English from Continental, and particularly French, life more sharply than the use of this newly adopted coal fire. During the reign of Louis XIII (1610–43) one could have visited the house of any poor man or rich man in Paris or almost any other French town, with the exception of Lyons and St. Etienne, or the peasants in nearly all their village homes, even in provinces where coal outcropped, without finding coals in the hearth or stove. French visitors to England sometimes wondered how people could work and eat and rest amid the suffocating fumes from this base mineral. They were equally astonished by its widespread use in manufactures. At home, they knew, it was burned, save for a few rare and unimportant exceptions, only to calcine limestones and to forge certain metal wares, not the artistic wares in which the French excelled.

For several centuries limeburners and smiths had employed coal locally to a small extent in those French provinces where the seams outcropped.

---

nearly 100,000 tons were burned in the local salt manufacture, and probably an additional 150,000 tons in glassmaking, metalworking, and other local industries and in domestic fires (*ibid.*, pp. 36, 208, and *passim*). It is improbable that more than 50 per cent of the British output was then produced in Durham and Northumberland (*ibid.*, p. 23).

[120] Cf. A. P. Usher, "Two Notable Contributions to Economic History," *Quarterly Journal of Economics,* XLVIII (1933), 177–78. Between 1540 and 1640 output probably increased seven- or eightfold, between 1740 and 1840 approximately sevenfold, from about 5,000,000 tons to something like 35,000,000 tons (Nef, *op. cit.*, II, 357; J. H. Clapham, *An Economic History of Modern Britain* [Cambridge, 1926], p. 431). In the earlier period most of the growth came after 1560; in the later period after 1760. But, as I have suggested elsewhere, the second sharp upturn in British coal production, and in industrial output generally, came, not in the mid-eighteenth century, as Macaulay and Toynbee the elder supposed, but in the 1780's (Nef, *Western Civilization since the Renaissance,* pp. 290–96).

During the sixteenth and early seventeenth centuries they used it more frequently and in larger quantities, and its use sometimes spread among limeburners and smiths outside the area of the actual diggings. By 1578, and probably somewhat earlier, packhorses began to carry part of the coal from small pits near Alais, in the Cévennes, down through the hills to limeburners in Nîmes, thirty miles to the south.[121] Coal from Rive-de-Gier, in Lyonnais, was shipped in increasing quantities up the Rhone to Lyons, a distance of some twenty miles. According to an *intendant,* who probably exaggerated, between 30,000 and 40,000 tons were consumed annually by the middle of the seventeenth century in this great city,[122] with its sixty or seventy thousand inhabitants, its rapidly multiplying silk looms, its bankers and its merchants who, together with those of Vienne, controlled the steel supplies of Dauphiné.[123] Lyons provided the most important market for coal in the whole of France.

There was also a growing demand for it at towns along the Loire. Local traders built a small storage house in Nivernais at Decize, conveniently situated for loading coal from the growing colliery of La Machine, and between 1560 and 1590 little boats began to move the fuel downstream as far as Gien and Orléans, and up the river Allier into Bourbonnais, to the thriving town of Moulins,[124] possibly to serve the cutlers whose wives besieged the traveler at his inn with their husbands' wares, if they had not already waylaid him on his arrival at the city gates.[125] The religious wars interfered with the progress of most industries, but, especially at St. Etienne in Forez, they stimulated the manufacture of arms, and indirectly, as coal was used there to some extent by smiths in forging weapons, the working of coal. The place grew from a medieval village, with a few hundred people, into a thriving town, with several thousands.

The increasing use of coal by smiths and limeburners during the late sixteenth and early seventeenth centuries explains the increasing activity of local peasants in digging for it in many new spots in several provinces. Tiny enterprises, generally employing less than half-a-dozen hands but in a few cases a dozen or more, multiplied in the Cévennes, in Provence, in

---

[121] A. Bardon, *L'exploitation du bassin houiller d'Alais* (Nîmes, 1898), pp. 15, 19.

[122] L. J. Gras, *Histoire économique générale des mines de la Loire* (St. Etienne, 1922), p. 156.

[123] Cf. Godart, *L'ouvrier en soie,* pp. 19–20; J. B. Giraud, "Les épées de Rives," in *Documents pour l'histoire de l'armement au Moyen Age et à la Renaissance,* II, 237–46.

[124] P. Destray, "Les houillères de La Machine au XVIe siècle," in J. Hayem, *Mémoires et documents pour l'histoire du commerce et de l'industrie* (4th ser.; Paris, 1916), pp. 177–82. Coal mining in Bourbonnais itself was of negligible importance until the eighteenth century (S. Claudon, "Etude sur les anciennes mines de charbon en Bourbonnais," *Bulletin de la Société d'Emulation et des Beaux-Arts du Bourbonnais,* VIII [1900], 47–48, 198).

[125] Camille Pagé, *La coutellerie depuis l'origine jusqu'à nos jours* (Chatellerault, 1896), I, 84–85.

Nivernais, in Anjou, in Forez, and especially in Lyonnais.[126] In the Cévennes leases of the same mines at different dates show that the rents paid increased a good deal more rapidly than the value of money fell, particularly during the last half of the sixteenth century.[127] The proprietor of a mine at Dauphin, a tiny village in the hilly country near the river Durance in Provence, sold about 500 tons of coal in 1603 to one buyer for use in smith's work at Manosque, a small town some five miles to the south.[128] At La Machine, according to Guy Coquille, the jurist and historian of Nivernais who died in 1603, large sums were spent at certain seasons in pumping out water.[129] But most French mines were still so shallow that drainage was not yet a serious problem.

Although a marked increase had evidently occurred in the production of coal in central and southern France, progress was slow compared to that in most English counties where coal was mined. Apart from Forez, Lyonnais, and Nivernais, there was no French province which produced a substantial volume of coal in the seventeenth century. In Anjou, according to a modern local authority, the output in 1600 was only some 2,000 tons,[130] about a fifth as much as was then obtained from a single colliery in southern Lancashire, with nothing but a local demand for its produce in Manchester —a place at that time of hardly more than four or five thousand people.[131] In Bourbonnais the output was even smaller than in Anjou,[132] and it could not have been much greater at the southern end of the Cévennes or even in Provence, where coal was dug in several districts.[133] Above all, the mineral resources of the north, which were to furnish most of the coal mined in France during the eighteenth and nineteenth centuries, were not tapped at all. The annual production of the entire kingdom at the end of Louis XIII's reign could hardly have been more than at the beginning of the eighteenth century, when a reasonable estimate would perhaps not greatly exceed 100,000 tons.[134]

---

[126] Bardon, op. cit., pp. 13–42; Inventaire des archives départementales, Basses Alpes, B. 1812, 2010, 2214; Destray, op. cit., pp. 162 ff.; O. Couffon, Les mines de charbon en Anjou du XIVᵉ siècle à nos jours (Angers, 1911), p. 564; L. J. Gras, Historique de l'armurerie stéphanoise (St. Etienne, 1905), pp. 2–3; Gras, Histoire des mines de la Loire, pp. 155–56.

[127] Bardon, op. cit., pp. 23, 42.

[128] Inventaire des archives départementales, Bouches-du-Rhône, B. 3444.

[129] Histoire du pays et duché de Niversnois (2d ed.; Paris, 1622), p. 353.

[130] 76,204 bushels (Couffon, op. cit., p. 564).

[131] Nef, Rise of the British Coal Industry, I, 64; A. P. Wadsworth and J. de L. Mann, The Cotton Trade and Industrial Lancashire (Manchester, 1931), p. 509.

[132] Cf. Claudon, loc. cit.

[133] H. de Gerin-Ricard, "Mines et mineurs autrefois et aujourd'hui," Société Statistique de Marseille, XLVII (1906–7), 217, 251 ff., 308; Inventaire des archives départementales, Basses Alpes, B. 1812, 2214; Bouches-du-Rhône, B. 3444. In addition to the provinces mentioned in the text, coal was mined in small quantities in Burgundy, Champagne, Brittany, and the diocese of Albi.

[134] Nef, op. cit., I, 125–26. My estimate is based on the reports made in 1709 by

In the reign of Charles I, England, with about a third the population of France, probably produced ten times as much coal, well over a million tons a year.[135] The English coal-mining industry dwarfed the French to an extent never equaled since the early eighteenth century. Compared with the "mountains" of coal, as astonished travelers described the piles beside the pits in some English counties, the mines of France, except those at Rive-de-Gier and La Machine, seemed no more than large anthills!

THE SMELTING OF ORES

The progress of deeper mining in England had made the problem of drainage so serious that thousands of pounds in seventeenth-century money, worth perhaps twenty or thirty times that of our own day, were frequently spent by a single enterprise on adits and pumps driven by horse or, less frequently, by water power. The pumping machinery was costly to operate. It was ineffective for raising water more than a hundred feet at a single flight. Inventors were busy trying to improve it. They were experimenting with steam as a force to substitute for horses and running water at the larger mines,[136] which were often worked to depths of three or four hundred feet. While the search for improved drainage engines of all sorts was caused mainly by the expansion in coal mining, inventors were offering their new machines, which rarely accomplished what was claimed for them, to adventurers in ore mines as well as to adventurers in collieries.

Ore mining, like coal mining, was extended down to greater depths in England during the late sixteenth and early seventeenth centuries, mainly because of an increase in the demand.[137] The market for metal in England might have grown scarcely less rapidly than the market for coal, had a technique been devised to make possible the substitution of the new fuel for charcoal in the furnaces, forges, and ovens where metals were extracted from their ores.[138] For England was confronted with a timber crisis. Be-

the *intendants* on the condition of French coal mining. The industry was seriously depressed at this time; for the output in Forez and Anjou was said to be a great deal less than it had once been (A. M. de Boislisle, *Correspondance des contrôleurs généraux* [Paris, 1897], Vol. III, No. 496). (But I am now less disposed than I was when I wrote this article to think these reports of the *intendants* gave a complete account of the output in 1709.)

[135] See above, p. 169. My conjecture that annual production on the eve of the Civil War reached something like a million and a half tons, includes Scotland. An estimate of the output of Scotland at that time is mainly guesswork, but it could hardly have been less than 200,000 tons per annum. (Nef, *op. cit.*, I, 45).

[136] See above, p. 132.

[137] This was not true in the case of tin mining. The tin mines were worked to greater depths in spite of a slight decline in the output of tin (cf. G. R. Lewis, *The Stannaries*).

[138] The market for ores did not, of course, expand in exactly the same proportions as the market for metals. In ironmaking the widespread introduction of the blast furnace (see below, p. 178) reduced the quantity of ore required to make a ton of

tween 1540 and 1640 the price of firewood and some kinds of lumber increased much more rapidly than the price of all other commodities in common use, about three times as rapidly.[139] As some forty cords of wood had to be converted into charcoal to make one ton of bar iron,[140] and as the extraction of other metals from their ores was not much less spendthrift of fuel, the costs of smelting, which might have fallen considerably as a result of more efficient technique,[141] were kept up. As early as 1606, when the ironmaking industry of southeastern England had begun to suffer from the growing shortage of fuel, plans were made to ship English iron ore and cinders to be smelted in Ireland, where the woods were thicker.[142] There were few regions in England where metallurgical enterprise was not hindered by deforestation at one time or another before the Civil War. There were probably places where smelting operations had to be temporarily abandoned.[143]

Notwithstanding this handicap, there was an increase in the production of all metals except tin. Calamine, the ore of zinc, which had hardly been dug in medieval England, was discovered first in Somerset in 1566, then in Gloucestershire and Nottinghamshire. These discoveries made possible the extensive development of a new manufacture of brass—an alloy of prepared calamine and copper.[144] The introduction of the brassmaking industry was probably the chief cause[145] for the falling-off in the output of tin, because brass wares were substituted for those of bronze—an alloy of tin and copper. But brass and wire, made of brass or latten, were wanted for many other articles—such as pins and cards for the carding of wool—besides those formerly made of bronze. The growth in brass manufacture, together

---

iron from about five to something like three tons (cf. Rhys Jenkins, "Iron-making in the Forest of Dean," *Transactions of the Newcomen Society,* VI [1925–26], 47) and also brought about, at least at some furnaces in the Forest of Dean, the use, in place of fresh ore, of cinders which had gone to waste at the medieval bloomery forges. There was probably less improvement in the methods of smelting other ores. The proportion of lead ore mined to lead produced early in the seventeenth century was about two to one (*Star Chamber Proceedings* [Public Record Office, London], James I, 75/10). Coppermaking was many times more spendthrift of ore than either lead- or ironmaking. Even in the eighteenth century the proportion of ore mined to copper produced was between thirteen and twenty to one (Henry Hamilton, *The English Brass and Copper Industries to 1800* [London, 1926], p. 351; A. H. Dodd, *The Industrial Revolution in South Wales* [Cardiff, 1933], p. 167). Consequently the production of copper in substantial quantities, which began in Elizabeth's reign (see below, p. 175) partially offset the reductions, caused by improvements in the smelting process, in the proportion of ores mined to metals produced.

[139] See below, pp. 261 ff.; Nef, *op. cit.,* I, 158 ff.
[140] *Ibid.,* p. 193. For a possible explanation of the course taken by charcoal prices, see below, p. 264.
[141] See above, p. 130.
[142] *Calendar of State Papers, Domestic,* 1603–10, p. 306.
[143] Cf. Nef, *op. cit.,* I, 193–95; *Calendar of State Papers, Domestic,* 1638–39, p. 276.
[144] For what follows concerning brass and copper see Hamilton, *op. cit., passim.*
[145] For other causes see Nef, *op. cit.,* I, 166–67.

with the greatly increased demand for copper in various forms, especially for the large kettles and boilers in which saltpeter and other products of the rapidly growing manufactures were cooked,[146] caused an expansion in the output of copper which much more than offset the decline in the output of tin.[147] Copper ore was smelted for the first time in England in more than negligible quantities. By the middle of the seventeenth century calamine was wanted not only in the domestic brass manufacture (which had declined somewhat in importance from a peak apparently reached in the reign of James I), but for export to foreign countries.[148] The two greatest joint-stock companies organized in connection with industry in the Elizabethan Age, the Society of the Mines Royal and the Society of the Mineral and Battery Works, were formed to exploit the newly found resources of copper ore and calamine and to convert these ores by a series of processes into copper and brass ingots, sheets, rods, and wire.[149] They had mines, smelting houses, and other equipment in a number of counties, and they provided work for several thousand laborers.

The manufacture of lead and iron, like the manufacture of tin, employed many workmen even in the Middle Ages, but the output of lead and iron, unlike that of tin, grew notably between 1540 and 1640. To judge from the increase in the number of miners employed, in the capital invested in mines, and in the royalties paid to local landlords, the production of lead ore and lead in Somerset and Derbyshire, the two chief lead-producing counties, grew several fold at the end of the sixteenth century and during the first two decades of the seventeenth.[150] In Charles I's reign the annual output of metallic lead in the whole country was estimated at about 12,000 tons, something like twenty times the output of tin.[151]

A comparison of the growth of metal production in France and England is possible only in the case of iron. But, if we are concerned with the volume of output, iron is much the most important metal to consider, be-

[146] Cf. below, p. 195.

[147] The output of tin fell from about 900 to between 500 and 600 tons per annum during the century from 1540 to 1640 (Lewis, *op. cit.*, pp. 253, 255).

[148] For the progress of calamine production in Somerset see J. W. Gough, *The Mines of Mendip* (Oxford, 1930), pp. 213–15.

[149] Cf. W. R. Scott, *The Constitution and Finance of English, Scottish and Irish Joint-Stock Companies to 1720* (Cambridge, 1910–12), II, 383–429.

[150] Gough, *op. cit.*, pp. 112–15; *Victoria County History, Derbyshire*, II, 231, 233. Lead ore was also mined and smelted in Yorkshire, Durham, and various parts of Wales.

[151] Nef, *op. cit.*, I, 167. The "fother" of lead was equivalent to about a ton (*ibid.*, II, 375). I did not profess to solve all the problems of weights and measures in sixteenth- and seventeenth-century Great Britain in Appendix C of my coal book. I simply tried to open up the subject with materials which, as I indicated at the time, were mostly inadequate if great precision is demanded. And, as I have tried to show elsewhere, the demand for precision was novel at this time in history, and is in itself an aspect of what I call the "early English industrial revolution" (Nef, *Cultural Foundations of Industrial Civilization* (New York, 1960), pp. 6–17).

cause in both countries the tonnage of iron produced was coming to exceed that of all other metals combined. Again iron is the most important metal if we are to show that the English output of metals was forging ahead of the French, because it is chiefly in connection with iron that England's advantage is open to doubt.

While tin, lead, and copper ore were all mined in the French kingdom to some extent, the supplies of metal extracted from them were inadequate to meet domestic needs. A memoir on foreign trade, drawn up about the middle of the sixteenth century, indicates that France imported large quantities of tin, lead, and copper. The first two metals came mainly from England, whose shipments of metal to France apparently exceeded in value those of wool and woolen cloth.[152] A century later the relative positions of the two countries remained much the same. Some two decades after the English Civil War, in 1669, 1671, and 1672, tin, lead, and copper in various forms were still among the most important items in the incomplete records of imports kept by the French government. According to these records France was importing 845 *milliers de livres* of tin annually, or about 407 tons (at a time when the whole English output scarcely reached 800 tons);[153] she was importing about 2,700 tons of lead and about 605 tons of copper and copper wares, including the species of brass wire known as latten.[154] There is no way of determining what proportion of the imports of lead and tin was English, but the proportion may have been considerable.[155] Just before the Civil War, England exported about 4,500 tons of lead annually[156] and a good deal more than half her yearly output of tin.[157]

---

[152] Boissonnade, *Le socialisme d'état*, pp. 11–13; cf. *Inventaire des archives départementales*, Bouches-du-Rhône, B. 3332, fol. 839.

[153] Lewis, *op. cit.*, p. 255.

[154] Archives Nationales (Paris), F[12] 1834[A]. It was through the kindness of M. Georges Bourgin that I was able to get copies of these interesting documents. The figures they contain somewhat understate the actual imports of tin, lead, and copper for two reasons. In the first place, they do not cover the whole of France. They include the imports into all provinces which formed part of the central customs division known as the *cinq grosses fermes* and also the imports into the *provinces réputées étrangères*, with the exception of Brittany and Dauphiné. As very little metal, except possibly iron from Savoy, was imported into Dauphiné, the only important omissions were Brittany and the few *provinces à l'instar de l'étranger effective*, most of which did not belong to France until after 1640. In the second place, some of the metal brought into the territory covered by the returns probably escaped entry, either because of smuggling or because of corruption on the part of the customs officials.

While the returns include some French commodities, such as soap from Marseille, which paid duties on entering the area of the *cinq grosses fermes* or at the toll stations of Valence and Lyons (cf. E. F. Heckscher, *Mercantilism* [London, 1935], I, 98–105), it is plain that virtually all the entries of tin, lead, and copper were of foreign origin.

I have reduced the figures given in the returns to tons on the assumption that the *livre* was equivalent to 0.49 kg (see below, p. 180, n. 175).

[155] A substantial portion of the wrought copper came from the Spanish Netherlands and was probably produced in the valley of the Meuse, at and around Namur.

[156] The English exports of lead increased from 2,900 "fothers," or nearly 3,000 tons,

While calamine was not included in the seventeenth-century records of French imports, we have no evidence of any discoveries of this ore in France before 1640 to match those which in England permitted the establishment of a notable brass manufacture. There were certainly no French supplies of calamine as abundant as those produced in the Duchy of Limbourg by the celebrated mines of Moresnet. The monopoly enjoyed by these mines in supplying the surrounding countries was strengthened by an order of the king of Spain in 1590, that no brass or copper wares made with any other calamine should be sold even in those parts of the Low Countries—Lille, Douai, and Orchie—which were eventually to become French.[158]

Iron ore was the only base material in which French resources were superior to English, and during the reign of Francis I ironmaking probably occupied a place of greater importance in France than in England. In both countries the ore was smelted at that time in many regions mainly for local consumption. Down to at least 1540 the smelting operations were apparently conducted on a larger scale in several French provinces than in any part of England, with the possible exception of Sussex. Blast furnaces put in an appearance at the end of the fifteenth century, if not before, in Burgundy and Champagne, at Laigle near Alençon, and perhaps in Nivernais.[159] The new process of ironmaking was probably introduced into England from France.[160] But, at the Reformation, blast furnaces were still scarce in France as well as in England, where we know for certain of only three until after 1540.[161] The French ironmaking industry derived its advantage from the steadily increasing use, since the thirteenth century or earlier, of water power for driving the hammers and bellows at the older types of mill where wrought iron was made directly from the ore. By the beginning of the sixteenth century, if not before, water power had come to be almost universally used in the manufacture of iron in Dauphiné, the upper Marne Valley, and many other parts of the French kingdom.[162] In

during the year ending at Michaelmas, 1593, to about 4,600 fothers annually on the eve of the Civil War, when the output was estimated at 12,600 fothers (*Calendar of State Papers, Domestic,* 1591–94, p. 556; *ibid.,* 1636–37, p. 305).

[157] Lewis, *op. cit.,* pp. 55–56.

[158] H. Pirenne, *Histoire de Belgique* (3d ed.; Brussels, 1923), III, 254; Archives du Nord (Lille), B. 1835, fols. 34–35.

[159] Ernest Straker, *Wealden Iron* (London, 1931), p. 40; Bulard, "L'industrie du fer dans la Haute-Marne," *Annales de géographie,* XIII (1904), 232; M. Leroux, *L'industrie du fer dans le Perche* (Paris, 1916), p. 59; A. Massé, *Monographies nivernaises* (Nevers, 1913), II, 358.

[160] Straker, *op. cit.,* p. 47.

[161] Nef, "Note on the Progress of Iron Production in England, 1540–1640," *Journal of Political Economy,* XLIV (1936), 398.

[162] T. Sclafert, *L'industrie du fer dans la région d'Allevard au Moyen Age* (Grenoble, 1926), pp. 46–47, 49–50, 63–64; Ernest Chabrand, *Essai historique sur la métallurgie du fer et de l'acier en Dauphiné et en Savoie* (Grenoble, 1898), pp. 19–20, 22; Bulard, *op. cit.,* p. 232.

England, where the annual output of the average bloomery forge at the beginning of the sixteenth century was probably about twenty tons,[163] water power was less generally employed. French forges were usually larger than English and were staffed by more workmen. They generally produced a somewhat greater quantity of iron.

Between 1540 and 1640 there was a notable development of the iron-making industry in the north of Europe. The blast furnace was widely adopted.[164] It generated a greater heat than the older forges and, by reducing the ore to a liquid form, made it possible to extract more metal. The pig iron obtained at these furnaces was carried to forges, where it was again heated and hammered into bars. Both the new furnaces and the forges were much larger establishments with heavier and more costly machinery than most of the older English iron mills which they superseded.

An idea of the growth in the output of iron in England can be obtained from records of the progress of the blast furnace. By the reign of Charles I the new furnaces, hardly known except in southeastern England before the dissolution of the monasteries, had spread to at least fourteen counties. There were probably between one hundred and one hundred and fifty of them in blast, and nearly twice as many large forges for converting the pig iron into bars. The national output of iron seems to have grown at least as rapidly as that of lead. It increased several fold—perhaps fivefold or even more—between 1540 and 1625. When Charles I succeeded to the throne, between 20,000 and 30,000 tons of bar iron were probably produced annually at the new forges, besides the wrought iron still made directly from the ore by more primitive methods and the finished articles, such as fire backs, cannons, and grave slabs, which were cast into final form at the blast furnaces.[165]

Between the death of Francis I and the accession of Louis XIV in 1643 there was nothing comparable across the Channel to this rapid expansion of the English ironmaking industry. The officials of the French crown do not seem to have been eager to encourage the progress of ironmaking. In 1543, a royal ordinance declared that, in the interest of conserving wood supplies, the number of iron mills should not be increased.[166] While the output of iron grew in central France, particularly during the religious wars when the demand for arms expanded, mills were decreasing in number in the Cévennes and in Champagne, where a revival of the manufacture at the beginning of the seventeenth century was cut short in the thirties by the invasions of foreign armies.[167] In Dauphiné, possibly the most important

---

[163] Nef, "Note on Iron Production," p. 402.

[164] Cf. Ludwig Beck, *Die Geschichte des Eisens* (2d ed.; Brunswick, 1891), I, 781.

[165] Nef, "Note on Iron Production," pp. 401, 403.

[166] Archives Nationales, X[1A] 8614, ff. 22–23; cf. Nef, *Industry and Government in France and England*, pp. 68–76.

[167] Bardon, *L'exploitation du bassin houiller d'Alais*, pp. 36–37, 41; Bulard, *op. cit.*, pp. 234–35.

iron-producing region, the progress of the industry in the late sixteenth and early seventeenth centuries was no more striking than it had been in the fourteenth century and again at the end of the fifteenth.[168]

The new processes of ironmaking were less developed in France than in England between the mid-sixteenth and the mid-seventeenth centuries. Blast furnaces had been fairly generally adopted as the basis for iron production by the 1630's in Perche and in Champagne and Nivernais, where they had been introduced before 1540, and also in Dauphiné, where they were apparently a novelty.[169] But they had not penetrated at all to at least two ironmaking areas of some importance, those of the Cévennes and the Comté de Foix.[170]

Not only was the blast furnace making slower headway in France than in England, but it was apparently increasing more slowly in size. While the scale of ironmaking operations had been greater in France at the time of the Reformation, the positions of the two countries seem to have been reversed during the hundred years which followed. By the middle of the seventeenth century there were probably furnaces in the Midlands which produced as much as 700 tons of pig iron in a year. The average output of an English blast furnace in the thirties possibly exceeded 200 tons[171]— about ten times as much iron as had been commonly made by the old-fashioned English bloomery forge at the beginning of the sixteenth century. Our knowledge of the output of French mills is meager. But in Nivernais, which became one of the most important ironmaking provinces in the seventeenth century, the first large blast furnace was built in 1645. Some decades later it was able to turn out annually about 400 tons of pig iron.[172] It replaced an older, much smaller furnace, apparently similar to the ones in Sussex which had produced about 100 tons or even less in Elizabeth's reign.[173] Such small-scale operations as were characteristic of sixteenth-century Sussex seem to have persisted in France longer than in England, in all those provinces where iron had come to be made mainly by the roundabout process. In other parts of France the output of the forges was probably smaller.

The annual production of pig iron in England and Wales on the eve of

[168] Sclafert, op. cit., pp. 103, 107; Giraud, "Les épées de Rives," pp. 198 ff. Boissonnade speaks of sixty-eight forges near Rives in 1660 (op. cit., p. 232), but these were not, as he apparently supposed, ironmaking forges but small mills for working iron into steel.

[169] Leroux, op. cit., p. 60; Coquille, Histoire du pays et duché de Nivernois, pp. 356–58; Chabrand, op. cit., p. 25; Giraud, op. cit., p. 218.

[170] Bardon, op cit., pp. 39–41; Henri Rouzaud, Histoire d'une mine en mineur: La mine de Rancié (Toulouse, 1908), pp. 93–94. The Comté de Foix was annexed to the French kingdom in 1589.

[171] Nef, "Note on Iron Production," p. 401.

[172] Corbier, "Notice sur les forges impériales de la Chaussade," Bulletin de la Société Nivernaise des Lettres, Sciences et Arts, 2d ser., 1869, pp. 357–58.

[173] Nef, "Note on Iron Production," p. 401.

the Civil War almost certainly exceeded 20,000 and may have reached 40,000 tons.[174] For France, I find no basis for an estimate of production before 1789, when the output of pig iron stood at about 136,000 tons, rather more than half of which came from the *généralités* of Strasbourg, Nancy, and Besançon—territory which had not belonged to the French kingdom under Louis XIII.[175] The whole of France as it was bounded in his reign, an area that contained nearly twenty million people in 1789, was then producing only about twice as much pig iron as had been made a century and a half earlier in England and Wales. Meanwhile, there had been a remarkable growth in the output and the scale of enterprise in central and western France.[176] Before this growth, in the reign of Louis XIII, the production of pig iron in England may possibly have been greater absolutely than in France; it was almost certainly much greater relative to population. France was then turning out more wrought iron (iron made directly from the ore), for the fashioning in France of artistic iron wares continued to flourish. Wrought ironwork was being adapted to the French classical style of life. It was in the quantity of iron produced that the English forged ahead of the French between the Reformation and the Civil War.

THE MANUFACTURE OF METAL WARES

The rapid growth in the output of English iron was probably hindered even before the death of Elizabeth, and perhaps brought to an end before the Civil War, by the shortage and dearness of wood. That difficulty did not interfere directly with the growth in the production of metal wares, because coal was successfully substituted for wood as fuel in almost every operation after the metals had been extracted from their ores.[177] Before Elizabeth's reign a good deal of the metal produced in England had been sent abroad to be worked by foreign craftsmen,[178] and the English had been dependent on Continental countries, especially Germany and the Netherlands, for many kinds of finished metal commodities. The introduction into England, during the reigns of Elizabeth and James I, of brass-

[174] *Ibid.*

[175] Cf. above, p. 149. The whole French kingdom produced 282,730 *milliers de livres* of pig iron, of which 146,615 *milliers* came from the *généralités* of Strasbourg, Nancy, and Besançon (H. and G. Bourgin, *L'industrie sidérurgique en France* [Paris, 1920], p. 463). The figures have been reduced to metric tons by Professor Heckscher on the assumption that the average weight of the *livre* was 0.49 kg. (Heckscher, *Mercantilism*, I, 201 n.). In this way he got "about 138,000 tons." If we reduce the figures rather to tons of 2,240 lb., the result is about 136,000 tons.

[176] It would require more space than is at my disposal to give the evidence on which this statement is based. I hope at some future date to discuss in detail the growth of French industrial output in the late seventeenth and eighteenth centuries. (For a beginning, see Nef, *Western Civilization since the Renaissance*, pp. 148–51, 276–85.)

[177] Nef, *Rise of the British Coal Industry*, I, 201–5; and see above, pp. 133 ff.

[178] Cf. above, p. 178.

making and new methods of steelmaking laid the foundations for a greater independence. The skill of English craftsmen, particularly the cutlery workers, increased so much that in the reign of James I an Englishman could boast, "The best and finest knives in the world are made in London." [179] They were probably less beautiful to contemplate than French cutlery, but they seem to have done more effective execution! Nails and pins, kettles and pans, and cutlery not only came into more general use at home, where the market for all of them was growing scarcely less rapidly than that for windowpanes and bottles, but they were exported in much more substantial quantities than in the reign of Henry VIII. English cast-iron cannon were in growing demand on the Continent.[180]

We have a partial record for the three years 1634–36 of English exports of iron and iron wares.[181] It shows that by this time the latter greatly exceeded the former in value and probably even in volume. In all, 629¼ tons of English-made iron were shipped to foreign parts, 444 tons of which went to Africa and the Canary Islands.[182] The exact volume of iron goods shipped cannot be determined because the entries are given in a variety of different quantities not susceptible of reduction to any common denominator. In addition to miscellaneous iron wares and tools to the value of £3,246 (two hundred thousand dollars or more in terms of today's money), the exports included 32 cannons and 26 tons of additional large ordnance, 9,636 pieces of small arms, 600 swords, and 56 tons of shot. They also included 5½ tons of wire, 30 or more tons of nails, and a fair quantity of such articles as anchors, chimney backs, locks, tacks, and rivets, axes, hatchets, hoes, puncheons, shovels, saws, and scythes, spurs, stirrups and bits, kettles, pots, and pans. England was sending andirons, smoothing irons, tacks, anchors, and rivets even to the Netherlands, one of the chief foreign sources for supplying the English market with metal wares.

A growth in the imports of metal from Flanders, Spain, Ireland and, above all, Sweden made possible a continued expansion of the metal trades, in spite of the handicap imposed on the native production of metal by the rising price of wood fuel. The records of commodities passing westward through the Danish Sound suggest that shipments of iron to England from

[179] G. I. H. Lloyd, *The Cutlery Trades* (London, 1913), *passim,* esp. p. 93; R. E. Leader, *History of the Company of Cutlers in Hallamshire* (Sheffield, 1905), p. 11 and *passim.*

[180] Nef, *Western Civilization since the Renaissance,* p. 37.

[181] British Museum, Sloane MSS, 2103, fols. 247–65. The record covers the period from February, 1633/34, to December, 1636, but it is not clear whether it is a record of exports from England and Wales as a whole or only of exports from certain places.

[182] The iron exports recorded in the document come to 1,010¼ tons, but 321 tons were re-exports of Spanish iron and 60 tons re-exports of Irish iron. For English imports of Spanish iron see also *Calendar of Exchequer Depositions by Commission,* p. 415.

the Baltic increased several fold between 1565 and 1635, and that the expansion in this trade was most rapid between 1624 and 1628. In the thirties England was probably importing many thousands of tons every year, chiefly from Sweden.[183] The ironmongers, carpenters, blacksmiths, and nailers of London, like the cutlery workers of Sheffield, became no less eager to prevent regulations designed to reduce or prohibit the importation of foreign iron than the owners of blast furnaces were eager to promote it.[184] That is because foreign supplies were becoming indispensable for the English artisans. Before Elizabeth's reign more metal had been produced at home than had been worked into finished commodities. On the eve of the Civil War more metal was probably worked into finished commodities at home than was produced at English furnaces and forges. The output of metal wares grew more rapidly during the century from 1540 to 1640 than the output of metal.

In France there was no general deforestation such as occurred throughout Great Britain, and timber prices were rising much more slowly than in England.[185] It was not, to the same degree as in England, a shortage of wood fuel which was holding back the smelting of ores;[186] it was the lack

[183] Bang, *Tables de la navigation et du transport,* II, *passim.* If we compare the average annual shipments of iron from the Baltic through the Danish Sound in the two five-year periods 1562–66 and 1635–39, we find that they increased about sixfold, from less than 900 to about 5,000 tons (allowing 6.4 *skippund* and 0.5 *laest* to the ton). Most of the expansion occurred between 1624 and 1628, when the traffic grew nearly fourfold in five years. At the same time there was a great increase in the proportion of iron coming from Sweden rather than from East Prussia, until, on the eve of the English Civil War, practically all the iron passing westward through the Sound was Swedish (cf. Eli F. Heckscher, *Sveriges Ekonomiska Historia Från Gustav Vasa* [Stockholm, 1935–36], I(i), 157, I(ii), 473–74). During the thirties the annual shipments of iron remained steady at about 5,000 tons, but they again increased during the forties and fifties and, when the traffic was not hampered by warfare, reached 10,000 tons and even more. These figures do not include the iron carried out of the Baltic in Swedish ships, which were exempted from paying the Sound tolls, and such shipments first became important in the thirties of the seventeenth century (*ibid.,* p. ix). Nor do the figures include, of course, the considerable quantities of Swedish iron which came to England directly without passing through the Sound.

We have, unfortunately, no record of the destination of the iron cargoes on which a toll was paid. Although the iron carried in English ships did not increase much in the first half of the seventeenth century, it is probable that a large portion of the Swedish iron exported both in Swedish ships and in ships from Dutch and German ports went to England; for in 1668 it was estimated, perhaps with some exaggeration, that during recent years the annual English imports of Swedish iron had amounted to 12,000 tons (see below, p. 183, n. 188).

[184] John Nicholl, *Some Account of the Company of Ironmongers* (London, 1851), pp. 178–80; *Victoria County History, Derbyshire,* II, 359–60; Straker, *Wealden Iron,* p. 62. Although the nailers at first supported a project presented in James I's reign to prohibit the import of Flemish iron, they afterward decided, "after better consideration of the busynes," to oppose it (Nicholl, *op. cit.,* pp. 177, 180–81).

[185] Nef, *Rise of the British Coal Industry,* I, 161–62.

[186] See Leroux, *L'industrie du fer dans le Perche,* pp. 60, 67; Rouzaud, *op. cit.,* p. 99, for evidence that the smelting of iron ore in the Perche and the Comté de Foix was not being held up by any shortage of wood. There were local complaints against

of new markets for metal, outside the demand for artistic wares. There is no evidence of any great increase in the imports of iron, such as occurred in England during the decades preceding the Civil War. I have found no records of the French trade in foreign iron during Louis XIII's reign. But some thirty years later, when it could hardly have decreased, French iron imports were greatly inferior to English. According to accounts kept by the French government, the average annual imports during the years 1669, 1671, and 1672 amounted to only 3,745 tons of bar iron, 334 tons of pig iron, and 701 tons of iron in other forms including steel and wire. Some of these supplies came, not from foreign countries, but from provinces like Dauphiné, whose products were treated by the customs officials as imports.[187] The English imports of iron from Sweden alone in favorable years for trade were estimated in 1668 at 12,000 tons.[188] Before the Civil War, England, with about a third the population of France, was apparently bringing from abroad a much larger volume of iron for use in her manufactures.[189]

There was only one group of metal commodities for which the French demand was increasing between 1540 and 1640 more than the English. These were the fine artistic wares—such as ornamental balustrades, window grills, entrance locks and knockers, and locks and decorations for strong boxes, with which the court and the nobility embellished their houses—and the more luxurious cutlery which they bought chiefly for display, alongside the glass mirrors, modeled by fugitive Venetians or their pupils, and the beautiful pottery and enamel work done by Bernard Palissy and his followers.[190] Some of these metal wares, like the glass and the pottery, have found their way in our own time into museums and private collections.[191] They were the products of artistic craftsmanship. The monu-

---

the smelters of iron ore for their causing a rise in the price of firewood in a number of French towns, especially at Grenoble and Nevers (Giraud, *op. cit.*, pp. 222–23; Massé, *Monographies nivernaises*, II, 198). But such complaints were not new at Grenoble, and, notwithstanding the alarm of the citizens of Nevers over a possible shortage of wood, both Guy Coquille, a native, and Thomas Coryat, an English traveler, wrote in Henri IV's reign of the abundant store of trees which they saw in Nivernais along the banks of the Loire where the iron mills were at work (Coquille, *op. cit.*, p. 337; *Coryat's Crudities*, I, 197).

[187] Archives Nationales, F¹² 1834ᴬ. A good deal more than two-thirds of the iron and at least three-fifths of the steel entered in these returns certainly came from foreign countries. The remainder was entered under the following customs divisions: *Caen par terre*, which apparently covered the land traffic from Brittany into Normandy, *Maine et Anjou, Chalons et Troyes, Bourges et Moulins, Dijon et Chalons-sur-Saône, Lyon Valence et Bresse,* and *Poitou.* It is not possible to estimate how much of the iron entered under these divisions came from French territory, but it was probably considerable. On the other hand, some imports of foreign iron probably escaped entry in the returns (cf. above, n. 39).

[188] *Calendar of State Papers, Domestic, 1668–69,* p. 140; cf. above, p. 182.

[189] Cf. above, p. 182.

[190] See below, p. 302.

[191] H. R. d'Allemagne, *La ferrurerie ancienne* (2 vols.; Paris, 1924).

mental locks, for example, with their groups of lifelike figures arranged in unified designs, show that the artisans who made them used iron as a medium for expressing their love of beauty, much as the Renaissance sculptors used stone. Some of their works seem to echo the marvelous groups of statues on the screen which surrounds the choir of Chartres Cathedral.[192]

While the fashioning of metal ornaments required much skill and patience, a fine sense of aesthetic values, elaborate and varied labor, the amount of metal consumed in the process was small. Three tons of pig iron were regarded as an adequate supply for the shop of a steelmaker in Dauphiné in 1660,[193] and such shops produced sickles, scythes, and swords, as well as fine steel for artistic cutlery. Following Racine, Diderot once said that the achievement of the artist consists in creating a world out of nothing; and, compared with the anchorsmith or even the nailer or blacksmith, the artistic metalworker of the age of Montaigne was certainly making much out of little. Nor was that little all metal. The cutlers, who forged the knives and razors for courtiers and for other very wealthy people, mounted them in exotic wood, tortoise shell, mother-of-pearl, and ivory, and had to master the craft of manipulating all these materials as well as iron and steel.[194]

In the production of common cutlery—sickles, scythes, and ordinary knives—where a keen cutting edge was of more importance than a beautiful appearance, the English were making more rapid progress than the French. Moulins and St. Etienne, alone among the chief cutlery-producing towns of France, showed a remarkable increase in the number of cutlers between 1540 and 1640. There was a rather rapid growth in the cutlery trade at Thiers, a slow growth at Paris and Chatellerault, the most famous French cutlery centers in the late Middle Ages, and something of a decline at Toulouse.[195] Nowhere in France was there, it seems, an expansion in the volume of cutlery manufacture comparable to that which occurred in London and in and around Sheffield and Birmingham.

Ways of living and standards of comfort were changing in England more rapidly than in France, especially among the common people. At least one of the changes—the adoption of the coal-burning fire—caused a demand for metal little felt across the Channel. To replace logs by coal in the domestic hearth, it was necessary to have an iron grate, and the growing use of coal by rich and poor alike in London, with its tens of thousands of new houses,[196] as well as in scores of provincial towns and villages, was accompanied by a demand for tens of thousands of grates. A

[192] Cf. *ibid.*, Pls. XXXVIII, XLVI, XCII, and CX.
[193] Giraud, "Les épées de Ríves," p. 245.
[194] Pagé, *La coutellerie*, I, 161.
[195] *Ibid.*, I, *passim*.
[196] See below, p. 189.

generation accustomed, like our own, to iron and steel construction would hardly suppose that the general adoption of grates could have caused an impressive increase in metallurgical enterprise. But it should be remembered that the seventeenth century was an age of wood. Metal was still used only where it was indispensable—as for the cutting edges and striking faces of tools and for objects which had to resist fire. Iron grates required more metal than sickles or scythes, shovels or plowshares, and their widespread adoption added substantially to the volume of English metal manufacture.

While metallurgical enterprise was stimulated by the growing demand for metal wares in housekeeping, the remarkable increase during the century from 1540 to 1640 in the tonnage of metal commodities produced in England was probably stimulated even more by the demands of rising industries such as mining, smelting, shipbuilding, and saltmaking.

Mining at depths of more than a hundred feet required what were, for the age, large quantities of metal. Besides the picks and other tools, used even in shallower pits, it involved the use of brass sockets, iron cogs and gears, axles, chains, and gimbals which formed part of the pumping and winding machinery.

The smelting of iron ore by the new roundabout process required metal parts for the machinery which drove the bellows, both at the furnaces and forges. The new forges had, in addition, machine-driven hammers, which were larger than those of the earlier mills and sometimes weighed hundreds of pounds.

Even in an age of wooden ships the builders needed so many metal parts that an Englishman could write shortly before the Civil War, "Navigation on Iron does stand." [197] Every new keel laid upon the stocks at shipyards in Ipswich, Harwich, and other ports not only required a large supply of small metal wares, such as nails, bolts, and clamps, but it had to be provided with heavy anchors and chains. In addition, many merchantmen were armed with cannon to protect them from foreign battleships in time of war and from pirates in time of peace. Still more metalwork was required in building naval vessels. Even before the Anglo-Dutch naval battles of the mid-seventeenth century, the ships of the line bristled with culverins and even larger cannon. Their hulls were sometimes sheathed with iron.

Saltmaking, as it developed in Great Britain after the dissolution of the monasteries, probably required almost as much metal as shipbuilding. The scores of pans in which seawater came to be heated in the north of England were large rectangular basins made of pieces of heavy iron riveted together, two or three feet high on each side and sometimes from twenty to thirty feet across.

As the output of mines, furnaces, forges, and shipyards was growing

[197] Nicholl, *op. cit.* (2d ed.; 1866), pp. 211–13.

more rapidly in England than in France,[198] the markets which these expanding industries provided for metal wares must also have grown more rapidly. By the reign of Charles I, England was probably producing as much iron, more ships, and nearly ten times as much coal as France. And in England coal mining probably required a much larger amount of metal machinery for a given output than in France, because the mines were deeper. The French still produced much more salt than the English, but saltmaking in France required little metal. Nearly all French salt was obtained without artificial heat from seawater at the marshes along the Mediterranean and the Bay of Biscay.[199] On both coasts even as late as the nineteenth century the earth itself formed the rectangular basins in which the saltwater evaporated in the sun; one basin was separated from another by a dyke of earth, and the water was brought to the reservoirs, whence it flowed into these basins, through pipes cut out of tree trunks.[200]

The demands for metal goods were obviously increasing in quantity much more rapidly in England than in France during the century following the Reformation. The hands engaged in hammering out metal wares multiplied in both countries, for French craftsmanship maintained and developed its leadership in the fashioning of artistic metal work, and the service of delight requires a great deal of time and pains. A comparison between the progress of the metal industries in the two countries must take account during this period, even more than in periods before the Reformation, of the differences in the objectives of the craftsmen and of the influence of these objectives on different techniques of workmanship.

Economic history is a recent phenomenon. Coming at a time when economists focused their attention on economic growth and on the value of reductions in labor costs, students of the subject have neglected the importance of beauty. Beauty has a capacity to endure which efficiency by itself lacks. The emphasis laid by French metal workers on delightful results, gives the French metal industries from 1540 to 1640 a distinction of their own which should not be lost sight of. It is no less a part of history than is "economic history," and both subjects suffer by being separated.

---

[198] The same thing was true of the output of breweries, soapworks, and alum and copperas plant (see below, pp. 197 ff.). Such enterprises, with their large cauldrons, sometimes required as large a volume of metal wares as the chief mines and smelting establishments.

[199] Where artificial heat was employed, in the manufacture along the coast of western Normandy (see above, p. 149, n. 17), the seawater was heated, not in great iron pans, but in tiny cauldrons of lead, such as had been used at the English brine springs at least as early as the thirteenth century (Boyé, *Les salines et le sel en Lorraine*, p. 5). In Franche-Comté and Lorraine large pans, similar to those adopted in England for manufacturing salt from seawater, were used to heat the brine from springs at Salins and other less important saltmaking centers. But Franche-Comté and Lorraine were not yet part of the French kingdom (cf. above, p. 105).

[200] Lefebvre, *Le sel*, pp. 77–78, 108–12.

THE BUILDING TRADES AND THE TEXTILE INDUSTRIES

With respect to building, the century from 1540 to 1640 was a period of greater activity in England than in France, especially during the French religious wars (c. 1562–89), when the Elizabethan English were working out their destiny under exceptionally peaceful conditions.[201] Social changes and changes in the technique of construction likely to promote new building were much more pronounced in England, and these changes were of significance in the genesis of the modern industrialized world. The dissolution of the English monasteries, which threw a considerable portion of the land on the market,[202] led to the replacement of old ecclesiastical buildings by new lay manor houses. Abandoned abbeys and priories, with their abundant supplies of dressed and undressed stone, provided cheap materials and became a happy hunting ground for local building contractors.[203] In England the population was increasing considerably, but in France it was practically stationary. There were much more extensive migrations of people from one part of the country to another in England than in France, and these were not altogether movements of vagabonds whose resources, even when they found work in the rising rural industries, only permitted them to build hovels or unpretentious cottages. Yeomen of substance, the younger sons of the landed gentry and even the nobility, were seeking their fortunes in provincial towns and especially in the capital. Between 1540 and 1640 the population of London grew five- or sixfold, while that of Paris increased much more slowly. Even the humble workmen who came to the capital had to be housed, and tenements were built for them in many parts of the city. The rise of the trader and moneylender to positions of affluence and power was carried further in England than across the Channel mainly because private enterprise developed more and more without effective government interference.[204] More wealth was available for expenditure at the private discretion of its possessors. This encouraged the building of new, expensive houses not only in the towns but in the country, where merchants were acquiring manors by the hundreds from the older landed classes, especially the clergy. Lands which had belonged to the church and others which belonged to the crown came on the market in profusion, at a time when the church and the crown retained their possessions in France. So in England property once firmly held by institutions was made available for sale and resale or for leasing on long terms to the advantage of those who were called "improvers." [205] The growing instability of wealth

[201] Nef, *Western Civilization since the Renaissance,* pp. 20–22.
[202] See below, pp. 231 ff.
[203] D. Knoop and G. P. Jones, *The Mediaeval Mason* (Manchester, 1933), p. 189.
[204] Nef, *Industry and Government in France and England,* esp. pp. 135–48.
[205] Cf. below, pp. 232 ff.; Nef, *Industry and Government,* p. 128; *Rise of the British Coal Industry,* pp. 133 ff.

and place in England, which accompanied the rapid rise of the mercantile classes, weakened one of the primary motives that had guided the great medieval builders—that of creating permanent monuments. Old dwellings were torn down and new dwellings built much more readily than in France.

On the technical side the spread of glass windows was more general in England than in France, and the introduction of new fireplaces and chimneys suitable for burning coal was confined almost altogether to England. Both changes encouraged the English to replace old dwellings by new ones, equipped with the new conveniences which were coming to be regarded as essential to comfort. As a consequence there were changes in the objectives of building, away from beauty and endurance in the direction of commodity and immediate satisfaction. The changes pointed toward the nineteenth and twentieth centuries, and were, it is necessary to repeat, a part of what I have called the "early English industrial revolution," which broke down in men's minds and habits barriers standing in the way of the triumph of industrialism.

The scarcity of timber might have checked the growth of building in England, had it not been possible to substitute stone and especially bricks.[206] Lime for solder sometimes had been made by a coal fire even in the Middle Ages, and after about 1610 a method was found which permitted, at least to some extent, the substitution of coal for wood in baking bricks.[207] Thus the amount of timber required in construction work was reduced, and the English building industry largely escaped the difficulties which began to hold back the progress of the metallurgical industries as early as the reign of James I.

When we think of the reigns of Francis I and his successors down through Louis XIII, we are likely to remember the marvelous harmony of the great châteaux along the lower Loire, in Berry, the Île-de-France, and many other parts of the French kingdom. They remain as monuments to the taste and skill of French architects and builders of the Renaissance. The Elizabethan manor houses like Wollaton or Knole, fine though they are, are not quite equal in beauty to castles like Azay-le-Rideau, Chambord, or Anet. We should remember that most of the finest French châteaux were started, and some completed, before 1540.[208] Nor should we forget that people living in Shakespeare's time, who knew both countries, must have been struck chiefly by the thousands of new, if more prosaic, dwellings of stone and brick with their chimneys, built in London, Norwich, Newcastle, Nottingham, and other towns, and also by the fine manor houses, set in newly laid-out parks and frequently paid for with the money of merchants who retired from trade or married their daughters into the gentry and the nobility. French merchants were acquiring many *fiefs* and *seigneuries* and

---

[206] Knoop and Jones, *op. cit.*, p. 190; Nef, *Rise of the British Coal Industry*, I, 187.
[207] *Ibid.*, I, 205, 216–17.
[208] Cf. Boissonnade, *Le Socialisme d'état*, p. 38.

were building expensive houses both in the country and in the towns, but these new houses were nothing like as numerous as those of English merchants.

In the days of Shakespeare and Milton, Londoners who sauntered out for an afternoon stroll were accustomed to the constant noise of saws and hammers and to the sight of dozens of new dwellings in various stages of construction, with carpenters, masons, plasterers, and bricklayers busy at their trades. As in the growing American cities of the late nineteenth and early twentieth centuries, houses were put up helter-skelter, often with a complete disregard of the building rules promulgated by the crown.[209] Early in 1637, no less than two hundred new buildings, erected in Wapping during the previous summer, were ordered to be torn down because they did not conform to the regulations.[210] London expanded in every direction into areas once meadows and woodlands, and absorbed old villages. The brickmakers were charged with spoiling the neighboring fields in their search for earth.[211]

The last years of the sixteenth century and the early part of the seventeenth were marked not only in London but in many parts of England by a greatly increased demand for new dwellings of all kinds. At the same time hundreds of sheds, barns, and houses to serve as workshops were put up in connection with the expanding industries. In France, to judge from the history of Rouen—the most important mercantile town after Lyons and Paris—this was probably a period of slower growth in building than the last half of the fifteenth and the first half of the sixteenth century.[212]

The period of Elizabeth I and the first two Stuarts was, then, an exceptionally busy time for the building trades, both compared to the English past and to contemporary France. The chief contrasts were to be found not in the scale of building operations, but in the quantity and the kinds of building which was done. Since at least the eleventh and twelfth centuries building in Europe had been capitalistic in the sense that the major construction works had required very heavy expenditures. The capital invested in one of the chief cathedrals strikes us even today as stupendous, when we allow for the small population of most cathedral towns and for the great value of money during Romanesque and Gothic times. The novelty of building activity in England during the late sixteenth and seventeenth centuries consisted in the extent to which the capitals employed in building were directed toward utility, both domestic and industrial. Never before in European history had there been in an area of equal size and

---

[209] For these rules see W. Cunningham, *The Growth of English Industry and Commerce: Modern Times* (6th ed.; Cambridge, 1919), pp. 315–17.

[210] *Calendar of State Papers, Domestic,* 1636–37, p. 542. The State Papers for the reigns of James I and Charles I are full of evidence concerning the extraordinary activity of the builders in London and the attempts of the crown to regulate it.

[211] *Ibid.,* 1637–38, p. 107.

[212] R. Quenedey, *L'habitation rouennaise* (Rouen, 1926), pp. 56–58, 77–78.

population such extensive investments in houses designed to serve for domestic commodity and in industrial structures needed to facilitate the progress of mining and manufacturing. The new directions taken by the construction industry in England prepared the way for the experiences of modern urbanization, where so much that is built is intended to be superseded. In the processes of concentrating to an unprecedented degree on utility, the English were removing obstacles in traditions and habits to the kinds of industrial expansion which the modern world takes for granted. The cities, towns, and villages, and the industrial centers within them, were rebuilt between the sixteenth and eighteenth centuries, to be rebuilt again and differently in the nineteenth and again in the twentieth century. The evolution of building which began in the age of the first Elizabeth and the early Stuarts helped to break down barriers to industrialization during a time when building in France was undergoing a slower, more traditional evolution.

There was perhaps less difference between the progress of the textile manufactures than between that of the building trades in the two countries. But the contrasts were of a similar kind. In some branches of textile work the French retained and increased their lead over the English. These were mainly the making of silk and lace goods and of tapestries, wanted as luxury articles and objects of art chiefly by the court, the nobility, the richer merchants, and churchmen. When it came to the production of more homely wares—woven out of cotton, hemp, flax, and, above all, wool—for which the demand was more widespread, the positions of the two countries were different. Of the more common textile fabrics, woolens were undoubtedly the most important, though in France the manufacture of woolen cloth did not exceed that of linen by as big a margin as in England.[213]

The great advantage held by the English over the French in the manufacture of woolen cloth of most kinds throughout the *ancien régime* is one of the commonplaces of economic history. Everywhere in France the growth of the manufacture was handicapped by a partial dependence on foreign countries for raw materials, for wool itself, and for the alum[214] needed in dyeing. While the woolens produced in a few provinces like

---

[213] Fagniez tells us that the production of linens in France was more important than the production of woolens. But, if he means that the output was greater, he offers no evidence in support of that view except a passage in Montchrétien, suggesting that linen goods formed a more valuable branch of exports than woolen (Fagniez, *L'économie sociale de la France*, pp. 138–42). The late M. Raveau's careful study only partly bears out Fagniez, insofar as Poitou is concerned. In one place Raveau says that *tisserands en toile* were more numerous than *tisserands en drap ou en serge*, but in another he speaks of the manufacture of woolen cloth as the most important industry of Poitou (Raveau, *Essai sur la situation économique et l'état social en Poitou*, pp. 28, 5).

[214] See below, pp. 202–3.

Poitou had some market in other parts of the kingdom,[215] there was no general concentration of the manufacture of ordinary cloth, such as had already taken place in England in the west country before our period, and such as was taking place during it in East Anglia and in Lancashire and the West Riding. French exports of woolen cloth were small compared with imports, and those came from Italy, Flanders, and, especially, England.[216]

It is not clear which of the two countries had an advantage in the output of cotton goods in the seventeenth century. But the use of cotton undoubtedly increased more rapidly between 1540 and 1640 in England than in France, where nothing occurred comparable to the remarkable extension of cotton manufacture in Lancashire. Throughout the period England imported some fustians from abroad, but by 1620 she had begun to export substantial quantities to France and also to Spain, Holland, and Germany.[217] Already in the reign of Henri IV the principal French centers of fustian manufacture at Rouen and Troyes suffered from foreign, and particularly English, competition.[218]

While the French had probably fallen behind the English in cotton manufacture, it is possible that they made more linen goods from flax and hemp than the English during the whole of our period. But if they had an advantage here, it could not have offset their heavy disadvantage in the woolen manufacture.

When wealthy Englishmen began to grumble toward the end of the seventeenth century over the prohibitively high duties levied by successive Parliaments upon imports, some of them complained that, if French clothing were effectively shut out, they would no longer be able to distinguish their wives from their chambermaids! Ladies of fashion were getting their fine dresses from Paris as they have done ever since. While these ladies often had most elaborate wardrobes, they were few in number. The amount of cloth in the dresses of ladies who could afford chambermaids was small compared with the volume of all kinds of cloth produced. By the mid-seventeenth century, if not before, the common people, who formed the overwhelming majority of the population in both countries, had come in all probability to be more amply provided with clothing, bedding, and hangings in England than in France.

It does not follow that nothing was being done for the people by the rather different evolution of work in France. The fashioning of artistic wares made a contribution of its own to civilization, a contribution which remains to be explored. The genesis of industrialism is not to be found simply in the collapse of those barriers in thought and habits which hin-

[215] Raveau, *op. cit.*, pp. 20–22.
[216] Fagniez, *op. cit.*, pp. 83, 137–38.
[217] Wadsworth and Mann, *Cotton Trade and Industrial Lancashire*, p. 21.
[218] Fagniez, *op. cit.*, p. 142.

dered quantitative progress, but also in qualitative hopes, such as a love of delight, which were fostered by the evolution of the artistic crafts, by the work fashioned by craftsmen and artists.[219]

More has probably been written during the past hundred and fifty years about the European textile industries than about any other subject of industrial history. By focusing attention on questions concerning the capitalistic organization of these industries, historical writers have fostered, in some ways, a misleading outlook upon the part played by clothmaking and its numerous auxiliary trades in the origins of industrialism. Karl Marx related the growth of these trades in England during the times of the first Elizabeth and the early Stuarts to what he singled out as an important stage in the evolution of a capitalistic society. What he called the regime of "manufactures"—a regime which he associated especially with the England of that time—consisted of large blocks of capital, raised by individuals or partnerships, in order to multiply not so much the workpeople they employed in a single plant, as those who labored for them for wages at home with wool, cotton, yarn, and cloth put out in various stages of production. Marx distinguished this form of capitalistic organization from "machinofacture," which gave rise to large factories and came, as he supposed, two centuries afterward at the time of what under the influence of Toynbee the elder, has been called *the* industrial revolution.

Since Marx wrote, further historical research has shown how extensive the form of capitalistic organization—which developed rapidly in English clothmaking, as he correctly observed, from Elizabethan times—had been on the Continent before the Reformation and even during the twelfth and thirteenth centuries, especially in Italy, the Low Countries, and northern France. In these areas, at the time of the Renaissance, textile materials were frequently put out by a single firm with central warehouses, to hundreds of workpeople engaged in various textile operations. These operations were designed, when skilfully interrelated by agents of the "capitalist" owners, to produce fine cloth of many descriptions and beautiful colors. Also, tidy sums were frequently invested in small plant for silk throwing, fulling, dyeing, and for many finishing processes where water-driven machinery was used.[220]

The rapid progress of many branches of clothmaking in England at the juncture of the sixteenth and seventeenth centuries was far from being "revolutionary," therefore, in so far as "capitalism" is concerned. Actually, in spite of the slower growth of industry in France, *ateliers*—considerable workshops—representing substantial investments of capital in a single establishment were probably more frequent in French than in English seventeenth-century clothmaking. These French workshops were usually under the tutelage of the crown. They formed part of an early French

[219] Nef, *Cultural Foundations of Industrial Civilization*, pp. 127–39, and *passim*.
[220] Cf. above, pp. 84–85.

"system of manufactures" different from that to which Marx gave the name. Their *raison d'être* was often the making of beautiful tapestries and other artistic wares in the fashioning of which the English seldom competed with the French. As fantasy and improvisation, together with formal artistic discipline, were essential to the results sought, there was relatively little pressure under the French "system of manufactures," except possibly in the throwing of silk, to supplant handwork by power-driven machinery such as was being done in England and Holland on a small scale with the stocking-knitting frame, invented by William Lee apparently about 1589, and with the so-called Dutch loom for making ribbons and other kinds of small wares.

In England, as elsewhere, the *basic* operations in textiles—spinning and weaving—were the last, not the first, great processes of manufacture to be invaded by machinery.[221] Artistic craftsmanship as practiced in the larger French workshops raised a barrier to the use of machinery.[222] During the depression of 1929–33, when there was a reversion to fine tapestry-making at Aubusson, in central France, hand looms were installed in the factories alongside the power-driven looms rendered temporarily silent.

What was novel about the progress of English textiles in Elizabethan and Stuart times, was the growing emphasis, in connection with almost every kind of clothmaking from hats to underwear, on the supply of homely and substantial warm commodities for larger numbers of consumers. As a consequence, clothmaking in England was much riper than in France for the eventual adoption, in order to increase output, of power-driven machinery. During the eighteenth century English mechanics almost invariably taught the French how to introduce machinery driven by water and horse power and eventually by steam. The utilitarian character of the industrial expansion which began in Elizabethan times in England created, in clothmaking as in many other industries, conditions more inviting to the coming of industrialism than had hitherto existed in Europe. The greater emphasis placed on quantity as compared with quality was the "revolutionary" element in the progress of English textile "manufactures" at the juncture of the sixteenth and seventeenth centuries. As a result of this new emphasis, brakes that interfered with the concentration of capital in machinery and furnaces for the sake of mass production were released.

THE "NEW" MANUFACTURES

Between the birth of Leonardo da Vinci, in 1452, and the death of Francis Bacon, in 1626, there was a remarkable development in Europe

---

[221] See the remarks of the late George Unwin quoted by Wadsworth and Mann, *op. cit.*, p. 97.

[222] I have assembled considerable material on this subject which I hope to treat in more detail in later work.

of industries like printing and tobacco-rolling, which were entirely novel; of others like the making of paper, soap, sugar, and gunpowder, for which the demand had been slight; and of still others like the making of alum, for which Europe had been mainly dependent upon the older civilizations in the Near and Far East. While none of these "new" manufactures employed as many workpeople in seventeenth-century Europe as the older industries such as building or textiles, the laborers employed in all of them, taken together, ran into a great many thousands in every important country.

Their development had a significance beyond that which can be measured by the number of hands engaged. Most of them required machinery or furnaces, cisterns, boilers, and other equipment which cost hundreds, and in some cases thousands, of pounds in money of that time, worth perhaps more than twenty times as much as English money now. Consequently the making of alum, soap, or gunpowder, unlike the weaving of cloth, the grinding of knives, or the forging of nails, called for much more capital than groups of small craftsmen could possibly muster. Nor was there as much opposition to the establishment of large-scale enterprise in the new industries as in the old. Regulations of the gilds and of municipal governments, inherited from the Middle Ages and designed to restrict the number of journeymen and apprentices who could work for a single master, were more difficult to apply and to enforce than in the older industries, where they had the support of long-established custom. In these new manufactures some of the enterprises employed many workmen—a dozen, a score, or even more—laboring in buildings reconstructed or built specially for manufacturing, instead of in the cellars or garrets or small shops which continued to serve most of the craftsmen in the textile and the metal finishing trades. Some of the new industries, such as alum- and copperas-making, developed mainly—like mining, smelting, and saltmaking—in rural areas, but there were others, such as printing, soap-boiling, sugar-refining, and brewing, which invaded the old towns.

In those towns homework had been the rule. During the Middle Ages they had been largely free from considerable establishments specially built or extensively remodeled for manufacturing purposes. By no means all the town ventures in these "new" industries broke with tradition in this respect. There were soapmakers, printers, and even gunpowder makers who carried on the business in their homes, and home brewing almost certainly remained the common form of enterprise in most English towns in the reign of Charles I. Nevertheless, the rise of the new industries did much to establish, in those ancient citadels of domestic work, more extensive workshops, in which, however, it was common for the master owner to maintain his residence and to work beside his employees—a method of industrial organization also favored in the artistic industries, such as tapestry-making.

Were the new manufactures growing more rapidly in England or in

France during the century following the Reformation? Did they occupy a more prominent place in the kingdom of Charles I or in that of Louis XIII?

Thomas More, who wrote in his *Utopia* about the harm done to men's morals by gold and silver and the benefits which mankind derived from iron, had practically nothing to say about the products of what I am calling the "new" manufactures. Even at his death, in 1535, these industries were carried on in Great Britain in a very small way, without the machinery or the large furnaces and boilers which were already common in some regions of the Continent. Their rapid development in the island kingdom began in the 1540's and 1550's and became most striking during and after the seventies.

A little gunpowder had been made in England as early as the reign of Henry VI.[223] In 1554 or 1555, not long after the introduction into Sussex of the method of casting iron cannons, a mill was established in Surrey,[224] and the manufacture of gunpowder, like that of saltpeter, which was indispensable in its production, grew under Queen Elizabeth I. She is said to have begun by putting the industry in the hands of Dutchmen and by paying one of them to teach two of her subjects how to produce saltpeter.[225] As early as 1561, it was being made in some quantities.[226] While the kingdom remained partly dependent a decade later upon imports of gunpowder, as well as of saltpeter,[227] the proportion of the supplies of both obtained from domestic manufactures increased during Elizabeth's reign. Commissioners for saltpeter were appointed by the crown, and in 1588 English powder mills were so important that these commissioners planned to supply them by a considerable manufacture of saltpeter in many counties.[228]

At a time when sewage disposal was still primitive, the saltpeter men appointed to obtain the raw materials came to be regarded everywhere as a nuisance by householders, particularly the poorer sort. Armed with a royal warrant, which permitted them to enter private as well as public property, they ransacked the incrustations of buildings and barns for peterish earth to boil in specially constructed copper kettles set in iron frames.[229] Their disregard of personal privacy was carried to such lengths, according to reports, that they entered even the bedchambers of the dying and of women in childbirth.[230] People became so incensed that they tried to prevent the growth of peterish earth in and near their homes.[231]

[223] British Museum, Sloane MSS, 1039, fol. 93.
[224] *Victoria County History, Surrey*, II, 246.
[225] For a fuller account of the progress of the saltpeter and gunpowder manufacture in England, see Nef, *Industry and Government*, pp. 89–98.
[226] *Calendar of State Papers, Domestic*, 1547–80, p. 172.
[227] *Ibid.*, p. 117; Addenda, 1566–79, p. 495.
[228] British Museum, Lansdowne MSS, 58, No. 63; Harleian MSS, 1926, No. 118.
[229] Cf. Star Chamber Proceedings (Public Record Office, London), 8/173/27.
[230] Lipson, *The Economic History of England*, III, 358–59.
[231] *Calendar of State Papers, Domestic*, 1628–29, p. 101.

Whether or not this tussle was responsible, the English saltpeter commissioners do not appear to have got impressive results in terms of output. Although saltpeter was manufactured at the end of the sixteenth and beginning of the seventeenth centuries in and around London, in the north and west of England, and in Wales,[232] the annual output in 1636 did not much exceed three hundred tons, a figure which apparently had been reached already in 1589.[233] The progress of the manufacture was held up by a shortage of wood ashes as well as of peterish earth.[234]

The output of gunpowder, unlike that of saltpeter, seems to have increased during the reigns of James I and Charles I. In 1600 the crown patentee, who had been granted a monopoly of the gunpowder manufacture, was bound to supply the queen every year with one hundred lasts, a shade more than one hundred tons.[235] By 1626, the holder of the patent—John Evelyn, an uncle of the diarist—was under contract to deliver twenty lasts a month.[236] Both he and his successor, Samuel Cordewell, sometimes fell short in their deliveries for want of adequate supplies of saltpeter. The restrictions placed on its importation to relieve the saltpeter commissioners from foreign competition were proving a handicap to the native manufacture of gunpowder;[237] and, as the crown, in preparation for war, was sometimes obliged to import considerable quantities of *that*,[238] the admiralty officials felt that neither the saltpeter nor the gunpowder monopoly was giving the desired results. On more than one occasion it was suggested that both be abandoned and that any man be allowed to manufacture gunpowder from foreign saltpeter.[239] That policy was not adopted until 1641.[240] But the attempts to enforce the saltpeter and gunpowder monopolies were not very successful.[241] Some saltpeter was imported,[242] and gunpowder was

[232] *Ibid.*, 1581–90, pp. 112, 607, 612, 623; 1591–94, p. 187; 1595–97, p. 153 1625–26, p. 490; 1627–28, p. 480; Star Chamber Proceedings, 8/128/18 and 19; *State Papers Domestic*, Charles I, Vol. CCCXLI, No. 68. By 1591 London was receiving shipments of saltpeter from Hull (Exchequer K. R. Port Books [Public Record Office], 9/3). For material on the subject, see also Nef, *Rise of the British Coal Industry*, I, 186 n.

[233] *Ibid.*, p. 211; cf. *Calendar of State Papers, Domestic*, 1595–97, p. 153, where there is a reference to an annual output of three hundred *lasts* of saltpeter. A *last* of saltpeter was apparently equivalent to about 2,100 lb., a *last* of gunpowder to about 2,400 lb. (*ibid.*, 1635, p. 57; 1598–1601, p. 471).

[234] See, e.g., *Calendar of State Papers, Domestic*, 1635–36, pp. 358, 433.

[235] *Ibid.*, 1598–1601, p. 471.

[236] *Ibid.*, 1625–26, p. 236.

[237] *Ibid.*, 1637, p. 188; 1638–39, p. 443; 1640–41, p. 313.

[238] *Ibid.*, 1625–26, p. 236. But there were occasions when the crown was over-supplied, and license was granted to export gunpowder (*ibid.*, 1580–1625, p. 522).

[239] *Ibid.*, 1625–26, p. 236; 1635–36, p. 20.

[240] Cunningham, *The Growth of English Industry and Commerce, Modern Times*, p. 61.

[241] *Calendar of State Papers, Domestic*, 1627–28, p. 492; 1633–34, p. 290; 1637–38, pp. 32, 150.

[242] Cf. *ibid.*, 1638–39, p. 443.

made outside the patent at Bristol, where there were three or four horse mills at the beginning of Charles I's reign, at Battle in Sussex, in Dorset where there were water mills,[243] and also on a smaller scale at various places in the west of England.[244] In the late thirties of the seventeenth century Cordewell managed to deliver most of the 240 lasts a year which he had promised.[245] As a good deal of powder was made outside the patent, the annual production in England probably exceeded three hundred lasts.

The mills of the patentees and their associates were all to the south of London, some along the Thames.[246] Those of the Evelyns at Long Ditton and Godstone, and the one built by Cordewell at a place called Chilworth in Surrey,[247] apparently took up almost as much space with their dams and waterwheels and the specially built buildings for drying the product, as the new smelting furnaces.

The brewing of beer, as distinct from ale, was also something of a novelty in the sixteenth century. Before the reign of Henry VIII, what little beer was drunk in England was either imported or brewed at home by foreign craftsmen from foreign-grown hops. Nor was this beverage then much esteemed. By the 1540's beer was still regarded by an Englishman as "a naturall drynke for a docheman." But its consumption was increasing; for the same writer adds, "of late dayes it is moche used in Englande to the detryment of many Englyshemen, speciyally it kylleth them the which be troubled with the Colyeke and the stone. . . ."[248] Rapid progress in the native manufacture of beer began with the domestic growing of hops, which were hardly cultivated at all in England until shortly before 1549. By the beginning of Elizabeth's reign the condition of the English brewing industry had changed so greatly that an appeal was made to the queen for license to export three thousand tons of beer.[249]

We do not know whether this beer really attacked those who suffered from "colyeke and stone." If it did, their health probably deteriorated rapidly under the first Elizabeth! By 1585 the annual production of the London breweries alone was estimated at 648,960 barrels—or upward of

[243] Ibid., 1627–28, p. 493.
[244] Ibid., 1628–29, pp. 118, 544. The saltpeter commissioners also made some gunpowder on their own account, and the East India Company apparently carried on a manufacture with Indian saltpeter (ibid., 1637–38, p. 242; 1627–28, p. 492).
[245] Ibid., 1637, p. 548; 1638–39, p. 118; 1639–40, p. 67; 1640–41, p. 303.
[246] On the Thames there were small works at Windsor, Henley, and other places, which were apparently in operation only once in every six or seven years (State Papers Domestic, Charles I, Vol. CCCXCIII, No. 13). Whether these works and the mills at a place called Halten, in Middlesex, and at another place called Redriffe (Star Chamber Proceedings, 8/128/18 and 19; 8/219/21) were operated under an agreement with the holder of the gunpowder patent is uncertain.
[247] Calendar of State Papers, Domestic, 1639–40, p. 512.
[248] Hubert H. Parker, The Hop Industry (London, 1934), pp. 5–7.
[249] Calendar of State Papers, Domestic, 1547–80, p. 119.

150,000 tons.[250] This was more than half the output in the capital nearly two centuries later,[251] when the population had almost certainly more than doubled. A decisive change in English drinking habits seems to have occurred between about 1540 to 1580. The Londoner in Shakespeare's time apparently drank at least as much beer as his descendants in the times of Johnson or of Dickens, and a good deal more than the Londoner today. English brewers, whose predecessors had learned their craft from the Dutch and the Flemish, had become so proficient by the 1590's that they were exporting beer in large quantities even to Ostend, Flushing, and other places in the Low Countries.[252] The annual exports to all foreign nations already amounted to many thousands of tons.[253]

During the early decades of the seventeenth century there was apparently a further development of brewing, especially in provincial towns,[254] where innkeepers and alehouse-keepers, who made their own beer, were frequently regarded as competitors by persons who specialized in the manufacture.[255] In the reign of Charles I, there were scores of brewers in most important counties. One table, apparently incomplete, listed 643 in England and Wales.[256] Their products were reaching even the humblest; for in the seventeenth century beer and ale had become, next to bread, the chief stay of the poor. As a gallon of "wholesome small beer" sometimes sold for as little as a penny, at a time when the diet of the ordinary person was changing toward the most reasonably priced foods,[257] it is no wonder that the consumption of beer per capita should have been greater than in our own time.

The "early industrial revolution" in England consisted partly in these changing material habits. Soon after the English began to drench their bodies with beer, they adopted another custom which stained their nostrils and lungs no less than the smoke from the multiplying seacoal fires. Before the end of the sixteenth century tobacco was being brought from America, and the manufacture of smokers' pipes had begun. During the first two decades of the seventeenth century tobacco growing spread scarcely less rapidly than hop cultivation through many English counties, to the despair of the king's advisers, who wanted the land reserved for growing grain. The king himself was strongly against the weed. But, in

---

[250] British Museum, Lansdowne MSS, 71, fol. 53. The barrel contained thirty-six gallons. Four of the sixteenth-century barrels appear to have been roughly equivalent to a ton (*Calendar of State Papers, Domestic, 1591–94*, pp. 136, 192).

[251] Parker, *op. cit.*, p. 45.

[252] *Calendar of State Papers, Domestic, 1581–90*, p. 693; 1591–94, pp. 115, 508, 574.

[253] *Ibid.*, 1598–1601, pp. 87–88.

[254] That is the impression conveyed by the *Calendar of State Papers, Domestic, passim*.

[255] E.g., *ibid.*, 1637, p. 49; 1637–38, p. 108.

[256] *Ibid.*, 1637–38, pp. 108–9.

[257] *Ibid.*, pp. 580–81.

spite of statutes and proclamations prohibiting its planting, and in spite of orders to the militia to tramp it down wherever they found it growing, tobacco raising was not completely stamped out until at least the end of the seventeenth century.[258] For all that, the supplies of homegrown tobacco never satisfied the increasing demands of smokers. Partly as a result of the original proclamation of 1619 against tobacco growing in England, and of another proclamation of 1625 prohibiting the importation of all tobacco except that of Virginia or the Bermudas,[259] the imports from Virginia increased from 20,000 pounds in 1619 to 1,300,000 pounds in 1631.[260] Before that year, tobacco-rolling[261] and the baking of pipes in London and in Shropshire had taken their places, along with saltpeter and gunpowder-making and beer-brewing, as established English manufactures.

By the beginning of the seventeenth century it had become an important objective of English economic policy to encourage the finishing processes in the textile industry—scouring, fulling, dyeing, and dressing—by restricting and even prohibiting the export of cloth undyed and undressed. The attempt, in James I's reign, to prohibit altogether the export of unfinished cloth would have proved a much greater calamity than it did for the spinners and weavers,[262] who were still partly dependent on foreign markets, had it not been for the growing domestic manufacture of four materials indispensable in the finishing processes: alum, which was needed for dyeing in all colors; copperas or green vitriol for dyeing in black; soap for scouring cloth as well as wool; and starch for dressing.

After the first important European alumworks had been established in 1462 in the lands of the popes,[263] the papacy set out to monopolize the supplies for Europe, partly, no doubt, as a means of maintaining and increasing the substantial revenue it obtained from the new industry. It also professed a holier motive. In their efforts to defeat the infidel, successive popes threatened to excommunicate, not only the traders who sold alum obtained from the Near East, but also the civil and religious authorities who tolerated such commerce. These threats never had much effect upon the English trade in Levantine alum; and, before the middle of the seventeenth century, the efforts of the papacy to furnish the English market were rendered futile by the rise of a native alum-making industry.

During the first part of Elizabeth's reign many attempts were made to develop the manufacture in England,[264] first on the Isle of Wight, where

---

[258] Lipson, *op. cit.*, III, pp. 169–71.

[259] *Calendar of State Papers, Domestic*, 1625–26, p. 7. Licenses were granted, however, permitting the import of some foreign tobacco (*ibid.*, p. 576; 1627–28, p. 58).

[260] C. M. MacInnes, *The Early English Tobacco Trade* (London, 1926), p. 134.

[261] Cf. *Calendar of State Papers, Domestic*, 1638–39, pp. 546–47.

[262] Cf. Friis, *Alderman Cockayne's Project*, esp. chaps. v and vi.

[263] See above, p. 74.

[264] *Calendar of State Papers, Domestic*, 1547–80, pp. 253, 277, 443, 534; W. H. Price, *The English Patents of Monopoly* (Cambridge, Mass., 1906), p. 82.

alumstones had apparently been discovered before 1346.[265] These attempts met with indifferent success, but they seem to have brought about an improvement in the quality and an increase in the quantity of the domestic product.[266] In 1581 Burghley felt that the English supplies were satisfactory enough for him to embark on a policy of levying duties on papal alum.[267] By the accession of James I, abundant fresh deposits of stones had been found in Yorkshire—near Whitby,[268] in Durham—at Hartlepool,[269] and probably in other counties. A proclamation prohibiting the import of all foreign alum was passed as early as 1609.[270]

Two years earlier the crown tried to establish a monopoly of alum manufacture in the hands of a group of royal patentees, who invested many thousands of pounds in building near Whitby a series of large alum houses, each of which contained brick cisterns and furnaces and large metal pans and employed about sixty workmen.[271] The output of all these houses did not ordinarily exceed 1,000 tons a year between 1609 and 1618,[272] and it fell to 313 tons on the average between 1619 and 1624.[273] But there was a great improvement in the productivity of the enterprise during the thirties.[274]

The Yorkshire works were not the only source of domestic supplies. Notwithstanding the exclusive patent granted to their owners, an alum factory, owned at one time by Lord Lumley, a great Durham landowner, and started at Hartlepool at least as early as 1600, was apparently in pretty continual operation during the reigns of James I and Charles I.[275] Between them the enterprises at Hartlepool and in Yorkshire produced upward of 2,000 tons a year in the late thirties of the seventeenth century,[276] and

[265] Salzman, *English Industries of the Middle Ages*, p. 208.

[266] *Calendar of State Papers, Domestic*, Addenda, 1566–79, p. 344.

[267] *Ibid.*, 1581–90, p. 16.

[268] Price, *op. cit.*, p. 83.

[269] Public Record Office, London: Exchequer K. R. Port Books, 185/10, which shows that coal was imported at Hartlepool for use at the alum pans in 1600.

[270] *Calendar of State Papers, Domestic*, 1603–10, p. 521. The proclamation was renewed later (*ibid.*, 1611–18, pp. 256, 527).

[271] For the history of the royal alumworks see Price, *op. cit.*, pp. 83–100.

[272] British Museum, Lansdowne MSS, 152, No. 6, fol. 17.

[273] Price, *op. cit.*, p. 95.

[274] Nef, *Rise of the British Coal Industry*, I, 209; Price, *op. cit.*, pp. 97–98; *Calendar of State Papers, Domestic*, 1637–38, pp. 33, 97.

[275] Public Record Office, London: Exchequer K. R. Port Books, 185/10, 186/2; Exchequer Depositions by Commission, 9 Charles I, Mich. 11 (testimony of Sir John Hedworth).

[276] This is partly based on our knowledge that the two enterprises consumed upward of 7,000 tons of coal annually during the decade preceding the Civil War (Nef, *Rise of the British Coal Industry*, I, 209). By 1637 the works in Yorkshire alone were apparently producing 1,800 or 2,000 tons of alum per annum (*Calendar of State Papers, Domestic*, 1637, p. 152; 1637–38, p. 97).

there were smaller alum producers elsewhere.[277] As the alum required to supply the whole realm had been estimated in 1595 at rather less than 500 tons,[278] it is plain that the domestic manufacture had made great strides since the death of Queen Elizabeth. The dyeing industry, which was said to be growing to perfection as early as 1593,[279] must have benefited. Although papal alum was still smuggled into the country during the reign of James I, in defiance of proclamations prohibiting its importation,[280] the aim of the crown to make England independent of foreign supplies seems to have been realized on the eve of the Civil War, when English production apparently exceeded that of the papal estates.[281] A small export trade, destined to grow considerably in the late seventeenth century, had begun.

A similar position was secured with regard to supplies of copperas. Most of the projectors who tried to develop the manufacture of alum in Elizabeth's reign proposed to combine it with the manufacture of copperas, and their efforts seem to have met with some success.[282] Copperas works were also started independently of alum houses.[283] In the seventeenth century a combination of the copperas with the alum manufacture proved impracticable, because copperas stones were found in different localities from alumstones. After Elizabeth's reign the two industries were carried on separately, the manufacture of copperas mainly in southeastern England, where one of the chief enterprises was at Queenborough in Kent.[284] But the industries were still linked together in the minds of many subjects. In 1655 the value of all the alum and copperas annually produced was estimated at £55,000,[285] many millions of dollars in terms of today's money.

Soap had been so scarce in England early in the sixteenth century that urine was widely used for cleaning wool preparatory to spinning and weaving. Along with the building of alum and copperas factories in rural areas during the reigns of Elizabeth and her two successors, went the establish-

---

[277] E.g., in Dorset (ibid., 1629–31, p. 553). There was an alum house in London near the Tower at the beginning of Charles I's reign, but it was suppressed in 1627 (ibid., 1627–28, pp. 269–70, 274). Alumstones were discovered near Newcastle-on-Tyne in 1612 (Lansdowne MSS, 152, No. 6, fol. 111), and in the twenties there was talk of transferring the royal works from Yorkshire to the Tyne valley (Price, op. cit., p. 97). Small quantities of alum were exported from Newcastle in the thirties (Exchequer K. R. Port Books, bdl. 191).

[278] I.e., 8,000 or 10,000 quintals (Calendar of State Papers, Domestic, 1595–97, p. 102).

[279] Ibid., 1591–94, p. 337.

[280] Nef, Rise of the British Coal Industry, I, 185.

[281] Jean Delumeau, L'Alun de Rome (Paris, 1962), p. 126.

[282] Calendar of State Papers, Domestic, 1547–80, pp. 253, 272, 277, 436, 440; 1581–90, p. 32.

[283] Ibid., 1591–94, p. 570.

[284] Nef, Rise of the British Coal Industry, I, 185.

[285] Public Record Office, London: State Papers Domestic, Interregnum, Vol. XCIV, No. 106.

ment of a number of soap factories in London, which became the principal center for supplying the entire kingdom.[286] Many starch houses of considerable size were started during the same period. Before the Civil War about forty were in operation, and one of them was said to consume annually fifteen hundred quarters or more of wheat.[287] The London soap factories were producing something like five thousand tons of soap a year in the thirties of the seventeenth century,[288] and soap houses in the western counties—some of the most important of them at Bristol and Exeter[289]—nearly again as much.[290]

The remarkable progress between 1540 and 1640 of these "new" manufactures—and of others such as printing, papermaking, sugar refining, and pottery-making—had greatly improved England's industrial position in Europe. Before the middle of the seventeenth century she had already established a striking lead over France in the manufacture of alum, beer, tobacco, and smokers' pipes.

France was apparently producing little alum.[291] The French dyers, in the sixteenth century, were dependent mainly upon that which came from the Levant or from Italy or Spain.[292] Before the end of Louis XIII's reign France had probably begun to import supplies from England and from the neighborhood of Liège, where the alum manufacture, helped no doubt by the local supplies of coal, was developing at about the same time as in Yorkshire and Durham.[293] Savary des Bruslons, who was not given to minimizing the importance of his country's industries, wrote early in the eighteenth century that France was still entirely dependent upon foreign alum. England, together with Italy and the principality of Liège, had come

---

[286] *Calendar of State Papers, Domestic,* 1547–80, pp. 605, 692.

[287] British Museum, Cotton MSS, Titus B. V. fol. 388. This document, which deals with the consumption of wheat in starchmaking, is undated, but it apparently belongs to the reign of either James I or Charles I.

[288] The figure is for 1637 (Public Record Office, London: Exch. K. R. Accts., Various 634/15).

[289] *Calendar of State Papers, Domestic,* 1635, pp. 62, 69; 1638–39, p. 240.

[290] Scott, *Joint-Stock Companies to 1720,* I, 211, 213–14; S. R. Gardiner, *History of England* (London, 1901), VIII, 72, 75. Cf. *Calendar of State Papers, Domestic,* 1636–37, p. 51. For soapmaking at various places in the west country, see *ibid.,* 1637–38, p. 142. Some soap was also made at York and Newcastle-on-Tyne (*ibid.,* 1639, pp. 5, 363–64; 1639–40, p. 602).

[291] In 1611 and again in 1615 the crown, by decree and letters patent, granted a certain Jérôme Comens the right to manufacture alum anywhere in the kingdom where he could find stones (*Inventaire des archives départementales,* Haute-Garonne, B. 1913, fols. 165, 169). But little apparently came of the grant.

[292] *Inventaire des archives départementales,* Bouches-du-Rhône, B. 3326, fols. 150, 155; Archives du Nord (Lille), B. 1834, fols. 22–24, 48–51. I am very grateful to M. Georges Espinas and to M. de Saint Aubin, the chief archivist at Lille, for helping me to obtain copies of these and other documents in the archives départementales.

[293] Archives du Nord (Lille), B. 1835, fols. 173–76, 178–80, 229–48.

to furnish the bulk of French supplies, although a small portion still came from Asia Minor.[294]

Little beer was made anywhere in France except in the north. In Flanders, Artois, and Picardy, brewing was carried on extensively in the sixteenth and early seventeenth centuries at Lille, Cambrai, Arras, and a number of other towns and in some villages.[295] But Flanders and Artois were not annexed to the French kingdom until the reign of Louis XIV. Inns or alehouses dispensing beer and ale, which were to be found every few doors in London and most English provincial towns, were practically unknown in the greater part of France. Wine took the place of both beverages except in Normandy, where cider was drunk. The wealthy alone could afford the fine vintages, but nearly every region provided *vin ordinaire* in such abundance that it formed a part of the nourishment not only of craftsmen and peasants but of their children down to those of a very tender age.

This sharp difference in drinking habits between the two countries is indicative of industrial changes which were drawing England farther than France along the road to industrialism. Like the making of salt, the preparation of the daily drink of the greater proportion of the inhabitants in France remained, for the most part, an agrarian pursuit, at a time when, in England, the preparation of drink, like the making of salt, became an industrial vocation.[296]

One of the few English habits which astonished French travelers before the middle of the seventeenth century more than the wholesale drinking of beer was the immoderate desire for tobacco that prevailed throughout the kingdom.[297] Thick clouds of tobacco smoke greeted them whenever they entered English inns and taverns, and they spoke with contempt of the new weed which they sometimes associated with scenes of drunken debauchery. Smoking was fast becoming a consolation in England of "the base vulgar sort," who labored for wages in the new mines and workshops, carried sacks of coal, or worked at looms and hearths in village cottages or in town garrets and cellars. It had been taken up before the end of the seventeenth century even by peasant women in Cornwall.

It was not, of course, a habit from which the French were altogether free. Michelet deplored the use of tobacco in the early seventeenth century among the sailors of Bayonne and Saint-Jean-de-Luz, who were the first Frenchmen to be introduced to this product of the new world.[298] Accord-

[294] *Dictionnaire universel de commerce* (Geneva, 1742), Vol. I, article on "Alun." (The account given in the text is confirmed by Delumeau, *op. cit.,* pp. 43–52.)

[295] Archives du Nord (Lille), B. 1835, fols. 15–16; B. 4032, fols. 179–82; Archives de l'Aisne (Lens), E. 451 (min. de Floury); *Inventaire des archives communales de Cambrai,* AA. 103, fol. 83; BB. 1, fol. 24; BB. 2, fol. 86; CC. 220, fol. 16; DD. 5; DD. 39; EE. 101.

[296] See above, p. 138.

[297] *Calendar of State Papers, Domestic,* 1627–28, p. 58.

[298] *Histoire de France,* Vol. XIII, chap. xvii.

ing to him it befouled their breath to the point often of rendering loathsome to their wives and mistresses their kisses and lovemaking! Compared with the English, the French had hardly been tainted as yet by what Michelet called the new "demon." When, in 1626, the *parlement* of Normandy registered the king's letters-patent authorizing experiments with tobacco growing near Rouen, it was on condition that the product should be released for consumption only if the physicians of the town had made a favorable report upon its effects on the health of the smokers.[299] The manufacture of tobacco and the baking of smokers' pipes were not taken up with such avidity in the France of Louis XIII as in the England of James I and Charles I, because there was a much smaller demand for the products.

There was probably no other industry among the new manufactures, unless it was the making of copperas, in which England had gained as decisive a lead over France on the eve of the Civil War as in brewing, tobacco-rolling, pipemaking, and the production of alum. In printing and in the manufacture of paper France retained its lead as late as the middle of the seventeenth century. This lead she owed largely to the remarkable progress made by her printing industry during the last decades of the fifteenth century, when the introduction of the press and movable type made it possible to pour out multiple copies of written matter by machinery. The first French printing press was set up in Paris in 1470. Thirty years later the capital had at least thirty printing establishments, a few with four or five presses; Lyons, which was becoming one of the most famous centers for printing in Europe, had almost as many establishments as Paris; and the new industry was carried on in at least forty other French towns.[300]

During the hundred years covered by this essay, the output of books and other printed matter continued to increase in France, but at a slow pace. The period from 1540 to 1590 was one of strikes among the journeymen printers of Paris and Lyons and of religious wars;[301] it was not favorable to the progress of the French printing industry. It was a period during which the production of books in London grew considerably. Although the first English press had been set up as early as 1478, little printing was done in England at the beginning of the sixteenth century, and most of the books sold were imported, mainly from Paris and Rouen.[302] In Henry VIII's

[299] E. Gosselin, *Documents pour servir à l'histoire de la marine normande* (Rouen, 1876), p. 131.

[300] P. Mellottée, *Histoire économique de l'imprimerie* (Paris, 1905), pp. 453–54. Mellottée's list includes Paris and forty other towns, but it is incomplete. He does not mention Bordeaux, although it has been shown that a printing establishment was started there in 1486 (Ernest Gaullieur, *L'imprimerie à Bordeaux en 1486* [Bordeaux, 1869]). For Lyons, see also H. Hauser, *Ouvriers du temps passé* (5th ed.; Paris, 1927), pp. 178–79; Lucien Romier, *Le royaume de Catherine de Médicis* (Paris, 1925), II, 80.

[301] Mellottée, *op. cit.*, p. 454; Hauser, *op. cit.*, pp. 179 ff.

[302] E. Gordon Duff, *A Century of the English Book Trade* (London, 1905), pp. xi,

reign attempts were made to reduce the imports.[303] While many books for the English market continued to come from abroad during Elizabeth's reign, London had begun to overtake Paris as a center for printers. A survey made in 1583 put the number of presses at fifty-three,[304] distributed among about twenty-five printing houses,[305] more than half as many as were then to be found in Paris[306] with its larger population.

During the first quarter of the seventeenth century printing in Paris and in the French provinces increased in importance.[307] In 1645 Paris had seventy-six houses with 183 presses.[308] The growth of the business in London, and also in Oxford and Cambridge, was impeded in 1586 by a decree of the Star Chamber forbidding any further increase in houses or presses.[309] It was only after 1640, when these restrictions were relaxed, that the industry grew rapidly. By 1649 London had upward of sixty printing houses and was very nearly abreast of Paris.[310] But little had been done in English provincial towns to overcome the great lead which had been won for French provincial printing by the beginning of the sixteenth century. There seems to have been some decline in the number of provincial houses in England from 1557 to 1582, and in the latter year Christopher Barker, the queen's printer, said an estimate of "8 or 10 at the most would suffice for all [provincial] England, yea and Scotland too." [311] While the proportion of English books printed abroad had been substantially reduced between 1540 and 1640, and while the French share in the English import trade had also diminished, the output of printed matter per capita in France in Louis XIII's reign still exceeded that in England.

In many parts of France corn mills, turned by waterwheels rotating in the moving streams, had been successfully converted into paper mills during the late fifteenth and early sixteenth centuries in response mainly, it would seem, to the new demand for paper brought by the rapid growth of printing. Until the 1580's little paper of any kind had been made in England; for it was not until the middle of Elizabeth's reign that its manufac-

---

xiii; also *The English Provincial Printers, Stationers and Bookbinders to 1557* (Cambridge, 1912), p. 125.

[303] *The Cambridge History of English Literature,* IV (1910), 458.

[304] *Calendar of State Papers, Domestic,* 1581–90, p. 111.

[305] *Cambridge History of English Literature,* IV, 441–42.

[306] We have no record of the printing houses in Paris at this time, but information given by Mellottée (*op. cit.,* pp. 454, 456) concerning the number of booksellers and printers, taken together, suggests that there were probably not more than forty houses.

[307] Mellottée, *op. cit., passim; Inventaire des archives départementales,* Bouches-du-Rhône, B. 3340, fol. 779; B. 3444, fol. 1848.

[308] Mellottée, *op. cit.,* p. 455. Less than eighty of the presses were in continual operation. The others were used casually to print speeches, decrees, poems, etc.

[309] Cf. *Calendar of State Papers, Domestic,* 1581–90, p. 336.

[310] *Cambridge History of English Literature,* IV, 442.

[311] *Ibid.,* pp. 441, 467.

ture by means of water-driven mills was permanently established.[312] Before that time paper was being produced in many French provinces—in Provence, Auvergne, Dauphiné, Languedoc, Limousin, Poitou, Anjou, Champagne, and Normandy,[313] as well as in Franche-Comté, which was not yet part of the kingdom.[314] The French manufacturers were anxious to thwart attempts to introduce the Continental methods of papermaking into England. According to Richard Tottell, the well-known London printer and stationer who tried to set up a paper mill in the seventies or early eighties, they bought up all the English rags that he needed to get his enterprise under way.[315]

Shortly after Tottell's failure the English papermaking industry was successfully established. At least three mills—one near London, another at Cambridge, and a third at Worcestershire—are said to have been already in operation[316] when shortly before 1588 John Spilman, a naturalized German who had become the queen's jeweler, started his famous paperwork at Dartford in Kent, where two great waterwheels, one of which cost something like the equivalent in modern money of $100,000, drove the stamping machinery and the hammers for beating the cloth.[317] The Lord Mayor of London complained in 1601 that Spilman had authorized "great numbers of poor people, especially girls and vagrant women," to range "abroad in every street, begging at men's doors" for the rags to be brought to his mill.[318]

Papermaking increased in importance in England during the first half of the seventeenth century, and in the reign of Charles I there were at least ten and probably more fairly large mills at work.[319] England was catching up with France in the production of paper as well as in the production of

[312] Rhys Jenkins, "Early Attempts at Paper-Making in England, 1495–1680," *Library Association Record,* II, Part II, 581–85.

[313] Emile Isnard, "Les papeteries de Provence," in Hayem, *Mémoires et documents pour servir à l'histoire du commerce et de l'industrie,* IV, 39; *Inventaire des archives départementales,* Bouches-du-Rhône, B. 3332, fol. 855; Fagniez, *L'économie sociale de la France sous Henri IV,* p. 160; H. Blanchet, *Rive et ses environs* (Grenoble, 1861), pp. 34–35; Paul Raveau, *Essai sur la situation économique et l'état social en Poitou,* p. 17; G. H. Overend, "Notes upon the Earlier History of the Manufacture of Paper in England," *Huguenot Society of London, Proceedings,* VIII (1905–8), 200.

[314] Jules Gauthier, "L'industrie du papier dans les hautes vallées franc-comptoise du XVᵉ au XVIIIᵉ siècles," *Mémoires de la Société d'Emulation de Montbéliard,* XXVI (1897), 41–44.

[315] *Calendar of State Papers, Domestic,* 1581–90, p. 296. According to Duff, Tottell's attempt was made in 1573 (*A Century of the English Book Trade,* p. 157), but his account of the venture in the State Papers has been dated tentatively 1585. At the time of writing it, Tottell still hoped to succeed.

[316] *Calendar of State Papers, Domestic,* 1601–3, pp. 43–44.

[317] *Ibid.,* 1581–90, p. 556; Thomas Churchyard, *A Description and Playne Discourse of Paper* (1588), reprinted in John Nichols, *The Progresses of Queen Elizabeth* (1788), Vol. II; cf. above, p. 125.

[318] *Calendar of State Papers, Domestic,* 1601–3, pp. 43–44.

[319] See above, p. 125.

books. But the English mills apparently were used almost exclusively for making the crude, so-called brown paper, wanted for wrapping and, to some extent, for blotting. The watermarks on English manuscripts and the pages of English books indicate that the country remained dependent upon imports for its white paper until after the middle of the seventeenth century.[320] Shipments from the chief paper-exporting towns of France—Caen, Morlaix, and La Rochelle—probably increased during the reigns of Henri IV and Louis XIII; for the mills in the north and west of France, a few of which were owned by Englishmen,[321] gained something of a monopoly over the export trade to England as the use there of Italian, Swiss, and German paper diminished.[322] In France during the reign of Louis XIII mills were to be found in almost every province. They were much more numerous than in England. But like French glassworks, French paper mills seem to have been generally smaller. Unlike the enterprise of Spilman at Dartford, described in 1588 as "a house of some estate," [323] the little mills near Troyes in Champagne, one of the principal papermaking provinces, were not imposing enough to attract the eyes of travelers. Some of those built at the beginning of the seventeenth century were no bigger than corn mills.[324]

If, under the stress of more warfare, the French almost certainly produced in state managed enterprises[325] much more saltpeter and gunpowder than the English during the late sixteenth and early seventeenth centuries, it is by no means certain that the English remained behind on the eve of the Civil War in the output of soap and starch. The beginnings of rapid progress in the manufacture of all these commodities go back, as is true of printing and papermaking, to an earlier period in France than in England. This may be illustrated by the history of soapmaking in Provence, which was a great center for supplying the rest of France. The manufacture was definitely established there in the last half of the fifteenth century—at Toulon, Hyères, and Marseille. By 1525 there were at least two workshops in operation at Marseille and probably more before 1540.[326] By that time the industry was clearly well on its feet. It grew at Marseille during the

---

[320] In 1640 the art of making writing paper was said to be "a new invention not heretofore used in [England]," (*Calendar of State Papers, Domestic,* 1640, p. 226).

[321] A. de Montchrétien, *Traicté de l'Économie politique* (1615), ed. Funck-Brentano (n.d.), p. 95.

[322] Edward Heawood, "Paper Used in England after 1600," *Library,* 4th ser., XI (1930–31), 292.

[323] Churchyard, *loc. cit.*

[324] *Inventaire des archives départementales,* Aube, E. 366. The same was apparently true of the mills in Picardy (*Inventaire des archives départementales,* Aisne, H. 67).

[325] See, e.g., Archives de l'Aisne, B. 503, B. 3545; *Inventaire des archives départementales,* Bouches-du-Rhône, B. 3553, fol. 165.

[326] *Encyclopédie départementale. Les Bouches-du-Rhône,* III, 168; L. Barthelemy, *La savonnerie marseillaise* (reprint from *La Revue de Marseille*) (Marseille, 1883), pp. 9–10, 12, 20.

second half of the sixteenth century,[327] but this growth appears to have been caused partly by a concentration of the manufacture at the expense of soapmaking in other Provençal towns. There was some development of the industry in Languedoc in the time of Henri IV. Two small factories were started at Gignac, west of Montpellier, one in 1602, the other in 1609.[328]

We do not know how much soap was produced at Marseille in Louis XIII's reign, but the output seems to have been less than that of London, where the English manufacture tended to concentrate.[329] In 1669, when production at Marseille had apparently declined somewhat since 1640, the town had seven factories, most of them with more and probably larger boilers than those started before 1540.[330] Four of the factories were in operation, and the recorded shipments of Marseille soap to western, central, and northern France, mainly by way of the Rhone, amounted to about 1,310 tons.[331]

By the reign of Charles I the new manufactures, taken together, almost certainly employed a larger number of hands relative to the total population in England than in France. The great lead obtained by the English in alum-making, brewing, tobacco-rolling, and pipemaking much more than offset their disadvantage in gunpowder-making, in printing, and in papermaking. And in France the progress of the new manufactures had been spread over two centuries, while in England it had almost all been crowded into the hundred years following the dissolution of the monasteries.

CONCLUSION

This comparison of industrial growth in France and England makes no pretense at completeness. It is sufficient, nevertheless, to bring out great differences between development in the two countries. In France there was no sharp break with the past insofar as industrial growth was concerned. New industries were introduced, and the output of old industries increased. But that had happened before, particularly during the late fifteenth and early sixteenth centuries. Between the mid-sixteenth and the mid-seventeenth centuries there was no wholesale introduction of new manufactures,

---

[327] *Ibid.*, p. 22.
[328] *Inventaire des archives départementales,* Hérault, C. 2660.
[329] See above, pp. 201–2.
[330] *Encyclopédie départementale,* III, 195.
[331] Archives Nationales, F¹² 1834ᴬ. The figure given in the document is 2,714,950 *livres.* I have converted this into tons on the assumption that the livre was 0.49 kg. (see p. 176). It is possible that the designation *savon de Marseille* included soap made in other Provençal towns besides Marseille. But that is not necessarily the case, for the record also includes imports of *savon blanc,* most of which, like Marseille soap, came up the Rhone. This *savon blanc* may have been manufactured in Provence, but it may have come from abroad. In 1669, the imports of *savon blanc* amounted to 914,619 *livres,* or about 440 tons.

no unprecedented growth in the volume of salt, glass, ships, coal, iron, metal wares, and building materials, such as led many English traders during Shakespeare's lifetime to hope for a doubling of their business almost every decade. The output of coal, iron, glass, and many other products continued to increase, especially in central France, around Lyons and along the Loire and in the lower Rhone valley, even during the religious wars from 1560 to 1593. But this period was marked by a general slowing down of industrial progress, except perhaps in parts of southern France. Nor was the recovery in the rest of France during the half-century following the religious wars fast enough to bring an increase in the volume of industrial production at all comparable to that north of the English Channel during the hundred years 1540-1640. In some regions—such as Poitou, Champagne, and Provence—the reign of Louis XIII proved an even less favorable period for industrial development than the more troubled reigns of Charles IX and Henri III. The century which ended in 1640 appears to have been an age of slower growth in industrial output in France than the preceding century.

In England the later century was marked by a remarkable speeding up of production. A number of manufactures flourished for the first time. The output of the older industries, except tinmaking, multiplied four-, five-, or sixfold and in at least one case eight- or tenfold. A spurt in the rate of industrial growth, revolutionary compared with previous centuries, got under way during the reign of Elizabeth I, and was perhaps most rapid after about 1580. There have been two periods in the history of Great Britain when a much more rapid rate of industrial growth was established. The first began after the dissolution of the monasteries. The second began more than two hundred years later, in the 1780's, which is to say on the eve of the French Revolution.[332]

Before the dissolution of the monasteries England was industrially in a backwater compared with the chief Continental countries, especially northern Italy, southern Germany, and the Belgian provinces. While England already produced more coal, tin, lead, and woolen cloth relative to her population than France, she was far behind in the output of nearly all other industrial products. The growth in mining and manufacturing in England during the next hundred years changed the economic map of Europe. Foreigners who visited London in the reign of Charles I were astonished by the coal smoke from tens of thousands of domestic fires and from hundreds of small factories and workshops. To them the city with its breweries, its soap and starch houses, its brick kilns, sugar refineries, earthenware works, and glass furnaces seemed hardly fit for human habitation. There were plenty of Londoners who agreed with them. In 1627 a complaint was brought "full cry" to the Privy Council that an alum house near the

---

[332] See Nef, *Western Civilization since the Renaissance*, pp. 290-93.

Tower caused great annoyance to the inhabitants within a mile compass. The "loathesome vapour" from the factory was said to poison the very fish in the Thames, and an appeal was made to the College of Physicians to pronounce the smoke damaging to the health of the citizens.[333] London had taken her place in Charles I's reign as the leading industrial city of the world.[334]

By that time the volume of industrial output, relative to population, had almost certainly become much larger in England than in France. England had gained an enormous absolute advantage in the production of coal, alum, and beer. Relative to her population, she was turning out many more ships, much more tobacco and many more tobacco pipes. Her leadership in woolen cloth and lead production had increased. She was now also manufacturing, relative to her population, a larger volume of iron, copper and brass, of finished metal commodities, and of building materials—such as bricks and lime. She had drawn abreast of France in the production of common glass, soap, and starch. She had reduced the lead which France had held before the Reformation in the output of salt, paper, and printed matter. It was only in the making of wares which the very wealthy alone could afford to acquire—such as lace, silks, tapestries, and works of art modeled in glass, metal, clay, and stone—that the French increased the advantage they had always had over the English. Artistic craftsmanship consolidated a position in France which it had inherited from the age of gothic cathedrals and the age of the Renaissance at a time when Englishmen were coming to be interested primarily in technical progress designed to lower costs of production and increase output.[335]

Did the revolutionary speeding up in the rate of English industrial growth bring with it revolutionary changes in the structure of industrial enterprise and a revolutionary development in the use of power-driven machinery? There had been before, especially in Continental Europe, large capital investments in industrial plant, enterprises with hundreds of workers on their payrolls. Those ventures had been comparable in size to the largest collieries, metallurgical establishments, salt- and alumworks started in England between 1540 and 1640. In the 1630's the Yorkshire alumworks had no more employees than those in the papal estates at Tolfa had had almost a hundred years before; no English shipyard on the eve of the Civil War seems to have had a concentration of capital and labor equal to that in the Venetian arsenal in the times of Giorgione and Titian. Large assemblies of workpeople in single centers were no seventeenth-century novelty. Machinery driven by water and horse power was even less so.

The great industrial expansion in England during the hundred years fol-

---

[333] *Calendar of State Papers, Domestic,* 1627–28, pp. 269–70.
[334] Cf. Nef, *Rise of the British Coal Industry,* I, 157.
[335] See above, chap. iii.

lowing the Reformation had increased the place of both large-scale enterprise and power-driven machinery in the economy. On the eve of the Civil War assemblies of workpeople in enterprises of more than a hundred, together with heavy capital investments in mines and furnaces and other plant with appropriate machines and conveyances, had become more common, in all probability, than ever before in Europe, in the sense that no other country of the size and population of England had ever had as many. If all the laborers in English mines and workshops with more than a dozen employees had been mustered out around 1635, they could have been counted in tens of thousands. There were possibly nearly as many of them as there had been in the whole of Europe, with some sixty million people, in the times of the Emperor Charles V.[336]

But statistical comparisons of this kind do not bring out the deeper meaning of the English industrial expansion for the genesis of industrialism. The revolutionary character of that expansion is found in the shift in the objectives for which considerable industrial capital and numerous workpeople were employed: the shift in the major resources of capital and labor away from production primarily for the sake of beauty, of delight in contemplation, toward production primarily for the sake of usefulness in the purely economic sense of substantial comforts in greater quantities.[337] The revolutionary character is found in the concentration of inventive effort less upon art and more upon utility—in the sense of laborsaving machinery, cheaper raw materials, more economical furnaces and means of transport.[338] The revolutionary character is found also in the steady strengthening of private enterprise at the expense of government regulation and participation in mining and manufacturing.[339] While individualism and utility had always been present to some extent wherever there had been economic progress in the past, no people before had centered their energies upon them to the same extent as those of England had begun to do by the early seventeenth century.

Industrialism is a phenomenon of recent times. The conquest of the material world as we know it is without precedent in connection with any of the societies that formerly peopled the earth. It is the creation primarily of Europe and North America. Today when people in all regions are eager to become industrialized, we often fail to realize that industrialism did not come easily, let alone automatically, that its coming was not an inevitable process as the endless followers of a Marxian view of history are inclined to suppose. Actually, the ways of living and thinking, of feeling and worshiping, that once prevailed in western Europe, as in other parts of the

---

[336] Cf. above, p. 112.
[337] Nef, *Cultural Foundations of Industrial Civilization*, pp. 6–16, 50–53, and *passim*.
[338] *Ibid.*, pp. 54–61; Nef, "Coal Mining and Utilization," *A History of Technology*, III (Oxford, 1957), C. Singer, E. J. Holmyard, and A. R. Hall (eds.), pp. 72–88.
[339] Nef, *Industry and Government in France and England, passim.*

world, stood mainly in the way of the coming of industrialism. That depended upon a transformation of these ways of living and thinking, feeling and worshiping—upon revolutionary changes in the basic purposes for which the adventure of life on earth is undertaken.

All the European peoples had a part in these revolutionary changes. What happened during the century following the Reformation, especially in the north of Europe and foremost in Great Britain, was a change in the terms on which individuals conducted their lives. This change is symbolized by the appearance of newly built cities and towns, chimneys and coal smoke, plain glass windows and grates with coal-burning fires in the homes of the moderately well off as well as in those of the rich, the saturation of human bodies of all classes with beer and tobacco. The change was expressed in an agrarian upheaval which set what contemporaries called "rogues and vagabonds" moving from village to village and from village to towns and other growing industrial centers in search of any kind of work that would give them a livelihood.[340] They found it, more than workmen had ever before, in mines and workshops catering to production for the sake of quantity, in the interest of private profits. The stimulus of profits, calculated more and more exclusively in quantitative monetary terms, was heightened by the novel independence from government interference successfully claimed by private adventurers in a considerable way of business.[341]

These are the senses in which England underwent, during three generations of living prior to the Civil War, an early industrial revolution. This revolution helped to prepare the way for all Europeans gradually to break through the sturdy and pervasive barriers which blocked the road to industrialism.

So the contribution to the conquest of the material world of English historical development from 1540 to 1640 was not negligible. The pages that follow show how the meanings for our age of the industrial history of those times can be understood better if its relation to other sides of history is recognized, if history is seen as a whole.

[340] A theme which my colleague and friend, Dr. Eric Kerridge, is developing. It is foreshadowed in Nef, *Rise of the British Coal Industry*, I, 284–318; II, 145–68.
[341] Cf. *ibid.*, II, 3–134, 267–99

PART 3

Studies in Historical Interrelations, ca. 1540–ca.1787

5

The Protestant Reformation
and the Birth of Industrial Civilization

The problem of the interrelations between religious history and the rise of capitalism has engaged much attention during the past half-century. Among the most valuable contributions to an understanding of it have been works by the editor of the journal *Economia e Storia*.[1] I share Professor Fanfani's view that the attention paid to Max Weber's essay—*The Protestant Ethic and the Spirit of Capitalism*—has led students to limit the problem too narrowly to particular aspects of religious history.[2] I would go farther than Fanfani by suggesting that the concern with "capitalism" has also led students to limit too narrowly the forces which have brought the modern industrialized world into being.

The term "capitalism" is not found, I am told, in Karl Marx's *Das Kapital*. But it was mainly through the influence of Marx and his followers that the rise of capitalism came to be identified with the origins of the industrialism established in Europe and the United States before the end of the nineteenth century. At the beginning of the twentieth, "capitalism" was widely regarded as the distinguishing feature of contemporary civilization. The word was variously defined. Weber wrote that ". . . capitalism is identical with the pursuit of profit, and forever *renewed* profit, by means of continuous, rational, capitalistic enterprise." [3] In mining and manufacturing, "capitalistic enterprise" generally implied production in plant specially constructed for an industrial purpose by persons seeking profit on their investments, persons who employed laborers and sold their output in a

[1] From *Economia e Storia*, No. 2 (April–June 1955), pp. 1–28. This essay appeared in that review under the editorship of the former Prime Minister, in Italian translation, with the title "La Riforma Protestante e l'Origine della Civiltà Industriale."
[2] Amintore Fanfani, *Catholicism, Protestantism and Capitalism* (London, 1935) (first published in Italian in Milan in 1934).
[3] *The Protestant Ethic and the Spirit of Capitalism*, trans. Talcott Parsons (London, 1930), p. 17.

free market with a minimum of government interference. The study of economic history, something of a newcomer among scholars' subjects in 1904 when Weber's essay appeared, has been preoccupied with the historical origins of capitalism. His essay aroused special interest because he suggested that the triumph of capitalism, as a system of economic enterprise, had been brought about in no small measure by a new spirit of thrift and hard work among individuals, introduced and fostered by Calvinism and particularly by Calvin's statement of the doctrine of predestination.

THE ESSENCE OF INDUSTRIAL CIVILIZATION

I suggest elsewhere that the birth of the industrial civilization in the midst of which we are living, has been erroneously identified with the origins of capitalism, the "spirit of capitalism," and with class struggle, to the exclusion of other elements more important. The direct forces behind industrial civilization are to be found, I suggest, not only in the spirit of capitalism but in a novel emphasis on quantity as the principal purpose of production and on precise measurement and mathematical statement as the major methods in scientific inquiry.[4] Men and women in all societies have counted, they have calculated in numbers; such skills have not even been beyond the mental powers of what have been called primitive peoples. But, before the genesis of industrial civilization, counting and calculating in numbers were matters of convenience, carried on to satisfy other ends than the maximization of scarce means or the statement of scientific laws. The use of figures derived from quantitative surveys as guides to economic and political action or on behalf of what may perhaps be called social purposes is a modern phenomenon.

The notions of establishing precisely the population of a town or country, or the volume of its trade, and of trying to determine the rate of growth over periods of years hardly go back beyond the late sixteenth century. In the seventeenth century, we meet for the first time, and especially in England, ancestors of present-day demographers and economists. Sir William Petty estimated in 1682 that if the population of London and the population of England and Wales continued to increase at the rates which he thought prevailed in his time, by 1840 practically the entire population, which he calculated at 10,917,389, would be living in the metropolis! So he predicted the growth of the city would stop about 1800 when London would have a population of rather more than five millions![5]

The growing prestige attaching to precise and ever more precise meas-

[4] See above, pp. 211–12 and below, chap. vii, p. 275; Nef, *La Naissance de la civilisation industrielle et le monde contemporain* (Paris, 1954), esp. chaps. i–iii. (I have developed this theme still more recently in *Cultural Foundations of Industrial Civilization* (New York, 1960), esp. chap. i.

[5] *Another Essay in Political Arithmetick* (London, 1682), quoted in *The Economic Writings of Sir William Petty*, ed. C. H. Hull (Cambridge, 1899), II, 464.

urements and to mathematical speculations in connection with intellectual life has led us to measure human happiness in terms of general life expectancy, the multiplication of production, and the increase in the material standard of living. Men have been influenced indirectly by modern scientific speculations to estimate values in terms of numbers, because scientists and other scholars came to deal with matters subject to measurement and with problems subject to mathematical formulation, and because their methods of reasoning have been contagious. Furthermore the emphasis on quantitative methods and on new mathematical ideas in the natural sciences, together with the emphasis which accompanied it on tangible evidence derived from positive observation and experiment, by providing keys to scientific laws and to the advance of every kind of scientific knowledge, have helped to make possible the technical progress that has transformed the material conditions of life during the past century and a half and especially during the past fifty years. With figures collected by governments and private business enterprises dancing upwards before our eyes, sometimes in geometrical progression, we are almost hypnotized into considering our public and private problems in terms of quantitative hopes or nightmares.

Our distant ancestors were not as much inclined as we are to think and talk in numbers. This suggests they were probably disposed to lay less store than our contemporaries on increases in quantity. The reader of Pliny's *Natural History,* written in the first century A.D., when the Mediterranean lands all formed part of the Roman Empire, will be struck by the fact that in dealing with the products of the subsoil—ores and other minerals—Pliny is more concerned with maintaining scarcity than with multiplying output. He regarded it as evil, as sacrilegious, to ransack the earth, to rob it of its underground treasures.[6] The reduction by any and every means of the labor costs of production, together with the multiplication of output, as sufficient ends in themselves, are features of modern societies. The habits of measuring happiness in terms of the rate of growth in output and consumption, and in terms of increased average life expectancy, are new. Before our times, in sophisticated societies, the fashioning of durable commodities, which were of great importance to the economy, was undertaken much less for quantitative ends and much more for aesthetic results. Energy and effort, which have now come to be concentrated on mass production, transportation, and communication, were often husbanded for the fashioning of beautiful buildings and decorations. Industrial enterprise had as a central purpose the creation of durable objects for contemplation and delight. This was true in ancient Greece in the fifth century B.C. It was true in the European society of the later Middle Ages from the eleventh to the early sixteenth century, at a time when many of the greatest buildings were erected as testimonies to Christian religious faith.

[6] Cf. above, chap, i, p. 4.

Of course there are now hosts of artists, particularly amateur artists, even (perhaps we should say especially) in the United States, but art and artistry no longer provide the principal driving forces in the daily industrial economy of a town or country. Quality is always to some extent the concern of the mass-producer. But it is not the quality sought in a work of art for the sake of permanent beauty; one might say that what is sought is quality for the sake of quantity.[7] The objects are *made* to be superseded. For example, automobiles have been manufactured increasingly for selling in ever greater numbers, and this has led during the past fifty years in the United States, whence has come the greatest initiative in this movement, to the reduction in the number of essentially different designs to almost a single standard type. It has become increasingly difficult at any distance to distinguish a Ford from a Cadillac.

I recently asked the small son of a gifted painter what he thought of an exhibition then being held of his father's canvases. "Oh, they're all alike," roared the eight-year-old somewhat irreverently. "Of course," his mother told him, deftly turning the irreverence to the best account, "they are all your father's." There is a vital sense in which every work of a great artist bears the mark of a single human inspiration. His image reveals itself in his pictures with all the individuality which can characterize a face one knows. So a lover of beauty has little difficulty in recognizing a Giotto or a Rembrandt, a Rubens or a Renoir, a Derain or a Chagall, the moment he sees one. But the inspiration of the great artist is on the highest level of universality, with its appeal to what is most permanent in mankind, because his work reflects the range and the profundity of one almost infinitely varied personality.

The common stamp of the contemporary automobile is of a different order. Automobiles appear "all alike," not because they are the work of a single human brain, but because they are the work of many brains bent to conform to a purpose dictated by mechanics and aiming at the production, not of one or a few or even a few hundred works of art, but of millions of cars—smart in line, serviceable to operate, comfortable to ride in, each for a short space of weeks and months, or at the very most a few years. The automobile of 1954–55 may be more agreeable to look at than the earlier and more numerous types of automobile of say 1920–21 (though that is debatable), but looking at it can hardly provide an aesthetic and spiritual experience comparable to that sometimes evoked by a thirteenth-century cathedral, a painting by Botticelli, or a passage from one of Shakespeare's plays. In each of these, many most varied impressions are distilled in a universal one. If the work is lost something precious is torn out of human experience. In the case of mass production, any element of this universal one, which may exist in a planner or designer, is largely lost in the imper-

---

[7] Cf. Nef, *Cultural Foundations*, pp. 137–38.

sonal process of conforming to the specifications for making cheaply things in large quantities to be quickly superseded.

A quantitative outlook on worldly matters, a disposition to treat larger and larger quantities as self-justifying ends, and to use quantitative methods in the treatment of intellectual problems, are features of industrial civilization. It might be that Weber had something of this kind in mind when he wrote in his celebrated essay of "the specific and peculiar rationalism of Western culture." [8] But he linked this peculiar rationalism with the capitalistic spirit and with capitalistic enterprise, whereas it is partly independent of both. It is no less prevalent in the collectivist and totalitarian societies of the mid-twentieth century than in the relatively free enterprise economy which prevailed in North America and western Europe at the beginning of this century, and which still prevails to some extent. In the publication of books, for example, the quality of the content and style is of less moment to the publishers, generally speaking, than in the heyday of "capitalism." What counts is the probable sales, or, in a totalitarian country, conformity to the dicta of the rulers.

The capitalist spirit was certainly a factor behind the triumph of industrialism. But so was access to abundant coal seams and deposits of iron ore.[9] So was the rise of modern science, with its eventual influence on technology.[10] If we are seeking the essence of modern industrialism which now pervades most parts of the world, it is to be found less perhaps in capitalism and the capitalistic spirit than in quantitative goals and quantitative means. What we have to explain as students of the origins of industrial civilization is the novel and growing emphasis on these goals and means.

When did a decisive shift in emphasis occur from the goal of making commodities to endure and to delight, toward the goal of making them in ever larger numbers? When did a decisive shift in emphasis occur in science from speculations derived from theology, philosophy, and art toward speculations based on precise measurement, mathematical rigor, and demonstration, buttressed by tangible evidence derived from positive observation and experiment? If the essence of industrial civilization is found, as I am suggesting, first and foremost in a quantitative approach to production and on mathematical considerations as of primary importance in science, we can say with some confidence that industrial civilization came into existence after the time of Rabelais, who died apparently in 1553.

There is a great deal of dispute as to when he was born; dates have been given all the way from 1480 to 1495. As Professor Lucien Febvre seems

---

[8] *Op. cit.*, p. 26.
[9] Cf. Nef, *La Naissance de la civilisation industrielle et le monde contemporain*, pp. 86–90, 92–93.
[10] See below, chap. vii.

to have established by his recent book, *Le Problème de l'incroyance au XVIᵉ siècle où La Religion de Rabelais,* this suggests that it was probably uncommon in Rabelais's time for people to remember just when they had been born, although records of births were kept, as were records of tax assessments and of shipments of goods from seaports. The outlook of men on the problem of time was essentially different then from what it has now become. Time was a process for the ripening of fruits and animals and human beings. Duration was not a matter of precise measurement but of fulfilment, as is true also of works of art which demand the time needed to obtain a result bordering on perfection.

The rhythm of economic life, the rhythm of work, at the beginning of the sixteenth century resembled that of the artist more than that of the modern employee, which is partly determined by exact recording instruments—clocks, watches (which were little used), or even calendars (which had still to be made exact according to our modern notions). So in the age of Rabelais it was much less usual than now to be certain even about one's own age, a fact about which a lack of precision has its advantages and not only for women! Of course some people had the quantitative outlook on existence—which we are suggesting is the essence of industrial civilization —but that outlook was not yet characteristic of any side of European life or of any country.

MEANING OF THE PHRASE EARLY INDUSTRIAL REVOLUTION

What might perhaps be called a major rehearsal for the industrial revolution which began across the British Channel in the 1780's occurred in the north of Europe, particularly in Great Britain and above all in England, during the late sixteenth and early seventeenth centuries, or roughly from 1540 to 1640 and especially from 1580 to 1640. Insofar as the speeding up of industrial growth and the accompanying progress of technology[11] at this time bears on the coming of industrial civilization, the early "revolution" consisted not only in the development of *private* capitalist enterprise, which was impressive, but also in a remarkable new emphasis on quantity as the major goal of industrial production.

This was the period when coal was becoming the basic fuel in the economy of two leading states—England and Scotland. By its nature coal is a more noxious and more plentiful fuel than wood; its adoption put a premium on the production of commodities—such as bricks, sheet glass, anchors, nails, fire grates, pots, and pans—which were valuable primarily because their production was easily susceptible to rapid multiplication.[12]

This was also a period when, in Great Britain, the Low Countries, and

[11] Compare above, chaps, iii and iv.
[12] See above, pp. 134–36.

Sweden, cast iron began to replace wrought iron as the principal product of iron metallurgy.[13] In northern Europe the melting of the iron ore to form pig iron during the times of Shakespeare and Milton, Francis Bacon and Descartes, Gustavus Adolphus and his daughter Christina, made it possible to use inferior iron ores, to diminish the waste in metallurgy, and to provide metal bars and rods of standard types, more susceptible to multiplication than to the fashioning of ornamental locks and keys, fine armor, and other products of craftsmanship, in which beauty and style were the principal objectives of the craftsmen, and to which the older wrought iron, obtained more slowly and directly from the ore, with a greater waste in metal, was better suited.

As a number of historians of science (Whitehead, Koyré, Weizsäcker, Butterfield) have now established, the period of this "early industrial revolution" was also the period of the scientific revolution. The preparation for industrial civilization at this time (apart from the growth of private capitalistic enterprise) was therefore a twofold phenomenon. It consisted of changes in the goals of industrial enterprise in the direction of quantity production, and of changes in the methods of scientific investigation in the direction of controlled experiments and accurate measurement.[14] The revolution, of which I started years ago to write in terms of the spread of capitalist industry in private hands, was even more a revolution in men's ways of working and of thinking. The question we have to answer then, when we consider the interrelations between industrial and religious history, is less what the Protestant Reformation did for the spirit of capitalism than what it did to stimulate quantity production, large-scale private enterprise, and quantitative thinking.

CALVINIST DOCTRINES AND THE EARLY INDUSTRIAL REVOLUTION

The great nineteenth-century German historian, Ranke, chose 1540 as a decisive date in the Protestant Reformation. By that year it had become inevitable, he wrote, that the original object of the reformers to retain a single worship would not succeed. By that year it had become inevitable, he believed, that Europeans would embrace several different kinds of church, in place of the single worship and the single Church which had enlisted their ancestors for what seemed to persons then living "time out of mind." What were the connections between these momentous changes in ecclesiastical history and the genesis of industrial civilization during the hundred years that followed?

These connections are not to be found *mainly,* in my judgment, in the religious thought and the moral teaching of the early Protestants. The views

[13] See above, p. 178.
[14] See below, chap. vii.

which seem to have originated with Sir William Ashley, concerning the influence of Calvin on interest-taking, the views which seem to have originated with Weber, concerning the influence of Calvinist thought in promoting individualism, in encouraging economic activity and accumulation among capitalists, managers, and workers, were not meant by their authors to apply primarily to the period 1540–1640. Nor were they meant to apply to the revolutionary changes in economic objectives and intellectual methods which make that period, as we have learned recently, so significant for the genesis of the atomic age. At the time when Ashley and Weber wrote, economic history was dominated by the idea that the coming of modern industrial society, in which the rise of modern "capitalism" was considered the essential element, should be identified with an "industrial revolution" which they supposed, following the thesis of Toynbee the elder, had taken place between about 1760 and 1832 in Great Britain. What Ashley and Weber were trying to understand in terms of religious history was *that* industrial revolution. They were hardly aware of an earlier industrial revolution; they were not concerned with the scientific revolution of the period 1580 to 1640. Both the earlier industrial revolution and the scientific revolution were, according to my view, among the important forces leading to industrial civilization.

Subsequent attempts by others to extend the theories of Ashley and Weber to the rise of capitalism and the capitalistic spirit, striking as we now see especially in England and Holland during the hundred years following 1540, have not, in my opinion, been successful. In this opinion I am borne out, at least in part, not only by the work of Fanfani, but also by that of Hauser, Tawney, and Brentano. Hauser found that the teaching of Calvinist churchmen concerning interest-taking did not show any novel characteristics of leniency, likely to stimulate saving and capital accumulation, before the mid-seventeenth century.[15] So Ashley's thesis concerning Calvinism and capitalism hardly fits the period 1540 to 1640. What of Weber's thesis?

Predestination was certainly a major pillar in Calvin's thought, and in that of his Scottish and Dutch, as well as his English, disciples. But, as Weber himself recognized, predestination was invariably combined in Calvinism with an emphasis on moral rectitude, on the living of a Christian life in this world. Brentano argued that the early influence of Calvinist doctrines in the realm of economic conduct was conservative. All the reformers turned to the text of the Bible, emphasizing to a greater or a lesser degree, as Luther did, the passages that suited their own ideas concerning the major tenets of the Christian faith. Calvin and the early Calvinists concerned themselves pre-eminently with conduct here and now, as the ground

---

[15] Henri Hauser, "Les Idées économique de Calvin," in *Les Débuts du capitalisme* (Paris, 1927), pp. 70–72, 77–78.

on which the hopes of future life were tested. The words of Christ as recorded in the Gospel were by no means a tonic to capital accumulation and investment here and now.[16] Riches and even worldly activity devoted to the making of profits appear in the New Testament not infrequently as a *danger* to salvation. During the late sixteenth and early seventeenth centuries the teachings of clergymen who followed Calvin seem to have stressed the hazards of material accumulation even more than the virtues of economic activity. It was only gradually that the values of such activity were taken to outweigh the hazards, only gradually that the disciplined economic life, organized primarily for technical efficiency rather than for fashioning objects of beauty, affected industrial development.

The changes in religious teaching on behalf of saving and hard work, which Weber traces to the rise of Calvinistic Protestantism, could hardly have been responsible for the first remarkable speeding up in the rate of economic growth in England. That got under way between 1540 and 1560,[17] before Calvin's English and Scottish disciples had made an important mark on individual conduct. The new discipline of the calling came into prominence toward the mid-seventeenth century, as was true of the growing leniency in the matter of interest-taking. The Calvinist idea of predestination can hardly be regarded, therefore, as a major factor in the revolutionary changes in industrial objectives and scientific methods, or in the spread of private capitalist enterprise, which occurred in Elizabethan and early Stuart England. Weber's thesis, while probably not unrelated to the ultimate triumph of industrial civilization, is largely irrelevant to its sixteenth- and early seventeenth-century origins.

As Tawney was perhaps the first to suggest, it is at least as plausible to regard economic development at that time as modifying Christian ethical doctrine and molding the thought and the moral teaching of Protestant clergymen and laymen as to regard that economic development as a response to the teachings of Calvin's disciples.[18] The emergence of a new economic discipline connected especially with Calvinism in the mid-seventeenth century was apparently most striking in Holland and England, the two countries where the growth of industrial output and the progress of modern industrial technology and private capitalist enterprise had been most notable during the hundred years 1540 to 1640. It is possible, therefore, that revolutionary developments in industrial life which immediately followed the Reformation were a positive factor in fostering the capitalist spirit among Calvinists, less perhaps because they were Calvinists than because capitalist enterprise and individualism made great headway in countries where Calvinist worship was becoming widespread.

[16] Cf. L. Brentano, *Der Wirtschaftende Mensch in der Geschichte* (Leipzig, 1923), pp. 363–425.
[17] See above, chap. iv.
[18] R. H. Tawney, *Religion and the Rise of Capitalism* (London, 1926), pp. 319–20.

The capitalist spirit has been no monopoly of Calvinist or even of Protestant teaching in modern times. There was a lot of it before the Reformation. And a gospel of thrift and "rational calculation" spread eventually to Roman Catholic countries. With the speeding up of industrial growth in France and other Catholic countries that began in the early eighteenth century, moral teachings among the Roman clergy were also bent to absorb the practices of modern business as consistent with Christian faith and communion. Nor was this perhaps evil in the sight of God! After all, it was not a negligible achievement of the Europeans and their descendants overseas that commerce was replacing piracy. As Montesquieu pointed out, gentle manners usually accompanied commerce. The civilization of which Europeans were aware in the eighteenth century was in many ways more Christian than the violence and cruelty which it superseded.[19] Why therefore should priests and pastors treat the business enterprise which accompanied it as primarily sinful?

If the significance of the Reformation for the genesis of industrial civilization during the times of Francis Bacon and Descartes is not to be found mainly in the religious *doctrines*—moral, spiritual, and intellectual— of the early Protestant fathers, is there some other sense in which the Reformation should be associated with the speeding up in the rate of industrial growth and the new emphasis on quantity production that began in the sixteenth century in England and in the north of Europe generally? Most surely there is. It is to be found in the conceptions of the Protestant fathers as to what is a church, what is the proper scope and nature of priestly intervention in secular life. The early Protestants were trying to get men and women to think and to behave in the ways of Christ by means different from those which the Roman church had employed for centuries, and which it renewed by the Counter Reformation. Along with Protestantism, the Counter Reformation swept over Europe during and after the Councils of the church at Trent, 1545–63. What bearing have the contrasts between the success of the older church in some parts of Europe, and of the various reformed churches in other parts, upon the new economic configuration which emerged from 1540 to 1640, and which gave the north of Europe a position of leadership on the road to modern industrialism? [20]

THE CHURCH AND MEDIEVAL ECONOMIC DEVELOPMENT

The medieval church, as it existed for at least some four or five centuries before the Reformation, was an institution whose influence penetrated to

[19] See below, pp. 229–37.
[20] For the nature of this industrial configuration, I refer the reader to my *Western Civilization since the Renaissance* (New York, 1963), pp. 6–14. (Now translated into French as *La Guerre et le Progrès Humain* [Colmar and Paris, 1955].)

the smallest village and to every aspect of life. It played an economic role of immense importance. During the two hundred and fifty years following 1050, down to about 1300, the scope of its activities widened because of its increasing authority, not only in religion but indirectly in political matters. With this growth in authority went a remarkable increase in the number of the clergy and in the property held and developed by ecclesiastical foundations, an increase upon which the growth in authority partly rested.

Modern scholars, with their passion for statistics, have provided quantitative evidence of the growth in the secular clergy and in the religious of both sexes, monks and nuns, during those two hundred and fifty years. In the case of England, figures derived from two independent inquiries have been published concerning this increase after the Norman Conquest. These figures bear out the statement made in 1940 by Dom David Knowles that "the numerical increase and diffusion of the monastic body" during the first hundred and fifty years after the Domesday Survey of 1086, "had been truly prodigious." [21] The estimated number of all monks and nuns in England in 1066 is 1050. For the period 1216 to 1350 the estimated number is 16,892 to 17,411, a growth of sixteen or seventeen fold during the century and a half following 1066.[22] To the religious we should add the secular clergy which was more numerous still, and which had perhaps grown almost as rapidly. After the Black Death of the mid-fourteenth century, in 1377 (when a poll tax was taken which has provided the historian with quantitative data), the secular clergy are said to have numbered 24,900 and the religious 10,600.[23] If we assume that the secular clergy had been proportionately hardly less reduced than the religious by the ravages of the Black Death after 1345, the entire English clergy may have reached a high point in numbers of nearly 60,000 early in the fourteenth century.

What proportion of the inhabitants does this figure represent? According to the leading authority on English population in the Middle Ages, Professor J. C. Russell, there were about 1,100,000 people in England and Wales in 1086 and perhaps just over three and a half millions in 1300.[24] At the time of the Domesday Survey, then, perhaps one person in a thousand was a religious. The number of the secular clergy in 1086 is uncertain. Assuming they then outnumbered the religious by two to one, hardly one person in three hundred then belonged to the clergy. At the beginning of the fourteenth century the proportion appears to have in-

[21] *The Monastic Order in England, 943–1216* (Cambridge, 1940), p. 679.

[22] David Knowles and R. Neville Hadcock, *Medieval Religious Houses* (London, 1953), p. 364. Professor John Cox Russell gives a slightly greater number for the religious in the early fourteenth century, viz., 18,431 ("The Clerical Population of Medieval England." *Traditio*, II [1944], 212).

[23] *Ibid.*, p. 179.

[24] Russell, *British Medieval Population* (Albuquerque, N.M., 1948), p. 235. According to Russell, a maximum of 3,700,000 was reached in 1348.

creased to about one in sixty. When we reflect that the average age of all persons living at that time was perhaps 20 to 25, hardly a third what it now is in the most prosperous countries, and that persons rarely entered orders or joined any branch of the clergy before adolescence, we see that the percentage of churchmen and nuns in the *adult* population was, in all probability, at least two in every hundred.

I am not familiar with any figures for Continental countries, which would enable us to compare the growth of churchmen there and in England. It may perhaps be assumed that the increase of the religious was exceptionally rapid in Great Britain after the Conquest. If this is so, it was largely because the rapid spread of monasteries on the Continent began somewhat earlier, and because the population of England perhaps grew rather more rapidly than that of the principal Continental countries— especially France and Italy—in the twelfth and early thirteenth centuries. The place of the churchmen of all kinds among the inhabitants of the Continent could hardly have been much less prominent than in Great Britain.

During the epoch when the greatest gothic cathedrals were conceived and built, from the mid-twelfth to the early fourteenth century, the religious and the secular clergy combined formed apparently one of the most important elements numerically in European society. The peasants alone greatly outnumbered them.

In such a society, without newspapers or organized entertainment for profit, the religious exercised an enormous influence on daily living. Their example was impressed on the secular priests and it often determined the ways they dealt with their lay charges. According to Knowles, "As a great and formative influence on the civilization of the West, the monasteries of Europe are perhaps the most important factor in the spiritual and cultural life of the Church and society from the days of Gregory the Great to those of Bernard.[25]

There was apparently no marked reduction in the *proportion* of the English inhabitants who were churchmen even after the Black Death. At that time, according to Professor Russell, the population of England and Wales fell from about 3.7 in 1345 to about 2.2 millions in 1377.[26] In England and Wales there was apparently some slight increase in the number of religious during the fifteenth century,[27] when the English population as a whole probably increased very slowly. On the eve of the Reformation, about 1530, the percentage of the inhabitants belonging to both the religious and the secular clergy was probably still much the same as in the early fourteenth century.

[25] *The Monastic Order in England,* p. 692.
[26] *Traditio,* II, 179.
[27] Knowles and Hadcock, *op. cit.,* p. 364.

The economic power of the churchmen was actually much greater than their numbers suggest. Here again we may cite the principal authority on English monasticism, Dom Knowles. What he says of England and Wales probably applies, subject to differences in time, to western Europe generally. "The possessions of the monasteries in land and in every kind of wealth and influence were even greater than their numbers might seem to warrant. . . . The share of the monks [and nuns] in the whole was without doubt greater in 1170 than in 1066, and perhaps amounted to a quarter or even to a third of the total wealth of the country in lands, rents and dues. Above all, they had grown in wealth and influence, in ecclesiastical property, and were the owners or patrons of perhaps a quarter of the churches in England. To this must be added the ownership of so many great fabrics and groups of buildings stored . . . with precious objects of all kinds and housing almost all the artistic treasures and books of the land." [28]

For centuries, therefore, the church exercised everywhere in Europe considerable, and in some regions preponderant, influences on the ways in which the soil and the resources of the subsoil were exploited. Through their possession of land, their income from all kinds of property, and through the immense contributions which they obtained in various ways from laymen (at a time when what we now call charitable contributions almost always took the single form of contributions to the church), churchmen determined to a large extent what building should be done. They provided the principal orders for many durable goods, especially works of art in stone, glass, wood, cloth, iron, and other materials. Persons who had, by their vows, renounced the life of the world to devote themselves to the service of Christ, persons whose primary obligations were spiritual, whose proper allegiance was not to Caesar but to God, made the decisions which settled the purposes of a large proportion of all economic efforts.

Criticisms of the vices and luxury of the religious go back at least to Saint Bernard, who lived in the early twelfth century; no doubt they go farther back. I am not suggesting that all the men and women who enlisted as religious or served as secular priests lived up to their vows of chastity, poverty, and obedience. Nor am I suggesting that churchmen had any monopoly of such virtues as were manifested by our medieval European ancestors. Bishop Stubbs wrote of the inhabitants of the monasteries, that, from the end of the twelfth century to the Reformation: they were "bachelor country gentlemen, more polished and more charitable, but little more learned or more pure in life than their lay neighbours. . . ." Their lay neighbors were certainly not always pure.[29] Nor, according to the standards which came to prevail in western Europe and North America during the eighteenth and nineteenth centuries, were they gentle. Violence and torture

---

[28] *The Monastic Order in England,* p. 680.
[29] William Stubbs, *Epistolæ Cantuarienses* (London, 1865), pp. cxix, xiv.

were companions which the most civilized Europeans and Americans of later centuries hoped were disappearing once and for all from human relations.

But the rough manners and morals of medieval religious are not the essential matters upon which to fix attention if we are concerned with the changes in supply and demand which their disappearance in some countries at the time of the Reformation encouraged.

The economic objectives of medieval churchmen were different from those which predominate in modern life. Many of them, especially the religious, were grouped in small communities, each subject to the discipline of the church. They were forbidden to marry. Consequently they did not share the family obligations and preoccupations of the lay population. They lacked a motive for amassing individual private fortunes to pass on to their children, or to spend on themselves and their families. The eternal happiness they sought constituted an obstacle to quantitative progress, but, within the limits of religious needs, a stimulus to qualitative progress, because of the importance given to the arts in connection with the building and furnishing of all religious edifices.

Much emphasis has been laid, by some historians, on the profound influence of St. Augustine not only upon scholastic thought from St. Anselm to Duns Scotus, but also upon the structure of society as it developed from the mid-eleventh to the early fourteenth century, during and after the times of Hildebrand. Centuries after it was conceived, Augustine's idea of two cities, the city of God and the city of man, seems to have had a great effect upon the activities of the religious and the secular clergy, and particularly upon the policies of ecclesiastical foundations, with their immense economic influence. The period of late Romanesque and early Gothic architecture, from about 1050 to 1325, was marked by an extraordinary development of ecclesiastical building and of many forms of art and craftsmanship under church guidance. It was as if the Europeans set about in those centuries to build for every village and town—with their monasteries, churches, and cathedrals—a splendid and permanent ascent from the city of man toward the city of God. Piercing the skies, these religious buildings, with their colored glass windows, their statues in stone, their great pillars and spires, were made of the raw materials provided by the immediately surrounding soil and subsoil. The thought that they could be superseded hardly occurred to the masons, the carpenters, the glaziers, and the sculptors who worked daily at their tasks of building and embellishing churches. Much of the work they did was intended to endure, at least until the Day of Judgment, which was often expected before the passage of many centuries! The goals of production were, above all, to provide spiritual guidance with the help of the buildings, the Bibles, and the other works of art on which so much time and labor were expended.

While religious demands seem to have contributed to the economic progress of Europe from the eleventh through the thirteenth centuries,[30] these goals stood in the way of multiplication for its own sake, in the way of production primarily for the sake of quantity, which is so essential a part of industrial civilization.

Even on the eve of the Reformation, the ecclesiastical demands for works of beauty were strong. The humanism of Erasmus and Rabelais did not aim at austerity, for all the criticism of the religious and the secular clergy which they expressed in their works and their lives. Indeed the period still frequently spoken of as the Renaissance, from *ca.* 1450–1530, was marked by increasingly lavish expenditures by great princes of the church on works of art. In the times of Leonardo da Vinci and Botticelli, Raphael and Grünewald, a large part of the demand for what the modern economist would call "durable goods" still came directly or indirectly from churchmen. And "durable goods" to please the senses were in more demand than ever.

THE ECONOMIC VACUUM CREATED BY THE REFORMATION

The Reformation and the spread of various forms of Protestantism in western Christendom were of notable importance in changing the goals for which people worked. There were a variety of reasons for this. The Protestants had very different ideas from the Catholics concerning the proper nature and functions of a church. They attacked the Roman church on the ground that it was too rich, that its ecclesiastical foundations, especially the monasteries, possessed more land and property than was good for religious discipline. The leading reformers wanted to abolish sacerdotal celibacy, to get rid of the religious of both sexes, to dissolve the monasteries and use the buildings for lay purposes (making them into schools or workshops). They wanted to diminish the size of the secular clergy in the interest of a more immediate and direct relationship between the individual's conscience and God. The Bible was to be put in the hands of the laity as a plain book (rather than as a scarce object sometimes fashioned by generations of monks). The plain Bible was to take the place of the priest and of the massive and beautiful Bibles which appeared as works of art in the service of the mass. Holy days were to be reduced in number, until, apart from daily prayers and in some cases daily reading of the Bible, all religious observances were to be concentrated on Sundays. Nearly all the reformers treated as idolatrous the images and much of the religious art created by their forefathers in churches and cathedrals as well as in monasteries. In their zeal, Protestants and particularly Calvinists rose up and tore down images and trampled on them.

[30] Nef, *A Search for Civilization*, Chicago, 1962, pp. 52, 94.

In many parts of Europe, particularly in the south—in Austria, Italy, southern France, and Spain—such uprisings were unsuccessful. While the activities of the Roman church were reconsidered, in the light of the reformers' criticisms, at the Council of Trent, monastic life was not abolished. The demands for religious buildings and works of art were little curtailed. But where the Reformation succeeded, the changes in the nature of supply and demand were pronounced. The leaders of the new churches were committed to reduce the size of the clergy, to favor the secularization of church property, especially the lands and buildings of monasteries, to discourage the construction of expensive religious edifices and especially their embellishment. Orders for glass, stone, iron, copper, bronze, wood, and other materials to be fashioned into works of art diminished wherever the Reformation triumphed; they almost vanished where extreme Calvinist austerity prevailed. In their enthusiasm for the return to rigorous Christian virtues as described in the Bible, for the elimination of much priestly intervention between man and God, the reformers were favoring the abolition of most tangible expressions of a heavenly city built on earth reaching to heaven. So they were abolishing what had once served their ancestors, especially during the eleventh, twelfth, and thirteenth centuries, as a mainspring for different kinds of economic development.[31] In so far as the Protestants were successful during the sixteenth century in supplanting the papists, their success created a kind of economic vacuum.

The greatest success of the reforms which the Protestants advocated were not in the countries where the original reformers—Luther, Zwingli, and Calvin—had been born and had first made a mark on religious history. The first confiscations of ecclesiastical landed property on a national scale were carried out in Sweden, Denmark, England, Scotland, and also in Holland. These confiscations were not dictated by profound religious convictions such as moved some of the martyrs in the age of religious warfare which followed. They were mainly political moves undertaken to strengthen the financial position of the sovereign authorities. At a time when princes everywhere in Europe sought increased power, princes in the north were exploiting the spirit of the Protestant Reformation, with its opposition to the worship, the wealth, and the government of the Roman church.

As a result of the dissolution of the English monasteries by enactments of 1536 and 1539, and subsequent acts involving lesser religious gilds, "The religious life as such was . . . swept from the country," almost at a

---

[31] I am aware that it is possible to hold, as my colleague Robert S. Lopez does, a different view of the economic influence of the medieval church, namely that it was little stimulus to *any* kind of economic development. I have devoted some attention to his thesis, in advancing which he seems to me to have missed the part played by qualitative progress in laying the foundations of industrial civilization, in my "L'art religieux et le progrès économique au 12e ou 13e siècles," *Association pour l'histoire de le Civilisation* (Toulouse, 1952–53), 23–29, to which I refer the reader.

stroke.[32] Only a few individual religious passed into exile "and continued to follow [that] life." While few of the others were executed, all were dispossessed of the properties belonging to their orders, though many were pensioned off. But, as the death rate was high, these pensions soon ceased to be a charge on the state.

In England and Wales ten thousand religious or more were eliminated in these ways by the dissolution of the monasteries and religious gilds between 1536 and 1550. The size of the secular clergy relative to population was much reduced in the sixteenth and seventeenth centuries.

What strikes the historian who looks at conditions a century after the dissolution, on the eve of the English Civil War, is the poverty of the Anglican church. In spite of the remarkable growth in the wealth of Great Britain, the churches were falling into ruin. The bishops and the parsons had not sufficient revenue to repair them.[33] The efforts of Laud, the Archbishop of Canterbury and Charles I's principal minister, to find revenue to restore these buildings, added to his unpopularity, and was not without its influence in causing the rebellion which cost him his head, as well as that of his sovereign.

FILLING THE VACUUM

After the dissolution of the monasteries and other religious gilds, something like a fourth of all the land in Great Britain is said to have passed out of church control and ownership into the possession of the crown and of laymen. A major portion of this property came on the market. What were the connections between the disappearance of this ecclesiastical wealth and the changes in industrial life which characterized the late sixteenth and early seventeenth centuries? How was the vacuum, brought about by the shrinkage of the wealth and influence of the clergy, filled?

The elements in the population which replaced the clergy in controlling supply and demand were represented by individuals who had different ideas from those of medieval churchmen concerning the uses to which the resources of the kingdom should be put. Their purpose was private profit and commodity derived primarily from multiplication of output rather than from beauty and permanence in the commodities created. A concentration of resources upon progress of this kind was novel in European history. It was encouraged by many other conditions besides the dissolution, among them the abundant supplies of easily accessible coal and iron ore, the peaceful relations which prevailed within the island of Great Britain from the accession of Elizabeth in 1558 to the Civil War in 1642, and the increasing

[32] Knowles, *The Religious Houses of Medieval England* (London, 1940), p. 58.
[33] H. R. Trevor-Roper, *Archbishop Laud, 1573–1645* (London, 1940), pp. 195–96.

difficulty experienced by the crown in regulating or participating in the industrial enterprise carried on by private persons.[34]

After the dissolution, two new political institutions—the Office of Augmentation, an administrative body, and the Court of Augmentation, a judicial body—were created to deal with the confiscated lands. Some extensive properties were handed over at once to powerful royal favorites. The *sale* of religious lands began, moreover, immediately after the dissolution. During the hundred years that followed, 1540–1640, the crown, in its efforts to raise revenue, disposed bit by bit of most of the holdings once possessed by the church, together with a substantial proportion of all other crown possessions.

Much of the confiscated land was rich in coal and iron ore. When extensively exploited, those resources tended to orient production in the direction of quantitative progress. Whether the land was retained by the crown (whose officials were disposed to lease it out on terms favorable for its economic development) or sold to subjects, the change of ownership encouraged its exploitation for purposes such as coal mining, the conversion of iron and other ores to metals, the making of salt, etc. It is surprising to what an extent the principal collieries, ironworks, and salt manufactures in England, Wales, and Scotland were founded in landed properties lost by the church. These were either leased out by the crown to rich private adventurers, generally joined in partnership, or worked by the new landed proprietors.[35]

An example gives an idea of the scope of the new coal mining enterprises. In the native country of Adam Smith, on the north shore of the Firth of Forth, was the large manor of Culross. It had once belonged to the Abbey of Culross. From early documents we learn that coal had been dug there in a small way, but that almost all efforts to get the mineral had been abandoned before the Reformation. The last abbot declared that the monastery had "neither large nor small coal for our own house fire." [36]

Culross then came into the hands of the Bruce family. Sir George Bruce, a contemporary and friend of James VI of Scotland who succeeded Elizabeth on the English throne in 1603 as James I, revolutionized its economy. He set to work to find the capital and the enterprise to make it an important coal-producing manor. He was challenged by the fact that a great proportion of the richest available seams were below water at high tide. At Culross the tides are formidable, rising some forty feet, which was more water

---

[34] For a discussion of these and other factors in the early English industrial revolution, see Nef, *La Naissance de la civilisation industrielle; Industry and Government in France and England, 1540–1640; Western Civilization since the Renaissance.*

[35] For evidence see Nef, *Rise of the British Coal Industry* (London, 1932), I, 143–56; "Note on the Progress of Iron Production in England, 1540–1640," *Journal of Political Economy,* XLIV, No. 3 (1936), 398–401.

[36] A. S. Cunningham, *Mining in the Kingdom of Fife* (Edinburgh, 1913), p. 5.

than most ships drew in Bruce's time. It occurred to someone, perhaps it was Bruce himself, that he might exploit this situation, if he was daring and adventurous enough to provide a wharf at which the coal could be loaded directly into the seagoing vessels rather than rowed out to them by lighter-men and shoveled aboard. Accordingly shafts and headways were cut for more than a mile under the sea. Horse- and water-driven pumping machin-ery was set up on shore to drain the shafts and headways where the pitmen hewed coal. The decisive advantage over other collieries for loading the bulky mineral fuel was gained by sinking to these undersea veins a shaft in a reef, free from water at low tide and artificially protected at high tide by the building of what a contemporary document describes as "a round circular frame of stone . . . joined together with glutinous and bitumous matter, so high withall, that the sea . . . can neither dissolve the stones, so well compacted in the building, or yet overflow the height of it." At high tide the ships could anchor beside this frame of stone, which was built as a wharf. The coal brought up the shaft could be conveniently dumped into their holds.

Contemporaries considered this colliery a tremendous feat of ingenuity. A widely-traveled Englishman of humble origin, Taylor, the London water poet, who had rowed lighters on the Thames in his youth, described Culross colliery in 1618, saying: "I did never see, read or heare of any worke of man that might parallell or bee equivalent with this unfellowed and un-matchable worke." [37] At about this time the king is said to have paid Bruce a visit, spending the night in the castle at Culross, according to the un-verified story. Knowing of James's interest in improvement, Bruce thought he would give him a pleasant surprise. He persuaded the king to rise be-fore dawn, led him in the dark from the shore down into the highways and byways of the prodigious mine with the men at work, and then hours later, without warning, after day had broken, brought him up the shaft in the reef. On emerging suddenly into light, the king found himself surrounded by the sea. Aware as James was of the violent characteristics of his Scottish ancestors and kinsmen and not conspicuous for his courage, it is little wonder that he shouted "Treason!"

Can we suppose that if Culross had remained in the possession of the Abbey, such a colliery would have been founded there?

The effect of the Reformation was to place the control of natural re-sources—coal, ores, and salt—in the hands of country gentlemen and mer-chants. They were less preoccupied than the monks with cultural and chari-table pursuits, and more likely in consequence to concentrate their energy and their thought, when the conditions were ripe, upon the exploitation of

---

[37] John Taylor, *The Pennyless Pilgrimage* (1618), quoted in P. Hume Brown, *Early Travellers in Scotland* (Edinburgh: D. Douglas, 1891), pp. 115–17.

minerals which provided raw materials for the manufacture of cheap commodities in greater abundance.

Wherever in England or Scotland lands were transferred through the dissolution of the monasteries, leases for the development of coal mines or ironworks could be obtained by venturesome enterprisers on much more favorable terms than in the past.[38] This was not in the main because Protestants taught different economic doctrines from Catholics. It was apparently no less difficult to get advantageous terms from the Anglican than from the Roman church. As late as the eighteenth century, Daniel Defoe, with his immense knowledge of economic conditions in England, explained the backwardness of building near Wolverhampton by the fact that "the land, for the chief part, being the property of the Church . . . the tenure [is] not such as to encourage people to lay out their money upon it.[39]

In most Continental countries, where the confiscation of church lands was carried out in only a small way, or where, as in France and the Spanish Netherlands, the Roman church retained as much landed property after the Reformation as before, coal mining and iron ore smelting by means of the blast furnace made slower progress than in Great Britain from 1540 to 1640. It can hardly be doubted that the far more extensive ownership of landed property by the Roman, as compared with the Anglican, church after the Reformation was a factor in holding back quantitative progress in France. A survey of 1788 was published years ago by the brothers Bourgin, giving particulars concerning many French ironworks on the eve of the Revolution. In all the provinces where it is possible to distinguish ironworks in lands belonging to the church from those in the lands of laymen, the output of the furnaces was notably less. In some provinces the difference was very great. In Champagne, for example, the average annual production in 1788 of an enterprise in the land of laymen was apparently about 380 tons, the average annual production of an enterprise in land of the clergy was only about 75 tons.[40]

The influence of the Reformation upon the "early industrial revolution" was not confined to the stimulus which confiscations provided for the exploitation of base minerals. The changes in the conception of the religious life introduced by Protestantism contributed also to the supply of laborers. It would be easy to exaggerate the stimulus which the abolition of sacerdotal celibacy provided. Monasticism had not always been incompatible with an increase in the human species, for the rise of sacerdotal celibacy and the

---

[38] For evidence relating to the coal mines, see Nef, *Rise of the British Coal Industry,* I, 143–56.

[39] *Tour thro the whole Island of Great Britain* (1769 ed.), London, II, 411.

[40] H. and G. Bourgin, *L'Industrie sidérurgique en France* (Paris, 1920), and the figures derived from this in Nef, *The United States and Civilization* (Chicago, 1942), pp. 158–59.

rapid spread of the religious life during the eleventh and twelfth centuries were accompanied almost everywhere by a high birth rate among the laity and a remarkable increase in the population as a whole. But the existence of a richly endowed celibate religious life, however grievously some of its practitioners fell from grace, was not a stimulus to childbearing! The elimination of the religious, combined with the general permission granted the secular clergy to marry, almost certainly contributed to the notable increase of the English population which accompanied the speeding up of industrial development between about 1540 and 1640. There were more persons than before without property or a settled occupation inherited from their parents, and such persons were readily available for work in industries of new kinds like the refining of sugar, the making of tobacco pipes, and the manufacture of cheap paper to be used in wrapping, and also for work in industries which expanded greatly in England for the first time, such as coal mining and the manufacture of salt and cheap glass.

With the growing importance of Puritanism in England and Presbyterianism in Scotland, there was a notable tendency to concentrate all religious observances on the Sabbath, a fact to which Weber refers as contributing to the rational organization of life. Laborers were more readily available than in the past for continuous work at routine tasks. Routine labor, as distinguished from artistic craftsmanship which lends itself to a less routinized organization of work, was encouraged still more by the fact that Puritanism and Presbyterianism denied that it was to any large extent the function of the religious life to create or encourage works to delight the senses or even to nourish beauty at all.

By diminishing the proportion of all wealth in ecclesiastical hands, the Reformation created a vacuum on the side of economic demand as well as of supply. The medieval religious, to repeat the judgment passed on them by Bishop Stubbs, had been "more polished and more charitable" than their lay neighbors. A similar distinction may perhaps be made between the Roman clergy generally and the Protestant clergy which succeeded them in some parts of Europe, nowhere more as time went on than in England and Scotland. Austerity and sternness in the pursuit of righteousness were keynotes of the Puritans and Presbyterians, and austerity and sternness on the part of the clergy, which sets an example by its activities as well as by its preaching and its teaching, are no less contagious in a lay community, which takes seriously the Christian faith, than are polish and charity. The Calvinist clergy could not command anything like as large financial resources as the Roman Catholic clergy, nor were they disposed to employ the resources they retained in the interest of polish and charity. Such encouragement of beauty as was provided by the English church during the century following the Reformation came from those in the priesthood who adhered to the orthodox Anglican communion, and who conceived of a church much as Hooker did in his *Laws of Ecclesiastical Polity*. That great book, partly published in 1593 or 1594, warned Hooker's contemporaries of the dangers of a Puritan domination of the Church of England. Among these dangers he stressed the abandonment of decoration, ceremony, music, and other forms of beauty as an accompaniment to prayer and communion. During the half-century following the appearance of Hooker's book, the Puritan influence, distrusted by Hooker, waxed and produced a religious crisis. That portion of the demand for artistic works which had come from ecclesiastics during the Middle Ages largely dried up.

With Calvinist austerity there went also what Tawney calls "the new medicine for poverty." Material provision for the unemployed, for the maimed, and even for the sick and old was left in England to government with its poor law. Charity in tangible forms of *gifts* to the needy ceased to have the place in religious life it had once occupied.

In France, the influence of reformed Roman Catholicism was thrown, with a new vision and a new humanity, into the support of polish and of charity. The two religious leaders whose influence affected French and even European history most during the early seventeenth century were St. François de Sales and St. Vincent de Paul. The intellectual and cultural movement in France which we call "classicism" is associated with the spread of more polite manners and gentler conduct. The humanism of St. François de Sales and his followers was intimately associated with both, through the enormous influence which the renewed Christian life had upon the aristocracy and especially among women of noble birth. At the same time the endless labor of "Monsieur Vincent" on behalf of the poor, the sick, and the old, enlisted extraordinary material support from these same rich women of the nobility. The charitable efforts of the "filles de charité" spread through France, through Continental Europe, and even overseas.[41]

Next to the increasingly strong and wealthy monarchical government, no institution in seventeenth-century France commanded such spending power as the reformed Roman church. Unlike the crown, that church was not obliged to spend for national defense and conquest. Its influence was used on behalf of qualitative progress: the extension of elegance, beauty, and consolation to laymen. By retaining its wealth, and by renewing and developing in novel forms its relation to beauty and to charity, the post-Reformation Roman church, especially under French leadership, encouraged an economic evolution in which beauty, elegance, moderation, and gentleness provided the principal goals.

The kind of vacuum created in Great Britain and other northern countries by the Reformation hardly existed on the Continent, except in Holland. Central Europe, where the Reformation met in certain countries with much

---

[41] See Nef, *La Naissance de la civilisation industrielle et le monde contemporain*, chap. ix; *Cultural Foundations of Industrial Civilization*, chaps, iv, v, vi.

success, was plunged into religious strife and economic decadence during the first half of the seventeenth century, and the people there were in no position to assume the leadership in quantitative progress which we associate especially with the Dutch and the English, or the leadership in qualitative progress which we associate with the French even more than with the Dutch.

CONCLUSION

The Reformation contributed to the speeding up of industrial growth during the late sixteenth and seventeenth centuries in England and Scotland, and in all countries of the north of Europe which went over to Protestantism especially in its Calvinistic forms. Brakes which had hitherto been applied by religious government and religious habits to rapid industrialization, to the use of laborsaving machinery, were gradually released. A wider field was opened in economic life for the production of comforts and conveniences of many kinds in the making of which art played a smaller role than in the religious economy of the Middle Ages and the Renaissance.

It will be presumably the disposition of nearly all contemporary historians and sociologists, as well as of contemporary economists, if they partly agree with the account given in these pages, to leave the subject there. They will see in the reduction in the number and the enormous reduction in the wealth of the clergy, which occurred in the Protestant countries of northern Europe, only instruments of progress. They will regard the maintenance in the number and the wealth of the clergy in Catholic countries much as it was regarded already in the late seventeenth century in some quarters in northern Europe and as it has come to be regarded by scholars and writers since the time of Weber, even to some extent since the time of William Petty and Josiah Tucker, as a handicap to economic growth.[42] "In the King of England's Dominions," wrote Petty in 1690, "there are not twenty Thousand Church-men. But in France . . . there are about Two Hundred and Seventy thousand, viz. Two Hundred and Fifty thousand more than we think are necessary. . . ."[43]

There may have been idle monks and priests sustained by the Roman church in France and throughout post-Reformation Europe. But this was not the basis of Petty's and Tucker's criticism of Catholicism. The view of

[42] Nef, *A Search for Civilization* (Chicago, 1962), p. 90.
[43] *Economic Writings of Sir William Petty*, I, 291–92. Petty makes this last calculation, forgetting apparently that the population of France in 1690 was much more than twice that of England. Sixty years later Tucker put the number of French churchmen at 300,000, and regarded the French clergy as "a great Burden, and consequently a Disadvantage to the Trade of France." (*A Brief Essay on the Advantages and Disadvantages which respectively Attend France and Great Britain with Regard to Trade* [2d ed.; London, 1750], p. 25.)

Petty, which was also that of some "Hollanders" whom he quotes in another place, was that the religious functions performed by the Roman clergy were a "superfluous charge" in France and Spain. This view reveals a bias that dominates the outlook of modern people, preoccupied as they have come to be with production measured by size and volume. They fail to recognize that the direction of inventive ingenuity and administration to ever greater increases in material production depended not only on modern science and technology and capitalistic initiative, but on the development of a more civilized outlook on man and of more civilized conduct among human beings than had prevailed in the past.

The supreme achievements of modern scientists have been inspired by a wider culture than that provided by scientific inquiry, by the use of rational processes which transcend quantitative methods and involve intuition of the same genius which inspires the artist and the man of faith.[44] The unrestrained application of new scientific results to modern technological progress depended on the development of a reassuring confidence, novel in history, that human nature was improving so that the new knowledge would be used mainly not for destructive but for constructive purposes. This confidence, in its turn, depended on the realization of more harmonious relations between and within independent nations than had ever existed before, on the development of a concept of limited warfare among all the European peoples and potentially among all peoples throughout the globe.[45]

Without humane and gentle relations such as had never prevailed before, the rapid economic progress of the nineteenth century which brought about the triumph of industrial civilization would hardly have been possible.[46] At the roots of these improved relations was the qualitative economic progress characteristic of France and also of Holland in the seventeenth century. This progress had an immense influence throughout Europe, and even in Great Britain, during the late seventeenth and early eighteenth centuries. Insofar as the renewed Roman church contributed after the religious wars to this qualitative progress, it was not interfering with the rise of industrial civilization, nor was it a "superfluous charge." It was helping to make industrial civilization possible. We begin to see, therefore, how misleading for the historian has been the outlook of economic history and of sociology, insofar as these disciplines have confined the problem of the coming of contemporary industrial society to the origins in religious thought and doctrine of the "spirit of capitalism" and of rapid economic growth. A much broader hope in man, because of the belief in him inspired by his divine origin through the testimony of Christ, made the Christian

[44] See below, chap. vii.
[45] See Nef, *Western Civilization since the Renaissance*, esp. chaps. vi, vii, Part II generally, and chap. xvii.
[46] Nef, *Civilization, Industrial Society, and Love*, Center for the Study of Democratic Institutions, Santa Barbara, Calif., Occasional Paper No. 118, 1960.

faith, in spite of all the iniquities and violence done in the name of Christianity, a great civilizing force.

Historians of the nineteenth century who, like Buckle, saw the church and even the Christian faith as one of the most formidable obstacles to economic progress, have also put us on a wrong track. Our Christian history, before as well as after the awful ordeal and aberration of a century of religious wars, provided an integral part of the preparation for the remarkable material achievements of the Western peoples during the past hundred and fifty years. There is of course no necessary connection between a large clergy and the influence of Christian morality and Christian love. There is nevertheless a connection between the morality and the love to which, as Christ taught, all human beings have access and the rise of civilization. And the Roman church, in spite of all the shortcomings and vices of the clergy, helped to foster this morality and love.[47] It would not be inconsistent with the views put forward in this book concerning the birth and triumph of industrial civilization to suggest that, even from an economic standpoint, the world today is suffering less from too many than from too few true followers of Christ.

[47] Nef, *A Search for Civilization* (Chicago, 1962), pp. 101–8. Cf. Nef, "A New Christian View of History?" *Thought,* XXXVII, No. 146 (1962), 351–55; and below, chap. ix.

6

Prices and Industrial Capitalism
in France and England, 1540–1640

Throughout western Europe during the second half of the sixteenth century, peasants, craftsmen, and shopkeepers, as well as princes and bishops, all shared one novel experience of some importance for their daily lives. In each decade they found that any standard coin, even if it contained precisely the same quantity of precious metal as in the previous decade, would buy less of almost any commodity bought and sold.

This "price revolution," as it has come to be called, was caused mainly by the abundant supplies of precious metals which poured into Europe from South and Central America. Prices—measured in silver—rose in the various European countries, we are told, from two- to more than threefold between 1520 and 1650.[1] The prices which people actually paid rose much more, because princes everywhere were debasing the currency.

For some time historians and economists have been disposed to regard the price revolution as an important cause for the rise of modern capitalism. But, until recently, no one attempted to show concretely how the inflow of treasure from America promoted the development of large-scale enterprise in industry, commerce, and finance. In 1929 Professor E. J. Hamilton, to whom we owe our exact knowledge of the price revolution in Spain, suggested that the rapid increase in prices stimulated the growth of capitalism mainly by cheapening labor costs, and thus making possible exceptionally large profits during a period of many decades.[2] These profits

From *Economic History Review,* VII, No. 2 (May, 1937), 155–85.
[1] Georg Wiebe, *Zur Geschichte der Preisrevolution des 16 und 17 Jahrhunderts* (Leipzig, 1895), pp. 376–77, 379, 382; Earl J. Hamilton, *American Treasure and the Price Revolution in Spain* (Cambridge, Mass., 1934), pp. 205–10, 403. Cf. François Simiand, *Recherches anciennes et nouvelles sur le movement général des prix du XVI° au XIX° siècle* (Paris, 1932), pp. 167–68.

[2] Hamilton, "American Treasure and the Rise of Capitalism," in *Economica,* XXVII (1929), 338–57.

brought about an unprecedented accumulation of wealth in the hands of enterprising merchants and other rich men, who could afford to invest in large-scale enterprises, and who were tempted to do so by the prospect of abnormally large returns. Later, in his *Treatise on Money,* Lord Keynes used his great authority to support and interpret Dr. Hamilton's thesis.[3]

Dr. Hamilton observed that the effect of the price revolution upon the material welfare of the wage-earner was not the same in all countries. In Spain, he found, rising wages did not lag behind rising prices anything like as much as they apparently did in England.[4] He concluded that the differences between the course of wages in the two countries provided a very important explanation for the greater progress made by capitalist enterprise in England than in Spain, especially during the first two or three decades of the seventeenth century. At that time wages caught up with prices in Spain, and the Spanish wageworkers regained all they had lost in earning power during the previous eight decades.[5] But in England wages apparently lagged further than ever behind prices, and the wageworkers were able to buy only about half as much with the money they received as at the beginning of the sixteenth century.[6] The greater fall in the standard of living of the English laborer was a part of the cost which he had to pay for great national progress.[7] Without the price revolution, an extensive and prolonged decline in real wages could hardly have occurred. Therefore, according to this theory, the price revolution was the principal driving force behind capitalistic enterprise during the late sixteenth and early seventeenth centuries.[8]

THE PROGRESS OF LARGE-SCALE INDUSTRY DURING THE PRICE REVOLUTION

A comparison of French with English industrial history during the century from 1540 to 1640 suggests that there is a danger of exaggerating

[3] J. M. Keynes, *A Treatise on Money* (New York, 1930), II, pp. 152–63.

[4] Dr. Hamilton's calculations concerning the course of real wages in Spain, as announced tentatively in his article in *Economica* (*loc. cit.,* pp. 253–54), were borne out by his further researches (*American Treasure and the Price Revolution in Spain,* p. 273).

[5] *Ibid.,* pp. 273, 279–82.

[6] Hamilton, "American Treasure and the Rise of Capitalism," pp. 350–52.

[7] Cf. Keynes, *op. cit.,* II, p. 163.

[8] Hamilton, "American Treasure and the Rise of Capitalism," pp. 338, 344, 349. Cf. Keynes, *op. cit.,* II, p. 159. Dr. Hamilton's argument about the influence of the discoveries in promoting capitalism was not concerned exclusively with the role played by the price revolution in reducing the cost of labor. He also wrote of the phenomenal profits made by merchants in the East India trade, and of the probable decline in the real cost of renting land, as further factors which increased the accumulation of capital and encouraged investments in large-scale enterprise ("American Treasure and the Rise of Capitalism," pp. 347–50). But it was to the fall in real wages that he attached the most importance (*ibid.,* pp. 349, 355–56), and it was to this aspect that Lord Keynes drew attention.

the role played by the price revolution, and the decline of real wages that it made possible, in stimulating the progress of capitalist enterprise in industry.[9] At the time Dr. Hamilton wrote it was assumed that the progress of industrial enterprise in France was similar to that in England during these hundred years.[10] But it now seems that there were important differences. In England from 1540 to 1640 there occurred a great speeding-up in the rate of industrial growth for which there was no equivalent in France. There was no increase in the output of coal, glass, salt, alum, building materials, metal wares, and ships comparable in rapidity to that which raised England from an industrial backwater to the most advanced industrial country in the world.[11] Technical changes in the methods of mining and manufacturing which greatly increased the amounts of capital needed to set up in industry were less widely introduced.[12] The progress of private enterprise in English industry was very much more rapid than in France.[13] What we have to explain in the case of France is not, as in that of England, why industrial capitalism made so much progress in the age of the price revolution, but why it made so little.

The explanations arrived at for France have a special interest, because the case of France was more representative of European countries generally than the case of England. In southern Germany and the Spanish Netherlands, the age of the price revolution was, as compared with the age of the Renaissance, a period of slow industrial development. Only in Holland, in Scotland, in Sweden, and perhaps in the principality of Liège, was there a speeding-up in the rate of industrial development resembling to some extent that which occurred in England.

Were there any differences between the course of wages in England and France from 1540 to 1640 which help to account for the great differences in the progress of industrial capitalism? The only index numbers of wages and commodity prices in the two countries available when Professor Hamilton wrote his article in 1929, were those compiled in 1895 by Georg Wiebe, who used the voluminous records of wages and prices, collected by Thorold Rogers[14] and the Vicomte d'Avenel,[15] as a basis for the first comprehensive inquiry into the price revolution.[16] Dr. Hamilton reprinted these index numbers in order to compare the course of real wages in Andalusia and in

[9] In this article we are not concerned, as Dr. Hamilton was, with the influence of the price revolution upon commercial and financial, as well as industrial, organization.

[10] Hamilton, "American Treasure and the Rise of Capitalism," pp. 338, 356.

[11] See above, chap. iv.

[12] Cf. above, chap. iii, for England.

[13] Nef, *Industry and Government in France and England* (Ithaca, N.Y., 1957).

[14] *A History of Agriculture and Prices in England* (7 vols.; Oxford, 1866–1902).

[15] *Histoire économique de la propriété, des salaires, des denrées et de tous les prix,* (7 vols.; Paris, 1894).

[16] Wiebe, *op. cit.,* pp. 374–79.

England and France.[17] Lord Keynes derived from them tables of what he called "profit inflation." These tables give for successive periods during the sixteenth and seventeenth centuries the ratio of commodity prices to costs of production, on the assumption that in both England and France money wages accounted for half the costs of production, and that the other half rose exactly as commodity prices.[18] For the convenience of the reader in following our argument, Lord Keynes' tables are reproduced below.

LORD KEYNES' TABLES[19]

England			France		
Period	Price/Costs Ratio		Period	Price/Costs Ratio	
1500–1550	. . .	100	1500–1525	. . .	100
			1525–1550	. . .	103
1550–1560	. . .	116			
1560–1570	. . .	112	1550–1575	. . .	110
1570–1580	. . .	116			
1580–1590	. . .	120	1575–1600	. . .	139
1590–1600	. . .	137			
1600–1610	. . .	139	1600–1625	. . .	118
1610–1620	. . .	135			
1620–1630	. . .	141			
1630–1640	. . .	134	1625–1650	. . .	128
1640–1650	. . .	133			

His results suggest that the behavior of real wages in the two countries was similar. The standard of living among laborers apparently fell in France nearly, if not quite, as much as in England.[20] On Wiebe's showing, there were at least two generations of French workers whose wages would buy only about half the quantity of commodities that the wages of their ancestors in the late fifteenth century would have bought.[21] While France belongs, like Spain, to a group of countries where industrial capitalism made comparatively slow progress from 1540 to 1640, it seems to belong, as England does, to a group of countries where the fall in real wages was much greater and more prolonged than in Spain.

As can be seen from Lord Keynes' tables, Wiebe's index numbers were

[17] Hamilton, "American Treasure and the Rise of Capitalism," pp. 352–54.
[18] Keynes, op. cit., II, pp. 159–60.
[19] Taken from Keynes, op. cit., II, pp. 159–60.
[20] Wiebe compiled two sets of index numbers for commodity prices in England, based on different methods of weighting the commodities (op. cit., pp. 374–76, 383). If Dr. Hamilton had reprinted not the first but the second set, which shows prices rising a good deal more slowly, it would have appeared that the workers' standard of living fell more in France than in England.
[21] Hamilton, "American Treasure and the Rise of Capitalism," p. 353.

worked out by decades for England and by twenty-five-year periods for France. If we are to study the relations between price changes and industrial development, it is important to know not only that industrial capitalism made much slower progress in France than in England during the century from 1540 to 1640 as a whole, but also to know in which portions of the century the contrasts were greatest.

For the purpose of comparing the progress of industrial capitalism in the two countries, the century can be divided into four fairly well-defined periods.[22] The first ran from 1540 into the 1560's. In France this period was probably marked by some slight slowing down in the rate of industrial growth, which had been rather rapid since the end of the Hundred Years' War. In England it was marked by a speeding-up in the rate of growth. The rapid increase in the output of cloth, which had begun in the reign of Henry VII, was accompanied after the dissolution of the monasteries, in 1536 and 1539, by a rapid increase in the output of other industrial commodities, such as beer, coal, and iron. Blast furnaces, costing with their water-driven bellows and hammers thousands of pounds, multiplied in Sussex, and large foundries for casting iron cannons were introduced from the Continent. The amount of capital invested in new mines and small factories was probably much larger—relative to population—than in France.

The differences between development in the two countries during this first period were slight compared with those during the next, which began in the 1560's and ran into the 1590's. During the seventies and eighties in England many new industries, like the manufacture of brass, paper, sugar, alum, and copperas, were introduced, and the output of older industries, like mining, smelting, shipbuilding, salt- and glassmaking, grew at a more rapid rate than during the forties and fifties. The phenomenal growth in industrial output, together with the widespread adoption of costly horse and water mills, hitherto little employed in Great Britain compared with many other European countries, produced an unprecedented demand for industrial capital. Hundreds of new mines and small factories were started. But in France the seventies and eighties were decades of religious warfare and civil strife. While the effects of the wars upon economic life have been represented by contemporary writers and even by modern historians as more disastrous than they were,[23] they did hold back investments in new enterprises. Much less capital was probably invested in large-scale industry during the seventies and eighties than during the forties and fifties. This was probably the period when the contrasts between industrial progress in the two countries were greatest.

[22] What follows is derived mainly from material referred to above in chap. iv. It is intended to be a tentative statement, which I hope to correct and amplify with the help of a study of further documents.
[23] See above, pp. 146–48.

The third period began in the 1590's and lasted until about 1620. In England it may be regarded from the point of view of industrial history as a continuation of the previous period. The rate of growth in industrial output after 1604 was possibly even greater than during the 1570's and 1580's. New inventions cheapened the products and increased the scale of enterprise in industries like glass- and steelmaking. Horse- and water-driven engines and large furnaces and kilns, which had been adopted in many ventures during Elizabeth's reign, replaced the older more primitive tools and ovens even more extensively, both in manufacturing and mining, in centers of population like London and centers of industry like the Tyne valley. Except in Sussex, Surrey, and Kent, where the exhaustion of the forests interfered with the progress of the iron and glass manufactures, more capital found investment than during the previous period in new mines and small factories and in the expansion of old ones. This was also in France a period of expanding industrial output and of marked technical development. A large number of new enterprises were started in many provinces, especially after the publication of the Edict of Nantes in 1598 had brought to an end the most destructive phases of the religious wars. In comparison with the twenty-five years from 1570 to 1595, those from 1595 to 1620 were a bright period for the progress of French manufactures, at any rate north of the Loire and the Rhone. Though progress was less rapid than in England, the contrasts were less remarkable than during the religious wars.

The fourth period, from about 1620 until the outbreak of the English Civil War and the death of Louis XIII, in 1643, was marked in both countries by some slowing down in the rate of industrial development. In England there were serious depressions in industry during the twenties. These were followed, however, by renewed rapid expansion in the thirties, and, according to Lord Clarendon, the English people on the eve of the Civil War "enjoyed . . . the fullest measure of felicity, that any people in any age . . . have been blessed with." [24]

In France, the depression in the Levant trade, which began about 1620, proved a serious blow for industry at Marseille, and elsewhere in the south. Throughout Provence and Languedoc many enterprises in such manufactures as soap-boiling, shipbuilding, iron- and glassmaking shut down for lack of markets. Nor was the depression confined to the south. Manufacturing was on the decline in Poitou, and, at least insofar as the building of merchant ships and the production of iron was concerned, in Brittany and Champagne.

The depression of the twenties was not followed in France, as it was in England, by a substantial recovery during the early thirties. We can find

[24] Clarendon, *The History of the Rebellion and Civil Wars in England* (Oxford, 1843), p. 30.

nothing in France to rival the rapid expansion which occurred at that time in English merchant shipbuilding, in the manufacture of alum in Yorkshire and Durham, and in the building trades of London. The depression in the French Levant commerce, which began in the twenties, was followed by a collapse in the thirties. While the output of iron in England probably did not increase rapidly, new and larger furnaces were built during the thirties in the Midlands and the Forest of Dean to replace the older ones in southeastern England.[25] It was not until the reign of Louis XIV that a similar development of large new blast furnaces and forges occurred in central and western France to offset the decline of the iron manufacture in Champagne and the Cévennes.[26] The picture painted by Voltaire of the deplorable condition of French industry and trade at the great king's accession, while overdrawn, contains much truth.[27] England continued to maintain a striking lead over France with respect to industrial growth as had been true of the two previous periods.

When we consider the growth in the volume of industrial output in England and France during these four periods in relation to the course of profit inflation as shown in Lord Keynes' tables, what do we find? While there is nothing in the tables to account for the depression which came in England at the end of James I's reign (1619–24), there is certainly a remarkable coincidence between profit inflation, which reflects the fall in real wages, and the speeding-up of industrial growth. Conditions appear to have been increasingly favorable for exceptional profits throughout the hundred years 1540–1640.[28] Except for three decades, 1560–70, 1610–20, and 1630–40, the openings for profits were greater in every decade than they had been in the previous one.

With these figures before us, there is a temptation to regard the price revolution as the principal explanation of the early English industrial revolution. There is a temptation to believe that the new shipyards, the hundreds of new mines, smelting furnaces and forges, the numerous soap, starch, and sugar houses, the glass furnaces, breweries, brick- and limekilns, and the alum and copperas factories were built, equipped, supplied with raw materials, and staffed by workmen, largely because the exceptional profits ob-

[25] Nef, "Note on the Progress of Iron Production in England," *Journal of Political Economy*, XLIV (1936), 402–3.

[26] See above, pp. 178–80.

[27] Voltaire, *Le siècle de Louis XIV* (1751), chap. ii.

[28] Lord Keynes' tables give the impression that in England prices began to rise more rapidly than wages only after 1550. But Wiebe's index numbers show that the fall in real wages began much earlier, as soon as prices started upward. Prices actually began to rise in the second decade of the sixteenth century, and the rise became rather rapid during the forties. The real situation has been obscured because Wiebe's index numbers, which give prices in terms of their silver values, make it appear that prices *fell* during the forties (Wiebe, *op. cit.*, pp. 70, 376–77). This point was called to my attention by John Saltmarsh.

tained by the wealthy as real wages fell, had created great new reservoirs of capital awaiting investment, and because the cheapness of labor made investments exceptionally attractive.

But in France, after 1550, according to the tables, labor was hardly less cheap than in England; yet no comparable expansion of privately owned industrial enterprise occurred. It is true that from 1550 to 1575, according to the table, profit inflation was slightly less in France than in England. But from 1575 to 1600 profit inflation reached its zenith in France, and was even greater than in England. Theoretically this was the period in France when price conditions seem to have been most favorable for investments in new enterprises; it was a period when they were more favorable in France than in England. But, in fact, this was of all four periods (with the possible exception of the last) the one during which the least new capital flowed into industrial enterprise in France. It was the period during which English development was in most striking contrast to French.

According to the tables, real wages in France were a good deal higher in the first quarter of the seventeenth century than in the last quarter of the sixteenth. Theoretically this should not have been as good a time for the expansion of industrial enterprise as either the preceding or the succeeding period. But, in fact, it proved to be a better time.

Some years ago Monsieur André Liautey wrote, in a study of the price revolution in France, that a rise in prices "is . . . compatible with the most dissimilar economic conditions." [29] The same thing seems to be true of a fall in real wages. Periods of profit inflation coincided with periods of industrial expansion; they also coincided with periods of industrial depression.

THE COST OF INDUSTRIAL LABOR DURING THE PRICE REVOLUTION

Since Wiebe compiled his index numbers, several sets of price and wage records, not contained in the volumes of Rogers and d'Avenel which he used, have been published. A brief examination of these records and of new data collected by the International Scientific Committee on Price History,[30] together with the old data on which Wiebe's work was based, suggests that the decline in the material welfare of the English workers from 1500 to 1642 was much less than Wiebe's index numbers suggested. Be-

[29] *La hausse des prix et la lutte contre la cherté en France au XVIe siècle* (Paris, 1921), p. 337.

[30] Made possible through the generosity of Lord Beveridge, once Chairman of the English Price Committee. My work was greatly facilitated by the kind help of Miss M. E. Rayner, the Secretary of the Committee, who not only found for me the relevant material, but made some calculations of the price averages for timber purchased by the Royal Navy. I am much indebted to both of them. Since my essay was published in 1937 much new material has appeared concerning prices and wages in Europe from 1540 to 1640. I hope to be able to make use of it later.

fore the studies of Thorold Rogers were published, some writers claimed that the mechanic could get more wheat for a day's work on the eve of the Civil War, in 1640, than at the beginning of Elizabeth's reign, about 1560.[31] Rogers' transcription of thousands of price and wage records made that position untenable. But he and some other scholars who used his volumes seem to have exaggerated the losses which the workers suffered from rapidly rising prices almost as much as ill-informed persons, who had no reliable statistics to establish their case, once exaggerated the gains which the same workers obtained from increases in wages.

To begin with, wage rates apparently rose appreciably more than Rogers' data indicated. His data did not concern the wages of mechanics like smiths or cutlers, or the wages of spinners and weavers, or those of miners, smelters, and workers in other rising manufactures. They related entirely to the wages of laborers in the building trades, such as masons, carpenters, tilers, and bricklayers. According to the averages worked out from Rogers' tables by Wiebe and others, wage rates rose a shade less than two-and-a-half-fold between the first decade of the sixteenth century and the decade preceding the Civil War.[32]

We now have a number of new, rather complete series for the money wages paid to the same kinds of workmen in connection with building enterprises at several places in southern England. Three are for London.[33] The others are for Eton, Winchester, Dover, Canterbury, Cambridge, and Exeter.[34] The new data indicate that—on the average—wage rates rose nearly, if not quite, threefold between 1510 and 1640, or something like 20 per cent more than Wiebe's tables show. It is mainly for the sixty years from 1580 to 1640, the period during which according to Wiebe's index numbers the building workers suffered most from rising prices, that his figures understate the increase in their money wages. According to these figures, wage rates rose about 39 per cent between the period 1571–82 and

[31] E.g., William Playfair, *A Letter on our Agricultural Distresses* (London, 1821), charts facing pp. 50 and 44, and also pp. 48, 29. I am grateful to my colleague, Professor Jacob Viner, for calling my attention to this tract.

[32] If we take the average wages in the decade 1501–10 as 100, then, according to Wiebe, the average in the decade 1633–42 (not in silver, but in English money) was 248 (Wiebe, *op. cit.*, pp. 377, 70). According to Steffen, the average was 237 (Gustaf F. Steffen, *Studien zur Geschichte der Englischen Lohnarbeite* [Stuttgart, 1901], Vol. I). Professor Knoop and G. P. Jones have worked out from Rogers' data separate averages for Oxford and Cambridge. The result for the decade 1633–42 is 200 for Oxford and 266 for Cambridge (Douglas Knoop and G. P. Jones, *The Mediæval Mason* [Manchester, 1933], p. 236).

[33] From one of these—the London Bridge series—averages have been derived and published (Knoop and Jones, *op. cit.*, p. 236). The other two—for the Royal Works and for Westminster College and Abbey—are among the MSS. of the Price Committee at the London School of Economics.

[34] MSS. of the Price Committee at the London School of Economics. So far as I know, index numbers have not yet been worked out from these records.

the decade 1633–42.[35] The new data suggest that they rose more than 50 per cent.[36]

If we are to estimate the effects of the price revolution upon the laborers' standard of living, we ought to know whether unemployment among the building workers increased or diminished. We ought to know what the workers bought with their wages. We ought also to know whether they made their purchases from the same kinds of tradesmen and on the same terms as did the crown and the municipalities, and the colleges, hospitals, and other institutions, since most of the price records that have been collected have been taken from the account books of such authorities and establishments. No satisfactory answer can be given to these questions. But, in dealing with them, certain rather misleading assumptions have been made by nearly all the authorities who have discussed the standard of living among wageworkers during the period of the price revolution. It has been assumed that money wages were all that workmen received for their labor, and that these wages were spent almost exclusively on the purchase of certain foodstuffs and foods.

First of all, we have to consider whether the foodstuffs and foods have been selected in such a way as to give a true picture of the rise in the cost of diet among the laboring classes. Englishmen early in the seventeenth century were fond of saying that bread, and after bread, ale or beer, were the chief "stay" of the poor. But cereal products were not by any means the only nourishment of working people, as has been often assumed in attempting to determine the standard of living. Since Rogers' time authorities who have tried to estimate the rise in the price of food during the sixteenth and seventeenth centuries have never been able to include in their computations the prices of either bread or beer. They have got around this difficulty by substituting the prices paid in towns for the various grains from which bread and beer were produced. But in the principal towns at the beginning of the seventeenth century home-brewing had largely disappeared, so that most of the townsfolk bought their beer, and even home-baking was of less importance than it had been before the Reformation.[37]

Can we assume that the prices of drink, bread, and meal were rising as

[35] Wiebe, loc. cit. According to Steffen's averages, also obtained from Rogers, wages rose only about 27 per cent (Knoop and Jones, loc. cit.).

[36] According to the averages worked out by Knoop and Jones, wage rates for building work at London Bridge increased between the decades 1501–10 and 1633–42 practically threefold—from 8 d. to about 23d. a day. Between 1571–82 and 1633–42 wage rates increased from about 14d. to about 23d. (Knoop and Jones, op. cit., p. 236). My examination of the new records collected by the Price Committee indicates that these averages are more typical than those worked out by Thorold Rogers and used by Wiebe and Steffen (Rogers, History of Agriculture and Prices, IV, 518–23; V, 664–67).

[37] Cf. Sylvia Thrupp, A Short History of the Worshipful Company of Bakers (London, 1933), pp. 74–75, 79.

much during the price revolution as the prices of the grains from which they were produced? The matter is of importance, because the prices of grains, grain products, and grasses rose almost twice as much between the first decade of the sixteenth century and the decade preceding the Civil War as the prices of most foods. Wheat increased about six-and-a-half-fold in price, oats and malt between seven- and eightfold, hay and straw more than eightfold.[38] Meanwhile peas increased about fivefold in price, butter about four-and-a-third-fold, hens and eggs a shade under four-and-a-third-fold, and pigeons about three-and-a-third-fold.[39] There was at least one food—herrings—which apparently increased in price somewhat less rapidly than the wages of building craftsmen rose. It is possible that, with the enactment of laws to encourage fish-eating, herrings came to occupy an even more important place in the diet of the common people than before the Reformation. We have not as yet any index numbers for the prices of meat until the reign of Elizabeth. But between the decades 1580–89 and 1630–39, when the price of grain almost doubled, the price of beef and mutton rose less than 50 per cent,[40] hardly more than the wages of carpenters.[41] During this half-century the price of foods, other than cereal products, appears to have risen only about as rapidly as wage rates in the building trades.

The prices of bread and drink were determined by the cost of making them as well as by the prices of the grains and grain products from which they were made. When it is assumed that bread and drink rose in price as rapidly as wheat, oats, rye, barley, malt, and hops, it is also assumed that the price of labor and the price of materials other than grain employed in milling, baking, malting, and brewing increased as rapidly as the price of grain, and that there was no reduction in the quantity of either labor or grain used in these processes. It seems to me that none of these assumptions is warranted.

To judge from conditions in the building trades, wage rates rose only about threefold between the first decade of the sixteenth century and the decade preceding the Civil War.[42] The cost of labor in baking and brewing probably increased somewhat more than these figures indicate, because the workmen were frequently supplied with food in addition to their wages,[43]

[38] These figures are taken from Lord Beveridge's MS. "Provisional Index Numbers of Food and Fuel—1500–1800," 1932, the London School of Economics.

[39] As Lord Beveridge did not have index numbers for these foods covering the whole period from 1500 to 1640, I have used Steffen's ten-yearly average prices (*op. cit.*, I, 254–55, 365–66).

[40] MS. "Provisional Index Numbers," *loc. cit.* Cf. Steffen, *op. cit.*, I, pp. 255, 366.

[41] As these were shown in the records of the Price Committee at the London School of Economics.

[42] See pp. 247–49.

[43] See p. 253.

but it could not have increased anything like as rapidly as the price of grain.

Firewood alone among the materials needed in making bread or beer, rose in price more than grain.[44] But in brewing, coal, which was cheap, was widely substituted for wood fuel during the reigns of Elizabeth and her two successors, so that by 1637 only one of the five brew houses in Westminster had a log-burning furnace.[45] In baking, coal was still little used,[46] but even as late as 1619, when logs and faggots were extremely dear, wood accounted for only about one-tenth of the costs of the baker in London.[47] It is unlikely that any of the other costs increased as rapidly as the price of grain.

Nor can we assume that the quantity of labor or of grain which went into making a loaf of bread or a gallon of drink remained constant during the sixteenth and early seventeenth centuries. Although the equipment and the staff of the London baker, with his small oven and his three or four journeymen, did not alter much between the reigns of Henry VII and Charles I,[48] the equipment of the miller improved. More efficient mills for grinding corn were introduced throughout the country, especially toward the end of the sixteenth century,[49] and a new class of capitalist millers, upon whom the bakers were coming to depend for their meal and even for their flour, arose in the neighborhood of London.[50] The growing use of better machinery and the increase in the scale of operations undoubtedly reduced the labor required in milling. The price of bread probably rose appreciably less rapidly than the price of wheat.[51]

If the course of grain prices is an imperfect guide to the course of bread

[44] See pp. 262–64.
[45] Nef, *Rise of the British Coal Industry* (London, 1932), I, 213–14; *Calendar of State Papers, Domestic*, 1636–37, p. 415.
[46] Nef, *op. cit.*, I, 216; Thrupp, *op. cit.*, pp. 17, 115.
[47] *Ibid.*, p. 17.
[48] *Ibid.*, pp. 98–99.
[49] This is an impression I have derived from the calendars and indexes of the Exchequer Special Commissions, the Exchequer Depositions by Commission, the Chancery and Star Chamber Proceedings.
[50] Thrupp, *op. cit.*, p. 27.
[51] In 1619–20, when wheat was selling in London for between 25s. and 28s. a quarter (Rogers, *op. cit.*, VI, 32), the expenses of converting this quantity into bread —including apparently the miller's charge—was estimated at 13s. (Thrupp, *op. cit.*, p. 17). We may perhaps infer that the expense of milling and baking accounted for nearly, if not quite, a third of the price of white bread on the eve of the Civil War. If, as seems possible, the expense of making meal and bread did not increase more than fourfold between the first decade of the sixteenth century and the decade preceding the Civil War, then the price of bread would not have increased, like the price of wheat, six-and-a-half-fold, but only about five-and-a-half-fold. In the conversion of inferior grains into bread, milling and baking doubtless accounted for a larger proportion of the cost. Bread made from rye or maslin probably rose in price slightly less rapidly than bread made from wheat.

prices during the sixteenth and early seventeenth centuries, it is no guide at all to the course of drink prices. Technical changes in methods of production affected the costs much more in brewing than in breadmaking. As a result of the introduction of hop cultivation in Henry VIII's reign and the discovery of improved methods of drying malt, small beer replaced ale during the sixteenth century as the common beverage of the English people.[52] In Elizabeth's reign, for the first time, Englishmen could take pride in their native beer. It had come to rival in quality the best Continental brews.[53] The quantity obtained from a given amount of grain had increased, for small beer was not as strong as medieval ale had been, and the use of hops was a great economy in malt.[54] Costs of brewing had been further reduced by the growth in the scale of enterprise, and the substitution of coal for wood fuel. Some large breweries, with expensive copper boilers, brass siphons, and new coal-burning furnaces, were built in London at a cost of what would amount in terms of today's money to tens of thousands of pounds.[55]

These changes in manufacturing methods prevented the price of the cheapest brews from rising anything like as rapidly as the price of malt between 1500 and 1640. In every town and in many large villages by the beginning of the seventeenth century poor workmen obtained a part of the daily nourishment for themselves and their families by purchase of small beer from brewers, innkeepers, and victualers.[56] They probably drank much more beer than their descendants in the age of Dickens and Thackeray. They could hardly have consumed all this beer if it had been expensive. They appear to have seldom paid more than 3d. a gallon for small beer before the Civil War.[57] As the cheapest ale had rarely cost less than a penny a gallon in the last half of the fifteenth century,[58] the rise in wage rates during the price revolution seems to have covered fully the increase in the price of drink.

If bread was rising in price appreciably less rapidly than wheat, and

---

[52] Cf. above, pp. 134, 197.

[53] Michael Combrune, *The Theory and Practice of Brewing* (London, 1762), p. x.

[54] Cf. Rogers, *op. cit.*, IV, 550.

[55] Above, p. 138; cf. Rogers, *op. cit.*, V, 705–6.

[56] Cf. *Calendar of State Papers, Domestic, 1637–38*, pp. 580–81.

[57] The indications are that small beer usually cost about 2d. a gallon during Elizabeth's reign, and that under her two successors the normal price was 2d. or 2½d. (Sir George Shuckburgh Evelyn, in *Philosophical Transactions*, LXXXVIII (1798), 176—a reference for which I am indebted to my colleague, Professor Jacob Viner—and M. Combrune, *An Inquiry into the Prices of Wheat, Malt . . . etc.* [London, 1768], p. 107). Sixteen inhabitants of the villages of St. Neots and Eynesbury, west of Cambridge, claimed in 1638 that they had been accustomed to buy small beer from local innkeepers and victualers at a penny a gallon and a farthing a quart (*Calendar of State Papers, Domestic, 1637–38*, pp. 580–81).

[58] W. Fleetwood, *Chronicon Preciosum* (London, 1745), pp. 88–89, 92; Rogers, *op. cit.*, III, 249.

drink hardly as rapidly as the wages of masons and carpenters, it is misleading to work out costs of living mainly or even partly on the basis of grain prices. By doing so, all authorities since Rogers' time have exaggerated the rise in the price of subsistence during the sixteenth and early seventeenth centuries. Men did not eat hay or straw, or even oats or wheat. In the towns seven or eight times as much money may have been required to feed a horse in the reign of Charles I as in the reign of Henry VII. But it would be surprising if even five or four-and-a-half-times as much was needed to nourish a man.[59] Except for green vegetables, which were probably little eaten by town laborers, and bread, there was apparently not a single article in the poor man's diet which rose in price as much as four-and-a-half-fold. As the price of bread apparently increased more than that of other foods, it is possible that the poor replaced bread, cakes, and porridge to some extent by other kinds of nourishment, such as herrings, beef, mutton, eggs, cheese, and small beer, which, unlike bread, could be had it seems, even when we allow for the great changes in the value of money, for less in Shakespeare's time than today.[60] While there was a marked decline in the purchasing power of the building craftsman's wages in terms of food until the 1560's, it is by no means certain that this decline continued thereafter.

The decline in the English laborer's standard of living would still be exaggerated by comparing the course of wage rates with the course of town food prices, even if we were able to substitute the prices of bread and beer for the prices of grain and to determine what changes took place in the diet of the workers. In the first place, the practice of feeding workers was common in the sixteenth and seventeenth centuries. Journeymen bakers in London were provided by their masters with their meat and drink in addition to their money wages.[61] Coal miners also frequently had an allowance for food and drink.[62] We cannot be sure that money was all the reward received by the building artisans.[63] Professor Knoop and Mr. Jones think it conceivable that the practice of providing these craftsmen with some nourishment in addition to their money wages became more common in the sixteenth century than it had been before.[64] Insofar as an employer supplied his workmen with food, the rise in the price of diet bore down on him. His costs of production increased more than we should infer from a study of wage rates.

[59] Cf. Knoop and Jones, *op. cit.*, p. 213.
[60] A. V. Judges, "A Note on Prices in Shakespeare's Time," in *A Companion to Shakespeare Studies,* ed. H. Granville-Barker and G. B. Harrison (Cambridge, 1934), p. 384.
[61] Thrupp, *op. cit.*, pp. 17–18.
[62] Nef, *Rise of the British Coal Industry,* II, 187.
[63] Cf. Rogers, *op. cit.*, IV, 501; V, 637–38.
[64] Knoop and Jones, *op. cit.*, p. 212.

Nor is it probable that wageworkers engaged in industrial occupations, particularly in rural districts, had to buy all their food, even when their employers did not provide it for them. Men lived closer to the earth in the sixteenth century than today. Most laborers—particularly the multitudes who spun or wove or forged metal wares in their cottages under the putting-out system, and even many of those who found work in the new mines and metallurgical plants—held a plot of land capable of furnishing them with a part of what they needed to live.[65]

The prices of such foodstuffs and foods as the village laborer had to buy could hardly have risen as fast as the prices of the same articles in the towns. Town prices were forced up partly by the need which arose during the Elizabethan age to draw on the supplies of distant farms. London was growing from a large town of some 50,000 or 60,000 people to a metropolis of more than 300,000.[66] Its inhabitants, nourished before the Reformation almost entirely by the produce of the home counties, became increasingly dependent on grain, meat, milk, butter, cheese, and salt brought by wagon, packhorse, and small ship from more remote parts of the realm.[67] The increase in prices in the capital and in some other growing towns must be attributed partly to the cost of driving livestock for slaughter and carrying foodstuffs and foods greater distances, and also to the multiplication of the profit-making middleman through whose control the commodities passed on their way from the husbandman to the consumer. On the whole the industrial laborer in rural areas probably escaped paying many of the new charges which fell heavily upon some items in the diet of his fellow in the largest towns.[68]

Three main points emerge from this discussion of English food prices. In the first place, the index numbers hitherto compiled exaggerate the increase in the cost of subsistence during the price revolution. Secondly, the increase in the cost of the workmen's diet was borne to some extent not by them but by their employers. Thirdly, many workmen held small plots of land from which they obtained some of their necessary supplies. It follows that they were probably able to spend a more than negligible portion of the money wages they received on commodities other than food.

Were the prices of these commodities rising faster than wage rates? After

[65] Cf. R. H. Tawney, "The Assessment of Wages in England by the Justices of the Peace," *Vierteljahrschrift für Sozial- und Wirtschaftsgeschichte*, XI (1913), 535–37. Knoop and Jones tell us that some of the masons must have had agricultural holdings (*op. cit.*, p. 214).

[66] N. S. B. Gras, *The Evolution of the English Corn Market* (Cambridge, Mass., 1915), p. 75.

[67] F. J. Fisher, "The Development of the London Food Market, 1540–1640," *Economic History Review*, V (1935), 46–51.

[68] Cf. A. P. Usher, "The General Course of Wheat Prices in France, 1350–1788," *Review of Economic Statistics*, XII (1930), 165.

food, fuel was the most costly item in common housekeeping. But not all workers had to buy their fuel. The practice of granting fire coal to coal miners was universal, and the number of regularly employed coal miners increased many fold between 1540 and 1640.[69] It is impossible to determine whether the majority of the workers who had to buy their own fuel were worse off on the eve of the Civil War than industrial workers had been on the eve of the Reformation, because coal replaced logs and charcoal in the housekeeping of a great number, perhaps the majority, of Englishmen during the reigns of Elizabeth and James I.[70] The change was brought about chiefly by the phenomenal rise in the price of firewood.[71] Up to the time when a workman installed an iron grate in his home and adopted a coal-burning fire, the price of his fuel undoubtedly rose much more rapidly than his wages. But once he had made the change, the price of his fuel rose more slowly than his wages. According to some provisional index numbers worked out by the Price Committee, coal in the south of England was not appreciably dearer in the decade 1620–29 than in the decade 1570–79, and was only about 15 per cent dearer in the decade before the Civil War.[72] Wage rates in the building trades had risen during these sixty years 50 per cent or more. This is just the period when it has been assumed, from comparisons between the course of grain prices and wage rates, that the workers' standard of living fell precipitately.

We know nothing about the costs of lodging. But it is by no means certain that industrial workmen had to spend a larger proportion of their wages on housing in the reign of Charles I than in that of Henry VII. Employers in the new capitalistic industries often built cottages for their workmen, many of whom had migrated from distant counties.[73] The costs of building probably rose rapidly during the price revolution because of the phenomenal increase in timber prices.[74] But in the Elizabethan Age, all observers were struck by the widespread substitution of brick and stone for wood as building materials. To judge from conditions in the building trades, wage rates rose during the reigns of Elizabeth and her two Stuart successors at least as rapidly as the prices of bricks and lime,[75] which were coming to be made mainly with coal fuel. If grain prices are not a satisfactory guide to the cost of subsistence during the price revolution, neither are timber prices a satisfactory guide to the cost of housing.

What was happening to the cost of such manufactured commodities as

[69] Nef, *Rise of the British Coal Industry,* II, 187, 136–40.

[70] Nef, *op. cit.,* I, 196–98.

[71] See below, p. 263.

[72] MS. "Provisional Index Numbers of Food and Fuel Prices in England," at the London School of Economics.

[73] Cf. Nef, *op. cit.,* II, 187.

[74] See p. 263.

[75] MS. of the Price Committee: "Chairman's Report on English Naval Stores," September, 1933; cf. Wiebe, *op. cit.,* p. 375.

workers and their families were likely to need? While the price of candles rose more rapidly than wage rates in the building trades between 1540 and 1640,[76] the price of ordinary textile wares, nails, and paper rose much less rapidly,[77] the price of some kinds of glass apparently did not rise at all [78] and the price of smokers' pipes fell a great deal, at least after 1601.[79] While wage rates increased less rapidly than the prices of most foods, they increased more rapidly than the prices of most industrial products. If a workman was able to spend as large a proportion of his wages upon manufactured commodities on the eve of the Civil War as on the eve of the Reformation, he could in all probability have bought substantially larger quantities.

Without more knowledge concerning yearly earnings as distinct from wage rates, and concerning the expenses which money wages covered, prices in rural districts, and wages in other industries than building, we cannot hope to make an accurate comparison between the standard of living among industrial workmen at the beginning of the sixteenth century and on the eve of the Civil War. No doubt their real earnings fell with each rapid rise in prices. But there was also a persistent tendency throughout the period for earnings to overtake prices during the intervals between these rapid rises. The indications are that this tendency was especially marked after the accession of Elizabeth. Starting with the second decade of the sixteenth century, the general trend of the wageworkers' standard of living was almost certainly downward until at least the sixties, and the fall in their real earnings was probably most rapid during the forties and fifties. But it is doubtful whether, as has been generally believed, the downward trend in their standard of living persisted during the four or five decades of most rapid industrial expansion from about 1575 to 1620. Changes were introduced both by the Statute of Artificers of 1563 and by a later Statute of 1603, in the principles and the methods used by local authorities in assessing wages. The new legislation, and the policy followed until the Civil War by the Privy Council in enforcing it, made the raising of wages by law, especially in the textile industry, more easily possible than it had been. And when, as was often the case, the regulations under the Statutes were evaded, the market rate of wages was usually above the legal rate.[80] Partly perhaps as a result of the new government policy, wageworkers seem to have been at least as well off materially in the reign of Charles I as on the eve of the Armada. During the half-century preceding the Civil War, their wages had probably risen on the average less rapidly than the price of bread, but

---

[76] MS. "Provisional Index Numbers of Food and Fuel Prices in England."

[77] Wiebe, *op. cit.*, pp. 375–77, 383.

[78] MS. "Chairman's Report on English Naval Stores."

[79] *Historical Manuscripts Commission, Report on the MSS. of the Duke of Rutland,* IV, 437, 526, 542.

[80] Tawney, *op. cit.*, pp. 311, 321, 534–35, 542–52, 561–64.

about as rapidly as the prices of other foods and drink, and more rapidly than the prices of coal and the products of manufactures. The contrasts between the movements of real wages in England and Spain throughout the period of the price revolution were much less striking than Wiebe's index numbers suggest.

In considering the influence of labor costs upon the progress of industrial capitalism, we are more interested in the wages paid to workmen in mines, at smelting furnaces and forges, and in other small factories than in those paid to masons, carpenters, and other workmen in the building trades,[81] in connection with which the expansion of large-scale enterprise was less novel in England from *ca.* 1540 to 1640. And we are more interested in the prices obtained for the products of these mines and factories than in the prices paid for grains, grasses, livestock, and foods, commodities which were given heavy weight in Wiebe's index numbers. The fact that wage rates in the building trades rose more slowly than the town prices of foodstuffs and foods, did not offer any special inducement to draw an enterprising country landlord to sink shafts to his coal seams or a wealthy city merchant to enter a partnership for smelting iron ore or manufacturing glass or paper.

Wage rates could hardly have risen much less in the new industries than in the building trades. It is even possible that special bait in the form of good pay had to be sometimes offered to induce men to enter more novel and disagreeable occupations like coal mining and sheet-glass manufacturing.[82] As wage rates in the building trades rose much more rapidly between 1560 and 1640 than the prices of coal, ordinary textile wares, and most manufactured articles, wage rates in other industries probably also rose more rapidly. But if wage rates were rising in most industries more rapidly than the prices of the products, how could industrial ventures have been exceptionally profitable during the reigns of Elizabeth and James I?

When, more than forty years ago, Wiebe advanced our knowledge of the price revolution by publishing his book, he warned us against assuming that the cheapness of manufactured goods could be explained entirely, or even primarily, by the slow rise in wages. Further investigation, he believed, might show that mechanical improvements were a more important factor than cheap labor.[83] We now know that labor was dearer in England than his calculations suggested, and that the improvements in industrial technology were more sweeping than he suspected. The openings for profits arose mainly because costs of production were reduced by the widespread adoption of better machinery and improved kilns and furnaces, by the increase in the scale of industrial enterprise, and by the discovery and use

[81] Cf. Wiebe, *op. cit.,* p. 240.
[82] Cf. Nef, *op. cit.,* II, pp. 192, 194.
[83] Wiebe, *op. cit.,* pp. 239–43.

of new supplies of raw materials such as calamine, alumstone, and, above all, coal.[84]

Labor in France, as well as in England, was no doubt dearer than Wiebe's index numbers indicate. These index numbers were worked out in terms of silver in order to show the effects of the inflow of treasure upon prices. But during the century from 1540 to 1640, the *livre tournois* lost about half, and the shilling between a third and a fourth, of its silver content.[85] Prices rose rather more in France than in England, not less as might be supposed from a glance at Wiebe's tables. If, in these tables, we substitute prices and wages actually paid for prices and wages in terms of silver, the absolute spread between prices and wages which occurs as we proceed through the sixteenth and early seventeenth centuries is increased considerably more in the case of France than in that of England, but the ratio between the two remains the same. In the case of England, as we have seen, that ratio exaggerates the decline in the real earnings of the wageworker during the sixteenth and early seventeenth centuries. Is this equally true in the case of France?

The most important work done on French wages and prices since Wiebe wrote is the study of Poitou by the late Monsieur Raveau.[86] Comparisons are difficult between his results and those which Wiebe obtained from d'Avenel's data, partly because the periods selected by Raveau are not the same as those selected by Wiebe, and partly because Raveau's averages are computed from wage records for a single province, while Wiebe's are computed from a miscellaneous mixture of sparse records for several provinces.[87] But the two results do not differ widely. Both show that although money wages rose rapidly, their purchasing power in terms of food, fuel, and some other commodities fell continually from the accession of Francis I, in 1515, down to the passage of the Edict of Nantes, in 1598, when they were worth hardly half as much as at the beginning of the sixteenth century. Both suggest that real wages rose at the beginning of the seventeenth century. They rose in Poitou more than they are represented by Wiebe's index numbers as rising, but even in Poitou the wageworkers still seem to have been worse off in the reign of Louis XIII than their ancestors in the reign of Louis XII.

The results obtained by the Commandant Quenedey for Rouen suggest

[84] Cf. above, chap. iii.

[85] A. Dieudonné, *Manuel de numismatique française* (Paris, 1916), II, 314, 351; H. Hauser, Introduction to *La réponse de Jean Bodin à M. de Malestroit* (Paris, 1932), pp. xxvii ff.; Wiebe, *op. cit.*, pp. 30 n., 70; (cf. A. E. Feaveryear, *The Pound Sterling* [Oxford, 1931], esp. pp. 56–65, 78–79).

[86] P. Raveau, "La crise des prix au XVI⁰ siècle en Poitou," *Revue historique*, CLXII (1929), 16–24; cf. his *L'agriculture et les classes paysannes dans le haut Poitou* (Paris, 1926), p. xxxii.

[87] Wiebe, *op. cit.*, pp. 378–79, 417–19; cf. d'Avenel, *Histoire économique*, II, 491 ff.

that workmen in the building trades fared better there than in Poitou throughout the period of the price revolution.[88] While food prices apparently rose less in Normandy than in Poitou during the sixteenth century,[89] wage rates rose more. In Poitou, masons were apparently earning about twice as much money in 1578 as during the last half of the fifteenth century; at Rouen they were apparently earning appreciably more than twice as much.[90] After the Edict of Nantes, the workmen in Poitou gained on their fellows at Rouen. In both cases money wages continued to rise. But food prices were apparently rising in Normandy more than in Poitou,[91] where there was a sharp fall in the price of grain and wine at the end of the sixteenth century.[92] In spite of the gain made by the laborers in Poitou during the second half of Henri IV's reign, they were probably still somewhat worse off under Louis XIII than those at Rouen.

The new wage data collected by the Price Committee for the Île-de-France are too scanty to serve as a basis for generalization. So far as they go, they suggest that during the sixteenth century the course of real wages in the neighborhood of Paris differed from that at Rouen as well as from that in Poitou. Workmen appear to have suffered nearly if not quite as much as in Poitou, but the fall in the purchasing power of their wages seems to have been more pronounced during the first half of the century and less pronounced during the second.[93]

It is even more difficult to generalize concerning the material welfare of wageworkers in France than in England, not only because we have much less data, but because conditions apparently varied more from region to region.[94] This is not surprising in view of the economic self-sufficiency that persisted in French provinces during the sixteenth and early seventeenth centuries, when it was breaking down in England.[95] What little we know suggests that Wiebe's index numbers exaggerate the decline in the material welfare of the wageworkers in most French provinces, as well as in England, but probably not quite as much.

As in England, wage rates in the building trades appear to have risen nearly everywhere between 1540 and 1640 appreciably more than has been

---

[88] R. Quenedey, *Les prix des matériaux et de la main-d'œuvre à Rouen* (offprint from *Bulletin de la Société du commerce et de l'industrie de la Seine-Inférieure*), (Rouen, 1927), pp. 23–25.

[89] For Normandy: Quenedey, *op. cit.*, p. 26; Wiebe, *op. cit.*, p. 378; R. Jouanne, "Report on Prices at Caen," among the MSS. of the Price Committee at the London School of Economics. For Poitou: Raveau, *L'agriculture et les classes paysannes,* p. xxxii, and *passim*.

[90] Raveau, "La crise des prix," pp. 17, 20–21; Quenedey, *op. cit.*, p. 24.

[91] Jouanne, *loc. cit.;* Wiebe, *op. cit.*, p. 378; Quenedey, *op. cit.*, p. 26.

[92] Raveau, *L'agriculture et les classes paysannes,* p. xxxii.

[93] Reports by Yvonne Bézard and Jean Mallon among the MSS. of the Price Committee at the London School of Economics.

[94] Cf. Usher, *op. cit.*, p. 165.

[95] Cf. above, p. 164.

supposed. As in England, they rose more slowly than the prices of food-stuffs and food. We have no means of knowing whether employers pro-vided their workmen with food and drink, in addition to wages, less fre-quently in France than in England. The French workman who had to sup-port himself and his family mainly out of his wages seems to have suffered more from rising prices than the English workman, in at least two respects. Technical improvements designed to reduce the costs of manufacturing were less widespread in France than in England during the hundred years from 1540 to 1640. It is therefore probable that the costs of milling were not reduced as much to offset the great rise in grain prices common to both countries. When it came to drink, the French workmen, except to some extent in northern France, continued to depend on wine as their ancestors had done from time immemorial. And the price of wine, like that of food, but unlike that of the Englishman's common drink, was rising in some provinces substantially more rapidly than wage rates.[96]

That was also true of the price of logs and faggots, which remained almost the only fuels burned in hearths and stoves, except around Lyons and St. Etienne. Until the period of the religious wars (1560–1589) the French workman had an advantage over his English fellow, because fire-wood was rising in price more slowly in most parts of France than in England.[97] But after the English workman had substituted coal for logs and faggots, the advantage lay with him, because the price of coal in Eng-land increased much more slowly than the price of wood in France. It is not possible to say in which country the workman had to spend a larger proportion of his wages on fuel at the eve of the English Civil War, but for at least half a century in England the proportion had been diminishing.

In France as in England, manufactured articles, such as plain cloth, were rising in price more slowly than wage rates in the building trades. If the French workman in the reign of Louis XIII had as large a portion of his wages as the English workman to spend in buying these wares, he could have got almost as much for his money.[98] But we know that the output of mines and manufactures was increasing between 1540 and 1640 at a much more rapid rate in England than in France, and it is probable that on the eve of the Civil War the volume of cloth, metal wares, tobacco pipes, and windowpanes produced was greater, relative to population, in England.[99] The English manufacturer excelled in the making of plain cloth and other

[96] Raveau, *L'agriculture et les classes paysannes*, p. xxxii.

[97] See p. 265.

[98] It might be supposed that the cost of manufactured goods would have risen more in France than in England, as technical improvements which reduced the quantity of labor needed in manufacturing were less widespread. But the advantage which the English employer enjoyed in this respect was offset by the fact that the prices of the lumber and firewood (and possibly the price of the labor) needed in industry were rising more in England than in France (see p. 265).

[99] See above, chap. iv.

homely wares, which found some sale even among the poorer subjects. This suggests that the purchases of the industrial workmen may have increased more in England than in France, and that by the reign of Charles I the Englishman may have been able to lay out a larger part of his wages than the Frenchman upon the products of the rising industries.

The effects of the price revolution upon the poor man's standard of life were similar in the two countries. Such differences as we have found seem to have been mostly unfavorable to the French workmen. Their real earnings had almost certainly fallen more than those of English workmen by the last quarter of the sixteenth century, as Wiebe's own figures indicated.[100] During the next twenty years their position improved somewhat in many provinces. But from what we now know, it seems unlikely that the English workmen lost ground after about 1600.

Wiebe's index numbers did not indicate that the fall in real wages favored the English much more than the French employer of labor.[101] The new evidence collected since Wiebe's time suggests that the cost of hiring workmen may have decreased more, not less, in France than in England. If cheaper labor had been the principal driving force behind the flow of capital into expanding industries, the pace of industrial growth should not have been much slower in France than in England; it should have been as fast or even faster.

THE COST OF TIMBER DURING THE PRICE REVOLUTION

Money wages, Lord Keynes rightly pointed out, formed only a part of the expenses of carrying on an enterprise in the sixteenth and seventeenth centuries. In constructing his tables of profit inflation in France and England, he assumed that money wages accounted for half the expenses of production. He further assumed that in both countries all other expenses rose just as rapidly as, according to Wiebe's index numbers, general commodity prices rose. Is this second assumption justified? Did the materials needed in mining and manufacturing rise in price no more and no less rapidly than the average price of all commodities? Were the costs of materials rising equally rapidly in France and in England, or were there differences in the behavior of these costs which help to explain why more capital should have been invested in new kinds of industrial enterprises in England than in France?

After wages, the chief expenses borne by the owners of mines and large workshops in the sixteenth century were probably the sums spent on timber, firewood, and charcoal. In the development of large-scale industry at this time, wood largely took the place occupied during the nineteenth

[100] See p. 243.
[101] See p. 243.

century by both iron and coal. Metal was used only for the cutting or striking face of tools, for the gears and axles of machinery, and for the cauldrons and boilers in which various raw materials were heated. Stone and brick were commonly used only for the furnaces and kilns. In spite of the poor resistance wood afforded to the frequent fires, the rest of the plant was nearly all of timber.[102] And, in many industries, the plant was extensive. The clusters of alum and salt houses and the metallurgical works often formed so impressive a phalanx of buildings that contemporaries compared them to villages and even to small towns. At the larger mines, the houses and barns were hardly less numerous than at the alumworks, and hundreds of pounds in the money of the time (worth at least twenty times today's money) were often spent to obtain the additional deal boards and oaken bars required to timber the shafts. By the middle of the seventeenth century, and possibly even earlier, payments for lumber and planks of various sizes accounted for more than half the cost of building and launching a ship.[103]

Logs, faggots, and charcoal were almost the only fuels used in manufacturing in France throughout the period of the price revolution. In England they were the principal fuels until perhaps the reign of James I, for it was not much before the end of the sixteenth century that coal began to replace wood extensively in processes other than the forging of crude metal wares and the calcining of limestones, for which it had served to some extent even in the Middle Ages. The cost of fuel was considerable in most manufactures; in some, such as glassmaking and the smelting of ores, it greatly exceeded the cost of lumber for construction work. Scores of acres of woods were consumed every year in supplying one of the large blast furnaces. Farmers of ironworks in the Forest of Dean were legally entitled in 1639 to an annual wood supply of 13,500 cords,[104] and they probably used a much larger quantity.

In some industries, therefore, more was spent for lumber, charcoal, and firewood than for labor at the plant. In very few industries did the cost of obtaining wood form a negligible proportion of the costs of production. If we are to discover whether price conditions were more favorable for the development of large-scale industry in England than in France, we must consider the course of timber prices as well as the course of wage rates.

Everywhere in England the manufacturer was burdened during the reigns of Elizabeth I and James I by the phenomenal rise in the price of firewood and lumber. In county after county trees were felled in such profusion to feed the rising industries, that lands once thick with forests could be con-

[102] Cf. W. Sombart, *Der Moderne Kapitalismus* (1916), II, 1138–40; Nef, *Rise of the British Coal Industry*, I, 191.

[103] R. G. Albion, *Forests and Sea Power* (Cambridge, Mass., 1926), p. 94.

[104] *Calendar of State Papers, Domestic,* 1638–39, p. 557; Nef, *op. cit.,* I, 193–96, for the inroads of the glass- and ironmaking industries upon the supplies of wood.

verted into runs for sheep and cattle, or broken by the plow to supply the new demands for grains.[105] Lumber, logs, and faggots, once available in abundance just beyond the town gates, had to be hauled or carried by wagon and packhorse for miles over rough ground and along miserable pathways full of ruts, or brought in ships from the Baltic countries. Between the decade following the dissolution of the monasteries and the decade preceding the Civil War (between the 1540's and the 1630's), while the price of grains increased little more than fourfold and the price of textile wares and various other manufactured goods much less than doubled, the price of firewood increased almost seven times over. Before the second decade of Elizabeth's reign (the 1570's) had ended, firewood was already more than twice as dear as it had been in the last decade of her father's reign (the 1540's). On the eve of the Civil War (*ca.* 1635–40), it was nearly three times again as dear. About eleven pounds were often needed at this time to buy as many logs and faggots as had sold for a pound at the beginning of the sixteenth century.[106]

The rise in the price of some kinds of lumber was no less startling, as is revealed by the accounts of the Admiralty for the purchase of naval stores. Continuous records of these purchases do not go back beyond the first decade of Elizabeth's reign (the 1560's). But between this time and the outbreak of the Civil War, planks and timber, mainly of oak, were growing dearer as rapidly as firewood. Four-inch planks cost the navy more than four times as much in 1632 as in 1567, and timber more than three times as much. In 1637 timber was almost five times, and in 1641 four times as dear as in 1567.[107] Meanwhile the prices of ordinary textile wares and some manufactured goods remained practically stationary,[108] and the price of coal increased only about 20 per cent.[109] Scattered figures covering a longer period [110] suggest that the navy paid at least fifteen times as much for oak in Charles I's reign as at the accession of Henry VIII in 1509. Meanwhile the general price level, according to Wiebe's imperfect calculations, had not risen much more than fourfold.[111] In spite of the rising costs of the basic material used in shipbuilding, the shipyards grew in number and importance. The tonnage of the Royal Navy doubled and that of the merchant marine nearly quintupled.[112] Many conditions, besides

[105] Cf. Nef, *op. cit.*, I, 158–61.
[106] Wiebe, *op. cit.*, pp. 70, 375.
[107] The data on which these statements are based was kindly supplied by Miss Rayner, who worked out for me, from the Admiralty Accounts (Treasurers' Ledgers), five-year samples of the average price paid for timber and planks from 1567 to the Civil War.
[108] Wiebe, *op. cit.*, pp. 375, 383.
[109] MS. "Chairman's Report on Naval Stores," cited above.
[110] Collected by Professor Albion, *op. cit.*, p. 91.
[111] Almost exactly fourfold if we take Wiebe's second set of index numbers rather than his first (see above, p. 243, n. 20).
[112] See above, pp. 159 ff.

cheap labor, favorable to the progress of industry must have been present to produce a great speeding-up in the rate of industrial growth under such unfavorable price conditions.

With firewood and timber mounting in price much more rapidly than other commodities, it is natural to suppose that charcoal followed suit. But, in fact, charcoal prices do not seem to have increased more rapidly than the average prices for all commodities. Charcoal was scarcely four times as dear on the eve of the Civil War as at the beginning of the sixteenth century.[113] At first sight this is very puzzling. The price of charring wood was of course an important element in the price of charcoal. It is certain that the price of charring wood rose very much more slowly than the price of timber, probable that as a result of technical improvements in the process it rose less than fourfold. But this can hardly provide an adequate explanation of the great differences between the course of charcoal and timber prices. A more important one is possibly to be found in the fact that charcoal was cheaper to transport than logs. Our prices for both firewood and charcoal are town prices. The rise in timber prices in the towns was undoubtedly caused more by the necessity for hauling wood from greater and greater distances than by the rise in the prices paid where the trees were felled. Costs of transportation were of less, costs of production of more, importance in determining the price of charcoal than in determining the price of logs.

But charcoal was not widely used for fuel by any manufacturer save the smelter, and the prices he paid were not town prices. He bought or leased large tracts of woodlands and hired colliers to char his logs. His blast furnaces and forges exhausted the neighboring supplies of timber, and the local price of charcoal probably rose nearly as fast as the local price of firewood.[114] The inevitable result was to force the smelter eventually to move to another wooded site at a greater distance from the chief markets for metal and metal wares. While this kept the price of his fuel from rising rapidly, it made it necessary for him to abandon old equipment and invest large sums in new furnaces and forges and in water-driven machinery to operate the bellows and the hammers. The rise in charcoal prices in the towns is a poor guide, therefore, to the rise in the costs of producing metal caused by the exhaustion of the forests.

In the age of Elizabeth, England was faced with a timber crisis, brought about partly by the increase in population but mainly by the remarkable growth of production. This crisis increased the expenses of mining and manufacturing so much that the average rise of commodity prices is no index to the rise in the costs of industrial materials.

---

[113] Wiebe, *op. cit.*, pp. 70, 375.

[114] Cf., e.g., *Historical Manuscripts Commission, Report on the MSS. of the Marquis of Salisbury*, XII, 20–23.

The course of wood prices, like that of grain prices and wages, varied more from region to region in France than in England. But except in a few regions such as the densely populated Île-de-France,[115] firewood did not become conspicuously dearer, it seems, than other commodities between 1540 and 1640. Wiebe's index numbers for France, which were compiled from data collected by d'Avenel for several provinces, show no very great deviation between the trend of firewood and general commodity prices.[116] Raveau's more recent and more detailed work shows that in Poitou between 1515 and 1598 the price of firewood rose less than the price of grain and about as much as that of wine.[117] We have a new series of prices from 1558 to 1640 for logs and faggots bought at Château-Gontier, on the Mayenne.[118] While faggots were about three and a half times as dear in the last decade of Louis XIII's reign (1633–43) as in the decade preceding the religious wars (1550–60), logs were rather less than two and a half times as dear. They had not risen in price more than such commodities as beans, butter, salt, and red wine. In most French provinces, the rise in the price of wood is explained almost entirely by the increase in the supply of silver and the debasement of the currency.

The costs of fuel and doubtless also of lumber, the principal materials needed in manufacturing and in mining, were rising in England much more than in France until at least the beginning of the seventeenth century. After that coal replaced firewood and charcoal in many English industries so extensively that most English manufacturers, except the smelters, began to have an advantage in the costs of fuel. The shift from a wood-burning to a coal-burning economy eventually relieved much of the pressure on the English forests.

If industrial enterprise proved less profitable in France than in England during the price revolution, this cannot be explained on the ground that wood or labor were dearer. In fact wood, and probably also labor, were cheaper. The immediate explanation seems to be that in France technical changes which reduced the quantity of labor required in mining and manufacturing were less extensive than in England, that there was no such growth in privately controlled enterprises producing cheap commodities in larger quantities, and no such exploitation of new supplies of raw mate-

[115] Reports of Yvonne Bézard and Jean Mallon among the MSS. of the Price Committee at the London School of Economics.
[116] Wiebe took 100 as the price of all commodities during the last half of the fifteenth century. With this base, his index numbers for the first half of the seventeenth century —which express prices in terms of silver—show firewood at 212·5, general commodity prices at 216 in France. For England, they show firewood at 554 and general commodities at 282, or 245 if Wiebe's second, differently weighted table is the basis of comparison (Wiebe, op. cit., pp. 278–79, 375, 377, 383).
[117] L'agriculture et les classes paysannes, p. xxxii.
[118] Report of René Gauchet among the MSS. of the Price Committee at the London School of Economics.

rials, like calamine, alum, and coal, the widespread use of which cheapened production in many industries.

Neither the sweeping changes in technique and in the objectives of industrial enterprise, nor the exploitation of new raw materials, were an inevitable result of the inflow of American silver, or of the decline in real wages that often accompanied it. If they had been, a speeding-up in the rate of industrial growth should have occurred in France to match that in England.

CONCLUSION

A comparison of prices and industrial capitalism in France and England from 1540 to 1640 does not prove that the price revolution failed to stimulate industrial development. It shows that the influence of price changes was complex rather than simple, and it warns us against the tempting assumption that the remarkably long period of rising prices, common to all European countries, was of compelling importance in connection with the revolutionary developments which, especially under British initiative, were orienting economic enterprise toward industrialism.[119]

By raising prices, the inflow of treasure from America helped to keep down the costs of the labor and perhaps the costs of the land [120] needed for mining and manufacturing, and thus encouraged the investment of capital in new industrial enterprises, as Professor Hamilton and Lord Keynes have pointed out. But the decline in the real earnings of wageworkers was nothing like as great as has been supposed since the time of Rogers and d'Avenel. Had the standard of living among the English working people really fallen by anything approaching half, the advantages which employers derived from hiring labor cheaply might have been offset by the reduction in the amount workmen could have spent on manufactured goods. The expansion of the mining, the metallurgical, the glass, and the textile industries in Elizabethan England was brought about to some extent by the growth of home markets among the common people. If the earnings of nearly all wageworkers had been cut to the bare minimum required for subsistence according to medieval standards, the demand for grates,

[119] See above, pp. 210–11, 220–21.

[120] As I remarked above (see pp. 241, n. 8), Professor Hamilton suggested that cheap land as well as cheap labor probably stimulated investments in industrial enterprises. We do not know whether land rents rose more slowly than did the prices paid to mine owners and manufacturers for their products. But the dissolution of the monasteries, which occurred on the eve of the early English industrial revolution, was probably of more importance in England than the inflow of silver and the debasement of the coinage in making it possible for adventurers to acquire land for mining and manufacturing on favorable terms (see above, pp. 231 ff.). Unlike the price revolution, the dissolution of the monasteries helps to explain why industrial development in England should have been more rapid than in France.

windowpanes, cloth, bedding, tobacco, and crude tableware could hardly have grown as rapidly as it did.

The moderate fall in real wage rates that occurred in England with every rapid rise in prices tended to increase profits, to promote the accumulation of wealth, and to encourage the investment of funds in mining and manufacturing, especially perhaps during the 1540's and 1550's, the only period of considerable duration in which wage rates may have risen more slowly than the prices of manufactured products. But the discoveries had little to do with the rise in prices which made possible this decline in real wages just before the accession of Elizabeth. More commodities could be bought with the same quantity of silver when Edward VI became king, in 1547, than in the reign of his grandfather, Henry VII (1485–1509). The rise in prices during the first half of the sixteenth century in England was caused by debasement of the coinage.

The rapid increase in the real costs of the indispensable supplies of timber provided a stimulus of a different kind from the fall in real wage rates. It helped to bring about changes in industrial technique, outstanding among them the shift from wood to coal fuel, which might have been less widespread had the need for them been less urgent. Without these changes in the technology of production, the increasing costs of materials must have slowed down the growth of English industries, no matter how cheaply labor could have been hired.

French history suggests that a prolonged decline in the real wages of labor, while undoubtedly an incentive to enterprise, is not by itself a sufficiently powerful influence to cause a great speeding-up in the rate of industrial growth. It is possible that during the last quarter of the sixteenth century the fall in the workmen's standard of living in France was so great as to prevent increases in the demand for some industrial products and that the misery of the poor hindered more than it helped the progress of manufactures during the religious wars.

Industry was responding in different ways in the various European countries to the strains and the stimuli provided by the inflow of treasure from America and by debasements of the coinage. Whether or not the response took the form of greatly increased activity in sinking mining shafts and setting up new manufacturing enterprises, depended mainly on conditions independent of the price revolution. Further comparisons between French and English history help to reveal these conditions.

7

The Genesis of Industrialism
and of Modern Science, 1540–1640

THE COINCIDENCE OF THE EARLY INDUSTRIAL WITH THE SCIENTIFIC
REVOLUTION

Both industrialism and the methods of scientific investigation which we
Westerners are now inclined to take for granted are novel in history.

No earlier societies than those which have emerged in Europe were
dominated by power-driven machinery and by large-scale enterprise in
industry and communications. Societies everywhere on earth are now
adopting industrialism. Never before has this planet been so thickly
populated, never has it been so urbanized, with a million or more inhabitants in hosts of cities. Never before has any large proportion of the
people gained their livelihood in mechanized occupations, away from the
soil and from handicrafts; never before have their leisure hours been
filled by mechanized entertainment. In no earlier societies have learned
men looked at nature and at man himself mainly through the eyes of the
experimental scientist. Alfred North Whitehead, whose philosophical inquiries opened a fresh historical interest in the subject, called the rise of
modern science "the most intimate change in outlook which the human
race has yet encountered. . . . The quiet growth of science has practically
recoloured our mentality so that modes of thought which in former times
were exceptional are now broadly spread through the educated world." [1]

It is a commonplace that the coming of industrialism and of modern
science are connected. A better understanding of the nature of the connections might help to clarify the changes in human outlook and purpose
which have resulted from the combined triumph of industrialism and modern science. A better understanding of the connections might also con-

From *Essays in Honor of Conyers Read,* ed. Norton Downs (Chicago, 1952), pp.
200–269.
[1] *Science and the Modern World* (New York, 1925), p. 2.

tribute to knowledge concerning a fundamental issue for philosophy and theology: How far have economic institutions determined thought? How far has the mind itself determined the nature and history of economic institutions?

While it is taken for granted that industrialism and modern science are interrelated, it is not realized how closely their beginnings are linked in time. The conventional view of the industrial revolution has led the learned man and the public alike, in western Europe and the United States, to relate the origins of industrial civilization to the reign of the English king George III, which began in 1760. Every schoolboy is told about Arkwright's water frame, Watt's new steam engine, and many other mechanical inventions of the late eighteenth century. These inventions are represented as transferring English industry from the home to the factory in the period covered by the once widely read books of J. L. and Barbara Hammond. The schoolboy takes it as axiomatic that "the rise of modern industry" occurred between 1760 and 1832.

The same schoolboy is taught to relate the rise of modern science to an earlier period. It is hardly necessary to emphasize the spectacular nature of the discovery associated with the Polish astronomer Copernicus (1473–1543), that the earth is not flat and fixed as the center of the universe; that it is instead a revolving sphere moving through space along with a myriad of other spheres. Such a change in man's view of the physical world today catches the imagination of all but the dullest in the industrialized countries, for there almost every child has been impressed with modern scientific knowledge and has had his thinking colored by the scientific outlook. So it is not difficult to make the early history of modern science popular. The teacher can explain that, as a result, above all, of the work of Galileo (1564–1642), Kepler (1571–1630), and Newton (1642–1727), what were to be long regarded as the correct views of the motion of the spheres and the correct laws of all motion superseded older, incorrect, and, as it has been made to seem, childish views which possessed the learned men of antiquity and the Middle Ages.

Newton died a generation before the time when, as we were taught, the industrial revolution began. His major scientific work was done a generation before his death, and so before the end of the seventeenth century. In point of time, therefore, the scientific revolution appears separate from the industrial revolution.

During the last fifty years, much that is new has been learned about economic history and the history of ideas. The view of both which prevailed in the late nineteenth century has been altered. One consequence is to bring the origins of industrialism and of modern science closer together.

According to the new view, what was the course of European economic history during the two hundred years or so that followed the childhood of

Copernicus, the period which was marked by the birth of modern science? In 1453, the Hundred Years' War ended with the expulsion of the English from most of the possessions on the Continent which their kings had held. For almost a hundred years following that protracted conflict between France and England, economic growth was characteristic of most Continental European countries. All the way from Poland and the Balkans to the toe of Italy and the Portuguese coast of the Spanish peninsula, there were remarkable increases between 1460 and 1540 in the yield of the soil and the subsoil—more grains and ores of every kind, more sheep and goats and other cattle—remarkable increases in the volume of industrial products —more metal, more cloth, more books and paper, more guns—and remarkable increases in the commercial prosperity from which many shopkeepers and traders, and also merchants in a considerable way of business, reaped profits.[2] When this period of nearly a hundred years drew to a close about the middle of the sixteenth century, Europeans were, as it has since seemed, irretrievably split for the first time over the appropriate forms of Christian religious worship.[3]

During the next hundred years or so, during the century that followed the Reformation, the prosperity characteristic of Continental Europe in the late fifteenth and early sixteenth centuries was on the wane. The wars of religion from 1562 to 1648 were in many countries a period of industrial retrogression, brought about partly by the fighting. In the mid-sixteenth century, Spain, what is now Belgium, Germany, Bohemia, and much of Austria—all at least nominally under the rule of Charles V (who combined the thrones of Spain and the Holy Roman Empire)—were in the vanguard of a remarkable industrial expansion. A century later, when the Thirty Years' War ended with the collapse of the Empire, all these countries, with the possible exception of Belgium, had been reduced in population and industrial productivity, until a good many regions had hardly as many inhabitants or as large an output of ores, metals, and most manufactured goods as two centuries before, when the Hundred Years' War ended.[4]

The rest of Continental Europe fared better than Spain and the Empire from 1562 to 1648. In point of population and production, Italy and Switzerland more than held their own until at least the early seventeenth century. So did France, in spite of the religious disputes and the wars which set neighbor against neighbor during the second half of the sixteenth century.[5]

A different kind of industrial development began as the first movement of expansion played itself out. The new development occurred mainly in the

[2] See above, chap. ii (also chap. i, pp. 43–47).
[3] See above, p. 221.
[4] Cf. Nef, "Silver Production in Central Europe, 1456–1618," *Journal of Political Economy,* XLIX, No. 4 (1941), 586–91.
[5] See above, pp. 146 ff.

north of Europe, in countries which had not shared fully in the industrial prosperity of the late fifteenth and early sixteenth centuries, in countries which broke most decisively in the sixteenth century with the authority of the church of Rome: in Sweden, Denmark, Holland, Scotland, and Wales and, above all, in England, where striking industrial expansion continued with few interruptions for a hundred years, from the dissolution of the English monasteries in 1536 and 1539 to the outbreak of the Civil War in 1642. Copper exports from Sweden increased twenty-five fold from 1548 to 1650.[6] In Holland, as in England, the expansion was most rapid during the last two decades of the sixteenth century and the first two decades of the seventeenth, a great era in Dutch painting and in English literature. The cloth production of Leiden, for example, increased more than fourfold in thirty-five years, from 26,620 pieces in 1584 to 109,560 pieces in 1619, when the ten-year-old Rembrandt left this town of his birth for Amsterdam.[7] Shipments of coal from the north of England grew at least ten times over in a span of seventy years, and possibly much more.[8] Describing the condition of the English people before the "great rebellion," as he called the Civil War, the Earl of Clarendon spoke of them as "the wonder and envy of all the parts of Christendom."

What was no less singular than this "felicity," of which Clarendon wrote,[9] was its character. In Roman Britain and in medieval Europe, at places where coal seams outcropped, some use had been made of these black stones as fuel, especially by limeburners and by smiths in rough ironwork, such as the forging of anchors or horseshoes. But, if we except an early industrial revolution in China during the tenth and eleventh centuries, which did not lead to an industrial civilization as we know it, it was not until the seventeenth century that the people of any nation attempted to build an economy on coal. In Great Britain on the eve of the Civil War coal was becoming the prevailing fuel for heating rooms, for cooking, and for laundry work. Coal was beginning to be widely used in industry—not only at limekilns and at a few of the forges where iron was made into the crudest iron wares such as horseshoes, but at saltworks, alumworks, in soap boiling, in making saltpeter and gunpowder, in brewing beer, in baking bricks, tiles, and tobacco pipes, and in making glass and steel.[10]

Among our European ancestors, as among other economically advanced

---

[6] Figures derived from Eli F. Heckscher, *Sveriges Ekonomiska Historia Frän Gustav Vasa* (Stockholm, 1935–36), I, Part I, 28, 30. Appendix; Part II, 443–44.
[7] N. W. Posthumus, *De Geschiedenis van de Leidsche Lakenindustrie* (s'Gravenhage, 1939), II, 304.
[8] See above, pp. 163, 169–70.
[9] See above, chap. iv, *passim.*
[10] See above, chap. iii, *passim;* cf. Nef, *Rise of the British Coal Industry* (London, 1932), I, 200–23.

peoples, gathering firewood, kindling, peat, and turf had been the ordinary means of obtaining fuel. These occupations had rarely lent themselves to a capitalist organization of labor, and the making of charcoal, which alone among them required heat, had been largely annexed to the metallurgical industries, the principal consumers of charred wood. With the rise of coal mining in Great Britain, the provision of fuel changed its nature. It became necessary often to dig deep for supplies; shafts of thirty or forty fathoms became common. The capital required for starting and maintaining a colliery, already of some consequence in the chief coal-mining districts during the later Middle Ages, multiplied many fold.[11]

Coal played an even more important part in the genesis of industrial civilization by its influence upon the industries it was coming to serve. The composition of most coals made their fires more harmful than the fires of firewood or charcoal to most of the industrial materials touched by the flames and fumes. That is one reason why, during the Middle Ages and the Renaissance, coal fuel was used only in making crude products. But coal was more plentiful than either firewood or turf; once coal began to be seriously exploited, its very abundance stimulated a desire to multiply the output of manufactures. With the rise of the British coal industry, a source of heat was opened below the earth's surface capable of supplying manufacturers on a scale without precedent, a source of heat destined to discourage production for the sake of beauty but to encourage production for the sake of quantity.[12]

In earlier societies than those of western Europe iron had been almost always obtained directly from its ore, in the form of a pasty mass, in a forge with a charcoal fire. To rid the metal of its impurities, this pasty mass was subjected to repeated heatings and hammerings on the anvil. Small-scale operations alone were possible, and much of the iron present in the ore was lost as slag and scale. A strong heat had, on occasion, reduced iron ore to liquid. But, except in China during the remarkable eleventh-century industrial expansion which proved abortive, nothing intensive had been done to exploit the discovery that iron ore would melt, any more than to exploit the discovery that the earth contained black stones that would burn.

In the Middle Ages, certainly before the end of the fourteenth century and possibly earlier, a primitive form of blast furnace was introduced in northeastern France, the Rhineland, and northern Italy. The greater heat obtained at such furnaces, by means of more powerful bellows and a taller structure, reduced the ore to liquid iron. The carbon was absorbed by the reduced iron, forming, when it cooled, an alloy, cast iron or pig iron, of much lower melting point than the pure metal.

[11] *Ibid.,* pp. 347–79.
[12] See above, pp. 135–36.

The consequences of this change in the method of making iron were eventually no less revolutionary and no less fundamental to the triumph of modern industrial civilization than the consequences of substituting coal for wood, charcoal, turf, and other fuels derived from surface vegetation rather than out of the bowels of the earth. Industrialism is linked historically to cheap metal as well as to cheap fuel, and the introduction of cast iron paved the way for a phenomenal growth in the output of metal, once means were devised for using coal in place of charcoal in smelting. But cast iron did not become suddenly the principal product derived from iron ore. In spite of the introduction of blast furnaces in the fourteenth and fifteenth centuries, older methods of producing iron had a tenacious hold on the Europeans. Even after the considerable growth of industrial output in the era preceding the Reformation, very little of the iron ore, which was being dug in hundreds of districts in Europe, was melted at blast furnaces. Cast iron played no significant role, any more than coal, in the industrial growth of the late fifteenth and early sixteenth centuries.[13]

A decisive change in the methods of making iron first came in the hundred years following the Reformation, and then mainly in the north of Europe—above all, in the principality of Liège and in Great Britain. In the 1630's, on the eve of the English Civil War, there were probably between one hundred and one hundred and fifty blast furnaces in operation in England and Wales. For the first time in history the major portion of all the iron produced in a great country either passed through the pig-iron stage or was used in the form of cast iron.[14]

As a result of the adoption of the blast furnace, the metallic ore was purged of impurities which persisted in the pasty masses of wrought iron obtained at the older types of forge or furnace. Consequently, the adoption of the new method of smelting reduced the quantity of iron lost as slag and scale. It became feasible to exploit less pure ores than in the past. This, combined with the reduction in the costs of production, encouraged the manufacture of larger quantities of iron products.

In Great Britain, in Sweden, and in Holland—the chief scenes of industrial expansion during the late sixteenth and early seventeenth centuries—cast iron itself was used for a wide range of products, among them cannon and firebacks. But a larger quantity of the iron ore melted in the blast furnaces was cast into pig shapes to be treated usually at two forges—the "finery" and the "chafery." There the pig iron was reheated under oxidizing conditions and hammered into bars. Certain types of bar iron were then carried to slitting mills to be rolled and cut into rods. The new forges and slitting mills, like the new blast furnaces, had to be equipped with ma-

---

[13] Cf. above, pp. 40–41.
[14] Nef, "Note on the Progress of Iron Production in England, 1540–1640," *Journal of Political Economy*, XLIV (1936), 401–3.

chinery and supplied with water power to drive it. Each new forge and slitting mill, like each new blast furnace, required more capital and a larger labor force than had been commonly needed at the old forges, where wrought iron was extracted gradually but directly from the ore. The making of iron for the metal-finishing trades, which had been in earlier times an operation requiring only one principal establishment, and that frequently a small one, came to be carried on in three and sometimes four stages. Thus the spread of the roundabout method of iron manufacturing, like the general adoption of coal as fuel, marked an important step in the direction of large-scale industry and production for the sake of quantity.

The bars and rods derived from pig iron by the new methods of treatment provided an equivalent for the older wrought iron, which proved superior for the purposes of modern industry and eventually of mass production. While it was not until the end of the eighteenth century, when coal was first widely substituted for charcoal in iron metallurgy, that the new kinds of iron were made available in much larger quantities, we can trace to the late sixteenth and early seventeenth centuries in Great Britain the beginning of a historical process which was to turn the emphasis in connection with industrial work from the goals of quality and beauty to the goals of quantity and lower costs of production.[15]

The twentieth-century observer almost invariably looks back at the Elizabethan period with a mentality that the triumph of industrialism and of modern science has created. For him, *invention* relates to technical discoveries which reduce the death rate or the labor costs of production and so make it possible to prolong life and to multiply output tremendously. This very outlook prevents him from recognizing the full significance of industrial history in the late sixteenth and early seventeenth centuries. He is inclined to take for granted that his outlook always prevailed, whereas it was novel, a part of what I have called an "early industrial revolution."

Notable reductions were actually made at that time in the north of Europe in labor costs of production, and not only in the manufacture of iron. In glass- and steelmaking a new kind of furnace was devised in which the materials were separated in closed pots from the flames. This enabled the workmen to replace dear wood and charcoal by cheaper coal. The spread of coal and cast iron also provided many other industries with cheaper fuel and cheaper metal than would otherwise have been available. Further reductions in costs of transportation and production were effected by the introduction of railed ways with horse-driven wagons; of ships with more hold space; of boring rods for testing the underground strata before sinking shafts; of coke for drying malt to be used in brewing; of more mechanical looms for weaving stockings, ribbons, and various small wares.

[15] Cf. above, pp. 211–12.

Horse power and water power were coming to be more extensively used for driving machinery, and this also tended to cheapen production.[16]

Yet, when all is said—and more might be said—the saving of labor effected in the north of Europe during the lives of Shakespeare and Rembrandt was not spectacular if it is judged by the statistical mind of the twentieth century, proud of the fact that "steel is now cheaper than dirt," as a head of the United States Steel Corporation once remarked in a speech. The new railed ways and the boring rods were little used until the end of the seventeenth century. And such substantial saving of labor as there was before the Civil War resulted less from new inventive ideas than from the exploitation of old ones; cast iron and coal had an earlier history especially in China, and a considerable use of crude water-driven machinery can be traced back in Europe to at least the eleventh century.

The important matter which the twentieth-century mind misses is that neither the magnitude of the changes nor the originality of the inventive ideas is decisive in estimating the significance of the period which began in England around 1580, for modern industrialism. What seems decisive is that, especially in the north of Europe and, above all, in Great Britain, men came to attach a *value* that was novel to inventive ideas whose main purpose was to reduce labor costs and to multiply production. The technical problems whose solution in the 1780's led to the industrial revolution—with its coal-burning smelting furnaces, its steam power, and its railroads—were raised more acutely than ever before in history between about 1580 and 1620.[17]

The novel *emphasis* in the time of Shakespeare and Francis Bacon on quantity as the purpose of industrial effort provides a striking analogy to developments which were taking place at much the same time in the realm of scientific speculation. Science, like industry, was beginning to emancipate itself from a dependence on the experiences of the artist and the craftsman who worked with matter. Science, like industry, was beginning to be concerned with quantities more and with qualities less than in the earlier centuries of Western civilization. A kinship exists between the spirit of industrial change and the spirit of scientific change manifested in Europe during the late sixteenth and early seventeenth centuries.

Were the changes in industrial outlook sufficiently widespread during this period to be compared to the changes in scientific outlook? Even in the England of Charles I the industrial world—the world of coal mining, of metallurgy, and of other rising heavy industries, such as salt, alum, sugar, and soap manufacturing—was a small world. The numbers employed in these industries ran into some tens of thousands, but the English people

[16] See above, chap. iii.
[17] Nef, "Coal Mining and Utilization," in C. Singer, E. J. Holmyard, and A. R. Hall (eds.), *A History of Technology*, III (London, 1957), pp. 72–88.

numbered, in all probability, between five and six million. The country was still primarily agricultural,[18] though less predominantly so than a hundred years before, when Henry VIII had broken with Rome. The "early industrial revolution" of the late sixteenth and seventeenth centuries—involving decisive changes in economic purpose—was mainly confined, moreover, to Great Britain, to the United Provinces, and to Sweden.

Central Europe was apparently as innocent of blast furnaces for ironmaking in 1640 as in 1540. There is little evidence of a growing use of coal on the Continent, except in Holland, which got coal increasingly from England and Scotland. In the principality of Liège, where coal mining had been more important perhaps during the Middle Ages than in any part of Great Britain,[19] the output of the local mines stopped increasing after the middle of the sixteenth century.[20] The output of iron perhaps grew little from 1550 to 1650 even in what is now Belgium. In Spain, where the ironmakers were apparently as slow in adopting the roundabout process as in Central Europe, the output of iron almost certainly diminished during the first half of the seventeenth century.

France, Italy, and Switzerland (countries which suffered much less economically from 1550 to 1650 than did Spain and the Empire) were moving industrially in directions different from those characteristic of the north of Europe.[21] After the worst phases of the French religious wars had ended in 1589, the art of statesmanship was practiced with greater success in France than in any other European country. During the Thirty Years' War, Cardinal Richelieu established French political hegemony in Europe. There is a story that he was once asked what was his principal passion and that, instead of answering as his interlocutor had expected—the welfare of the French people—he said: "Writing verses." However that may be (he was certainly not a good poet), his predilections were for art. What pleased him most in connection with the products of manufactures, as well as with the products of craftsmen's workshops and artists' studios (which the French were incorporating in their "manufactures"), was the delight that the objects gave rather than reductions in the costs of making them.[22]

In this outlook Richelieu reflected the predilections of the most influential of his countrymen. He carried out an economic policy which he inherited from Sully, the remarkably gifted chief minister of Henri IV. The records of the Conseil d'État for Henri IV's reign suggest that the French government was less interested in encouraging inventions which aimed at

[18] J. E. Neale, *The Elizabethan House of Commons* (London, 1949), chap. i.

[19] Nef, *Rise of the British Coal Industry*, I, 13.

[20] Jean Lejeune, *La Formation du capitalisme moderne dans La Principauté de Liège au 16ᵉ siècle* (Paris, 1939), pp. 133 and *passim*.

[21] Cf. above, chap. iv, *passim*.

[22] Nef, *Western Civilization since the Renaissance* (New York, 1963), pp. 280–81.

abridging labor than in encouraging others which promised novelty in the service of beauty. The treatment accorded Claude Dangon, a craftsman of Lyons, is characteristic. In 1606 Dangon claimed to have invented a loom which could weave more beautiful silks. Royal officials encouraged him to make three trips to Paris to demonstrate before the Conseil d'État. He was then granted a substantial subvention by the crown to help him in spreading his loom among the craftsmen of Lyons, the chief center of the French silk manufacture.[23]

The silkmaking industry, the weaving of tapestries, the making of fine glass and pottery, and similar artistic manufactures were the main concern of the French state, at the time when the state in France was increasing its power over economic life. In all the arts and crafts, as in the arts of painting, music, and architecture, France owed much to Italian models and to the revival of the interest manifested especially in Italy during the fourteenth and fifteenth centuries in the models provided by classical Greece and Rome. Under French leadership the traditional values of beauty, splendor, and elegance were renewed and given fresh life, at a time when French ways of craftsmanship, like French manners, were influencing the economic development of Continental Europe more than the new industrial outlook exemplified by the English. In the industrial life of most of Europe, considerations of quality retained their ascendancy.

We must not be misled by the persistence among the Europeans of older values, which provided scope for a different kind of progress, also valuable for the rise of civilization,[24] into minimizing the significance of the new industrial outlook—the emphasis on quantity—which was manifested especially in Great Britain. That was as revolutionary in its way as the new scientific outlook. It is a part of our purpose in this essay to try to discover how and to what extent the two changes in outlook were related, how far the early industrial revolution contributed to the scientific revolution and how far it was brought about by the scientific revolution. Between them, these two revolutions made almost inevitable the eventual triumph of industrialism. After the middle of the seventeenth century, when the religious wars ended, the new industrial economy, which had evolved mainly in England and to some extent in Holland (which had in a way the best of both these worlds), gradually attracted the Continental countries. After about 1740–50 its attractions became irresistible. But during the hundred years from 1540 to 1640, the century preceding the English Civil War, the industrial changes which prepared the ground for the triumph of industrialism were confined mainly to the northern countries and especially to Great

[23] Nef, *Industry and Government in France and England* (Ithaca, N.Y., 1957), p. 84.
[24] See above, pp. 238–39; cf. Nef, *Cultural Foundations of Industrial Civilization* (New York, 1960), pp. 128 ff., 149 ff.

Britain. The scene, therefore, is the same as that which has attracted Professor Read in his principal historical studies.[25]

Fundamental changes in human outlook are written large only by the later generations, whose state of mind is derived from the ideas of earlier innovators. The new emphasis which, as we shall see, distinguished the science of early modern Europe from earlier science was confined to a very few. The scientific revolution was even less a mass movement than the early industrial revolution. Most sixteenth- and seventeenth-century Europeans were not innovators in their thought. The intellectual changes which now seem, and which were in fact, momentous were at the time inconspicuous. In writing of the scientific revolution, Whitehead remarks: "Since a babe was born in a manger, it may be doubted whether so great a thing has happened with so little stir."

It may be granted, then, that the changes in emphasis before the English Civil War in connection with industrial values were comparable in magnitude to the changes in emphasis in connection with scientific values and procedures. The general reader is likely to say, however, that the scientific revolution came first. He thinks of the scientific revolution as occurring in the time of Copernicus. And Copernicus' life was contemporary with an earlier movement of industrial development which was less "revolutionary" in its implications for industrial values than the "early English industrial revolution," because the earlier movement brought no decisive break from an emphasis on beauty to an emphasis on quantity.[26]

Must we not also distinguish the scientific outlook and the scientific results of Copernicus' time, however, from the outlook and results of the late sixteenth and early seventeenth centuries, the time of Galileo, Kepler, and Harvey? Ought we not to regard the later period as revolutionary for science, as well as for industry, in a sense that the earlier period was not?

The work of Sir Charles Sherrington and Professor Herbert Butterfield indicates that there were two periods in the history of science, as in the history of industry, during the two centuries which began, roughly speaking, with the birth of Leonardo da Vinci in 1452 and ended with the death of Galileo in 1642. Each of the periods occupied approximately a hundred years. The first lasted from the mid-fifteenth to the mid-sixteenth century; included the great epoch in painting associated with Botticelli, Titian, Giorgione, Raphael, Michelangelo, Leonardo, Dürer, Cranach, Grünewald, and Fouquet; included also the discovery of America, the conquests of Mexico and Peru, and the Reformation; and so was contemporaneous with the industrial expansion of the Renaissance. The second period lasted from the

[25] This essay was published in honor of Conyers Read (see above, p. 268).
[26] See above, chap. ii, *passim*.

mid-sixteenth to the mid-seventeenth century; included the wars of religion, the art of El Greco, Shakespeare, Cervantes, Rubens, Poussin, Velasquez, Hals, and Rembrandt, the settlement in North America of the Atlantic seaboard; and so was contemporaneous with the early industrial revolution.

Among the major figures in the history of science during the earlier period were Leonardo (1452–1519); Copernicus (1473–1543); Vesalius (1514–64), the celebrated Italian professor of anatomy; Jean Fernel (1497–1558), the French doctor and physiologist; and Paracelsus (1493–1541), the Swiss physician. Let us examine the nature of their achievements and the sources of these achievements in order to compare their work with that of the greatest scientists of the late sixteenth and early seventeenth centuries.

The inventiveness of the scientific mind in the earlier period—the period of the Renaissance—was more closely related to the inventiveness of the artist than in the period of the religious wars and the early industrial revolution. What the artist seeks to achieve is works which will endure because of the impression of beauty and truth concerning every side of man's experience which they convey to human beings of his own and future generations. What the modern natural scientist seeks to achieve is knowledge, and ever more knowledge, concerning the nature of the physical world and of all kinds of matter. The part played by direct meaning in determining the value of a work of art varies from a prose essay, where what is actually expressed in words is of the first importance, to a piano concerto, where an interpretation of the meaning in words is likely to dim the beauty. Yet form and content are inseparable in all works of art; the success of every artist's effort depends in no small measure upon an approach to perfect unity between the two. Form is not irrelevant to the success of the works of the scientist, but the decisive question is whether the results obtained are in accord with tangible evidence relating to a precise problem, evidence which other scientists can verify beyond peradventure by repeating the observations or the experiments.

Works of art have to be verified in a different way, because authentic results depend upon a successful unification of far more complicated subject matter, in which intangibles always play some part and frequently the dominant part. That is why Marcel Proust speaks of this artistic verification as "la rencontre fortuite avec un grand esprit" [27]—the accidental meeting which a serious reader, or observer, or listener has with a book, a painting, or a symphony, a meeting in which his assent is enlisted with abiding enthusiasm. This kind of assent by many other persons besides the author is what establishes a work of art. Artistic verification is a compound of a far greater variety of elements than are involved in scientific verification, including the humanity of the artist and that of his audience. There can be

[27] John Ruskin, *La Bible d'Amiens* (Paris, 1947), preface by Marcel Proust, p. 92 n.

no objective test of the verification; instructed artists may and often do make grievous mistakes in judging the merits of their own works or those of others, mistakes which are less likely to occur when a leading scientist judges his own work or that of another scientist. This is not because science is superior to art; it is because the natural scientist deals with far more limited categories than the artist, because questions of human nature and destiny hardly enter into his judgments, and because, until very recently, he dealt only with phenomena which could be directly observed.

The emergence of this special world of science, where men have detached certain categories of material problems for examination, especially for quantitative examination, and have brought the entire arsenal of human genius to bear upon their solution, is a novel achievement of the modern mind. To it men owe their great new powers of construction, of survival, and of destruction.

During the late fifteenth and the early sixteenth centuries, the search for scientific knowledge remained a by-product of the vision of the artist and the philosopher, or a by-product of the experience of the mine, of the workshop, and of the practice of some traditional profession like that of the physician. If we examine the careers of Leonardo, Copernicus, Vesalius, Fernel, and Paracelsus, I think we shall conclude that none of them made the decisive break away from tradition that characterized the scientific revolution. Science did not occupy a special world of its own in the mid-sixteenth century such as it had begun to occupy a hundred years afterward.

Leonardo's notebooks show us a self-educated natural scientist, whose adventures in the world of matter and space were a part of his efforts to use the experience of his senses in fresh ways in the service of drawing and painting. Under the influence of the ancients, Archimedes in particular, he began to ask questions about the first principles of dynamics, about motion in itself; and he then went on to ask questions which seem never to have been asked before concerning winds, clouds, the age of the earth, generation, and the nature of the human heart. Of his contributions to the work of later scientists there can be no doubt. But what were most important were the questions he asked, not the results he achieved. One of the leading art critics of our age, Sir Kenneth Clark, has suggested that the burden Leonardo assumed of trying to be at the same time a universal artist and a universal scientist proved too heavy for him to carry. The weight of this burden partly explains the small quantity of Leonardo's artistic output and its fragmentary character.[28]

The experiences of the artist, which Leonardo employed in scientific speculation, were making possible new visions for future ages to explore and verify, but the conversion of the visions into accepted realities, into new systems of scientific truth, was not accomplished by the Renaissance

[28] Kenneth Clark, *Leonardo da Vinci* (New York, 1939), pp. 56–59.

mind. We think of Copernicus as a supreme innovator concerning the structure of the physical universe, and so he was. But the establishment of his innovation as positively true demanded a different kind of investigation from his. The new system of the movement of the heavenly bodies, which Copernicus invented, was not derived from "a rational dynamical explanation of those movements." It was derived from art and theology, from the classical aesthetic concept that "the most perfect curve . . . is the circle," and from the religious concept that in God's universe heavenly bodies must move in the most perfect ways. Therefore, Copernicus believed erroneously that "heavenly bodies can move only in perfect [circles.]" [29]

In his recent book, *The Origins of Modern Science,* Professor Butterfield suggests that during the late fifteenth and early sixteenth centuries the chief factor in the progress of anatomical knowledge "was the actual development of the visual arts and the sharpening kind of observation which the eye of the artist was able to achieve." Art was the principal source of Vesalius' contributions to anatomy,[30] and of all the men of the age that was closing, he contributed most, through *De fabrica,* which was published in 1543, to a correct understanding of the structure of the human body.

The work of the two physicians, Fernel and Paracelsus, shows how it was possible to derive in Europe at the time of the Reformation new views concerning the functions of human organisms (as distinguished from their structure) and the nature and treatment of disease, from the practice of medicine and from the industrial experience of the mines and workshops. Fernel has been called the greatest French doctor of his time. It was the knowledge he acquired in the sickrooms of Paris, especially his observations of patients who died before his eyes, which led him to issue in 1542 his book *The Natural Part of Medicine.* Later he changed its name to *Physiology.* After more than thirteen centuries it supplanted Galen's treatise on the subject.[31]

Paracelsus' adventures in medicine are inseparable from his many travels among the developing mines and metallurgical works of Central Europe and his participation in some of these enterprises. As a young man he was employed for five years in the smelting plants at Schwaz, in the valley of the Inn, one of the most productive centers of the age for copper and silver. Later he spent some time at another leading metallurgical plant, the one at Villach in Carinthia, which was operated under the direction of the celebrated German merchant family, the Fuggers of Augsburg.[32] It seems to be agreed that Paracelsus' monograph, *On the Miners' Sickness and Other*

[29] C. F. von Weizsäcker, "The Spirit of Natural Science," *Humanitas,* III, No. 1 (1947), p. 3.
[30] Herbert Butterfield, *The Origins of Modern Science, 1300–1800* (London, 1949), pp. 34–35.
[31] Charles Sherrington, *The Endeavour of Jean Fernel* (Cambridge, 1946), *passim.*
[32] Cf. above, pp. 35, 49–50.

Miners' Diseases, grew out of these experiences. He studied the poisonous effects of metals and the morbid conditions of mercury poisoning. Paracelsus' works cannot be understood completely without his Galenic background—his familiarity with the medical writings which had survived classical antiquity—plus a strong dose of mysticism. But his extensive practical knowledge of mining and metallurgy was of immediate importance to him in the composition of all his treatises, including the one which dealt with mental diseases.[33]

It is not difficult to understand why historical students have been frequently led to treat the period of the late fifteenth and the early sixteenth centuries as the true starting point of modern science. The scientists of that age were attracted by their great classical predecessors, especially the Greeks and Romans, but they were also looking on nature and the human body afresh. With the development of perspective and of painting in oils since the fourteenth century, artists acquired a new curiosity concerning the physical structure and functions of men, animals, plants, mountains, forests, and the heavens. Their curiosity led them to see and record phenomena which had escaped their ancestors. The medieval mind had been more concerned with the abstract world that it could create by means of its inner resources, with what the greatest English theologian of Queen Elizabeth's reign, Richard Hooker, called "things that are and are not sensible," [34] with the Christian's vision of man's nature and destiny. That destiny transcended the world of matter, space, and time and so led men to look within themselves beyond all these tangibles. During the fifteenth and early sixteenth centuries, men began to look more directly at the material world than their ancestors had looked from the tenth through the thirteenth centuries. A new interest, derived from art, arose "in natural objects and in natural occurrences, for their own sakes." [35] This helped Vesalius to see more exactly the actual structure of the bodies of men and animals as he dissected; it led Leonardo to examine more exactly the nature of a bloody battle between two armies; it helped Copernicus to see the heavens anew and Fernel to look on his patients with more attention than his medieval predecessors to the actual physical circumstances of disease and death.

This disposition to look at man, the earth, and the rest of the visible universe with fresh eyes, to tune all the senses more to the tangible nature of things, was the main source of Renaissance visions of reality. The novelty of those visions was partly a product of the industrial development which accompanied the Renaissance, because this industrial development increased the scope of observation. It drew men to work in new surroundings

---

[33] *Four Treatises of Theophrastus von Hohenheim called Paracelsus,* ed. Henry E. Sigerist (Baltimore, 1941), pp. 46–47, 49, 52, 54, 135, 139, 188–89, 198, and *passim.*
[34] *Of the Laws of Ecclesiastical Polity* (1592–94), B. I, chap. vii, sec. 1.
[35] Whitehead, *Science and the Modern World,* p. 16; cf. pp. 14, 42.

in Europe, at the very time when explorers were sailing to new islands and continents. Men in search of a livelihood went deeper into the earth, farther among the mountains. They were introduced to natural substances and to natural phenomena that had been little observed before. Mineral resources were tapped which had been little touched during the Middle Ages, for example, cinnabar, the ore of mercury, and calamine, the ore of zinc. The discovery during the fifteenth century of abundant supplies of calamine in the Tyrol and Carinthia and especially at Moresnet, near Aachen, made possible the extensive manufacture of brass, an alloy produced by heating prepared calamine with copper in a charcoal fire.[36]

Thus the picture of the material world opened by men of the Renaissance differed from that which their medieval ancestors had seen. It also differed from that which the classical Greeks and Romans had seen, although the Renaissance has been persuasively described and explained as mainly "a classical revival." Yet, however we describe or explain the Renaissance in the time of Copernicus (it is well known that this "renaissance" began before his birth and that there had been still earlier renaissances), it is important for the historian to recognize that this was not the first time that civilized men had looked at nature more directly than had their ancestors of immediately preceding generations.

An experience with groups of statues from the Parthenon, as these are preserved in London in the British Museum, shows that Attic art presented the human body with a reality, as well as a splendor, which has never been excelled and which was hardly approached among the Mediterranean or the European peoples for a millennium after Christ. An experience with the scenes portrayed in stone in the cathedrals of western Europe from the early twelfth through the thirteenth centuries suggests that the artists of that age were looking at animals, landscapes, and human bodies much more closely than the artists of the tenth and early eleventh centuries had. Yet, in spite of the fresh outlook of the artists and craftsmen, neither the great age of Greek, nor the great age of Gothic, art led directly to the scientific revolution.

What distinguishes modern science from science of the past, is not the observation of nature but a peculiar purpose and method in the examination of nature. On the side of purpose, it is an effort to solve particular problems of the physical and the biological world which had eluded earlier minds, and, on the basis of these solutions, to formulate, at least as hypotheses, scientific laws. On the side of method, it is, first, the persistent use of the experiment or of controlled observation as the final arbiter in reaching any result and, second, the employment of quantitative measurements and calculations as the major means of achieving the results which are subject to the control of positive evidence.

[36] See above, chap. i.

The eye of the artist can discover an immense amount about nature and about the behavior of the human body. What the artist's eyes and other senses seek, above all, are not exact measurements but the entire atmosphere surrounding the things observed and the transfiguration of these things into enduring forms by means of the inner life vouchsafed the human being. In the interest of truth and delight the artist seeks, not quantities or precise space relationships, but qualities which transcend analysis and measurement. The exact dimensions of Chartres Cathedral and the surrounding landscape were not the concern of Corot when he painted the version of the scene which now hangs in the Petit Palais in Paris, and the mind accustomed to precise measurements will be startled by Corot's picture. He reveals qualities in the cathedral which would escape an architect's drawing. But he is not concerned, any more than were the artist-scientists of the Renaissance, with the abstractions that have enabled modern scientists better to understand the nature of the physical world and of living matter.

The discoveries of a mind that is primarily artistic in outlook are not irrelevant to modern knowledge of the physical and the biological world. No modern has perhaps excelled the great Greek physician, Hippocrates, in the acuteness of his observations of the behavior of the body during illness, observations carried out nearly twenty-five hundred years ago. It would seem that these observations of the human being in a morbid state were similar in their nature to the observations which guided Phidias in his portrayal of the human being in a state of health. We may speak of Hippocrates as a great artist. But I do not think we can speak as legitimately of Lister or of Claude Bernard as great artists, though neither lacked those imaginative faculties without which no important work of the mind is possible. It is not the experience of the artist but a use of the mind and senses in some ways antipathetic to art which characterizes modern science. The Renaissance delight "in natural objects and natural occurrences for their own sakes" was insufficient to bring about the scientific revolution. That earlier delight had to be supplemented and to some extent supplanted by what Sherrington describes as "new-found delight in natural observation for its own sake," [37] and by observation for the sake of quantities and precise space relationships, even at the expense of a knowledge of qualities. What was needed for the birth of modern science was less art than a breaking away from art. Fancy, mystery, and the disciplined imagination with which the artist draws on both, had to be brought under the rigid control of tangible, positively demonstrable facts and logically demonstrable mathematical propositions.

The leading scientists of the late fifteenth and early sixteenth centuries by no means made such a break away from art or from the sources of

[37] Sherrington, *op. cit.*, pp. 144–45.

artistic imagination. They hardly seem to have been interested in exact quantitative statements concerning biological or physical phenomena. Paracelsus' last treatise was devoted to nymphs, sylphs, pygmies, and salamanders, which he conceived of as the makers and guardians of the treasures in the mines. Much as Grünewald in some of his paintings, now in Colmar, by a return to medieval abstraction, combined the more direct art of the Renaissance with an abstract art which almost suggests twentieth-century surrealism, Paracelsus combined his new medicine with medieval folklore and mysticism.[38] For all his insight, Copernicus studied within the framework of an ancient set of ideas. While his world system differed from the world systems of Aristotle and Ptolemy, it was mystical like theirs, with its insistence that the spheres, being heavenly bodies and therefore perfect, must move in perfect circles. Vesalius deliberately accommodated his anatomical results to the teachings of Galen, and he failed to realize the need for a new account of the movements of the heart and blood.[39] Working at the functions, rather than the structure, of the body, Fernel was as far as Vesalius from establishing a firm basis for the modern biological sciences. Sherrington has written of Fernel, "he and the Renaissance, with all their zest for doing and for progress, were still in reality little forwarder than were the Middle Ages. . . . Far more were wanted than comment, conciliation and mere systematization," the achievements which made it possible for Fernel's physiological treatise to supplant Galen's. "There had to be re-foundation." [40]

Re-foundation involved a use of the intellect that was novel because of a twofold *emphasis,* which it is perhaps desirable to repeat. There is, first, the emphasis upon the systematic pursuit of experiments and observations (which are not a by-product of the artist's interest in objects and occurrences for their own sakes and which have no immediate practical purpose, whether it be the purpose of the artist or the modern engineer), for the sake of discovering physical and biological laws. There is, second, the emphasis upon the quantitative method of treating all phenomena, with the object of discovering these laws. The quantitative method, which extends the range of *scientific* certainty, brings with it ever more precise and ever more ingenious scientific statements with the progress of the mathematical knowledge which such emphasis helps to inspire. These crucial changes in emphasis, which were to lead eventually to the triumph of the scientific outlook, came in the late sixteenth and early seventeenth centuries, in the age of the early industrial revolution.

The contrasts between the industrial experience of different European countries during that period help to bring the early English industrial revo-

[38] Paracelsus, *op. cit.,* p. 220.
[39] Butterfield, *op. cit.,* pp. 30, 38–39.
[40] Sherrington, *op. cit.,* p. 96.

lution into relief.[41] It is natural, therefore, to compare the development of science in different parts of Europe during the same period, both as a means of understanding the nature of the scientific revolution and as a means of inquiry into the genesis of industrialism. The scientific revolution of those times was an indispensable preparation for obtaining theoretical results which, when applied, much later, especially during the past hundred years, to technological innovations helped to make possible the conquest of the material world in recent times.

Lack of historical knowledge has obliged me to concern myself mainly with the contrasts, during the late sixteenth and seventeenth centuries, between Great Britain and France. This historical limitation is unfortunate. Yet, in view of the course taken by European history down to the mid-nineteenth century, there is some justification in concentrating, if one has to concentrate, upon England and France. All the great European countries had a share in producing the unique civilization of modern times. But, at least until after 1850, the strongest elements in the compound were British and French.

THE STUDY OF THE BODY

In the biological sciences the re-foundation of which Sherrington spoke was provided by William Harvey. He carried out, in the early seventeenth century, fundamental work concerning the movements of the heart and blood, and he managed to discover what is still regarded as the correct explanation of these movements. In the older physiology of Fernel and Galen, the heart was a kind of "hearth supporting a vital fire." Harvey showed it to be "a little hydraulic power-plant," [42] and, by so doing, he "released physiology for a new start in the study of living creatures." [43] From the appearance, in 1628, of his Latin treatise, *Exercitatio anatomica de mortu cordis et sanguinis in animalibus,* "we may date the beginning of experimental medicine." [44]

How did Harvey's approach to physiology differ from the approaches of his predecessors? Experimenting in itself was no great novelty. It was the persistent use of experiment which distinguished Harvey's work from that of scientists of the Renaissance, as well as of the Middle Ages and antiquity. He cut the arteries and veins of living things, from large animals to tiny insects, observing and recording with unending care and patience the flow of the blood and the motion of the heart. He had recourse to the new

[41] Cf. above, chaps. iv and vi.
[42] Sherrington, *op. cit.,* p. 144.
[43] Butterfield, *op. cit.,* p. 47.
[44] William Osler, "Harvey and his Discovery," *Alabama Student* (1908), 330, as quoted in J. F. Fulton, *Physiology* (New York, 1931), p. 13.

magnifying glass, produced by progressive glassmakers, to observe wasps, hornets, and flies.[45]

Like Fernel, Harvey was a physician. This makes the contrasts in the methods of the two the more striking. There is no evidence that Fernel experimented at all; his knowledge of physiology was gained mainly from his practice. But Harvey derived little or no data from his practice. Almost all of them came from planned experiments, carried out with extraordinary persistence over a period of more than two decades.

With Harvey, experiment became the arbiter in reaching every conclusion. Old experiences were abandoned as a basis for knowledge, in favor of new ones. These new experiences were not the product of any traditional intellectual discipline, of any craft, or even of any new industry. The entire inquiry was devised without practical purpose, solely for the sake of solving specific problems in the biological sciences. As the English poet, Abraham Cowley, wrote in an ode composed on the occasion of Harvey's death:

> . . . Harvey sought for Truth in Truth's own Book,
> The Creatures, which by God himself was writ,
> And wisely thought 'twas fit
> Not to read Comments only upon it,
> But on th' Original it self to look.[46]

Such energy and assiduity in vivisection, as a means of reaching generalizations concerning the physical nature of life, had never before been equaled. While Galen had made some experiments on living animals,[47] in Greco-Roman times and in the Middle Ages the learned men of the Mediterranean countries and of Europe apparently felt that it was illegitimate and repulsive to penetrate the living body as an experiment, an analogue perhaps to the notion prevalent among the Romans in the time of Pliny the Elder that it was thievish and sacrilegious to take ores or other minerals in large quantities from the subsoil. The first restraint stood in the way of modern biology. The second stood in the way of industrialism, for the rise of industrialism depended upon new economic values which would make a virtue of production for its own sake, as well as for the sake of the consumer, even if more production made it necessary to ransack ruthlessly the resources of the earth.

In recent times it has become usual to regard these restraints as prejudices. (Although antivivisection societies have been organized in the nineteenth and twentieth centuries, they are not taken seriously in respectable intellectual circles.) History shows that the accepted procedures of one age sometimes seem only prejudices to another, and the methods and values

---

[45] *The Works of William Harvey*, ed. Robert Willis (London, 1847), p. 29.
[46] Cowley, *Works* (London, 1721), II, 524.
[47] Butterfield, *op. cit.*, p. 36.

associated with modern science and modern economics may not prove to be immortal. It is possible that the scientific and industrial outlook of our times, which puts experiment, quantitative statement, and material productivity almost beyond criticism as values in science and industry, which makes these methods and values touchstones by which all other methods and values are judged, may seem prejudiced in future times. However that may be, the astounding progress of experimental science and heavy industry in the modern world depended partly on a collapse of the restraints, now widely treated as prejudices, which once stood in the way both of planned experiments and of the exploitation of the natural resources of the earth. Like the increased emphasis placed on *quantity* in production, the increased emphasis placed by Harvey on vivisection was indicative of the revolutionary character of changes in modes of thought in the late sixteenth and early seventeenth centuries.

No fundamental changes are brought about easily in the conventional ways in which men regard life and the universe and use their minds trying to understand them. At the time of the Renaissance, with the revival of learning and the introduction and spread of printing, the scientific knowledge possessed by the famous men of antiquity gained a new prestige. One effect was to give the learning of the past even greater authority than it had possessed among the Europeans of the twelfth and thirteenth centuries. As we shall try to show later in this essay, the scientific revolution derived a stimulus from the Renaissance as a classical revival, especially from the new interest which arose in geometry as a result of the increase in the knowledge of Plato and Archimedes. Yet there were other aspects of the classical revival which were more of a handicap than a help to the scientific revolution. The Renaissance gave an increasing prestige to the actual scientific theories of antiquity, many of which were to appear misguided or definitely false to the modern scientist. Thus the classical revival often intrenched the mind in erroneous views concerning the nature of material phenomena. The old ideas of Galen concerning the circulation of the blood gained new adherents in the fifteenth and sixteenth centuries and pervaded the thought of even the most advanced students of physiology.

Harvey learned much from past knowledge in biology. He was familiar with the great classical authorities, especially Hippocrates, Aristotle, and Galen. As a young man studying in Italy at the close of the sixteenth century, he was introduced to the works of Vesalius. From these and from the lips of Fabricius, Vesalius' successor in the famous chair of anatomy at the University of Padua, Harvey became familiar with the additions recently made to anatomical knowledge. But his discovery depended on a break with the teachings of his masters as well as with earlier authorities, and not simply a break of the kind that men of genius always make, even when they proceed within an established tradition, whether in science, art, or philosophy, but a break into a new mode of procedure in seeking results.

The systematic attack on living creatures in search of evidence, which Harvey conducted after he returned to England at the age of twenty-four in 1602, involved special difficulties on account of its novelty. These difficulties, which confronted all the natural scientists of Harvey's time, did not arise mainly from the danger that, in a period of religious controversy and war, the church might take sanctions against learned persons who employed the new experimental method to obtain unorthodox results. That danger existed, but there has been a tendency to exaggerate it, because of the just horror felt by our immediate ancestors for religious persecution. In any event, this particular danger was hardly present in seventeenth-century England, to which Harvey returned to live the rest of his long life. The difficulties that are of greater moment in connection with original work of the kind he did arose because it was necessary for the experimenter to proceed as none of his predecessors had done, without any guidance or ready recognition from his contemporaries, from past knowledge, or from faith, to proceed more and more as experimental evidence dictated and to put his final faith in experimental evidence. It was not until 1616, at least fourteen years after he began his experiments, that Harvey's labors bore fruit in his lectures to students of the Royal College of Physicians in London. It was another twelve years before he published any of his results. By that time King James I was dead, so that Harvey's researches concerning the motion of the heart and blood, begun under Elizabeth, stretched into a third reign. During the whole time, Harvey was ceaselessly moving along untrodden ways.

Today these ways seem to most men the only rational roads for the mind to follow. But we must remember that, in Harvey's time, what most men regarded as rational was different. According to Hooker, who was much older than Harvey, reason is the means by which "man attaineth a knowledge of things that are and are not sensible." It has now become the custom to think of sensible verification as the only guaranty of reason, but in Harvey's time that was a revolutionary idea. The methods adopted by Harvey subjected him, therefore, to an agonizing emotional ordeal. He tells us so himself:

> When I first gave my mind to vivisections as a means of discovering the motions and uses of the heart, and sought to discover these from actual inspection, and not from the writings of others, I found the task so truly arduous, so full of difficulties, that I was almost tempted to think with Fracastorius that the motion of the heart was only to be comprehended by God.

This reference to the intellectual capitulation of the Italian physician, Fracastoro (1483–1553), the first Western writer on syphilis,[48] suggests

[48] Girolamo Fracastoro, *Syphilis sive Morbus Gallicus* (Verona, 1530).

both how arduous were the problems confronting the earliest experimenters and how much more difficult it was for the generation of Fernel than for the generation of Harvey to surmount them. Harvey proceeds:

> At length, and by using greater and daily diligence, having frequent recourse to vivisections, employing a variety of animals for the purpose, and collating numerous observations, I thought that I had attained to the truth, that I should extricate myself from this labyrinth, and that I had discovered what I so much desired, both the motion and the use of the heart and arteries.[49]

From the success of his long labors, Harvey drew a general conclusion about the value of the new method he had been employing. He observed:

> True philosophers . . . never regard themselves as already so thoroughly informed, but that they welcome further information from whomsoever and from whencesoever it my come; nor are they so narrow-minded as to imagine any of the arts or sciences transmitted to us by the ancients, in such a state of forwardness or completeness, that nothing is left for the ingenuity and industry of others; very many, on the contrary, maintain that all we know is still infinitely less than still remains to be known.[50]

Harvey's enthusiasm for observation and experiment hardly flagged until after he was sixty. In 1636, on a visit to Germany, accompanied by the English ambassador, he caused his companions much anxiety by wandering alone into the woods to observe strange trees, plants, soils, etc. Sometimes he was "like to be lost," reported the artist Hollar, who was of the party, "so that my lord and ambassador would be really angry with him, for there was not only danger of wild beasts, but of thieves."[51] His new quest, once begun, was not easily forsaken. As physician to Charles I, Harvey visited the royal deer parks and accompanied the king on stag hunts. He took advantage of the opportunity to cut up the doe at different stages in gestation, in an endeavor to understand the process as accurately as he understood the circulation of the blood.

These experiments led him to write his *Anatomical Exercises on the Generation of Animals*. This book was published late in his life, in 1651, when he was seventy-three, and, according to one account, without his permission. The new treatise marked no such sharp break with the past as had his book on the heart and blood. As Harvey grew old, he seems to have fallen back upon the training he had received in the schools and universities, to have returned to the habits of the generations of learned men who had preceded him. While vivisection and observation enabled him to correct a number of errors in the views of ancient authorities concerning generation,

---

[49] *Works of William Harvey,* p. 19.
[50] *Ibid.,* p. 6.
[51] *Ibid.,* pp. lxxiii–lxxiv.

he depended much more than in his earlier treatise upon old scholastic views and methods. After the age of sixty or sixty-five most men find nature compelling them to follow well-beaten paths, and the paths which Harvey had been schooled to follow in his youth were dug deep in the European tradition.

In embryology, as well as in physiology, Harvey had shown that the new road of observation and experiment was the only one likely to lead to satisfactory results, if men were to correct the views of ancient authority concerning the real nature and functions of the body.[52] With the heavy weight of authority still bred into the learned during the sixteenth century, more of a break than Harvey made away from traditional methods of scientific procedure could hardly be expected from a single man.

Such a successful expedition into the unknown as Harvey conducted depended, it may be suggested, both upon his natural genius and upon the attitude of his colleagues and countrymen to a novel emphasis on experiment. It seems that the kind of researches conducted by Harvey would have been more difficult for a contemporary Frenchman.

Support for this hypothesis comes from two lines of historical inquiry. First, the reception accorded Harvey's discovery in France suggests that, during the late sixteenth and early seventeenth centuries, French minds moved less readily toward the intelligent use of the experimental method in biology than did English or Dutch minds. Secondly, the somewhat earlier career of the great French surgeon, Ambroise Paré (ca. 1510–ca. 1590), who died when Harvey was twelve, suggests that conditions in France made it more natural than in England for the mind to depend for scientific knowledge mainly upon older, more traditional ways of following occupations or of observing the experiences of practical life.

These differences between conditions in the two countries persisted during the whole of Harvey's lifetime. No man of that time in any country broke more sharply away from the prejudices of ancient authorities in the domain of *ideas* than did Descartes. Unlike other Frenchmen touched by genius who were his contemporaries—among them Mersenne, Poussin, Claude Lorrain—Descartes was not drawn to Italy; the only foreign countries besides Holland that tempted him as a place of residence were England and later Sweden. His choice of Holland as a congenial setting for his mature thought is indicative of the ardent desire that he had to free himself from all past misconceptions and to found the true philosophy; for in Descartes's time (1596–1650) the United Provinces, along with Great Britain, provided the most revolutionary intellectual atmosphere in the world. Yet even Descartes, who was in so many ways independent of his native France, was unable to liberate himself, to the extent that Harvey

[52] *Ibid.*, pp. lxix–lxx.

did, from a priori deductions in the domain of *facts*.[53] He lacked genius for observation and experiment, and this was partly a result of his nationality. It appears that the France of his time was a less congenial country than England for the systematic development of the experimental method.

At the very time when Harvey published his first treatise in 1628, the parlement of Paris issued an edict forbidding all instructors in France to teach anything concerning the circulation of the blood contrary to the accepted doctrines of classical and medieval authority.[54] It is not surprising, therefore, that the first printed attack on Harvey's new theory of the motion of the heart and blood should have come from France. This was written by a pupil of Joannes Riolanus, professor of anatomy in the University of Paris, and it appeared in 1630. So far as evidence was concerned, Riolanus' pupil thought it sufficient to set against Harvey's new explanation of the circulation of the blood the ancient theory of Galen, according to which the blood passed from the right to the left ventricle through the septum. Before the time of Harvey, Galen's view had already been questioned in some particulars by Vesalius, Fabricius, and others, but their criticisms had apparently made little impression in the lecture rooms of Paris. Two decades passed before any university lecturer in France expressed open agreement with Harvey. The first to do so was a professor of medicine in the University of Montpellier, famous at least down to the times of Rabelais for the strength of its medical faculty. When this Montpellier professor defended and taught Harvey's physiology, he created such a scandal that his colleagues called on him to resign his chair.[55] Not until several decades later did the new description and explanation of the circulation of the blood win general acceptance in France. Not until the last half of the eighteenth century, when learned Frenchmen began to give the new scientific methods pre-eminence among rational procedures and when France rivaled England in the progress of machines and heavy industry,[56] was Harvey's achievement enthusiastically received, for example by writers on economic subjects such as Turgot and Quesnay. They compared the circulation of wealth through the nation to the circulation of blood through the body.[57] By this time, enlightened opinion in France would have fully indorsed the lines which Cowley had penned a hundred years earlier.

In most European countries the university faculties were hardly less backward than in France about accepting the validity of Harvey's methods and the accuracy of his results. The notable exceptions were England itself

---

[53] See Etienne Gilson's notes to his edition of Descartes's *Discours de la méthode* (Paris, 1925), pp. 280–82, and also Gilson, "Descartes, Harvey et la scolastique," *Etudes de philosophie médiévale* (Strasbourg, 1921), pp. 244–45.

[54] T. C. Allbutt, *Science and Medieval Thought* (London, 1901).

[55] For these attacks on Harvey's results, see *Works of William Harvey*, pp. xlii ff.

[56] Nef, *Western Civilization since the Renaissance* (New York, 1963), pp. 276–86.

[57] C. Gide and C. Rist, *Histoire des doctrines économiques* (4th ed.; Paris, 1922), pp. 20–21.

and, after England, Holland, industrially the two most prosperous states of Europe during Harvey's lifetime and those which had moved farthest in the direction of modern economic values. Harvey met with no serious opposition at home. It is true that some rival medical practitioners, jealous more of his success as a physician than as a scientist, took advantage of the appearance of his unorthodox treatise to spread a rumor that he was crackbrained. This seems to have cost him some patients, for the income from his practice apparently fell off. But his associates in the College of Physicians and his scientific contemporaries in England generally sided with him. His methods and his results were immediately taken up by contemporary philosophers, for example by Hobbes, and by contemporary men of letters, for example by Dryden.

Descartes was hardly less enthusiastic about the new explanation of the circulation of the blood than was Hobbes. In the Holland of his adoption, Descartes wrote and published in 1637 his agreement with the main conclusions of Harvey's treatise.[58] Two years after that, in 1639, a young Englishman, Roger Drake, successfully maintained before the faculty of the new University of Leiden a thesis in support of the fresh explanation of the circulation of the blood.[59]

The revolutionary methods of supporting rational arguments and reaching new explanations of physical phenomena by means of the experimental method evidently received a more sympathetic hearing in England than in France. Support for this view comes from the history of other sciences besides physiology. At the end of the sixteenth century the resistance to the Copernican hypothesis concerning the movement of the heavenly bodies appears to have been less strong in England than in most other countries.[60] It was in England, too, that the first steps were taken toward making a science of chemistry, which even before modern times was, in a crude and mystical sense, "experimental" among the alchemists. The establishment of chemistry as a science is usually regarded as primarily the work of Robert Boyle (1627–91). Of all European countries, England seems to have provided the most favorable intellectual, economic, social, and political conditions during the late sixteenth and seventeenth centuries for the systematic application of the experimental method, purged, insofar as the actual results are concerned, of mystical and superstitious elements.

It is true that Boyle and Newton, as well as Kepler, had sides that strike the modern scientist as hardly less mystical and superstitious than the writings of Paracelsus.[61] The important difference is that the scientific principles stated by the great seventeenth-century scientists, unlike the theories of

[58] Descartes, *Discourse de la méthode,* Part V; cf. Gilson, "Descartes, Harvey, et la scolastique," pp. 217–23.
[59] *Works of William Harvey,* p. xliv.
[60] Butterfield, *op. cit.,* p. 50.
[61] Nef, *Western Civilization since the Renaissance,* pp. 195–96.

Paracelsus, were independent, insofar as proof is concerned, of these expeditions into the supernatural.

When we consider the contributions made in France to knowledge of the human body, we find that they came less from any revolution in the emphasis of the mind itself than from the pursuit of knowledge by old traditional methods, which were extended into new spheres as a consequence of economic and technical developments. The French may be said to have prolonged the ancient methods of assembling scientific data. In the biological sciences there was no such sharp break with the Renaissance as occurred in England. During the hundred years from 1540 to 1640 France had no physiologist or embryologist fit to rank with Harvey as an innovator. Great achievements like his were dependent partly upon the collapse of the prejudice against combining creative learning with manual work. This prejudice, which may have arisen partly out of the ancient association of manual labor with slavery, was prolonged, after slavery had almost disappeared in western Europe, by the medieval distinction (to which the scholastic philosophers of the twelfth and thirteenth centuries contributed) between the "liberal" and the "servile" arts, between work done with the mind alone and work which involved a change in matter.[62] Like the work of poets, logicians, or mathematicians, the work of the physician produced no such change. It was therefore "liberal." Like the work of sculptors, glaziers, or ironworkers, the work of the surgeon produced a change in matter. It was therefore "servile."

During the late sixteenth and early seventeenth centuries this distinction seems to have retained greater strength in France than in England. It was generally a handicap to the progress of the experimental method, because that involved a combination of intellectual with manual work for no more practical purpose than speculative inquiry, a combination for which little support existed in the medieval learned tradition of Europe.

There was one side of inquiry into the condition of the body, nevertheless, in which the French surpassed the English, partly because the very separation of manual from purely intellectual work reflected a greater concern with excellence in craftsmanship, at a time when much manual work was artistic, and when it involved, consequently, subtle and tasteful decisions by the mind controlling the hands. Trained not in the schools and universities but as craftsmen in their gilds, the barber-surgeons were not restrained, as French physicians and learned scientists were, from working with matter, from manipulating and operating upon living human beings. Barber-surgeons, who wore short robes as a sign of social inferiority, were not accorded the same positions in society as were members of the medical faculties in the universities or surgeons of the long robe. But the barber-

---

[62] Jacques Maritain, *Art et scolastique* (3d ed.; Paris, 1935), p. 33.

surgeons had the advantage of expert manual training in an age when the manual dexterity of the workshop carried more esteem than it does today and when the standards of craftsmanship were higher. Because the surgeons of the long robe would not condescend to operate and incur the loss of prestige involved, the barber-surgeons took over practically all the increasing surgical practice of an age of war, such as the sixteenth century proved to be for Continental Europe.[63] It was an age in which England had less war than France, as well as less craftsmanship.

French surgery was more skilful than English during the sixteenth and early seventeenth centuries. England had no surgeon whose advances in his art could equal those made by Ambroise Paré.[64] During the period from 1560 to 1640 no one in France made more important contributions to our knowledge of bodily processes than he. So it is not capricious to select Paré for comparison with Harvey. In doing this, however, it is necessary to remember that Paré was some sixty years Harvey's senior and that the European world in which he worked was different from the world in which Harvey worked. The time of Paré's mature life, the fifty years from about 1540 to 1590, should be regarded as a period of transition from the older science of the age of Fernel and Copernicus to the new science of the age of Harvey and Galileo. Paré was working in that older tradition. In the fifty years following his death, 1590–1640, the time of Harvey, the French mind developed scientifically in novel ways which, as we shall see, helped, through mathematics, to make possible a revolution in scientific methods. But this development of mathematics in France seems to have had little or no influence on the study of the body until after the mid-seventeenth century. That is why it is perhaps legitimate to select Paré as the leading French figure in the development of the biological sciences in the period of the scientific revolution.

As a barber-surgeon, Paré was not a learned man. But he had behind him the medieval craft tradition; he cut the body with a skill equal to that exercised by the greatest French sculptors of his time, when they cut stone to fashion, for example, the cloisters which surround the choir of Chartres Cathedral. During Paré's early years, before he was admitted in 1541 to mastership in the Paris gild of barber-surgeons, cannon, culverins, arquebuses, muskets, and pistols were coming into widespread use for the first time, in the battles between the armies of the French king Francis I and the Emperor Charles V.[65] The balls, bullets, and shot sprayed from these firearms tore new kinds of wounds in human flesh, of which neither Hippocrates nor Galen had had any knowledge. By virtue of his craft, the

[63] Francis R. Packard, *Life and Times of Ambroise Paré* (New York, 1926), pp. 15–16.
[64] T. C. Allbutt, *The Historical Relations of Medicine and Surgery* (London, 1905), pp. 99–100.
[65] Nef, *Western Civilization since the Renaissance,* pp. 24–32.

barber-surgeon was confronted with novel problems which called imperatively for solution. Unlike the founders of the experimental method, he did not have to construct the problems in order to answer questions which had no immediate practical purpose. In caring for the wounded in the campaigns of the French army in Italy, Paré's skill and genius in the surgeon's craft were demonstrated with remarkable effect by his exercise of what seems little more than good sense. The accepted method of treating gunshot wounds was to pour on hot oil. In one of the battles in which Paré was engaged as army surgeon, the wounds came so fast that he was left without this "remedy." Next morning, when he examined the wounded, he found the men he had been unable to treat, for want of supplies, more comfortable and further on the road to recovery than those he had subjected to the prescribed treatment.[66] So he abandoned hot oil.

His work with the army soon attracted the attention of Francis I, who made him his own surgeon, and he served as royal surgeon to five successive French sovereigns, the last of whom was Henri III. This position gave him special advantages in instruments and in conditions for making discoveries. He observed the harm done after amputations by applying hot irons to wounds to staunch the blood. He established the use of the ligature for the control of hemorrhages. He promoted the use of artificial limbs. Having found on the field of battle, in connection with novel problems of surgery, that accepted methods of treatment could be improved upon, he proceeded to try, as part of his craft, new methods in connection with perennial problems. In obstetrics he showed the advantages of inducing artificial labor by manipulations, when the natural process of birth was so delayed as to endanger the mother's life.[67]

Latin was still the preferred language of the learned, and Harvey wrote his celebrated treatise on the circulation of the blood in that ancient tongue. As a barber-surgeon, Paré had no knowledge of Latin. So he began to publish in French the results derived from his practice. This made his conclusions doubly offensive to a learned French audience. He challenged accepted knowledge, and he challenged it in uncouth language. On both counts, Paré's daring outraged the French faculties no less than had Harvey's unorthodox methods and results.

For a long time learned circles refused to adopt Paré's methods or accept his results. The appearance in 1575 of the first collected edition of his works drew a warning from the School of Medicine of the University of Paris that the writings of this "imprudent man, without any learning," should not be put on sale until they had been submitted to the medical faculty for approval.[68] Five years afterward the dean of the School of Medicine, Étienne Gourmelen, attacked Paré's work. Gourmelen found it

[66] Packard, *op. cit.*, pp. 27–28.
[67] *Ibid.*, pp. 92–93.
[68] *Ibid.*, pp. 106 ff.

enough to show that no ancient medical and surgical writers had used the ligature in place of hot irons in amputations or had employed any other of the more gentle practices introduced by Paré in treatment of wounds.[69] Against Paré's methods, Gourmelen had nothing to say which seems at all convincing to our age, because frequent innovations in matters of technique are now as expected as they were then suspect.

Gourmelen's comments were characteristic of learned authority on the Continent. When Athanasius Kircher (1601–80), the German philosopher and mathematician, tried to get a Jesuit professor to look through the telescope, an invention of the late sixteenth century, at the newly discovered sunspots, the professor brushed him aside with the remark, "It is useless, my son. I have read Aristotle through twice and have not found anything about spots on the sun in him. There are no spots on the sun. They arise either from the imperfections of your telescope or from the defects of your own eyes." [70]

It was easier to challenge ancient authority by the exercise of the surgeon's craft than by the establishment of new speculative sciences, such as biology or astronomy. This was partly because the eventual practical significance of discoveries in those sciences was apparent only to a rare genius like Descartes, who drew attention in his *Discours de la méthode* to the possibility that the new scientific methods might eventually prolong life, multiply commodities, and reduce the burden of manual labor.[71] What made the criticism of Paré's work ineffective was the immediate demonstrable effectiveness of his novel treatments among his patients. These included some of the most powerful members of the royal family. Paré retained his ascendancy at court, notwithstanding the attacks made on him by the faculties and notwithstanding the suspicion that he was a Huguenot, at a time when religious hatred and violence reached their peak in France. Catherine de Medici and Charles IX apparently intervened to save him from being massacred in Paris, along with other Protestants, on St. Bartholomew's Day. French royalty was not so stupid as to throw away, in a fit of zeal for religious orthodoxy, a man with unique gifts for relieving their physical sufferings. Paré had obtained solid results in the realm of surgery, which were destined to be valuable to medicine, once medicine adopted the experimental method. But his methods represented no such break with the past as did Harvey's. He was working in the Renaissance craft tradition.

While English conditions were more favorable than French to the progress of experimental science, they were less favorable to such scientific

[69] *Ibid.*, p. 25.
[70] Cited by B. Hessen, "The Social and Economic Roots of Newton's 'Principia,'" *Science at the Crossroads* (London, 1931), pp. 167–68.
[71] Cf. below, p. 327.

progress as was exemplified by the work of Paré. During the Middle Ages and still more during the hundred years following the Reformation, the French surpassed the English in the visual arts. Painting can serve as an example. In spite of Leonardo's claim that it was a "liberal" and not a "servile" art, painting, as carried on in early modern times, required exceptional manual dexterity and skill in mixing and manipulating materials. Where are the English painters to rival the French before the eighteenth century, before the time of Hogarth and Gainsborough? There are no English equivalents for Fouquet, Clouet, Le Nain, Georges de La Tour, Poussin, Philippe de Champagne, or Claude Lorrain. The miniature portraits of Nicholas Hilliard (1537–1619) are memorable for the famous men who provided the subjects: Sir Francis Drake or Sir Walter Raleigh, for example. As works of art they are insignificant beside the paintings of any one of fifty of Hilliard's great Continental contemporaries.[72] Down well into the sixteenth century in France, art was inseparable from the ancient crafts; during the hundred years that followed, the artist became a species of supercraftsman, often under the patronage of the French court. Surveys preserved in documents of the Châtelet in the Archives Nationales suggest that in many quarters of Paris the proportion, among the gainfully employed, of artist-craftsmen—sculptors, painters, silk-workers, tapestry-makers, etc.—was remarkably large, at least until after the middle of the seventeenth century. The strength of tradition in France, with its emphasis on beauty, combined with the lack of a striking rise in the rate of industrial growth such as occurred in contemporary England, with its emphasis on quantity, to make it more natural for Frenchmen than for Englishmen to excel in craftsmanship. Barber-surgeons were craftsmen. Consequently, it was more natural for the French than for the English to make contributions to surgery which were of scientific importance.

THE STUDY OF THE PHYSICAL WORLD

The contrasts between England and France in the physical sciences seem, at first sight, almost as striking as the contrasts between the two countries in the biological sciences. It is frequently forgotten that the first modern man to found a science on the experimental method was probably William Gilbert of Colchester. As Gilbert was born in 1544, he was a generation older than Harvey. He was also much older than either Galileo or Kepler, and his discoveries, which had an influence on them, preceded their more momentous discoveries.

Gilbert showed that the behavior of the compass, which had come to be used extensively by seamen from Colchester and other ports, is explained

[72] Nef, "Industry and Art in France and England, 1540–1640," *The Thomist*, V (1943), 281–307.

by the fact that the earth is itself a great magnet. Before Gilbert's time it had been supposed that amber alone could be excited by friction to attract other bodies, but Gilbert showed that many commonplace substances, such as glass, sulphur, and resin, had the same properties of attraction. While he found that virtually all bodies could be made electric, he discovered that only bodies containing iron could be made magnetic. Thus he founded the sciences of magnetism and electricity. Before his work no accurate knowledge existed concerning these subjects, and it is perhaps justifiable to follow a recent scientist in calling Gilbert "a prodigy of originality." [73]

Gilbert's manner of obtaining his results has been described by one of his followers, Sir Kenelm Digby, the author, diplomatist, and naval commander, who was born in 1603, the year that Gilbert died. According to Digby, Gilbert's curiosity led him to form "a little load-stone into the shape of the earth. By which means he compassed a wonderful designe, which was, to make the whole globe of the earth maniable; for he found the properties of the whole earth in that little body; which he therefore called a terrella, or little earth; and which he could manage and try his experiences upon at his will." [74] Here was an almost perfect setting for his persistent application of the experimental method.

Gilbert was conscious of the revolutionary nature of his procedure—in putting exclusive faith in the experimental method—and he was confident of its superiority to the procedures hitherto in use for understanding natural phenomena. "We have no hesitation," he wrote in *De magnete,* a Latin treatise published in 1600, "in setting forth in hypotheses that are provable, the things that we have through a long experience discovered." He denounced with assurance and considerable contempt the common practice of depending on written authority for knowledge of natural phenomena, at a time when books were becoming more abundant than ever before and when most writers simply repeated the views found in ancient authorities, particularly those in the surviving works of Aristotle. He asked:

> Why should I, in so vast an ocean of books whereby the minds of the studious are bemuddled and vexed; of books of the more stupid sort whereby the common herd and fellows without a spark of talent are made intoxicated, crazy, puffed up; are led to write numerous books and to profess themselves philosophers, physicians, mathematicians, and astrologers . . . why . . . should I submit this noble and (as comparing many things before unheard of) this new and inadmissible philosophy to the judgment of men who have taken oath to follow the opinions of others, to the most senseless corrupters of the arts, to lettered clowns, grammatists, sophists, spouters, and the wrong-headed rable, to be denounced, torn to tatters and heaped

[73] L. L. Woodruff (ed.), *The Development of the Sciences* (New Haven, 1923), p. 51.
[74] *William Gilbert of Colchester,* trans. P. Fleury Mottelay (New York, 1893), p. xviii.

> with contumely? To you alone, true philosophers . . . who not only in books but in things themselves look for knowledge, have I dedicated these foundations of magnetic science—a new style of philosophizing.[75]

Gilbert advised those who pretend to inform and instruct others to give up dialectics and betake themselves immediately to this "new style of philosophizing," to betake themselves to the experimental method.

On the Continent in Gilbert's time such diatribes as he (and, soon after him, Bacon) directed at the neoscholastic philosophers were hardly possible. Paré, for example, never thought of meeting head-on the attacks made upon him by the faculty of the University of Paris. He was satisfied to pull the dean's leg, by describing what Gourmelen regarded as his objectionable manner of amputating a gentleman's limb without the use of a hot iron: "I dressed him, and God cured him. I sent him to his house, merry, with a wooden leg, and he was content, saying that he had got off cheap, not to have been miserably burned to stop the blood, as you write in your book, *mon petit maistre.*" [76]

The "wrong-headed rable," who attacked the new scientific discoveries, seem to have been at the time less numerous and less articulate in England than in other European countries. If a Frenchman had felt the inclination and found the courage to write against dialectics as vigorously as Gilbert wrote, it is unlikely that he would have been rewarded. He would probably have been attacked in the universities and perhaps even at court, where he might have been welcomed as a physician, but hardly as a physical scientist. Gilbert was treated handsomely. Queen Elizabeth saw to it that he got a pension to provide him with the leisure he needed for his researches.[77] Like the treatises of Harvey, *De magnete* made a strong impression among a wide circle of learned Englishmen. Its influence extended to the mercantile class and the gentry, for many rising merchants and squires were coming to be interested as amateurs in scientific progress, sensing perhaps what Bacon and Descartes recognized so vividly, the implications of such progress for the multiplication of commodities and the prolongation of the human span of life.

The favorable treatment accorded Gilbert by the English crown provides further evidence that the new methods of observation and experiment were becoming congenial to the English scene. Dryden celebrated Gilbert's achievements, along with Bacon's, Harvey's, and Boyle's, as enthusiastically as Cowley celebrated the achievements of Harvey or as Pope was to celebrate the still greater achievements of Newton. Dryden spoke against the tyranny of the ancient Aristotelian philosophy with as much vigor as Macaulay two centuries later:

---

[75] *Ibid.,* pp. xlviii–xlix.
[76] Packard, *op. cit.,* p. 189.
[77] W. C. Dampier–Whetham, *A History of Science* (New York, 1929), p. 137.

The longest tyranny that ever sway'd,
Was that wherein our ancestors betray'd
Their free-born reason to the Stagyrite,
And made his torch their universal light.
So truth, while only one supply'd the state,
Grew scarce, and dear, and yet sophisticate.
Still it was bought, like emp'ric wares, or charmes,
Hard words deal'd up with Aristotle's arms.

.   .   .   .

Among th' asserters of free reason's claim,
Our nation's not the least in worth or fame.

.   .   .   .

Gilbert shall live, till loadstones cease to draw,
Or British fleets the boundless ocean awe. [78]

For Dryden the word "reason," which to Hooker and his predecessors was the instrument for achieving agreement in matters that "are not sensible," has come to be identified with experiences which are subject to sensible verification. The mind has turned full circle in its concept of the nature of firm truth. At the very time when Hooker lived, "reason" in its older sense was beginning to be undermined. The work of Gilbert bore a share of the responsibility.

Such disparagement of the Aristotelian "tyranny" as Dryden's lines express and such enthusiasm for the experimental method would hardly have been possible for a French poet of Dryden's time. It was not until the age of Voltaire, nearly a century after Dryden, that French poets or men of letters began to identify reason as definitely as Dryden had identified it with the new work of the natural scientist, in which proof by tangible demonstration in terms accessible to sensory verification becomes the final arbiter. In the age of Louis XIV "reason" still meant to the French mind much the same as it had meant to the Greek. It was common sense raised to an art. As Pascal explains in one of the most celebrated passages of Les Pensées, an approach to perfection in reason enlists not only the mathematical mind, the esprit de géométrie, which proceeds logically from principles artificially created, but also the esprit de finesse, the nimbly discerning mind, which enables one at "a single bound" to grasp intuitively something of the infinitely complicated and delicate world in which human beings move by virtue of their inner selves, the world of common experience which confronts us all.

Frenchmen were not emphasizing, to quite the same extent as were some Englishmen, the experimental method or any form of inductive reasoning. Nevertheless, the French made valuable direct contributions to knowledge

[78] Dryden, Epistles, II, "To My Honoured Friend Dr. Charleton," in Miscellaneous Works (London, 1767), II, 117–18.

of the physical world during the period from 1560 to 1640. It is interesting to find that these contributions resulted from the same kinds of inquiry which brought French contributions to knowledge of the body. The contrasts between the methods of Harvey and Paré are of much the same kind as the contrasts between the methods of Gilbert and a French contemporary of Paré—Bernard Palissy, who was the greatest French naturalist born between 1500 and 1615. Everybody called him "Maître Bernard." His life, like that of Paré, stretched clear across the sixteenth century. Both men were born between 1510 and 1520, and both died in 1589 or 1590. Most of those who think of Palissy today (and their number outside France is not large) think of him as the rediscoverer of enamel and the father of the French art of pottery. We are filled with delight by the color and charm of his works, as they are displayed for us in Paris in the Musée de Cluny and in provincial museums, notably at Dijon and Agen. There are his graciously proportioned pitchers and his great plates, filled with fantastic scenes in many colors, always conceived in the Italian manner, like most French art of the time. Rather overloaded with animal figures, his pitchers and plates nevertheless leave an impression of much beauty, enhanced by the clear luster of the enamel. They reveal in their author a life full of taste, imagination, and extraordinary vigor.

Conditions for work with matter were changing rapidly in Palissy's time, and circumstances combined with his remarkable energy and long life to carry him into many kinds of labor. He served his apprenticeship as a glazier. As the demand for beautiful painted glass windows died out in France after 1540, he turned to other occupations. When he was about thirty, he was shown an enamel cup which had been made in Italy, and he set himself the task of experimenting with materials in order to find out how this glassy composition could be produced and embodied in pottery. After years of labor he began to get the results for which he remains renowned.[79] He was called on by the royal officials in his native province of Saintonge, north of Bordeaux, to make plans for new salt marshes along the Bay of Biscay at Brouage, Marennes, and Soubise, wanted by the government at the time of the reorganization of the gabelle, which was to increase notably the financial resources of the crown.[80] His skill in making plans of this kind became so great that his help was sought in planning fortresses, at a time when fortress building was still mainly an art.[81] He planned the beautiful gardens of Chenonceaux, one of the finest French

[79] Mrs. Mark Pattison, The Renaissance of Art in France (London, 1879), II, 256–57, and passim.
[80] On the financial importance of the gabelle, see Nef, Industry and Government, pp. 78, 83.
[81] See Nef, Western Civilization since the Renaissance, pp. 51–53, 128, on the art of fortress building.

châteaux, and thus became a predecessor of Le Nôtre, the most renowned of all landscape architects.

Palissy was no more a doctor of philosophy than was Paré. There was nothing in his schooling, as there was in that of learned Frenchmen like Descartes, to keep him from handling matter and acquiring manual dexterity; all his schooling as a craftsman was designed to help him in such tasks. In his extraordinarily resourceful work as a glazier and potter, he obtained an insight into the nature and properties of many mineral and vegetable substances. In his hardly less skilful work in laying out salt marshes, gardens, and fortresses, he obtained much knowledge of the behavior of water. He incorporated this learning in his published writings and probably in the public lectures which he inaugurated in the open air near the Louvre. His treatises show that he obtained an understanding of the behavior of matter novel in many respects. He seems to have worked out the law that water will always seek its own level. He commented upon the force of steam. He attacked some of the chemical theories of the alchemists. In geology he gave an explanation of petrified wood, fossil fuel, and mollusks that proved correct.[82] The cabinet of natural history that he collected was perhaps the first of its kind.

The difference between the scientific work of Palissy and that of Gilbert was fundamental, because it was a difference of aim as well as of emphasis. Palissy's work represents no such break with Renaissance science as does Gilbert's work or Harvey's. Palissy was not concerned, as Gilbert was, with bringing about a change in the basic principles of knowledge as these were taught in the schools and universities. He did not set out, as Harvey did, to devise experiments for the sake of discovering general laws to supplant the generalizations of medieval and classical authorities. The scientific discoveries of Palissy, like those of Leonardo, were a by-product of his career as an artistic craftsman. What he said that has scientific value was not said with the precision which, in modern times, has come to be associated with scientific results.

Although Palissy was much less revolutionary as a scientist than Gilbert, the scientific implications of his work provoked a storm among learned Frenchmen. During the religious wars Palissy's open-air lectures in Paris drew a distinguished audience. Paré came, and with him other surgeons and a sprinkling of doctors and apothecaries. There were also some representatives of the gentry and of the reformed church, to which Palissy belonged, like many of the innovators in modern science. Unlike the merchants, the men of letters, and the rising squires in England, who applauded the discoveries of Gilbert and Harvey, the band who listened to Palissy was not

---

[82] Woodruff, *op. cit.*, p. 198. Palissy has even been called the founder of the science of geology (Allbutt, *The Historical Relations of Medicine and Surgery*, p. 64).

in a position to influence learning in the face of the tough prejudices that prevailed in France against the notion that the schools of liberal arts could learn from craftsmen anything that would be of value to knowledge. Palissy spoke outside the university because its portals were closed to him, untrained as he was in the liberal arts. Although the comment of Michelet on these lectures is not sufficiently laudatory to suit Palissy's biographers, it is close to the truth. Michelet writes of this "good potter" who "teaches with so little emphasis, so humbly, in so low a voice, that he is scarcely heard." Beside the self-confidence of Harvey and the strident assertiveness of Gilbert, the tone of Palissy's writings is almost one of self-abnegation. Palissy begged his readers to examine his work "without regard to the weak, abject condition of the author, and the rustic, unadorned character of his language." The knowledge he expounded did not involve any attempt to bring the material world within the focus of the experimental mentality. Palissy was not a theorist and systematizer. The advances he made in knowledge were arrived at, as if by accident. He obtained novel results because his work as an artist-craftsman brought him novel experiences.

Palissy's work, like that of Paré, was pleasing to the royal family. It contributed to their delight, as Paré's contributed to their physical well-being. He helped to lay out gardens for Catherine de Medici. But Palissy was less essential to the health of sovereigns and other princes than Paré, and he seems to have been less wary about concealing his religion. What most learned and powerful Frenchmen of the age heard or read of his scientific views was not to their taste, because some of his views ran counter to the teaching of the schools. He was eventually arrested and imprisoned in the Bastille. In spite of his advanced age, Palissy was apparently kept a prisoner until he died of want and ill-treatment.

It will have been noted that Dryden, in his poem, applauded Gilbert for having broken away from the tyranny of Aristotelian thought. But, in France, one learned Protestant was ordered to be cut in pieces in the massacre of St. Bartholomew because he had spoken ill of Aristotle. After 1589, with the end of the worst phases of the religious wars, violence diminished in France, but the attitude of the Sorbonne and even of the courts of justice toward natural science changed slowly. The older ways of looking at the material universe persisted not only in the sixteenth century but during much of the seventeenth. The past of western Europe (including the Renaissance) was prolonged into modern times more in France than in England.

Was this prolongation of the past an insuperable barrier, as long as it persisted, to new scientific methods and discoveries, such as were exemplified by the work of Gilbert and Harvey? The contrasts which the French scene presented to the English in the late sixteenth and early seventeenth centuries were characteristic of that in most Continental European states.

Yet anyone acquainted with the history of science will realize that the methods and discoveries which are properly associated with the beginnings of modern science were no monopoly of Great Britain or of the group of countries in the north of Europe which moved in new industrial directions after about 1580 and which included the United Provinces, Sweden, and perhaps Denmark, as well as England and Scotland.

The re-foundation of man's knowledge of the physical world before the advent of Newton has been represented correctly as the achievement, above all, of two great scientists, neither of whom belonged to the industrially progressive countries: the German Kepler, who spent some of his most productive years at the imperial court in Vienna, and the Italian Galileo, whose adventures in an atmosphere hostile to his researches provide one of the most widely commented upon chapters in scientific history. The sympathetic reception that England accorded "the new philosophy" was evidently not indispensable for those revolutionary intellectual innovations which, as Donne wrote in one of his most famous poems, "called all in doubt."

It was in the time of Donne, between about 1580 and 1630, that the new views of the architecture of the physical universe actually replaced the Ptolemaic and Aristotelian views. Unlike the concepts of Copernicus, who made few fresh observations and who based his factual knowledge mainly upon old observed data hitherto differently interpreted, Kepler's laws of planetary motion were based on new observations obtained with the help of better instruments. The data were gathered chiefly from 1573 to 1595, above all by the Danish astronomer Tycho Brahe (1546–1601), who was an almost exact contemporary of Gilbert. Like Gilbert, but unlike Palissy and De Caus, Brahe secured government support for his researches. He was lavishly subsidized by King Frederick II of Denmark, who provided him with an island in the Danish Sound for his observatory, together with a handsome income to meet all his scientific and personal needs. The fame of Brahe's observations rapidly spread, and the Scottish king, who later reigned as James I in England and who was always anxious to appear as a prince remarkable for his learning, paid a visit to the observatory in 1590. It was only after Frederick's death, when the major work had been done, that Brahe, faced by the withdrawal of Danish royal support, left for Bohemia and was installed by the Emperor Rudolph II in a castle near Prague, where the young Kepler joined him in 1600, on the eve of Brahe's death.

Gilbert's role in the foundation of astrophysics has received much less attention than Brahe's, perhaps less attention than it merits. Gilbert's experiments with magnetism led him to conclude that gravity is a form of magnetic attraction and that the movements of the planets, which Copernicus had described, could be accounted for on the principles of the magnet, of which Gilbert had made himself the master. This view became the basis for a doctrine of almost universal gravitation and an integral part of the system of the heavenly bodies, as that system was expounded by Kepler.[83]

It appears, therefore, that the voluminous data on which Kepler founded his laws were gathered partly by observers and experimenters from those countries where conditions seem to have been most favorable to the establishment of the experimental method as the arbiter in scientific knowledge. On the basis of tangible evidence, Kepler sacrificed the Copernican view that the motion of the planets is in perfect curves, becoming to the Christian mind of medieval times, to an orderly universe designed by the Heavenly Father. Kepler substituted the view of a general movement of the planets along an elliptical orbit.[84] His greatest innovation consisted, not in assembling new data, but in the mathematical treatment of data. As Professor E. A. Burtt wrote some years ago, "The exactness or rigour with which the causal harmony must be verified in phenomena is the new and important feature in Kepler." [85] It was a combination of systematic observations and experiments with the concepts of measurement and periodicity, encouraged by the progress of mathematical theory, that made Kepler the founder of modern astronomy.

At much the same time Galileo was working out, in Italy, the laws of gravity and inertia and was laying the foundations of mechanics. Galileo has been frequently called "the real father of the experimental method in physics." But Professor Butterfield has drawn our attention to the fact that, "in one of the dialogues of Galileo, it is Simplicius, the spokesman of the Aristotelians—the butt of the whole piece, who defends the experimental method of Aristotle against what is described as the mathematical method of Galileo." [86] Whether or not, as Professor Alexandre Koyré has recently suggested, Galileo made a determined attempt to apply the principles of mathematical philosophy to physics,[87] it seems to be agreed that it was by submitting to mathematical treatment the tangible observations he made in his experiments that he reached his epoch-making conclusions. It was Galileo's use of mathematics, even more than his observations and experiments, that made him the founder of modern physics.

The work of Kepler and Galileo brings out the two-sided nature of the "scientific revolution." Without the rigor and exactness in connection with observations, without the quantitative concepts encouraged by the development of mathematical thought, especially the application of algebraic meth-

---

[83] Butterfield, *Origins of Modern Science*, p. 56.

[84] *Ibid.*, pp. 53 ff.

[85] *The Metaphysical Foundations of Modern Physical Science* (London, 1925), p. 53.

[86] Butterfield, *op. cit.*, p. 68.

[87] "Galileo and Plato," *Journal of the History of Ideas*, IV, No. 4 (1943), 17 and *passim*. Exception has been taken to this argument of Koyré's (Hiram Haydn, *The Counter-Renaissance* [New York, 1950], p. 249, n. 319).

ods to geometry, the mathematical approach so necessary to modern astrophysics, astronomy, and physics would hardly have been possible.[88] This mathematical approach was essential to establish the ascendancy and prestige of experiment, of materially verifiable results. By means of the mathematical ideas of recurrence, of precise repetition, of geometrical similitude, it became possible to apply simple materially demonstrable propositions to the entire physical universe and to inflate man's knowledge of the very small until it seemed almost to explain the infinite.

THE STUDY OF MATHEMATICS

Revolutionary advances in mathematical knowledge were hardly less essential, then, to the scientific revolution than were the revolutionary advances in the biological and the physical sciences which have already engaged our attention. But the revolution in the mathematical sciences which took place in the early seventeenth century depended mainly on different procedures. Little equipment was required beyond the brain of man and the materials for sketching and writing. It was not necessary to dissect animals and insects, to form a loadstone into the shape of the earth, or to drop objects from a height (as Galileo did). The processes of reasoning depended very little upon the exact observation of phenomena of the external world, for the essential problems were formulated artificially in the mind, with the help of a knowledge of what earlier mathematicians had done.

Before the usefulness in technology of the new theoretical mathematics of the seventeenth century began to be seriously exploited (which is to say before the mid-eighteenth century), these mathematical speculations were in a class of activities which is widely treated today (partly through the influence of "economic science"), as "futile," as unproductive. Yet in the traditional thought of Europe—derived from the Greeks, from Plato and his followers and also from Archimedes—the very "futility" of the creative work of the mind gave it a special dignity and lifted it above the work of the craftsman, even above the work of those artists whose callings obliged them to labor with matter. Plutarch wrote that for Plato it was "utterly corrupt" to make "Geometry . . . discende from things not comprehensible, and without body, unto things sencible and materiall, and to bring it to a palpable substance, where the vile and base handie work of man is to be employed." [89]

Among our medieval ancestors there was a recognized and dignified

---

[88] Whitehead, *Science and the Modern World*, pp. 31–33; Nef, *Cultural Foundations*, pp. 29–31.

[89] Plutarch, "The Life of Marcellus," *The Lives of the Noble Grecians and Romans*, trans. Thomas North (Oxford, 1928), III, 75; cf. Nef, "L'Universalité française," *The French Review*, April, 1956.

place for mathematics among the "liberal arts," because the mathematician had no need, any more than the poet, to manipulate matter in order to achieve his results. Mathematics derived its most compelling problems from what were regarded as pure, "uncorrupt" speculations of the mind, until Thomas Hobbes, in the mid-seventeenth century, suggested that the motions of the mind itself might be nothing more than the products of sense-impressions.

Possibly the eight men born between 1500 and 1615 who made the most important contributions to mathematical knowledge were Cardan, Tartaglia, Rhetius, Vietà, Napier, Desargues, Descartes, and Fermat. Among them Napier, the Scot, was the only representative of Great Britain. Four of the other seven were French. Francis Vietà (1540–1603), who started life as a lawyer and became a privy counselor under Henri IV, denoted general quantities in algebra by letters of the alphabet, solved equations of the third and fourth degree, and applied algebraic transformations to trigonometry. Gérard Desargues (1593–1662), an engineer and architect of Lyons, laid the foundations of projective geometry at about the time that Descartes (1596–1650) laid the foundations of analytical geometry. Pierre de Fermat (1601–65), another lawyer and government official, who served in the provincial parlement at Toulouse, expounded many of the laws of numbers and founded the calculus of probabilities. During the early English industrial revolution, France established a leadership in the mathematical sciences that she was far from possessing in the biological or the physical sciences. France contributed more than any other nation to the theoretical progress which made possible later, in the times of Newton and Leibnitz and afterward, a more comprehensive and refined mathematical treatment of natural phenomena than could be achieved when Kepler and Galileo worked.

A historian concerned with the meaning of history is led, not unnaturally, to inquire whether the pursuit of mathematical speculations was particularly congenial to the French mind, especially in the early seventeenth century, and, if that was so, why it should have been so. It is perhaps significant that Pascal (1623–62), whose mathematical genius declared itself at a surprisingly early age and whose short life coincided with the ascendancy in France of a great mathematical school full of fresh ideas, should have said nothing in his celebrated passage on the rational processes about the experimental method or the direct observation of natural phenomena. For him scientific reasoning seems to have been mainly identified with mathematical reasoning, and he spoke of the conclusions reached by such reasoning as "palpable." If we consider closely the sense of this passage of Pascal's, we find that he seems to have thought of mathematics almost entirely as geometry. The late H. F. Stewart, who devoted most of his life to the study of Pascal, published a most carefully considered translation of *Les Pensées*. As a consequence, this work can be read in English for the first time with confidence. It is not accidental that Stewart translated Pascal's famous phrase, *l'esprit de géométrie,* as "the mathematical mind," for this conveys a true impression that for Pascal, as for the Greeks, the realm of mathematics was largely occupied by geometry.

When we consider the character of the revolutionary mathematical discoveries of the French school, which reached its full maturity in Pascal's time, we find that they were based mainly on geometrical concepts and on geometrical reasoning and that in France mathematicians seem at this time to have laid greater stress on geometry than they did in the sixteenth century. For example, Vietà, the oldest of the group of four great French mathematicians of the period, whose work began at least as early as 1580, seems to have been more interested than the others in the algebraic side of mathematics. But his results were obtained primarily by the application of geometry to algebraic problems. In working under the influence of Italian mathematicians, the greatest European mathematicians of the *early* sixteenth century, Vietà seems to have stressed the qualitative sides of the subject, and he advanced on his Italian predecessors mainly by the greater generality of his algebraic speculations. The most important mathematical contributions of both Descartes and Desargues were to geometry; Descartes searched "for geometrical constructions of classical problems" and managed to solve many questions left unanswered by the ancients, particularly by the Greeks. Fermat, perhaps the greatest mathematical genius of the four, is most famous for his anticipation of the differential calculus, which we associate with Isaac Newton. This work of Fermat's represents an application of analytical geometry that was beyond the powers of Descartes. It was Fermat's method of tangents, which he discussed at length in his correspondence with Descartes, that gave Newton his idea for the development of the calculus.[90]

The influence of the Greeks—Apollonius, Diophantus of Alexandria, and especially Archimedes—is apparent in many aspects of the work of this French school. Its members were attracted by geometry and geometrical reasoning in no small measure because of the purity and sublimity of the subject matter and the methods of thought to which the Platonic philosophy gave such great prestige. The attraction for these Frenchmen of unsolved

[90] For the content of this paragraph I am heavily indebted to one of our graduate students at the University of Chicago, Marshall Kaplan. In connection with a course of mine on the interrelations of intellectual and economic history, he undertook a comparison of French and English mathematics from 1540 to 1640 and obtained what seem to me to be interesting results. Much of Kaplan's material was obtained from Julian Coolidge, *History of Geometrical Methods* (Oxford, 1940). I hope to return to this subject in more detail at a later time.

problems left by the Greeks seems to have been at the root of the revolution in mathematics, which was to prove so fruitful for the development of modern science.

As the words we have quoted from Plutarch suggest, the peculiar fascination of geometry lies in the purity of the ideas, their abstract character, their freedom from contamination with all that has body, all that is material substance. No question of personal interest or practical purpose can impede the search for truth. We have seen how much stronger than in England the traditional separation between the liberal (the nonmaterial) and the servile arts remained in France during the hundred years or so from the mid-sixteenth to the mid-seventeenth centuries. This separation gave French science advantages when it came to progress through the intellect alone, as in geometry. The leading French mathematicians were not craftsmen like Paré or Palissy. They were all the sons of men of higher social rank. In the schools and universities they were trained in the principles of knowledge inherited from the Gothic age and from classical antiquity. Their education was that of a small number of Frenchmen who were not brought up in the crafts or on the land but who were admitted to the liberal arts.

The French mathematicians seem to have set about consciously, especially from about 1619 or 1620 (when the classical and mainly geometrical rules of art were also being formulated in French painting, music, poetry, and prose[91]), to take full advantage of the opportunities opened to them by the Greek and the medieval learned traditions, with their veneration for pure speculation. Descartes, the greatest philosopher of the age, became almost a disembodied mind. Together with the other leading French mathematicians, he held the view that, among his French predecessors, mathematics had fallen too much into the hands of craftsmen and had been debased by its association with manual labor and mechanics.

In this connection it is instructive to examine the work of one of these predecessors, an obscure Frenchman named Jacques Besson, professor of mathematics at Orléans in the mid-sixteenth century. Besson was much interested in the practical applications of his subject. He left behind a treatise, which must have aroused considerable interest, for it was reprinted several times. In it are many drawings of machines. These machines are not of the kind which came into more widespread use in England during the seventy years following Besson's death in *ca.* 1569. Besson was not trying to substitute horse power and water power for manual labor, one of the principal objects of technicians in Great Britain.[92] Almost all his machinery was designed to be operated by the hands and feet. In several

[91] Nef, "Art in France and England," *The Thomist,* V (1943), pp. 296, 298–300, 306–307.
[92] Cf. above, chap. iii; Nef, *Rise of the British Coal Industry,* I, 350–79.

cases his designs called for a substitution of manpower for water power or horse power. He depended for his results upon a skilful transmission of muscle, by the multiplication of gears and pulleys and the use of better geometrical principles of balancing.[93]

Descartes and the other extraordinary French mathematicians of his age looked upon work of that kind as beneath their dignity. It was part of Descartes's purpose to lift mathematics out of the slough to which it had descended as a mere craft at the service of mechanics. He reacted against the instruction he had received in his youth from a Jesuit teacher in mathematics at the college of La Flèche, a certain Father François, who talked, as Besson wrote, in terms of applied mathematics about land surveying, topography, hydrography, and hydrology. For Descartes the proper application of mathematics, which captivated him by what he called "the certainty of its demonstrations and the evidence of its reasoning," was not to mechanics but to philosophy.[94] Thus he and his French contemporaries in the science of mathematics were undertaking speculative inquiries which, like the inquiries of the founders of the modern experimental method, served no practical purpose.

The mathematicians built on the learned tradition of the past more directly than did the great innovators who were their contemporaries in the biological and even in the physical sciences. But they worked in a similar spirit, in the sense that they were no less confident than were Gilbert or Harvey of their power to achieve a certainty which they felt that all earlier scientists and philosophers, including the greatest Greeks, had failed to reach. Descartes built up his philosophy by means of mathematical reasoning. He confidently expected that his new method, which he set forth in 1637 in his celebrated *Discours de la méthode,* would enable men for the first time to obtain a clear and distinct view of the nature of the physical universe and even of its metaphysical foundations. The new mathematical relationships, which he and his contemporaries discovered, were no less demonstrable by the appeal to mathematical proof than Harvey's new explanation of the circulation of the blood was demonstrable by the appeal to experimental proof. All trained mathematicians who agreed on their premises were bound to reach identical conclusions. A way seemed to be opening to the intellect, unaided by revelation or even by grace, to reach the truth, a way that the medieval Christian thinkers had neglected. Plato and Archimedes had been on the right track in their insistence upon the priority of mathematical reasoning to the more common-sense reasoning of Aristotle, who had been hitherto the preponderant influence in European

---

[93] Jacques Besson, *Théâtre des instruments mathématiques et méchaniques* (Lyons, 1579), *passim.*

[94] Etienne Gilson, *The Unity of Philosophical Experience* (New York, 1937), pp. 133–34.

philosophy, but they had not gone far enough. Now the fresh mathematical discoveries made it possible to push beyond the conclusions of the wisest Greeks.[95] As Professor Gilson has written, Descartes's purpose was not to revise Aristotle but to replace him.

Apart from the emphasis on rigorous mathematical proof, what distinguished the abstract mind of most of the new mathematicians from the abstract mind of most of the scholastic philosophers of the twelfth and thirteenth centuries was this: The mathematicians treated the abstractions of the mind as both their starting point and their end rather than linking their powers of abstraction to God's grace. In retaining God, as nearly all of them did, they came perilously near to making Him a mathematician whose secrets they could discover, and so they came perilously near to identifying their own powers as mathematicians with ultimate Truth.

It is curious to observe the eventual consequences of the new mathematical knowledge in the realm of technology. The very desire to keep the mind free from materialism (which was characteristic of French learning) contributed no less to the genesis of modern science, by its effects on the study of mathematics, than the same desire hindered the genesis of modern science, by its effects in discouraging the learned man from experimenting. One of the eventual consequences of the scientific revolution was to produce a no less complete revolution in the very mechanical pursuits—in the handling of matter—from which the French mathematicians of the early seventeenth century sought to free the study of mathematics. Machinery has now replaced most manual labor in industry, in transport, and even in agriculture; and, contrary to the tendencies exemplified in the work of Jacques Besson, artificial power of various kinds has now replaced manual force in setting the machinery agoing. All these practical developments lay in the distant future, but the advances in mathematics in France, which were contemporary with the early industrial revolution in England, represented a step toward the technological upheaval that has come in our times. The turn taken by men's minds in the seventeenth century was part of the genesis of industrialism.

Whether the prospect of such developments would have disturbed Descartes is doubtful. There is a celebrated passage in the *Discourse on Method,* where he wrote: "It is possible to acquire knowledge most useful for life . . . [by means of which] we can make ourselves lords and possessors of nature." [96] Such a statement is not in the least Platonic.

There was obviously a conflict between the social aspirations of Descartes, as expressed in this passage, and the abstract and impractical nature of the speculations in the realm of mathematics, which he encouraged and

---

[95] Alexandre Koyré, *Descartes after Three Hundred Years,* "University of Buffalo Studies," 1951, *passim.*

[96] *Discours de la méthode,* ed, Etienne Gilson, Part IV, pp. 62–63.

in which he participated. While the mathematical discoveries of the French school in the early seventeenth century were essential to modern science, in order to use these discoveries for the ends which Descartes foresaw and welcomed, it was necessary in connection with science itself to stress the quantitative sides of mathematical inquiry. Professor Koyré has suggested that Kepler was prevented from formulating, as Newton was later able to formulate, the law of universal gravitation because of the persistence in his mind "of a *qualitative* conception of the universe." [97] The British mathematicians of the late sixteenth and early seventeenth centuries were far from equal to the French in the fundamental realm of mathematical theory, but the British seem to have been more interested than the French in algebra, in numbers, in precise numerical calculations, and in the invention of tangible mathematical instruments which could be employed practically in the scientific and even the economic life of the age.

The contrast between the British and the French outlook on mathematical studies, until the influence of the new mathematics became strong in England especially with Newton (1642–1727), is brought out in a remark that an Englishman, John Wallis (1616–1703), made in 1635. "Mathematics were scarce looked upon as Academic studies," he wrote, "but rather Mechanical." [98] Newton was to carry the new pure mathematics into a great English university, but it would almost appear that in Great Britain, during the first half of the seventeenth century, mathematicians stressed the very sides of mathematical inquiry which their contemporaries in France eschewed as unworthy of the dignity of the science.

There is a danger undoubtedly of making this juxtaposition between the leading mathematicians of the two countries too sharp. Yet there can be little question that, in Great Britain (and perhaps also in Holland) at the juncture of the sixteenth and seventeenth centuries, the leading mathematical minds looked on the study of mathematics from a more practical standpoint than did the French geometers. This was true of Henry Briggs (1561–1630) and of William Oughtred (1575–1660). It was also true of Adrian Vlacq (1600[?]–1667), a Dutchman. These men were all interested in facilitating numerical computations.

The difference in mathematical emphasis stands out in the mathematical work of John Napier (1550–1617), who, with the possible exception of the much less-well-known Thomas Hariot (1560–1621), was the leading mathematician of the period from 1540 to 1640 in Great Britain. Napier had a decidedly practical bent in the direction of modern machinery, which was not equaled by any leading mathematician of the early seventeenth

[97] "La Gravitation universelle de Kepler à Newton," lecture delivered by Koyré at the University of Paris, April 7, 1951, p. 8. (I have forgotten where this lecture was published.)
[98] Martha Ornstein, *The Role of the Scientific Societies in the Seventeenth Century* (Chicago, 1928), p. 241.

century in France. He designed an armored car, or tank, which was apparently in advance of most of the numerous engines of this kind which were conceived during the two centuries following the Hundred Years' War. He also wrote of an extraordinary explosive, of which he had the secret, capable, he claimed, of clearing the earth of life in an area some four miles in circumference.[99] He devised an engine, driven by horse power or water power, for draining coal pits.

A modern authority, W. R. MacDonald, has remarked that "towards the end of the sixteenth century, the further progress of science was greatly impeded by the continually increasing complexity and labor of numerical calculation." [100] He suggests that Napier's discovery of logarithms in the early years of the seventeenth century was made, at least partly, to get around that difficulty. That the discovery of logarithms contributed, at the same time, to quicker practical mathematical calculations is a fact too obvious to require emphasis. Napier's discovery was useful alike to students of the heavenly bodies and to merchants in keeping their accounts. Napier's practical bent in mathematics is brought out also by an invention less stressed by historians than his logarithms, by a device which came to be known as "Napier's bones." This was a group of rods upon which the multiplication table was placed. Of their immediate practical usefulness we have evidence in Napier's own little *Rabdologia,* first published in 1617. In it the rods are described, and Napier tells his readers that the "bones" were already in common use. This book of Napier's was reprinted in Latin in England; it was translated into Italian (1623), Dutch (1626), and German (1623 and 1630); so it is safe to assume that the "bones" were soon known throughout Europe. They retained a place even after Pascal and Leibnitz had introduced new adding and calculating machines later in the seventeenth century.[101]

This difference of emphasis in mathematical inquiry between France and England has persisted. France has generally excelled in "pure" mathematics, England in the "applied" variety. As Western civilization became more utilitarian at the end of the eighteenth century and during the nineteenth, French mathematicians were sometimes drawn into practical paths —as Gaspard Monge and Lazare Carnot were drawn into the trade of destruction at the time of the French Revolution.[102] Yet the distinction between the work of the two countries, which was manifested in the early seventeenth century, was deeply ingrained,[103] as is shown by a comparison of

[99] Nef, *Western Civilization since the Renaissance,* pp. 57–58, 121–24.
[100] W. R. MacDonald, *The Construction of Logarithms* (Edinburgh, 1889), p. xv.
[101] For the information about "Napier's bones," I am indebted to another graduate student in my course, Robert A. Meier.
[102] Nef, *Western Civilization since the Renaissance,* pp. 19–21.
[103] A point called to my attention by my colleague Professor S. Chandrasekhar, for whose help in connection with this essay I am most grateful.

the mathematical work of A. L. Cauchy (1789–1857) in France with that of G. G. Stokes (1819–1903) in England. It is shown also by the stress laid on general culture in the curriculum of the École Polytechnique, the great French school of advanced mathematical study, founded by Monge. General culture can be less easily dispensed with in theoretical than in applied mathematics.

For the triumph of modern industrial civilization, both the geometrical and theoretical and the more practical and mechanical sides of mathematics were indispensable. The forms of mathematical speculation and reasoning in which the French excelled in the early seventeenth century provided fundamental ideas which have been of great use to scientists and even to inventors ever since. For the full exploitation of these fundamental ideas in science, and especially for their relentless practical application in finance, commerce, industry, agriculture, transport (in short, in every side of mechanical technology), there was a need for a greater emphasis on algebra and numerical calculation than was characteristic of the French school in the early seventeenth century. There was a need for the more quantitative approach to mathematics and the unyielding concern with material results and with the multiplication of such results, exemplified by the English school.

Whatever Descartes's scientific mistakes may have been, whatever were the practical limitations of French mathematics in his time, Cartesian modes of thought were of predominant interest in France and throughout much of seventeenth-century Europe. Every cultivated person had to take account of Descartes; it was possible to take issue with him, but it was not possible to be ignorant of his views and methods. In the custody of most seventeenth-century Cartesians, mathematics was non-utilitarian in its objectives. There was no desire to overturn the old hierarchy of workmanship; as we have seen, the great French geometers were anxious to maintain the superiority of pure speculation over work with matter; consequently, they encouraged the ancient separation between the liberal and the servile arts. Among all the learned men who played a leading part in the scientific revolution, the geometers were those who retained the closest relations between science and art—a relation which, as we have seen, was retained also, in a different way, by Paré and Palissy in their capacity of artist-craftsmen.

Desargues, who was an architect and a student of architectural engineering, offers the historian a most direct link between the new school of mathematics and the visual artistic tradition. A modern inquirer into mathematical history has written of Desargues, "he composed more like an artist than a geometer." [104] By suggesting, as he does, that a sharp antithesis has always existed between geometry and art, the writer, Dr. E. T. Bell, betrays

---

[104] E. T. Bell, *The Development of Mathematics* (New York, 1945), p. 158.

a modern outlook which is historically false. In the Platonic tradition, geometry, through its close concern with all matters of form and repetition, had always been an essential part of art, especially in architecture and music, but also in painting and in poetry. A close connection existed between the transition from Romanesque to Gothic architecture and the revival of the geometrical sides of Platonism, especially in the school of Chartres during the twelfth century.[105] Throughout the later Middle Ages, geometry and geometrical ideas seem to have played a fundamental role in architecture. Dürer's interest in geometry is well known. He was responsible for the first printed work on plane curves, published in 1525.

The Cartesian influence—through its emphasis on clarity, purification, and simplification—upon the rational nature of French "classicism" in the seventeenth century is a commonplace. The new elegance exemplified in French mathematics contributed to the orderly, precise, and subtle languages invented in France for painting, music, poetry, and prose. These four tongues of delight were the instruments of all the great artists of the reign of Louis XIV. Without these instruments, which owed a good deal to geometrical concepts, French "classical" art could not have attained its great perfection, nor could it have influenced the entire art of Europe— the baroque and the rococo—as profoundly as it did. There was, therefore, an important sense in which French seventeenth-century mathematics, in its inspiration and its methods of work, was the ally of art. This alliance provides further evidence that the scientific revolution resulted from the renewal of tradition, as well as from new experiences and from a break with earlier methods of reasoning.

Insofar as the new mathematics, in which France played the leading part, served the artist without making him its slave, the progress of mathematical science partly offset the influence inherent in the scientific revolution to narrow the range of intellectual activity to the establishment of palpable conclusions, positively demonstrable. Yet the very certainty which the Cartesians sought, and which has served the natural scientists so well ever since, was founded on a separation of the mind from the body and, indeed, from all experience, that sometimes makes the modern quantitative approach to phenomena almost inhuman and, in itself, hostile to art. Professor Koyré, whose admiration for the Cartesian philosophy is great, has observed justly that "the distinctness of an idea makes it *valid for our mind*. But how can we be certain that the real world conforms itself to the demands of our reason? Could it not happen that the real [is], on the contrary, something obscure and irrational, something which reason cannot penetrate and make clear?" [106]

[105] For this information I am indebted to my colleague, Professor Otto von Simson. See his *The Gothic Cathedral* (New York, 1956).
[106] Koyré, *Descartes after Three Hundred Years*, p. 26.

That very concept of the real as something obscure and inaccessible to statement in precise, palpable terms had predominated in European history before the scientific revolution. The ways of art and the ways of faith, which were not the ways of modern science and which depend on what Pascal called "nimble discernment" (on the power to reach conclusions in the presence of innumerable experiences which cannot be reduced to clearly provable propositions), were ways men had followed for centuries in order to obtain approximate truths. The same dependence had been laid on nimble discernment in rational judgments, in "reason" as this word was understood by Aristotle and his followers and by the scholastic philosophers. The consequence of ignoring this side of the mind, as the more rigid Cartesians were inclined to do, was to narrow the range of human experience of which the mind takes account. Such an emphasis on mathematical rigor as Descartes advocated was, in the long run, a serious danger to the imagination and to all qualitative judgments. That is of concern even to scientific progress, which has always depended to some extent on fundamental ideas that are intuitive, and which in the twentieth century seems to depend less than in the nineteenth on quantities and precise measurements.

Insofar as mathematics, with its emphasis on "clear and distinct ideas," has banished the real world in which we actually live, it has been inclined along with the experimental method to make science one-sided and narrow. Since the sixteenth century, scientific modes of thought have so largely recolored man's outlook on life that men have forgotten the limitations inherent in the modern concept of "reason," as covering only what is positively verifiable.[107] Now only a great poet can reveal the contradiction between the palpable knowledge which governs us and the creatures that we are. "One had to be Newton," wrote Paul Valéry, "to observe that the moon is falling when anyone can see for himself that it is not falling." [108] There is a sense in which the scientific revolution focused the minds of men on an unreal world which is of little concern in their lives, which may have little to do with their nature and destiny. Whitehead has written that the whole system of organizing the pursuit of scientific truth, which dominates modern learning in the universities throughout the world, "is quite unbelievable. This conception of the universe is surely framed in terms of high abstractions, and the paradox only arises because we have mistaken our abstraction for concrete realities." [109]

What has made this unreal world of the modern scientist seem of the utmost concrete importance has been the success of science in supplying those values which were given philosophical emphasis at the time of the early industrial revolution by two philosophers whose fame has endured,

[107] Nef, *A Search for Civilization* (Chicago, 1962), pp. 41–45, 68–79.
[108] Cited by Louis de Broglie, *Savants et découvertes* (Paris, 1951), p. 34.
[109] Whitehead, *Science and the Modern World,* p. 56.

Francis Bacon and Descartes—the success of science in lengthening lives, lightening labor, and multiplying output. Without the scientific revolution, the infant industrialism which was generated in the north of Europe during the same period could hardly have led to the fantastic command men have now achieved over nature. By virtue of their consequences, therefore, the scientific revolution and the early industrial revolution are two aspects of a single story. Both were essential parts of the genesis of modern industrial civilization.

CONCLUSION

If the two revolutions—in scientific procedures and in industrial values —are aspects of a single story, as we suggest, it is not unnatural to assume that one was the cause of the other, or at least that the two were joint products of the same economic conditions. But the comparisons we have made between English and French history warn us against these ready assumptions. The dialectics of history are not so simple or so geometrical. Unlike many of the phenomena of the physical world, historical cause-and-effect relationships, which are the outcome of the thought and activity of living men in societies, are not susceptible to mathematical statement.

It is obvious that the coincidence in time of the early industrial revolution and the scientific revolution was not merely fortuitous. The speed of industrial, commercial, and financial development after about 1580, in the north of Europe, in Holland, and especially in Great Britain, by increasing the need for complicated numerical calculations, perhaps helps to explain why English (and Dutch) mathematicians should have been more concerned with algebra than with geometry, and why they should have stressed the practical mechanical applications of mathematics more than French mathematicians. The novel directions taken by industrial progress in northern Europe seem to have helped also to provide an intellectual atmosphere in England favorable to experiments and observations. In draining mines, driving hammers, moving bulky commodities (coal in particular), and in devising furnaces which would make it feasible to substitute coal for firewood and charcoal as fuel in such industries as glassmaking and steelmaking, inventive problems, unrelated to beauty and concerned almost exclusively with cheapening labor costs, arose in a more urgent form in Great Britain than elsewhere. By the middle of the seventeenth century, the reciprocal advantages to "natural philosophers" (as scientists then were called) and industrial technicians of a knowledge of each other's work were beginning to be recognized. Robert Boyle referred to the reductions in labor which might be obtained through the naturalist's insight into trades. The scientists played the central role, through the newly formed Royal Society, in encouraging and co-ordinating efforts in every occupation throughout the country to acquire curious data which might help to reveal nature's secrets and laws. In 1667 or thereabouts, the members noted with satisfaction: "All places and Comers are now busy and warm about this Work and we find many noble Rareties to be every Day given in [to the Society] not only by the hands of learned and professed Philosophers; but from the Shops of Mechanics; from the voyages of Merchants; from the Ploughs of Husbandmen; from the Sports, the Fishponds, the Parks, the Gardens of Gentlemen." [110]

When, in the sixteenth century, men with scientific interests, like Agricola, Paracelsus, Paré, or Palissy, derived helpful information from the occupations of their times, they got it directly as part of their own professional work in mines, saltworks, or metallurgical establishments, in the treatment of the sick, or in arts and crafts. A clearing-house, such as the Royal Society presented in the 1660's, for data which might have scientific significance, was novel. Through the elaborate correspondence which the members established with foreigners and newly formed foreign societies, and also through the election of foreigners to associate membership, the clearing-house became international in scope. New technical problems, whose solutions were made more urgent as a result of the early industrial revolution which placed a new pressure on available natural resources, had a bearing on the scientific researches of Newton, Boyle, and other members of the Royal Society during the later seventeenth century. The scientists, in their turn, were glad to have their knowledge used for practical purposes,[111] though they were sometimes reticent out of an anxiety lest science should contribute to destruction. Boyle actually sought to steer the work of one practical inventor away from destructive toward productive ingenuity.[112]

The symbiosis between the progress of modern science and of industrial technology which was seen to be possible in Great Britain as early as the 1660's does not seem to have had great practical consequences for nearly a hundred years. Beginning in the mid-eighteenth century, men of learning, like Réaumur, in Continental Europe, as well as in Great Britain, began to apply fresh scientific knowledge to problems of production and destruction. The interrelations between science and technology multiplied during and after the Napoleonic wars. In more recent times, especially since the end of the nineteenth century, the symbiosis between the two has become a reality that can hardly escape anyone. This symbiosis has had and is having an immense effect upon productivity and upon the multiplication of the species, until the nature of material existence has been profoundly altered

---

[110] Thomas Sprat, *History of the Royal Society* (London, 1667), pp. 71–72.
[111] Nef, *Rise of the British Coal Industry,* I, 240–56; Hessen, *Science at the Crossroads,* pp. 157–74.
[112] Nef, *Western Civilization since the Renaissance,* pp. 193–98.

in many parts of the world. In a sense, therefore, the striking changes in direction taken by both science and industry in the late sixteenth and seventeenth centuries laid an essential basis for the atomic age.

It would be an error to push this economic determinism further than the conditions will bear. It has been shown that Newton and Boyle derived their inspiration, their data, and their methods from many sources besides industrial experience. Among these sources, the inspiration provided by the love of truth for its own sake was important.[113] Furthermore, the work of Boyle and Newton began after the period that mainly concerns us in this essay.

It would be rash to assume that practical problems, raised in a more acute form than ever before by the early industrial revolution, were of much importance in bringing about the fundamental changes in scientific procedures during the critical decades when the scientific revolution actually started, between 1570 or 1580 and 1640. The work of Galileo and Kepler was done in parts of Europe which were little affected by that industrial revolution. Gilbert and Harvey were living much closer to it. What consequences had it for their work?

The loadstone, which had been known from time immemorial, is a variety of magnetite, the magnetic oxide of iron, and Gilbert's interest in the subjects of magnetism and electricity may have been increased by the remarkable expansion of the English ironmaking industry in his time. In *De magnete,* he refers frequently to the multiplication of iron mills, and he describes the roundabout process for manufacturing iron.[114] He studied the behavior of all kinds of iron, but what interested him most was the behavior of the ship's compass with its magnetic needle. That had been in use for many generations, and the voyages of discovery, at the time of the Renaissance, had increased its importance.

Harvey's treatise on *The Motion of the Heart and Blood in Animals* contains less evidence of industrial experience than does *De magnete*. It is true that there are at least two references to bellows. There is also a comparison of the two motions of the ventricles and the auricles with that "in a piece of machinery, in which, though one wheel gives motion to another, yet all the wheels seem to move simultaneously; or in that mechanical contrivance which is adapted to firearms." [115] But bellows were an exceedingly ancient device, and no early industrial revolution was required to bring either the machines or the guns, whose mechanical actions Harvey compares to consecutive motions of the blood, to his attention.

The more one considers the direct connections between the scientific and

[113] G. N. Clark, *Science and Social Welfare in the Age of Newton* (Oxford, 1937), pp. 68–91.
[114] *William Gilbert of Colchester,* p. 48.
[115] *Works of William Harvey,* pp. 18, 29, 37–38.

the early industrial revolution, the more they seem to be superficial. Our inquiry in this essay has shown that the use for scientific purposes of data and ideas derived from the arts, crafts, and manufactures was no distinctive feature of the new sciences. Galileo was a great observer; yet what distinguished his scientific work from that of earlier scientists was not the practice of making observations but the way he correlated his observations for purposes of his own intellectual devising. He studied the methods of work employed in building and repairing warships at the famous arsenal in Venice. He observed the loading and firing of guns. He derived material from the work of building craftsmen who were constructing churches, palaces, and fortifications. But his procedures differed from those of artists or craftsmen like Palissy or Paré. His discoveries were not, as theirs were, a by-product of experience with crafts which he followed as a professional. He took his material wherever he could find it—from the movements of a swinging lamp while he was at Mass in the cathedral at Pisa, for example—and, in all he took, he was guided by systematic plans of his own devising for answering fundamental problems of the physical sciences. There is no evidence that the theoretical issues which Gilbert and Harvey set about to solve, in a similar spirit, or their modes of procedure owed anything substantial to the remarkable speeding-up in the rate of industrial growth which occurred in their times in England. All these men were examining bodies and conditions of the universe which had been there from time immemorial, and their methods owed little or nothing to practical inventors like De Caus and Worcester, who tried to make a steam engine, or like Platt and Rovenzon, who tried to purge coal of its noxious properties and make it more suitable as fuel.

The coming of modern science and the coming of industrialism had a momentous characteristic in common: Both represented a disposition on the part of man to face the problems of existence—which are spiritual and intellectual as well as material—in a new way, in which the emphasis in human happiness is upon quantity and mathematical precision more than upon quality and transcendence. Yet, at the same time, in making the break in new directions, the scientific genius of the late sixteenth and early seventeenth centuries turned from all practical industrial experience, whether it was the experience of the ancient arts and crafts, that had furnished scientists of the Middle Ages and the Renaissance with material and ideas, or the experience of the growing heavy industries, that began to flourish in the north of Europe. The "new philosophy," as modern science was called in seventeenth-century England, created a world of its own. The outstanding characteristic of this world was its independence of practical experience, new as well as old, for its basic intellectual decisions. At the period when a decisive change occurred in rational procedures, the mind itself, and not the economic institutions of sixteenth- and seventeenth-century Europe, called the new tunes and encouraged most of the variations that the greatest scientists were playing on them.

According to an old, often repeated saying, necessity is the mother of invention. The validity of the saying depends largely upon the kind of invention to which it is applied. If we are concerned with the invention of the artist or if we are concerned, as in this essay, with the fundamental invention of the scientist which has been behind almost every important step forward in scientific knowledge and which has provided the basis for the most sensational practical inventions of recent times, the saying is mainly false. We are nearer truth when we say that complete independence, complete intellectual disinterestedness, which is close to what the practical modern citizen regards as laziness, is the mother of invention. Freedom, rather than necessity, was the power behind the scientific revolution. The only slavery was the slavery of the new scientists to a search for fresh truth concerning matter, space, and time.

It is true, of course, that laziness of every kind, including the laziness conducive to constructive freedom, is impossible without leisure and that leisure is dependent on at least a minimum of wealth. It is also true that the rapid growth of wealth made for more leisure in Great Britain, Holland, Denmark, and Sweden toward the end of the sixteenth century and during the early seventeenth. In Great Britain especially, this growth of wealth resulted mainly from the early industrial revolution and the conditions which produced it, among them a large measure of peace in a warring world.[116] By its contribution to wealth, the speeding-up in the rate of industrial growth played an indirect part in the scientific revolution. How important was the part?

It was in Denmark that Brahe received the financial support necessary to build and equip his observatory. The remarkable progress in Great Britain and northern Europe generally of new industries outside the older crafts apparently facilitated the manufacture of scientific instruments, which were new and costly, such as the microscope and the telescope. These instruments were of help in the great discoveries which revolutionized the biological and the physical sciences. Both were introduced before 1600. The first telescope was made either in Holland or in England; the first microscope in Holland. At the juncture of the sixteenth and seventeenth centuries, these and other scientific instruments were more readily obtainable in England and Holland than in other countries.

What was fundamental to their discovery and subsequent manufacture, however, was a novel desire to use them. That, in turn, depended upon a fresh interest in the actual structure and content of matter and space and upon a desire to undertake quantitative observations and experiments

[116] Nef, *Western Civilization since the Renaissance*, p. 88.

which were of no immediate use. Neither the microscope nor the telescope was of much help in a coal mine, in the conversion of coal to coke, or in constructing the closed pots which made it possible to adopt coal as fuel in the manufacture of glass and steel. The revolutionary scientific discoveries of Gilbert, Harvey, Galileo, and Kepler were of little immediate practical use, and the contribution of the new science to the rapid growth of production in the north of Europe was small.

By its effect in reducing costs of production, industrial progress in northern Europe and, above all, in Great Britain tended to reduce the proportion of the time of men and women that had to be devoted to getting the bare necessities of life,[117] in a period when, in the Protestant countries of the north, the reduction of holidays left the workmen with more time to give to economically productive pursuits.[118] Economic development in Great Britain was providing little opportunity for the kinds of constructive craftsmanship and art which were at the disposal of the French and other Continental peoples in the small workshops of artisans and in the studios of artists, some of which were subsidized by the French crown. The human energy released by economic progress and by changes in religious worship in England was likely to be put, therefore, to novel purposes. What these purposes should be depended on the predilections of individuals, on the leadership provided by writers, by the government, and by rich men. Human energy might have been drawn mainly into idle and vapid trifling, as in the twentieth century with the spread of motion pictures, picture papers, radio advertising, and television. Or it might have been drawn exclusively into magical fancy of the sort exemplified by the alchemists.

Progress was insufficient to make it possible to fill people's time with such mechanized entertainment as scientific discovery has provided in the twentieth century, while the fancy of the writer in an age of literary genius was not encouraging the Elizabethan in the study of the occult. In fact, the whole band of alchemists, with their costly drugs and equipment, was becoming a subject of ridicule. During the years when Harvey was busy with vivisection and with his estimates of the precise quantity of blood flowing from the heart, Ben Jonson's *Alchemist* (with its lampoons at the expense of the magic formulas of the pseudo-scientist) delighted London audiences even more than Shakespeare's comedies.

As time went on, a growing conflict between the English crown and the wealthy merchants of the kingdom developed over political and economic policies.[119] But when it came to the use of the leisure time of Englishmen and Scots, the influences of the court and of wealthy individuals were often

---

[117] Cf. above, chaps. iii, vi.

[118] Cf. above, chap. v.

[119] Nef, *Rise of the British Coal Industry*, II, 267 ff., and *passim;* Nef, *Industry and Government*, pp. 35 ff., 149 ff., and *passim.*

thrown in the same direction, toward encouraging independent speculative work.

On the Continent, except perhaps in Holland and Denmark, there was no country where the learned man who wanted to try new methods of scholarship and research, without any practical purpose, could count as much as in England on sympathetic recognition and authoritative support. For several generations the universities and the ecclesiastical foundations, including the churches set up by the Reformers, had been generally hostile to revolutionary intellectual innovations. Queen Elizabeth's patronage of Gilbert was a symptom of a new attitude among the mighty toward the experimenter and his efforts. Isaac Casaubon (1559–1614), the French classical scholar, could not find satisfactory conditions for his work either at Geneva or at Paris, and in 1610 he finally sought asylum at the English court and became a naturalized Englishman. Casaubon's biographer, Mark Pattison, tells us that the court of James I, for all the king's pedantry, was the only court in Europe where the learned professions were in any degree appreciated.[120] It is significant that Kepler, who must have known of James I's visit to the observatory of Brahe in Denmark in 1590, should have thought enough of the king's scientific interests to dedicate to him *De harmonice mundi,* a work published at Augsburg in 1619, in which the great scientist announced his third law of motion. During James I's reign, with Francis Bacon in office as solicitor-general and later as attorney-general, the outlook on experimental inquiry by learned men was more liberal in England than in other parts of Europe. So the English court provided new experimental work with official approval such as could be obtained almost nowhere else.

Nor was this approach to scientific innovations limited to a favored few surrounding the king. On the eve of the Civil War, England was becoming a country full of amateur "inventors," a title given both to searchers after natural information to satisfy idle curiosity without immediate purpose and to projectors seeking to construct new kinds of clocks or new machines for draining mines. In her delightful essay, "Rambling round Evelyn," the late Virginia Woolf gives us a view of the passionate enthusiasm with which these men sought natural knowledge by amateur vivisection and close inspection of tangible objects, alive and dead. Mrs. Woolf writes of Evelyn:

> No one can read the story of Evelyn's foreign travels without envying in the first place his simplicity of mind, in the second his activity. To take a simple example of the difference between us—that butterfly will sit motionless on the dahlia while the gardener trundles his barrow past it, but let him flick the wings with the shadow of a rake, and off it flies, up it goes, instantly on the alert. So, we may reflect, a butterfly sees but does not hear; and here no doubt we are much on a par with Evelyn. But as for going into the house

---

[120] *Isaac Casaubon* (2d ed.; Oxford, 1892), pp. 263–64.

to fetch a knife and with that knife dissecting a Red Admiral's head, as Evelyn would have done, no sane person in the twentieth century would entertain such a project for a second.[121]

How much this naive curiosity, widely diffused, must have encouraged the more learned and systematic inquiries of a Harvey! The circumstances which produced this curiosity, the conditions which determined that a considerable part of the new-found leisure of the English should be spent in idle reflections and pursuits which were encouraging to the new scientific outlook and research—these circumstances are elusive. For the historian the final explanation of the conditions lies not only beyond John Evelyn's knife but beyond the methods which are a part of modern science. Doubtless the rapid growth of production contributed to the amount of leisure available in England for such pursuits. But what was behind the speeding-up of output?

I have discussed some of the circumstances which made for it, in various books of mine.[122] The period from 1540 to 1640 and especially a period which began about 1580 seems to occupy a special place in the genesis both of industrialism and of modern science. It is natural therefore to ask how far the birth of one accounts for that of the other, and to what extent both are explained by a breaking away from the traditions surrounding workmanship and scientific inquiry in medieval and Renaissance Europe.

It would be easy to exaggerate the connections between industrial history and the history of scientific thought during the decades immediately following 1580. The "scientific revolution" does not explain the "early industrial revolution," nor does the "early industrial revolution" explain the "scientific revolution," although each touched the other at many points and although eventually in recent times a union between scientific and industrial progress, through technology, has been a basic force in the triumph of industrialism.

What about the relations to earlier history of modern industry and modern science, as these emerged in the late sixteenth and early seventeenth centuries? We should hardly be justified in regarding European traditions only as barriers to the new directions taken by industry and science, directions which were to have in the long run such momentous consequences not only for Europe and North America but for the whole world. A break away from the past *was* an important element in the progress of private industrial enterprise and in the new emphasis on production for quantity in the north of Europe during the age of Elizabeth I and the early Stuarts. But it needs to be recognized that many discoveries and inventions essen-

---

[121] *The Common Reader* (New York, 1925), pp. 114–15.
[122] See *Rise of the British Coal Industry*, esp. II, 319–30; *La Naissance de la civilisation industrielle et le monde contemporain*, Part II and chap. x; cf. above, chap. v.

tial to that industrial progress—such as great wheels driven by horse power and water power to drain mines and to drive bellows at blast furnaces—were products of earlier European experience during the Middle Ages and the Renaissance.[123]

If the early industrial revolution cannot be understood apart from earlier European experience, the scientific revolution is altogether inexplicable without it. The most startling progress of the physical and the mathematical sciences in the sixteenth and early seventeenth centuries occurred in parts of Europe which did not participate directly in the speeding-up of industrial growth which occurred in Great Britain and other countries of northern Europe. While a fundamental break in emphasis from previous experience did mark the genesis of modern science, it needs also to be recognized that the scientific genius of Galileo, Kepler, Desargues, Fermat, and Descartes, even the scientific genius of Harvey and Gilbert, derived inspiration and sustenance from the traditions of earlier science, philosophy, and religion.

If the mind was to create, as it actually created, a way of looking at the world unique in its emphasis, abstract but antirationalist in that it eventually denied all rationality to the intellect unless the conclusions could pass the test of palpable experience, the mind had to possess immense confidence in its own powers. Men had to believe that their minds gave them the capacity to reach judgments that were valid for all creation. This confidence was derived from generations of habit in exact abstract thought, which go back at least to Aristotle. It was derived from the belief in the dignity and reality of pure ideas, independent of palpable experience, which goes back especially to Plato. It was derived from the powers of observation demonstrated in visual form by the great art of Europe and of classical antiquity, which continued to play an important role in the scientific advances of the sixteenth and seventeenth centuries, as the discoveries of artist-craftsmen, such as Palissy and Paré, show in the realm of the skilled manipulation of materials, and as the discoveries of geometers, like Descartes, Desargues, and Fermat, show in the realm of forms and space relationships. The new confidence in the mind was derived perhaps most of all from the Christian faith, as expounded especially by Augustine, Aquinas, and other great scholastic philosophers (and presented in the Judeo-Christian Scriptures) that God is supremely *rational,* that not only is He the Truth, but that man, by virtue of being made in His image, has the intellectual power to participate dimly in the Truth.[124] It was out of their confidence that man's origin provided him with an instrument independent of all temporal circumstances, an instrument capable of revealing secrets hitherto known only to God, that the great scientists of the early seventeenth century turned to the experimental method, to mathematics, and to

---

[123] See above, chap. i.
[124] Cf. the argument in Whitehead, *Science and the Modern World.*

the mathematical treatment of observed phenomena. It was not any dependence of the mind upon industrial experiences but a striking independence which was responsible for the genesis of modern science.

In more recent times, beginning with the late eighteenth century, the spread of the "new philosophy" has tended to weaken each of the traditional ingredients out of which it had emerged. The scientific outlook has now so completely "recoloured our mentality" that it threatens to undermine the philosophy and the faith[125] without which there would have been no scientific revolution.

The emphasis that was new during the late sixteenth and seventeenth centuries on quantity as an economic end had eventually an important influence in bringing the modern world into being. As new economic values, which emerged in the north of Europe during the late sixteenth and seventeenth centuries, came into ascendancy after the mid-eighteenth century and especially during the nineteenth and twentieth centuries, science was provided with an unparalleled opportunity to achieve practical results. The modern scientific mind, which had also originated during the late sixteenth and early seventeenth centuries in a sense of intellectual freedom from all material circumstances, lost some of the liberty associated with its birth.

With the phenomenal material progress made during the last century and a half, it has become usual to attribute all the blessings which this progress has brought, to the scientific and economic values whose ascendancy among an important minority of learned men can be traced to the age of Bacon and Descartes. There is a sense in which it is true that these values are responsible for the condition of the world today. But our inquiry shows that the new scientific speculations themselves would hardly have been possible without the prior existence of a rich world of the mind and spirit which emphasized other intellectual values that learning today too often has come to treat as obsolete.

The part of these older values in bringing into being the modern world, with its unique facilities for production and destruction, has not been confined to their role in forming the scientific mind. One thing that helped to make possible the early industrial revolution was the increasingly peaceful conditions which came to prevail during the late sixteenth and early seventeenth centuries in the north of Europe and especially in Great Britain. Rapid industrial progress everywhere depended upon limitations on war and violence, while limitations on war and violence depended, in their turn, upon a novel attempt to realize in actual living the traditional values of tenderness and love as well as justice, an attempt which the modern world seems disposed to forsake.[126] These values imposed a brake upon the rapid progress of industrialism and the application of modern science to useful

[125] Cf. Nef, *A Search for Civilization*, chap. iv.
[126] The relation of limited warfare to the triumph of industrialism is a leading theme of Nef, *Western Civilization since the Renaissance*.

objectives. But they also provided conditions necessary to the progress of both modern science and industrialism.[127] Without restraints on the economic growth which Europeans and Americans since the eighteenth century have come to identify with progress, this very progress which the world now worships would have been hardly possible.

During the last fifty years the researches of great scientists (such as Sherrington, Whitehead, Whittaker, Rutherford, and Einstein) have revealed the limitations inherent in the peculiar scientific view of the physical universe and of man, whose origins have concerned us in this essay. These researches suggest that the future of civilization may depend upon new efforts to realize the very values and procedures that modern science and industrialism have pushed into the background. Does not the history of Europe during the late sixteenth and early seventeenth centuries add to the testimony that recent scientific research itself is bringing forward on behalf of a wider, more comprehensive view of man and the universe? The new emphasis in science and industry which began in that period provided material conditions for a great increase in human happiness. But happiness itself depends on hopes and on services that the new emphasis, in triumphing, has obscured.

[127] Cf. Nef, *Cultural Foundations of Industrial Civilization.*

8

English and French Industrial History
after 1540 in Relation to the Constitution
of the United States

Our ancestors found this country rich in the mineral wealth necessary for the progress of industry. They found it peopled with Indians. As the Indians could not tell them how to exploit this wealth, they naturally turned back on occasion to the experience of the old Europe whence they had come.

One of many objectives of the founding fathers in preparing and recommending the adoption of the Constitution was to provide favorable conditions for the development of industry. This was partly a matter of self-interest. As Dr. Beard showed in 1913, a few of the leading delegates to the Convention were part-owners of textile mills and shipbuilding companies, while a much larger number, engaged as they were in trade and in the lending of money, stood to profit from an increase in the output of mines and factories.[1] The concern of the delegates over the future of American industry, in its infancy at the time of the Convention, reflected concern for the future strength of the nation. For generations in Europe statesmen had regarded it as one of their duties to foster the birth of new industries and the expansion of old. The diversity of the private interests which influenced government policies and the conflict between different objectives which always confronted statesmen had prevented any statesman from devoting himself single-mindedly to encouraging industrial *growth;* there had been great differences of opinion concerning the policies most likely to stimulate it; there had even been writers who thought their countries would be better off without too much of it. But before the end of the eighteenth century there was pretty complete agreement, in America as well as in Europe, that industrial *productivity,* when not obtained

From Conyers Read (ed.), *The Constitution Reconsidered* (New York, 1938), pp. 79–103.
[1] C. A. Beard, *An Economic Interpretation of the Constitution* (New York, 1913), esp. pp. 40–42, and chaps. ii and v generally.

artificially at the expense of the more basic occupation of agriculture, was bound to strengthen the state and to increase the welfare of its people.[2] As early as 1774, Alexander Hamilton had written: "If . . . manufactures should once . . . take root among us, they will pave the way still more to the future grandeur and glory of America."[3] Americans in 1787 expected industry to develop rapidly, now that the artificial restrictions imposed by the British government on manufactures in the colonies were no longer in force. "The time is not distant," Gouverneur Morris remarked at one of the meetings of the Federal Convention, "when this country will abound with mechanics and manufacturers . . ."[4]

In England and France, the two greatest powers of the eighteenth century, various policies designed to stimulate the growth of industry had been tried out. From English and French experience since the Reformation lessons could be drawn concerning the policies most likely to permit and foster such growth. What could the industrial history of these two nations have taught the more learned delegates who assembled in Philadelphia in 1787?[5] What could it have taught James Madison, James Wilson, and Alexander Hamilton, fresh from their study of history, law, and political economy? Madison and Wilson were among the few men chiefly responsible for the form the Constitution finally took, and Hamilton did as much as any man to bring about its ratification by the states. Were the opinions which they might have formed from their knowledge of history[6] likely to coincide with the private interests of wealthy textile manufacturers and financiers, like Robert Morris of Pennsylvania or Jacob Broom of Delaware, and of merchants, like Thomas Fitzsimons of Pennsylvania or John Langdon of New Hampshire?

The merchants, the financiers, and the manufacturers, as well as the

[2] Let me make clear again that no serious statesman seems to have been against industrial *progress*, but there had been differences over whether progress consisted mainly in better *quality*, or whether *growth in quantity* was the proper *end* of policy. Cf. the remarks by Alexander Hamilton in his *Report on Manufacturers*, written in 1790 (A. H. Cole (ed.), *Industrial and Commercial Correspondence of Alexander Hamilton* [Chicago, 1928], pp. 247 ff.). Even the French Physiocrats looked on industrial growth as desirable, provided it did not interfere with agriculture (cf. C. Gide and C. Rist, *Histoire des doctrines économiques* [4th ed.; Paris, 1922], pp. 14–15). While Benjamin Franklin believed it was possible for a country to become "fond of manufactures beyond their real value," he felt that the United States would probably grow richer if they discouraged the importation of manufactured goods and thus fostered native industries (A. H. Smyth, *The Writings of Benjamin Franklin* [New York, 1905], I, 149; X, 122).

[3] John C. Hamilton (ed.), *The Works of Alexander Hamilton* (New York, 1851), II, 12.

[4] Max Farrand, *Records of the Federal Convention* (New Haven, 1911), II, 202.

[5] See Nef, *Industry and Government in France and England* (Ithaca, N. Y., 1957), for an attempt to answer the question insofar as French and English history from 1540 to 1640 is concerned.

[6] Cf. A. C. McLaughlin, *A Constitutional History of the United States* (New York, 1935), pp. 149–51.

scholars, may have known that England's industrial leadership over the Continent in the use of labor-saving machinery, and in the per capita output of coal, metal wares, woolen cloth, and most manufactured goods, was no new thing. It was probably not until the 1830's or 1840's that many historians and businessmen began to think England's supremacy had been produced by an "industrial revolution," which started after the accession of George III, in 1760.[7] As a matter of fact, this "revolution," which really got going about 1785[8] at the time of the American constitutional debates, only increased a lead in mining and heavy manufacturing that England had secured as the result of an earlier industrial growth, which became rapid at the end of the reign of Henry VIII, after 1540, which was most remarkable in the reigns of Elizabeth I and James I, from about 1580 to 1620, and which continued, though perhaps at a somewhat slower rate, after the Civil War and Interregnum (1642–60). The chief Continental countries participated in this "early industrial revolution" much less than in the later one. In France, which became the mightiest political power on the Continent, the progress of mining between about 1540 and 1730 and of almost all manufactures, except the artistic and luxury trades, was much less impressive than in England. In the reign of Henry VIII England had been industrially a backwater compared with nearly every Continental country. By the Peace of Utrecht, in 1713, if not seventy-five years earlier, on the eve of the Civil War, she had become the foremost nation in Europe in mining and heavy manufacturing, that is to say in production mainly for the sake of quantity.[9]

How had she done it? This was a question that eighteenth-century mechanics, tradesmen, and financiers, economists, scientists, and even men of letters were asking themselves with increasing interest and increasing frequency. It was a question that Frenchmen were asking more often even than Englishmen, because they stood in greater need of an answer. The question first took on a compelling importance for them after the death of Louis XIV, in 1715, when they began to lay less exclusive emphasis upon the qualities of the age of the great monarch—good form, elegance, and taste in the fine arts and in the art of living, reason and moderation in thought, high standards of moral conduct, combined with a belief in the

[7] This idea did not become a commonplace among scholars until the 1880's, after the publication of Arnold Toynbee the elder's lectures, but it was expressed in an embryonic form long before that time. The use of the word "revolution" in connection with industrial changes goes back at least to the beginning of the nineteenth century in France, and the phrase "industrial revolution" was common in French books of the twenties and thirties (Anna Bezanson, "The Early Use of the Term Industrial Revolution," *Quarterly Journal of Economics,* XXXVI [1922], 343–46). The first case I have found in which the phrase was used to suggest that the development of English industry had been phenomenally rapid as compared with Continental, occurs in the early 1840's.

[8] Nef, *Western Civilization since the Renaissance* (New York, 1963), pp. 290–93.

[9] Cf. above, chaps. iii and iv.

church and in the divine right of kings—and began to concern themselves more with wealth, health, and the discovery of the secrets of the material world.

Echoes from discussions relating to the question were probably heard in America. Benjamin Franklin, who played an influential part in the Convention at his great age of eighty-one, had met ministers, *intendants,* and inspectors of manufactures, all of whom were much concerned in trying to overcome the economic superiority of the English. French merchants who came to America, like John Holker, were hardly less concerned. Holker's father had migrated from Lancashire to introduce English textile machinery into France, and had been made Inspector of Foreign Manufactures. The younger Holker was for six years, from 1778 to 1784, a business partner and associate of Robert Morris, who, as delegate to the Convention from Pennsylvania, played an important part in private negotiations. Holker also had close relations with Thomas Fitzsimons, and with the most influential of all the Pennsylvania delegates, James Wilson, the famous lawyer.[10] Wilson and Morris had been born abroad, and their interest in the question may have been enhanced by the direct knowledge of economic conditions in Great Britain which they had obtained in their early years. Delegates born in America, who had neither traveled abroad nor associated with foreign merchants at home, were not likely to escape the question if they read widely in French and English books. Various aspects of it were often mentioned not only by writers on industrial subjects like Gabrielle Jars, the French mining engineer, and Dean Tucker, who devoted an essay to "the Advantages and Disadvantages which respectively attend France and Great Britain with Regard to Trade," [11] but by great men of letters, like Voltaire, who were helping to mold European thought, and whose correspondence is full of admiring comments about English scientific and mechanical discoveries.

To the question why had English industrial production grown more rapidly than French there are many answers which contain a measure of truth.[12] In the eighteenth century many answers, not all of which contain even a measure of truth, were being given. Those who believed that the form of government and the policies of statesmen had an influence upon industrial progress could find important contrasts between the constitutional history of the two countries to help them in explaining the backwardness of France. Tucker, in an essay which was published in 1750, wrote that

[10] From an unfinished thesis by Marion Rice (now Mrs. Charles Darwin Anderson), "John Holker, French Man of Business in the American Revolution: an Economic Biography."

[11] *A Brief Essay on the Advantages and Disadvantages which Respectively Attend France and Great Britain with Regard to Trade* (London, 1750).

[12] For an attempt to give tentatively some of the answers, see Nef, *La Naissance de la civilisation industrielle et le monde contemporain* (Paris, 1954), chaps. ii–viii and x; cf. above, chaps. v–vii.

"The first Disadvantage . . . is the Government, which is arbitrary and despotick; and therefore such as a Merchant would not chuse to live under, if he knows the Sweets of Liberty in [England] . . . [where he] can go to Law with the Crown, as easily as with a private subject." [13] During the two previous centuries the English people, by a number of stages, had moved away from the absolute monarchy of Henry VII and Henry VIII, when the king had governed without having his prerogative seriously challenged, to the establishment and the strengthening of parliamentary government, and to a position where the crown was impotent in fundamental matters of policy without the support of the House of Commons. Meanwhile in France the monarchy had continued to increase its power, at least from the accession of Henri IV in 1589 to the death of Louis XIV, and the representative assembly, the estates general, had not been summoned to meet since 1614. Tucker's opinion that an authoritarian government had handicapped France in her economic development was held by many Englishmen. It was coming to be shared by many Frenchmen, including some of the greatest men of the age. On what historical facts was it based?

In France the crown had used its authority to interfere increasingly with the freedom of industrial development. Thousands of decrees, edicts, ordonnances, *règlements,* and letters patent re-enacted, elaborated, and extended medieval regulations and established new ones. As the powers of the provincial estates and *parlements* diminished during Louis XIV's long reign, the enactments of the king were made more and more effective. They were prepared, interpreted, and enforced by the central government, with the advice and help of an elaborate hierarchy of local officials appointed by the crown, especially the powerful *intendants* who governed the provinces, the *subdélégués* whom they appointed as their representatives in the *départements,* and the inspectors of manufactures, who were also to some extent subject to their authority.

As a result, at the beginning of the eighteenth century, the central government exercised control in varying degrees over all industrial enterprises, including those of the village craftsman who labored with his family in a humble cottage in parts of the kingdom remote from Paris. More and more master workmen everywhere, in some villages as well as in towns, were brought under the authority of the corporate gilds, whose number was increased by the crown and whose rules were subject in large measure to its approval. These rules generally limited the master to one or two apprentices, and thus hindered the growth of large enterprises. Royal enactments fixed the size and the quality of all kinds of cloth and leather goods, and even of soap and paper. Industrial products had generally to be marked in a specified way, and this caused trouble when the makers were

---

[13] *A Brief Essay on the Advantages and Disadvantages . . . with Regard to Trade* (2nd ed.), pp. 23, 33.

illiterate. If any of the wares did not conform to all the regulations concerning them, the traders and merchants, who had put out the raw materials or partly finished goods to be worked on by craftsmen in their homes or at small water-driven mills along the streams, were not allowed to sell them. This obliged the traders and merchants to refuse to accept and pay for them when they were delivered at the warehouses.

Private persons with capital were seldom at liberty to start a new enterprise employing a dozen or more laborers without the permission of the central government. If a landlord, even in distant provinces, like the Comté de Foix in the shadow of the Pyrenees, wanted to mine within his lordship or to build a large forge for smelting ore, or if he proposed to lease his land for these purposes, he or his lessees had to seek a grant of letters patent, or some other sort of authorization, from the crown. This might be refused if the applicant could not prove, by ancient documents or by the testimony of old inhabitants, that an enterprise of the same kind had existed at the same place in earlier times. It might be refused if the new enterprise conflicted with one of the monopolies of mining in one or more provinces which the crown had been in the habit of granting for a term of years to rich noblemen and other persons, who sometimes claimed a special knowledge of the mineral arts and of the existence of minerals. It might also be refused if the new enterprise could be shown to jeopardize the future of some local mine or forge already in operation, or if there seemed to be no adequate market for the product.[14]

At the beginning of the eighteenth century nearly all the large industrial enterprises in metallurgy, clothmaking, sugar refining, papermaking, soap- and glassmaking, were either royal manufactures or so-called privileged manufactures. Very few of them were owned directly by the crown and managed by its officials. But many had been started with the help of government capital, almost all with the help of government privileges, such as grants of land and exemptions from various taxes for the owners, managers, and workers. In return for such favors, the owners were bound to conform to the regulations of the governing authorities. These regulations were hardly less complicated than those enforced by the gilds. In many industries even the machinery used in workshops had to be approved and marked by government agents. This sometimes led to absurd rules. The paper mills of Annonay, the largest in France when they were started early in Louis XV's reign, were subject to the control of the local *subdélégué*.

---

[14] These two paragraphs are based mainly on documents in various French *Archives départementales* and in the *Archives nationales* in Paris; cf. Henri Hauser, "Les Pouvoirs publics et l'organisation du travail dans l'ancienne France," in *Travailleurs et marchands dans l'ancienne France* (Paris, 1920); P. Boissonnade, *Le Socialisme d'état* (Paris, 1927), and *Colbert* (Paris, 1932); E. F. Heckscher, *Mercantilism* (London, 1935), I, 137 ff. I have treated the subject in more detail since this chapter was first published in 1938 (see Nef, *Industry and Government in France and England*, chaps. ii and iii).

He was stationed at Tournon, a little town on the right bank of the Rhone, facing the slope of Hermitage with its famous vineyards. Before the large wooden frames for papermaking, fashioned at Annonay, could be installed in the factories there, they had to be carried to Tournon to be marked, a journey there and back of some forty miles along the precipitous paths of the Cévennes. As the frames were delicate, they were frequently broken. It cost several thousand francs in the money of the time to replace one of them.[15] In this way and in many other ways, the French regulations governing manufactures added to the expenses of production and hindered the growth of output.

The control exercised by the central government over industry was at least partly maintained in France throughout the seventeenth century, in spite of efforts by Richelieu and Colbert to encourage individual initiative within the system and to improve the status of the private merchant.[16] But in England government regulation and control was frequently challenged before the Civil War.

During the century following the Reformation many attempts were made by the English crown to establish and extend its authority over manufacturing and even mining. Queen Elizabeth successfully challenged the Earl of Northumberland in the celebrated case of mines in 1566, when he claimed the ownership of a mine of argentiferous copper ore within his lands. As Dr. Read has remarked, the Tudors and early Stuarts made an effort to guard the social interest from exploitation at the hands of the profiteer and the capitalist, by statutes and proclamations designed to regulate industrial conditions.[17] An act of 1555 aimed to prevent country weavers and clothmakers from keeping more than one or two looms. The Statute of Artificers of 1563 was enforced longer than any of the other industrial enactments. While it did not actually limit the number of apprentices a master could keep, it empowered the justices of the peace to fix wage rates and to enforce the obligation of a seven-year apprenticeship for all handicraft workers in existing industries.[18] Following the precedents set by Continental princes, Elizabeth and her two Stuart successors established the right of the crown, through its agents and patentees, to license and control the new manufactures of saltpeter and gunpowder. Monopolies of the manufacture of glass, alum, and soap were granted to royal patentees.[19] Any project for state control that promised the crown a revenue

---

[15] *Inventaire-sommaire des Archives départementales, Hérault,* série C, III (1887), 188.

[16] Nef, *Western Civilization since the Renaissance,* pp. 215–17.

[17] *The Constitution Reconsidered,* pp. 66 ff.

[18] Cf. M. R. Gay, "Aspects of Elizabethan Apprenticeship," in E. F. Gay, *Facts and Factors in Economic History* (Cambridge, Mass., 1932), pp. 135–36, 142, 162–63.

[19] Cf. W. H. Price, *The English Patents of Monopoly* (Cambridge, Mass., 1906), *passim;* S. R. Gardiner, *History of England* (London, 1901), VIII, 71 ff., 284.

independent of parliamentary grant was likely to find favor at court. By the reign of Charles I the coal trade had become of vital importance to the people of London, because coal had generally replaced wood as fuel. The king and some of his ministers toyed with the idea of making the trade a royal monopoly in the hands of a small group of projectors who offered to pay £50,000 or £60,000 annually for the privilege, sums representing at least twenty times as much in today's money.[20]

These attempts were more and more effectively challenged in England by private merchants, and after the middle of the seventeenth century any serious control by the national government over industrial life was lost. Even before the Civil War a decision given as far back as Elizabeth I's reign, in 1566, in favor of the crown in the case of mines, was interpreted to mean that all minerals, except those containing large quantities of precious metal, belonged not to the crown but to the private landlord, who was free to work or lease them as he chose. The Civil War put an end to the system of royal monopolies and left the field of mining and manu-facturing open to the private capitalist. New privately owned enterprises could be set up almost anywhere without the special permission of the state; mines and small factories were not subjected to any effective control by the government. Although the provisions under the Statute of Artificers which called for a seven-year apprenticeship retained some vitality until the middle of the eighteenth century,[21] most of the penal statutes had be-come a dead letter more than fifty years earlier. The laws remained on the statute books, but they were less and less effectively enforced. As one Eng-lish writer put it in 1766, "the difference between us and France consists chiefly in this; that they take no less care in the execution of their laws, than in making them; we are remarkable for good laws, but are shamefully neglectful in their execution." [22]

If private enterprise was much more extensively regulated in France than in England, especially after the middle of the seventeenth century, it was also subjected to heavier financial burdens. The power of the French king to govern without a representative assembly made it easier to impose direct taxes on wealth. The *tailles,* the *capitation,* and the *dixième* (which even-tually became the *vingtième*) lent themselves to great abuses. The clergy, the nobility, and most of the royal officials, when not exempted from pay-ing them at the time they were first levied, managed to gain exemption before they had been long in force. But neither the French clergy nor the

[20] Nef, *Rise of the British Coal Industry* (London, 1932), II, 273 ff.

[21] I owe this information to Miss M. R. Gay, who has in hand an interesting thesis entitled "The Statute of Artificers with Special Reference to Apprenticeship Regula-tion." (This work has been published since her marriage. It is now contained in Margaret Gay Davies, *The Enforcement of English Apprenticeship; a study in applied mercantilism 1563–1642* (Cambridge, Mass., 1956).

[22] M. Postlethwayt, *The Universal Dictionary of Trade and Commerce* (3d ed.; London, 1766), p. iii.

French nobility took much part in the development of large-scale mining and manufacturing during the two centuries following the Reformation. Their incomes were largely devoted to building, to caring for their parishioners, to adorning themselves and their followers with fine apparel, to ordering sumptuous repasts prepared by chefs who were sometimes ready —like the famous Vatel—to commit suicide rather than to serve an imperfect dish, to ornamenting their châteaux with carved railings and grills, beautiful furniture, plate, tapestries, oil paintings, and sculptures which were the chief glory of the royal workshops. Most of the money to finance large mines and manufactures came from the mercantile classes. But the members of these classes who most frequently escaped from paying direct taxes were the crown officials and the owners of royal and privileged manufactures. They had an interest in maintaining the system from which they derived much of their income, and were not anxious to use their capital to set up new workshops. The private merchant who was eager to develop enterprises outside the established system had frequently to bear, along with the peasant and the craftsman, a heavy load of direct taxes.

In England he was much better off. Before the Civil War the House of Commons challenged the right of the crown to impose taxes without parliamentary consent, and during the late seventeenth and eighteenth centuries, the funds raised by taxation were usually obtained, not from taxes levied on income or personal property, but from a land tax, hearth and window taxes, and a great variety of indirect taxes and duties. These impositions left the fortunes of rich merchants largely intact; they did not greatly reduce the resources of the rising squirearchy, whose members were generally of mercantile origin and were more disposed than the French nobility to invest in large industrial ventures.[23]

After the Restoration in 1660, the wealth of many English merchant families was increased by the new opportunities they were offered to lend money to the government. In France private merchants were also becoming the creditors of the crown for much larger sums than in the past. But in France the creditors were less secure than in England against the risks of default and debasement. Between 1602 and 1740 the pound sterling lost only about a third, the *livre tournois* more than half, its value in terms of gold. At one time, in 1720, the *livre tournois* was worth less than a fourth as much in gold as in 1602.[24] The principle of maintaining a fixed gold standard for the national currency was more firmly established in England than it has ever been in France, partly as a result of the English recoinage of 1696, and the public discussions connected with it. The gold value of the English coins, which had recently fallen by about a fifth, was restored.

---

[23] The subject is treated in greater detail in Nef, *Industry and Government in France and England,* pp. 121, and *passim.*

[24] A. Dieudonné, *Manuel de numismatique française,* II (1916), 340, 344, 350–51, 363; A. E. Feaveryear, *The Pound Sterling* (Oxford, 1931), p. 376.

Largely through the influence of John Locke (supported, it is said, by Newton) £3 17s. 10½d. an ounce came to be regarded as the magic and unalterable price for gold. Locke argued, as Alexander Hamilton was to argue during and after the Constitutional Convention concerning the repayment of the public debt, that the "public faith," the "establishment of the national character" as Professor McLaughlin has called it, was at stake.[25] The establishment of the English national character in 1696 did no harm to the financial and the landed interests, for rich men were given the opportunity to unload upon the exchequer all the bad money they held. They benefited in so far as they purchased bad money at a discount from those who were less fortunately placed to get rid of it,[26] and insofar as they were creditors of the state. The policies of the English government were encouraging the accumulation of capital by the persons most willing and able to invest it in private industrial ventures. The state took less money from them than in France; it gave back more.

Within France the mine owner and the manufacturer were handicapped in obtaining raw materials and in reaching markets by the great number of land and river tolls, a relic of feudalism, levied by local lords and towns on commodities passing through their territory, and also by the duties imposed, in most cases by the crown, on interprovincial commerce. In spite of many attempts by statesmen to abolish the local tolls and to reform the public duties, little was accomplished to facilitate domestic trade. If the position of the trader was no worse in the eighteenth century than it had been at the Reformation, it was not conspicuously better. In 1701 commodities passing down the Loire from Roanne, where the river first became easily navigable, to Nantes, at the mouth, paid thirty separate local tolls; commodities passing down the Sâone and Rhone from Gray, in Franche-Comté, to Arles paid twenty-eight in 1786. Road tolls were hardly less common than river tolls. The producer in one province was frequently at several additional removes from the consumer in another on account of the public impositions. Dealers in commodities sent from Languedoc to Paris by the easiest route—the Rhone and the Sâone—had to pay, besides all the local land and river tolls, at least three interprovincial tolls, the foraine, which was levied on goods leaving Languedoc, and two douanes at Valence and Lyons, before their shipments reached the boundary of the northern customs union, the cinq grosses fermes, where another duty was collected. The bill for tolls on a consignment of goods often greatly exceeded the bill for freight.[27] The effect was to hold back industrial concentration. Thus, in 1728 and again in 1738, we find the subdélégué at Tournon complaining that the expansion of the paper mills at Annonay

[25] Feaveryear, op. cit., pp. 136–37; McLaughlin, Constitutional History, p. 225.
[26] Feaveryear, op. cit., pp. 128–29.
[27] Cf. Heckscher, op. cit., I, 78–109, esp. 94–95, 84, 86, 99–102, 103.

was being prevented by the collection of the *foraine* and the *douane de Valence* on shipments of paper. These tolls, he pointed out, in effect subsidized the smaller and less efficient mills in neighboring provinces, as well as those in Switzerland and Germany.[28]

In contrast to France and other Continental countries, England and Wales (and after 1707 the whole of Great Britain) offered the mine owner and manufacturer an area of almost complete free trade. Most of the medieval tolls levied by landlords on land and river traffic had disappeared before the Reformation.[29] The national government refrained from levying duties on domestic commerce, except in the case of the coastwise traffic in coal, which bore an increasingly heavy burden of impositions during the seventeenth and early eighteenth centuries.[30] These duties hindered the expansion of colliery enterprise near the coasts; but the domestic market was open without much interference to the mine owner elsewhere and to the manufacturer everywhere. When Adam Smith compared the tolls levied in France and England, he remarked that the "freedom of interior commerce . . . is perhaps one of the principal causes of the prosperity of Great Britain; every great country being necessarily the best and most extensive market for the greater part of the productions of its own industry." [31] This was an opinion that his American readers were bound to share after their experience with impositions on interstate commerce under the Articles of Confederation.

Adam Smith could not regard English policy concerning foreign trade with the same satisfaction. England had been no more backward than France in laying tariffs upon imports and some exports; so economists were unable to find, in comparisons between the history of the two countries, support for a policy of international free trade, as they could for a policy of interprovincial free trade. It was possible to argue, as the free traders did, that England's prosperity had been secured in spite of tariffs. It was also possible to argue, as Alexander Hamilton did in America and as Friedrich List did in Germany, that tariffs were essential for the development of manufactures in industrially backward countries.

The lessons which could be most readily derived from French and English history seemed to be favorable to certain kinds of government interference with the freedom of economic enterprise, and unfavorable to other kinds. They were not clearly opposed to regulation of trade by the state, provided the regulations took the form of laying tariffs on imports and clearing away obstacles to the freedom of commerce within the country. They were opposed to the maintenance of industrial and commercial

---

[28] *Inventaire-sommaire des Archives départementales, Hérault,* série C, III, 184–86.
[29] Cf. Heckscher, *op. cit.,* I, 46–56.
[30] Cf. Nef, *Rise of the British Coal Industry,* II, 268 ff., 289 ff., 305–15.
[31] *Wealth of Nations,* Bk. V, Chap. II, Part II, art. iv (Rogers ed., II, 499).

monopolies, and to a minute control over methods of manufacturing. But they seemed to be favorable to a government policy of encouraging inventors and scientists and of bringing in skilled mechanics from foreign countries. Until after the death of Louis XIV, the English government did more than the French to stimulate technical improvements which aimed to reduce costs in mining and manufacturing. The system of granting patents for new inventions, as distinct from the granting of industrial monopolies, originated in England in Elizabeth's reign and secured the support of parliament in the celebrated Statute of Monopolies of 1624.[32] During the late seventeenth and early eighteenth centuries, this system had done something to help English inventors to enjoy the fruits of their discoveries for a limited term of years.[33] At the same time the crown, especially after the Restoration, encouraged the experimental sciences. Charles II and his ministers showed much interest in the activities of the Royal Society, which was incorporated in 1664, and which included among its members most of the great scientists of the age.

In France the Académie des Sciences was founded only two years after the incorporation of the Royal Society. But French thought, in its main currents, remained less favorable than English to experimental science and technical improvement until the eighteenth century. Teaching and discussion were more dominated than in England by the scholastic philosophy. Alchemy and magic were taken more seriously. While statesmen like Richelieu sometimes saw the value of machinery designed to reduce labor, in practice they showed the inventor and the scientist little sympathy. If, as has been suggested, Richelieu had De Caus locked up as a madman for pestering him about the power of steam,[34] he was reflecting the French distrust for the value of new forces, a distrust which persisted throughout the reign of Louis XIV. This distrust is to be found in the philosophy of Malebranche and the letters of Madame de Sévigné, as well as in the teachings of the Jesuits, who played a great part in educating the youth, and in the writings of Pascal and other Jansenists, whose books were widely read by the cultured nobility, as well as by the clergy. Statesmen of the French classical age were much more at home with the Académie Française, which Richelieu had fostered, with the Académie de Peinture et de Sculpture, founded by Le Brun in 1648, and with the French theater, than they were with the Académie des Sciences.

To many French writers of the eighteenth century, who were more ma-

---

[32] E. W. Hulme, "The History of the Patent System," *Law Quarterly Review,* XII (1896), 144, 153–54; XVI (1900), 44; Price, *op. cit.,* p. 7; 21 Jac. I, cap. 3, secs. v, vi.

[33] There is some doubt as to whether the patent system actually helped the genuine inventor very much until after the Civil War (cf. Hulme, *op. cit.,* xii, 152; XVI, 53; Price, *op. cit.,* pp. 65–66).

[34] Nef, *Western Civilization since the Renaissance,* p. 280.

terialistic in their thinking than their ancestors of the classical age, it seemed that their country had mistaken the ornaments for the substance of living. Impatient with his countrymen for their inability to understand Newton, Voltaire wrote in 1735, "In truth, we are the whipped cream of Europe." [35] For him, the grace, the precision, the gentleness, and the finesse of French culture could not make up entirely for what he called the more masculine virtues in which the English excelled.[36]

If, as seems to be the case, some eighteenth-century economists believed that England's leadership over France in production for the sake of quantity could be explained mainly by the difference between the economic policies of the French and English governments, they were wrong. The study of constitutional history in England and France helps us to understand the more rapid growth of industry in England, but it should also put us on our guard against exaggerating the importance of government policies as an aid or a handicap to industrial expansion. The contrasts between industrial progress in the two countries were greatest before the triumph of parliamentary government in England, when the crown was attempting, with a measure of success, to regulate economic life along lines similar to those tried in France. England's industrial supremacy in the early eighteenth century had been gained as the result of a multitude of forces interacting upon each other. It was mainly the result of forces upon which government policies had little or no effect.[37] The changes in English economic policies were more a result of the industrial expansion than a cause for it.

Our inquiry into the possible influence of industrial history upon certain clauses in the Constitution is concerned, not with the relative importance of forces making for industrial growth, but with the opinions held in the eighteenth century about the role of government policies in that growth. It is true that, even in England, there were still writers, such as Postlethwayt, who argued that the enforcement of all kinds of rigid laws regulating the freedom of industrial enterprise was beneficial.[38] But by 1750, in France as well as in England, such views were less commonly held and less influential than they had been in the seventeenth century. A majority of writers had come to doubt the value of granting industrial monopolies, or of forcing mine owners and manufacturers to conform to a strict legal code. There was a disposition in France to exalt the English form of government and English economic policies, along with most things English.

These new views concerning the proper place of the state in economic

---

[35] Letter of Nov. 30, 1735, to Abbé d'Olivet (*Œuvres complètes de Voltaire* [Paris, 1880], XXXIII, 556).

[36] Letter of Nov. 11, 1738, to Abbé Le Blanc (*ibid.,* XXXV, 41).

[37] For a discussion of some of these forces, see Nef, *La Naissance de la civilisation industrielle et le monde contemporain,* chaps. ii–viii and x; *Cultural Foundations of Industrial Civilization* (New York, 1960), chaps. iv and v.

[38] Postlethwayt, *Universal Dictionary of Trade and Commerce,* p. iii.

life were strengthened by the history of the half-century preceding the Constitutional Convention. This is the period when, it is still widely believed, the "industrial revolution" began in England. The "revolution" is supposed to have spread to the Continent later, after the United States Constitution had been working for some time. But we must push back the beginnings of rapid industrial change in France as well as in England further than has been customary. Judged by the rate of increase in the volume of industrial output and in the number of workpeople employed in considerable mines and factories, the fifty years from 1735 to 1785 were possibly a period of even more rapid development in France than in England.[39] The output of coal and probably of iron grew at a more rapid rate. While the output of cotton and woolen cloth probably grew more slowly, English machinery, English workmen, and English capital were being introduced in the textile industry, as in mining, metallurgy, paper- and glass-making, and nearly all other manufactures. France, in her turn, was borrowing technical skill from England, as England in the Elizabethan Age had borrowed from the leading Continental countries. By the eve of the French Revolution several very large plants, each employing more than a thousand workmen and many millions of francs in capital, were in operation for mining coal at Anzin in the north, for metallurgy at Le Creusot in central France, and for making glass at Saint-Gobain in Picardy.[40] Establishments of this size, entirely controlled by private adventurers, were still a novelty in the second half of the eighteenth century. Mines and factories of that kind employing more than a hundred workmen were no novelty.[41] But the number of these increased very rapidly in France during the last fifty years of the *ancien régime*. By 1787 there were several score. While parts of the country were not touched by this remarkable industrial development, and while England remained in 1787 the most important industrial nation in Europe, her lead over France in the volume of output per capita from mines and manufactures was possibly less striking than it had been half a century before.[42]

The French industrial expansion of the eighteenth century was accompanied by some modification in the economic policies of the crown, fore-

[39] The case for this position is now stated more fully in Nef, *Western Civilization since the Renaissance*, pp. 276–86.

[40] I owe this information about Saint-Gobain to Warren Scoville.

[41] It is common, however, to exaggerate the number of such establishments in the reign of Louis XIV. Many of the "royal manufactures," employed most of the workmen in their own homes under the putting-out system.

[42] The remarkable progress of French industry after about 1735 perhaps explains why there were Englishmen, like Postlethwayt, who believed in 1766 (erroneously, I feel sure, unless the statement is confined to the artistic and luxury industries) that "France has hitherto surpassed and out-rivalled all the world in their manufactures" (*op. cit.,* I, iii). On the importance, for the establishment of industrial civilization, of the development of the luxury and artistic industries, see now Nef, *Cultural Foundations of Industrial Civilization*, pp. 128–39.

shadowed by Richelieu and Colbert in their fostering of individual initiative on the part of the private merchant.[43] During the eighteenth century many writers on economic subjects began to express the opinion that industrial enterprise was too much fettered by the government for the good of the country. We must not exaggerate the practical results obtained by this new movement in French thought. It was not strong enough to bring about, before 1789, any general suppression of the tolls imposed on the transport of raw materials and commodities within the country.[44] In spite of widespread opposition to the control exercised by the gilds over industry, which culminated in an edict of 1776 designed to throw all crafts and professions open to everyone, whether or not he had served an apprenticeship or joined a gild, the edict was withdrawn after the fall of Turgot. The gilds were re-established and the corporate regime was even extended to certain crafts which had been free.[45] But there was a disposition on the part of public officials, in Paris and in the provinces, to disregard the old regulations, both of the gilds and of the central government, when they interfered with the introduction of cheaper methods of mining and manufacturing intended to increase the volume of output.

We can see the process at work in Languedoc. Restrictions on the production of the chief textile enterprises there were withdrawn early in the eighteenth century, and each merchant or group of merchants was allowed to decide how much cloth should be turned out for the market in the Levant.[46] The construction of large coal-burning factories for the manufacture of glass bottles was encouraged, even though this was clearly an infringement of the privileges of a closed craft, the gentlemen glassmakers, whose rights had been established by letters patent of 1436 and confirmed by subsequent letters patent of 1475, 1655, and 1727.[47] A decree of 1744 revoked the exclusive right to refine sugar in the province, which had been granted earlier to two successive companies of Montpellier merchants, and the decree threw the industry open to anyone.[48]

Similar changes in policy may be observed in all provinces. The manner of leasing coal mines throughout the realm was radically changed by a decree of 1744. In the past the crown had granted widespread monopolies, often covering a number of provinces, to various noblemen and others.

[43] Nef, *Western Civilization since the Renaissance*, pp. 215–18.
[44] Heckscher, *Mercantilism*, I, 85–87, 106–7.
[45] Cf. Henri Sée, *L'Évolution commerciale et industrielle de la France sous l'ancien régime* (Paris, 1925), pp. 194–99.
[46] *Archives départementales de l'Hérault*, C. 2949 (*Mémoire sur le commerce général de la province de Languedoc*, 1744).
[47] *Inventaire-sommaire des Archives départmentales de l'Hérault*, série C, III, 384.
[48] *Archives départementales de l'Hérault*, C. 2698 (*Mémoire des intéressés à la raffinerie royale de Sete and Mémoire pour le Sieur Sabatier, propriétaire de la raffinerie de sucre, à Montpellier*). For transcripts of these documents, I am indebted to M. de Dainville, the chief archivist at Montpellier, and to his assistant, M. L. Maury.

Now concessions for starting new collieries at particular places could be obtained by any persons with sufficient capital.[49] Traders, merchants, and landlords, whose only passport was their financial resources, found it increasingly easy to enter every industry.

At the same time, the burdens imposed by the financial policies of the crown upon the resources of the private merchant were somewhat lightened. Industrial capital and the profits from industries were largely relieved after 1725 from the obligation to pay the *vingtième*. This impost became almost exclusively a tax on land.[50] After 1740 the gold value of the *livre tournois* was maintained until the French Revolution, so that the risks to creditors of the crown from debasement, if not from default, were diminished.

There was only one aspect of industrial life with which government officials concerned themselves more than in the past. Experience seemed to show in this case that government interference was needed to promote prosperity. Ministers, *intendants, subdélégués,* and inspectors of manufactures all worked to introduce new machinery, new kinds of furnaces, and new chemical processes into manufacturing and mining.[51] The government advanced capital more freely than in the past to help in the establishment of new industrial processes. The immigration of foreign technicians and capitalists was welcomed as never before. Although a patent system, modeled on that of England, was not adopted until 1791, much was done by the state before the Revolution to encourage the scientist and the inventor. Persons were no longer locked up as insane when they sought support for their inventions; slightly insane persons were kept at liberty if they could help to introduce labor-saving machinery![52]

As the French Revolution approached, men began to speculate about the causes for the growing industrial prosperity of France. Progressive-minded Frenchmen were seldom, if ever, satisfied with the progress that had been made for, while the margin of England's advantage was perhaps reduced between about 1735 and 1785, England still seemed to be ahead of France in 1785 in the volume of her industrial output relative to her population. Many Frenchmen felt that if France were to overtake England as an industrial power, she must copy English economic policies in almost every respect. The changes in the relation of the government to economic life, introduced toward the close of the *ancien régime,* fell far short of such a goal, but they were sufficiently notable to be sometimes regarded on the

[49] Marcel Rouff, *Les Mines de charbon en France* (Paris, 1922), Part I, chap. vi, and Part II.

[50] Cf. A. Esmein, *Cours élémentaire d'histoire du droit français* (15th ed., Paris, 1925), pp. 550–51.

[51] Cf. A. P. Wadsworth and J. de L. Mann, *The Cotton Trade and Industrial Lancashire* (Manchester, 1931), pp. 197–99.

[52] Nef, *Western Civilization since the Renaissance,* p. 281.

eve of the Revolution as a cause for the expansion of French industrial output. It is doubtful whether they had in fact more to do with this expansion than the changes in English economic policies in the seventeenth century had had to do with the industrial supremacy England had established at that time. But those delegates at Philadelphia who had kept up with recent French history could find in it fresh reasons for believing that the adoption of English economic policies was desirable for the prosperity of the United States.

The Constitution seems to embody the lessons which were being derived in the late eighteenth century from French and English history by a majority of statesmen and writers on economic questions. There were no specific provisions for the setting-up of government-operated mines and manufactures, for the granting of industrial monopolies, or for the direct regulation of industry by the state. There was, of course, the famous clause by which Congress received authority to regulate commerce.[53] In the eighteenth century the word "commerce" was often used in a much wider sense than is customary today, to cover nearly all branches of economic activity. It has been suggested that the founding fathers intended, by the commerce clause, to grant Congress power to formulate a policy for the national economy, a power which was to extend to manufactures, internal improvements, and the creation of corporations.[54] But in 1787 "commerce" was an ambiguous word. It was also used in its narrower, modern sense. Savary des Bruslons, in the 1742 edition of his *Dictionnaire universel de commerce,* which formed the model for at least one English dictionary on the same subject, defined the word as "exchange, sale, purchase, traffic, or trade in merchandise." [55] The principal definition in most English eighteenth-century dictionaries was similar.[56] These definitions do not differ substantially from the first one in our American *Century Dictionary and Cyclopedia* of 1889: "Interchange of goods, merchandise, or property of any kind; trade; traffic. . . ."

If the delegates to the Constitutional Convention had wanted "commerce" to be understood in its broader sense, as covering industry or manufacturing, they could easily have made their meaning plain by adding one or the other of these words. From the beginning of the eighteenth century,

[53] Article I, sec. 8.
[54] Walton H. Hamilton and D. Adair, *The Power to Govern* (New York, 1937), *passim* and esp. pp. 119–20.
[55] I, Part II, 8. The full title of this work is *Dictionnaire universel de commerce, d'histoire naturelle, et des arts et métiers.* If the author had thought that "commerce" would inevitably be understood to include "arts et métiers," he would hardly have troubled to add these words.
[56] Cf. Hamilton and Adair, *op. cit.,* pp. 206–7.

if not earlier,[57] the word "industry" had been increasingly used, at least in France, in its modern sense of mining and manufacturing.[58] Thus we find the duc de Saint Simon referring to Vauban's proposed tax "sur les terres . . . sur le commerce et l'industrie," and John Law writing in 1719 that the people of England and Holland are happy because "les terres sont bien cultivées, l'industrie et le commerce sont étendues." [59] In both passages industry and commerce are treated as separate phases of economic activity. Alexander Hamilton used the word industry a number of times with the same meaning in his *Report on Manufactures,*[60] and it is not likely that he discovered this usage during the two or three years which elapsed between the sittings of the Convention and the writing of that document. Such a usage was also known to Franklin.[61] Even if, as is possible, it was uncommon in English in 1787, by that time the word "manufactures" was frequently used in its modern sense. Madison spoke, at one of the early meetings in the Convention, of "the landed, the manufacturing," and "the commercial interests." Some of the delegates actually drafted a clause granting Congress power for "the promotion of agriculture, commerce, trades, and manufactures." [62] Like the clauses authorizing Congress to establish "public institutions" and to grant "charters of incorporation," it was not included in the Constitution.[63] The only clause which clearly gave the national government power to embark on business enterprise was the one providing for the establishment of post offices and post roads. When Franklin proposed to extend this clause to cover the cutting of canals, "where deemed necessary," his motion was defeated by a vote of eight states to three.[64]

We may perhaps conclude that a majority of the delegates were not anxious to establish government-owned or government-controlled industrial enterprises.[65] Nor is there any evidence in the debates that a majority

[57] In a French ordinance of 1543, dealing with ironmaking, the word "industrie" is apparently used in the modern sense (*Archives nationales,* X¹ᴬ8614, fol. 22); cf. A. de Montchrétien, *Traicte de l'économie politique* (1615), ed. Funck-Brentano (Paris, n.d.), p. 56.

[58] Paul Harsin, "De quand date le mot 'Industrie'?" *Annales d'histoire économique et sociale,* No. 6 (1930), pp. 237–42.

[59] *Ibid.,* pp. 237, 240.

[60] For example, Cole (ed.), *Industrial and Commercial Correspondence of Alexander Hamilton,* pp. 276–77.

[61] Smyth (ed.), *The Writings of Benjamin Franklin,* I, 149.

[62] Hamilton and Adair, *op. cit.,* pp. 109, 116.

[63] Cf. Farrand, *Records of the Federal Convention,* II, 321–22, 325, 615, 616, and *passim.*

[64] *Ibid.,* pp. 615–16.

[65] It is true that two delegates, Mason and Gerry, refused to sign the Constitution, partly because they feared that the commerce clause might be interpreted as authorizing Congress to create monopolies and companies (Hamilton and Adair, *op. cit.,* pp. 118, 225). But this does not prove that a majority of the delegates intended that the clause should be interpreted in this way. James Wilson, who thought that the power

wanted Congress to enact elaborate regulations for the conduct of mining and manufacturing, such as had been enacted in France. A majority were apparently in favor of the relative freedom of industrial enterprise which already existed in England, in spite of old statutes rusty for want of execution.

That a majority of the delegates favored the full repayment of the public debt is not open to doubt.[66] The financial clauses of the Constitution were bound to help wealthy persons to become still more wealthy. Against the danger of a government default, the payment of the nation's debts was made, by section 8 of Article I, the first objective of raising revenue, before the other two objectives, the "common defense" and the "general welfare." Revenue was to be raised mainly by duties, excises, and indirect taxes, which would fall less heavily on the financial and mercantile classes than would the "capitation or other direct tax," which the French king still levied and which the Constitution expressly forbade.[67]

Free trade within the United States was assured and the basis laid for the protection of American industries, by several clauses, in sections 8, 9, and 10 of Article I, which granted Congress the power to regulate foreign trade and trade between the states, but prohibited the levying of taxes or duties, either by Congress or the states, on interstate commerce.

Congress was given the authority, in section 8 of Article I, "to promote the progress of science and useful arts, by securing for limited times to authors and inventors the exclusive right to their respective writings and discoveries."

How far a knowledge of English and French economic history actually guided the founding fathers in drafting these economic sections of the Constitution, is a question to which no precise answer can be given. The objectives of the delegates were numerous, complex, and to some extent contradictory, like the motives behind each objective. The future progress of industry was only one among a number of aims which they had at heart. Economic considerations generally were of less compelling importance in statecraft than they were to become in the nineteenth century. It is probable that the decision to confer upon Congress the power to regulate commerce was determined, less by economic considerations, than by the belief that this power, exercised by the British parliament until the Revolution, would strengthen the political authority of the federal government.[68] It is probable

to create mercantile (he did not say industrial) monopolies was included in the meaning of the commerce clause, did not believe that the clause gave the national government the power to cut canals. It was he who seconded Franklin's motion to add a specific phrase granting this power (Farrand, *op. cit.*, II, 615–16; cf. III, 463, 465).

[66] Cf. Beard, *An Economic Interpretation of the Constitution, passim.*

[67] ". . . unless in proportion to the census or enumeration herein before directed to be taken" (Article I, sec. 9).

[68] Cf. A. C. McLaughlin, "The Background of American Federalism," *American Political Science Review,* XII (1918), 215–40.

that the widely felt need for establishing the national credit, and the private interests of the delegates as men of property,[69] played a greater part in determining the nature of the clauses governing taxation and the payment of the public debt, than the dimly perceived relationship between the encouragement of private accumulation and industrial prosperity. The fragmentary records left us of the constitutional debates suggest that, when the delegates talked about economic history, it was more often American than European. We find, for example, in the debates which resulted in the prohibition of taxes on commerce between the states, no reference to the tolls levied on French interprovincial trade, but several references to the duties recently levied by some states, under the Articles of Confederation, on interstate trade.[70]

American history was closer to the delegates than European, but, as Gouverneur Morris remarked in the Convention, it did "not savour much of real wisdom" "to draw from our short and scanty experience rules which are to operate through succeeding ages." [71] On economic questions, the lessons derived by the founding fathers from the more immediate experience of America were almost invariably re-enforced, and on a few occasions even modified, by lessons derived from the experience of Europe since the Reformation. European precedents were often cited in the debates, and the economic thought of some of the most famous delegates was plainly influenced in important respects by English and, to a lesser extent, by French history. In commenting on the activities of European governments in regulating economic life, Franklin wrote as early as 1764: "At present most of the Edicts of Princes, Placaerts, Laws and Ordinances of Kingdoms and States for that purpose, prove political Blunders. The Advantages they produce not being *general* for the Commonwealth; but *particular,* to private Persons or Bodies in the State who procur'd them, and *at the Expense of the rest of the People.*" [72] Madison thought it should be the general rule among statesmen to leave "to the sagacity of individuals, and to the impulse of private interest, the application of industry and capital." But the industrial experience of prosperous European countries, and particularly the experience of Great Britain with the development of some branches of her textile manufacture in the late sixteenth and seventeenth centuries, had led him to believe it was necessary to foster the introduction of new manufactures, by liberal support of the government or the aid of skilled immigrant workers or both.[73] Some of the principal arguments in Hamilton's *Report*

---

[69] Cf. Beard, *op. cit., passim.*

[70] James Madison, *Journal of the Federal Convention,* ed. E. H. Scott (Chicago, 1898), I, 46–47; II, 622.

[71] Farrand, *op. cit.,* II, 126.

[72] Smyth (ed.), *The Writings of Benjamin Franklin,* IV, 244.

[73] *Letters and Other Writings of James Madison* (Philadelphia, 1867), III, 42–43, 160, 653–54.

on Manufactures were supported by appeals to European, and especially to English, history. In dealing with public finance, he said it was "the prevailing opinion of the [English] men of business, and of the generality of the most sagacious theorists," that the funding of the public debt in England, by helping to provide capital, had contributed to the extraordinary prosperity of "every species of [British] industry." A similar handling of the public debt of the United States, he suggested, would be likely to produce the same results.[74] In *The Federalist*,[75] he argued that the raising of revenue mainly by direct taxes was even less practicable in the United States than in England, and, as a justification for the financial sections of the Constitution, he pointed to the success of Great Britain in raising the greatest part of its national income by excises and duties on imports. Again, in the *Report on Manufactures*, Hamilton referred to the immense utility of the various societies organized in Great Britain for the encouragement of arts, manufactures, and commerce, and also to the protection afforded to industrial inventors in various European countries. He hoped that the federal government, in addition to fostering the patent system, would set up a commission "to induce the prosecution and introduction of useful discoveries, inventions, and improvements. . . ." [76] In advocating the creation of a Society for Establishing Useful Manufactures, he was undoubtedly influenced by the methods adopted by the French government during the last half-century of the *ancien régime* for helping new industrial ventures by advancing capital.[77]

If some of the leading delegates to the Constitutional Convention were accustomed to turn to European experience as a guide to economic policy, it cannot be entirely accidental that the economic sections of the Constitution were written almost exactly as many students of English and French history would have been disposed to write them. Whenever English or French industrial history was consulted by Americans, it seemed to justify the very policies which were favorable to the private material interests of the majority of the delegates at Philadelphia and of the social classes which they represented. Thus the Convention could find in industrial history support for one of the most important innovations of eighteenth-century thought, that by seeking one's own financial advantage in the marketplace one increased the general welfare, that in economic matters self-love and social were identical.

[74] Cole (ed.), *Industrial and Commercial Correspondence of Alexander Hamilton*, p. 277; cf. pp. 274–79. The same argument concerning the role played by public credit in promoting manufactures is contained in a communication of Hamilton to the house of representatives, Jan. 14, 1790 (Hamilton, *The Works of Alexander Hamilton*, III, 5–6).

[75] Number XII.

[76] *Industrial and Commercial Correspondence*, pp. 294, 296, 319.

[77] *Ibid.*, p. 202; cf. pp. xxvii, 183–228.

This belief found expression in the Constitution. In the nineteenth century, it came to be a more influential guide to private and public conduct in the United States than in any other country. It owed its origin partly to European industrial history.

Truth, Belief, and Civilization

9

Epilogue: Truth, Belief, and Civilization

For more than a century there have been among the learned those who have tried to extend the outlook and the methods of the natural sciences to the study of man and to the behavior of human societies. Their efforts have raised issues which are of vital concern in the thermonuclear age which we have entered.

Can the desires and forces which play about inside individual men and women be studied with a confidence in the reliability of the results comparable to that which is now felt in tracing the movements of the heavenly bodies through space, measuring the speed of sound or light, or analyzing the consequences of mixing chemical compounds? Are there laws concerning human behavior, concerning the course of history, which can be used for practical purposes by administrators and statesmen in ways analogous to those in which they exploit technical knowledge derived from the natural sciences? Can the secrets of the mind and even of the heart be mastered by scientific methods of inquiry so that men and women can be treated to their advantage as if they were inanimate objects?

Confronted with such questions, many sensitive persons will answer instinctively "no." Yet in universities and research institutes much study is carried on as if the answer might eventually be "yes." The issues are not new, but they have taken on a new importance at our time in history.

These issues have been central to much of the study done, and to many of the discussions held, under the auspices of the Committee on Social Thought which I have directed since it was founded twenty-two years ago. More recently some of my European and American friends and I have founded, also under the auspices of the University of Chicago, a Center for Human Understanding with its headquarters in Washington. The pos-

From *The Review of Politics,* XXV, No. 4 (1963), 460–82.

sible contributions which the human sciences might make to a strengthening of moral, spiritual, and artistic values was raised by Charles Morazé at our first meeting in April, 1962.[1]

Hitherto, it would seem, the progress of science has worked mainly in the other direction. The triumphs of modern science, which have been accompanied by a growing prestige for any results which bear the stamp "scientific," have tended to diminish in recent times the importance men attach to the search for permanent values as a basis for their decisions. I take an example at random. The late dean of a leading university divinity school told me that he had been reading books for one of the most reputable publishing houses ever since he had entered a theological faculty in about 1890. At that time his employers wanted to know whether the manuscripts they submitted would, in his judgment, make good books. But by 1930 all they wanted to know was whether a manuscript could be made into a book which would readily sell. There has been a growing disposition to forget the intrinsic merit of any work or any action.

A good physician is one who knows the limits as well as the possible scope of his knowledge. This paper is written in the belief that there are limits to scientific knowledge even in this age when so many are disposed to think we can solve all our problems by increasing, if possible in geometrical progression, the time devoted to scientific training and research.

In recent decades there has been some approach toward agreement, among a few of the most distinguished physical scientists, about the qualities of scientific knowledge and the limitations of the search for scientific truths in their fields. I have in mind the published views of such men as Whitehead, Eddington, Sherrington, Whittaker, Schrödinger, Hubble, Heisenberg. All agree that scientific statements are never an expression of the whole human being, that science cannot pronounce authoritatively on the issues that mean most to a sensitive individual: the existence or non-existence of God and eternity; the nature and meaning of love and of hatred; the issues of good or bad, beautiful or ugly. In large parts of the world modern science, as has been suggested in these pages, especially in chapter vii, has produced a revolutionary improvement in the human material condition, by lightening labor, diminishing bodily illnesses, and pro-

---

[1] See "A New Conception of Grandeur" (1962), unpublished paper of the Center. I myself have tried during the past four years to consider this subject from a somewhat different point of view than Morazé's, in two essays. One is contained in a chapter called "Religion and Man" in a book called *A Search for Civilization* (Chicago, 1962). The other is the Smith Lecture in History which I gave in 1960 at the University of St. Thomas in Houston, published as a brochure with the title *Religion and the Study of Man* (Houston, 1960).

A sample of the work of the Center for Human Understanding has now been published. See Nef (ed.), *Bridges of Human Understanding* (New York: University Publishers Inc., 1964).

longing life. But nowhere has it helped us to deal justly with the matters that are closest to our hearts. We seek a firm staff on which to lean when we are in trouble (and who of us is not?), we seek a certainty which will help us to decide what actions we cannot and what actions we must take. And by virtue of its very qualities, scientific knowledge has been provisional and always in a state of flux so far as approaches to final truths are concerned.

The scientific methods of examining and analyzing phenomena, which have brought such astounding and interesting and in many ways such helpful results, tend to give the persons who use them a particular and, in the main, an inhuman view of our bodies and of everything accessible to our senses, including space and time as well as matter. One of my scientist friends recently pointed out that there is often beauty in objects seen through microscopes or telescopes, that the scientist, both because of his instruments and his ways of looking at phenomena, may have access to fresh artistic material. Yet, as scientific *investigators,* bent on obtaining results within the scope of modern science, men see objects mainly in a special, abstract, artificial light. As *scientists,* they do not look at what is there with the eyes of an artist, they look at the particular aspects of the object or the subject which for the special purposes of their scientific inquiry they need to know. They may even abstract these aspects into the form of mathematical formulae. As *scientists* their experience (which may seem to them passionately interesting) differs from that derived from the various visions—with flaws, blemishes, and beauties—which the same objects present when they are contemplated directly and intimately without scientific purpose, or when they are fashioned by the human hand and mind into works of art touched by genius.[2]

The characteristic scientific analysis presents examples of what Whitehead has called, in a revealing phrase, "misplaced concreteness." These particular views of objects, of space, of time gained ground rapidly during the eighteenth and nineteenth centuries. The growing scientific training, which has characterized education in recent decades, has tended to warp our outlook in connection with the very matters about which some of the greatest scientists have told us science has nothing really helpful to communicate.

The inquiries undertaken in this book suggest how important have been those realms in human thought and conduct in the cultivation of which scientific investigation has been no guide. These inquiries indicate that the very progress of the experimental sciences since the Reformation, together with the applications of the results of modern science to the technological triumphs, depended in no small measure upon a new confidence in humans

[2] See above, chap. vii, *passim.*

as individuals capable of serving values which faith teaches are external. It is with this faith, and this confidence in man, that we are concerned in this chapter.

SCIENCE AND FAITH

In judging experience which lies outside the range of the truths which physical and biological scientists reveal, we depend on opinions and beliefs. Beliefs have played and are playing compelling parts in history. All of us believe in something. If we believe in error or in evil, that is still a belief, and such a belief can become overwhelmingly strong. Even if we believe in nothing, that is a belief and its consequences may be as insidious, if not as vicious, as those of believing in evil. It matters mightily therefore what it is that we believe.

While wise physical scientists have recently pointed to pitfalls in trying to employ scientific knowledge as a guide to beliefs, during the past century and a half or so—since the Constitutional Convention which concerned us in the last chapter—persons all over the globe, usually without knowing it, have derived from the human sciences some of the major beliefs which influence their conduct. How has this happened?

During these recent times learned men have tried to extend the outlook and the methods of the natural sciences to the behavior of man and to the study of human societies. Belief in the validity of scientific laws concerning the behavior of societies has taken on a pseudo-religious character at least since Auguste Comte brought forward, over a hundred years ago, his positive philosophy with its religion of humanity. More recently dogma derived from a supposedly scientific inquiry into history—that of Karl Marx—has led a great number of persons in many parts of the world—anti-Marxians as well as Marxians—to treat the inevitability of class struggle as an article of faith. It is as beliefs, rather than as unchallenged scientific laws, that widely disseminated views concerning historical change command assent, but these beliefs carry more conviction because of the scientific evidence that is assumed to be behind them.

By their outlook on man, by the methods they employ in studying societies, and because of the administrative framework into which they have fitted as part of universities and research institutes, the learned men who apply scientific categories and principles to human behavior have helped to create new dogmas. It is true that these are almost always disputed by other scientists. But when the supposedly scientific views of one among them spread to a wide public and command emotional support, most of the supporters ignore the challenges. The intensity with which belief in the inevitability of class struggle is now held on both sides of a world allegedly divided into two hostile camps bears a resemblance to the condition of

Europe in the late sixteenth and early seventeenth centuries when issue was joined over religious beliefs between Roman Catholics and Protestants. It is sobering to reflect that, if the warring elements in those times had been armed with the devastating weapons now devised in this thermonuclear age, none of us might be alive.

If belief is an inevitable part of individual experience, nothing is perhaps of greater moment than the question whether men and women generally have accessible any belief capable of uniting rather than dividing them, any belief that will nourish the gentle virtues and help justice, charity, compassion, and love, rather than hatred, jealousy, fear, and the lust for power, which if now given rein would almost inevitably destroy the world. There is the further interrelated question: What beliefs are true, true both to human nature and to the physical universe in which men and women find themselves with a control over natural processes such as our ancestors never possessed? Is truth in conflict with the gentle virtues? Does truth lead to the destruction of our race? Or have all people beliefs in common that could enable them to husband, in the interest of what is good for the individual, the advantages which men's new control over nature offers?

The widely diffused opinion that discoveries of modern scientists have destroyed the basis for Christian belief has left the universities and institutes peopled by large majorities of teachers and researchers who suppose that science has rendered absurd the faith that God became a man, as the Christian Gospel proclaims. The opinion plays havoc with the belief that the words of Christ, as reported by the four saints in the New Testament, are not merely human but also divine and so eternal.

The critical attitude toward all beliefs which prevails in universities has become a form of faith. So, in a very different way, has the Marxian conception of progress, which treats Christianity as obsolete. At the same time many of us have been confronted in our education with accounts of the terrors of the several inquisitions in medieval and early modern Europe and with the horrors of conflict, hatred, and frustration produced by religious beliefs, leading, as they have sometimes, not only to bigotry and calumny between sects but to most cruel warfare, and to barbaric slaughters. So, apart from the question of the truth of the Gospel, men are readily alarmed by the possible consequences of spreading a belief in the supernatural order, and even of faith in Christ as God.

Two years ago in Cincinnati, at a gathering of clergymen and humanists, I presented a paper on the need for a new Christian view of history.[3] I suggested that historically there seems to have been a connection between belief in Christ and the coming of a relatively humane civilization which many of our grandfathers, like some of their forebears in the eighteenth

---

[3] A revised version has now been published, Nef, "A New Christian View of History?" *Thought*, XXXVII, No. 146 (1962), esp. 349–55.

century, considered capable of winning over the human race to a higher level of decency in thought and conduct than had prevailed in any earlier societies.[4] My paper was received with dismay. A Swedish Lutheran minister, professor in one of our most respectable divinity schools, had been appointed to discuss it. My *new* Christian view of history alarmed him. He said my thesis was more dangerous than the hydrogen bomb! Later, in a private letter which touched me very much, he retracted most of what he had said. That's easier to do when no one's there to hear you. What he had feared, I presume, was this: If people generally came to believe, as I did, that Christian belief had been a great civilizing factor in history, that might strengthen the Christian faith and thereby lead to a revival of the Inquisition and the religious wars. We see in his views an example of the curious paradox that professors in what are nominally Christian divinity schools feel impelled to be lukewarm in their faith, to take refuge in critical analyses of religious documents and of the conduct and thought of saints and sinners, as if the Christian religion, when really believed, is a threat to the welfare of mankind.

In searching for human understanding and for the truths without which understanding is hardly possible, is it not important to compare beliefs based on science with those based on religion? Are beliefs derived from science truer than beliefs founded on faith? Are they safer? Can beliefs founded upon the scientific study of human societies provide the individual with hopes and means of regeneration comparable to the ones Christ inspires in those who believe that He is God? Are the two kinds of beliefs actually in conflict? If not, how can they be reconciled?

THE TESTIMONY OF HISTORY: GOBINEAU AND TOCQUEVILLE

One of the most destructive doctrines of modern times—the doctrine of superior races—was brought forward a century ago in the name of science by Count Gobineau in his now famous book, *Essai sur l'inégalité des races humaines,* which first appeared in two volumes in 1853 and 1855. The doctrine had much to do with the peculiar inhumanities which we associate with the rise of the Nazis, the Second World War and its sequels, with the liquidation in concentration camps of millions of men and women whose only crime was that they were supposed to belong to a particular non-Aryan race. So alarming was the alleged scientific origin of this doctrine to some members of UNESCO following the war, that this new international organization assembled a number of leading social and biological scientists in 1949 in the hope that they would be able to make a unanimous declara-

[4] See also Nef, *Cultural Foundations of Industrial Civilization* (New York, 1960); *Civilization, Industrial Society, and Love,* Center for the Study of Democratic Institutions, Santa Barbara, Calif., Occasional Paper No. 118, 1960.

tion that science proves all races are equal. Although a few of the scientists agreed on a rather innocuous statement tending to support such a thesis,[5] several others expressed the view that it is no less unscientific to declare that all races are equal than to declare they are unequal.

In effect these others extended to genetics, anthropology, paleontology, and every human science the views of the distinguished physical scientists whose names I mentioned at the outset of this chapter concerning the limitations of science. They said, in effect, that the humanistic sciences, like the physical sciences, can give no valid answers on questions which are close to our hearts. "I do not believe," wrote Professor Walter Landauer, "that ethical values can ever be directly derived from scientific data. . . . The declaration that 'all men are created equal' was a fine one and remains so, even though and in the best sense because it is untrue in the biological sphere."(!)[6]

In the light of this experience of UNESCO, Gobineau's doctrine about the inequalities of human races may serve as a starting point for a comparison between the value of science and religion as a basis for beliefs with regenerative possibilities. We have an important documentary basis for making this comparison. The rival claims of science and religion as approaches to truth were discussed over a century ago by Tocqueville and Gobineau in their correspondence before and after the publication of Gobineau's book.

Tocqueville had long been a friend of the younger man. He had helped Gobineau with both his diplomatic and his literary career. There was a fundamental difference between them in religious and in scientific outlook, which the appearance of Gobineau's essay intensified. The debate which they carried on by letter directs attention to the historical influences of belief in scientific truth as a basis for conduct as compared with the historical influences of belief in Christ.

Christ had entered the world some eighteen hundred years before Gobineau explored early archeological and anthropological studies, which had begun to be made around 1800, with the intention of reaching scientific generalizations concerning the role played by races in building civilizations. Now, more than a hundred years after the appearance of his book, we are in a position to consider how far the dismay felt by Tocqueville over its implications has been justified by history.

According to Gobineau's thesis scientific inquiry shows that the various races of the earth are unequal in their potentialities. Because of their nature some are predestined to fail, others to succeed, in bringing civilization. If the blood of a superior race is mingled with that of inferior races, the civilization which the superior race has built is doomed. For Gobineau this

[5] UNESCO, *The Race Concept* (Paris, 1952), pp. 11–16.
[6] *Ibid.*, p. 19.

was a scientific law resembling the law of political economy according to which the introduction of bad money will always drive out good. In the writings of some of Gobineau's followers (prominent among them the Anglo-German Houston Stewart Chamberlain) this thesis eventually became a dogma among groups in several countries. Nowhere was it more strongly held than in Germany, where the young Gobineau had found a kind of intellectual home to such an extent that Tocqueville depended on him for knowledge of German philosophy and letters. Later, racial doctrine took a most powerful *political* turn in Germany. It became an essential part of the Nazi belief in Teutonic destiny as based on a master race. It also had a pronounced influence, in a somewhat different direction. Oswald Spengler and other expounders of cycle theories of history were confirmed in their belief that societies are bound to perish after a life span which is as inexorably fixed as that of a man, and that Western society has been, and is, evolving toward natural and inevitable disintegration.

Tocqueville had long been aware of Gobineau's views. In 1843, ten years before the first volume of the *Essai* appeared, in a letter written to his young friend he had taken a position from which he never retreated. He asked that we judge Christianity of itself, above all as it is revealed in the four Gospels, and not by the instruments through which, like any religion, it has had to pass, and which have frequently deformed it. It had been put to terrible uses, contrary to its spirit, by kings and princes including ecclesiastics during what Tocqueville described as "centuries of profound ignorance and cruelty." [7] Against the harm human beings who professed the Christian faith have done through the evils born of power, barbarous manners, and intolerance, Tocqueville asks us to weigh the contributions of Christianity to thought and conduct.

Christianity presents, Tocqueville wrote, a view of right thought and conduct different from that derived from any other religion or moral philosophy. It seemed to him "to have brought about a revolution, or if you prefer a considerable change, in men's ideas concerning the obligations and rights which are the subject matter of any healthy ethics."

He went on to describe three basic changes which Christianity has introduced into the moral order.

First, although Christianity did not create any new obligations, it introduced a new hierarchy of the virtues. Before the coming of Christ, Tocqueville explains, "rough and half savage virtues had stood at the top of the list. Christianity placed them at the bottom." The gentle virtues, "such as humanity, pity, indulgence, the forgetting of injuries, were the last. Christianity placed them ahead of all the others." [8]

And, in fact, do we not read in Saint Matthew, "Ye have heard that it

[7] Alexis de Tocqueville, *Oeuvres Complètes* (Paris, 1959), IX, 57.
[8] *Ibid.*, p. 45.

hath been said, Thou shalt love thy neighbor, and hate thine enemy. But I say unto you, Love your enemies, bless them that curse you, do good to them that hate you, and pray for them which despitefully use you, and persecute you. . . . Whosoever therefore shall humble himself as this little child, the same is greatest in the kingdom of heaven." [9] With these words before us, it is difficult to doubt that Tocqueville was right in saying that, in the inner lives of individuals, Christ helped lift love and humility to a primacy that it is more difficult to obtain for them unaided. Is there anything quite as total in its love in the teachings of Buddha, Confucius, Mohammed, or other prophets ancient or modern?

The second change introduced by Christ and ever present with Him was an enlargement of the scope of virtuous conduct. "The domain of moral obligations was limited," Tocqueville proceeds in his letter to Gobineau, "Christianity extended it. It had hardly gone beyond fellow citizens. Christianity opened it to all men. It had been chiefly confined to masters; Christianity introduced slaves. It placed in an incandescent light the virtues of human equality, unity and fraternity."

Of the truth of Tocqueville's view do we not read in Saint Matthew, "But, be not ye called Rabbi: for one is your Master, even Christ, and all ye are brethren."? [10] All human beings are brothers under God.

The third change was to provide *ultimate* sanctions for moral law as amended and extended by the first two changes. Formerly sanctions had rested more with this world than with the next. Christianity gave life an object beyond tangible life itself, and placed the accounting on a higher plane, where the struggles and the turmoil of the material existence in which we all live have ceased. "It placed the purpose of life beyond life, and thereby gave a purer, more immaterial, more elevated character to ethics." Issues of right or wrong inner thought, of right or wrong conduct, could no longer be settled by any earthly power, even the power of priests and prophets.

We read again in Matthew: "And call no *man* your father upon the earth: for one is your Father, which is in heaven." [11] So there is a final appeal from the intolerance of human beings, even from intolerance exercised in the name of Christ. Our Lord lifted moral questions above all earthly authority, beyond the mere *opinions* of men, no matter how armed with worldly might the men might be. The grandeur of Christianity consists, Tocqueville concluded, in making possible "a human society beyond all national societies." [12] Might this be the just world society for which today so many yearn?

The difficulty in the way of actually creating such a society was and is,

[9] Matt. 5:43–44; 18:4.
[10] Matt. 23:8.
[11] *Ibid.*, 23:9.
[12] Tocqueville, *op. cit.*, IX, 45–46.

of course, one of which Tocqueville was aware. The supreme authority "is not of this world," and men's opinions and beliefs are. Imperfect and sometimes evil human beings have had Christianity in their keeping. The question was, and is, whether the influence of Christianity in its pure form, as brought into the world by Christ, has outweighed the evils born of power, barbarous manners, and intolerance in the hands of those acting in His name.

Gobineau's essay was a blow to two positions concerning the human condition as it had been understood by idealistic Europeans increasingly since the sixteenth century. Both were derived partly from the Christianity in its pure form toward which these letters of Tocqueville direct our thoughts. One concerned race; the other civilization. The first position is that all races have historically a common origin, that every one of us is descended, not from several men and women, but from one. It followed that no individual is necessarily condemned by reason of race to inequality of achievement. For example, a black man is entitled to the same opportunities and to the same recognition for his qualities as a white man. This concept of brotherhood became a cornerstone of civilization as it emerged in Europe. According to a present-day statesman that concept was part of the early Portuguese projects of colonization.[13] However that may be, the hierarchy of values created by the world outlook of the European mind in the seventeenth century, under French leadership, recognized no higher category of individual than the "honnête homme."

This phrase is untranslatable. It refers to a man whose fundamental integrity is absolute, and who has consequently the highest claim on our admiration in and for his moral qualities, without respect to his success or his worldly position. A statement attributed to Madame de Rambouillet, the first leader of polite, European society, suggests that no one was excluded in her mind from this category for reasons of race. She is said to have remarked that she would welcome a black man to the inner circle of her drawing room if he were an "honnête homme." The concept of brotherhood which is inherent in Christ's words provides a basis for the equal opportunities which all peoples of the world now legitimately seek.

The other position held by Europeans, and also derived from the hope Christianity inspired, related to civilization. The word was apparently introduced into the French and English languages about the middle of the eighteenth century. For the early users of the word, "civilization" was a new phenomenon; civilization was in the making, and the Europeans were taking the lead in making it. It united them all in what Burke called a "great republic," blotting out national frontiers. The achievement of civilization, in this sense, was not a matter of race or nationality; the Euro-

---

[13] Adriano Moreira, *Portugal's Stand in Africa* (New York, 1962), pp. 156–57 and *passim*.

peans claimed no monopoly for it; the doors were wide open for other peoples to adopt it. As with the League of Nations, apparently first conceived by an obscure French monk Emeric Crucé in 1623, all the peoples of the earth were free to join as *they* became civilized. According to Gibbon a consequence of the spread of civilization was to leave the civilized without the ambition to conquer and subjugate, so why should we fear the spread of civilization to all mankind?

Gobineau challenged these positions concerning race and civilization as scientifically unsound. For some decades explorers such as Humboldt had brought evidence that what seemed to the investigators *advanced* societies had developed only to disappear. The Aztecs and the Mayas in Central and South America provided examples. Similar evidence was being derived from other parts of the world. For the ordinary intelligent man at the beginning of the nineteenth century history had not gone back far. As late as 1825, Stendhal had written of "the two thousand years of recorded world history," [14] a span of time which hardly covered all the events recorded by Bossuet in his *Histoire Universelle*. But archeologists were changing this view in the times when Gobineau grew up. Excavators of ancient ruins and historical researchers looked further back into the past for advanced conditions of human life in the Near and Far East, North Africa, and Asia. They found that large, populous and sophisticated societies had developed there before the progress of the Persians, the Greeks, the Romans, and the Mohammedans, peoples who had been of primary interest to earlier European historians, philosophers, and other men of letters.

It seemed to follow that, contrary to what Europeans who had coined the word supposed, civilization was no new thing. The word changed its meaning. Learned men now spoke not of civilization but of civilizations. Through Gobineau's efforts and those of other speakers and writers, the new usage became dominant, until the first meaning given the word was almost forgotten, to be rediscovered during the past fifty years, without causing much stir in popular or even in learned conversation. Most of those who are aware of the origins of the word, seem to think that the meaning first attached to it is better discarded. This view is by no means confined to persons who share Gobineau's outlook on race.

The Decline and Fall, a title Gibbon had given to what has been since its publication in the 1770's and 1780's the history most read in the English-speaking countries, was taken as evidence that the Greeks and Romans were not our direct ancestors in the building of societies. In connection with the Roman Empire, Gibbon treated the Christian religion as a principal cause for its decay. Yet in his optimism he, unlike Gobineau, regarded European society as a new species destined to survive and to be joined by all mankind.

[14] *Racine et Shakespeare,* ed. Edouard Champion (Paris, 1925), I, 91.

Under the influence of Gobineau and others, later Europeans became more and more pessimistic concerning the future of this society. The pessimism existed long before Paul Valéry published his oft-quoted sentence just after the First World War: "Nous, civilisations, nous savons désormais que nous sommes mortelles." I remember my first meeting with this outlook. When I was a child of perhaps nine, I was introduced to an old nineteenth-century story called *Masterman Ready*. It was written expressly for boys by an English sailor and novelist, Frederick Marryat (1792–1848), and first published in 1841 some years before Gobineau's *Essai*. What *Masterman Ready* suggests is that *our* civilization may be destined to perish. Fifty years later, at the end of the nineteenth century, some writers had become certain this would happen, that modern European and American society could not survive any more than had earlier great societies like the Graeco-Roman. In 1895 Brooks Adams published a book called *The Law of Civilization and Decay*. While there were archeologists, anthropologists, and geneticists who took a less discouraging view of our possible future, and while the more optimistic Americans shut their eyes to the gloomier interpretations of anthropology and history, the idea that mankind is incapable of rising to a higher level of understanding and love of the neighbor than ever before entered the American universities more and more as the alleged fruits of scientific study of society, at a time when scientific results were coming to possess a prestige that left many with the impression that there could be no appeal from them.

Among historians who have been widely read, Guizot (1787–1874) was one of the last to regard civilization as something unique, enduring, and potentially universal, to retain in short the original meaning of the word. For him, as for Tocqueville, who was his younger contemporary, civilization was the product not of any particular race but of Christianity. He wrote of "the barbarous indifference for the lives and deaths of [our] fellow men and women which Christianity alone succeeded in rooting out of human societies." [15]

Years ago when I was in the process of getting a French education in the best way: in France and with a woman my own age whose French was almost perfect, a middle-aged Frenchman contributed to our instruction concerning the religious state of the French people. He was in the iron and steel business and even then looking toward what has become the "common market," about which we read almost every day in the newspapers. A practicing Roman Catholic, he explained that in his country there were only two religious positions, those of "catholics and freethinkers"! Through my later friendship with André Siegfried, I was to discover how far from inclusive this industrialist's classification was. It provided no place for Siegfried or Guizot, who was an ardent influential Protestant, and unlike Sieg-

[15] *Histoire de France* (Paris, 1872), I, 415.

fried (who was also a Protestant) a firm believer in the truth of Christian Revelation. Nor did our iron and steel friend really provide for Tocqueville, who remained outside the Roman Catholic Church all his creative life, yet would hardly have qualified as a sound freethinker for he took its sacraments on the eve of his death. What about Gobineau's religion? His letters show that this father of a "scientific" theory of superior and inferior races considered himself a Roman Catholic in good standing. Only for him religion and science were in separate compartments, and as a scholar his allegiance was to science.

Tocqueville saw the issue raised by Gobineau's essay between science and Christianity, between religion and what my colleague Hayek calls "scientism," with a clarity which astonishes a sympathetic reader today by its foresight no less than do his much earlier observations on the condition and the future of democracy in America. What above all separated him from Gobineau, was a growing conviction that the faith in science, which the younger man adopted as the final arbiter in thought, threatened the advances in human societies which he, like Guizot, attributed to Christianity. (In my judgment there are times when the old are young and the young are old, and this is one of them.)

Tocqueville believed there had been a close connection between the good in Christianity and the progress of tender manners and of liberty. As a young traveler in the United States, he had been encouraged about the Americans because he thought the words of the Christian Gospel were taken here with greater seriousness than in Europe, above all in connection with family relations. What also encouraged him about democracy and the overthrow of kingly power, as he wrote in a later book, *L'Ancien Régime et la Révolution,* was this: The French Revolution was not fundamentally anti-Christian. It was only anti-clerical. It attacked the power exercised by political authorities with the sanction of priests. Tocqueville seems to have hoped that the Revolution had eliminated some of the barriers to a spread of the gentler, the compassionate sides of Christ's teaching. It is consistent with the contents of his letters to Gobineau, and I think he would have said, that since God had offered Himself through Christ to *all* human beings, the doors of Western civilization, because of what he believed to be its Christian origins, were open to the peoples of all nations. That is what he had in mind when he wrote that Christianity had "placed in an incandescent light the virtues of equality, unity and human brotherhood."

Tocqueville's historical position resembles one I had taken independently, before I read this correspondence.[16] What is my position? Essentially this: The rise particularly during the seventeenth and eighteenth centuries in Europe of a society transcending national and even European boundaries,

---

[16] Nef, *Cultural Foundations of Industrial Civilization,* esp. pp. 105-8 and chap. vi generally.

putting the tender virtues in the forefront as ideals to be sought after, a society bent for a time on settling by *limited* warfare the issues that divided parts of it, a society open to all the peoples of the world, cannot be accounted for without the attempts made to realize in the world something of the love emanating from Christ. That is what I was trying to express to those theologians and humanists in Cincinnati. I was trying to say that, as I read history, something of the hope confirmed in men by the coming of Christ filtered into the world of affairs and action, and helped commerce to replace piracy.[17] In the rise and triumph of modern industrialism Christianity, in this sense, outweighed as a historical factor all the bigotry and persecution of other men, often associated not unnaturally or unrealistically with men and women belonging to all the Christian churches. In spite of the bigotry and persecution of churchmen, it helped some human beings to feel greater confidence in the love they sometimes find for one another.

Let me summarize my position, and Tocqueville's, as I understand them. To account for civilization, in the original meaning of that word, solely in terms of Christianity would be to present a caricature of history. But to claim that civilization has been historically entirely independent of Christianity would be, in Tocqueville's view and mine, to miss an essential element.

Yet that is exactly what Gobineau did in his book. And he did it in the name of science. As if in answer to letters he had received from Tocqueville years earlier, Gobineau wrote, "I think I should be allowed to confess, that I have never understood the doctrine, *which is entirely modern* [my italics], and which consists in identifying the law of Christ with the interests of this world to such a point that an order of relationships is artificially made to appear and is called *christian civilization*" [Gobineau's italics].[18] Gobineau did not deny that human beings were influenced by religion or that the Christian religion had had special influences of its own. But, for him, there was no connection between Christianity and civilization. His view in this matter seems to be essentially related to his claim that there is not one civilization, but that there are many, and that, if I understand his argument, the distinctive contribution of Christianity is that its influence has not been confined to any one. (The gap between the two views of the meaning of "civilization" seems to make it impossible for him to treat Tocqueville's argument as rational.)

Gobineau wrote:

> There is unquestionably a pagan civilization; there are brahmanic, buddhistic and judaistic civilizations. There have existed, there exist, societies based on religion; religion has given them their form, composed their laws, regulated their civil rights, defined their limits, determined their hostilities.

[17] Cf. above, pp. 238–39.
[18] *Essai sur l'inégalité des races humaines,* p. 64.

Yet the fundamental force in civilization has been not religion but race. ". . . During its eighteen hundred years of existence, the Church has converted many nations. . . . But one cannot see that it has ever provided the world with a unique type of civilization, to which it has claimed believers should attach themselves." As the result of what Gobineau regards as an inexorable scientific law, all civilizations are mortal; consequently for him, as a Christian, it would be a mistake for Christianity to identify itself with any one, for then it might die with that one. He winds up the chapter in his book where the matter is discussed with these words, "Once again, Christianity is not a civilizing factor; it has good reason not to be." [19]

These words are an expression of a position widely held by practicing members of all churches founded in the name of Christ throughout Christian history. Human nature is too base to be redeemed in the actual world in which we live. Therefore the emphasis in all religious effort is properly to achieve salvation in the world to come by following the rules of the church to which one belongs. What above all separates Gobineau's from Tocqueville's position and mine, is that he takes a fundamentally pessimistic view of human nature and sees no possibility for even the partial achievement on earth of the perfection that Christ exemplified. Because of the meaning Gobineau gave to the word "civilization," Gobineau's racial theories were coupled with another allegedly scientific historical law, according to which industrial society is foredoomed to extinction in a foreseeable future. This view, which has come to be held independently of any racial theory of progress, was put forward most vigorously and persuasively by Spengler.

The consequence of adopting either Spengler's or Gobineau's "scientific" interpretation of history is the same in at least one respect. Each leaves little hope on earth for those who wish to help human beings to guide their conduct by what ought to be.

If faith abdicates its responsibilities in the temporal realm, the field is left to science. In a letter Gobineau wrote to Tocqueville in March 1856, he defended his book from Tocqueville's concern over its probable immoral consequences, on the ground that it was concerned only with what is, not with what ought to be. "If the truth is not in itself a superior ethics," he wrote, "I am the first to agree that my book altogether lacks morality, but then it is not the opposite—immoral—any more than are geology, medicine or archeology. It is a search, an exposition, a quarrying of facts. Either these exist or they don't. Nothing more can be said." [20]

But Tocqueville continued to believe that more could be said, and that this was so important that it must be said. His affection for the younger

---

[19] *Ibid.*, pp. 65, 67, 75.
[20] Tocqueville, *op. cit.*, p. 261.

man alone held him back, and at times his conviction broke through this restraint.

> I must confess [he wrote nine months later, in January 1857] that you do not seem to appreciate the difficulty in reconciling your learned theories with the letter and even the spirit of Christianity. As for the letter: Is anything made clearer in *Genesis* than the unity of the human race and the descent of all men from one man? And as for the spirit of Christianity: Is not its distinctive trait the desire to abolish all the racial distinctions which the Jewish religion had allowed to subsist, and to make a single human race, all of whose members are equally capable of perfecting themselves and of resembling one another? How can this spirit . . . be reconciled with an historical doctrine which makes separate races, unequal, more or less able to understand, to judge, to act, and this as a consequence of certain original conditions which cannot be altered and which impose insuperable limits to the perfecting of some of them? Christianity has obviously tended to make all men brothers and equals. Your doctrine makes them at most cousins whose common father is only in Heaven; here below there are only victors and vanquished, masters and slaves by right of birth, and this is so clear that your doctrines are approved, cited and commented upon . . . by whom? By the owners of negroes in favor of eternal slavery based on a radical racial difference. . . .[21]

> Like you I think our contemporaries are pretty badly brought up . . . but I believe we can make something of them, as of all human beings, by skillful appeals to their natural honesty and common sense. I want to treat them like men, it is true. Perhaps I'm mistaken. But I adhere to my principles, and what is more I find a deep and noble pleasure in doing so. You hold the human race in profound contempt, . . . you not only believe in its fall but in its incapacity ever to rise. Its constitution condemns it forever to serve. . . .

> In my eyes human societies, like individuals, are of value only by the use they make of liberty. That such liberty is more difficult to establish and to maintain in democratic societies like ours than in certain aristocratic societies of the past, I have always recognized. That this is impossible, I could never be so rash as to believe. That we must lose all hope of succeeding, I pray God never to let me entertain such an idea. No, I shall never believe that this human race, which is at the head of all visible creation, has become the degenerate flock you maintain, and that there is nothing for it but to surrender it, without a future and without resources, to a small number of shepherds who are, after all, no better animals than we and sometimes worse.

Tocqueville follows these words with a devastating phrase: "You will allow me to have less confidence in you than in the goodness and the justice of God!"[22]

[21] *Ibid.*, p. 277.
[22] *Ibid.*, pp. 280–81.

It seems that Gobineau with his confidence in science as our only key to truth (like Marx and Spengler and others who set forth what they regarded as scientific laws which govern societies) ignored a most important fact. Men are believing creatures, and if they *believe* in the truth of scientific laws which predestine them to a particular course of development, the belief leads them, as it were, to obey the laws. What Tocqueville feared was that Gobineau's belief would supplant the faith and hope which Christ's presence has sometimes inspired, and thus cause men and women, and through them societies, to become those very degenerate flocks Gobineau claimed they are.

Is not the behavior of peoples during the last hundred years, insofar as it supports Gobineau's thesis, less a proof of the validity of the thesis, than of the power of beliefs to make over the world in their image? Insofar as the work of learned men has had an influence, it is more the *belief* in scientific laws governing human behavior, than the truth of these as laws, that has furnished evidence on behalf of them as suitable approaches to the study of man. During the past hundred years history has demonstrated much less the truth of laws put forward by social and behavioral science than the consequences of *believing* that the course of human development is predetermined and that our minds are capable of telling us how, in a way similar to an astronomer's prediction of an eclipse. If that is so, then these consequences are of little *scientific* value. As human beings, the scientists participate by their choices in the laws they proclaim, they help as men to determine whether these laws shall or shall not be, to a much greater extent than has been true of the physical scientists in their discovery of laws concerning the behavior of matter, space, or time.

THE SIN OF CYNICISM

The reader may have noticed that Gobineau wrote of the view that there is a Christian civilization as *modern*. And this leads me back to my suggestion that the older of these two correspondents was in spirit the younger. The partial eclipse during the past hundred years of the hope of realizing a society based on the hierarchy of virtues affirmed by Christianity is no stronger evidence of the invalidity of Tocqueville's thesis than it is of the validity of the allegedly scientific law of civilization and decay or of the inevitability of class struggle. That eclipse, like the class struggle, is rather evidence of the vital importance of belief in determining the course of human development.

The cynicism concerning human nature, which Tocqueville detected in Gobineau, fed not only on the realities which are certainly behind it, but on an exaggerated distortion of these realities in the minds and emotions of men. In his *Souvenirs de la Troisième République,* André Siegfried has described the habit, among the public men of the late nineteenth century whom he met in his father's circle, of attributing all actions and thoughts to base motives. While wariness may sometimes forestall evil actions, the exaggerated pessimism which is properly called cynicism feeds on itself. It is capable of helping to produce the kind of emotional mass slaughter which characterized the Nazi dictatorship in Germany of which Gobineau was unintentionally an intellectual ancestor.

Men and women have not yet determined to an appreciable extent the nature of the physical universe or the structure of matter even insofar as it relates to human bodies. Have they determined the course of history? To a much greater extent, it would seem. Yet as much of what human beings do is unpredictable, the efforts of scientists to discover the laws of history have not led to anything like the certainty which exists for us concerning the movement of planetary bodies. It is common nowadays to assume that Gobineau's theories were scientifically unsound, that the social and behavioral sciences have made much progress during the hundred years since he lived, that the study of biology is on the point of helping the psychologist to set forth sound knowledge of human behavior which our ancestors ignored.

Important progress has been made with the social and behavioral sciences since the mid-nineteenth century. But the tragic consequences of the racial theories, invoked by Gobineau in the name of science, have occurred in the very epoch when we like to think these theories are being scientifically disproved. The dangers seem to remain that beliefs derived from allegedly scientific truths may lead to no less inhuman dogmas than those which alarmed our Lutheran minister in Cincinnati and which he associated with Christian beliefs. That they may lead to greater slaughters than have ever been committed in the name of religious dogmas. I do not think he was right in fearing that belief in the love Christ personified is more dangerous than beliefs that make possible unlimited recourse to the hydrogen bomb.

There would seem to me to be an important difference between faith in science and the faith in Christianity expressed by Tocqueville. The allegedly scientific doctrines concerning race and civilization, brought forward by Gobineau, lead legitimately to a cynicism and despair concerning human nature which cannot be legitimately associated with the words of Christ as reported in the New Testament. This is what Tocqueville recognized, this is what so profoundly dismayed him.

In the passages I have quoted from his letters, has he misinterpreted Christ's message? Do Our Lord's words, does His spirit working within us, justify any one among us in holding "the human race in profound contempt"? Should not faith in Christ have led Christians "to make all men brothers and equals," as Tocqueville wrote it had tended to do? What other meaning can be legitimately attached to the words I have cited from the Gospel: "But be not ye called Rabbi, for one is your Master, even Christ, and all ye are brethren. And call no man your father upon the earth: for one is your father, which is in heaven."? [23]

In their search for brotherhood which might prevent the destruction of the human experiment here on earth, many outside the churches turn to Christ's words. At the same time they find much that is done in the name of Christ by churchmen blocking their hopes. Twenty years ago Georges Bernanos wrote from Brazil to a French nun, "For many years now people have tried to fix the blame for the decadence of Christianity. They have failed because they looked in the wrong place; they looked outside Christianity, when those who are primarily responsible are within. Mediocre Christians, mediocre priests are losing the world. . . ." [24]

In losing it, they have been helped partly by developments for which they have no direct responsibility, by the spread during the past hundred years and more of beliefs that men are bound by scientific laws, that their very nature, together with the circumstances of history, render them incapable of even partial redemption here on earth, that there is nothing they can do but further their own self-interest as members of professions, of nations, of religions, accepting the written and unwritten rules of groups and institutions, much as they accept the rules of clubs they have joined, and resigning themselves in the world itself to the trends which economists and others have discovered from examining data, much of it statistical. This leaves room for power founded on the basest interpretations of human nature.

Men and women everywhere are now confronted with dangers and blessed with opportunities greater than any that existed in the times of Gobineau. The way in which they meet these dangers and opportunities depends not only upon the scientific and technological knowledge they possess but upon the beliefs they hold. They can hardly put forward what is best in them unless they acquire faith in the value, in the beauty, of the human experience as it is lived by individual men and women who prefer life to death, goodness to evil, beauty to ugliness, love to hatred, who do not regard our deal with fate as predetermined and sealed, as settled entirely by inexorable scientific laws based on our violent origins. Scientific laws concerning human behavior can be based only on the way men and societies have behaved in the past. If science settles everything about human conduct, then men's moral condition is frozen once and for all. All possibility of improvement is denied.

It seems probable that the future of the human race rests with conduct based on higher ethical and aesthetic standards than have ever prevailed in

[23] Matt., 23:8–9.
[24] Nef, *A Search for Civilization* (Chicago, 1962), pp. 12–13.

either private or public relations. If this is so, how can we reject Tocqueville's testimony concerning Christianity? If, as Landauer holds, "ethical values can never be directly derived from scientific data;" there is nothing wrong with seeking them in Christ's example, and applying them to the new circumstances about which so much can be learned from science. It is for us to serve the hierarchy of values which Tocqueville tells us Christianity introduced and which corresponds to the aspirations and hopes of others besides Christians in every country. This hierarchy is not outdated; it has open to it, perhaps for the first time, the possibility of coming into its own.

No one should be *forced* to believe in Christian revelation. The implications of Christianity for human hope are, not infrequently, better seen by persons outside than within the Christian churches. It is for all those who have the spirit of Christianity, as evoked by Tocqueville, in their being, whether or not they belong to a religious group, to show by example that the justice of which they are the custodians is enlightened, not blind, that toleration and tenderness will have to become more human than harshness and force. Salvation does not rest with the mediocre Christians of whom Bernanos wrote. It rests with all those, whether or not they are Christians, who believe, as Tocqueville did, in the human experiment, with all who believe that the old ways can be supplanted to an extent that will matter by new, that the hierarchy of the virtues introduced by Christianity can influence the conduct alike of the mighty and the humble as they have never done before. These are matters not of science but of faith. They depend on hope and on charity.

However dangerous dogmatism based on religious faith may be, it is less dangerous than dogmatism based on the extension of science to matters upon which science cannot legitimately pronounce. It is possible that, as Ardrey suggests,[25] man obtained his place at the head of creation as a killer. But man's glory has come from his recognition that killing is in its nature evil, that he has access to a higher power, the power of love. His future on earth, as in heaven, rests more with loving than with killing. It is from faith, more than from science, that we derive the truth and the hope, which this history of man's conquest of the material world sustains, that man can be better than he has been. Inner faith more than science can inspire men to be better than they are. The younger in spirit of the two men whose correspondence we have discussed must have the last word or all that is human on this earth may be reduced to eternal silence.

Having conquered the material world, men and women have now the mission of making it a more decent place for human beings to live in. In order to do this, they will have to conquer themselves.

[25] *African Genesis* (1961).

Bibliography

Books

AGRICOLA, GEORGIUS. *De re metallica.* Ed. HERBERT HOOVER. London, 1912.

D'AJANO, R. BROGLIO. *Die venetianische Seidenindustrie . . . bis zum Ausgang des Mittelalters.* Stuttgart, 1893.

ALBION, R. G. *Forests and Sea Power.* Cambridge, Mass., 1926.

ALLBUTT, T. C. *The Historical Relations of Medicine and Surgery.* London, 1905.

———— *Science and Medieval Thought.* London, 1901.

D'ALLEMAGNE, H. R. *La ferrurerie ancienne.* 2 vols. Paris, 1924.

ARDREY, ROBERT. *African Genesis.* New York, 1961.

ARNOULD, G. *Le bassin houiller du couchant de Mons.* Mons, 1877.

ASHTON, T. S. *Iron and Steel in the Industrial Revolution.* Manchester: Manchester University Press, 1924.

———— and SYKES, J. *The Coal Industry of the Eighteenth Century.* Manchester: Manchester University Press, 1929.

ATKINSON, STEPHEN. *The Discoverie and Historie of the Gold Mynes in Scotland,* 1619. Edinburgh: Bannatyne Club, 1825.

D'AVENEL, VICOMTE. *Histoire économique de la propriété, des salaires, des denrees et de tous les prix.* 7 vols. Paris, 1894.

BANG, NINA. *Tables de la navigation et du transport des marchandises passant par le Sund, 1497–1660.* Copenhagen, 1922.

BARDON, A. *L'exploitation du bassin houiller d'Alais.* Nîmes, 1898.

BARREY, P. "Le Havre transatlantique, 1571–1610," *Mémoires et documents pour servir à l'histoire du commerce et de l'industrie,* ed. J. HAYEM. 5th ser., 1917.

BARTHÉLEMY, L. *La Savonnerie marseillaise.* Marseille, 1883.

BEARD, C. A. *An Economic Interpretation of the Constitution.* New York, 1913.

BEAUPRE, M. *Les gentilshommes verriers . . . dans l'ancienne Lorraine.* 2d ed. Nancy, 1846–47.

BECK, LUDWIG. *Die Geschichte des Eisens.* 2d ed. Brunswick, 1890–1903.

BECKMANN, JOHN. *A History of Inventions.* 4th ed. London, 1881.

BELL, E. T. *The Development of Mathematics*. New York, 1945.

BESSON, JACQUES. *Théâtre des instruments mathématiques et méchaniques*. Lyons, 1579.

BIRINGUCCIO, V. *Pirotechnia*. Ed. CYRIL S. SMITH. New York, 1942.

BLANCHET, H. *Rive et ses environs*. Grenoble, 1861.

BOISLISLE, A. M. DE. *Correspondance des contrôleurs généraux . . . avec les intendants*. Paris, 1897.

BOISMÊLÉ, J. B. T. DE. *Histoire générale de la marine*. Amsterdam, 1746.

BOISSONNADE, P. *Colbert*. Paris, 1932.

——— *Le Socialisme d'état, 1453–1661*. Paris, 1927.

BOURGIN, H. AND G. *L'industrie sidérurgique en France*. Paris, 1920.

BOUTILLIER, ABBÉ. *La verrerie et les gentilshommes verriers de Nevers*. Nevers, 1885.

BOYÉ, P. *Les Salines et le sel en Lorraine*. Nancy, 1904.

BRENTANO, L. *Der Wirtschaftende Mensch in der Geschichte*. Leipzig, 1923.

BRERETON, SIR WILLIAM. *Travels in Holland, the United Provinces, England, Scotland and Ireland*. "Chetham Society Publications," Vol. I. London, 1844.

BROGLIE, LOUIS DE. *Savants et découvertes*. Paris, 1951.

BROWN, P. HUME. *Early Travellers in Scotland*. Edinburgh, 1891.

BRUSLONS, SAVARY DES. *Dictionnaire universel de commerce, d'histoire naturelle, et des arts et métiers*. Geneva, 1742.

BÜCHER, KARL. *Die Bevölkerung von Frankfurt am Main*. Tübingen, 1886.

BURTT, E. A. *The Metaphysical Foundations of Modern Physical Science*. London, 1925.

BUTTERFIELD, HERBERT. *The Origins of Modern Science, 1300–1800*. London, 1949.

The Cambridge Economic History of Europe, Vol. II. Ed. M. POSTAN AND E. E. RICH. Cambridge, 1952.

The Cambridge History of English Literature, Vol. IV. Ed. A. W. WARD AND A. R. WALLER. Cambridge, 1910.

CAMDEN, WILLIAM. *Britannia*. Ed. GOUGH, 1753.

CARUS-WILSON, E. M. "The Iceland Trade," *Studies in English Trade in the Fifteenth Century*, ed. E. POWER AND M. POSTAN. London, 1933.

——— "The Overseas Trade of Bristol," *Studies in English Trade in the Fifteenth Century*, ed. E. POWER AND M. POSTAN. London, 1933.

CHABRAND, ERNEST. *Essai historique sur la métallurgie du fer et de l'acier en Dauphiné et en Savoie*. Grenoble, 1898.

CHAMBERS, J. D. *Nottinghamshire in the Eighteenth Century*. London, 1932.

CHAMPION, EDOUARD (ed.). *Racine et Shakespeare*. Paris, 1925.

CHARLIAT, P. *Trois siècles d'économie maritime française*. Paris, 1931.

CHURCHYARD, THOMAS. *A Description and Playne Discourse of Paper*, 1588. Reprinted in John Nichols', *The Progresses of Queen Elizabeth*, II. London, 1788.

CLAPHAM, J. H. *An Economic History of Modern Britain*. Cambridge, 1926.

CLARENDON, LORD. *The History of the Rebellion and Civil Wars in England*. Oxford, 1843.

CLARK, G. N. *Science and Social Welfare in the Age of Newton*. Oxford, 1937.

CLARK, KENNETH. *Leonardo da Vinci*. New York, 1939.

CLÉMENT, PIERRE. *Jacques Cœur et Charles VII*. Paris, 1866.

COLE, A. H. (ed.). *Industrial and Commercial Correspondence of Alexander Hamilton*. Chicago, 1928.

COLLINGWOOD, R. G., AND MYRES, J. N. L. *Roman Britain and the English Settlements*. 2d ed. Oxford, 1937.

COLLINGWOOD, W. G. *Elizabethan Keswick*. "Cumberland and Westmorland Antiquarian and Archaeological Transactions," Tract No. VIII; Kendal, 1912.

COMBRUNE, M. *An Inquiry into the Prices of Wheat, Malt . . . etc*. London, 1768.

———— *The Theory and Practice of Brewing*. London, 1762.

CONSITT, FRANCES. *The London Weavers' Company*. Oxford, 1933.

COOLIDGE, JULIAN. *History of Geometrical Methods*. Oxford, 1940.

COORNAERT, E. *La Draperie-sayetterie d'Hondschoote*. Paris, 1930.

COQUILLE, GUY. *Histoire du pays et duché de Niversnois*. 2d ed. Paris, 1622.

CORYAT, THOMAS. *Coryat's Crudities Hastily Gobled Up . . .* New ed. Glasgow, 1905.

COUFFON, O. *Les mines de charbon en Anjou du XIVe siècle à nos jours*. Angers, 1911.

COULTON, G. G. *Art and the Reformation*. Oxford, 1928.

COWLEY, ABRAHAM. *Works*. London, 1721.

CUNNINGHAM, A. S. *Mining in the Kingdom of Fife*. Edinburgh, 1913.

CUNNINGHAM, W. *The Growth of English Industry and Commerce: Modern Times*. 6th ed. Cambridge, 1919.

DAMPIER-WHETHAM, W. C. *A History of Science*. New York, 1929.

DARTIGUE-PEYROU, C. *Le vicomté de Béarn, 1517–55*. Paris, 1934.

DAVIES, MARGARET GAY. *The Enforcement of English Apprenticeship: a study in applied mercantilism, 1563–1642*. Cambridge, Mass., 1956.

DECAMPS, G. *Mémoire historique sur l'origine et les developpements de l'industrie houillère . . . de Mons*. "Société des Sciences des Arts et des Lettres du Hainaut Publications," 4th ser., V; 1880.

DELUMEAU, JEAN. *L'Alun de Rome XVe–XIXe siècle*. Paris, 1962.

DESCARTES. *Discours de la méthode*. Ed. ETIENNE GILSON. Paris, 1925.

DESTRAY, P. "Les houilleres de la Machine au XVIe siècle," *Mémoires et documents pour l'histoire du commerce et de l'industrie,* ed. J. HAYEM. 4th ser. Paris, 1916.

DIEUDONNÉ, A. *Manuel de numismatique française*. Paris, 1916.

DIGBY, SIR KENELM. *William Gilbert of Colchester*. Trans. P. Fleury Mottelay. New York, 1893.

A Discourse of the Common Weal of This Realm of England. Ed. ELIZABETH LAMOND, 1893.

DODD, A. H. *The Industrial Revolution in South Wales*. Cardiff, 1933.

DOREN, A. *Die florentiner Wollentuchindustrie vom XIV. bis zum XVI. Jahrhundert*. Stuttgart, 1901.

DRYDEN, JOHN. *Epistles,* II, in *Miscellaneous Works,* II. London, 1767.

DUFF, E. GORDON. *A Century of the English Book Trade*. London, 1905.

DUVAL, PIERRE. *Description de la France*. Paris, 1663.

EHRENBERG, RICHARD. *Capital and Finance in the Age of the Renaissance*. Trans. H. M. Lucas. London, 1928.

Encyclopédie départmentale. Les Bouches-du-Rhône, III. Ed. PAUL MASSON, 1920.

The English Provincial Printers, Stationers and Bookbinders to 1557. Cambridge, 1912.

ESMEIN, A. *Cours élémentaire d'histoire du droit français*. 15th ed. Paris, 1925.

ESPINAS, GEORGES. *Sire Jehan Boinebroke*. Lille, 1933.

FAGNIEZ, G. *L'économie sociale de la France sous Henri IV*.

FANFANI, AMINTORE. *Catholicism, Protestantism and Capitalism*. London, 1935.

FARRAND, MAX. *Records of the Federal Convention*. New Haven, 1911.

FEAVERYEAR, A. E. *The Pound Sterling*. Oxford, 1931.

FFOULKES, CHARLES. *The Gun-Founders of England*. Cambridge, 1937.

FILLON, BENJAMIN. *L'art de terre chez les Poitevins*. Paris, 1864.

FLEETWOOD, W. *Chronicon Preciosum*. London, 1745.

FORMEVILLE, H. DE. *Les barons fossiers et les férons de Normandie*. Caen, 1852.

FRACASTORO, GIROLAMO. *Syphilis sive Morbus Gallicus*. Verona, 1530.

FRANCOTTE, HENRI. *L'industrie dans la grèce ancienne*. Brussels, 1900.

FRIEND, J. NEWTON. *Iron in Antiquity*. London, 1926.

FRIIS, ASTRID. *Alderman Cockayne's Project and the Cloth Trade*. London, 1927.

FULTON, J. F. *Physiology*. New York, 1931.

GARDINER, S. R. *History of England*. London, 1901.

GAULLIEUR, ERNEST. *L'imprimerie à Bordeaux en 1486*. Bordeaux, 1869.

GAY, E. F. *Facts and Figures in Economic History*. Cambridge, Mass., 1932.

GERBIER, SIR BALTHAZAR. *Counsel and Advice to All Builders*. 1663.

GIDE, C., AND RIST, C. *Histoire des doctrines économiques*. 4th ed. Paris, 1922.

GILSON, ETIENNE. "Descartes, Harvey et la scolastique," *Etudes de philosophie médiévale*. Strasbourg, 1921.

―――― *The Unity of Philosophical Experience*. New York, 1937.

GIRANCOURT, A. DE. *Notice sur la verrerie de Rouen, 1598–1664*. Rouen, 1867.

―――― *Nouvelle étude sur la verrerie de Rouen . . . au XVIe et XVIIe siècles*. Rouen, 1886.

GIRAUD, J. B. "Les épées de Rives," *Documents pour l'histoire de l'armement au Moyen Age et à la Renaissance*. Lyons, 1904.

GIRAUDET, E. *Histoire de la ville de Tours*. Tours, 1873.

GOBINEAU, JOSEPH ARTHUR. *Essai sur l'inégalité des races humaines*. 1853–1855.

GODART, J. *L'ouvrier en soie*. Lyons, 1899.

GOLLUT, L. *Les Mémoires historiques de la République Séquanoise*. Arbois, 1846.

GORIS, J. A. *Etude sur les colonies marchandes méridionales à Anvers de 1488 à 1567*. Louvain, 1925.

GOSSELIN, E. *Documents pour servir à l'histoire de la marine normande.* Rouen, 1876.

GOUGH, J. W. (ed.). *Mendip Mining Laws and Forest Bounds.* London, 1931.

——— *The Mines of Mendip.* Oxford, 1930.

GRAS, L. J. *Histoire économique générale des mines de la Loire.* St. Etienne, 1922.

——— *Historique de l'armurerie stéphanoise.* St. Etienne, 1905.

——— *Notes historiques sur l'industrie de la verrerie en Forez et Jarez.* St. Etienne, 1923.

GRAS, N. S. B. *The Evolution of the English Corn Market.* Cambridge, Mass., 1915.

GRÉAU, E. *Le Fer en Lorraine.* Nancy, 1908.

GRIFFITH, G. T. *Population Problems of the Age of Malthus.* Cambridge, 1926.

GUIZOT. *Histoire de France.* Paris, 1872.

HÄBLER, K. *Die Geschichte der Fugger'schen Handlung in Spanien.* Weimar, 1897.

HAGEDORN, B. *Entwicklung der wichtigsten Schiffstypen.* Berlin, 1914.

HAMILTON, E. J. *American Treasure and the Price Revolution in Spain.* Cambridge, Mass., 1934.

——— *Money, Prices and Wages in Valencia, Aragon, and Navarre, 1351–1500.* Cambridge, Mass., 1936.

HAMILTON, HENRY. *The English Brass and Copper Industries to 1800.* London, 1926.

HAMILTON, JOHN C. (ed.). *The Works of Alexander Hamilton.* New York, 1851.

HAMILTON, WALTON H., AND ADAIR, D. *The Power to Govern.* New York, 1937.

HARRISON, W. *An Historical Description of the Island of Britain.* 1587 ed.

HARTSHORNE, ALBERT. *Old English Glasses.* London, 1897.

HARVEY, WILLIAM. *The Works of William Harvey.* Ed. ROBERT WILLIS. London, 1847.

HAUSER, H. "Les idées économiques de Calvin," *Les Débuts du capitalisme.* Paris, 1927.

——— "Introduction," *La réponse de Jean Bodin à M. de Malestroit.* Paris, 1932.

——— *Ouvriers du temps passé.* 5th ed. Paris, 1927.

——— "Les Pouvoirs publics et l'organisation du travail dans l'ancienne France," *Travailleurs et marchands dans l'ancienne France.* Paris, 1920.

——— "Le sel dans l'histoire," *Les origines historiques des problèmes économiques actuels.* Paris, 1930.

HAYDN, HIRAM. *The Counter-Renaissance.* New York, 1950.

HEATON, HERBERT. *The Yorkshire Woollen and Worsted Industries.* Oxford, 1920.

HECKSCHER, ELI F. *Mercantilism.* London, 1935.

——— *Sveriges Ekonomiska Historia.* Stockholm, 1936.

HESSEN, B. "The Social and Economic Roots of Newton's 'Principia'," *Science at the Crossroads*. Papers presented to the International Congress of the History of Science and Technology. London, 1931.

HEWITT, H. J. *Mediæval Cheshire*. Manchester: Manchester University Press, 1929.

HITZINGER, P. *Das Quecksilber-Bergwerk Idria*. Ljubljana, 1860.

HOOKER, RICHARD. *Of the Laws of Ecclesiastical Polity*. 1592–94.

HOPPE, OSWALD. *Der Silberbergbau zu Schneeberg bis zum Jahre 1500*. Freiberg, 1908.

HOUDOY, JULES. *Verreries à la façon de Venise*. Paris, 1873.

HOUGHTON, T. (ed.). *Laws and Customs of the Miners in the Forest of Dean*. 1687.

HUE, OTTO. *Die Bergarbeiter*. Stuttgart, 1910.

HUIZINGA, J. *The Waning of the Middle Ages*. London, 1927.

HULME, T. E. *Speculations*. London, 1924.

ISNARD, EMILE. "Les papeteries de Provence," *Mémoires et documents pour servir à l'histoire du commerce et de l'industrie*. Ed. J. HAYEM, IV.

JARS, G. *Voyages métallurgiques*. Paris, 1781.

JASTROW, J. *Die Volkszahl deutscher Städte zu Ende des Mittelalters*. Berlin, 1886.

JENKIN, A. K. H. *The Cornish Miner*. London, 1927.

JUDGES, A. V. "A Note on Prices in Shakespeare's Time," *A Companion to Shakespeare Studies*, ed. H. GRANVILLE-BARKER AND G. B. HARRISON. Cambridge, 1934.

KEYNES, J. M. *A Treatise on Money*. New York, 1930.

KNOOP, D., AND JONES, G. P. *The Medieval Mason*. Manchester, 1933.

KNOWLES, DOM DAVID. *The Monastic Order in England, 943–1216*. Cambridge, 1940.

────── *The Religious Houses of Medieval England*. London, 1940.

────── AND HADCOCK, R. NEVILLE. *Medieval Religious Houses*. London, 1953.

KOCH-STERNFELD, J. E. R. VON. *Die deutschen Salzwerke zunächst im Mittelalter*. Munich, 1836.

KOYRÉ, ALEXANDRE. *Descartes after Three Hundred Years*. "University of Buffalo Studies," 1951.

KRETSCHMAHR, HEINRICH. *Geschichte von Venedig*. Gotha, 1920.

LANE, F. C. *Venetian Ships and Shipbuilders of the Renaissance*. Baltimore, 1934.

LEADER, R. E. *History of the Company of Cutlers in Hallamshire*. Sheffield, 1905.

LEFEBVRE, E. *Le sel*. Paris, 1882.

LEJEUNE, JEAN. *La Formation du capitalisme moderne dans La Principaute de Liège au 16ᵉ siècle*. Paris, 1939.

LEPAGE, H. "Recherches sur l'industrie en Lorraine," *Mémoires de la Société des sciences, des lettres, et des arts de Nancy*. Nancy, 1849.

LEROUX, M. *L'industrie du fer dans le Perche*. Paris, 1916.

LE VAILLANT DE LA FIEFFE, O. *Les verreries de la Normandie*. Rouen, 1873.

LEVASSEUR, E. *Histoire du commerce de la France*. Paris, 1911.

────── *La population française*. Paris, 1889.

LEWIS, G. R. *The Stannaries*. Cambridge, Mass., 1907.

LIAUTEY, ANDRÉ. *La hausse des prix et la lutte contre la cherté en France au XVIᵉ siècle*. Paris, 1921.

LIPPMANN, EDMUND O. VON. *Geschichte des Zuckers*. Berlin, 1929.

LIPSON, E. *The Economic History of England*. London, 1931.

MACAULAY, T. B. *History of England*. 1866.

MACDONALD, W. R. *The Construction of Logarithms*. Edinburgh, 1889.

MACINNES, C. M. *The Early English Tobacco Trade*. London, 1926.

MADISON, JAMES. *Journal of the Federal Convention*. Ed. E. H. SCOTT. Chicago, 1898.

———— *Letters and Other Writings of James Madison*. Philadelphia, 1867.

MAREZ, G. DES. *L'Organisation du travail à Bruxelles au XVᵉ siècle*. Brussels, 1904.

MARITAIN, JACQUES. *Art et scolastique*. 3d ed. Paris, 1935.

MASSÉ, A. *Monographies nivernaises*. Nevers, 1913.

MASSON, P. *Histoire du commerce français dans le Levant au XVII ᵉ siècle*. Paris, 1896.

MCILWAIN, C. H. "Medieval Estates," *The Cambridge Medieval History*, VII. Cambridge, 1932.

MCLAUGHLIN, A. C. *A Constitutional History of the United States*. New York, 1935.

MELLOTTÉE, P. *Histoire économique de l'imprimerie*. Paris, 1905.

MILET, A. *Histoire d'un four à verre de l'ancienne Normandie*. Paris, 1871.

The Mischief of the Five Shillings Tax upon Coal. London, 1699.

MONTCHRÉTIEN, A. DE. *Traicté de l'Economie politique*, 1615. Paris: Funck-Brentano, n.d.

MOREIRA, ADRIANO. *Portugal's Stand in Africa*. New York, 1962.

MÜLLNER, ALFONS. *Geschichte des Eisens in Krain, Görz und Istrien*. Vienna, 1909.

NEALE, J. E. *The Elizabethan House of Commons*. London, 1949.

NEF, JOHN U. (ed.). *Bridges of Human Understanding*. New York, 1964.

———— *Civilization, Industrial Society, and Love*. "Center for the Study of Democratic Institutions," Occasional Paper No. 118; Santa Barbara, Calif., 1961.

———— "Coal Mining and Utilization," *A History of Technology*, ed. C. SINGER, E. J. HOLMYARD, AND A. R. HALL, III. London, 1957.

———— *Cultural Foundations of Industrial Civilization*. New York, 1960.

———— *Industry and Government in France and England, 1540–1640*. Ithaca, N. Y., 1957.

———— *La Naissance de la civilisation industrielle et le monde contemporain*. Paris, 1954.

———— *Religion and the Study of Man*. Houston, 1960.

———— *Rise of the British Coal Industry*. London, 1932.

———— *A Search for Civilization*. Chicago, 1962.

———— *The United States and Civilization*. Chicago, 1942.

———— *War and Human Progress*. Cambridge, Mass., 1950.

———— *Western Civilization since the Renaissance*. New York, 1963.

NEUBURG, CLAMOR. "Der Zusammenhang zwischen römischem und deutschem Bergbau," *Festgaben für Wilhelm Lexis*. Jena, 1907.

NICHOLL, JOHN. *Some Account of the Company of Ironmongers*. 2d ed. 1866.

NICHOLS, H. G. *Iron Making in . . . the Forest of Dean*. 1866.

OPPENHEIM, M. *A History of the Administration of the Royal Navy*. London, 1896.

ORNSTEIN, MARTHA. *The Role of the Scientific Societies in the Seventeenth Century*. Chicago, 1928.

PACKARD, FRANCIS R. *Life and Times of Ambroise Paré*. New York, 1926.

PAGÉ, CAMILLE. *La coutellerie depuis l'origine jusqu'à nos jours*. Chatellerault, 1896.

PALISSY, BERNARD. *Œuvres*. Ed. B. Fillon. Niort, 1888.

PARACELSUS. *Four Treatises of Theophrastus von Hohenheim called Paracelsus*. Ed. HENRY E. SIGERIST. Baltimore, 1941.

PARKER, HUBERT H. *The Hop Industry*. London, 1934.

PATTISON, MARK. *Isaac Casaubon*. 2d ed. Oxford, 1892.

PATTISON, MRS. MARK. *The Renaissance of Art in France*. London, 1879.

PETTUS, SIR JOHN. *Fodinae Regales*. 1670.

PETTY, SIR WILLIAM. *Another Essay in Political Arithmetick* (London, 1682). Included in *The Economic Writings of Sir William Petty*. Ed. C. H. HULL. Cambridge, 1899.

PHOLIEN, F. *La verrerie et ses artistes au pays de Liège*. 1899.

PIRENNE, HENRI. *Economic and Social History of Medieval Europe*. Trans. I. E. Clegg. New York, 1937.

——— *Histoire de Belgique*. 3d ed. Brussels, 1923.

PLAYFAIR, WILLIAM. *A Letter on our Agricultural Distresses*. London, 1821.

PLOWDEN, EDMUND. *The Commentaries or Reports*. 1818.

PLUTARCH. "The Life of Marcellus," *The Lives of the Noble Grecians and Romans*, trans. Thomas North, III. Oxford, 1928.

POSTAN, M. M. "The Economic Relations of England and the Hanse 1400–1475," *Studies in English Trade in the Fifteenth Century*. Ed. E. POWER AND M. POSTAN. London, 1933.

POSTHUMUS, N. W. *De Geschiedenis van de Leidsche Lakenindustrie*. s'Gravenhage, 1939.

POSTLETHWAYT, M. *The Universal Dictionary of Trade and Commerce*. 3d ed. London, 1766.

PRICE, W. H. *The English Patents of Monopoly*. Cambridge, Mass., 1906.

PRINET, MAX. *L'Industrie du sel en Franche-Comté avant la conquête française*. Besançon, 1900.

PUCKLE, JAMES. *A New Dialogue between a Burgermaster and an English Gentleman*. 1697.

QUENEDEY, R. *L'habitation rouennaise*. Rouen, 1926.

——— *Les prix des matériaux et de la main-d'œuvre à Rouen*. "Bulletin de la Société du commerce et de l'industrie de la Seine-Inferieure"; Rouen, 1927.

RANKE, LEOPOLD. *The Ecclesiastical and Political History of the Popes of Rome*. Trans. Sarah Austin. London, 1841.

────── *History of the Reformation in Germany.* Trans. Sarah Austin. London, 1905.

RAVEAU, P. *L'agriculture et les classes paysannes dans le haut Poitou.* Paris, 1926.

────── *Essai sur la situation économique et l'état social en Poitou au XVI*ᵉ *siècle.* Paris, 1931.

READ, CONYERS. *Bibliography of British History, Tudor Period, 1485–1603.* Bloomington: Indiana University Press, 1933.

────── (ed.) *The Constitution Reconsidered.* New York, 1938.

Recueil général des anciennes lois françaises. Paris, 1825.

Revue des sociétés savantes, 7th ser., II. 1880.

RIVIÈRE, J. *Le Problème de l'église et de l'état.* Louvain, 1926.

ROGERS, J. E. THOROLD. *A History of Agriculture and Prices in England.* 7 vols. Oxford, 1866–1902.

ROMIER, LUCIEN. *Le royaume de Catherine de Médici.* Paris, 1925.

RONCIÈRE, CHARLES DE LA. *Histoire de la marine française.* Paris, 1910.

ROSTOVTZEFF, M. *The Social and Economic History of the Hellenistic World.* Oxford, 1941.

────── *The Social and Economic History of the Roman Empire.* Oxford, 1926.

ROUFF, MARCEL. *Les mines de charbon en France.* Paris, 1922.

ROUZAUD, HENRI. *Histoire d'une mine au mineur.* Toulouse, 1908.

RUSKIN, JOHN. *La Bible d'Amiens.* Paris, 1947.

RUSSELL, JOHN COX. *British Medieval Population.* Albuquerque, N. M., 1948.

SALIN, ED., AND FRANCE-LANORD, ALT. *Le Fer à l'époque mérovingienne.* Paris, 1943.

SALZMAN, L. F. *English Industries of the Middle Ages.* 2d ed. Oxford, 1923.

SCHMIDT, ALFRED. *Das Salz.* Leipzig, 1874.

SCHRÖTTER, F. VON. *Wörterbuch der Munzkunde.* Berlin, 1930.

SCHUERMANS, H. *Verres "façon de Venise" ou d'Altare fabriques aux Pays-Bas.* Letters published 1884–93. Paris: Bibliothèque nationale.

SCLAFERT, T. *L'industrie du fer dans la région d'Allevard au Moyen Age.* Grenoble, 1926.

SCOTT, GEOFFREY. *The Architecture of Humanism.* London, 1914.

SCOTT, W. R. *The Constitution and Finance of English, Scottish and Irish Joint-Stock Companies to 1720.* Cambridge, 1910–12.

SÉE, HENRI. *L'Évolution commerciale et industrielle de la France sous l'ancien régime.* Paris, 1925.

SHERRINGTON, CHARLES. *The Endeavour of Jean Fernel.* Cambridge, 1946.

SIMIAND, FRANÇOIS. *Recherches anciennes et nouvelles sur le movement général des prix du XVI*ᵉ *au XIX*ᵉ *siècle.* Paris, 1932.

SIMSON, OTTO VON. *The Gothic Cathedral.* New York, 1956.

SMYTH, A. H. (ed.). *The Writings of Benjamin Franklin.* New York, 1905.

SOMBART, WERNER. *Der moderne Kapitalismus.* 4th ed.; 4 vols. Munich and Leipzig, 1922.

SPRAT, THOMAS. *History of the Royal Society.* London, 1667.

STEFFEN, GUSTAF F. *Studien zur Geschichte der Englischen Lohnarbeite.* Stuttgart, 1901.

STERNBERG, KASPAR. *Umrisse einer Geschichte der böhmischen Bergwerke.* 2 vols. Prague, 1836, 1838.

STRAKER, ERNEST. *Wealdon Iron.* London, 1931.

STRIEDER, JAKOB. *Zur Genesis der modernen Kapitalismus.* Leipzig, 1904.

———— *Studien zur Geschichte Kapitalistischer Organisations-formen.* 2d ed. Munich, 1925.

STUBBS, WILLIAM. *Epistolæ Cantuariensis.* London, 1865.

SUDHOFF, KARL. *Beitrage zur Geschichte der Chirurgie im Mittelalter.* Leipzig, 1914.

SUE, EUGÈNE. *Correspondance de Henri de Sourdis.* Paris, 1839.

SWANK, JAMES M. *History of the Manufacture of Iron in All Ages.* Philadelphia, 1892.

TAWNEY, R. H. *Religion and the Rise of Capitalism.* London, 1926.

THRUPP, SYLVIA. *A Short History of the Worshipful Company of Bakers.* London, 1933.

TOCQUEVILLE, ALEXIS DE. *Oeuvres Complètes.* Paris, 1959.

TOMASCHEK, J. A. *Das alte Bergrecht von Iglau.* Innsbruck, 1897.

TREVOR-ROPER, H. R. *Archbishop Laud, 1573–1645.* London, 1940.

TUCKER, JOSIAH. *A Brief Essay on the Advantages and Disadvantages which respectively attend France and Great Britain with Regard to Trade.* 2d ed. London, 1750.

UNESCO. *The Race Concept.* Paris, 1952.

UNWIN, GEORGE. *Industrial Organization in the Sixteenth and Seventeenth Centuries.* New York, 1904.

USHER, A. P. *The History of the Grain Trade in France, 1400–1700.* Cambridge, 1913.

UTSCH, RICHARD. *Die Entwicklung und volkswirtschaftliche Bedeutung des Eisenerzbergbaues und der Eisenindustrie im Siegerland.* Gorlitz, 1913.

VASARI, GIORGIO. *De la peinture,* 1551. French Trans. Charles Weiss. Paris, n.d.

Victoria County History: Cornwall, I; *Derbyshire,* II; *Surrey,* II.

WADSWORTH, A. P., AND MANN, J. DE L. *The Cotton Trade and Industrial Lancashire.* Manchester, 1931.

WEBER, MAX. *The Protestant Ethic and the Spirit of Capitalism.* Trans. Talcott Parsons. London, 1930.

WHARTON, EDITH. *French Ways and Their Meaning.* New York, 1919.

WHITE, LYNN. *Medieval Technology and Social Change.* Oxford, 1962.

WHITEHEAD, ALFRED NORTH. *Science and the Modern World.* New York, 1925.

WIEBE, GEORG. *Zur Geschichte der Preisrevolution des 16 und 17 Jahrhunderts.* Leipzig, 1895.

WOLFSTRIGL-WOLFSKRON, M. R. VON. *Die Troler Erzbergbaue, 1301–1665.* Innsbruck, 1903.

WOODRUFF, L. L. (ed.). *The Development of the Sciences.* New Haven, 1923.

WOOLF, VIRGINIA. *The Common Reader.* New York, 1925.

ZYCHA, ADOLF. *Das böhmische Bergrecht des Mittelalters auf Grundlage des Bergrechts von Iglau.* Berlin, 1900.

———— *Das Recht des ältesten deutschen Bergbaues bis ins 13. Jahrhundert.* Berlin, 1899.

Periodical Articles

ANDRÉ, AUGUSTE. "De la verrerie et des vitraux peints dans l'ancienne province de Bretagne," *Bulletin et mémoire de la société archéologique du département d'Ille et Villaine,* XII (1878).

BARBOUR, VIOLET. "Dutch and English Shipping in the Seventeenth Century," *Economic History Review,* II (1930).

BEALES, H. L. "Historical Revisions: The Industrial Revolution," *History,* XIV (1929).

BEAUNE, HENRI. "Note sur le régime des mines dans le duché de Bourgogne," *Mém. de la société des antiquaires de France,* XXI (1869).

BELOCH, JULIUS. "Die Bevölkerung Europas zur Zeit der Renaissance," Zeitschrift für Sozialwissenschaft, III (1900).

BEZANSON, ANNA. "The Early Use of the Term Industrial Revolution," *Quarterly Journal of Economics,* XXXVI (1922).

BESNIER, MAURICE. "L'interdiction du travail des mines en Italie," *Revue archéologique,* 5th ser., X (1919).

BITTNER, L. "Das Eisenwesen in Innerberg-Eisenerz," Archiv für österreichische Geschichte, LXXXIX (1901).

BLOCH, MARC. "Une matière première au moyen âge: la pierre de taille," *Annales d'histoire économique et sociale,* XXVI (1934).

BRAUDEL, FERNAND. "Monnaies et civilisations," *Annales: Economies, Sociétés, Civilisations,* I, No. 1 (1946).

BULARD, MARCEL. "L'industrie du fer dans la Haute-Marne," *Ann. de géog.,* XIII (1904).

CALHOUN, G. M. "Ancient Athenian Mining," *Journal of Economic and Business History,* III (1931).

CLAUDON, S. "Etude sur les anciennes mines de charbon en Bourbonnais," *Bulletin de la Société d'Emulation des Beaux-Arts du Bourbonnais,* VIII (1900).

CORBIER. "Notice sur les forges impériales de la Chaussade," *Bulletin de la Société nivernaise des lettres, sciences et arts,* 2d ser. (1869).

DOBEL, F. "Ueber den Bergbau und Handel des Jacob und Anton Fugger in Karten und Tirol, 1495–1560," *Zeitschrift des historischen Vereins für Schwaben und Neuburg,* IX (1882).

EVELYN, SIR GEORGE SHUCKBURGH. *Philosophical Transactions,* LXXXVIII (1798), 176.

FINK, E. "Die Bergwerksunternehmungen der Fugger in Schlesien," *Zeitschrift des Vereins für Geschichte und Altertum Schlesiens,* XXVIII (1894).

FINOT, JULES. "Le commerce d'alun dans les Pays-Bas," *Bulletin historique et philologique du comité des travaux historiques et scientifiques,* 1902.

FINSTERWALDER, P. W. "Die Gesetze des Reichstags von Roncalia von 11 November 1158," *Zeitschrift der Savigny Stiftung für Rechtsgeschichte,* Germanistische Abteilung, XLI (1931).

FISHER, F. J. "The Development of the London Food Market 1540–1640," *Economic History Review,* V (1935).

GAUTHIER, JULES. "L'Industrie du papier dans les hautes vallées franc-comptoise," *Mémoirs de la société d'émulation de Montbéliard,* XXVI (1897).

GERIN-RICARD, H. DE. "Mines et mineurs autrefois et aujourd'hui," *Société Statistique de Marseille,* XLVII (1906–7).

GOTHEIN, E. "Beiträge zur Geschichte des Bergbaus im Schwarzwald," *Zeitschrift für die Geschichte des Oberrheins,* N.S., II (1887).

HAMILTON, E. J. "American Treasure and the Rise of Capitalism," *Economica,* XXVII (1929).

HARSIN, PAUL. "De quand date le mot 'Industrie'?" *Annales d'histoire économique et sociale,* No. 6 (1930).

HEAWOOD, EDWARD. "Paper Used in England after 1600," *Library,* 4th ser., XI (1930–31).

HUGHES, EDWARD. "The English Monopoly of Salt in the Years 1563–71," *English Historical Review,* XL (1925).

HULME, E. W. "English Glass-Making in the Sixteenth and Seventeenth Centuries," *Antiquary,* XXX (1894).

———— "The History of the Patent System," *Law Quarterly Review,* XII (1896).

INAMA-STERNEGG, K. T. VON. "Zur Verfassungsgeschichte der deutschen Salinen im Mittelalter," *Sitzungsberichte der Kaiserlichen Akademie der Wissenschaft,* CXI (1866).

JENKINS, RHYS. "Early Attempts at Paper-making in England, 1495–1680," *Library Association Record,* II, Part II (1900).

———— "Iron Making in the Forest of Dean," *Transactions of the Newcomen Society,* VI (1925–26).

———— "Notes on the Early History of Steel Making in England," *Transactions of the Newcomen Society,* III (1922–23).

———— "The Rise and Fall of the Sussex Iron Industry," *Transactions of the Newcomen Society,* 5th ser., I (1920–21).

KOCH, ERNST. "Geschichtliche Entwickelung des Bergbaues und Salinenbetriebes in Elass-Lothringen," *Zeitschrift für Bergrecht* (1874).

———— "Das Hütten- und Hammerwerk der Fugger zu Hohenkirchen bei Georgenthal in Thüringen, 1485–1549," *Zeitschrift des Vereins für Thüringische Geschichte,* N.S., XXVI (1926).

KOYRÉ, ALEXANDRE. "Galileo and Plato," *Journal of the History of Ideas,* IV, No. 4 (1943).

KROKER, ERNST. "Leipzig und die sächsischen Berkwerke," *Schriften des Vereins für die Geschichte Leipzigs,* IX (1909).

LANE, F. C. "Venetian Shipping during the Commercial Revolution," *American Historical Review,* XXXVIII (1933).

LLEWELLIN, W. "Sussex Ironmasters in Glamorganshire," *Archaeologia Cambrensis,* 3d ser., IX.

LUCE, S. "De l'exploitation des mines et de la condition des ouvriers mineurs en France au XV e siècle," *Revue des questions historiques,* XXI (1877).

MacAdam, Ivison. "Notes on the Ancient Iron Industry of Scotland," *Proceedings of the Society of Antiquarians, Scotland,* XXI.

Marchegay, P. "Une verrerie dans la Fôret de Roche-sur-Yon en 1456," *Annuaire de la Société d'Emulation de la Vendée,* IV (1857).

McLaughlin, A. C. "The Background of American Federalism," *American Political Science Review,* XII (1918).

Meister, A. "Die Anfänge des Eisenindustrie in der Graftschaft Mark," *Beiträge zur Geschichte Dortmunds und der Graftschaft Mark,* XVII (1909).

Mott, J. R. "The London and Newcastle Chaldrons for Measuring Coal," *Archaeologia Aeliana,* 4th ser., XL.

Nef, John U. "L'art religieux et le progrès économique au 12 e ou 13 e siècles," *Association pour l'histoire de la Civilisation* (Toulouse, 1952–53).

—— "Industry and Art in France and England, 1540–1640," *The Thomist,* V (1943).

—— "A New Christian View of History?" *Thought,* XXXVII, No. 146 (1962).

—— "Note on the Progress of Iron Production in England, 1540–1640," *Journal of Political Economy,* XLIV (1936).

—— "Silver Production in Central Europe," *Journal of Political Economy,* XLIX, No. 4 (1941).

—— "L'Universalité française," *The French Review* (April, 1956).

Overend, G. H. "Notes upon the Earlier History of the Manufacture of Paper in England," *Proceedings of the Huguenot Society of London,* VIII (1909).

Pirenne, Henri. "Les Dénombrements de la population d'Ypres au XV e siècle," *Vierteljahrschrift für Sozial- und Wirtschaftsgeschichte,* I (1903).

Raveau, P. "La crise des prix au XVI e siècle en Poitou," *Revue historique,* CLXII (1929).

Ropp, Goswain van der. "Zur Geschichte des Alaunhandels im 15. Jahrhundert," *Hansische Geschichtsblätter,* X (1900).

Roubet, L. "La verrerie d'Apremont," *Bulletin de la Société nivernaise des sciences, lettres, et arts,* 3d ser., II (1886).

Russell, John Cox. "The Clerical Population of Medieval England," *Traditio,* II (1944).

Saint-Quirin. "Les verriers du Languedoc," *Bulletin de la société languedocienne de geographie,* XXVII (1904), XXVIII (1905), XXIX (1906).

Schmoller, Gustav. "Die geschichtliche Entwickelung der Unternehmung," *Jahrbuch für Gesetzgebung, Verwaltung und Volkswirtschaft im deutschen Reich,* XV (1891).

—— "Die wirtschaftlichen Zustände im Herzogthum Magdeburg," *Jahrbuch für Gesetzgebung, Verwaltung und Volkswirtschaft im deutschen Reich,* XI (1887).

Sieveking, Heinrich. "Die genueser seidenindustrie im 15. und 16. Jahrhundert," *Jahrbuch für Gesetzgebung, Verwaltung und Volkswirtschaft,* XXI (1897).

Stein, Henri. "La Papererie d'Essonnes," *Annales de la société historique et archéologique du Gâtinais,* XII (1894).

TAWNEY, R. H. "The Assessment of Wages in England by the Justices of the Peace," *Vierteljahrschrift für Sozial- und Wirtschaftsgeschichte,* XI (1913).
―――― "Studies in Bibliography: Modern Capitalism," *Economic History Review,* IV (1944).
USHER, A. P. "The General Course of Wheat Prices in France, 1350–1788," *Review of Economic Statistics,* XII (1930).
―――― "Two Notable Contributions to Economic History," *Quarterly Journal of Economics,* XLVIII (1933), 171–80.
WEIZSACKER, C. F. VON. "The Spirit of Natural Science," *Humanitas,* III, No. 1 (1947).
WUTKE, KONRAD. "Die Salzerchliessungsversuche in Schlesien in vorpreussischer Zeit," *Zeitschrift des Vereins für Geschichte und Altertum Schlesiens,* XXVIII (1894).
―――― "Die Versorgung Schlesiens mit Salz während des Mittelalters," *Zeitschrift des Vereins für Geschichte und Altertum Schlesiens,* XXVII (1893).

Published Documents

ENGLAND

Calendar of State Papers, Domestic.
Calendar of State Papers, Spanish.
Exchequer Depositions by Commission. London: Public Record Office.
Exchequer K. R. Customs Accounts. London: Public Record Office.
Historical Manuscripts Commission. Report on the MSS of the Duke of Rutland, IV.
Historical Manuscripts Commission. Report on the MSS of the Marquis of Salisbury, XII.
Star Chamber Proceedings. London: Public Record Office.
State Papers, Domestic.

FRANCE

Inventaire des archives communales de Cambrai.
Inventaire des archives départementales, Aisne.
Inventaire des archives départementales, Aube.
Inventaire des archives départementales, Basses Alpes.
Inventaire des archives départementales, Bouches-du-Rhône.
Inventaire des archives départementales, Haute-Garonne.
Inventaire des archives départementales, Hérault.
Inventaire sommaire des archives départementales du Gard.
Inventaire sommaire des archives départementales de l'Hérault.
Inventaire sommaire des archives départementales du Nord.

Unpublished Documents

ENGLAND

British Museum. Cotton MSS.
British Museum. Harleian MSS.

British Museum. Lansdowne MSS.
British Museum. Sloane MSS.
London School of Economics. Lord Beveridge MS.
London School of Economics. Price Committee MSS.
Public Record Office, London. Exchequer K.R. Port Books.

FRANCE

Archives de l'Aisne.
Archives départementales de la Loire Inférieure.
Archives Nationales. MSS Collections: K.876; F^{12} 1834; X^{1A} 8614, 8624, 8644; XIX, 152.
Archives du Nord (Lille).

Other Unpublished Works

Center for Human Understanding. "A New Conception of Grandeur." Washington, D. C.
Hartwell, Robert M. "Iron and Early Industrialism in Eleventh-Century China." Ph.D. dissertation, University of Chicago, 1963.
Koyré, Alexandre. "La Gravitation universelle de Kepler à Newton." Lecture, University of Paris, April 7, 1951.
Roover, Raymond de. "A Florentine Firm of Cloth Manufacture." Unpublished essay.

Index